The Greenwood Encyclopedia of
American Poets and Poetry

Advisory Board

The Greenwood Encyclopedia of

AMERICAN POETS AND POETRY

Volume 3

H – L

Jeffrey Gray, Editor
James McCorkle and Mary McAleer Balkun,
Associate Editors

GREENWOOD PRESS
WESTPORT, CONNECTICUT • LONDON

Library of Congress Cataloging-in-Publication Data

The Greenwood encyclopedia of American poets and poetry / Jeffrey Gray, editor ; James McCorkle and Mary McAleer Balkun, associate editors.
    p. cm.
  Includes bibliographical references and index.
    ISBN 0–313–32381–X (set : alk. paper) — ISBN 0–313–33009–3 (v. 1 : alk. paper) — ISBN 0–313–33010–7 (v. 2 : alk. paper) — ISBN 0–313–33011–5 (v. 3 : alk. paper) — ISBN 0–313–33012–3 (v. 4 : alk. paper) — ISBN 0–313–33013–1 (v. 5 : alk. paper)
  1. American poetry—Encyclopedias. 2. Poets, American—Biography—Encyclopedias.
I. Gray, Jeffrey, 1944– II. McCorkle, James. III. Balkun, Mary McAleer.
PS303.G74   2006
811.00903–dc22   2005025445

British Library Cataloguing in Publication Data is available.

Library of Congress Catalog Card Number: 2005025445
ISBN: 0–313–32381–X (set)
      0–313–33009–3 (vol. 1)
      0–313–33010–7 (vol. 2)
      0–313–33011–5 (vol. 3)
      0–313–33012–3 (vol. 4)
      0–313–33013–1 (vol. 5)

First published in 2006

Greenwood Press, 88 Post Road West, Westport, CT 06881
An imprint of Greenwood Publishing Group, Inc.
www.greenwood.com

Printed in the United States of America

The paper used in this book complies with the Permanent Paper Standard issued by the National Information Standards Organization (Z39.48–1984).

10 9 8 7 6 5 4 3 2 1

Copyright Acknowledgments

The author and publisher gratefully acknowledge permission to use the following material:

"Four Motions for the Pea Vines," "Motion," "Small Songs," and "Still" from *Collected Poems 1951–1971* by A. R. Ammons. Copyright © 1972 by A. R. Ammons. Used by permission of W. W. Norton & Company, Inc. "Easter Morning," from *A Coast of Trees* by A. R. Ammons. Copyright © 1981 by A. R. Ammons. Used by permission of W. W. Norton & Company, Inc.

"Paradise and Method" from *Paradise and Method: Poetics and Praxis* by Bruce Andrews (Evanston, IL: Northwestern University Press, 1996). Reprinted by permission of Northwestern University Press.

"Anti-Short Story" from *Veil: New and Selected Poems* by Rae Armantrout. Copyright © 2001 by Rae Armantrout. Reprinted by permission of Wesleyan University Press.

"Spain 1937" (© 1940, renewed 1968 by W. H. Auden), "In Praise of Limestone" (© 1951 by W. H. Auden, William Meredith, and Monroe K. Spears, Executors of the Estate of W. H. Auden), and "Bucolics" (© 1976 by Edward Mendelson, William Meredith, and Monroe K. Spears, Executors of the Estate of W.H. Auden) from *Collected Poems* by W. H. Auden. Used by permission of Random House, Inc. and Faber & Faber, Ltd.

Excerpts from Charles Bernstein's *Republics of Reality: 1975–1995* (Los Angeles: Sun & Moon Books, 2000), *With Strings* (Chicago: University of Chicago Press, 2001), *Controlling Interests* (New York: Roof Books, 1980, rpt. 2004), *My Way: Speeches and Poems* (Chicago: University of Chicago Press, 1999) and *Dark City* (Los Angeles: Sun & Moon Press, 1992). Used by permission of Charles Bernstein.

Excerpts from Frank Bidart's *Desire: Collected Poems* (© 1997 by Frank Bidart), *In the Western Night: Collected Poems 1965–1990.* (© 1990 by Frank Bidart), and *Star Dust* (© 2004 by Frank Bidart). Reprinted by permission of Farrar, Strauss and Giroux, LLC. Excerpts from *Desire: Collected Poems* also used with the permission of Carcanet Press Limited.

Excerpts from "Gerontion" from *Collected Poems 1909–1962* by T.S. Eliot. Reprinted by permission of Faber & Faber.

"Build Soil" from *The Poetry of Robert Frost*, edited by Edward Connery Lathem. Copyright 1969 by Henry Holt and Company, copyright 1936 by Robert Frost, copyright 1964 by Leslie Frost Ballantine. Published by Jonathan Cape. Reprinted by permission of the Random House Group Ltd. "Coming" from *The Mill of Particulars* by Robert Kelly (Los Angeles: Black Sparrow Press, 1972). Copyright © 1973 by Robert Kelly. Reprinted by permission of Black Sparrow Books, an imprint of David R. Godine, Publisher, Boston.

"A Theory of Prosody" from *A Walk with Tom Jefferson* by Philip Levine. Copyright © 1988 by Philip Levine. Used by permission of Alfred A. Knopf, a division of Random House, Inc.

Excerpts from *Representative Works* by Jackson MacLow (New York: Roof Books). Reprinted with permission of Anne Tardos. Excerpts from "1st Dance-Making Things New…" Reprinted with permission of Anne Tardos and Barrytown/ Station Hill Press.

Excerpts from Pablo Neruda, *Canto General*, 50th Anniversary Edition (The University of California Press and Pablo Neruda). Reprinted with permission.

Extracts from *Collected Poems* by Frank O'Hara. Copyright © 1971 by Maureen Granville-Smith, Administratrix of the Estate of Frank O'Hara. Used by permission of Alfred A. Knopf, a division of Random House, Inc.
Excerpts from *Selected Writings of Charles Olson* (© 1951, 1966 by Charles Olson). Reprinted by permission of New Directions Publishing Corp.

"1930s" from *New Collected Poems* by George Oppens. Copyright © 1934 by The Objectivist Press. Reprinted by permission of New Directions Publishing Corp.

Hannah Weiner texts used by permission of Charles Bernstein, for Hannah Weiner in trust, and by Mandeville Special Collections Library, University of California, San Diego.

"Sunday in the Park" from *Paterson* by William Carlos Williams. Copyright © 1948 by William Carlos Williams. Reprinted by permission of New Directions Publishing Corp. and Pollinger Limited.

Every reasonable effort has been made to trace the owners of copyright materials in this book, but in some instances this has proven impossible. The author and publisher will be glad to receive information leading to more complete acknowledgments in subsequent printings of the book and in the meantime extend their apologies for any omissions.

Contents

List of Entries

Strand, Mark
Stryk, Lucien
Stuart, Ruth McEnery
Sublime
Swensen, Cole
Swenson, May
Sze, Arthur
Tabb, John Banister
Taggard, Genevieve
Taggart, John
TallMountain, Mary
Tapahonso, Luci
Tarn, Nathaniel
Tate, Allen
Tate, James
Taylor, Bayard
Taylor, Edward
Teasdale, Sara
Terry, Lucy
Thaxter, Celia
Thayer, Ernest Lawrence
Thomas, Edith Matilda
Thomas, Lorenzo
Thompson, Dunstan
Thoreau, Henry David
Tillinghast, Richard
Tolson, Melvin
Tomlinson, Charles
Tompson, Benjamin
Toomer, Jean
Translation
Trask, Katrina
Trumbull, John
Tucker, St. George
Tuckerman, Frederick Goddard
Turner, Frederick
Tyler, Royall

Updike, John
Valentine, Jean
Van Duyn, Mona
Vangelisti, Paul
Variable Foot
Vazarini, Reetika
Verse Drama
Very, Jones
Villa, Jose Garcia
Violi, Paul
Visual Poetry
Voigt, Ellen Bryant
Vorticism
Voss, Fred
Wagoner, David
Wah, Fred
Wakoski, Diane
Walcott, Derek
Waldman, Anne
Waldrop, Keith
Waldrop, Rosmarie
Walker, Margaret
Ward, Diane
Ward, Elizabeth Stuart Phelps
Ward, Nathaniel
Warren, Mercy Otis
Warren, Robert Penn
Warren, Rosanna
Waters, Michael
Watten, Barrett
Webb, Charles Harper
Weiner, Hannah
Weiss, Theodore
Welch, James
Welish, Marjorie
Wells, Carolyn
Whalen, Philip

Wharton, Edith
Wheatley, Phillis
Wheeler, Susan
Wheelwright, John
Whitman, Sarah Helen Power
Whitman, Walt
Whittier, John Greenleaf
Wieners, John
Wigglesworth, Michael
Wilbur, Richard
Wilcox, Carlos
Wilcox, Ella Wheeler
Williams, C.K.
Williams, Jonathan
Williams, Roger
Williams, William Carlos
Willis, Nathaniel Parker
Wilson, John
Winters, Yvor (Arthur)
Wolcott, Roger
Wood, William
Woodworth, Samuel
Woolsey, Sarah Chauncey (also Chauncy)
Woolson, Constance Fenimore
Work, Henry Clay
Wright, C.D.
Wright, Charles
Wright, James
Wright, Jay
Wright, Susanna
Wylie, Elinor
Yau, John
Yiddish Poetry
Young Bear, Ray
Young, David
Zukofsky, Louis

List of Poets

Pre–Twentieth-Century Poets

Abbey, Henry
Adams, Henry Brooks
Adams, John
Adams, John Quincy
Albee, John
Alcott, Amos Bronson
Alcott, Louisa May
Aldrich, Anne Reeve
Aldrich, Thomas Bailey
Allen, Elizabeth Akers
Allston, Washington
Alsop, George
Austin, Mary
Balbuena, Bernardo de
Bangs, John Kendrick
Barlow, Joel
Bates, Charlotte Fiske
Bates, Katharine Lee
Beers, Henry Augustin
Belknap, Jeremy
Bell, Robert Mowry
Bierce, Ambrose
Bleecker, Ann Eliza
Bloede, Gertrude
Blood, Benjamin
Bodman, Manoah
Boucher, Jonathan
Brackenridge, Hugh Henry
Bradford, William
Bradley, Mary Emily Neeley

Bradstreet, Anne Dudley
Braithwaite, William Stanley
Brooks, Charles Timothy
Brooks, Maria Gowen
Bryant, William Cullen
Byles, Mather
Byrd, William, II
Carleton, Will
Cary, Alice
Cary, Phoebe
Cawein, Madison
Chandler, Elizabeth Margaret
Channing, William Ellery
Channing, (William) Ellery
Child, Lydia Maria
Church, Benjamin
Cleghorn, Sarah Norcliffe
Colman, Benjamin
Cooke, Ebenezer
Cooke, Rose Terry
Coolbrith, Ina
Cotton, John
Cradock, Thomas
Cranch, Christopher Pearse
Crane, Stephen
Dana, Richard Henry
Dandridge, Danske
Danforth, Samuel
Davies, Samuel
De Vere, Mary Ainge

Deland, Margaret
Dickinson, Emily
Doane, George Washington
Dodge, Mary Mapes
Drake, Joseph Rodman
Dreiser, Theodore
Duché, Jacob
Dudley, Thomas
Dunbar, Paul Laurence
Dwight, Timothy
Eastman, Elaine Goodale
Emerson, Ralph Waldo
English, Thomas Dunn
Equiano, Olaudah
Evans, Nathaniel
Faugeres, Margaretta Bleecker
Fenollosa, Ernest
Fenollosa, Mary McNeil
Fergusson, Elizabeth Graeme
Field, Eugene
Fields, Annie
Fields, James Thomas
Fiske, John
Fordham, Mary Weston
Forten, Sarah Louisa
Freneau, Philip
French, Mary
Fuller, Margaret
Garland, Hamilin
Garrison, William Lloyd

Gilman, Charlotte Perkins
Godfrey, Thomas
Goodhue, Sarah Whipple
Gorton, Samuel
Gould, Hannah Flagg
Grainger, James
Green, Joseph
Griffits, Hannah
Grimké, Angelina Weld
Grimke, Charlotte L. Forten
Guiney, Louise Imogen
Hale, Sarah Josepha
Halleck, Fitz-Greene
Hammon, Jupiter
Harper, Frances Ellen Watkin
Harris, Joel Chandler
Harte, Francis Bret
Hartman, Sadakichi
Hawthorne, Nathaniel
Haynes, Lemuel
Higginson, Thomas Wentworth
Hoffman, Charles Fenno
Holmes, Oliver Wendell
Hopkins, Lemuel
Horton, George Moses
Howe, Julia Ward
Howells, William Dean
Humphreys, David
Jackson, Helen Hunt
Jewett, Sarah Orne
Johnson, Edward
Josselyn, John
Juana Inés de la Cruz, Sor
Kemble, Fanny (Francis Anne)
Key, Francis Scott
Knight, Sarah Kemble
Lanier, Sidney
Larcom, Lucy
Lathrop, Rose Hawthorne
Lazarus, Emma
Leland, Charles Godfrey
Lewis, Richard
Lili'uokalani, Queen (Lydia
    Kamaka'eha)
Lincoln, Abraham
Livingston, William
Lodge, George Cabot
Longfellow, Henry Wadsworth
Longfellow, Samuel
Lowell, James Russell

Lowell, Maria White
Manwell, Juana (Owl Woman)
Markham, Edwin
Martí, José
Mather, Cotton
Melville, Herman
Menken, Adah Isaacs
Miller, Alice Duer
Miller, Cincinnatus Heine (Joaquin
    Miller)
Mitchell, Jonathan
Monroe, Harriet
Moody, William Vaughn
Moore, Clement Clarke
Moore, Milcah Martha
Morton, Sarah Wentworth
Morton, Thomas
Murray, Judith Sargent
Norton, John, II
Noyes, Nicholas
Oakes, Urian
Odell, Jonathan
Odiorne, Thomas
O'Hara, Theodore
O'Reilly, John Boyle
Osgood, Frances Sargent Locke
Page, Thomas Nelson
Paine, Thomas
Parke, John
Parker, Theodore
Pastorius, Francis Daniel
Paulding James Kirke
Peabody, Josephine Preston
Peck, Samuel Minturn
Pérez de Villagra, Gaspar
Phelps, Charles Henry
Piatt, Sarah Morgan Bryant
Pierpont, John
Pike, Albert
Plato, Ann
Poe, Edgar Allan
Posey, Alexander Lawrence
Ray, Henrietta Cordelia
Realf, Richard
Reese, Lizette Woodworth
Ridge, John Rollin
Riley, James Whitcomb
Rose, Aquila
Saffin, John
Santayana, George

Sargent, Epes
Schoolcraft, Jane Johnson (Bame-
    wa-wa-ge-zhik-a-quay)
Sears, Edmund Hamilton
Seccombe, Joseph
Selyns, Henricus
Sewall, Samuel
Sigourney, Lydia Huntley
Sill, Edward Rowland
Simms, William Gilmore
Smith, Anna Young
Smith, Captain John
Smith, Elizabeth Oakes Prince
Smith, Samuel Joseph
Spofford, Harriet Prescott
Stansbury, Joseph
Stedman, Edmund Clarence
Steere, Richard
Sterling, James
Stickney, Trumbull
Stockton, Annis Boudinot
Stoddard, Elizabeth
Stuart, Ruth McEnery
Tabb, John Banister
Taylor, Bayard
Taylor, Edward
Terry, Lucy
Thaxter, Celia
Thayer, Ernest Lawrence
Thomas, Edith Matilda
Thoreau, Henry David
Tompson, Benjamin
Trask, Katrina
Trumbull, John
Tucker, St. George
Tuckerman, Frederick Goddard
Tyler, Royall
Very, Jones
Ward, Elizabeth Stuart Phelps
Ward, Nathaniel
Warren, Mercy Otis
Wells, Carolyn
Wharton, Edith
Wheatley, Phillis
Whitman, Sarah Helen Power
Whitman, Walt
Whittier, John Greenleaf
Wigglesworth, Michael
Wilcox, Carlos
Wilcox, Ella Wheeler

Williams, Roger
Willis, Nathaniel Parker
Wilson, John
Wolcott, Roger

Wood, William
Woodworth, Samuel
Woolsey, Sarah Chauncey (also Chauncy)

Woolson, Constance Fenimore
Work, Henry Clay
Wright, Susanna

Twentieth- and Twenty-first–Century Poets

Ackerman, Diane
Adair, Virginia Hamilton
Adams, Léonie
Addonizio, Kim
Ai
Aiken, Conrad Potter
Alexander, Elizabeth
Alexander, Meena
Alexander, Will
Alexie, Sherman
Algarín, Miguel
Ali, Agha Shahid
Alvarez, Julia
Ammons, A.R.
Anania, Michael
Andrews, Bruce (Errol)
Angelou, Maya
Antin, David
Arensberg, Walter Conrad
Armantrout, Rae
Ash, John
Ashbery, John
Atwood, Margaret (Eleanor)
Auden, W.H.
Baca, Jimmy Santiago
Baker, David
Bang, Mary Jo
Baraka, Amiri
Barnes, Djuna
Becker, Robin
Bell, Marvin
Benedikt, Michael
Benét, Stephen Vincent
Bennett-Coverly, Louise
Berg, Stephen
Bernard, April
Bernstein, Charles
Berrigan, Ted
Berry, Wendell
Berryman, John
Berssenbrugge, Mei-mei
Bidart, Frank

Bierds, Linda
Birney, Earle
Bishop, Elizabeth
Bishop, John Peale
Blackburn, Paul
Blackmur, R.P.
Blaser, Robin
Bly, Robert
Bogan, Louise
Bök, Christian
Boland, Eavan
Bontemps, Arna
Booth, Philip
Boyle, Kay
Brainard, Joe
Brathwaite, Edward Kamau
Brautigan, Richard
Brock-Broido Lucie
Brodsky, Joseph
Bromige, David
Bronk, William
Brooks, Gwendolyn
Brossard, Nicole
Broumas, Olga
Brown, Sterling A.
Bruchac, Joseph
Buckley, Christopher
Bukowski, Charles
Burkard, Michael
Byer, Kathryn Stripling
Bynner, Witter
Cage, John
Campo, Raphel
Carroll, Jim
Carroll, Paul
Carruth, Hayden
Carson, Anne
Carver, Raymond
Cassity, Turner
Castillo, Ana
Cather, Willa
Ceravolo, Joseph

Cervantes, Lorna Dee
Cha, Theresa Hak Kyung
Chandra, G.S. Sharat
Chappell, Fred
Chin, Marilyn
Chrystos
Ciardi, John
Clampitt, Amy
Clifton, Lucille
Codrescu, Andrei
Cofer, Judith Ortiz
Cole, Henri
Coleman, Wanda
Collier, Michael
Collins, Billy
Coolidge, Clark
Cooper, Jane
Corman, Cid
Corn, Alfred
Corso, Gregory
Cortez, Jayne
Coulette, Henri
Cowdery, Mae Virginia
Crane, Harold Hart
Crapsey, Adelaide
Crase, Douglas
Creeley, Robert
Crews, Judson
Cruz, Victor Hernández
Cullen, Countee
cummings, e.e.
Cunningham, J.V.
Dahlen, Beverly
Davidson, Michael
Davison, Peter
Delgado, Juan
Dennis, Carl
Dent, Tory
Derricotte, Toi
Deutsch, Babette
De Vries, Peter
Dewdney, Christopher

Di Prima, Diane
Dickey, James
Digges, Deborah
DiPalma, Ray
Disch, Tom
Dobyns, Stephen
Donaghy, Michael
Dorn, Edward
Doty, Mark
Dove, Rita
Dragonette, Ree
Drucker, Johanna
Dubie, Norman
DuBois, W.E.B.
Dugan, Alan
Duhamel, Denise
Dumas, Henry Lee
Dunbar-Nelson, Alice
Duncan, Robert
Dunn, Stephen
DuPlessis, Rachel Blau
Dylan, Bob
Eady, Cornelius
Eberhart, Richard
Economou, George
Edson, Russell
Eigner, Larry
Eliot, T.S.
Elmslie, Kenward
Emanuel, Lynn
Enslin, Theodore
Equi, Elaine
Erdrich, Louise
Eshleman, Clayton
Espada, Martín
Evans, Abbie Huston
Evans, Donald
Everson, William (Brother
   Antonious)
Everwine, Peter
Fairchild, B.H.
Fearing, Kenneth
Feldman, Irving
Ferlinghetti, Lawrence
Field, Edward
Finch, Annie
Finkel, Donald
Finkelstein, Norman
Fitzgerald, Robert
Forché, Carolyn

Foster, Edward Halsey
Francis, Robert
Fraser, Kathleen
Friebert, Stuart
Friend, Robert
Frost, Carol
Frost, Robert
Fulton, Alice
Galassi, Jonathon
Gallagher, Tess
Galvin, James
Gander, Forrest
Gardner, Isabella
Garrigue, Jean
Geisel, Theodore (Dr. Seuss)
Gerstler, Amy
Gibran, Kahlil
Gidlow, Elsa
Gilbert, Jack
Gilbert, Sandra
Ginsberg, Allen
Ginsberg, Louis
Gioia, Dana
Giovanni, Nikki
Giovannitti, Arturo
Gizzi, Michael
Gizzi, Peter
Glatt, Lisa
Glück, Louise
Goldbarth, Albert
Goldsmith, Kenneth
Gonzalez, Ray
Goodison, Lorna
Graham, Jorie
Grahn, Judy
Greger, Debora
Gregg, Linda
Gregor, Arthur
Grenier, Robert
Grimké, Angelina Weld
Grossman, Allen
Guest, Barbara
Guest, Edgar A.
Gunn, Thom
Gwynn, R.S.
H.D. (Hilda Doolittle)
Hacker, Marilyn
Hadas, Rachel
Hagedorn, Jessica
Hahn, Kimiko

Haines, John
Hall, Donald
Hamby, Barbara
Harjo, Joy
Harper, Michael S.
Harrison, Jim
Harryman, Carla
Hartman, Charles
Hass, Robert
Hayden, Robert
Heaney, Seamus
Hecht, Anthony
Hejinian, Lynn
Heller, Michael
Herrera, Juan Felipe
Heyen, William
Higgins, Dick
Hilbert, Donna
Hillman, Brenda
Hirsch, Edward
Hirschman, Jack
Hirshfield, Jane
Hoagland, Tony
Hogan, Linda
Hollander, John
Hollo, Anselm
Holman, Bob
Hongo, Garrett
Honig, Edwin
Howard, Richard
Howe, Fanny
Howe, Susan
Hudgins, Andrew
Hughes, Langston
Hugo, Richard
Ignatow, David
Inada, Lawson Fusao
Jackson, Richard
Jacobsen, Josephine
Jarrell, Randall
Jeffers, Robinson
Johnson, Fenton
Johnson, Georgia Douglas
Johnson, Helene
Johnson, James Weldon
Johnson, Ronald
Jones, Rodney
Jordan, June
Joris, Pierre
Joseph, Allison

Joseph, Lawrence
Justice, Donald
Kaufman, Bob
Kees, Weldon
Kelly, Robert
Kennedy, X.J.
Kenyon, Jane
Kerouac, Jack
Kilmer, Alfred Joyce
Kim, Myung Mi
Kinnell, Galway
Kinzie, Mary
Kirby, David
Kiyooka, Roy (Kenzie)
Kizer, Carolyn
Klein-Healy, Eloise
Kleinzahler, August
Klepfisz, Irena
Kloefkorn, William
Knight, Etheridge
Knott, Bill
Koch, Kenneth
Koertge, Ron
Komunyakaa, Yusef
Kooser, Ted
Kostelanetz, Richard
Kowit, Steve
Kramer, Aaron
Kroetsch, Robert
Kumin, Maxine
Kunitz, Stanley
Kyger, Joanne
Lansing, Gerrit
Laughlin, James
Lauterbach, Ann
Laux, Dorianne
Lax, Robert
Lea, Sydney
Lee, Li-Young
Lehman, David
Leib (Brahinsky), Mani
Leithauser, Brad
Levertov, Denise
Levin, Phillis
Levine, Philip
Levis, Larry
Lewis, Janet
Lieberman, Laurence
Lifshin, Lyn
Lindsay, Vachel

Locklin, Gerald
Loden, Rachel
Logan, John
Logan, William
Lorde, Audre
Louis, Adrian C.
Lowell, Amy
Lowell, Robert
Loy, Mina
Lummis, Suzanne
Lux, Thomas
Mac Cormack, Karen
Mac Low, Jackson
Mackey, Nathaniel
MacLeish, Archibald
Major, Clarence
Mariani, Paul
Martin, Charles
Masters, Edgar Lee
Mathews, Harry
Matthews, William
Matthias, John
Maxwell, Glyn
Mayer, Bernadette
McCaffery, Steve
McClatchy, J.D.
McClure, Michael
McGrath, Campbell
McGrath, Thomas
McHugh, Heather
McKay, Claude
McPherson, Sandra
Menashe, Samuel
Meredith, William
Merrill, James
Merton, Thomas
Merwin, W.S.
Messerli, Douglas
Mezey, Robert
Miles, Josephine
Millay, Edna St. Vincent
Miller, Vassar
Mills, Ralph J., Jr.
Miłosz, Czesław
Momaday, N. Scott
Montague, John
Moore, Marianne
Mora, Pat
Morgan, Robert
Morley, Hilda

Moss, Howard
Moss, Stanley
Moss, Thylias
Muldoon, Paul
Mullen, Harryette
Mura, David
Muske-Dukes, Carol
Myles, Eileen
Nash, Ogden
Nelson (Waniek), Marilyn
Nemerov, Howard
Nichol, b(arrie)p(hilip)
Niedecker, Lorine
Nims, John Frederick
Noguchi, Yone
Norse, Harold
North, Charles
Notley, Alice
Nye, Naomi Shihab
Oates, Joyce Carol
O'Hara, Frank
Olds, Sharon
Oliver, Mary
Olson, Charles
Oppen, George
Oppenheimer, Joel
Ortiz, Simon J.
Ostriker, Alicia
Padgett, Ron
Paley, Grace
Palmer, Michael
Pankey, Eric
Parini, Jay
Parker, Dorothy
Pastan, Linda
Patchen, Kenneth
Peacock, Molly
Perelman, Bob
Perillo, Lucia
Phillips, Carl
Phillips, Dennis
Piercy, Marge
Piñero, Miguel
Pinkerton, Helen
Pinsky, Robert
Plath, Sylvia
Plumly, Stanley
Ponsot, Marie
Pound, Ezra Loomis
Pratt, Minnie Bruce

Prunty, Wyatt
Purdy, Al
Rabbitt, Thomas
Rakosi, Carl
Ramke, Bin
Randall, Dudley Felker
Rankine, Claudia
Ransom, John Crowe
Ratcliffe, Stephen
Rector, Liam
Reece, Byron Herbert
Reed, Ishmael
Retallack, Joan
Revard, Carter
Revell, Donald
Rexroth, Kenneth
Reznikoff, Charles
Rich, Adrienne
Riding [Jackson], Laura
Ríos, Alberto Alvaro
Roberson, Ed
Robinson, Edwin Arlington
Roethke, Theodore
Rolfe, Edwin
Ronk, Martha
Rose, Wendy
Rothenberg, Jerome
Rukeyser, Muriel
Ryan, Kay
Salinas, Luis Omar
Salter, Mary Jo
Sanchez, Sonia
Sandburg, Carl
Sanders, Ed
Saner, Reg
Saroyan, Aram
Sarton, May
Scalapino, Leslie
Scarbrough, George
Schnackenberg, Gjertrud
Schulman, Grace
Schultz, Susan M.
Schwartz, Delmore
Schwerner, Armand
Seeger, Alan
Seidel, Frederick
Selva, Salomón de la
Service, Robert W.
Seth, Vikram
Sexton, Anne

Shapiro, Alan
Shapiro, David
Shapiro, Karl
Shomer, Enid
Shore, Jane
Silko, Leslie Marmon
Silliman, Ron
Simic, Charles
Simon, Maurya
Simpson, Louis (Aston Marantz)
Smith, Dave
Smith, Joan Jobe
Snodgrass, W. D. (pseudonym S.S. Gardons)
Snyder, Gary
Sobin, Gustaf
Song, Cathy
Sorrentino, Gilbert
Soto, Gary
Spencer, Anne
Spicer, Jack
Spires, Elizabeth
Spivack, Kathleen
St. John, David
Stafford, William
Starbuck, George
Steele, Timothy Reid
Stein, Gertrude
Stepanchev, Stephen
Sterling, George
Stern, Gerald
Stevens, Wallace
Stewart, Susan
Stone, Ruth
Strand, Mark
Stryk, Lucien
Swensen, Cole
Swenson, May
Sze, Arthur
Taggard, Genevieve
Taggart, John
TallMountain, Mary
Tapahonso, Luci
Tarn, Nathaniel
Tate, Allen
Tate, James
Teasdale, Sara
Thomas, Lorenzo
Thompson, Dunstan
Tillinghast, Richard

Tolson, Melvin
Tomlinson, Charles
Toomer, Jean
Turner, Frederick
Updike, John
Valentine, Jean
Van Duyn, Mona
Vangelisti, Paul
Vazarini, Reetika
Villa, Jose Garcia
Violi, Paul
Voigt, Ellen Bryant
Voss, Fred
Wagoner, David
Wah, Fred
Wakoski, Diane
Walcott, Derek
Waldman, Anne
Waldrop, Keith
Waldrop, Rosmarie
Walker, Margaret
Ward, Diane
Warren, Robert Penn
Warren, Rosanna
Waters, Michael
Watten, Barrett
Webb, Charles Harper
Weiner, Hannah
Weiss, Theodore
Welch, James
Welish, Marjorie
Whalen, Philip
Wheeler, Susan
Wheelwright, John
Wieners, John
Wilbur, Richard
Williams, C.K.
Williams, Jonathan
Williams, William Carlos
Winters, Yvor (Arthur)
Wright, C.D.
Wright, Charles
Wright, James
Wright, Jay
Wylie, Elinor
Yau, John
Young Bear, Ray
Young, David
Zukofsky, Louis

List of Topics

Topical Entries Grouped
by Subtopics

American Poetics
Closure
Deep Image
Intentional Fallacy
Line
Linear Fallacy
Objective Correlative
Open Form
Poetic Forms
Prosody and Versification
Sentimentality
Sublime
Symbolism
Variable Foot

Ethnic, Cultural, and Political Influences
African American Poetry
African American Poetry
   Collectives
African American Slave Songs
Angel Island Poetry
Asian American Poetry
Black Arts Movement
British Poetry
Canadian Poetry
Caribbean Poetry
Chicano Poetry

Chinese Poetry
Corridos
East European Poetry
Feminist Poetics
French Poetry
Gay and Lesbian Poetry
Harlem Renaissance
Hawai'ian Internment Camp Poetry
   of Japanese American Internees
Irish Poetry
Japanese Poetry
Latin American Poetry
Latino Poetry
Minstrelsy
Modernismo
Native American Poetry
Negritude
Poetry and Politics, including War
   and Anti-War Poetry
Puerto Rican Poetry
Yiddish Poetry

Genres, Movements, and Schools
Agrarian School (the Agrarians)
Almanac Poetry (Seventeenth-
   Century)
Beat Poetry
Black Arts Movement

Black Mountain School
Children's Poetry
Concrete Poetry
Confessional Poetry
Corridos
Dada
Devotional Poetry
Digital Poetry
Ecopoetics
Ekphrastic Poetry
Elegy
Epic
Ethnopoetics
Expatriates
Experimental Poetry and the
   Avant-Garde
Feminist Poetics
Fireside Poets
Fluxus
Free Verse
Fugitives
Genteel Versifiers
Graveyard Poetry
Ideogram
Imagism
Language Poetry
Light Verse
Literary Independence Poem

Preface

Content and Structure

The Greenwood Encyclopedia of American Poets and Poetry is the largest reference work on American poetry ever assembled. Its span extends from the earliest appearance of poetry in what was to become the United States (and to some extent the Americas at large) to poetry at the beginning of the twenty-first century. Within this compass we include more than nine hundred essays, not only on the most recognized names but also on hundreds of others: early poets whose work was significant but little-known at the time, and later poets who, in a world of poetry now unrecognizably expanded, are emerging into prominence, either regionally or nationally.

The reader will also find topical entries on key schools, movements, poetic theories, practices, and terms. Since the *Encyclopedia* is not a dictionary of general literary terms, literary terms are included only if they were coined in the New World, or if they apply to American poetic practice. Thus, the entry on **sublime** will address the American sublime rather than the general concept. Similarly, the reader may assume that an entry on **ekphrastic poetry** or the **long poem**, for example, will principally concern instances and practitioners of these genres or approaches within American poetry. This is also true of entries such as **British poetry**, **Irish poetry**, and the like, which do not address all poetry from Ireland but rather Irish poetry's influence on and relation to American poetry and poetics.

Access

Entries are presented alphabetically regardless of period or type. While this is the simplest and perhaps most convenient arrangement, we also offer a total of five lists of entries that give readers other ways to get their bearings within this large encyclopedia:

1. An alphabetical list of all entries
2. A list of pre–twentieth-century poets
3. A list of twentieth-century poets
4. A list of topics
5. A list of the topics grouped under sub-headings

In this way, readers who may be interested, for example, only in those poets writing before the twentieth century may scan the list of names featured. For readers interested in certain American poetry subjects, the topics list prevents those entries from escaping notice among the hundreds of poet entries, and the reader can thus easily locate information on **Native American poetry**, **negritude**, **New Criticism**, **New Formalism**, the **New York School**, and many more subjects.

Following the A–Z entries in the volumes is a comprehensive bibliography of general sources on American poetry. Each entry in the A–Z section also includes further reading resources.

As further navigational aids, words or names in **boldface** indicate cross-references to guide the reader to related entries, and an index provides extensive access to the encyclopedia's contents.

Scope

A canon becomes a canon by leaving something out. Although copiously inclusive (if not canon-averse), *The Greenwood Encyclopedia of American Poets and Poetry* is nevertheless not "complete." If our inclusions are greater than any reference work on the subject thus far, our exclusions are equally, and inevitably, legion.

The problem is not so much the past, which, precisely because it recedes, appears mappable, but the present, which is vast, vibrant, and uncontainable, perhaps particularly so in America where few constraints remain to limit voices that demand hearing. Even if the editors attempted to represent all of the several thousand living, English-writing poets listed in the current *Directory of American Poets*, the *Encyclopedia* would still not be complete, since many more thousands of poets—hardly mute or inglorious—are writing in little magazines and on the Internet, some of whom will eventually assume prominent places in the landscape of poetry.

As examples of this uncontainability, consider the two categories in our title—"American" and "poetry"—and their tempting but slippery slopes. First, we live in the "Americas," and while even the Anglophone world increasingly understands "America" to mean what José Martí called "Nuestra America"—that is, an entity much larger than the United States—our purpose has been to represent predominantly Anglophone poetry, poetry of the Northern Hemisphere and parts of the Caribbean. While we have also attempted to account for important inter- and intra-American influences in all directions, the *Encyclopedia* is designed for English-speaking readers, who would not expect to find full treatments of Brazilian and Peruvian poets, for example, in an encyclopedia of American poetry.

Constructions of the Americas aren't the only geographical/cultural problem. Most Americans are by definition immigrants, and to understand their writing is to examine their histories and ethnicities. Thus, we have included entries that attempt to account for influences from abroad—for example, **Irish poetry**, **French poetry**, **Chinese poetry**, **Japanese poetry**, and so forth. This too is a nearly limitless slope; our choice was to do some of it as well as we could and leave much undone, or not to do it at all. We chose the former path.

The second category of the title—poetry—is not geographical but literary and generic. What constitutes "poetry"? For an encyclopedia that, initially at least, will appear in print, we should begin by acknowledging a bias toward that medium. The problem is, again, not the past but the present: poets now emerging who present their work principally on sound recordings or who are principally performers, and whose audiences know their work largely through performance, are underrepresented here. Song and performance are not neglected, however, in such entries as **performance poetry**, **jazz**, **minstrelsy**, **slam poetry**, **sound poetry**, **African American slave songs**, and so on. While we may not agree with Whitman that "the singers do not beget, only the Poet begets," with some musical exceptions, our leaning has been toward the enormous tradition of *printed* poetry from America's beginnings to the present time.

The other area that a print bias may only obliquely acknowledge is not sonic but visual: the Internet. If there are tens of thousands writing poetry in print, there may be several times that number writing online. Among poets with a very large Internet presence, one would have to list, among many others, Richard Denner, Luis Garcia, John Oliver Simon, Belle Randall, Paul Hunter, Charles Potts, John Bennett, Mark Halperin, and Joe Powell. These poets, while not represented here, may be Googled readily. (And we do include an entry on **Digital Poetry**.)

A last comment is necessary on the most interesting problem of all: the synchronic leaning of the twenty-first–century world. Our sympathies as writers and editors may tend toward the diachronic, but the culture at large and literature studies in particular, as college class enrollments reveal, show a much greater interest in the present than in the past. The *Encyclopedia*'s imbalance in the number of twentieth-century and contemporary poets represented here vis-à-vis those of earlier periods reflects this interest–existing as much among established scholars as among students—along with several other factors:

> The enormous growth in both population and in print technology and distribution over the past century
>
> The pronounced flourishing of poetry following the upheavals of literary modernism early in the twentieth century, and the successive waves of poetry since then, particularly from the 1960s, often extending but sometimes challenging the precepts and practices of modernism
>
> The burgeoning of poetic practice in the United States over the past forty years as a result of poetry workshops at universities across the nation, a situation earlier poets, for good or ill, could not avail themselves of

Because of this "excess" (as William Carlos Williams called poetry), our criteria for inclusion of twentieth-century poets have had to be different from those of earlier periods. Where now tens of thousands of writers publish books, formerly only a handful did. Some of our entries are on early poets who published only a few poems and never a book, a circumstance that seems quaint from today's perspective, suggesting either humility, a different set of priorities, or simply a level of economic and technological constraint difficult to comprehend in our own time.

Acknowledgments

In compiling the *Greenwood Encyclopedia of American Poets and Poetry*, we have often received counsel–from our advisory board but also from many colleagues and contributors, who offered suggestions about inclusions, exclusions, and lengths of entries. While we have not been able to accommodate all such suggestions, many suggested entries *have* been included to the greater benefit of the work as a whole.

Among our contributors are the most distinguished scholars, critics, and poets of the field. We owe thanks to our advisory board, some of whom are also contributors, for their many suggestions and helpful leads over the past couple of years, often connecting the right entry to the right writer. At Greenwood, we are much indebted to George Butler, who got the project off the ground, and to Mariah Gumpert and Anne Thompson for keeping this vast mission on track. For support from Seton Hall University's English Department, we thank former chair Martha Carpentier and secretary Rebecca Warren. We are particularly grateful for the work of our assistants from that department: Jocelyn Dumaresq, Sherry Chung, Peter Donahue, and Caitlin Womersley. We are indebted to our editorial staff, including colleagues such as Jeanne McNett, John Wargacki, and Robert Squillace, who helped in reading and editing entries; and Melissa Fabros, who was indispensable in creating and maintaining the EOAP website. We also wish to thank John A. Balkun, Lei Jun, and Cynthia Williams. There are far too many contributors to thank in this small space but among those who wrote a great many entries, helped critique entries, or matched writers with entries, we must mention Steven Gould Axelrod, Charles Bernstein, Burt Kimmelman, Don Marshall, Marjorie Perloff, Tad Richards, Linda Russo, and John Shields.

The Greenwood Encyclopedia of
American Poets and Poetry

H

H.D. (HILDA DOOLITTLE) (1886–1961)

H.D.'s work reflects the major project of literary **modernism**: the questioning of traditional certainties and the deliberate effort to remake literary form in ways that reflect the quest for new meanings. Using "H.D." as her nom de plume, Hilda Doolittle was an American poet, novelist, memoirist, essayist, and translator who lived most of her life in England and Switzerland. In her varied oeuvre, she responded to an age characterized by the violence of two world wars, rapid technological development, and advances in the status of women. Her work was also informed by other important intellectual currents such as psychoanalysis, anthropological and archaeological research, avant-garde cinema, and hermeticism. H.D.'s particular contribution grew out of her perspective as a woman contemplating the impact of public events upon private lives. Her work is comparable in its importance to that of other major modernist writers on both sides of the Atlantic—such as **Ezra Pound**, **Marianne Moore**, **William Carlos Williams**, **T.S. Eliot**, W.B. Yeats, **Amy Lowell**, D.H. Lawrence, **Gertrude Stein**, the Sitwells, and Dorothy Richardson, all of whom H.D. knew personally—as well as to the work of her companions, Richard Aldington, Bryher, and Kenneth MacPherson.

H.D.'s early poetry and her long poems of the 1940s and 1950s (*Trilogy* [1973], *Helen In Egypt* [1961], and *Hermetic Definition* [1972]) are among the defining works of modernism in their experimentation with lyric form, revisionary myth making, and critique of patriarchal culture. Her novels—*Hedylus* (1928), *HERmione* (1981), *Asphodel* (1992), *Paint It Today* (1992), *Palimpsest* (1926), and *Bid Me To Live* (1960)—belong with the prose fiction of Gertrude Stein, Virginia Woolf, James Joyce, and Dorothy Richardson, all of whom experimented, as H.D. did, with conventional narrative structure. H.D.'s **translations** from the Greek (mainly Euripides and Sappho) represent a lifelong engagement with classical texts, art, religion, and mythology, studies which informed her response to cultural catastrophe. Her memoirs and essays—such as *Tribute to Freud* (1974), *Notes on Thought and Vision* (1982), *The Gift* (1982), "H.D. By Delia Alton"(1986), and *End to Torment* (1979)—are also invaluable to the gendered study of modernism in their documentation of intersections between self-perception and the social forces that determine identity. H.D.'s work was widely recognized both by her peers and by the next generation of poets. The most extensive and influential discussion of its importance is **Robert Duncan**'s *H.D. Book*, published in parts in several "little magazines" between 1966 and 1988.

H.D. was born September 10, 1886, in Bethlehem, Pennsylvania, among the Moravian community of her mother, Helen (Wolle) Doolittle. Her mother's family had been influential in this pietist Protestant sect since its establishment in America in the eighteenth century. H.D.'s maternal grandfather, Francis Wolle, was the director of the Moravian seminary, and H.D.'s mother taught music and painting to the children there. H.D.'s father, Charles Leander Doolittle, whose Puritan ancestors had come from England, was a professor of mathematics and astronomy at Lehigh University. Although the family moved to Upper Darby, a suburb of Philadelphia, when Charles Doolittle became director of the Flower Observatory, H.D.'s Moravian background remained vital to her. In *The Gift*, an account of several generations of her family, H.D. connected her poetic gift with the mystical religious Gift of the Moravians, finding in their elevation of the female principle and espousal of racial tolerance the secret of world peace and understanding.

Hilda Doolittle grew up among five brothers. She was the sixth child and only daughter to survive in Charles Doolittle's large family, which included three children from an earlier marriage. With Helen Wolle there were five more: Gilbert, Edith (who died as a baby), Hilda, Harold, and Melvin. Hilda was her father's favorite child. She alone was permitted to play in his study, and a fascination with stars and astrological symbols would carry over into her poetry. Although drawn to her artistic mother, Hilda felt separated from her by her mother's open favoritism towards Hilda's brother Gilbert. Hilda identified with Gilbert, who would become the prototype of many brother figures in her later novels and poems. Also, Helen Wolle Doolittle's self-effacing manner provided a problematic model for her aspiring daughter. As H.D. would put it, "the house in some indescribable way depends upon father-mother. At the point of integration or regeneration, there is no conflict over rival loyalties" (*Tribute to Freud*, 146).

Hilda entered Bryn Mawr College in 1905 as a day student but withdrew in her second year, having experienced an identity crisis around the conflicting demands of sexuality, gender, and vocation. As she later put it in her autobiographical novel *HERmione*, "She only felt that she was a disappointment to her father, an odd duckling to her mother, an importunate overgrown, unincarnated entity that had no place here" (110). Yet these years were vital to her artistic development, which took place outside the family and college classroom. Although she would later remember meeting Marianne Moore at Bryn Mawr, most important among her friends at this time were Ezra Pound, William Carlos Williams, and Frances Josepha Gregg. By 1903, both Pound and Williams were students at the University of Pennsylvania and, according to Williams, both were attracted by Hilda's angular beauty (she was almost six feet tall) and by her "provocative indifference to rule and order" (*Autobiography*, 68).

Ezra Pound, not Williams, was Hilda's first love, however. She had first met him when she was fifteen and she later credited him with dragging her "out of the shadows" and awakening her as a poet (*End to Torment*, 4). During the period of their romance, 1905–1907, they exchanged poems and together read William Morris, Algernon Swinburne, Balzac's *Séraphita*, and Yoga books. Despite her father's disapproval—Pound was a fledgling poet with poor prospects—the two became engaged, but by 1908, when Pound sailed for England, the engagement had been broken. Hilda had grown increasingly uncomfortable with the idea of marriage, fearing that her role as Pound's muse would prevent her own artistic development. As she put it, "he would have destroyed me and the center they call 'Air and Crystal' of my poetry"(*End*, 35). By then she had formed an intense friendship with Frances Gregg, a young woman she considered a self-affirming alter ego: "I am HER. She is HER. Knowing her, I know HER. She is some amplification of myself like amoeba giving birth, by breaking off, to amoeba" (*HERmione*, 158).

In 1911 Hilda accompanied Frances and her mother on a four-month trip to Europe. In Hilda's case, it was a voyage that extended to a lifetime. She returned to the United States for visits only four or five times until her death. Introduced by Pound to his literary circle in London, Hilda met many of the writers who became her community of fellow artists—especially Richard Aldington, W.B. Yeats, T.S. Eliot, F.S. Flint, John Gould Fletcher, Ford Madox Hueffer (later Ford), Violet Hunt, May Sinclair, John Cournos, Brigit Patmore, George Plank, and Dorothy Shakespear. Hoping to live with Frances Gregg in a household of their own fashioning, Hilda was devastated when Gregg returned to the United States and married Louis Wilkinson. Pound's engagement to Dorothy Shakespear compounded this shock. Hilda turned to Richard Aldington, a British poet and translator six years her junior, whose persistent attention replaced the attentions of Pound and Gregg. She and Aldington studied Greek together at the British Museum, wrote poetry, and read widely in the French Symbolists and neo-Latin poets. They were married in London in 1913.

During World War I, H.D.'s life was permanently shattered by a series of traumatic events. In 1915, a year before the publication of *Sea Garden*, her first book of poems, H.D.'s first child was stillborn, a loss she believed was precipitated by the news of the *Lusitania*'s sinking. She suppressed her private grief because London was staggering under the shock of British army casualties, later writing in *Bid Me to Live* that her new friend, D.H. Lawrence, was the only one who understood it. In 1916 Aldington enlisted in the British army to avoid conscription. His experiences at the front changed him, estranging him from her. He was now "rather hearty and too loud . . . a great over-sexed officer on leave," H.D. wrote (*Bid Me to Live*, 46–47). Having been warned after the stillbirth not to get pregnant until the war ended, she began to dread Aldington's leaves, associating his frequent sexual demands with death. By 1917, with H.D.'s consent, Aldington began an extended affair with Dorothy Yorke, an American acquaintance. When this situation became untenable, the couple agreed that H.D. should leave London, live with music historian Cecil Gray in Cornwall, and return to Aldington at the end of the war. H.D.'s resulting pregnancy upset Aldington, who would not allow her to register the baby in his name. During this second pregnancy, H.D.'s brother Gilbert was killed in France, and her father, overcome with grief, died shortly thereafter. H.D. also caught the deadly influenza of 1919 and, lacking adequate medical care, was not expected to survive. She was rescued by the British writer and editor, Bryher (Winifred Ellerman), daughter of shipping magnate Sir John Ellerman, who supported her and promised her a trip to Greece if she got well. Both H.D. and her daughter Perdita, born March 31, 1919, lived, and H.D. began a new life with Bryher. Their relationship survived until H.D.'s death, spanning Bryher's two marriages of convenience (to Robert McAlmon and Kenneth MacPherson, respectively), in circumstances that included significant travel to Greece and Egypt in the early years and, after World War II, separate residences.

By the time of these traumatic events, H.D.'s literary career was well under way. **Imagism**, the influential literary movement of 1913–1917, was launched in the tea shop of the British Museum in 1912 when H.D. handed Ezra Pound three new poems. So impressed was he with their hardness, clarity, and intensity—qualities of diction that he advocated to replace the excesses of Georgian Romanticism—that he signed them "H.D. Imagiste" and sent them to **Harriet Monroe**, who published them in *Poetry* in January 1913. More poems by H.D. rapidly appeared in *Poetry* and other little magazines with the Imagist label. Pound edited the first imagist anthology, *Des Imagistes* (1914), and three more anthologies edited by **Amy Lowell** followed. The devastating impact of the war and a disagreement between Pound and Lowell led to the official abandonment of the anthologies in 1918, but by then the Imagist movement had gathered about it writers on both sides of the Atlantic who pioneered modernism in English poetry.

The Imagist principles that H.D.'s poems exemplified were rooted in French philosophy (particularly the work of Henri Bergson) and in the work of T.E. Hulme, whom Pound had come to know in London. The principles were also influenced by French Symbolist poetry, the Japanese haiku, the art of the Postimpressionists and Cubists, and the new Freudian psychoanalysis filtered through the work of Bernard Hart. In the March 1913 issue of *Poetry*, Pound and Flint had published a list of three rules for the writing of Imagist poems: (1) "Direct treatment of the 'thing,' whether subjective or objective; (2) To use absolutely no word that did not contribute to the presentation; (3) As regarding rhythm: to compose in sequence of the musical phrase, not in sequence of a metronome." Pound defined the image, in the "Doctrine of the Image," as "that which presents an intellectual and emotional complex in an instant of time" (reprinted as "A Retrospect"). The goal of the imagist poem was a sudden sense of liberation achieved through the exact rendering of particulars.

"Oread," H.D.'s most frequently anthologized poem, first published in 1914, demonstrates why she is regarded as the finest Imagist:

> Whirl up, sea—
> Whirl your pointed pines,
> splash your great pines
> on our rocks,
> hurl your green over us,
> Cover us with your pools of fir.

As the title indicates, this poem dramatizes the perception of a mountain nymph aroused in passion as she regards the sea. The imagery of the reiterated commands, all projections of her own wooded environment, blurs the boundary between subject and object, suggesting that potency and receptivity are internally coexistent. The irregular but distinctly musical cadences are built on patterns of repetition and internal rhyme that project intensity.

Most important, like the other poems in *Sea Garden* (1916), this is a poem about female identity. Written when women had almost won the struggle for suffrage, it imagines a pastoral realm on the borderline of civilization. As the title suggests, the book's main theme is homage to a particular kind of rugged, natural beauty: a beauty of fierce struggle and endurance, which the poet contrasts, in the five flower poems, with the cloying "beauty without strength" of conventional gardens (in "Sheltered Garden") or with the urban blight of modern cities. The natural world itself is not the subject of any given poem. It serves as the vehicle through which the poet explores consciousness (Friedman, *Psyche Reborn*).

Since many of the poems in *Sea Garden* were written during the years between H.D.'s wartime marriage to Richard Aldington and the immediate aftermath of their stillborn child (spring 1915), H.D.'s objectification of human passion in a revisionist language of flowers is particularly poignant. The anguish of a poem like "Storm," for example, where the speaker accuses the storm of crushing the green out of the trees' live branches, burdening them with "black drops," is undoubtedly rooted in H.D.'s historical circumstances. Between 1921 and 1931, H.D. published three full-length volumes of poetry and one verse drama: *Hymen* (1921), *Heliodora and Other Poems* (1924), *Red Roses for Bronze* (1931), and *Hippolytus Temporizes* (1927). As these titles suggest, she continued to situate herself in a classical landscape. In many of these poems she employed the **lyric** form to revise classical myths from a female perspective, often giving subjectivity and voice to heroines, such as Eurydice, Helen, Cassandra, and Demeter, whose stories have been elided in a predominantly male literary and religious tradition. Not only does she reinterpret myth here, but she also often uses it as a distancing mask for her own life. Predominant in the background of these poems is the legendary Greek poet Sappho, whose influence on H.D. is evident in her re-creation of full-length poems from extant fragments and in her essay "The Wise Sappho," written in 1920 and published in *Notes on Thought and Vision*.

Although H.D.'s *Collected Poems* (1925) was well reviewed by poets such as Moore and Williams, her work was often misunderstood by critics, who, dwelling on the "crystalline" surfaces of her early poems or her distancing Greek masks, found it escapist. That H.D. herself became frustrated with the Imagist label is evident in her 1940s essay "Some Notes on Recent Writing" (excerpted in *Bid Me to Live*), in which she connects the concentrated energy of her early poetry with the personal narrative encoded in such early works of fiction as *Palimpsest, Hedylus,* and *Pilate's Wife* (composed 1924–1934; published 2000):

> The Greek, or the Greek and Roman scenes and sequences of the prose studies are related to the early poems. I grew tired of hearing these poems referred to as crystalline. Was there no other way of criticizing, of assessing them?

At the same time that she masked her personal life in her poetry and in the historical novels mentioned above, H.D. made her personal life the center of other prose fiction, most of which she did not publish during her lifetime. These autobiographical novels are *Paint It Today* (written in 1921), *Fields of Asphodel* (written in 1921–1922), and *Bid Me to Live (A Madrigal)*, begun in 1939 and completed in 1950. H.D. later regarded the first two novels as early drafts of the third. However, although all three selectively record the rise and fall of a marriage and the death and birth of a child in wartime, each text emphasizes different aspects of the past. *Paint It Today* focuses on lesbian love and downplays the heroine's broken engagement and marriage. *Asphodel* begins with an appeal to lesbian sisterhood in Part I and then skips,

in Part II, to the aftermath of the traumatic stillbirth of the heroine's child. It then explores the dissolution of her marriage and the unfolding of the affair that leads to her second pregnancy and ends with the birth of her child and her new lesbian relationship. In *Madrigal*, by contrast, H.D. drops the lesbian frames of the earlier novels and focuses mainly on two stories of heterosexual love experienced by her heroine (the second unconsummated): with her soldier-husband (based on Aldington) and with a fellow artist (based on D.H. Lawrence). Although the stillbirth is a crucial memory and her affair with Gray is recorded, in *Madrigal* H.D. cuts off her life story well before the birth of Perdita. Her emphasis is rather on her heroine's consolidation as an artist. Taken together, these three novels form a palimpsest in which intertextual resonances and dissonances reflect a struggle between repression and expression (Friedman, *Penelope's Web*).

The metaphoric possibilities of the palimpsest (a parchment from which one writing has been imperfectly erased to make room for another) were resonant for H.D. as a way of layering personal and collective histories. In *Palimpsest* (1926) her first published fictional attempt to connect her personal story with her poetic identity, H.D. takes this archaeological metaphor as the principle of coherence for three related stories, each set in a different place and historical period: "War Rome" (the ancient city she associated with London), seventy-five years before Christ's birth; "War and Post-war London," the time and place of her personal trauma; and "Excavator's Egypt," a timeless modernist locale. These linked stories imply a mythopoetic view of history, the tendency to see parallels in historical evidence from disparate periods, which then become the basis for claims of a formal identity that is interpreted to reflect universality. In *Palimpsest* H.D. overtly combines autobiography with history, creating a new narrative strategy to dramatize the insight gained from her wartime experience.

The setting of the third story in *Palimpsest* is based on H.D.'s trip with her mother and Bryher in 1923 to Egypt, where they were present at the opening of King Tutankhamen's tomb. The Egyptian hieroglyphs uncovered there, emblems of a world older than Greece, fascinated H.D., who would return to Egypt as a symbol of spiritual resilience in important later works such as *Trilogy* and *Helen In Egypt*. This trip was the last of several important voyages H.D. took with Bryher between 1919 and 1923, voyages that set the scene for visionary experiences that she felt compelled to interpret. In July 1919 they spent a month in the Scilly Isles off Cornwall, where H.D. had the "jelly-fish" and "bell-jar" experiences she described in *Notes on Thought and Vision*, an experimental essay about the interconnections between creativity and procreativity. In the spring of 1920, H.D. and Bryher set off with Havelock Ellis on the ocean voyage to Greece that Bryher had promised. On board the ship, H.D. had a hallucinatory experience that she shared with a scarred fellow passenger (Peter Rodeck), who, in her vision, became an unblemished fellow witness. Attributes of this experience would inform the figure of the idealized male lover in the third story in *Palimpsest* and in *Helen In Egypt*. On the Greek island of Corfu, H.D. saw what she called the "writing-on-the-wall," a series of light pictures projected onto the wall of her hotel room. She described them in *Tribute to Freud* as having occurred in two stages. The second stage culminated in the following vision that she shared with Bryher: "a circle like the sun-disk and a figure within the disk; a man . . . reaching out to draw the image of a woman (my Nike) into the sun beside him" (56). In retrospect H.D. interpreted these visions as inspired emblems of personal destiny, rejecting Freud's suggestion that they were a dangerous symptom. They do, in fact, prefigure the power of her later long poems and even her success in the poetry establishment. She became the first woman to win the Award of Merit in Poetry in 1960 from the American Academy of Arts and Letters, a ceremony she dramatized in the central section of her last poem, "Hermetic Definition," in a way that echoes the culminating vision.

On a third journey, to America in the fall of 1920, H.D. introduced Bryher to Marianne Moore in New York before she and Bryher traveled to the California coast. H.D.'s and Bryher's friendship with Moore was to be an important source of creative exchange and validation for all three women. Although this trip produced no new visions, it did result in Bryher's marriage to the writer Robert McAlmon, whom she married in order to gain freedom from her family. She and H.D. returned with him to Europe, where Bryher funded McAlmon's press, Contact Editions. Through McAlmon, H.D. and Bryher met such artists as Gertrude Stein, Ernest Hemingway, James Joyce, Nancy Cunard, Man Ray, Berenice Abbott, and Mary Butts.

H.D.'s exposure to the avant-garde continued throughout the 1920s. In 1926 she fell in love with Kenneth MacPherson, a young artist and writer with whom she lived for a time (with Bryher and Perdita), chiefly in Switzerland. In this unusual ménage à trois, the three adults pursued mutual interests in cinema, psychoanalysis, and literature, starting the film journal *Close Up*. During the journal's publication from 1927 to 1933, H.D., Bryher, MacPherson, and others reviewed films from all over the world. In addition, MacPherson directed three films in which H.D. acted and participated in the editing: *Wing Beat* (1927), *Foothills* (1928), and *Borderline* (1930). Probably influenced by writers of the **Harlem Renaissance**, the last film is a dramatization of interracial sex and violence starring Paul and Essie Robeson along with Bryher and H.D. In the essay "Borderline," which she wrote about the film, H.D. demonstrates the importance to her of issues of racial and sexual discrimination.

Psychoanalysis was a key element in H.D.'s artistic development. Feeling on the brink of emotional and artistic paralysis in the late 1920s, she sought psychiatric help, first from several analysts in London and ultimately from Freud himself in Vienna in 1933 and 1934. Though she would continue to consult other analysts throughout her life, her work with "Papa," as she called Freud, helped her to achieve the sought-after shift in perspective that would bring about her greatest poetry. In *Tribute to Freud*, H.D. emphasizes the didactic dimension of her analysis more than the therapeutic one. She shows how Freud taught her to explore the truth of her own experience by free association upon memories, dreams, and visions, and she explains how he validated her sense of the connection between her inner life and the universal world of dream embodied in the master plots of myth. She presents her interaction with him as a creative collaboration in which she subtly transforms his theories to serve the requirements of her vision. For example, while she found comfort in Freud's view that her psychic experiences represented a desire to reestablish the pre-Oedipal bond between mother and daughter, she did not agree with his theory of penis envy. In "The Master," a poem written during her analysis but not published until after her death, H.D. records more overtly not only her reverence for Freud but also her anger at his theory of "the man strength." In the poem she asserts that "*woman is perfect*" and celebrates woman's independent spiritual power. Her memoir is both a tribute to Freud's place in twentieth-century intellectual history and a key to her own mature religious vision.

H.D.'s interest in psychoanalysis was paralleled by extensive research into hermeticism. Originating with the *Hermetica* attributed to Hermes Trisgmegistus, this occult, heterodox tradition was a feature of the works of such writers as Walter Pater, to whose "Alexandrian Hellenism" H.D. felt drawn (Gregory). Alienated from orthodox religion and yet possessed of a religious sensibility shaped by her Moravian heritage, H.D. found in the syncretism of ancient mystical traditions a concept of the Divine that incorporated woman as a symbol. The androgynous One of esoteric tradition paralleled the psychic integration she sought with Freud (Friedman, *Psyche Reborn*). Not only did she read books on the hermetic tradition by such writers as Denis de Rougemont, W.B. Crow, Jean Chaboseau, and Robert Ambelain, but she also joined the London Society for Psychical Research and attended spiritualist lectures, and during the final years of the war, she participated in weekly séances with a medium, through whom she claimed to be in touch with the spirits of dead Royal Air Force pilots.

A key figure in this period was Lord Hugh Dowding, Chief Air Marshal of the Royal Air Force during the Battle of Britain, who had turned to spiritualism for the same purpose. She modeled the character of Lord Howell on Dowding in her *The Sword Went Out to Sea* (unpublished), the first book of a second trilogy of novels that would lead to such major poems as *Helen in Egypt*, in which Dowding is the model for Achilles.

H.D. was extremely productive during the World War II period. Between 1939 and 1944, having chosen to remain with Bryher in London during the Blitz, H.D. drafted a number of important texts, including *The Gift*, "Writing on the Wall," *Magic Ring* (an unpublished novel based on her occult experiences), and, most important, the **long poem** she came to call her "war trilogy." *Trilogy* begins with "The Walls Do Not Fall," which is dedicated to Bryher "for Karnak 1923 / from London 1942." In it H.D. confronts the aftermath of the bombing of London directly, connecting it with the opening in 1923 of King Tut's tomb, where ancient buried treasure was uncovered along with the dead king's remains. In her desolation, she marvels at her survival and assumes the task of determining what meaning lies beneath the rubble: "we passed the flame: we wonder / what saved us? What for?" Through a process she calls "spiritual realism," she enters the realm of oracular vision, finding at the heart of modern destruction an apocalyptic pattern that incorporates regeneration.

With the publication of "The Walls Do Not Fall," H.D. dispelled the unfavorable critical impression that her work was detached from the historical moment. When he reviewed it, Osbert Sitwell mentioned that more of this kind of work was needed, and H.D. responded by writing "Tribute to the Angels" (dedicated to him) in May 1944, calling it a "premature peace poem" (Guest). In "Tribute to the Angels," H.D.'s immersion in Hermeticism is evident: Hermes Trismegistus provides the speaker with a syncretic religious philosophy that enables her to reintegrate Christianity with pagan myth and also provides a metaphor for a poetic method (an alchemy of the Word) with which to purify culture of its misogyny. The result is the creation of what Susan Gubar has termed a "feminist revisionary theology" replete with iconography. Symbols of salvation occur, followed by a vision of a Lady who represents the divine in a new form. Matriarchal goddesses from across the cultural spectrum merge in the speaker's newly liberated psyche. The Lady is "Psyche, the butterfly, / out of the cocoon" and the pages of the book that she carries are blank, from "the unwritten volume of the new."

This poem was followed in December 1944 by "The Flowering of the Rod," in which H.D. dramatizes the speaker's renewal by retelling the story of the Nativity. She does so through two peripheral characters in the gospel, the mage Kaspar, who is an Arab merchant in her version, and Mary Magdalene, the adulteress who, in her poem, comes to Kaspar to buy myrrh, which will be her gift to the Christ child. An example of feminist revisionary theology, this poem is inspired by H.D.'s conception of her analysis with Freud as a creative collaboration. Kaspar (Freud) finds Mary's behavior "unseemly" in a woman until a fleck of light in her hair reveals a glimpse of the lost Atlantis, the power of love embodied in woman that has been falsely desecrated by orthodox religious tradition. Mary's psychic renewal is the product of a moment of recognition between these two. H.D. dedicated the poem to Norman Holmes Pearson, the Yale professor who became her confidante, in acknowledgment of his important role in her creative resurrection. When he was based in London during the war, Pearson had responded to drafts of H.D.'s work with great sensitivity, and after his return to Yale, he continued to take an active role in her creative process. Besides influencing the composition of such important later works as *Helen in Egypt* and *End to Torment*, he elicited various autobiographical notes from H.D. and prompted her to write the retrospective commentary "H.D. By Delia Alton," in which she explained the purposes, goals, and underlying themes of her work. He also established the H.D. archive at Yale, ensuring her manuscripts and letters a future audience.

At the end of World War II, H.D.'s mental and physical condition deteriorated again. In 1946 she suffered a severe emotional breakdown and was flown to Klinik Kusnacht in Switzerland, where she recovered after six months. She then began another fourteen years of extraordinary creative productivity, living in Switzerland apart from Bryher, mainly in hotels, until she returned in the 1950s to Kusnacht, where she remained until the end of her life. In this period, she especially enjoyed the company of her friend and analyst Erich Heydt, whose interest in the poets of her circle prompted her to review the patterns underlying her past experiences with Pound, Aldington, Lawrence, and Dowding. H.D.'s work of this last phase includes *By Avon River* (1949), an essay about Shakespeare and the Elizabethan poets; a cycle of three prose romances (still unpublished) that reflect her second war experience and its parallels in history; *Helen in Egypt* (composed 1952–1954); a lyric romance, "Vale Ave" (composed in 1957 and not published until 1982), which draws on occult lore; and the three long poems "Sagesse," "Winter Love," and "Hermetic Definition," collected in *Hermetic Definition*.

The main creative event in this last phase was the composition of *Helen in Egypt*, a lyric **epic** in which H.D. retells the story of Helen of Troy from Helen's perspective, revising the epic's traditional focus on a male hero. H.D. employs the constellation of myths surrounding Helen—that irresistible avatar of female sexuality who became the despised symbol of the Trojan War—in order to acknowledge and counter this negative image of woman in the dominant culture. She takes her moral direction from Stesichorus and Euripides, post-Homeric poets who were "restored to sight" after they exculpated Helen in their late work. In their account, Helen did not go to Troy with Paris: She was "transposed or translated from Greece into Egypt. Helen of Troy was a phantom. . . . The Greeks and the Trojans alike fought for an illusion." Unlike the revisions of her ancient predecessors, whose exculpations posit an alternative Helen who is faithful to Menelaus but asexual, H.D.'s poem has a more radical objective. By making Helen's consciousness her subject, H.D. shows the painful self-division caused by woman's internalization of culture's traditional ambivalence toward her sexuality and dramatizes a search for wholeness.

Helen's quest for psychic integration through memory and dream constitutes the epic's main action. H.D.'s extraordinary use of sound in the poem is itself a style of thought (Morris). There is a sense that H.D. is unleashing repressed powers, dispensing with rationality. As she puts it in the opening lyric, "the old enchantment holds." She organizes Helen's story into three main parts, "Pallinode [sic]," "Leuké," and "Eidolon," which are divided into sections and subsections of semi-dramatic lyrics (mostly monologues). Each section also includes a prose introduction, in which a "narrator" comments on the poetry, creating a multilayered effect. Although set in the classical world, the poem is an example of palimpsestic thinking in that it is directly influenced by the rise of fascism in Europe. H.D. uses words such as "dictator," "allies," and "Command" that are not Homeric, even in translation (Friedman, *Psyche Reborn*). *Helen in Egypt* is both an extended psychodrama in which communal memories are worked through and a profound meditation on the psychosocial situations of women and men in a war-centered patriarchy. It marks the zenith of H.D.'s career. The three late poems collected in *Hermetic Definition* consolidate and refine the vision represented there.

Further Reading. *Selected Primary Sources:* H.D., *Asphodel,* ed. Robert Spoo (Durham, NC: Duke University Press, 1992); ———, *Between History and Poetry: The Letters of H.D. and Norman Holmes Pearson,* ed. Donna Krolik Hollenberg (Iowa City: University of Iowa Press, 1997); ———, *Bid Me to Live (A Madrigal)* (Redding Ridge, CT: Black Swan Books, 1983); ———, *Collected Poems: 1912–1944,* ed. Louis Martz (New York: New Directions, 1983); ———, *End to Torment: A Memoir of Ezra Pound* (New York: New Directions, 1979); ———, *The Gift* (New York: New Directions, 1982); ———, "H.D. by Delia Alton" (*Iowa Review* 16 [Fall 1986]); ———, *Helen in Egypt* (New York: New Directions, 1961); ———, *Hermetic Definition* (New York: New Directions, 1972); ———, *HERmione* (New York: New Directions, 1981); ———, *Paint It Today,* ed. Cassandra Laity (New York: New York University Press, 1992); ———, *Palimpsest* (Carbondale: Southern Illinois University Press, 1968); ———, *Pilate's Wife,* ed. Joan A. Burke (New York: New Directions, 2000); ———, *Tribute to Freud* (Boston: David R. Godine, 1974); Pound, Ezra, *Literary Essays* (New York: New Directions, 1935); Williams, William Carlos, *Autobiography* (New York: New Directions, 1951). ***Selected Secondary Sources:*** Friedman, Susan Stanford, *Psyche Reborn: The Emergence of H.D.* (Bloomington: Indiana University Press, 1981); ———, *Penelope's Web: Gender, Modernity, H.D.'s Fiction* (New York: Cambridge University Press, 1990); Gregory, Eileen, *H.D. and Hellenism: Classic Lines* (New York: Cambridge University Press, 1997); Gubar, Susan, "The Echoing Spell of H.D.'s *Trilogy*," in *Signets: Reading H.D.*, ed. Susan Friedman and Rachel Blau DuPlessis (Madison: University of Wisconsin Press, 1990); Guest, Barbara, *Herself Defined: The Poet H.D. and Her World* (New York: Doubleday, 1984); Hollenberg, Donna Krolik, *H.D. and Poets After* (Iowa City: University of Iowa Press, 2000); Morris, Adalaide, *How to Live, What to Do: H.D.'s Cultural Poetics* (Chicago: University of Illinois Press, 2003).

Donna Krolik Hollenberg

HACKER, MARILYN (1942–)

Marilyn Hacker writes almost exclusively in received forms such as the sonnet, the villanelle, the pantoum, and the sestina. Rather than constraining Hacker, these forms provide apt frameworks for the irony, brashness, playfulness, and sexuality that distinguish her poetry. In a 1996 interview on form with Annie Finch, Hacker suggested that perhaps "form can at least make a poem more accessible." It can both make it "'recognizable' as a 'poem'" and "tak[e] the power of definition out of the hands of the canonmakers" (24). This notion of accessibility seems particularly contemporary, and Hacker's poetry consistently evokes the contemporary and the immediate.

Born and educated in New York City, Hacker, the daughter of Jewish immigrants, earned a BA from New York University. She married and divorced African American novelist Samuel R. Delaney, and they have one daughter. In her exploration of the relationships among and between women, Hacker often writes to and about her daughter Iva as well as to and about her own mother and mother-in-law.

Hacker has published eleven books of poetry and a **translation** of Venus Khoury-Ghatas's poetry, *Here There Was Once a Country* (2001); she edited the *Kenyon Review* and *13th Moon,* a feminist **literary magazine**;

and she has guest-edited *Ploughshares.* Several of Hacker's volumes have won awards: *Winter Numbers* (1994), the Lenore Marshall Poetry Prize and a Lambda Literary Award; *Selected Poems, 1965–1990* (1994), the Poets' Prize; *Going Back to the River* (1990), a Lambda Award; and *Presentation Piece* (1974), the Lamont Poetry Selection of the Academy of American Poets and a National Book Award. Additional honors include the Bernard F. Conners Prize from the *Paris Review*, the John Masefield Memorial Award from the Poetry Society of America, and Guggenheim and Ingram Merrill foundation fellowships.

Besides detailing the various relationships that comprise women's lives, Hacker's work encompasses a variety of topics, including loss, death, aging, disease (HIV and breast cancer), lesbian lives, love, sex, poetry, and language. Her poems, simultaneously **narrative** and **lyrical**, often chronicle a process of living, dying, loving, mothering, and leaving. Many of her volumes contain sonnet sequences that provide a sustained treatment of these themes. In fact, *Love, Death, and the Changing of Seasons* (1987), often called a novel in sonnets, contains 175 sonnets, a few villanelles, and a rondeau all chronicling the development of a love relationship between two women, Hack, the narrator, and Rachel. As she does in most of her poems, Hacker uses the ordinary and the daily in order to reveal the complexities of living, and, as usually happens within a Hacker poem, the ordinary becomes awesome. The poems in *Love, Death, and the Changing of Seasons* reveal the passion, desire, and pain of falling into, being in, and falling out of love. This volume possesses a colloquial tone as the poems offer the details of loving—the day-to-day routines of building, sustaining, and ending a relationship. Hacker maintains the sense of immediacy in this book that marks her previous and subsequent volumes and also presents the graphic images of sexual love characteristic of Hacker's poetry.

Selected Poems, 1965–1990 gathers poems from *Presentation Piece, Separations* (1976), *Taking Notice* (1980), *Assumptions* (1985), and *Going Back to the River* (1990). The subjects of the poems reinforce Hacker's focus on women's lives. For instance, "The Regent Park Sonnets," "Iva's Pantoum," and "Against Silence" depict the intricacies of relationships between and among women (intricacies that involve strain as well as connection). "The Callers," "Somewhere in a Turret, "Living in the Moment," and "Shirland Road" reflect the intersections of loss, love, age, and change in the fabric of women's lives. These poems also reveal the range of this poet's voice: tender, bawdy, accusatory, conciliatory, angry, concerned, introspective, mournful, hopeful, and seductive. Hacker harnesses these tones with the tight structures of forms. The poet identifies a tension that arises between form and the response to a poem, and she sees "that tension as productive of [her] own best work" (Finch, 23). Hacker perceives this tension, when used by poets "with enough expertise to allow [an]

improvisatory counterform to come into play," as fruitful and daring (Finch, 23). The intensity of Hacker's voices and the sometimes subtle and sometimes blatant corporeality of the images strain against the poem's form to produce poetry that engages us intellectually, emotionally, and physically.

Throughout her oeuvre, Hacker relies upon the details of life in order to present the business of living. In *Winter Numbers*, she investigates the importance of numbers as we age. She asks, what do the numbers (ages, years, hours) mean? The sonnet sequence "Winter Cancer" reveals the numbers that mark the progress of breast cancer—the weight of a breast, the years one may or may not live. *Winter Numbers* continues Hacker's concern with death and endings, the death of friends and the ending of relationships: "Year's End" laments **Audre Lorde**'s too-early death from cancer while celebrating her life. As she looks beyond the literal meaning of numbers in our lives, Hacker seeks a language through which to make sense of change.

Her attention seldom wavers from the importance of finding the right word, the right vocabulary with which to present the process of living. *Squares and Courtyards* (2000) and *Desesperanto: Poems 1999–2002* (2003) highlight the significance of language. From the opening poem in *Desesperanto*, "Elegy for a Solider," dedicated to **June Jordan**, Hacker writes of the "power, terror / in words" (17), and she identifies poets as the voice and conscience of nations. The title of this volume combines the Spanish *esperar* (hope) with the French *desespoir* (to lose heart), a wordplay by which Hacker insists that words matter while simultaneously acknowledging the particularity, rather than the universality, of language.

Further Reading. *Selected Primary Sources:* Hacker, Marilyn, *Desesprenato: Poems 1999–2000* (New York: Norton, 2003); ———, *Going Back to the River* (New York: Random House, 1990); ———, *Love, Death, and the Changing of Seasons* (New York: Norton, 1986); ———, *Presentation Piece* (New York: Viking Press, 1974); ———, *Selected Poems 1965–1990* (New York: Norton, 1994); ———, *Separations* (New York: Knopf, 1976); ———, *Squares and Courtyards* (New York: Norton, 2000); ———, *Winter Numbers* (New York: Norton, 1994). ***Selected Secondary Sources:*** Finch, Annie, "An Interview on Form" (*American Poetry Review* 25.3 [1996]: 23–27); Honicker, Nancy, "Marilyn Hacker's *Love, Death, and the Changing of Seasons*: Writing/Living within Formal Constraints," in *Freedom and Form: Essays in Contemporary American Poetry*, ed. Esther Giger and Salska Agnieszka (Lodz, Poland: Wydawnictwo Uniwersytetut Lodzkiego, 1998, 94–103); Keller, Lynn, "Measured Feet 'In Gender-Bender Shoes': The Politics of Poetic Form in Marilyn Hacker's *Love, Death, and the Changing of Seasons*," in *Feminist Measures: Soundings in Poetry and*

Theory, ed. Lynn Keller and Christanne Miller (Ann Arbor: University of Michigan Press, 1994, 260–286).

Catherine Cucinella

HADAS, RACHEL (1948–)

One of the most prolific of the **New Formalists**, Rachel Hadas uses her ample gifts for meter and rhyme to explore mourning and memory in her poetry. In her witnessing of the death of parents and friends, Hadas testifies to the ways in which her life has been touched by those around her, and in her meditations on marriage and motherhood, she employs **poetic form** to unearth new facets of domestic life.

Born in 1948 in New York, New York, Rachel Hadas, the daughter of a classical scholar and a Latin teacher, was raised in Manhattan near Columbia University, surrounded by intellectuals. She attended Harvard, where she studied classics and took her first poetry writing course from **Robert Fitzgerald**. Between her undergraduate and graduate work, Hadas spent several years living on the Greek island of Samos with her then-husband Stavros Kondylis, with whom she ran an olive oil press. After the press was mysteriously destroyed in a fire, Hadas was tried for and acquitted of arson and then returned to the United States to pursue an MA in poetry from Johns Hopkins University and a Ph.D. in comparative literature from Princeton University. Since that time, Hadas has published nine volumes of poetry, as well as **translations** from Latin, French, and modern Greek poetry and two books of criticism, one on the poetry of **Robert Frost** and George Seferis, and the other titled *Merrill, Cavafy, Poems, and Dreams* (2000). In addition, Hadas published two collections of essays in the 1990s, *The Double Legacy* (1995) and *Living in Time* (1990), and an anthology of poems written by students in the poetry workshops she conducted for people living with AIDS. Hadas began teaching English at Rutgers University in 1980.

Hadas's sojourn in Greece heavily influenced her first poetry collection, the chapbook *Starting from Troy* (1975). These early poems, which already show Hadas's interest in poetic form, often allude to classical literature and incorporate Greek words. Dedicated to her father, who died suddenly when Hadas was seventeen, the poems in this collection begin the elegiac work for which Hadas is best known; as she writes in "Daddy," "Elegies / were all around me." Even posthumously, Hadas's father and his love of literature remain a strong influence on Hadas's work, as is evident in poems like "That Time, This Place," which compares her father to other "departed heroes," and "Daughters and Others," in which the words of Lucia Joyce echo Hadas's own sentiment: "They buried father, but he's not dead. / He's watching us all."

In the first section of *Slow Transparency* (1983), Hadas's first book-length work, Hadas continues to incorporate imagery and subjects acquired during her stay in Greece, which Hadas describes as "Eden, oasis, exile, island, desert." In the second section, Hadas considers language and poetry as subjects for poems before turning in the third section to a series of poems about life in rural Vermont, where Hadas lives when not teaching.

Dedicated to her son, Jonathan, Hadas's third collection, *A Son from Sleep* (1987), takes up themes of motherhood and domesticity in a language more accessible than that in her previous works. Though several poems in this book refer to Greece, most of the poems deal with more immediate emotional landscapes, as in "That Walk Away as One: A Marriage Brood." This ten-part poem is one of the first of Hadas's **long poems**, which grow increasingly prevalent in her later collections.

The title of Hadas's fourth volume of poetry, *Pass It On* (1989), refers to the ways in which knowledge is passed down through generations, whether through family ties or through books or classrooms. Meter and rhyme predominate in this collection, which begins with a thirteen-part sequence, "The Fields of Sleep (Summer)," and moves through three more seasonal poems.

Mirrors of Astonishment (1992) continues the work of the previous collection, this time in the form of a triptych in which the opening and closing sections consist of longer poetic sequences and the middle section offers mainly shorter lyrics. "Art" and "On Poetry," two of the poems in the first section, explore the role of the poet and the possible ways in which poetry may be made. Though the lyrics of the second section are less thematically unified, the focus of the final section is evident in the titles of the works: "Desire," "Happiness," "Love." Throughout the book, however, Hadas probes the wounds of loss and seeks in language some route to healing.

After witnessing the deaths of her mother, her friend David Kalstone, and several of her students from the Gay Men's Health Crisis Workshop, Hadas wrote *The Empty Bed* (1995), elegizing Hadas's lost loved ones while working through the loneliness of surviving so many deaths. These poems frequently deal with the practicalities of death, from retrieving her mother's body from the hospital to removing her mother's belongings. Though, in these poems, "Only for grief is our capacity / limitless," such grief is held in check by the formal craft of the poems, which are written in a variety of forms, many of them rhymed.

Halfway Down the Hall: New and Selected Poems (1998) provides a retrospective of the first twenty-three years of Hadas's career, as well as more than thirty poems making their first appearance in this collection. The new poems hint at the work that will come in *Indelible* (2001), in which Hadas returns to the **narrative** and **free-verse** forms employed in some of her earlier collections, incorporating them alongside rhymed quatrains, blank verse, and a sestina. As in earlier works, Hadas makes reference in these poems to classical literature and draws on reading and writing, love, and memories of her father as subject matter for this collection.

Laws, Hadas's 2004 collection, uses literary terminology and literature itself as a launching pad for many of the poems. In the book's first section, Hadas works through the significance of allegory, simile, synecdoche, and metaphor, among other poetic building blocks. In other poems, she takes the work of other authors, ranging from Homer to Cavafy to **Plath**, to decipher the importance of writing in her life. In the second section, Hadas returns to familiar territory: birth, elegy, and "my father writing letters against time."

Further Reading. *Selected Primary Sources:* Hadas, Rachel, *The Double Legacy* (Winchester, MA: Faber & Faber, 1995); ———, *The Empty Bed* (Middletown, CT: Wesleyan University Press, 1995); ———, *Halfway Down the Hall: New and Selected Poems* (Hanover, NH: Wesleyan University Press, 1998); ———, *Indelible* (Middletown, CT: Wesleyan University Press, 2001); ———, *Laws* (Lincoln, NE: Zoo Press, 2004); ———, *Living in Time* (New Brunswick, NJ: Rutgers University Press, 1990); ———, *Merrill, Cavafy, Poems, and Dreams* (Ann Arbor: University of Michigan Press, 2000); ———, *Mirrors of Astonishment* (New Brunswick, NJ: Rutgers University Press, 1992); ———, *Pass It On* (Princeton, NJ: Princeton University Press, 1989); ———, *A Son from Sleep* (Middletown, CT: Wesleyan University Press, 1987); ———, *Slow Transparency* (Middletown, CT: Wesleyan University Press, 1983); ———, *Starting from Troy* (Boston: David Godine, 1975). *Selected Secondary Sources:* Benfey, Christopher, "From the Greek" (*Parnassus: Poetry in Review* 16.2 [1991]: 405–414); Brame, Gloria Glickstein, "Rachel Hadas: A Poet's Life: An Interview with Rachel Hadas" (*ELF: Eclectic Literary Forum* 7.1 [Spring 1997]: 6–11); Helle, Anita, "Elegy as History: Three Women Poets 'By the Century's Deathbed'" (*South Atlantic Review* 61.2 [Spring 1996]: 51–68).

Jennifer Perrine

HAGEDORN, JESSICA TARAHATA (1949–)

An influential Filipino American writer, Jessica Hagedorn is a poet, novelist, playwright, musician, and performance artist. Her interests in music, theater, and film infuse her writing. Hagedorn writes from a postcolonial, diasporic aesthetic. Her work has been praised by critics for its rhythmic, voice-driven lyricism but criticized for inconsistent quality. Hagedorn's early career was nurtured in the frenzied and euphoric San Francisco literary and music scene during the late 1960s and 1970s. Her work is often set in raw urban settings and incorporates musical elements and pop culture references within its explorations of sexuality, gender, drug use, political corruption, and ethnic identity. Hagedorn's influences include diverse figures such as Gabriel García Márquez, Bienvenido Santos, **Amiri Baraka**, **Victor Hernandez Cruz**, **Nikki Giovanni**, **Allen Ginsberg**, and N.V.M. Gonzalez.

Jessica Hagedorn was born in Manila in the Philippines in 1949. She grew up under the Ferdinand Marcos dictatorship and describes her upbringing as "typically colonial and Catholic" ("Exile Within," 174). During her youth, Hagedorn's family supported her writing and other artistic pursuits even if they did not take them altogether seriously. Hagedorn's maternal grandfather was an author, and she frequently cites him as a factor in her own determination to become a writer. Hagedorn's early education in the Philippines was excellent, though traditionally Eurocentric, and she was well read in canonical literature by her teenage years. In 1963, at the age of fourteen, she immigrated to the United States with her mother after her parents separated. Hagedorn credits the move with allowing her the freedom and independence she did not have in the Philippines. Mother and daughter settled in San Francisco and Hagedorn finished high school four years later in 1967. She then studied acting and theater arts at the American Conservatory Theater in San Francisco for two years.

Hagedorn became active in San Francisco's Kearny Street Writers' Workshop and writes of 1973 as the year in which she began to think of herself as a Filipino American writer. The year 1973 also marked her first major publication. A selection of her poems, titled "The Death of Anna May Wong," appeared in the collection *Four Young Women: Poems by Jessica Tarahata Hagedorn, Alice Karly, Barbara Szerlip, and Carol Tinker.* Poet and translator **Kenneth Rexroth**, a leading figure of the **San Francisco Renaissance** and an important writer during the emergence of the **Beat** movement, edited the volume. Rexroth had become Hagedorn's friend and mentor soon after her move to San Francisco, and he encouraged her involvement with contemporary literary circles. During 1974–1975, Hagedorn became interested in the fusion of music and poetry and started a band called the West Coast Gangster Choir, with which she performed until 1978. In 1978 her friendship and theatrical collaborations with Ntozake Shange and Thulani Davis prompted her to move to New York City. She fell in love with New York and made the move a permanent one. Hagedorn reformed her band in the city and renamed it simply the Gangster Choir.

Hagedorn continued to experiment with different artistic forms including poetry, prose, music, film, and theater throughout the 1970s and 1980s, publishing *Dangerous Music,* a collection of poetry and short stories, in 1975, and *Pet Food and Tropical Apparitions,* which included the novella *Pet Food* and various poems, in 1981. When she decided to work seriously on her first novel, *Dogeaters*, Hagedorn disbanded the Gangster Choir and focused solely on her writing and her family. *Dogeaters*, which derives its title from a derogatory term for Filipinos, is set in Manila under the Marcos dictatorship and was published in 1990 to critical acclaim. The novel earned a nomination for the National Book Award and won an American Book Award. *Danger and Beauty*, a collection of new and previously published poetry and prose, followed in 1993. The volume was republished in 2002 with added material, including her response to the events of September 11, 2001. Hagedorn also edited and contributed to the important anthology *Charlie Chan Is Dead: An Anthology of Contemporary Asian American Fiction* in 1993. The anthology was unique in its eclecticism and was the first collection of its kind. Her next novel, *The Gangster of Love* (1996), addressed issues of cross-cultural identity and assimilation as it followed its Filipina protagonist Rocky from Manila to San Francisco and New York and back to the Philippines. Hagedorn's 2003 novel *Dream Jungle* explores Filipino identity as it details a young girl's sexual exploitation and a corrupt political regime's elaborate scheme to "discover" an invented lost tribe.

"Magic realism" and "surrealism" are terms often used to describe Hagedorn's writing style—dense, improbable, humorous, and authentic all at once. Her work employs collage, juxtaposing music and poetry with cinema and prose. Hagedorn views her pastiche style as emerging from the "hereditary mosaic" of Filipino culture and consciousness ("Exile Within," 175).

The colonial history of the Philippines (colonized first by Spain, then held as a U.S. territory) surfaces repeatedly in Hagedorn's work. Hagedorn weaves this history of colonization with vivid pop culture images in much of her early poetry. "Filipino Boogie," written in 1971 and originally published in *Four Young Women*, tackles the influence of Hollywood stereotypes and expectations for cultural assimilation. In the poem a youthful narrator rejects Hollywood's depiction of minorities on screen, cutting up a Dale Evans cowgirl skirt given to her by her mother: "(don't give me no bullshit fringe, / mama)." In her work, Hagedorn invokes images she encountered during her childhood in the Philippines: "Hollywood movies featuring yellowface, blackface, and redface actors giving me their versions of myself" (*Charlie Chan*, xxii).

Religion, especially the Catholicism brought to the Philippines by Spanish colonizers, comprises a major thematic element in Hagedorn's poetry. "Souvenirs," an important poem from her *Dangerous Music* collection, reveals a dark link between religion and colonization. This poem juxtaposes revisionist Eurocentric history with the fetishization of American popular culture in the Philippines and links the Marcos dictatorship and martial law of Hagedorn's childhood with the oppressiveness of colonization.

Hagedorn's writing becomes increasingly lyrical in *Pet Food and Tropical Apparitions*, and the surreal novella *Pet Food*, with its vivid cast of characters, has come to be seen as a precursor to Hagedorn's first novel, *Dogeaters*. The poems in this volume reflect her determination to wed music and poetry both in style and in references. "Motown / Smokey Robinson" joins the fate of a young Filipina immigrant who fails to find greater opportunities or a life less ordinary in the United States with the popular music of the time.

Some of Hagedorn's later poems are included in the final section of *Danger and Beauty*, titled "New York peep show: 1982–2001." These display both Hagedorn's familiar magic realism and her exploration of motherhood. "Skull Food #2" juxtaposes images of Ferdinand and Imelda Marcos hopping on a New York City bus with those of women rushing to meet their violent lovers; the prose piece "Notes from a New York Diary" compares the September 11 terrorist attacks to strife in the Philippines, "where the surreal and the real are one and the same . . . thirty years in New York has made me soft— . . . I thought I lived in the toughest city in the world and was therefore safe." Hagedorn continues to live and work in New York and has said she "will probably write about the culture of exile and homesickness in one form or another until the day I die; it is my personal obsession, and it fuels my work" ("Exile Within," 178).

Further Reading. *Selected Primary Sources:* Hagedorn, Jessica, ed., Introduction, in *Charlie Chan Is Dead: An Anthology of Contemporary Asian American Fiction* (New York: Penguin Books, 1993); ———, *Danger and Beauty* (New York: Penguin Books, 1993); ———, *Dangerous Music* (San Francisco: Momo's Press, 1975); ———, *Dogeaters* (New York: Pantheon Books, 1990); ———, *Dream Jungle* (New York: Viking, 2003); ———, *Four Young Women: Poems by Jessica Tarahata Hagedorn, Alice Karle, Barbara Szerlip, and Carol Tinker*, ed. Kenneth Rexroth (New York: McGraw-Hill, 1973); ———, *The Gangster of Love* (Boston: Houghton Mifflin, 1996); ———, *Pet Food and Tropical Apparitions* (San Francisco: Momo's Press, 1981). ***Selected Secondary Sources:*** Bonetti, Kay, "Interview with Jessica Hagedorn," in *Conversations with American Novelists: The Best Interviews from* The Missouri Review *and the American Audio Prose Library* (Columbia: University of Missouri Press, 1997); Evangelista, Susan, "Jessica Hagedorn and Manila Magic," (*MELUS* 18.4 [Winter 1993]: 41–52); Hagedorn, Jessica, "The Exile Within/The Question of Identity," in *The State of Asian America: Activism and Resistance in the 1990s*, ed. Karin Aguilar–San Juan (Boston: South End Press, 1994, 173–182).

Jessica Metzler

HAHN, KIMIKO (1955–)

Kimiko Hahn has published six collections of poetry, including the prize-winning *Earshot* (1992) and *The Unbearable Heart* (1996). Hahn's innovative and emotionally urgent poetry has been praised by Juliana Chang in her review of *Earshot* as among the most compelling **Asian American** writing of our time. Hahn's writing is strongly intertextual, responding to a large range of sources, from the Japanese classic *The Tale of Genji* to daily e-mail messages. By juxtaposing the modern and the classical, the personal and the literary, Hahn creates a poetic voice at once private and politically significant. Her poetics of intertexuality and multivocality illustrates how racism and sexism have been twinned in the representation of an orientalized femininity.

Kimiko Hahn was born on July 5, 1955, in Mt. Kisco, New York, to a Japanese American mother and German American father, both visual artists. She majored in English and East Asian Studies at the University of Iowa and graduated with a BA in 1977. Hahn pursued graduate study at Columbia University and received her MA in Japanese literature in 1982. Then she settled down in the New York City area, devoting herself to writing and teaching. Deeply interested in and influenced by her ethnic heritage and her undergraduate and graduate studies, Hahn, though writing primarily in English, often incorporates Asian languages, literatures, and philosophies into her work.

Hahn's poems were first collected in book form in *We Stand Our Ground* (1988), a collaboration with two other women poets, Gale Jackson and Susan Sherman. Beginning with her two independent collections *Air Pocket* (1989) and *Earshot* (1992), Hahn developed a style that combined the immediacy and directness of the **New York School** with a complexity derived from her concerns about the relationships among language, agency, and racialized female subjectivity. In *Earshot*, which won the Theodore Roethke Memorial Poetry Prize, Hahn interweaves and contrasts fragments from diverse sources. One of the sources inspiring Hahn most is *The Tale of Genji*, written by Lady Murasaki Shikibu. Hahn identifies her poetics with the female tradition of the Japanese Heian period (794–1192), the age in which Murasaki wrote *Genji*: "I connect to that century / as after breath is knocked out / we suck it in." However, with the narrator's comments and questions—"She made her his. . . . Why did a woman write this? Did she speak from the small heart?"—Hahn explicitly makes the distinction between "I" and "she," indicating her own suspicion and indignation that "she," the author Murasaki Shikibu, might not have spoken for "her," the girl whom the character Genji adopted and who later became his wife. *Genji* offers Hahn the opportunity to address the continuum of women's psychological and emotional experiences and to problematize the convoluted relationship among the contemporary female reader, the ancient Japanese woman writer, and the heroine.

Hahn's third volume *The Unbearable Heart*, a 1996 recipient of the American Book Award, consists of poems propelled by the sudden death of her mother in an automobile accident. It is a series of moving **elegies** with insightful meditations on motherhood and mortality. In the long prose poem "The Hemisphere: Kuchuk Hanem," Hahn incorporates Japanese literary texts and Western theoretical discourse and investigates the possibilities of language in undermining gender-power relations. The poem is comprised of short, discontinuous segments spoken by four voices, those of Edward Said, Gustave Flaubert, Kuchuk Hanem (an Egyptian prostitute who appears in Flaubert's travelogues), and a shape-changing Asian American female narrator. After the opening image of "I" as a four-year-old child seeking her mother, Hahn introduces excerpts from *Orientalism*, in which Said notes that Flaubert's privilege not only "allowed him to possess Kuchuk Hanem, but speak for her." This is followed by Kuchuk Hanem's first-person narrative ("Flaubert boasts on his own behalf. My image doesn't belong to me") that contrasts Flaubert's ("the oriental woman is no more than a machine"). This complex ordering of the poem, which entwines the personal experience of Hahn's mother's death with the experience of representing raced and gendered images in Orientalist texts (both involving the possibility of rendering absence through presence), creates a dialogue by which Hahn manages to resist the European male authors' reductive representations of Asian femininity.

The fourth collection, *Volatile*, and the fifth, *Mosquito and Ant*, were both published in 1999. In *Volatile*, one finds not only the personal echo of the lost mother but also political remonstration against male tyranny. Hahn quotes feminist writers **Adrienne Rich** and Elaine Showalter, questioning the status quo of any social or religious order promoted by men to enslave women. The title *Mosquito and Ant* refers to a secret script used by ancient Chinese women called "nushu" for private correspondence. In the title poem, Hahn tries to reclaim the lost text of women when she tells us, "I want my letters to resemble / tiny ants scrawled across this page" and "mosquitoes as they loop / around the earlobe with their noise." Some poems are written like adapted "nushu," taking the form of confidential letters to "L," a secret correspondent to whom the poet turns for counsel. Hahn's appropriation of Asian forms of women's writing like "nushu" and "suiyitsu" (casual notes of random private thoughts) in these two 1999 books carries her earlier themes into more intimate realms.

In her 2002 book of poetry *The Artist's Daughter*, Hahn seems to distance herself from Asian American concerns. This book fiercely examines extremes of human experience, from cannibalism to necrophilia. In sources that range from German fairy tales to the *New York Times*; she deploys Freudian psychoanalytic precepts, reflects on Lacanian poststructuralist images of "mirror" and "other," and quotes from Gray's *Anatomy*. Meanwhile, she sets mundane affairs of life side by side with monstrous behavior, enabling her to trace a shifting line between reality and imagination, love and perversity, bereavement and healing.

Further Reading. *Selected Primary Sources:* Hahn, Kimiko, *Air Pocket* (Brooklyn, NY: Hanging Loose Press, 1989); ———, *The Artist's Daughter* (New York: W.W. Norton, 2002); ———, *Earshot* (Brooklyn, NY: Hanging Loose Press, 1992); ———, *Mosquito and Ant* (New York: Norton, 1999); ———, *The Unbearable Heart* (New York: Kaya, 1995); ———, *Volatile* (Brooklyn, NY: Hanging Loose Press, 1999). ***Selected Secondary Sources:*** Chang, Juliana, "Review of *Earshot*" (*Amerasia Journal* 21.1 [1995]: 188–192); Yamamoto, Traise, *Masking Selves, Making Subjects: Japanese American Women, Identity, and the Body* (Berkeley: University of California Press, 1999); Zhou, Xiaojing, "Intercultural Strategies in Asian American Poetry," in *Re-placing America: Conversations and Contestations*, ed. Ruth Hsu, Cynthia Franklin, and Suzanne Kosanke (Honolulu: University of Hawaii Press, 2000, 92–100).

Jun Lei

HAINES, JOHN (1924–)

John Haines homesteaded in the wilderness seventy miles from Fairbanks, Alaska, for over twenty years beginning in 1947. Though Haines intended to live off the land and to paint or sculpt during the long winters, Alaska became instead the birthplace of his life as a poet. Closely identified with Alaska, Haines has been called a nature writer and a regional poet, yet his poetry has always been more than description of moose and caribou. Haines's work revolves around issues of community: the human relationship to nature—plants, animals, and geological and climatic forces—as well as each person's relationship to other humans and to the historical chain of social responsibility. Hanes is an accomplished critic and essayist, and much of his writing in both prose and verse expands upon his Alaskan experiences and discusses art, artists, and the life of the imagination, as well as poetry and politics.

Haines was born June 29, 1924, in Norfolk, Virginia, to John Meade Haines and Helen M. (Donaldson) Haines. Because Haines's father was an officer in the Navy, the family traveled extensively from port to port, residing in Hawai'i, California, and Washington, as well as in Rhode Island and New Hampshire. Following graduation from St. John's College High School in Washington, D.C., Haines enlisted in the Navy and served for three years during World War II. Haines studied both painting and sculpture at three East Coast art schools (National Art School in Washington, D.C., 1946–1947; American University, 1948–1949; and Hans Hofmann School of Fine Arts in New York City, 1950–1952). Haines then chose to return to his Alaskan homestead, where he lived a strenuous, frugal, and primarily solitary life, and where he remained until 1969. In 1969 Haines began serving as a visiting professor and lecturer at academic institutions across the United States and began acquiring numerous awards, including two Guggenheim fellowships, an NEA fellowship, and the prestigious Academy Award in Literature from the American Academy of Arts. He then settled into homes in Alaska and Montana.

The poems of *Winter News* (1966), Haines's first book publication, take hunting, trapping and skinning, gathering berries, the lore of old-time trappers and miners, and the solitude and loneliness of the long dark winters as their subjects. In "Poem of the Forgotten" Haines characterizes his Alaskan isolation as being "well quit of the world," while "Divided, the Man Is Dreaming" describes the paradox of a peaceful and contemplative man meeting the requirements of life as a hunter-gatherer, combining something akin to a primitive blood-lust with an almost monastic respect for the sanctity of life.

Like most of Haines's later work, the poems in *Winter News* are brief **lyrics** with short, breath-controlled lines. Replete with alliteration, they incorporate surrealistic or **deep images** and metaphors derived from myth and local history. During those Alaskan winters when Haines turned from painting to poetry, he read and was influenced by **Kenneth Rexroth**'s translations in *One Hundred Poems from the Chinese* and **Robert Bly**'s magazine *The Fifties*.

In an interview with Arthur Coffin, Haines reminisced that an attraction of the Alaskan wilderness was that it is imbued with "the silence in which it is possible to hear many things often disregarded" (54). "Listening in October" describes his cabin, the "quiet house," as a place where one can hear "the journeys of the soul." Sound, when it occurs in Haines's poetry, as in "And When the Green Man Comes," is frequently the "clamor of bedlam."

Haines's next books, *The Stone Harp* (1971) and *Cicada* (1977), were published after he left Alaska and expressed his dismay with conditions that he found in the lower states and the world, from environmental concerns to the Vietnam conflict. His references in "In the Middle of America" to "mass refusals, flag burnings, / and people who stand and fall" suggest Haines's anti-war sentiments. Poems such as "The Legend of Paper Plates" and "Dreams of a Cardboard Lover" suggest a deep dissatisfaction with America's disposable culture.

In "The Hole in the Bucket," an essay first published in 1975 and reprinted in *Living Off the Country* (1981),

Haines criticized late twentieth-century American poetry for its "thinness, sameness, and dullness," noting that it was **confessional**, that it promoted a cult of personality, and that it lacked the great imaginings and ideas found in the poetry of **Ezra Pound** or **Wallace Stevens**. Other essays and personal memoirs recounting the outdoor education and the human and animal encounters of his homesteading years have been collected in *The Stars, the Snow, the Fire* (1989) and *Fables and Distances* (1996).

New Poems, 1980–88 (1990) introduces **long poems** consisting of numbered sections. Contemplative sequences such as "Days of Edward Hopper," "Meditation on a Skull Carved in Crystal," and "Death and the Miser" explore the value, indeed the necessity, of art and the life of the imagination in a modern world of greed, impermanence, and superficiality. In the preface to *For the Century's End: Poems 1990–1999* (2001), Haines calls the political subject matter of many of his recent poems "inevitable, an element not to be refused." Though angry at the betrayal of the American Dream, the cataclysm of world wars, and the endless procession of refugees, Haines does not sink into total despair. "Poem for the End of the Century" concludes with an exhortation to "Awake!" because "tomorrow the sun will return." Haines's poems and prose trace an arc from a young man's idealism to an elder poet's considered contemplation of a troubled world.

Further Reading. *Selected Primary Sources:* Haines, John, *For the Century's End: Poems 1990–1999* (Seattle: University of Washington Press, 2001); ———, *The Owl in the Mask of the Dreamer: Collected Poems* (St. Paul, MN: Graywolf Press, 1993); ———, *Winter News* (Middletown, CT: Wesleyan University Press, 1966). *Selected Secondary Sources:* Bezner, Kevin, and Kevin Walzer, eds., *The Wilderness of Vision: On the Poetry of John Haines* (Brownsville, OR: Story Line Press, 1996); Coffin, Arthur, "An Interview with John Haines" (*Jeffers Studies* 2.4 [Fall 1998]: 47–56).

Diane Warner

HALE, SARAH JOSEPHA (1788–1879)

Sarah J. Hale was an eminent author, poet, and editor of the nineteenth century. Born Sarah Josepha Buell in New Hampshire on October 24, 1788, Hale was schooled primarily by her mother and older brother, studying everything from philosophy, Latin, and Greek to geography, although, like all women of the time, she was not allowed to attend college. She married David Hale in 1822, at the age of thirty-four, and together they had five children. She worked until the age of eighty-nine, retiring from the magazine *Godey's Lady's Book* in December of 1877, the year before her death.

Hale's broad intellectual interests helped make possible her varied and lengthy career. She spent fifty years as a magazine editor, editing the *Ladies' Magazine* of Boston from 1828 to 1836 and *Godey's Lady's Book* of Philadelphia from 1837 to 1877. As an editor, Hale was influential and successful. *Godey's Lady's Book* had 150,000 subscribers just before the Civil War, more than any other publication could claim at that time.

Hale's magazines published writers of such stature as **Edgar Allen Poe**, Harriet Beecher Stowe, **Lydia Sigourney**, and **Nathaniel Hawthorne**. Hale herself was widely published. She reviewed thousands of books and contributed her own poetry and fiction to magazines. As a poet, she penned seven volumes of poetry, two of which were written for children. She wrote six books of fiction; books on housekeeping and cooking; and a 900-page reference book on women in history.

A popular notion in the Victorian era was that of "separate spheres," which advocated women's dominion of (and restriction to) domestic, private space, while men were to occupy the public sphere. Hale's participation in politics and literature, and her leading role in the periodical industry, challenged the paradigm of "separate spheres," even as some of her writing promoted it. Hale was an avid believer in and proponent of essential gender difference, which she maintained and developed throughout her writing. Yet she found women capable, intelligent, and resourceful, rather than dependent. Her thoughts on the proper role of women in society were complex and in some cases changeable.

For example, Hale maintained that there was a biological basis for the difference between men's work and women's work, but wrote of the higher complexity of women's work in comparison to men's: Men "handle the spade or plough, but women must cook, clean, raise and husband animals, harvest, and provide clothing." Hale venerated domestic work as "art," with all the social and cultural significance of that word.

Hale mobilized women into various aspects of politics. She formed the Boston Women's Group in 1833, which worked to provide Boston's seamen, their wives, and their children with various basic necessities that had previously been missing. She and the other women members opened a cooperative that sold clothing made by the sailors' wives. Hale also championed women's roles and abilities as teachers and midwives, even declaring their natural skills ideal for becoming physicians. She liked the term "doctress," and indeed preferred the feminization of any word when it applied to women,, "mingling," she wrote, "the woman and her vocation, tenderness with respect." But she opposed women's suffrage and women's participation in political parties, calling in an 1872 *Godey's* editorial for "every woman who believes the mission of her sex to be in a sphere apart from politics to speak out."

Much of Hale's own writing works to validate, even exalt, the place of women in society, while setting forth an ideal of republican motherhood. Her poem "The Empire of Woman" is made up of five connected sonnets: The first serves as an introduction, while each of the following four explores a different role of Woman—Daughter, Sister, Wife, and Mother. Hale opens with "Woman's Empire Defined," in which she describes Woman as the gentler, purer complement to Man in a difficult and temptation-ridden world. Man's domain is "the outward World, for rugged Toil designed," whereas Woman's empire is "holier, more refined." Men battle in the "outward World," a public realm of work, politics, power, and war. But the "empire of Woman" is the soul, that most difficult and crucial locus. The soul, Hale thought,

Will Woman's sweet and gentle power obey . . .
Her love sow flowers along life's thorny way;
Her star-bright faith lead up towards heaven's goal.

The poem continues with examples of luminous and legendary women: Pocahontas, the Daughter, who "shook a soul where pity's pulse seemed dead"; Lazarus's sister, whose "winning smile . . . will bring / A change o'er all his nature"; the Wife, Lady Rachel Russell, who advocated staunchly for her husband during his imprisonment in the Tower of London ("she, angel-like, his sinking soul sustains"); and finally, the Mother, a more generalized category (the most exalted, but open to any woman who may strive for it). Through the love and care of the Mother, Hale writes, the Empire of Man is built. A mother's love can "fashion genius, form the soul for good, / Inspire a West, or train a Washington!" The "West" referred to here is the artist Benjamin West, who professed (as Hale footnotes), "My mother's kiss made me a painter." But, given the poem's provenance in the early nineteenth century, it is impossible not to feel a greater resonance in this line, reading it as referring to woman's role in shaping the future of America, the governance of her "deathless love" making the Empire great.

Many of Hale's poems touch on similar themes, in particular the special purity and innocence of soul present in young girls. For Hale, young women are a distilled, rarified form of Woman, an idea she followed in poems such as the now-famous "Mary's Lamb," sung by schoolchildren the world over, and "The Silk-Worm," in which a young girl cradles and admires an insect for which the author herself admits revulsion. This young girl is "Just at the age when childhood's grace / And maiden softness blend," and she innocently plays with the creature, allowing it even to crawl upon her cheek, both insect and author, apparently, moved by the girl's gentleness. Hale urges the reader to conceive a world wherein "every harmless thing" is viewed as bearing "the mighty Maker's seal." Ultimately, it is the tender compassion of a woman that, like the Mother in "The Empire of Woman," has the power to "form the soul for good."

Further Reading. *Selected Primary Source:* Hale, Sarah J., *The Genius of Oblivion* (Concord, NH: J.B. Moore, 1823). *Selected Secondary Sources:* Burt, Olive, *First Woman Editor: Sarah J. Hale* (New York: Messner, 1960); Okker, Patricia, *Our Sister Editors: Sarah J. Hale and the Tradition of Nineteenth-Century American Women Editors* (Athens: University of Georgia Press, 1995).

Andria Williams

HALL, DONALD (1928–)

For much of his career, Donald Hall established a reputation as the quintessential "man of letters" of his generation: a literary and cultural generalist, well connected, highly regarded, and sought after as editor, anthologist, reader, speaker, and fellow, able to support himself through writing while maintaining his commitment to poetry as the center of his output. In the later stages of his career, particularly after the death of his wife, the poet **Jane Kenyon**, he became known as one of the country's preeminent poets of grief and loss.

Hall was born on September 20, 1928 in New Haven, Connecticut, and educated at Phillips Exeter Academy and Harvard, where he edited the Harvard *Advocate* and cultivated friendships with a group of young poets who included **John Ashbery**, **Robert Bly**, **Kenneth Koch**, **Frank O'Hara**, and **Adrienne Rich**. He took his BA from Harvard in 1951, and a B.Litt. from Oxford University in 1953. At Oxford he edited a series of distinguished publications (including a stint as poetry editor of the *Paris Review*) and published the first books of Thom Gunn and Geoffrey Hill. From 1953 to 1954 he studied at Stanford with **Yvor Winters**. He taught at Harvard from 1954 to 1957 and at the University of Michigan from 1957 to 1975. He married Kirby Thompson in 1952, and they divorced in 1969. Hall then married **Jane Kenyon** in 1972; she died of cancer in 1995.

Donald Hall's awards for poetry include the Newdigate Prize from Oxford University in 1952, the Lamont Poetry Prize from the Academy of American Poets in 1955, the Edna St. Vincent Millay Award from the Poetry Society of America in 1956, the Lenore Marshall Prize in 1987, the National Book Critics Circle Award in 1988, the *Los Angeles Times* Book Prize in 1990, the Robert Frost Silver Medal from the Poetry Society of America in 1991, and the Ruth Lilly Prize in 1994. He was a National Book Award nominee in 1956, 1979, and 1993, and a Pulitzer Prize nominee in 1989. *The Oxford Book of Children's Verse in America*, which he edited, was included in the *Horn Book* Honor List for 1986. His other literary awards include the Sarah Josepha Hale Award for writings about New England in 1983, and the New England Booksellers Association Award in 1993. He was awarded

Guggenheim fellowships in 1963–1964 and 1972–1973. He was named Poet Laureate of New Hampshire in 1984–1989, and he took that title again, indefinitely, in 1995.

Hall was a youthful prodigy, publishing his first poetry at the age of sixteen. His first book, *Exiles and Marriages*, including the Newdigate Prize–winning **long poem**, *Exile*, came out as the Lamont Poetry Selection for 1955. Hall had already centered the locus of his poetic concerns on the self—home, marriage, fatherhood. In one of the most celebrated poems in the collection, he considers mortality from the point of view of a young father ("My Son, My Executioner"). He had developed a highly skilled formal style, following in the tradition of formal masters like **Robert Frost** and **Richard Wilbur**. At the same time, he was working with Robert Pack and **Louis Simpson** on an anthology, *New Poets of England and America*. Published in 1957, with a sequel in 1962, it became one of the most influential and controversial poetry books of its day, the first salvo in what became the war between the Academics and the **Beats**. It was promptly answered by Donald Allen's *The New American Poetry*. There was no overlap between the two books, but between them, they mapped the terrain of American poetry at mid-century. As all these poets moved into middle age and key Academics like Hall and **Robert Lowell** began experimenting with **free verse**, and as a younger generation emerged and drew from both preceptors, the distinctions became blurred.

His first children's book, *Andrew and the Lion Farmer*, came out in 1959; his first memoir, *String Too Short to Be Saved: Recollections of Summers on a New England Farm*, in 1961; his first book on art, *Henry Moore: The Life and Work of a Great Sculptor*, in 1966; and his first book on baseball, *Dock Ellis in the Country of Baseball*, in 1976. His publications also include numerous collections of essays on poetry and culture.

Hall was on his way to becoming one of America's foremost men of letters. He had three of the most important prerequisites: first, a wide range of interests covering both academic and popular culture; second, a fluid, intelligent, and readable style; and third, an agreeable presence and reading voice in front of an audience, at a time when public reading of poetry was becoming popular. Hall estimates that he has given as many as ten thousand public readings, and he discussed, in an interview, the effect of public **performance** on writing: "I remember a time—it was in 1959—when I was working on a poem, and there was a key word that I knew was wrong. 'Ah,' I heard myself say, 'but in a reading I can make it sound right.' And, fortunately, I caught myself. 'Uh-oh,' I remember thinking. 'Watch your ass. This can be dangerous.'"

In 1975 Hall gained a fourth and most desirable prerequisite for being a prominent man of letters: He no longer needed to be a professional at anything else. Taking the gamble that he could succeed in the literary life, he left his teaching job at the University of Michigan, where he had been since 1975, and moved to Eagle Pond Farm, the Wilmot, New Hampshire, family farm where his great-grandfather had first settled. He set up an office in the bedroom that he had used in boyhood visits to the farm and committed himself full-time to writing. He was, by that time, married to the poet Jane Kenyon, who had been his student, and she encouraged him to take the risk.

Hall's embrace of the life of letters was made no less of a gamble by the fact that his foremost commitment was always to poetry. He had produced five volumes of poetry before moving to Eagle Pond, and his reputation had been growing, but many people—including Hall himself—find his mature work from the Eagle Pond period to be his most satisfying. His 1975 poem, "Kicking the Leaves," which became the title poem of his first New Hampshire collection, originally appeared in the *New York Times*, over an author comment that the poet was taking a sabbatical from Michigan. It proved to be a lifelong sabbatical. The poem, written in the careful free verse that had become his style, takes him walking home from a Michigan football game, kicking leaves that turn over to reveal the colors of present, future, and especially the past of his family heritage. He recalls that his grandfather had died in March, at the age of seventy-seven, and thinks of his father, "dead twenty years / Coughing himself to death, at fifty-two." The death of his father, who had marked time in a job he hated, waiting for a retirement that never came provided a powerful impetus for Hall to make his move.

The transplant was successful; Hall and Kenyon made a life at Eagle Pond Farm, and Hall's following full-length poetry collection, *The Happy Man* (1986), was very much poetry of place, with the bucolic contentment of nature and farm life balanced against the predation of foxes, fishers, and coydogs. It was also the poetry of perspective: As Hall told interviewer Stephen Ratiner, "this landscape, these people, this place has been a vantage point from which to look at the place itself and at the rest of the world that I have known" (16). The vantage point was of a man, he said, living in the present moment for the first time.

In 1988 his book-length poem *The One Day*, in which sexuality, history, mortality, and spiritual fulfillment are brought together in one bed, won him the National Book Critics Circle Award. The fierce immediacy of Hall's language brought him out of the sphere of poetry and belles lettres and to the attention of rock and roll journalist Greil Marcus, who included an excerpt from the poem in his "Real Life Rock Top Ten," comparing Hall to rockers **Bob Dylan** and Johnny Rotten.

From the first, mortality had been a major theme in Hall's poetry, but it struck home with a vengeance in 1989, when he was diagnosed with colon cancer. He seemed to be in remission when the cancer metastasized to his liver in 1992. He was given scant hope of surviving, and in Hall's 1993 volume, *The Museum of Clear Ideas*, death is a close enough companion that Hall is able to treat it with grim humor, in his series of **elegies** to a fictional poet and in his baseball cycle ironically addressed to the late **Dadaist** Kurt Schwitters. Hall and Kenyon began to prepare for her life without him; one of her most celebrated poems, "Otherwise," is about the expected loss of her husband. But then, in 1994, as it began to appear that he would pull through, she was diagnosed with leukemia. Kenyon's cancer spread quickly, and in fifteen months she was dead.

The loss was devastating to Hall, especially since he and Kenyon had shared an unusual amount of their lives, even for a married couple: their rural seclusion in New Hampshire, their writing, their reading tours together. During her illness, Hall devoted himself to her. After her death, he took solace in poetry. His next book, *The Old Life* (1996), was dominated by the title poem, a tight and complex ninety-seven–page memoir in verse, which begins with his early childhood and heads inexorably toward death, though it encompasses marriage and friendship as well as loss. The book also contains the poem "Without," which was Hall's first sustained attempt to deal with the loss of Kenyon.

"Without" became the title poem of his 1998 collection of poems about Kenyon's illness, the hospital days, her death, and the experience of living without her. Written in a plain style ("He watched her chest go still. / With his thumb he closed her round brown eyes"), he charts the minutiae and the large feelings of loss and absence. While not considered by many critics to be his best work, it found a receptive audience. It became his best-selling collection and established his reputation as an elegist—a reputation not altogether unfitting; although *Without* is in many ways not representative of his generally more craftsman-like work, he has always had an elegiac strain running through his poetry.

In his next collection, *The Painted Bed*, Hall's ambivalence seemed deliberate. He began with an epigraph from the Urdu poet Faiz: "The true subject of poetry is the loss of the beloved," but in the book's first poem, "Kill the Day," he says "There is nothing so selfish as misery nor so boring, / and depression is devoted only to its own practice." The book followed both leads, containing poems of loss and grief, as well as poems of a fierce joy, including sexual joy, in the last part of life. In 2002 he published a prose memoir of Kenyon's last days, *The Best Day the Worst Day: Life With Jane Kenyon*.

Hall will be remembered for a wide range of poems and poetic voices, but probably mostly for the late ele-gies. And perhaps this will be, in the end, his preferred legacy. Hall said in an interview,

> I know that in the poems I've written since her death, I've incorporated her into me, both consciously and unconsciously. I address her, and I write about things I know she'd want to know about—the weather, the grandchildren. And she may be in the poems, too—my poems may sound more like her now. When a couple has been together for a long time, and they're close, the one that's left does tend to acquire the characteristics of the one that's gone.

Further Reading. ***Selected Primary Sources:*** Hall, Donald, *The Best Day the Worst Day: Life With Jane Kenyon* (Boston: Houghton Mifflin, 2005); ———, *Exiles & Marriages* (New York: Viking, 1955); ———, *The Happy Man* (New York: Random House, 1986); ———, *Kicking the Leaves* (New York: Harper & Row, 1968); ———, *The Museum of Clear Ideas* (Boston: Houghton Mifflin, 1993); ———, *The Old Life* (Boston: Houghton Mifflin, 1996); ———, *The One Day* (New York: Ticknor & Fields, 1988); ———, *The Painted Bed* (Boston: Houghton Mifflin, 2002); *Without* (Boston: Houghton Mifflin, 1998); Hall, Donald, Robert Pack, and Louis Simpson, eds., *New Poets of England and America* (New York: Meridian Books, 1962). ***Selected Secondary Sources:*** Gunn, Thom, "The Late Spring of Donald Hall" (*Los Angeles Times Book Review* [9 November 1989]: 10); Kelleher, Jack, ed., *Donald Hall: A Bibliographical Checklist* (Easthampton, NY: Warwick Press, 2000); McDonald, David, "Donald Hall" (*American Poetry Review* 31.1 [January/February 2002]: 17–20); Rector, Liam, ed., *The Day I Was Older: On the Poetry of Donald Hall* (Ashland, OR: Story Line Press, 1989); Richards, Tad, Interview with Donald Hall (2000), http://www.opus40.org/tadrichards/hall.html.

Tad Richards

HALLECK, FITZ-GREENE (1790–1867)

In the early nineteenth century, Fitz-Greene Halleck was America's premier poet, celebrated for his metrical elegance and good-natured satire. Associated with the "Knickerbocker" school, a loose aggregate of New York writers whose number included Washington Irving, **James Kirke Paulding**, and **Nathaniel Parker Willis**, he was—with **William Cullen Bryant**—the most accomplished figure to appear on the American scene between the Connecticut Wits (**John Trumbull, Timothy Dwight**, and **Joel Barlow**) and the younger of the **Fireside Poets**. Unlike Bryant, however, Halleck did not maintain his productivity after the 1820s. Never prolific and always diffident about publication, Halleck enjoyed a popularity based on a small number of works that saw print within a single decade, most notably "Fanny" (1819, expanded 1821), "On the Death of Joseph Rodman Drake" (1821), "Alnwick Castle" (1823), "Marco Bozzaris" (1825), the first half of "Connecticut" (1826), and "Red Jacket" (1828). Of his scanty later production, only the second half of "Connecticut" (1852) met the expectations of his public. Some attributed this near silence to a failure of ambition, others to a disaffection with the times, and still others to the responsibilities of employment. In 1832 Halleck became the personal secretary to John Jacob Astor, then the richest man in America; he was later a trustee of the Astor Library. After Astor's death in 1848, Halleck retired to his home state of Connecticut, surviving on a small annuity bequeathed him in Astor's will. A lifelong bachelor, Halleck spent his final nineteen years with his unmarried sister, Maria. In 1877, a decade after his death, his statue was erected in New York's Central Park; **Bayard Taylor** delivered the oration. Since then, Halleck's name has fallen into obscurity. Though he makes an appearance in Gore Vidal's historical novel *Burr* (1973), anthologists and literary historians have neglected his poetic contributions. Recent interest has focused instead on Halleck's conjectured homosexuality. Yet the language of his poetry remains fresh, and his disdain for high seriousness—out of fashion among the Victorians and under **modernism**—and his affection for social documentary find a twentieth-century echo in the work of the **New York School**.

Halleck was born in Guilford, Connecticut, on July 8, 1790, a descendant of the Puritan missionary John Eliot. After a perfunctory education, he became a clerk in a relative's store. In 1811, he moved to New York City, finding employment in the counting house of Jacob Barker, for whom he would work until the failure of Barker's business in the 1820s. In 1814, Halleck joined the Iron Grays, a militia comprised of men from well-to-do families, mustered to defend the city during the War of 1812. Through these business and social connections, Halleck discovered the subject of his first poetic success: the political, financial, and cultural life of New York City documented satirically in his "Croaker" poems (1819), written in collaboration with **Joseph Rodman Drake**. The series took its title from the poets' pseudonyms, adapted from Oliver Goldsmith's "The Good-Natured Man": "Croaker" (Drake), "Croaker, Junior" (Halleck), and "Croaker & Co." (Drake and Halleck together).

Halleck first met Drake in 1813; the two subsequently became known as the "Damon and Pythias" of American letters. The evidence for Halleck's homosexuality largely derives from this friendship (there is also a poem from 1811, "To Carlos Menie"—the earliest cited text in Robert K. Martin's *The Homosexual Tradition of American Poetry*). Particularly suggestive is Halleck's 1817 letter to his sister describing Drake as "perhaps the handsomest man in New York—a face like an angel, a form like an Apollo"; in this same letter, Halleck says of Drake's

wedding, where he served as groomsman, "I felt myself during the ceremony as committing a crime" (*Life and Letters*, 184). Drake's premature death (from tuberculosis) devastated Halleck, who later expressed a desire to be buried by Drake's side. His memorial poem, "On the Death of Joseph Rodman Drake," remains the most enduring reminder of either poet.

While Drake was still alive, Halleck brought out his **long poem** "Fanny" (fifty stanzas were added for a second edition). Praised a century later by **Ezra Pound**, the poem concerns a dry goods merchant who enters high society. The story, however, is but an excuse for a series of extravagant digressions in which the narrator (a bachelor, like Halleck, who prefers cigars to women) can comment freely on such topics as Tammany Hall, Wall Street, Weehawken, the tastes of the rich, and American achievements in the arts. For much of the poem, Fanny herself is "thrown / Where cheeks and roses wither—in the shade" (stanza 104), a hint of misogyny that John W.M. Hallock interprets as the poet's confession of "a lack of heterosexual identification" (77).

In 1822 Halleck toured Europe. Out of this experience came "Alnwick Castle," which contrasts "the romantic times / So beautiful in Spenser's rhymes" with Halleck's own more prosaic "age of bargaining." A few years later he published "Marco Bozzaris" (a favorite of **Emily Dickinson**), which recounts an episode from the Greek revolution. "Connecticut"—announced as a work in progress—extolled the democratic character of Halleck's home state (although, as Nelson Adkins notes, the poem contained "sufficient delineation of the harsher elements of the New England mind to make it acceptable to a New York audience" [165]). "Red Jacket" drew inspiration from Robert W. Weir's portrait of the Tuscarora chief Sagoyewatha. Other notable poems from these years include "Wyoming" (1821), a parody of Thomas Campbell's "Gertrude"; "The Discarded" (1821), a tribute to McDonald Clarke, "the mad poet of Broadway," written in Clarke's own manner; and the satires "Billingsgate McSwell" (1826) and "The Recorder" (1828) (the latter singled out by **Lydia Huntley Sigourney** in a poetic epistle celebrating Halleck's achievements). "The Field of the Grounded Arms" (1828), written in unrhymed quatrains, elicited mixed reviews but found favor in the twentieth century from **W.H. Auden**.

In his later years, Halleck resisted repeated calls to publish new poems. The rare exceptions include the second part of "Connecticut"—added after a quarter century to the abandoned first part—and "Young America" (1863), his final poem. Halleck's renewal of interest in "Connecticut" may be due to his return to Guilford after the death of Astor. The shock of return may also explain the poem's altered tone. Although run together in Halleck's *Poetical Writings*, the two parts of "Connecticut" are hardly continuous, forming separate fragments of a long poem that Halleck intended to write but never completed. The latter portion begins at stanza 13 with the remarkable lines "They burnt their last witch in CONNECTICUT / About a century and a half ago," and then continues with a rueful meditation on historical memory (including a denunciation of Cotton Mather, "who banned his living friends with shame" and then "made their death-beds beautiful with fame" [stanza 32]), before concluding with an ironical tribute to Peace and Glory. "Young America" is less successful: a heavy-handed allegory in which the eponymous hero, an adolescent boy, fends off the seductions of a preacher, a soldier, and a teacher before succumbing to marriage with a rich wife.

With the exception of the second part of "Connecticut," Halleck's best poems remain his satires. Like Byron, whose complete works he edited for the American public, Halleck had an ease with words that elevated trivialities and a gift for blending eloquence with jocularity. This genius for incongruities struck many readers, including **Edgar Allan Poe**, as a limitation or defect. Others were perplexed. William Cullen Bryant, who published many of Halleck's best-known works in the *New York Review* and *Talisman*, gave perhaps the best description of the poet's manner: "Sometimes [Halleck], with that aërial facility which is his peculiar endowment, accumulates graceful images in a strain of irony so fine that, did not the subject compel you to receive it as irony, you would take it for a beautiful passage of serious poetry" (1:383). Halleck's personality inspired no such perplexity. According to Evert A. Duyckinck, Halleck's "champagne-talk was fresh and sparkling, bubbling from the fount of his generous nature" (quoted in Adkins, 274), and Poe, who disputed Halleck's poetic achievements, nonetheless found him "a man to be admired, respected, but more especially beloved" (1158). A record of Halleck's personality survives in his correspondence; the wit of these letters partly compensates for the paucity of poems from Halleck's final years.

Further Reading. *Selected Primary Sources:* Wilson, James Grant, *The Life and Letters of Fitz-Greene Halleck* (New York: D. Appleton & Co., 1869); ———, ed., *The Poetical Writings of Fitz-Greene Halleck, with Extracts from Those of Joseph Rodman Drake* (New York: D. Appleton & Co., 1869). *Selected Secondary Sources:* Adkins, Nelson Frederick, *Fitz-Greene Halleck: An Early Knickerbocker Wit and Poet* (New Haven, CT: Yale University Press, 1930); Bryant, William Cullen, "Fitz-Greene Halleck," in *Prose Writings*, ed. Parke Godwin (New York: D. Appleton and Co., 1884, 1:369–393); Hallock, John W.M., *The American Byron: Homosexuality and the Fall of Fitz-Greene Halleck* (Madison: University of Wisconsin Press, 2000); Martin, Robert K., *The Homosexual Tradition in American*

Poetry (Iowa City: University of Iowa Press, 1998); Poe, Edgar Allan, "Drake and Halleck" and "Fitz-Greene Halleck," in *Essays and Reviews*, ed. G.R. Thompson (New York: Library of America, 1984, 505–539, 1154–1159); Slater, Joseph, "The Case of Drake and Halleck" (*Early American Literature* 8 [1974]: 285–297).

Benjamin Friedlander

HAMBY, BARBARA (1952–)

Barbara Hamby's poems are a confluence of humorous catalogues, duende, images, and wit that meld pop culture with antiquity. Her odes bridge the gap between high and low culture and open word playgrounds where she incorporates French and Italian words into her verse. Each of her full-length poetry collections has won a prestigious award, which posits Hamby as possibly one of the most influential **narrative poets** of the late twentieth century. By the time her second collection was published, Hamby had already gained fame for her satirical abecedarians, trademark odes, and long weaving stanzas.

Hamby was born in New Orleans, Louisiana, on June 29, 1952, but she lived in Honolulu, Hawai'i, from the time she was ten until she was eighteen. Her father was a great lover of poetry, and Hamby recalls his recitation throughout her childhood. Familial support and encouragement marked Hamby's childhood and adolescent writing forays. She published her first story at the age of three in the Frances Asbury Elementary School newspaper. This event spawned teacher encouragement for Hamby to nurture her writing talent. Throughout her school years she considered writing a great hobby, but she never considered a writing career until college.

In 1981 she received her MA in creative writing with a concentration in poetry from Florida State University (she later became a writer-in-residence at the same institution). Hamby indicates that during her collegiate career she learned how to write an intelligent, observant poem but nothing special. After graduating she worked as a freelance technical writer and editor on medical and social service projects. About seven years after graduation, her inherent desire to write resurfaced when a close friend went through a near-death experience. The event shocked Hamby and caused her to reevaluate her life, and it was around this time that she began writing regularly. The University of Pittsburgh Press published her chapbook, *Eating Bees* (1992), and it was followed by *Skin*, 1995 winner of the Gerald Cable Chapbook prize. Her husband of over twenty years, the poet **David Kirby**, is one of her greatest supporters, admirers, and editors.

Hamby's verse celebrates language in innovative word games that cross-reference human perversions with Italian frescos and piazzas. If she isn't begrudgingly commenting on "The Tawdry Masks of Women," then she's praising Catholic saints and French and Italian architecture. Her poems are as energetic as acrobats, but woven like tightropes. Published the same year as her second chapbook, Hamby's first full-length collection, *Delirium* (1995), won the Vassar Miller Prize, the Kate Tufts Discovery Prize, and the Norma Farber First Book Award from the Poetry Society of America. The first section of this volume is a bee sequence—reminiscent of **Sylvia Plath**'s bee sequence in *Ariel*—that glorifies femininity in "The Ovary Tattoo" and "Betrothal in B Minor." The second section chronicles a trip to Italy, which marks the first instance of an emblematic Hamby device, for many of her poems derive from living abroad, particularly in Florence and Paris. Hamby stretches her voice in the third section, aptly titled "The Autopsy of John Keats," where she imagines "two rather priggish Englishmen circa 1821" and chronicles the dying Keats's journey from London to Rome with the artist Joseph Severn. The book exhibits her now-signature long couplets, wordplay, and cultural-historical references.

The Alphabet of Desire (1999) exhibits an energy that *Delirium* (1995) lacks; the line arrangement is more controlled, marked by a particularity to indent a full five spaces, whereas many of the poems in her first collection were manually indented two spaces. *Alphabet* shows a more conceptualized vision in Hamby's craft and highlights her fondness for the abecedarian and odes that exemplify Horatian satires, such as "Ode on My Bitterness," "Ode on My Wasted Youth, "Ode to Money," and "Ode to Public Bathrooms." As the 1998 winner of the New York University Press Prize in Poetry, Hamby's second collection was also selected by the New York Public Library as one of the twenty-five best books of 1999, and poems from it were included in *Best American Poetry 2000* and the *2001 Pushcart Prize Anthology*. The poems illuminate Hamby's dexterous craft in their melding of English, Italian, and French words "soaring over the paltry world," exposing the gore of public bathrooms, cartoonish humor, and human biology, and referring to a cornucopia of literary greats, philosophers, artists, saints, dictators, and 1960s rockers—such as **T.S. Eliot**, Nietzsche, Galileo, Caravaggio, St. John, Hitler, Jimi Hendrix, and others. This is suggestive of Hamby's signature style of "hoodwinking [herself] with ideas" and simultaneously including everything of the "dark world of disorder" in her poems.

Chosen by **Stephen Dunn** as the 2003 winner of the Associated Writing Programs' Donald Hall Prize, *Babel* (2004) becomes a metaphor for her work, filled "with a barrage of words so cunningly fluent, so linguistically adroit" to suggest Hamby as a modern-day, femme-fatale polyglot. In this, her most recent collection, Hamby offers a poetic vision that redefines narrative poetry with her long sentences and that "girdles the globe," exposes the most "beautiful and hideous"

human psyche, and is sublimely "broadcasting the news, the blues, the death counts, the mothers wailing when everyone's gone home." Dedicated to her longtime friend and mentor, poet and translator **Richard Howard**, *Babel* features Hamby "rollicking through Paris" in the second section that hypothesizes "the sexual apparatus of the next thousand years," paying tribute to dialects and "dialogue, which is sometimes snappy or *très poétique*" and connecting the French's love for French fries with "the world's ravening gorge." In continuation with her affinity for odes, the third section is composed of "American Odes" that zip through "our porn-riddled galaxy of Walmarts," barbecues, Santa Claus and Satan, bubblegum and hardware stores.

Hamby documents the chaos of cultural consumerism, like "thoughts flitting across the television screen"; explores Italian and French lifestyles; and details "the artistic soul of creating." She glorifies the most demonic and pious aspects of human existence. Hamby's unique verse mixes linguistics with high culture and redefines ancient lyric forms.

Further Reading. *Selected Primary Sources:* Hamby, Barbara, *The Alphabet of Desire* (New York: New York University Press, 1999); ———, *Babel* (Pittsburgh: University of Pittsburgh Press, 2004); ———, *Delirium* (Denton: University of North Texas Press, 1995); ———, *Eating Bees* (Pittsburgh: University of Pittsburgh Press, 1992); ———, *Skin* (Eugene, OR: Silverfish Review Press, 1995).

Ashley Nicole Montjoy

HAMMON, JUPITER (1711–[BETWEEN 1790 AND 1806])

In 1760, with the publication of "An Evening Thought," Jupiter Hammon became the first **African American poet** to publish in America. Despite being a slave all of his long life, Hammon managed to write poems, essays, and sermons criticizing slavery in biblical code to escape censure or persecution. Unfortunately, the code was such that many scholars since have failed to understand what Hammon is saying. Only four of Hammon's poems have survived, though he is believed to have written more. Hammon's writing stands as an example of the triumph of the human spirit over extreme adversity.

Because the family that owned Hammon, the Lloyds, did not write complete records about their slaves, little is known about Hammon's personal life. However, from what information exists, it is known that Hammon was born on October 17, 1711, in Oyster Bay, Long Island, New York. His owners gave him his unique name from Jupiter, the Roman king of the gods, and Ham, the son of the biblical Noah, who supposedly started the African American race. Since the Lloyds only owned two slaves at a time, Hammon's father almost certainly was another slave named Opium, who unsuccessfully tried to escape a few times. Hammon's mother may have also been a slave who was sold when Hammon was young. There is no record of Hammon ever marrying or having children.

Little is known about Hammon's education, though he was obviously literate. He may have been privately tutored with the Lloyds' children and was possibly taught to read and write through the Society for the Propagation of the Gospel, an organization affiliated with the Church of England that provided education for African slaves, Native Americans, and whites who did not attend church.

In any case, religion was an important component of Hammon's life and work. After almost dying in 1830 from an illness, he eventually experienced a religious awakening. Buying a Bible in 1733 led to his life as an author and preacher who covertly fought from the inside against the very system that enslaved him. Words became his weapon of choice. Hammon made history on Christmas Day 1760, when his poem "An Evening Thought. Salvation by Christ, with Penetential Cries" appeared on a broadside. In it, Hammon specifically states his religious inclination, subtly indicting slavery and racism by suggesting that all people, even slaves, deserve salvation. He also states that if slaves were free from the "King" or slave owner, they would be saved not only spiritually but physically as well. He thus equates physical freedom with salvation. This poem demonstrates that Hammon followed the New Testament injunction to turn the other cheek and was willing to forgive those who were enslaving him and other African Americans—if they repented, of course. Hammon believed that everyone, regardless of the evil they had done, could receive God's grace.

During the Revolutionary War, the Lloyds, who supported the Revolution, fled to Hartford, Connecticut, when the British requisitioned their home. There Hammon learned about **Phillis Wheatley**, who would later become the first African American to publish a book. He was so impressed by her ability he dedicated a broadside poem to her entitled *An Address to Miss Phillis Wheatley*. In this poem, Hammon meditates upon biblical verses from Psalms and Ecclesiastes to refer to Wheatley's abduction from Africa into slavery at a young age. Hammon tells Wheatley not to be troubled by this trauma, for she has learned about the power and goodness of God; furthermore, God is the one that enslaved her so that she could receive his grace. Later in the poem, Hammon persuades Wheatley to heed God's call for inspiration in her own poetry:

Come you, Phillis, now aspire,
    And seek the living God,

So step by step thou mayst go higher,
    Till perfect in the word.

Besides telling Wheatley "to seek the living God," Hammon advises her "[t]o drink Samaria's flood," thereby suggesting that she be a good Samaritan to all people and that she forgive those who enslave her, just as he has done.

Wheatley was not the only person to whom Hammon dedicated his poetry. Hammon attached his third poem, "A Poem for Children with Thoughts on Death," to his prose sermon *A Winter Piece*, written in 1782. Hammon may not have had any children, but he felt that children alone could carry faith through to future generations. He encourages them in the poem to put their faith and trust in God, who will love them in return.

Hammon's last poem, "A Dialogue, Entitled, 'The Kind Master and Dutiful Servant,'" was published in 1783, after the end of the Revolutionary War. The poem appeared in his prose work *An Evening's Improvement: Shewing the Necessity of Beholding the Lamb of God, To which is added, a Dialogue, Entitled, The Kind Master and Dutiful Servant*. This poem is controversial, especially to those African American scholars who believe that Hammon equates bowing to God with bowing to slave masters. When, at the outset of the poem, the master enjoins the servant to follow him, "According to thy place," the servant answers that he will do so, praying that God will be with him. Hammon suggests that slaves must endure their bondage, relying on faith to see them through. He does not, however, equate slave masters with God. The poem's more subversive dimension is revealed when the servant responds to the master as follows:

Dear Master I shall follow then,
    The voice of my great King;
As standing on some distant land,
    Inviting sinners in.

And later,

'Tis God alone can give us peace.
    It's not the pow'r of man.

Thus, the servant's true master is God, his "great King," not the master whose physical needs he attends. Indeed, he states that he will listen only to God's word, not to the words of the man with whom he is having the conversation and who also must acknowledge God as ultimate authority. The master shows compassion by hoping that the servant receives God's grace, but he thinks that his comment will pacify his servant. Because of his slave background, Hammon knew that the masters promised slaves that faithful service would ensure their place in heaven. Thus, the servant in this poem is aware of what the master is trying to do, and he counters by going over his head directly to God.

Hammon's death was as obscure as his life. According to the Lloyds' records, he was alive in 1790. However, when the Quakers reprinted Hammon's poem "An Address to the Negroes in the State of New-York" in 1806, the references to him suggest that he had died by then. Even though the details of his life are sketchy, Hammon's contributions to literature and to the ending of slavery stand the test of time. He demonstrated that African Americans could be taught to read and write and that as a consequence they could be articulate and creative, contrary to the common beliefs of the era in which Hammon lived.

Further Reading. *Selected Primary Source:* Hammon, Jupiter, *America's First Negro Poet: The Complete Works of Jupiter Hammon of Long Island*, ed. Stanley Austin Ransom, Jr. (Port Washington, NY: Kennikat Press, 1970). *Selected Secondary Sources:* O'Neale, Sondra, "Hammon, Jupiter," in *The Oxford Companion to African American Literature*, ed. William L. Andrews, Frances Smith Foster, and Trudier Harris (New York: Oxford University Press, 1997); ———, "Jupiter Hammon," in *Dictionary of Literary Biography*, vol. 50, ed. Trudier Harris and Thadious M. Davis (Detroit, MI: Bruccoli Clark, 1986); ———, *Jupiter Hammon and the Biblical Beginnings of African-American Literature* (Metuchen, NJ: American Theological Library Association/Scarecrow Press, 1993).

Devona Mallory

HARJO, JOY (1951–)

A member of the prominent Creek Harjo family and distant cousin to poet **Alexander L. Posey**, Joy Harjo was born in Tulsa, Oklahoma, on May 9, 1951. She is of mixed European, Cherokee, and Creek descent and is an enrolled member of the Muskogee tribe. Coming from a family of artists convinced her that she too wanted to become an artist, so at age sixteen she left Oklahoma to study art and theater at the Institute of American Indian Art, a high school in Santa Fe, New Mexico. Later, she received an undergraduate degree from the University of New Mexico in 1976 and an MFA from the University of Iowa in 1978. It was around this time that she began writing poetry. Influenced by a diverse group of poets and writers such as **Galway Kinnell**, **Leslie Marmon Silko**, **Simon Ortiz**, Flannery O'Connor, **James Wright**, and Pablo Neruda, Harjo began to gain prominence, publishing her first book, *The Last Song*, in 1975. She published her tenth book in 2002. In addition to her numerous works of poetry, Harjo has also published a children's book, an anthology of Native women's writing, and many poems

in literary magazines. She has taught at a number of universities, such as Santa Fe Community College, Arizona State, University of Colorado, University of Arizona, University of New Mexico, and UCLA. Among her received awards are the Oklahoma Book Award, The American Book Award, and the Delmore Schwartz Memorial Award. Diversely talented, Harjo is a highly sought-after speaker, musician, and performance artist and has put out an acclaimed CD with her band Poetic Justice entitled *Letter from the End of the Twentieth Century* (1997), along with the recent *Native Joy for Real* (2004).

Born to a young mixed-race mother and a Creek father, Harjo grew up in a broken home in Tulsa, Oklahoma. She also suffered poverty as a single mother, giving birth at an early age to her children Phil and Rainy Dawn. She began writing her first poems while attending the University of New Mexico, at about the age of twenty-two. It was also at this time that her daughter Rainy Dawn was born. Readers can see the influence of Harjo's broken home, urban background, and young, single motherhood in her work, especially her early poetry, which is somewhat more alienated than her later work.

Her first poems also show a strong connection with her home state of Oklahoma, and her adopted state of New Mexico. Overall, however, these poems move from place to place, never staying in one place for long. Harjo explains the movement in her poetry in this way: "the reason I'm always traveling is so that Andrew Jackson's troops don't find me. You know, they moved my [Creek] family from Alabama to Oklahoma, and so I always figure I stay one step ahead so they can't find me" (*Spiral*, 23). This wry remark explains the role of travel in her poetry—it suggests her love of *all* places, urban or otherwise, but especially the Southwestern landscapes of her childhood and young adulthood. In addition, it refers to the Natives' ability to adapt to any set of circumstances for the sake of survival, and to their uneasy co-existence with the Euro-American.

Cities have an abiding presence in Harjo's poetry as well, possibly due to her having grown up in Tulsa. But while her cities can be alienating and surreal, they can also be redemptive places where beauty suddenly and mysteriously shines through. They highlight the idea of fragmentation for the Native, and for the Euro-American as well, for life in a city moves along rapidly, often offering little sense of community. Cities also mean a struggle for survival for the American Indian, for danger lurks in every window and at every street corner, in every encounter with a Euro-American.

Harjo's background as a visual artist has contributed to the imagery in her poetry, which is grounded in place and filled with images of horses, birds, cars, urban settings such as apartments or bars, historical figures such as DeSoto or Anna Mae Pictou, references to Creek material culture, fire, water, the sky, and, always, the red earth. Harjo's work is heavily influenced by the Native idea of the land as sacred and of time as circular; both ideas add up to what she calls "sacred space": a place of grace where there is no separation between worlds. In the end, however, as Harjo herself notes, her poetry is more about survival than anything; as she says in "Anchorage": "Because who would believe / the fantastic and terrible story of all our survival / those who were never meant/to survive?" (*Human*, 32).

Harjo admits to writing political poetry, citing influences such as **June Jordan**, **Carolyn Forché**, and **Audre Lorde**. To the novice reader her message can often seem harsh and unnerving. For example, in "A Postcolonial Tale" she describes her people as being stolen and stowed away "into a bag carried on the back of a white man who pretends to own / the earth and sky" (*Human*, 14). But poems such as "The Real Revolution is Love" make it clear that acknowledgment of one's difficult and marginalized past and present can only be overcome by love and that a journey to love is a journey of light.

Further Reading. *Selected Primary Sources:* Harjo, Joy, *The Good Luck Cat* (San Diego: Harcourt Brace, 2000); ———, *How We Became Human: New and Selected Poems* (New York: W.W. Norton, 2002); ———, *In Mad Love and War* (Middletown, CT: Wesleyan University Press, 1990); ———, *The Last Song* (Las Cruces, NM: Puerto Del Sol, 1975); ———, *A Map to the Next World: Poems* (New York: W.W. Norton, 2001); ———, *Reinventing the Enemy's Language: Contemporary Native American Women's Writings of North America* (New York: W.W. Norton, 1998); ———, *Secrets from the Center of the World* (Tucson: University of Arizona Press, 1989); ———, *She Had Some Horses* (New York: Thunder's Mouth Press, 1983); ———, *What Moon Drove Me to This?* (Berkeley, CA: Reed and Cannon, 1979); ———, *The Woman Who Fell From the Sky* (New York: W.W. Norton, 1994). ***Selected Secondary Sources:*** Cudlow, Jeannie, "Working the In-between" (*Studies of American Indian Literature* 6 [1994]: 24–42); Goodman, Jenny, "Politics and Personal Lyric in the Poetry of Joy Harjo" (*MELUS* 19 [1994]: 35–56); Holmes, Kristine, "This Woman Can Cross Any Line" (*Studies of American Indian Literature* 7 [1995]: 45–63); Lang, Nancy, "Twin Gods Bending Over" (*MELUS* 18 [1993]: 41–49).

Stephanie Gordon

HARLEM RENAISSANCE

Langston Hughes saw the Harlem Renaissance as beginning in 1920 and ending in 1929, an opinion confirmed by later scholars such as Henry Louis Gates, Jr. Others, however, see it as stretching from 1900 to 1940. An important movement in African American art, music, and literature it was characterized by diversity in theme, content, form, and technique, and involved both national and international influences in the representation of the African American experience. The Harlem Renaissance reflected the social, political, and economic forces transforming American culture during the period. The effects of the Harlem Renaissance may be seen in the emphasis on African American cultural expression in the Black Aesthetic Movement, or **Black Arts Movement**, of the 1960s and the neorealist movement of the 1970s as they may in the late twentieth and early twenty-first century emphasis on race, class, and gender themes in contemporary American literature in general.

Among the significant events that contributed to the Harlem Renaissance were World War I (1914–1918), the early phase of the great black migration, the publication of magazines aimed at a black audience such as *Crisis*, *Opportunity*, and the *Messenger*, the publication of *The New Negro: An Interpretation* (1925), the patronage of wealthy enthusiasts of literature and art, and Marcus Garvey's Back to Africa Movement. Although African American writers published in the eighteenth and nineteenth centuries, the Harlem Renaissance marked the emergence of a collective movement among African American writers and intellectuals to use literature as a means of social transformation. The social and political climate in the United States after World War I influenced the activism of the Harlem Renaissance. The return of African American soldiers from this war gave rise to a new type of militancy and agitation for civil rights among African Americans, particularly those who had risked their lives in war to promote freedom and democracy abroad. Demanding to be treated as equal citizens when they returned to the United States, the soldiers collectively engaged in the struggle for equal opportunity for black Americans. The great black migration north also influenced the Harlem Renaissance. In the twentieth century, millions of African Americans migrated from the South to the North in search of economic, social, and political opportunities. Due to economic devastation brought on by drought, flood, natural disasters, racial violence, and Jim Crow laws in the South, many African Americans relocated to urban centers in Boston, Philadelphia, Detroit, Chicago, and New York City, particularly Harlem. Many aspiring singers, writers, and artists were drawn to New York City for its preeminence in publishing, arts, and theater. The availability of affordable housing for African Americans in Harlem also influenced the settlement of blacks in the area. Harlem represented a lively cultural and arts scene for African Americans. As Nathan Irvin Huggins stresses in *Harlem Renaissance*,

Large numbers of blacks had streamed into northern cities in the first years of the new century, forced out by the poverty of southern agriculture and the mean brutality of southern racial bigotry. Harlem gained from that migration, as shortly after, in World War I, it gained from the waves of blacks who came to fill the war industries' labor needs that had been aggravated by the war-severed European immigration. (14)

African American writers of the Harlem Renaissance found opportunities for publishing in magazines that focused on civil rights and social justice, magazines such as *Crisis*, *Opportunity*, and the *Messenger*. An NAACP (National Association for the Advancement of Colored People) publication, *Crisis* featured fiction and nonfiction aimed at promoting African American rights. As editor of *Crisis* during the heyday of the Harlem Renaissance, **W.E.B. DuBois** used the magazine as a means of publicizing and promoting African American writers. Another magazine, the *Messenger*, was edited by Chandler Owen and A. Philip Randolph (Huggins, 27). Nathan Irvin Huggins notes, "The editors of the *Messenger* wanted to vie with DuBois as the most forthright and uncompromising in the Afro-American cause" (27). A third magazine, *Opportunity*, was created by the Urban League. The publication also promoted the ideas of advancement for African Americans (27).

The New Negro: An Interpretation, published in 1925, heralded the emergence of the New Negro Movement (also known as the Harlem Renaissance). An anthology featuring fiction, drama, poetry, and essays, this text exposed the world to the writings of many authors who would become major forces in the Harlem Renaissance. *The New Negro: An Interpretation* developed from a special March 1925 issue of *The Survey Graphic* (edited by Alain Locke), which focused on Harlem and African American culture (Hutchinson, 396). Among the important Harlem Renaissance poets featured in the book were **Countee Cullen**, **Claude McKay**, **Jean Toomer**, **James Weldon Johnson**, **Langston Hughes**, **Georgia Douglas Johnson**, **Anne Spencer**, **Angelina Grimké**, and Lewis Alexander. The book also includes an essay by Locke titled "The New Negro," which identifies the importance and significance of black culture and expression in Harlem in the twentieth century. In this essay, Locke states, "In Harlem, Negro life is seizing upon its first chances for group expression and self-determination" (7). Locke argued that Negro artists, heartened by the fact that white intellectuals welcomed their contribution, would provide what white American culture lacked. As a forum for aspiring writers, *The New Negro: An Interpretation* represented a sampling of African American poetry that engaged the themes of race, class, and gender that dominated the Harlem Renaissance.

The issue of patronage by wealthy individuals also influenced the Harlem Renaissance. The white New York socialite Charlotte Osgood Mason, for example, helped to provide funding for writers such as Langston Hughes and Zora Neale Hurston. In addition, philanthropists donated money for awards and fellowships for aspiring African American writers. The Harlem Renaissance also reflected the interest in Africa or pan-Africanism, a movement and philosophy focusing on the common struggle of people of African descent worldwide, and the influence of Marcus Garvey. Garvey, a Jamaican immigrant who moved to the United States, championed the idea of blacks returning to Africa during the Harlem Renaissance. Gloria T. Hull notes in *Color, Sex, and Poetry: Three Women Writers of the Harlem Renaissance*, "As seen most clearly with Garveyism, this attitude involved race solidarity and pride and a conscious connection with the African homeland" (2).

The Harlem Renaissance was non-monolithic in terms of ideology. Scholars and writers debated the representation of African Americans in literature during the period. Important texts that influenced aesthetic debates included Langston Hughes's "The Negro Artist and The Racial Mountain," DuBois's "Criteria of Negro Art," Richard Wright's "Blueprint for Negro Writing," and George S. Schuyler's "The Negro Art Hokum." The latter essay, which appeared in the *Nation* in 1926, is an example of a dismissive response. Schuyler saw little of merit in the Harlem Renaissance. For him, black American artistic productions were, at best, indistinguishable from those of white artists.

Negro art there has been, is, and will be among the numerous black nations of Africa; but to suggest the possibility of any such development among the ten million colored people in this republic is self-evident foolishness. Eager apostles from Greenwich Village, Harlem, and environs proclaimed a great renaissance of Negro art just around the corner waiting to be ushered on the scene by those whose hobby is taking races, nations, peoples, and movements under their wing. (51)

In contrast, in "The Negro Artist and The Racial Mountain" (*Nation*, 1926), Langston Hughes emphasizes the importance of African American writers connecting with black life and culture. He notes, "We younger Negro artists who create now intent to express our individual dark-skinned selves without fear or shame" (59). Others would also urge or promote the idea of African American literature connecting with the concerns of African Americans. In "Criteria of Negro Art" (*Crisis*, 1926) DuBois writes, "I do not care a damn for any art that is not used for propaganda" (66). Thus, DuBois favors the political implications of African American literature, and eschews the ideology of art for art's sake. For DuBois black literature of the Harlem Renaissance must advocate social change. For

Wright, the key issue is accurate representation of African American life. In "Blueprint for Negro Writing" (*New Challenge* [1937]), he critiques previous generations of black writers for not adequately depicting the African American experience in their writing. He contends, "For the Negro writer to depict this new reality requires a greater discipline and consciousness than was necessary for the so-called Harlem school of expression" (105).

The diversity of African American poetry of the Harlem Renaissance stems from the diverse perspectives and viewpoints of the writers and intellectuals associated with the movement. Nevertheless, common thematic concerns dominate the poetry of the period: identity, history, community, family, religion, sexuality, class, gender roles, and race. African American poets of the Harlem Renaissance appropriated African, African American, and European traditions in their writing. Most famously, Langston Hughes's poetry connects with the "folk aesthetic" and oral tradition in African American poetry, emphasizing working-class and lower-class characters, and the black vernacular. Hughes's poem "I, Too" focuses on the theme of racial discrimination and oppression. He writes, "I am the darker brother," calling attention to the kinship between Americans of all colors. The speaker desires to be treated as an equal and not as a second-class citizen. He states at the end of the poem: "I, Too, am America." His poem "The Negro Speaks of Rivers" exemplifies Hughes's treatment of black heritage through the use of nature imagery. The speaker recounts experiences in Africa and in the United States and compares his or her soul to rivers in those environments. The speaker states, "My soul has grown deep like the rivers." Another poem, "Dream Variation," represents a celebration of black identity and unity with nature. The speaker revels, rejoices, and identifies with the natural world. Hughes tackles the theme of appearance versus reality in the context of African American experience in the poem "Minstrel Man." The speaker notes the disconnection between his outside appearance and his inner feelings. Despite the fact that the speaker smiles, laughs, sings, and dances, he feels sadness and anguish. The speaker states, "You do not know / I die." The poem connects with the tradition in protest poetry among writers of the Harlem Renaissance who use literature as a means of critiquing race in America.

In contrast, Countee Cullen's poems show the influence of the British Romantics in form and structure. Nevertheless, his poems often connect with Afrocentric themes, thus representing a merger of the Eurocentric and Afrocentric traditions. His poem "Tableau" paints a portrait of the potential for positive race relationships between blacks and whites. The speaker describes two boys—one white and the other black—who walk together. Whites and blacks look at this scene with dislike, yet the two youths continue to walk. Cullen writes, "Oblivious to look and word / They pass, and see no wonder." Since many poets of the Harlem Renaissance use poetry as a means of promoting social justice, this poem fits in the tradition of poems about racial justice and equality.

Claude McKay represents the internationalism of the Harlem Renaissance. Born in Jamaica, he came to the United States after establishing himself as a poet in his native Jamaica. His poem "The Tropics in New York" focuses on the theme of memory and the significance of home. The speaker in the poem sees tropical fruit in a store window in New York City, reminding him of home. He notes, "And, hungry for the old familiar ways, / I turned aside and bowed my head and wept." The poem explores the loss and pain of cultural and geographical dislocation. McKay illustrates the range of Harlem Renaissance poets in theme, style, and content.

Jean Toomer's poetry, in some regard more **modernist** than that of the others, adds to the diversity of Harlem Renaissance poetry. His book *Cane* (1923), an experimental text that contains poetry and prose, focuses on the black rural and urban experience. "Georgia Dusk" focuses on the lives of workers in a rural setting, and "Song of the Son" focuses on the heritage of slavery in the south in the United States. Toomer writes, "O Negro slaves, dark purple ripened plums, / Squeezed, and bursting in the pine-wood air." Toomer's poetry during the 1920s expresses highly racialized themes connected to the history and heritage of African Americans.

Women writers also played a large role in the Harlem Renaissance. Although the tripartite race, class, and gender oppression mitigated their opportunities for publishing, their work is undergoing a critical reassessment and reevaluation. As Gloria T. Hull notes,

Yet, despite what appears to be full participation of women in the Harlem Renaissance, one can discern broad social factors and patterns of exclusion. One of the most basic is how male attitudes toward women impinged upon them, how men's so-called personal biases were translated into something larger that had deleterious effects. (7)

Women poets such as Anne Spencer, Angelina Weld Grimké, Alice Dunbar Nelson (wife of nineteenth-century African American poet **Paul Laurence Dunbar**), and **Helene Johnson** wrote during the Harlem Renaissance. For example, Anne Spencer wrote poetry connecting with the black female experience. As Hull states, "Anne Spencer is an arresting poet because of the originality of her material and approach" (13). In the poem "Lady, Lady," Spencer focuses on a black female figure to analyze the triple oppression of race, class, and gender discrimination faced by black women. African American women poets of the Harlem Renaissance laid the foundation for contemporary African American women poets such as **Sonia Sanchez**, **Nikki Giovanni**, and **Rita Dove**.

The Harlem Renaissance was a movement in which writers sought to depict the African American experience. Although the movement ended with the economic devastation to the publishing and artistic world caused by the Stock Market Crash of 1929 and the Great Depression of the 1930s, the legacy of the Harlem Renaissance poets continues in the focus on race, class, and gender in later twenty and twenty-first century poetry. Because of the establishment of African American Studies and Women's Studies programs in the academy in the 1960s and 1970s, more critical attention has been paid to the efforts of African American writers of the Harlem Renaissance, particularly the poets. The movement, by no means monolithic, served as an inspiration for the protest movements of the 1960s, the Black Aesthetics Movement (1960–1969), and the neorealism movement (1970s to present) in African American literature and continues to influence contemporary American poetry.

Further Reading. *Selected Primary Source:* Locke, Alain, ed., *The New Negro: An Interpretation* (New York: Johnson Reprint Corporation, 1968). ***Selected Secondary Sources:*** Huggins, Nathan Irvin, *Harlem Renaissance* (New York: Oxford University Press, 1971); Hughes, Langston, "The Negro Artist and the Racial Mountain," in *Within The Circle: An Anthology of African American Literary Criticism from the Harlem Renaissance to the Present*, ed. Angelyn Mitchell (Durham, NC: Duke University Press, 1994, 55–59); Hull, Gloria T., *Color, Sex, & Poetry: Three Women Writers of the Harlem Renaissance* (Bloomington: Indiana University Press, 1987); Hutchinson, George, *The Harlem Renaissance in Black and White* (Cambridge, MA: Harvard University Press, 1995); Schuyler, George S., "The Negro Art-Hokum," in *Within The Circle: An Anthology of African American Literary Criticism from the Harlem Renaissance to the Present*, ed. Angelyn Mitchell (Durham, NC: Duke University Press, 1994, 51–54); Wright, Richard, "Blueprint for Negro Writing," *Within The Circle: An Anthology of African American Literary Criticism from the Harlem Renaissance to the Present*, ed. Angelyn Mitchell (Durham, NC: Duke University Press, 1994, 97–106).

Sharon L. Jones

HARPER, FRANCES ELLEN WATKINS (1825–1911)

Living through the tumultuous period of slavery, the Civil War, and Reconstruction, Frances Harper found her imagination stirred by the struggle of African Americans to become a self-determining people. Born into a free black family in Maryland, she was initially sheltered from the trauma of physical bondage but soon learned to identify with those who had experienced physical and psychological humiliation first-hand. Dedicating herself to a life of public service, she labored strenuously to educate her nation about the horrors of racial injustice and to teach black people struggling toward freedom the importance of the new destiny they were carving out for themselves. One of the foremost black political leaders in America, Harper was actively involved with the abolitionist movement, the Underground Railroad, racial uplift activities during Reconstruction, the women's movement, and the National Woman's Christian Temperance Union. She traveled throughout the country, giving speeches to a wide range of audiences in both the North and South (an especially dangerous locale for a black activist after the Civil War). In her travels, she witnessed firsthand the anguish and hopes of runaway slaves, freed blacks, the victims of Klan violence, and families struggling to build new lives and communities. Her poetry, like her political speeches and fiction, shaped those experiences into powerful expressions that demanded her readers' sympathetic engagement. At the same time, Harper's writing provided a powerful vision of black history that allowed her readers into the lives and minds of the pivotal generation that passed from slavery through Emancipation into the dawn of a new era. Using materials from *Uncle Tom's Cabin*, the Bible, and recent events, she created one of the most moving poetic portraits of nineteenth-century black life that we have.

Harper is a poet of the people, who envisioned her writing as a moral and political force that might shape the values of both black and white communities. Didactic at their core, her poems model patterns of personal responsibility and social justice, measure deviations from such norms, and instill an enthusiasm for social change. Using conventional literary forms such as the ballad and blank verse, her texts depict unambiguous expressions of deeply held beliefs communicated through sentimental structures. Like other sentimental writers, Harper writes out of the conviction that *feeling* is the agent of motivation and political change. Like the author she describes in "To Mrs. Harriet Beecher Stowe" (1854), she uses a "pen of fire" that "thrilled upon the living chords / Of many a heart's deep lyre." Believing that moral action and political commitment depend upon energized emotions, she creates political sympathy for the victims of racial injustice as well as moral indignation at individuals who lose sight of their own higher selves. Motivating readers' identification with figures who suffer and struggle, her poems enact a process of community-building—a sense of solidarity molded out of felt connections to the characters and lives she depicts. Committed at various moments to the abolition of slavery, the forging of interracial political alliances, and the reconstruction of lives shattered by the Civil War, her poetry erases the barriers isolating society's victims. Challenging values that would hold them at arm's length, she fashions structures of emotional engagement that demand the recognition of the other's personal promise, whether that other is a runaway slave, a fallen woman, or the victim of alcohol abuse.

At the heart of Harper's poetics lies a profound religious sensibility, which Melba Joyce Boyd identifies as a black liberation theology committed to the images of both Moses and Jesus as models of African American identity and leadership. In its classic formulations, liberation theology highlights Jesus's ministry to the poor and outcast as a model of a political activism. Appealing to a higher authority than human law or institutions, Harper's poems express her conviction (as she phrased it in one of her speeches) that "God is on the side of freedom." Creating for herself a role that Carla Peterson identifies as the "poet-preacher," Harper frequently turned to well-known biblical narratives as analogues to help her analyze contemporary events. Some of her most powerful poems (such as "The Drunkard's Child" or "Saved by Faith") focus upon defining moments of religious conversion reorienting a person's values. Even more striking examples of Harper's religious commitment are found in her biblical paraphrases, poems that retell famous episodes of the Bible.

For example, the opening text in her 1854 volume *Poems on Miscellaneous Subjects* (1854), "The Syrophenician Woman," narrates an incident found in both Mark and Matthew: that of a Gentile woman who accosts Jesus and pleads that he cure her child possessed by a demon, a plea met with Jesus's surprising response that "it is not meet [right] to take the children's bread, and to cast it to dogs" (Matthew 15:26). But for the only time in scripture, Jesus loses a theological argument, as he acknowledges the mother's assertion that even "dogs" must be fed and he cures her child. Celebrated by later feminist theologians, this episode has been interpreted as one of the most powerful statements of female spiritual authority, as well as a striking paradigm of maternal love. Rather than focusing upon the demonic possession of the woman's child, Harper's retelling evokes a more generalized sense of disorder and pain, as the mother's anxiety and child's illness intertwine with "our griefs." For an 1850s audience attuned to the anguish of slave mothers (such as those depicted by Harriet Beecher Stowe), the mother's plea, "Master! Save, Oh! Save my child!" invokes both the brutal master-slave relationships of slavery and the abolition-

ist demand for racial justice in America. It is striking that Harper omits the ethnic slur that Gentile children are "dogs," beyond the purview of divine compassion, an omission that—for a reader versed in the Bible—powerfully underscores the relevance of this episode to the dynamics of racism. "But the humblest, meanest, may / Eat the crumbs they cast away," Harper's mother responds, shifting attention from racial differences toward economic and class differences. Demonstrating the power of a faith able to cross class and ethnic boundaries, she sways "th' astonished Lord," who tells her in the poem's final line: "Thou hast ask'd, and shalt prevail."

Linking Jesus's life to contemporary events, the second poem in *Poems on Miscellaneous Subjects* evokes one of the archetypes of abolitionist writing—"The Slave Mother." "Heard you that shriek?" the poem opens, a demand for perceptual and emotional response echoed in subsequent lines: "Saw you those hands so sadly clasped . . . ?" "Saw you the sad, imploring eye?" As in "The Syrophenician Woman," though not now in the form of dialogue, maternal anguish becomes the pivot for readerly response:

> Saw you the sad, imploring eye?
>   Its every glance was pain,
> As if a storm of agony
>   Were sweeping through the brain.

The powerful phrase "She is a mother," in the succeeding stanz, attempts to balance against but is overweighed by the brutal repetition (three times in five lines) of the observation "He is not hers." The concluding stanzas demonstrate Harper's strength as a poet of the people, as she measures an appeal to divine compassion ("Oh, Father! Must they part?") against the horrific recognition that the mother's "bitter shrieks" as her child is torn away are a common occurrence and "No marvel." At the poem's end, she is left with a role she is no longer allowed to fulfill: "She is a mother, and her heart / Is breaking in despair."

Equally powerful but politically more ambitious, "Eliza Harris" returns to one of the most famous episodes of *Uncle Tom's Cabin*—the pursuit of Eliza Harris, leaping across the ice floes of the frozen Ohio River toward freedom. As in "The Slave Mother," Harper deftly positions the reader as an emotionally engaged witness: "A woman swept by us, bearing a child," and, a few lines later, "It was a vision to haunt us, that innocent face." But then—in the central stanzas—she expands the poem's horizon to focus upon the national shame of slavery:

> Oh! How shall I speak of my proud country's shame?
> Of the stains on her glory, how give them their name?
> How say that her banner in mockery waves–
> Her "star spangled banner"–o'er millions of slaves?

As in Frederick Douglass's bitter speech "What to the Slave Is the Fourth of July?" Harper measures the suffering of the victims of slavery against a national idealism that seems horribly inappropriate. With her "shame" and "stains," Harper's America seems more a fallen woman than a glowing national icon. The iconoclastic quality of Harper's poetry is evident a few stanzas later, as she challenges the aestheticizing maneuver that would turn Eliza Harris into a literary character exempt from emotional or political engagement. Described as "fragile," "lovely," and "pale," Harper's Eliza seems to fit the mold of the beautiful, suffering woman idolized by American society. "You'd have thought her a statue of fear and despair," the poet observes, before she shatters the statue constructed by complacency in a series of stanzas that directly link a slave mother's anguish and release to the emotional lives of her readers:

> Did a fever e'er burning through bosom and brain,
> Send a lava-like flood through every vein,
> Till it suddenly cooled 'neath a healing spell,
> And you knew, oh! The joy! You knew you were well?

Suggesting that slavery is national "fever" that potentially infects everyone, Harper maps her readers' emotional lives onto the life of an escaped slave. Eliza's "rapture" at her successful escape maps the trajectory of a cure—the elimination of the brutal institution that has created "strange discord on Liberty's plains."

Other texts in *Poems on Miscellaneous Subjects* expand Harper's political and spiritual geography by contrasting the realm of human "anguish" with a heavenly realm transcending human divisions and pain. For example, the dying child in "The Drunkard's Child" facilitates his father's conversion by shifting his perception from "a dark and gloomy chamber" to a concluding vision of a radiant realm where they might meet again. Similarly, "The Dying Christian" concludes with the transfiguration of a dying woman into "A spirit pure and bright," and "The Tennessee Hero" (in the 1857 edition), killed because he would not reveal his fellow slaves' escape plot, ascends to "the throne of God." As in the poetry of Harper's precursor, **Phillis Wheatley**, heaven represents an idealized realm of spiritual fulfillment and political justice that stands in stark contrast to racial divisions on earth. But while the poet speaking in Wheatley's texts often found her imaginative ascension to such heights unstable and laborious, Harper easily opens the heavenly gates to provide a glimpse of paradise. While this difference in emphasis may reflect Harper's intense religious convictions (as well as the evangelical sensibility of mid-nineteenth–century America), it also suggests the different enunciative positions of a woman writing in bondage (Wheatley) and a

woman writing as a free black who had personally experienced the "paradise" longed for and pursued by fugitive slaves.

At the same time, Harper's passionate commitment to the abolitionist movement and her work with the Underground Railroad are evident in a number of powerful poems in which she identified with the anguish of slavery's victims. Brooding on the depth of human pain caused by slavery, "The Slave Auction" occupies a special status in *Poems on Miscellaneous Subjects*. Although most of the texts in this volume forge bonds of identification between Harper's readers and her subjects, this poem leads the reader to the emotional brink "of deep despair" and then seems to stop short. It depicts families torn apart by the auctioneer's gavel but then shifts from the representation of feeling to an emotional sublimity that transcends articulation and that may not cross racial lines:

> Ye who have laid your love to rest,
>   And wept above their lifeless clay,
> Know *not* the anguish of that breast,
>   Whose lov'd are rudely torn away.

The originality and importance of these lines is underscored when one remembers that Harriet Beecher Stowe concluded *Uncle Tom's Cabin* with an expression of the emotional analogy between the grieving white mothers of the North (who had lost children) and the slave mothers of the South. Departing from one of her most powerful literary models, Harper—like Harriet Jacobs a few years after her—insists that the specific suffering of African Americans in bondage cannot be subsumed under white categories of pain or grief. In order to comprehend the experience of those brutalized in slavery, one must acknowledge that their suffering surpasses anything imaginable in the secure home life of Northern readers.

Harper's commitment to the poetic representation of bondage and freedom is perhaps most evident in her longest production, the nearly 1,100-line-long blank-verse epic, *Moses: A Story of the Nile* (1869). As the biblical leader who led his people out of slavery, Moses played a central role in the nineteenth-century black imagination. Harper, especially, depicted the figure of Moses as an archetype of leadership, prefiguring her own sustained public efforts to define more liberated pathways of existence. As one of the leading African American leaders of her age, Harper knew firsthand the difficulty of motivating others to sustain an "exodus" (whether from chattel slavery or moral bondage) to the "promised land" of a new life. Both the story of Moses's leadership and the periodic recalcitrance of his people, spoke directly to Harper's experience of the laborious struggle of African Americans toward liberation. Visiting the South after the

Civil War, Harper recorded in her letters not only her sense of African Americans' enormous potential, "standing . . . on the threshold of a new era," but also the somber awareness that "the shadows of the past have not been fully lifted from the minds of the former victims of slavery."

In a striking amplification of a mere ten verses in Exodus, Harper focuses the first two chapters of *Moses: A Story of the Nile* (over one third of the entire text) upon Moses's relation to two maternal figures—the Egyptian princess who found Moses floating on the Nile and his Hebrew mother who had been forced to abandon him to save him from being killed. Opening with a dialogue between Moses and "Charmian" (Harper's name for his Egyptian foster mother), Harper expands the ideal of maternal love (which had oriented earlier anti-slavery poems) to include an ideal of racial responsibility. Attempting to hold onto Moses, Charmian lures him with the seductive image of an Egyptian life of material comfort and privilege, "beneath the radiance / Of our throne" as opposed to existence "in the shadow of those / Bondage-darkened huts." But like Harper herself, like Minnie and Louis in her 1869 novel *Minnie's Sacrifice*, and like Iola and Robert Johnson in *Iola Leroy*, Moses gives up a life of comfort "to join / The fortunes of my race." Although she stakes her claim to Moses upon the assertion of maternal love, Charmian is no match for Moses's memory of his mother, "the Hebrew nurse to whom thy gavest thy foundling." In contrast to Charmian's offer of a life of material comfort, his Hebrew mother offers a vision of political commitment. Instructing him in the Hebrews' history and religious traditions, she inspired him with the "promise, handed down from sire to son, / That God . . . / Would break our chains."

In Harper's retelling of the familiar biblical narrative, strong women are the source of both compassion and instruction, taking on an authority that rivals the power of God. Rejoining his race in Chapter II, Moses is reunited with his mother, who reminds him that she has woven "faith" into the "rushes of thine ark." Her words, Moses responds, shape the direction of his spirit. At the moment that he is ordered to reject his racial heritage and adopt the gods of Egypt, he "lived the past again," his soul "gathering / Inspiration" from her words, and he repudiates his identity as "the son / of Pharaoh's daughter."

In the biblical narrative, Moses's motivation to lead his people is centered upon his miraculous encounter with God's voice emerging from a burning bush. But in Harper's version, long *before* Moses's encounter with God, Moses's resolve is shaped by his Hebrew mother's angelic words and by his growing comprehension of the horror of slavery. In Chapter IV, fleeing to Midian after his killing of an Egyptian overseer, Harper's Moses

"nurse[s]" his faith in God and comes to recognize the destiny overshadowing his life. This phrasing recalls both his Hebrew mother's role as his nurse and the power of her angelic words. Only in the middle of Harper's poem does Moses encounter the burning bush and receive his commission from God. In contrast to the thirty verses of divine speech in Exodus, Harper gives God only two lines of indirect discourse.

At the same time that she emphasizes the influence of powerful women, Harper further revises biblical narrative by connecting her story to contemporary history. She omits Moses's dialogue with God at the burning bush, his increasingly frustrating interviews with Pharaoh, and even the Ten Commandments, in order to reshape the Exodus account into a poetic narrative that more closely resembles the American history of slavery, the Civil War, and Reconstruction. Moses's killing of the Egyptian overseer in Chapter III, for example, immediately follows Harper's description of slaves plotting rebellion, men whose eyes seem to say,

> we bide our time,
> And hide our wrath in every nerve, and only
> Wait a fitting hour to strike the hands that press
> Us down.

Similarly, in a scene that Harper adds to the biblical account, one of Pharaoh's counselors in Chapter V cautions him against the slaves' imminent rebellion. Dramatizing only Moses's first interview with Pharaoh, Harper turns her description of the plagues into an allegory of the Civil War, culminating in the moment when "Death! Was everywhere—in every home / A corpse—in every heart a bitter woe," a passage that emphasizes death and mourning and not Passover (which Harper omits from the story). Thus when "the last dread plague / . . . snap[s] in twain the chains on which/ The rust of ages lay," one reads these lines as a commentary on the Civil War and Emancipation.

In an even more amazing transformation of the Mosaic narrative, Harper leaves out the Ten Commandments, replacing them with "the primal truth of all," the truth that the recognition of "the unity of God" should "bind us closer to our God and link us / With our fellow man, the brothers and co-heirs / With Christ" (Chapter VII). If this truth could be learned, she expands, "war" would transform into "peace and freedom, love and joy"; and "light" would take the place of "bondage, whips / And chains." In Harper's powerful restatement of her abolitionist creed, the slave-owners of the world have lost sight of divine truth and have imposed "their selfish lives between / God's sunshine and the shivering poor." But the recently emancipated, in her historical allegory, still have important lessons to learn. She cautions that those "Born slaves" might love "their pots of flesh" more than "freedom," for "when the chains were shaken from their limbs, / They failed to strike the impress from their souls" (Chapter VIII).

Harper concludes *Moses: A Story of the Nile* with Moses's death. The promised land of Israel, despite its loveliness, "faded from his view" and is replaced with "another, fairer, vision"—that of a luminous paradise that his "ransomed soul" finally enters (Chapter IX). Conflating the escape from slavery with the movement from earthly obstruction to heavenly illumination, this passage both recapitulates the dynamic of Harper's earlier poetry and presents the dominant theme of her next volume, *Poems* (1871)—a book filled with references to heavenly light and assertions of the need to move from human injustice to illumination. Thus, the "bright and glowing visions" of the great anti-slavery Congressman Thaddeus Stevens have taught the poet that "There is light beyond the darkness" ("Lines to Hon. Thaddeus Stevens"). In similar terms, Harper alludes to Goethe in hoping that we may be "blessed with light, more light!" ("Let the Light Enter!"). In "The Dying Child to Her Blind Father," a daughter consoles her parent with visions of a heavenly realm where his "eyes will sparkle with rapture." Over a third of the poems in *Poems* deal directly with death or dying—a somber indication of the lingering shadow of the Civil War and of the turbulence of Reconstruction. Traveling and lecturing throughout the war-torn South, Harper had heard horrifying stories of brutality, violence, and lynching. She had seen firsthand the work of the Ku Klux Klan and knew the courage that was needed by both freedmen and freedwomen and their political leaders to resist the specter of racial terror and violence.

Out of these experiences emerged Harper's greatest poetic work—the 436-line "Aunt Chloe" sequence, which opened her next book of poems, *Sketches of Southern Life* (1872). Adapting the ballad stanza to the intonations of black folk-speech, she created one of her most memorable and important characters—Chloe Fleet, whose first-person account of slavery, Emancipation, and Reconstruction represents a groundbreaking act of historical imagination. "Aunt Chloe," the first poem in the sequence, focuses upon the trauma of slavery, represented by Chloe's memory of the day her children were sold to pay the debts of her widowed "Mistus." Despite being comforted by Aunt Milly, who also experienced the sale of a child, Chloe has "nursed" her sorrow. Instead of hearing God's voice in a burning bush, Aunt Chloe finds her sorrow alleviated by Uncle Jacob, who teaches her the consolation of a Christian faith. Learning to pray for the first time, she experiences a spiritual resurrection, as she feels her "heavy burden / Rolling like a stone away."

The next poem in the sequence, "The Deliverance," focuses upon the end of slavery, Emancipation, and the early days of Reconstruction. Chloe performs the expected emotional labor of sympathizing with old Mistus when her son enlists with the Confederate army but simultaneously opposes her mistress by praying for a Union victory. This oppositional stance grows even stronger after Emancipation, as the positions of the two women start to reverse. Mistus is now the one to mourn ("When she had to lose her servants, / Her heart was almost broke") while Chloe and the other emancipated slaves dance and march in the street in a "jubilee." Chloe recalls the difficult days after Lincoln's assassination when "another President,— / What do you call his name?" failed to fulfill the freedmen and freedwomen's dreams of social justice. In the face of political corruption and pressure from the Ku Klux Klan, some of the men lose heart and—like the Hebrews wandering in the wilderness—exchange their freedom for the equivalent of a golden calf and the "pots of flesh" of which Harper warned in *Moses*.

The foundations of a stable African American community, Harper argues in the remainder of her poem, are strong female leadership, honest voting practices, the expansion of literacy, and the establishment of a black church. Her vision of female political leadership comes into sharp focus in Chloe's account of how she and the other "women radicals" took on the Mosaic role of maintaining the moral and political compass of their community, in the face of men selling their votes for food. The story of "poor David Rand" adds an additional dimension: a scathing denunciation of the shallow and sugary promises of white politicians. Having sold his vote "for flour and sugar," Rand finds that "The sugar was mixed with sand."

Extending Harper's commentary on the sugary promises that enticed black men from their political responsibility, "Aunt Chloe's Politics" (the third poem) highlights the expense, in lost community resources, of succumbing to politicians who "honey-fugle round, / And talk so awful sweet."

The personal and communal climaxes of "Aunt Chloe" are the paired moments when Chloe achieves the foundation of personal independence by learning how to read the Bible at age sixty ("Learning to Read") and when the community establishes a "meeting place" by constructing a church ("Church Building"). Having glimpsed the promised land of a stable black community founded on religious principles, the religious leader Uncle Jacob is filled with a "mighty power" of prophecy; he blesses the church and then dies. Like Moses, he does not enter Canaan but is able to afford his followers a glimpse of the heavenly realm from afar. Only after the lives of Aunt Chloe and the community have been stabilized on solid religious foundations can Harper's poem end. Its final focus is upon the reuniting of black families torn apart in the diaspora of slavery and the

Civil War (a subject that Harper returned to in her 1892 novel *Iola Leroy*). Chloe's lost son, Jakey, returns (in "The Reunion"), bringing with him news of his brother Ben, who has married and is raising three children. The tables have entirely turned: Old Mistus has "no power" now to touch Chloe or her children, and Chloe feels "richer now than Mistus" because her own son has returned while Mistus's son Thomas has died in the Civil War. Planning to build a new cabin "that will hold us all," Chloe feels that now "like good old Simeon," she will be able "to die in peace" once she can "see 'em all." This closing image provides an apt summary of Harper's poetry for it fuses a moving vision of African American community, founded upon the restoration of black families, with a powerful Christian reference. In Luke 2:26, Simeon learns that he would not die before he had seen the Messiah; Chloe, in contrast, will die in peace after seeing her family reunited.

Displacing and merging biblical stories and the imaginative energy of Jesus into black communal life, Harper focused in subsequent books of poetry upon the moral dangers of personal and political corruption (such as alcoholism and racism), at the same time that she popularized familiar biblical episodes in the Old Testament and the life of Jesus. These poems consolidated Harper's position as one the most important religious poets and leading chroniclers of black life in the nineteenth century. Dramatizing the trauma of slavery, the struggle for freedom, and the necessity of maintaining ideals in the face of tragedy, her poems provided readers with important avenues of historical awareness at the same time that they offered models of personal and communal development. Functioning as the conscience of America and as the political superego of black readers struggling toward self-actualization, Harper's texts embody the promise of *popular* poetry: the works were written not as a record of moments of personal lyricism or insight but as an account of a people's past and a map of their future claims.

Further Reading. *Selected Primary Sources:* Harper, Frances Ellen Watkins, *A Brighter Coming Day: A Frances Ellen Watkins Harper Reader*, ed. Frances Smith Foster (New York: Feminist Press, 1990); ———, *Complete Poems of Frances E. Harper*, ed. Maryemma Graham (New York: Oxford University Press, 1988); ———, *Iola Leroy; Or, Shadows Uplifted* (Philadelphia: Garrigues Brothers, 1892); ———, *Moses: A Story of the Nile*, 2nd ed. (Philadelphia: Merrihew & Son, 1869); ———, *Poems* (Philadelphia: Merrihew & Son, 1871); ———, *Poems on Miscellaneous Subjects* (Boston: J.B. Yerrinton & Sons, 1854); ———, *Sketches of Southern Life* (Philadelphia: Merrihew & Son, 1872). ***Selected Secondary Sources:*** Andrews, William, ed., *Sisters of the Spirit: Three Black Women's Autobiographies of the Nineteenth Century* (Bloomington: Indiana University Press, 1986); Boyd, Melba Joyce, *Discarded Legacy: Politics and Poetic in the Life of Frances Ellen Watkins Harper 1825–1911* (Detroit, MI: Wayne State University Press, 1994); Carby, Hazel, *Reconstructing Womanhood: The Emergence of the Afro-American Woman Novelist* (New York: Oxford University Press, 1987); Foster, Frances Smith, "Introduction," in *A Brighter Coming Day*, by Frances Ellen Watkins Harper; Peterson, Carla, *"Doers of the Word": African-American Women Speakers and Writers in the North (1830–1880)* (New York & Oxford: Oxford University Press, 1995).

Jeffrey Steele

HARPER, MICHAEL S. (1938–)

Exploring history, race, art, and kinship, Michael S. Harper's poetry has distinguished itself as both a form of social action and a redemptive balm. At times difficult and nearly always improvisational, his work has resisted classification into any school. Rather, in linking personal life and loss to historical moments and sites, he has consistently demanded that his readers situate themselves in relation to the historical, including painful social injustices, in an effort to heal and to overcome what he has termed America's historical "amnesia." Frequently invoking jazz as a model for turning loss and pain into revelatory art, Harper's poetry also emphasizes the continuity and strength of African American culture and community.

Harper's first volume, *Dear John, Dear Coltrane* (1970), caught the attention of **Gwendolyn Brooks**, who urged its publication and in the process became one of Harper's poetic mentors, along with **Sterling Brown** and **Robert Hayden**. Opening with the poem "Brother John" and its refrain of "I'm a black man," *Dear John, Dear Coltrane* explores black culture and identity in relation to loss, suffering, and injustice in both the personal and the social arenas, realms that Harper's poetry has refused to see as separate. Using the life and career of jazz saxophonist John Coltrane as its central metaphor, the poems foreground personal and political struggle as what Harper termed in a 1972 interview as "a kind of cultural process" that in the end can be "redemptive." One example is the short poem "American History," which compares the 1963 bombing of a black church in Alabama, resulting in the death of four young girls, to the drowning of 500 "middle passage blacks" hiding underwater during the American Revolution. Although the poem emphasizes the disturbing notion of a continuing cycle of racial oppression and hate crimes, it can also be read as an affirmation of the need to revisit painful moments in the process of working for justice and equality. Similarly, the book's title poem explores both the racism of Coltrane's native south and his own personal pain as contributors to his vision of "a love supreme." A consistent theme is that the ability to move forward hinges upon an awareness of the struggles of history.

The title of Harper's second collection, *History Is Your Own Heartbeat* (1971), reveals his insistence on using personal experience to explore history. A fine example is the sequence "Ruth's Blues," based on the experience of the poet's mother-in-law. Separated from family members in part because of economic and social inequities, Ruth suffers health problems in solitude, without the support of family or community. Her illness is a metaphor for national ills, her blues also those of the nation. In a later interview, conducted in 1984, Harper referred to the blues as a form of art using "real things a person incorporates into his or her own life to fortify and sustain the living." In addition, *History Is Your Own Heartbeat* continued to explore the life and times of major jazz figures in poems like "Here Where Coltrane Is," which links the death of Coltrane to the assassinations of Martin Luther King, Jr., and Malcolm X. In "Movin' Wes" and "'*Bird Lives*': Charles Parker in St. Louis," Harper elegizes the musicians Wes Montgomery and Charlie Parker, in the latter poem exploring Parker's heroin addiction in relation to racism.

Harper extends his art in his next two volumes, *Song: I Want a Witness* (1972) and *Debridement* (1973). In addition to witnessing to racial strife, *Song* introduces a sequence of poems based on photographs. "Photographs: *Negatives*" traces the process of the emergence of photographs from negatives to their appearance in family albums and portfolios. Tracing love, conception, birth, and family as works of art that require time and effort, the sequence begins Harper's longstanding interest in photography and poems that he terms "photographic psychographs" in his acknowledgments for *Songlines in Michaeltree: New and Collected Poems* (2000). The volume *Debridement* begins with a sequence of poems headed "History as Cap'n Brown," which explore the history of resistance to slavery in America, using the historical figure of John Brown as central metaphor. In an interview published in 2000, Harper commented on his interest in "what John Brown meant to black people of his era." The title sequence, "Debridement," is loosely based on the actual experiences of a decorated black Vietnam War veteran who returns to his hometown of Detroit but is unable to find employment. Enduring health and financial hardship, he is ultimately shot and killed by a local store owner, then buried with full military honors at Arlington National Cemetery. Difficult and highly improvisational, "Debridement" is an important exploration of the social aftermath of the Vietnam conflict, and raises significant concerns about the role of people of color in the U.S. military system, as well as their return to society after service.

Harper's fifth major volume, *Nightmare Begins Responsibility* (1975), is one of his most wide-ranging and best-known collections. The title poem, which alludes to Delmore Schwartz's *In Dreams Begin Responsibilities*, returns to the death of Harper's two sons lost in infancy, a subject treated in a sequence of elegies in *Dear John, Dear Coltrane*. Harper presents himself working through his distrust of the white doctors caring for his son, his own sense of anger and helplessness described as "pane-breaking heartmadness." As in many other poems throughout his career, personal loss and pain are presented as an extension of racial tension and misunderstanding within the national culture. But by poem's end the speaker reaches a sort of reconciliation, recognizing the genuine efforts of the doctors, as well as his own responsibility to treat personal suffering within the larger context of the creative impulse. A major voice in the genre of the contemporary elegy, Harper uses his poems of personal loss to consistently look for ways of connecting his pain to larger historical and cultural patterns as a means of redemption and instruction.

Harper's work became known to an even wider audience after the publication of *Images of Kin: New and Selected Poems* (1977), which helped him earn a nomination for the National Book Award in poetry and to win the Melville Cane Award. Covering Harper's career to the publication date in reverse chronology, the volume begins with a sequence of new poems before moving into selections from his previous five volumes. Many of the new poems continue Harper's historical examination of forms of slave trade and racial oppression in the march of U.S. history. One of the new poems, "Psychophotos of Hampton," recalls the cost to Native American life and culture in the wake of "the fevered zeal of the government." As an archeologist of history, Harper has also performed significant editorial work that has been crucial to African American art and scholarship. *Chant of Saints: A Gathering of Afro-American Literature, Art, and Scholarship* (1979), co-edited with Robert B. Stepto, has been a very influential work. As editor of *The Collected Poems of Sterling A. Brown* (1980), Harper returned to print the work of a vital social poet working in the folk tradition. He also co-edited with Anthony Walton the anthologies *Every Shut Eye Ain't Asleep: An Anthology of Poetry by African Americans Since 1945* (1994) and *The Vintage Book of African American Poetry* (2000).

Harper's editorial work is best understood in relation to his notion of "ancestors," those forebears related to the artist not by biology but by choice. The jazz musicians so often honored in Harper's verse, as well as the writers from whom he draws his deepest inspiration, Sterling Brown, Ralph Ellison, and Robert Hayden, are often the subject or starting point for poems from *Healing Song for the Inner Ear* (1985) and *Honorable Amendments: Poems* (1995). A sequence of three poems from *Healing Song* pays tribute to Ellison's flexibility and exactingness as a literary mentor, a writer who "looks for the possible in things / unwritten." In an afterword to *Songlines in Michaeltree* titled "Notes on Form and Fictions," Harper characterizes these literary influences as "the interlopers, outsiders, systematic *makers* who have spent their mature lives producing the *force* that activates the material world with aesthetic energy and a new imagery of possibilities." In *Honorable Amendments* Harper continues to pay homage to influences and to engage contemporary social issues. The poem "Intentional Suffering" tells of an invitation by a black church to former Alabama governor George Wallace to appear before the congregation to ask and receive forgiveness for racist political policy. In a note for the poem, Harper asserts his belief that "Ethical teaching is the answer to a violent culture."

The new poems included in *Songlines in Michaeltree: New and Collected Poems* (2000) show Harper moving into dense but flexible shorter poems using shorter lines and stanzas than he used in much of his previous work. His subject matter continues to include family and community heritage, the spiritual force of jazz, sociopolitical issues, and occasional poems evoked by places and people he has visited and known. After the deaths of Gwendolyn Brooks and Ralph Ellison, Harper increasingly became recognized as one of the two or three most significant figures in African American letters, and his career as a teacher, primarily at Brown University, has allowed his influence to spread through the work of writers and scholars who have studied under him. In a 2000 interview he offered a useful thought on his aim as a poet: "What I strive for is a unique blend of eloquence and original phrasing as practiced by the best musicians, an equivalence of interior speech and historical wakefulness as a person alive in a dynamic reality."

Further Reading. *Selected Primary Sources:* Harper, Michael S., *Dear John, Dear Coltrane* (Pittsburgh, PA: University of Pittsburgh Press, 1970); ———, *Debridement* (New York: Doubleday, 1973); ———, *Healing Song for the Inner Ear* (Illinois, 1985); ———, *History Is Your Own Heartbeat* (Urbana: University of Illinois Press, 1971); ———, *Honorable Amendments: Poems* (Urbana: University of Illinois Press, 1995); ———, *Images of Kin: New and Selected Poems* (1977); ———, *Nightmare Begins Responsibility* (Urbana: University of Illinois Press, 1975); ———, *Song: I Want a Witness* (Pittsburgh, PA: University of Pittsburgh Press, 1972); ———, *Songlines in Michaeltree: New and Collected Poems* (Urbana: University of Illinois Press, 2000). ***Selected Secondary Sources:*** Bibby, Michael, *Hearts and Minds: Bodies, Poetry, and Resistance in the Vietnam Era* (New Brunswick, NJ: Rutgers University Press, 1996); Callahan, John F., "'Close Roads': The Friendship Songs of Michael S. Harper" (*Callaloo* 13.4 [1990]); Dodd, Elizabeth, "Another Version: Michael S. Harper, William Clark, and

the Problem of Historical Blindness" (*Western American Literature* 33.1 [1998]); Harris, Judith, *Signifying Pain: Constructing and Healing the Self Through Writing* (Albany: State University of New York Press, 2003); Stepto, Robert B., "Michael Harper's Extended Tree: John Coltrane and Sterling Brown," in *Twayne Companion to Contemporary Literature in English*, ed. R.H.W. Dillard and Amanda Cockrell (New York: Twayne, 2002).

Ernest Smith

HARRIS, JOEL CHANDLER (1848–1908)

Harris, a white collector of African American folktales and narratives, is best known as the creator of the character Uncle Remus, an elderly black storyteller who represents a white sentimentalized ideal of Southern slavery. Harris composed ten volumes of fiction and poetry utilizing black Southern dialect with Uncle Remus as the central narrator.

Born in the mostly African American town of Eatonton, Georgia, in 1848, Joel Chandler Harris started life in a good location to acquire knowledge of black folk customs and stories. His mother, who first inspired his literary interests, raised him until he was thirteen. At that age, he moved to a plantation called "Turnwold," where he wrote stories and worked as an apprentice on Joe Turner's newspaper, the *Countryman*. Harris befriended a runaway slave on the plantation, and in return, old slave storytellers like George Terrell and "Old" Harbert imparted their folktales to him. He developed a natural comfort level with black Southerners, and as an adult he even swapped with them some of the stories he had been told.

In 1866, Harris left Turnwold and built a career in journalism for the next ten years. Harris was extremely shy, which may account for his choice of a career in writing, and he avoided or struggled through public activities. He moved his family to Atlanta in 1876, to avoid a yellow fever outbreak, and there he immediately began work on the *Atlanta Constitution*, Atlanta's premier newspaper. Harris then initiated his first version of Uncle Remus—which ran for three years—a crude figure of a black beggar and mouthpiece for racist white critiques of postbellum Reconstruction. His second Uncle Remus, the one more popularly known, was a composite of a few black storytellers Harris knew. Stories featuring this second Uncle Remus, a teller of black folktales to a young white boy, ran regularly in the *Constitution* from 1879 to 1880. Although less a political representative than the first Uncle Remus, the second bordered on **minstrelsy** and embodied the archetype of "contented slave" within the Southern idealized myth of slavery. Simultaneously, however, the Uncle Remus tales present a utopia of social relations between a black man and a white boy, one in which social and racial differences are disregarded (Hemenway, 19). Uncle Remus functioned as a symbol of the white Southerner's coming to terms with Southern blacks and as a sign to white Northerners that the South had been rehabilitated from slavery. Harris published a collection of the folktales and songs, *Uncle Remus: His Songs and His Sayings*, in November 1880, and it met with immediate acclaim from critics.

The tales that Harris's Uncle Remus tells include the characters of the trickster Brer Rabbit, Brer Fox, and several other animals. These stories had a long tradition in African American and African storytelling, and all the animal tales he conveys through Remus were told to him by various black storytellers he had met. Although the mode of the stories' deliverance is biased from Harris's white perspective, research has proven that the tales were generally unchanged. Brer Rabbit, who represents the oppressed slave, continually uses his wit and cunning to outsmart, escape and ridicule Brer Fox, who often represents the white slave master.

Harris's primary accomplishment in the Uncle Remus tales is his incredible accuracy in capturing African American dialect. He admits that if his tales do not capture the genius, imagination, and "homely humor" of black Americans, he has "reproduced the form of the dialect merely, and not the essence" (40). In his first volume, *Uncle Remus: His Songs and His Sayings* (1880), Harris reproduces black vernacular for the tales and the poems told by Uncle Remus. Harris mentions that **African American slave songs** do not conform to regular meter; rather, they "depend for their melody and rhythm upon the musical quality of time, and not upon long or short, accent or unaccented syllables" (46). The songs closely reflect natural speech rather than the exactness of measured feet in high poetic verse. In "Revival Hymn," the first song in this collection, the narrator (presumably Uncle Remus) ponders who will go to heaven and who to hell when Judgment Day arrives. In the natural rhythm mentioned by Harris, the narrator warns, "Oh you nee'nter be a stoppin' ena lookin'; / Ef you fool wid ole Satun you'll git took in; / You'll hang on de aidge en get shook in, / Ef you keep on a stoppin' en a lookin'." The narrator concludes that one should "Fight de battles er de Lord," and then they will be able to "fine a latch ter de golden gate [of heaven]." Uncle Remus again urges others to follow God in the next poem, "Camp-Meeting Song." Camp-meetings were religious services attended by both masters and their slaves. Uncle Remus encourages his listeners to "cut loose fum de scoffin' crowd, / En jine dese Christuns w'at's a cryin' out loud / Fer de Lord fer ter come in de mornin'!"

The songs "Corn-Shucking Song" and "The Plough-Hand's Song," also presented by Uncle Remus, are both rhythmic work songs with recurring refrains. After each new verse in "Corn-Shucking Song," the refrain "Hey O! Hi O! Up'n down de Bango!" is repeated for an even

melody. The narrator lists several sounds—the hen, the crow, the calf, and so on—which indicate that dawn has arrived, and the workers must get to the fields because "boss'll be a wakin'." The narrator urges his coworkers to work faster and "let de w'ite foks year you singin'," and he slips in a story of Brer Rabbit, who gets clawed up by Mr. Fox for "sassing" him, likely a warning of the beating incurred for defying slave masters. In "The Plough-Hand's Song," the narrator expresses the few sources of relief a slave gets while out in the field: "we'n layin' by co'n," "we'n he year de dinner-h'on," and "we'n de night draws on." Throughout this song the repetition of the line "Dat sun's a slantin'" emphasizes the most comforting thought for a slave—going home to rest.

In "Christmas Play-Song," the narrator reflects upon illicit relations between slaves. The narrator implies a racial hierarchy when he says about black girls, "don't you take'n tell 'er name, / En den ef sumpin' happen you won't ketch de blame," but then he says about the "yallar," or mulatto, girl, "she may be yone but she oughter be mine!" He elaborates by saying "let de yaller gal 'lone; / Niggers don't hanker arter sody in de pone," and thus he implies an impropriety in interracial sexual relations. Additionally, in "Plantation Play-Song," the narrator admonishes the slaves to dance quietly—"hop light, ladies" (likely another sexual metaphor)—because the night is approaching, and they will all have to work again in the morning.

Harris's subsequent poetry collection, *The Tar-Baby and Other Rhymes of Uncle Remus* (1880), contains the songs mentioned previously plus several Brer Rabbit tales told in verse form. Harris mentions that Uncle Remus, to preserve the most melodic rhythm, "move[s] along the line of least resistance . . . the iambic four-beat movement, the simplest form of narrative verse" (Harris, ix). He finds this a more natural form than the controlled syllabic and accented poetry of "the professors of prosody, who seem to have not the slightest notion of the science of English verse" (ix). In the title story, "Brer Rabbit and the Tar-Baby," Harris reworks a short story from *Uncle Remus* into poetic verse. Harris asserts that "[t]he Tar-Baby story has been thrown into a rhymed form for the purpose of presenting and preserving what seems to be the genuine version" (ix). Harris convincingly conveys black dialect and the cadence of timed, rather than metrical, **free verse** in lines such as, "Dey wisht mighty strong dat der cants was coulds, / Twel de day Mr. Fox got back fum de woods." The animal characters experience a drought, ruined crops, and the threat of starvation. However, the exception is Brer Rabbit, the trickster, who is always able to survive hardship "wid his errytatin' tricks." Mr. Fox sets a trap in the muddy bed of a stream, where he forms an effigy, out of mud, of a dark child playing. This trap teaches Brer Rabbit a lesson in patience and caution; he tries to get the tar baby to talk, and when it doesn't, he hits it, getting his hands stuck, and then kicks it, getting his legs stuck; meanwhile, Mr. Fox hides and watches Brer Rabbit's errors. Harris uses dialectic onomatopoeia such as the sound of getting hit, "kerchuck," and he holds a steady rhythm with the recurring refrain, "Mr. Fox lay low!" After Brer Rabbit becomes fully stuck to the tar baby, Mr. Fox takes the opportunity of revenge on Brer Rabbit, apparently symbolizing the slave masters' anger at unruly slaves (Mr. Fox says he's "de patter-roller," referring to the patrol men who prevented slaves from escaping). However, Brer Rabbit escapes by using reverse psychology on Mr. Fox; he begs Mr. Fox not to throw him into the brier patch (perhaps a symbol of slavery), allowing any other type of death that Mr. Fox lists, but when Mr. Fox throws him in, Brer Rabbit triumphantly replies, "I ain't got a scratch! / *I was bred an' born in de brier-patch!*" (Harris's italics).

Also in *Tar-Baby*, "A Wishing Song" reveals Brer Rabbit's excessive sexual desire, a trickster trait, in the repetition of his "A-wish, wish, wishin'." The narrator issues a warning to the ladies about Mr. Rabbit, who stands "slicker dan sin," gawking at the girls, rubbing his chin.

"De Appile-Tree," another poem in *Tar Baby*, is a retelling of the Adam and Eve story from the slave's perspective. Adam's punishment for fooling around with Eve is that "De overseer gi' im a shovel an' a hoe, / A mule an' a plow, an' a swingletree." This poem reflects antebellum Southern Christian ideology, which explained and justified African American enslavement by condemning dark-skinned people as the fallen progeny of Adam ("Dey all got smeared wid de pitch er Sin . . . An' collogued wid Satan, an' dat what de matter").

Three of the narrative poems in *Tar-Baby* are myths of origin similar to Ovid's *Metamorphosis*. They are written in iambic pentameter with a basic *AA/BB* rhyme scheme, like all the other poems in the collection. The first, "How Brer Tarrypin Learned to Fly," explains why tortoises stay on the ground in a story (similar to that of Icarus) in which Brer Tarrypin nearly dies when, pursuing his impossible dream of flying, he rides Brer Buzzard's back too high. In "Why the Frog Has no Tail," Brer Rabbit, in trickster spirit, gets his revenge for Mr. Frog's luring and trapping him in a mire by ensnaring Mr. Frog in a tree and chopping off his tail. Brer Rabbit also out-tricks his enemy, Miss Buzzard, in "Why the Buzzard's Head Is Bald." In this tale, Miss Buzzard and Brer Rabbit fight over the same piece of land, and when Miss Buzzard plots to feed Mr. Rabbit to her starving younglings, Brer Rabbit burns her with fire, which he gets from "Mr. Man." These tales have roots in African storytelling, and slave storytellers adapted them to the setting of American slavery.

In "Baylor's Mail," Harris dramatizes a highly effective form of mass-communication used by slaves. The narrator urges young slave boys to run as hard as possible, avoiding all dangers and distractions as "a part er de frolic an' fun," to deliver a message by relay. Harris informs the reader that during the Civil War, every slave on a plantation learned of General Sherman's march through Georgia within twelve hours through this system.

Harris did not claim his literary success as his own; he considered himself only a journalist, not a literary man. He acknowledged that most of the appeal of his work came from African folklore, which he recorded for his primarily white readers. Until his death in 1908, Harris continued to write Uncle Remus stories, in addition to nineteen other books of fiction and essays.

Further Reading. *Selected Primary Sources:* Harris, Joel C., *The Tar-Baby and Other Rhymes of Uncle Remus* (New York: D. Appleton and Co., 1904); ———, *Uncle Remus: His Songs and His Sayings* (New York: Hemenway, 1982 [originally 1880]). *Selected Secondary Sources:* Hemenway, Robert, "Introduction," in *Uncle Remus: His Songs and His Sayings*, by Joel C. Harris (New York: Hemenway, 1982 [originally 1880]).

Kris Jensen

HARRISON, JAMES THOMAS (JIM) (1937–)

A prolific writer, Jim Harrison is the author of ten volumes of poetry, in addition to thirteen works of fiction, five collections of nonfiction, and numerous screenplays. The commercial and critical success of his fiction has often overshadowed his poetic achievements, though before publishing his first novel, *Wolf: A False Memoir* (1971), he had already established himself as a poet with two well-received collections, *Plain Song* (1965) and *Locations* (1968). In 1998 Harrison published *The Shape of the Journey: New and Collected Poems*, which spans more than thirty years. His poetry has consistently experimented with both inherited and non-traditional forms, and his work continues to search out and inhabit multiple vantages for detailing the moods and movements of the interior human realm and the natural world in which it lives and dies. Addressing equally the profane and the sacred, the poems gesture toward autobiography, though they are concerned less with the authority of personal experience and more with the potential knowledge latent in other, often non-human or non-Western ways of seeing. In his memoir, *Off to the Side* (2002), Harrison catalogues his seven obsessions: alcohol; stripping; hunting and fishing (and dogs); private religion; France; the road; and nature and natives. Harrison's interest in the spiritual possibility of place has been compared to the interests of prose writers Peter Matthiessen and Thomas McGuane, as well as of the poets **Gary Snyder** and **Ted Kooser**.

Harrison was born in Grayling, Michigan, in 1937, the second of five children. He grew up in rural northern Michigan, which has remained the spiritual center of his art. At the age of seven, an encounter with a girl and a broken bottle permanently blinded his left eye, a condition that is taken up in his poetry. As a young man, Harrison intermittently pursued an education at Michigan State University, taking leaves to explore the West and East coasts before eventually returning to earn both his BA (1960) and his MA (1964). His master's thesis was a critical essay concerned mostly with his first book, *Plain Song*, which was published with the help of the poet **Denise Levertov**, whom Harrison had befriended in Boston. In 1960 Harrison married Linda King, and the couple raised two daughters. He met two writers at the university who would eventually become lifelong friends and correspondents, the prose writer Thomas McGuane and the poet Dan Gerber, whom Harrison credits as his guide in the study of Zen Buddhism, and with whom Harrison edited the literary journal *Sumac* from 1968 to 1972. In 1962, Harrison's father and younger sister died in an accident when a drunk driver struck their car, a loss that pervades much of Harrison's early work. His two years as a professor at State University of New York at Stony Brook from 1965 to 1966 were an admitted failure. Eschewing the popular role of poet-teacher, Harrison supported himself early in his career with a variety of odd jobs before the commercial success of the novella collection *Legends of the Fall* (1979), which was followed by lucrative but emotionally destabilizing forays into Hollywood screenwriting. Following these ventures, Harrison continued to publish in all genres; his twenty-first–century works include the novel *True North* (2004); an epicurean's collection of essays, *The Raw and the Cooked: Adventures of a Roving Gourmand* (2004); and a collaboration with the poet Ted Kooser in a form similar to the *haika renga* (a Japanese linked sequence), *Braided Creek: A Conversation in Poetry* (2003).

Much of Harrison's work explores the dynamic between the outer world and the human interior. His poems often include naturalist details (birds, grasses, rivers, trees), though unlike traditional **pastoral** poetry, nature is not merely an object onto which the writer projects the pathetic fallacy; instead, the external world offers non-self perspectives through which the speaker can glimpse the whole of being, which includes the human. Harrison hints at this altered perspective in an interview from *Conversations with Jim Harrison* (2002): "You have to think of reality in terms of an aggregate of the perceptions of all creatures" (153). The blinding of his left eye as a boy is another way of locating this urge to perceive the world from different angles. "Sketch for a Job-Application Blank," one of the earliest poems in *Plain Song*, begins with the mildly surrealist description, "My left eye is blind and jogs like / a milky sparrow in its socket." What follows is a self-portrait composed of things the speaker saw, feared, and dimly understood as a boy growing up in a rural landscape: horses, snakes, water troughs, oil wells, and a salesman of glass eyes; the constitutional inheritance of his Nordic and German ancestry; and evangelical religion and an early erotic encounter. The end of the poem breaks apart syntactically, as if to challenge the supremacy of self-narrated knowledge or any singular vision.

Harrison's early poems, including *Locations* and *Outlyer and Ghazals* (1971), show traces of the **Deep Image** period style, influenced by Spanish and Latin American surrealism, and associated with American poets like **Robert Bly** and **James Wright**. With **Adrienne Rich**, Harrison popularized a late-twentieth-century interpretation of the *ghazal*, an ancient Arabic form of rhymed couplets and repeated phrases. The poems move from couplet to couplet by associative leaps rather than direct logic. Harrison's interpretation of the form drops the rhyme and meter, instead concentrating on the velocity and force of juxtaposed images and ideas. The long sequence of *ghazals* suits his wide range of perspectives, subjects, and moods, and Harrison's introductory comments to them prove an efficient summary for all of his work: "Crude, holy, natural, political, sexual." The *ghazals*, together with *After Ikkyu and Other Poems* (1996), as well as imagistic moments within longer poems and sequences, are indicative of Harrison's interest in Eastern epistemology and poetic forms.

Many critics consider the title sequence of *Letters to Yesenin* (1973) a high point in Harrison's poetry. Addressed to the early-twentieth-century Russian poet Sergei Yesenin, who hung himself, in the poem "23," the speaker speculates: "Perhaps if your old dog had been in the apartment that night / you wouldn't have done it. Everything's so fragile except ropes." The sequence is a sustained meditation within a spiritual underworld where the speaker wrestles despair—the possibility of death's simplicity and the world's meaninglessness—in order to find some necessary contract with the living. At the end of the sequence, in "Postscript," the speaker's apprenticeship to self-annihilation is postponed and he can say, plainly, "The world is so necessary."

The last section in *The Shape of the Journey* is a sequence called "Geo-Bestiary," the individual poems of which are more traditionally rhetorical and logical than the stations within Harrison's earlier experiments with long poems and suites. What remains consistent in Harrison's mature work, as in poem "34," the last in the book, is the speaker's instinct to stand outside of himself in order to more objectively—and wholly—comprehend the human drama: the promise of love, the failure of communication, rain and wind against the face. "Not how many different birds I've seen / but how many have seen me."

Further Reading. *Selected Primary Sources:* Harrison, Jim, and Ted Kooser, *Braided Creek: A Conversation in Poetry* (Port Townsend, WA: Copper Canyon, 2003); Harrison, Jim, *Conversations with Jim Harrison*, ed. Robert J. DeMott (Jackson: University Press of Mississippi, 2002); ———, *Just Before Dark: Collected Nonfiction* (Livingston, MT: Clark City Press, 1991); ———, *Legends of the Fall* (New York: Delacorte, 1979); ———, *Off to the Side: A Memoir* (New York: Atlantic Monthly, 2002); ———, *The Raw and the Cooked: Adventures of a Roving Gourmand* (New York: Grove, 2004); ———, *The Shape of the Journey: New and Collected Poems* (Port Townsend, WA: Copper Canyon, 1998); ———, *True North: A Novel* (New York: Grove, 2004); ———, *Wolf: A False Memoir* (New York: Simon & Schuster, 1971). *Selected Secondary Sources:* "James (Thomas) Harrison" (*Contemporary Authors Online* [3 June 2004]; *Literature Resource Center*, Thomson Gale [10 November 2004], http://infotrac.galegroup.com); Reilly, Edward C., *Jim Harrison* (New York: Twayne, 1996).

Mark Temelko

HARRYMAN, CARLA (1952–)

Carla Harryman is among the few women poets associated early on with **language** writing, a movement that took shape primarily in the Bay Area in the early 1970s, and which remains interested in disjunctive, opaque language and experimental forms as tools for interrogating the status quo. Concerned specifically with challenging and undermining hierarchies of gender and genre, Harryman's work juxtaposes narrative, poetry, drama, and critical theory in an effort both to subvert the prescribed limits of genre and to open new possibilities for thinking about literature as an intellectual and philosophical practice. Harryman's work is often grouped with that of **Beverly Dahlen** and **Lyn Hejinian**, and like these other language writers, Harryman focuses on showing the limitations of traditional narrative structures. At the same time, Harryman stands somewhat apart from many language writers for her refusal to completely deny or denounce narrative as a literary fact. As she writes in "Toy Boats," a piece from *Animal Instincts* (1989), "I prefer to distribute narrative rather than deny it. . . . Narrative exists, and arguments either for or against it are false."

Carla Harryman was born and raised in Orange, California, moving to San Francisco in the early 1970s. A co-founder of Poets Theater in San Francisco, Harryman has written, directed, and acted in her own experimental plays, in addition to performing in and directing the work of other playwrights. Her *Memory Play* was performed at The LAB in San Francisco in 1994, and *Fish Speech* was included in the PBS miniseries *The United States of Poetry* in 1996. She has given many poetry readings and talks on experimental poetics and has taught at the University of California–San Diego and the Detroit Institute of the Arts. In the mid-1990s, Harryman moved from Berkeley to Detroit with her husband, poet and critic **Barrett Watten**, and their son. Harryman joined the faculty of Wayne State University and became a co-organizer of Black Mouth Reader's Theater in Detroit. In 2005 she received a poetry award from the Foundation for Contemporary Arts.

Harryman's *Gardener of Stars* (2001) is a poetic novel charting the movement of two female characters through an apocalyptic, surreal landscape of oddball characters and impossible occurrences, wherein the focus is upon the two women trying both to make sense of what they see and to locate themselves and their own histories in context. Resonant with the work of postmodern novelist Kathy Acker, *Gardener of Stars* is an interrogation of the workings of narrative, drawing attention to the act of story telling ("I narrated all this to the near lifeless Babs, who moved only to swat flies from her pale limbs and morose little cheeks") and, more specifically, the workings of narratives of gender ("While I was missing Gardener, these creeps were trying to make me part of their harem. The harem was already made up of Bonnie, Mary, Eugenia, Patty. . . . Some of these are my favorite names staged and here presented as future Gold Rush brides."). With its inclusion of a detective figure and the backdrop of a postmodern wasteland, *Gardener of Stars* also recalls the work of **Alice Notley**, particularly the latter's *Disobedience* and *The Descent of Alette*. Throughout the novel, Harryman's narrator transgresses gender norms in her relation of her own sexual fantasies, her cynicism surrounding the prescribed roles of the feminine, and her frustration of traditional narrative structures, even as the overall work unfolds as a pleasurable meta-narrative on the acts of writing and staging.

Harryman's *There Never Was a Rose Without a Thorn* (1995) is perhaps her best-known work, frequently anthologized and included in Mary Margaret Sloan's *Moving Borders: Three Decades of Innovative Writing by Women*. In the preface, Harryman terms the work of this collection "hybrid writings, staged as they are between fiction and theory, the domestic and history, abstractions and androgyny, the rational and the non-rational, the creator and her artifact." "Portraits" from this collection begins with an invocation of DeQuincy as a female male, an androgynous early Victorian who "draws rings of discourse around the Victorian female's Cartesian viewpoint." At once summoning and mocking Cartesian logic, the text unfolds as a parade of disparate female types and archetypes ("a young woman in a novel," "the lady in white," "the ghost of the ghost of Clytemnestra," "the Amazon") blend with each other as an arc of time and, ultimately, an axis of interpretation itself. Theorizing the role of the (inherently unstable) feminine as fundamentally a figment of, or tool for, interpretation, Harryman has the piece end with the feminized interpretation "in her fixed position seated on the crossbeam in a construction site . . . Interpretation! . . . What will happen to you when the crane and shovel arrive with the crew?"—a comic visualization of the vexed relationship between textual construction and interpretation or analysis that tropes simultaneously on fetishes of gender.

Throughout her work, Harryman continually pushes at the limits of form as she searches for innovative, alternative means of expressing thought and intellectual connection in the post-Derridean age. In a prose poem from *Animal Instincts* (1989) entitled "What Is the Status of Narrative in Your Work?" Harryman's narrator begins in media res, "Oh the boats are large, are they not?" triggering a debate with an interlocutor about the phenomenological and the role of argument in creating nonce realities. As the piece unfolds, the impacted conversation touches on philosophy as the foundation of writing, on genre literature and the constructedness of narrative, and on the relationship of ideology to text. In closing, the text points outward, indicating Harryman's abiding concern with finding new forms to serve a dynamic intellectual landscape, at the same time that she acknowledges the significance of the quotidian in relation to the abstract: "A structure for writing that comes from anticipation relative to an elsewhere, which is to become somewhere—i.e., a writing—must borrow from the things of this world in their partiality."

Further Reading. *Selected Primary Sources:* Harryman, Carla, *Animal Instincts* (Oakland, CA: This, 1989); ———, *Gardener of Stars* (Berkeley, CA: Atelos, 2001); ———, *In the Mode of* (La Laguna: Zasterle, 1991); ———, *Memory Play* (Oakland, CA: O Books, 1994); ———, *The Middle* (San Francisco: GAZ, 1983); ———, *There Never Was a Rose Without a Thorn* (San Francisco: City Lights, 1995); ———, *Vice* (Elmwood, CT: Potes and Poets, 1986). *Selected Secondary Sources:* Harryman, Carla, Interview with Megan Simpson (*Contemporary Literature* 37.4 [Winter 1996]: 510–532); Perelman, Bob, "Facing the Surface: Representations of Representation" (*North Dakota Quarterly* 55.4 [Fall 1987]: 301–311); Vickery, Ann, *Leaving Lines of Gender: A Feminist Genealogy of Language Writing* (Hanover, NH: University Press of New England, 2000).

Amy Moorman Robbins

HARTE, FRANCIS BRET (1839–1902)

"Though I am generally placed at the head of my breed of scribblers in this part of the country," Mark Twain wrote from San Francisco in 1866, "the place properly belongs to Bret Harte" (quoted in Scharnhorts, x). Bret Harte is often seen both as a forefather of the "local color" movements in American literature and as

the one most responsible for the Western tradition of writing. Although mostly known for his short stories, such as "The Luck of Roaring Camp" and "The Outcasts of Poker Flats," Harte was also a prolific writer of poetry. His poetry, filled like his prose with miners, prostitutes, gamblers, and other assorted rogues, was just as influential in characterizing the California Gold Rush era as it was in supplying American poetry with one or two of our most popular humorous poems.

Francis Brett Harte was born on August 25, 1836, in Albany, New York. Harte moved West with the Gold Rush in 1854, where he put his literary talents to work, and he first settled in Union, California, but left after penning a scathing rebuke of an Indian massacre that irritated the populace. Relocating to San Francisco, Harte began to publish in the *Golden Era*. He next published his *Condensed Novels and Other Papers* (1867), which he followed with his first collection of poems, *The Lost Galleon and Other Tales* (1867).

Harte was later given the first editorship of the *Overland Monthly*, where he published most of his early work. With the success that followed, Harte moved back East after gaining a ten thousand dollar contract from the *Atlantic Monthly*. In 1878, with new debt mounting and little new literary success, he accepted a position as U.S. consul to Germany. Harte never returned to the United States. He transferred to Glasgow, Scotland, and finally retired to the London that he favored, where he would die in 1902 of throat cancer.

Henry Child Merwin sees the height of Harte's poetic talent in the dramatic quality his works possess. His poems "tell a story and depict a person" (309), but yet in this "tender simplicity" Merwin and others find heart-wrenching pathos, side-splitting humor, and an "exquisite impression of human nature" and feeling in masterful conciseness. But perhaps to the nineteenth-century reader it was not only Harte's coloring of the West that brought him notability but also his masterful use of satire and irony.

Much to Harte's own surprise, his most famous poem became "Plain Language from Truthful James" or "The Heathen Chinee" (1870). The sixty-line poem was one that Harte seemed never to have wanted to publish, but he placed it in the *Overland Monthly* as a last-minute filler. The poem was later published from coast to coast.

In the poem, Truthful James and Bill Nye sit down with "the heathen Chinee," Ah-Sin, to play a game of Euchre. As Ah-Sin claims to have no understanding of the game, the obvious intent is to take Ah-Sin's money. The irony begins when the egotistical and self-professed superior Nyes still must resort to cheating to beat the clueless mark. James claims to be shocked at the aces and bowers that Nye has stuffed in his sleeves, but is even more astonished when Ah-Sin continues to win hand after hand: "'Till at last he put down a right bower

/ Which the same Nye had dealt to me." In the melee that ensues, Nye and James find that Ah-Sin also had bowers stuffed in his sleeves and wax on his fingernails to mark the cards. In this ironic twist, it is the man of inferior race supposedly ignorant of the ways and customs of the American West who cons the self-appointed authority on those ways and customs. It is this turn of events that leads James to proclaim ironically "That for ways that are dark, / And for tricks that are vain / The heathen Chinee is peculiar."

Although unfortunately, and to Harte's chagrin, some have seen this poem as racist, most have seen the inherent satire. Gary Scharnhorst notes that Nye's complaint about being ruined by Chinese cheap labor was the "hypocritical slogan of the displaced workers" (36) of California of this time period. The anger of Nye, much like the anger of the displaced workers, stemmed from the fact that they were beaten at their own game.

In another widely published poem, "To the Pliocene Skull: A Geological Address," one could perhaps further see Harte's fondness for "plain language," concise writing, and the ironic twist. It is the cold, pretentious language of the scientist that Harte wishes to skewer in this poem. The poem's narrator and scientist begins with a lofty address to a skull recovered from a mine in Calaveras County: "SPEAK, O man, less recent! Fragmentary fossil! / Primal pioneer of Pliocene formation." The overblown language and the greeting itself last through nine of the poem's twelve stanzas. In the extended greeting, we see also the natural world that Harte loved stripped of its mythological majesty by being amended with the cold terms of scientific classification.

But it is the skull that gets the final laugh. The scientist stares in awe at the skull's "lateral movement of the condylois process, / With post-Pliocene sounds of healthy mastication." The skull grinds its teeth that are "Stained with expressed juices of the weed Nicotian" and finally speaks—in the Western dialect. The skull, who was actually from Missouri and not the Pliocene era, says his name was Bowers and that his "crust was busted" when he fell down the same mine in which he was found, showing that all of the scientist pomp was for naught.

Given Harte's use of satire and irony in the above two poems, along with the simplicity of language, pathos, and understanding of human nature, one can see why Twain heralded Harte not just as a writer of local color but as one of the best of the Western "scribblers."

Further Reading. *Selected Primary Sources:* Harte, Francis Bret, *East and West* (Boston: Osgood and Co., 1871); ———, *Echoes of the Foothills* (Boston: Osgood and Co., 1874); ———, *Her Letter, His Answer, and Her Last Letter* (Boston: Houghton Mifflin, 1905); ———, *The Lost Galleon and Other Tales* (San Francisco: Towne and Bacon, 1867); ———, *Poems* (Boston: Osgood and Co., 1871); ———, *Poems and Stories* (Boston: Houghton Mifflin, 1912); ———, *That Heathen Chinee and Other Poems* (Melbourne, Australia: George Robertson, 1871). *Selected Secondary Sources:* Merwin, Henry Childs, *The Life of Bret Harte* (Boston: Houghton Mifflin, 1912); Scharnhorst, Gary, *Bret Harte* (New York: Twayne, 1992).

Raymond Yanek

HARTMAN, CHARLES O. (1949–)

Poet, critic, and musician Charles Hartman's explorations are wide-ranging: they include considerations of the potential of computer-aided poetry, the connections between improvisation in music and poetry, scholarly discussions of **free verse** and the voice, and most importantly, an innovative body of poetry. In his essay "Verse and Voice" Hartman writes, "I began to write poetry after I began to play music, and poetry seems to me more instructively like music or dance than like painting. It deepens our awareness of being in time" (132). Hartman's poetry explores systems of understanding, beginning with the lyric voice and moving through complex computer-driven arrangements of language to fusions of varying modes of language and indeed languages. At the core, however, Hartman remains a **lyric** poet, unleashing, whether through automated means or not, incisive moments, as in this vision of mortality from "Retirement," from *The Long View*: "The way my head is turned I hear the knife / working its way through being, branch by branch."

Born on August 1, 1949, in Iowa City, Iowa, Hartman received his BA, magna cum laude, from Harvard University in 1971, and his Ph.D. from Washington University in 1976. He began teaching at Connecticut College in 1984 and became professor of English and poet-in-residence in 1991; he previously taught at University of Washington from 1979 to 1984, and at Northwestern University from 1976 to 1979. Hartman is the recipient of numerous awards, including fellowships from the Connecticut Council for the Arts (1994), The McDowell Colony (1992), Ingram Merrill Foundation (1988), National Endowment for the Arts (1984), and the National Endowment for the Humanities (1978).

A jazz guitarist, Hartman wrote on the connections between poetry and **jazz** in his 1991 *Jazz Text: Voice and Improvisation in Poetry, Jazz and Song*. His 1981 work *Free Verse: An Essay on Prosody* remains the seminal work on free verse. Here Hartman explores the tension between syntax and lineation, giving especial attention to **T.S. Eliot** and **William Carlos Williams**. His critical work—is *Virtual Muse: Experiments in Computer Poetry* (1996)—also in part a memoir of the generation of several of Hartman's most innovative texts—describes his own explorations of the possibilities and limitations of computer-generated poetry as well as his work with the poet **Jackson Mac**

Low and the **modernist** literary critic Hugh Kenner. He also created *the Scandroid* (2005), a metric scansion software. Hartman's works include five collections of poems: *The Pigfoot Rebellion* (1982), *True North* (1990), *Glass Enclosure* (1995), *The Long View* (1999), and *Island* (2004) as well as several limited editions of poems. Collaborating with Kenner, Hartman also created *Sentences* (1995), a text generated through a chain of computer programs.

The Pigfoot Rebellion contains poems, such as "Metrical Exercise," where formal rules such as syllabic count presage Hartman's rule-driven computer-generated poems; lyric meditations such as "To Shadow" or "Before My Father Before Me"; poems that turn from playful to disturbing, as in "Larry and Me"; and poems that are macabre, as in "The Pigfoot Rebellion." The poems of Hartman's second collection, *True North*, develop the collection's recurrent metaphor expressed in the title: the act of reading as a means of determining the truth or discerning one's bearings in the world. The three part poem "Catching a Ray," not unlike **Elizabeth Bishop**'s "The Fish," that examines the familiar made strange; Hartman's focus is on the narrator's unease at snagging a ray, as he asks, "Are these things meant to come / lurching out of the nowhere"? There is a final redemptive moment or communion, as the colors of sea, sky, and ray "fasten me" to them all. The collection's long concluding poem, "The Difference Engine," uses the metaphor of highways, whether interstate or neural, as a figure for a search for truth or solidity. The poem works through accumulation of names, geographic sites, snippets of fact, and observation, all attempting to keep "us from being / hopelessly lost."

Questions or metaphors of seeing, separation, containment, and exposure describe the poems of Hartman's third collection. While *Glass Enclosure* contains poems, such as "Monster with Stars" or "After Kuo Hsi," that continue the autobiographical lyric voice of Hartman's earlier volumes, it also contains poems that are disruptive and playful, such as the two long poems that open and close the collection: "Glass Enclosure" and "Monologues of Soul & Body." The title poem is taken from a jazz piece written by Bud Powell. The poem opens with three one-word lines, suggesting the materiality of language and the possibilities of assemblage. The ruptured opening word, "Sky- / light," forms a motif, with other repeated words, names, and phrases, through the poem. Different levels of language, ranging from the biblical, "Thy hands have made me" (from Psalm 119), to the colloquial, "What, hey," define each line. "Glass Enclosure" also juxtaposes typescript sections, including a trademark statement, with the collection's overall font, thus countering a "found" voice with the monologue of Hartman's version of Powell's voice.

Hartman explores the claim expressed in "Monologue of Soul & Body" that "language makes / three-quarters of your writing decisions / for you." The poem includes texts generated by the Travesty program (developed by Kenner and Joseph O'Rourke), which transforms statistical recurrences of letters into language. To these sections, as in most extended modernist poems, Hartman began to "add new sections, in different verse forms" so that by the end, as he writes in *Virtual Muse*, in "the computer output I saw the body constructing itself out of the material of the soul, working step by step back toward articulation and coherence" (58, 62). The process of decision—thereby free-will—is considered in the poem through references to chess, imperial design, warfare, information technology, and language.

Sentences, the 1995 collaboration with Hugh Kenner, extends the generative and procedural methods begun in *Glass Enclosure*. The book uses several computer programs (Travesty and Diastext, the latter of which, developed by Hartman, automates Mac Low's "diastic" writing) based on discerning recurrences and random selection of sequences that meet the preestablished procedural program. The found text selected for intervention was a mid-nineteenth–century elementary school grammar book. Each of the fifteen titled sections begins with a prose section that has been generated from the original text; this is again altered through programming, creating a fragmentary text, with lines often only a word long, repetitive lines, and fragments of sentences. Although the effect is often playful, the poem seduces us into attempting to create a narrative, and it yet also suggests a minimalist choral chant, thereby drawing us back to one of the roots of poetry.

Hartman moves away from the pure procedural or generated text in his fourth collection, *The Long View*. Divided into three sections, the first includes meditative poems that consider the known world and our limitations. At times, Hartman suggests, our abilities surpass our intentions, as in the poem "Joinery," and create surprise and delight. At other moments, there is a longing for a place of origin and retreat toward some larger connection with nature and the past, as in "The Clearing." The collection shifts in its second section, titled "*Except to Be:* First Quire," which consists of forty-eight prose works in the form of brief essays. The opening essay, "Accent," a meditation on voice and identification, establishes the theme of this section, the various forms of communication and communication's implied—and contained—desire, which is communion.

The final section of *The Long View* contains an example of Hartman's computer-generated poems, "Seventy-Six Assertions and Sixty-Three Questions." This "context-free grammar language generator," as Hartman describes it in a note upon its first publication in

Grist, creates wildly evocative, grammatically correct, but skewed sentences: "The court of color is atmosphere. Light in the spring marches, but place is the true science." This automated writing harkens back to **Dada** and surrealism's automatic writing; the computer has become a collaborator, or as Hartman notes in *Virtual Muse*, "It was helping me think about poetry . . . it was becoming a tool of discovery" (88). The long title poem, composed in tercets, combines history or temporal duration with seeing and with perception. Invoking Homer's Penelope, the art historian E.H. Gombrich, Bach, Zeno, and the anatomist Gray, among others, Hartman moves from distance toward sheer presence by the poem's end: "the bird a shadow on the hill / and then the bird."

Hartman's later collection, *Island*, is a hymn to the Greek island of Aegina (or Aigina, as Hartman, following the Greek, spells it). Divided into three sections, as well as a concluding prose essay "Where Am I," the collection maps the possibilities of representation. The form of the opening poem, "Tamborine," is dictated, writes Hartman in the notes, by "pi mnemonics," where "the length of each successive word is determined by the decimal digits of pi [3.1415]." The poem describes the island yet is also a reflection on being and the mystery of presence. Glimpses of the islanders' daily life and history are fused with descriptions of the landscape and abstract, often aphoristic, meditations: "when I seize X / X eludes." "X," the mysterious denominator, may be the island, the perceiving self, or the communicative presence. The second section of the collection, "Morning Noon & Night," consists of descriptive prose-like poems, recalling those of the Greek poet Yannis Ritsos. Dated from June through July of 1999, they form a diary of detailed observations. The final section consists of eight poems Hartman wrote originally in Greek and then translated. Arguably, translation becomes another system of coming to understanding the world. The poems of this collection reflect the double-bind of the lyric—the attempt to express presence when that presence is to be found always and already through the act of return, or as Hartman, in his final poem "Island," states, "When we finished what we went for we came back."

Further Reading. *Selected Primary Sources:* Hartman, Charles, *Glass Enclosure* (Hanover, NH: Wesleyan University Press, 1995; ———, *Island* (Boise, ID: Ahsahta Press, 2004); ———, *The Long View* (Hanover, NH: Wesleyan University Press, 1999); ———, *Pigfoot Rebellion* (Boston: Godine, 1982); ———, *True North* (Providence, RI: Copper Beech, 1990); ———, "Verse and Voice," in *Conversant Essays: Contemporary Poets on Poetry*, ed. James McCorkle (Detroit, MI: Wayne State University Press, 1990); ———, *Virtual Muse: Experiments in Computer Poetry* (Hanover, NH: Wesleyan University Press, 1996); Hartman, Charles, and Hugh Kenner, *Sentences* (Los Angeles: Sun and Moon, 1995).

James McCorkle

HARTMANN, SADAKICHI (1867–1944)

Sadakichi Hartmann wrote brief, imagistic, Asian-influenced poems earlier than just about any other modernist. His example helped generate **modernism**'s interest in Asian culture and its emphasis on objective imagery, verbal economy, and **free verse**. Hartmann had a palpable, though as yet unmeasured, influence on such poets as **Ezra Pound**, **H.D.**, **Amy Lowell**, and **Gertrude Stein**. Nevertheless, his name does not appear in any of the histories of modernism. A writer with a mixed-race background, he successfully resisted all attempts to pigeonhole him as he crossed national, racial, religious, and aesthetic boundaries. He associated with many of the greatest writers and artists of his time, helping bring not only East Asian but also Middle Eastern and European influences into the American mainstream. Pound commented that "If one hadn't been oneself, it wd. have been worthwhile to have been Sadakichi (not that my constitution wd. have weathered the strain)" (*Guide to Kulchur*, 310). Lowell called him "the most mysterious man in American letters" (Hartmann, *White Chrysanthemums*, vi). Stein remarked that "Sadakichi is singular, never plural" (vi).

Carl Sadakichi Hartmann was born in 1867, in Nagasaki, Japan, and died in 1944, in the United States, having spent his last years living in an isolated shack on the Morongo Indian Reservation in Banning, California. He was the son of a German trader and a Japanese mother, who died in childbirth. Brought up in Germany and the United States, he was to become an American citizen at the age of twenty-seven. He later wrote, "I personally never think of myself as a German or Asiatic. Others do it for me." As a teenager in Philadelphia, he attached himself to **Walt Whitman**, who said of him, "I have more hopes of him, more faith in him, than any of the boys" (*Whitman-Hartmann Controversy*, 27). Beginning at the age of nineteen, Hartmann made four trips to Paris and Germany, where he met important artists and studied the arts. Soon thereafter, he succeeded in publishing his Symbolist drama, *Christ* (1893), which despite its title promoted free love. Most copies of the play were burned, and Hartmann spent a brief time in jail. In subsequent years he wrote additional avant-garde dramas about Buddha, Confucius, Moses, and Muhammad, and he began to receive recognition as the author of revolutionary essays on art and photography. By 1908 Hartmann was living in New York, forging experimental alternatives to mainstream culture and assuming the role of "the King of Bohemia," as a friend labeled him. He wrote poems influenced by a multitude of international traditions and forms, publishing them in stray literary journals and then in books printed at his own expense. By 1923 Hartmann was writing unproduced film scripts and living in Los Angeles. By 1930 he was supporting himself by lecturing on art to small audiences across mid-America. In the 1940s he lived in seclusion, under surveillance by the FBI because of his Japanese-German background.

Hartmann's poetry includes bold images in the style of Ezra Pound and aphoristic language play similar to that of Gertrude Stein. Older than those writers, Hartmann was often ahead of them in such experiments. He composed haiku, for example, as early as 1898, about fifteen hears before H.D.'s and Pound's imagist poems. Hartmann introduced French symbolism, Japanese tanka and haiku, and medieval Persian lyric into American avant-garde poetic practice. By means of his poems and his essays, he put poetry into conversation with the latest developments in art, drama, music, photography, and cinema. Because Hartmann was noticed by his fellow artists, if not by poetry readers at large, he made a difference at a pivotal time. He helped American poetry modernize itself.

One of Hartmann's early poems, "Cyanogen Seas Are Surging" (1898), employs a scientific vocabulary to evoke a vivid dream landscape, perhaps forging links among metaphysical poetry, French symbolism, and incipient modernism. The image of "cyanogen seas"—cyanogen being a colorless, poisonous gas that turns pigment blue—might be said to forecast **Eliot**'s "patient etherised upon a table." The second line's "cinnabarine strands"—the adjective meaning bright red, like crystals of cinnabar—and the third line's "white Amazons" (later in the poem "white virgins") evoke the color contrast of Pound's "green arsenic smeared on an egg-white cloth." Moreover, the H.D.-like allusion to classical mythology, the Eliotesque metaphor of a red desert of sexual frustration, and the "Oread"-like image of surging sea of desire all tie the poem closely to a modernist rhetoric that was to come more than a decade later.

Perhaps even more startling is the way Hartmann's tanka and haiku, all invented despite their air of having been translated, resemble Asianist experiments by Pound and Lowell. Hartmann collected these poems in the self-published *Tanka and Haikai: Japanese Rhythms* (1916), but as Pound remarked, Hartmann had previously "scattered" them in various "lost periodicals" (*Guide to Kulchur*, 310) Lacking Pound's access to such mainstream journals as *Poetry*, Hartmann had a difficult time getting his poems distributed and read, but his experiments with tanka and haiku almost certainly preceded the productions of Pound and Lowell. Hartmann introduced the tanka form to his readers as "the most popular and characteristic of the various forms of Japanese poetry." He explained that the tanka "consists of five lines of five, seven, five, seven, and seven syllables—thirty-one syllables in all. The addition of the rhyme is original with the author" (*Tanka and Haikai: Japanese Rhythms*, 1):

Winter? Spring! Who knows!
White buds from the plumtrees wing
And mingle with the snows.
No blue skies these flowers bring,
Yet their fragrance augurs Spring.

Hartmann's direct treatment of the white flower buds mingling with the white snow in a season that is not quite winter and not quite spring evokes comparison to similar poems by Pound, H.D., Lowell, **Williams**, and Eliot. His interest in syllabics forecasts a similar aesthetic dimension in some of Williams's poems and all of **Moore**'s. We might say that Hartmann diverged from his cohorts, however, in his pursuit of rhyme—going so far as to impose it on a form that traditionally lacks it. But we can detect in Hartmann's combination of Japanese syllabics and English rhymes a formal analogue to his overarching project of putting eastern and western cultural practices into contact with each other, just as we glimpse his interest in hybridity in the poem's mingling of winter and spring.

Along with his fascination with phenomenological and linguistic play, Hartmann evidenced a strong awareness of social problems as well. He worried about the "sinister" aspects of "the machine age, the capitalist era, and the gold standard." He deplored Western imperialism, whereby "the white devils claim that they come as benefactors as they relieve the natives of the tsetse fly, when they themselves are worse than any plague of flies." He expressed such anxieties in his imitation of the *Rubáiyát of Omar Kayyám*, a twelfth-century Persian text famously translated into English by Edward FitzGerald in 1859. In 1913 Hartmann rewrote the Persian poem, revising it even more freely than Pound did *Sextus Propertius*. Hartmann explained that his meter was "a combination of Whitman's free rhymeless rhythm, the *vers libre* that changes with every subject and mood, and the vague alliteration of sound in quarter tones characteristic of Japanese poetry" (*My Rubaiyat*, 3). Hartmann renounced his predecessors' rhymes, substituted six-line stanzas for the original quatrains, and in other ways made the sequence entirely his own. From the predecessors he retained only a tone of philosophical melancholy. He made the personal aspect of his text clear by re-titling the poem *My Rubaiyat*. Hartmann used the revision as a forum for expressing his personal and political philosophy—his hopes and fears, his sense of marginality and sadness. Publishing the poem the year before World War I began, he particularly emphasized his horror of war, in which "mangled bodies strew the plains," and "o'er the corpse the mother wails."

Hartmann brought aesthetic experiment, international perspectives, and social awareness to the modernist enterprise. His introduction of new and hybridized forms showed the way to the first modernist generation in the second decade of the twentieth century, and his empathy for the poor, the marginalized, and the suffering foreshadowed the work of the second modernist generation in the 1930s. Hartmann was never in the limelight. But he was usually in the vanguard.

Further Reading. *Selected Primary Sources:* Hartmann, Sadakichi, *My Rubáiyát*, Author's Edition (St. Louis, MO: Mangan Printing, 1913); ———, *Tanka and Haikai: Japanese Rhythms*, Author's Edition (San Francisco: 1916); ———, *White Chrysanthemnums*, ed. George Knox and Harry Lawton (New York: Herder and Herder, 1971); ———, *The Whitman-Hartmann Controversy*, ed. George Knox and Harry Lawton (Frankfurt, Germany: Peter Lang, 1976); Pound, Ezra, *Guide to Kulchur* (New York: New Directions, 1938). *Selected Secondary Sources:* Knox, George, Introduction to *The Life and Times of Sadakichi Hartmann, 1867–1944: An Exhibition*, ed. Wistaria Hartmann Linton (Riverside: University of California Library, 1970, 1–9); Van Deusen, Marshall, "Sadakichi Hartmann," in *Dictionary of Literary Biography*, vol. 54 (Detroit, MI: Gale, 1987).

Steven Gould Axelrod

HASS, ROBERT (1941–)

Robert Hass's poetry fuses sensuality with the meditative, the political with the philosophical, the world of daily human activity with the natural world. His poetry often parallels that of the **lyric essay**, for a ruminative quality runs through the work, along with the tautness or economy of expression associated with poetry. To no small degree, Hass has from his earliest works insisted on the mutual pleasures of poetry and life. His work is grounded in the intimacy of everyday life, yet Hass refuses to remain restricted to either description or narrative, but opens the poem to speculation. Hass has received considerable acclaim not only for his poetry but also for his essays and his translations, notably those of the works of Nobel Laureate **Czesław Miłosz**. Hass's work, while usually located within the landscapes of California, portrays the complex interior life of the poet.

Born in San Francisco on March 1, 1941, Hass has remained a resident of California for almost his entire life. After growing up in the suburbs of San Rafael and attending a private Catholic school, Hass received a BA from Saint Mary's College of California in 1963. He then received his MA in 1965, from Stanford University, where he studied with the poet and critic **Yvor Winters**, whose influence as a proponent of **New Criticism** can be seen in Hass's work. Hass briefly taught at SUNY–Buffalo, accepting a position there in 1967. He returned

to California to complete his Ph.D. at Stanford in 1971; Hass then taught at his alma mater Saint Mary's College until 1989, when he began teaching at the University of California at Berkeley. While a student at Saint Mary's College, he married Earlene Lief, and their three children, Leif, Kristin, and Luke were all born while Hass attended graduate school. After the couple's divorce in 1989, Hass married the poet **Brenda Hillman**. From 1995 to 1997, Hass served as the United States Poet Laureate.

Field Guide, Hass's first book, was selected in 1973 by the poet **Stanley Kunitz** for the Yale Younger Poets competition. Ecco Press published his three subsequent books: *Praise* (1979), *Human Wishes* (1989), and *Sun Under Wood* (1996), which won the National Book Critics Circle Prize in Poetry. His collection of essays, *Twentieth Century Pleasures: Prose on Poetry* (1984), also received the National Book Critics Circle Prize for Criticism upon its publication. The recipient of a MacArthur fellowship, Hass served as the nation's poet laureate for two years, beginning in 1995. As part of his service, he published a weekly column on poetry, introducing each Sunday a new poem. These selections were subsequently collected in his *Poet's Choice: Poems for Everyday Life* (1998). Hass rendered deft versions of haiku and collected them in his *Essential Haiku: Versions of Bash, Buson, and Issa* (1994) and edited editions of translations of the Swedish poet Tomas Tranströmer and of the Slovene poet Tomaz Salamun; however, it is Hass's translations of Czesław Miłosz, often in collaboration with Miłosz, Renata Gorczynski, and **Robert Pinsky**, that have been the most ongoing and influential of his translations. Writing in his introduction to *Field Guide*, Stanley Kunitz observed,

> Reading a poem by Robert Hass is like stepping into the ocean when the temperature of the water is not much different from that of the air. You scarcely know, until you feel the undertow tug at you, that you have entered another element. Suddenly the deep is there, with its teeming life. (xi)

The poem "Letter" suggests this movement from the prosaic and conversational diction of the opening lines to an attentiveness to the natural world that transcends the ordinary. The poem then quickly moves to a meditation on the ability to transpose the act of acute observation into language. That awareness of loss when describing what was seen, Hass reflects, is the absence of human companionship, that of his family. The sense of desire and loss becomes part of the structure of the poem, which concludes as a love poem—an epistolary to Earlene—"I miss you, love. Tell Leif / you're the names of things."

The fusion of family, desire, and the acute observation of nature are especially present in the poems of *Field*

Guide. The collection is divided into three sections: "The Coast," "A Pencil," and "In Weather." The first section is situated in California, often balancing the immediacy of observation with an awareness of history. The second section invokes other writers, notably **Robinson Jeffers**, Bash, Buson, and Issa, and concludes with a series of poems imagining a pornographer, so as to provide a critique of art and pleasure in the United States as facile and hollow. The third section returns to evocations of landscape and family, but also to forms of displacement.

While Hass in various interviews has mentioned **Kenneth Rexroth**, **Ezra Pound**, and William Wordsworth as favorite and influential poets for him, it is **Gary Snyder** who often comes to mind when reading Hass's early work with its fusion of intimacy, politics, and the natural world. In "Black Mountain, Los Altos," Hass evokes the physical landscape with his opening lines "Clumps of ghostly buckeye bleached bones / weirdly gray in the runoff" and parallels Snyder's own, even more tautly sounded, lines. Also like Snyder, Hass reads the place as a palimpsest where different histories of oppression— that of the colonial Spanish and the United States' neo-colonial role in Vietnam—are overlaid. As much as Hass recognizes the pleasures of his California, he recounts other events as well. In "Palo Alto: The Marshes," Hass records the multiple histories of seizure and loss that define California: "'We take no prisoners,' John Fremont said, / and took California for President Polk," which is the same California where the Klamath tribe was routed and disappeared, and which has seen the loss of indigenous species. This palimpsestic approach is found in the long concluding poem of the collection, "Lament for the Poles of Buffalo." Here Hass's natal landscape and language are displaced: "These green New York summers— / foreign and magical to me," writes Hass in the opening lines of the poem. Occasioned in part by Hass's subpoena by a grand jury convened to investigate anti-war activities at SUNY–Buffalo in 1970, where Hass was teaching, the poem explores the poet's sense of loss that comes with distance, of dismay at the culture that has cut itself off from its origins and at the historical displacements and losses of his Polish neighbors, the Iroquois, and the landscape itself.

The collection is itself a field guide. One of the persistent qualities of Hass's poetry is his attention to the natural world. This may stem from the early influence of Rexroth and, in particular, Rexroth's poem "Time Spirals," from his first collection *In What Hour* (1940). In "Some Notes on the San Francisco Bay Area as a Culture Region: A Memoir," Hass describes his first reading of "Time Spirals" as seizing him with the presence of his own landscape—Papermill Creek and Tomales Bay— recast into poetry. Hass writes,

Art hardly ever does seem to come to us at first as something connected to our world; it always seems, in fact, to announce the existence of another, different one, which is what it shares with gnostic insight. That is why, I suppose, the next thing that artists have to learn is that this world is the other world. (222–223)

The presence of the natural world and the mapping of topographies through the Adamic process of naming defines much of Hass's work, as exemplified in these lines: "Chanterelles, puffballs, chicken-of-the woods" (from "Fall"); "sea-otter, sandal-wood, and bêche-de-mer" or "Olema / Tamalpais Mariposa / Mendocino Sausalito San Rafael" or "clams, abalones, cockles, chitons, crabs" (from "Maps"); and "Casting, up a salt-creek in sea-rank air, / fragrance of the ferny anise, crackle of field grass" (from "San Pedro Road").

Hass's next book, *Praise*, contains several of his most discussed poems: "Heroic Simile," "The Yellow Bicycle," "Against Botticelli," "Songs to Survive the Summer," and especially "Meditation at Lagunitas." Containing twenty-four poems, the collection is divided into two sections, the second composed entirely of the **long poem** "Songs to Survive the Summer." Many of the poems of the first section are composed in long prose-like lines, often opening with declarative statements: "In the life we lead together every paradise is lost" (from "Against Botticelli"); "This is a letter of apology, unrhymed. / Rhyme belongs to the dazzling couplets of arrival" (from "Not Going to New York: A Letter"); and perhaps most famously, "All the new thinking is about loss. / In this it resembles all the old thinking" (from "Meditation at Lagunitas"). If Hass's first collection was a guide to the sensual and physical world—both of pleasure and of violence—then *Praise* is a guide to metaphysical conditions, those of language, love, and the imagination.

The much-anthologized "Meditation at Lagunitas" continues the acute observations of the natural world that won Hass acclaim for his first collection, yet here the observation is tied directly to both philosophical and theological meditations. Hass suggests that the loss of an idealized connection between all things occurs through the mediation of language and specifically the act of naming and describing. Hass extends this to a critique of much contemporary philosophy and linguistics, particularly those philosophies of Saussure and Derrida, who hold that language is an arbitrary construction: Because there is no correspondence between word and object, "a word is elegy to what it signifies." Without some integral or essential connection between things and language, Hass argues in this poem, everything is in danger of dissolving. At the end of the poem, Hass rejects the postmodernist condition of language as limited and produced, asserting a fusion of the written and spoken or the abstract and physical word through the incantatory repetition of the word "blackberry."

It is this particularity of both *thing* and *word* that Hass praises. The physical and sensual world is where revelation exists, as he writes in "Santa Lucia": "as if the little song / *transcend, transcend* could get you anywhere." Abstract statements, and indeed the desire for transcendence, are viewed finally with skepticism. In such poems as "The Origin of Cities," "Winter Morning in Charlottesville," and "Monticello," where Hass addresses events of history, the poems insist upon a grounding in the colloquial and observed. In "Weed," Hass meditates on the natural history of the horse parsnip, not botanical but associative ("Horse is Lorca's word, fierce as wind, / or melancholy, gorgeous, Andalusian") and observed. The use of specific botanical descriptors such as stalks, bracts, and flowerets gives a sense of exactness and authenticity to Hass's writing. Hass emphasizes the sense that language is about human relations and how we move through the world, as he states near the conclusion of "Songs to Survive the Summer," that what he has to give are "stories, /songs, loquat seeds." Addressed to his child and set in unrhymed tercets, the poem is a meditation on mortality and transience; yet it also suggests that language names those relationships and that naming is "the frailest stay against our fears."

Ten years after the publication of *Praise*, Hass's third book, *Human Wishes*, was published. In the intervening years, Hass published his collection of essays *Twentieth Century Pleasures* (1984), which included long essays on **Robert Lowell**, **James Wright**, Miłosz, and Rilke, as well as on images and form. Divided into four sections, *Human Wishes* continues Hass's meditations on human desire and suffering, language and abstraction, art and sexuality. Composed in single line stanzas, the poems of the first section tend to have long lines, usually extending past the margin several times over. In the second section, Hass included prose meditations; like the Japanese form *haibun*, sections which traditionally form transitions from haiku, these texts focus on the transience of daily life. The poems of the third and fourth sections are composed in long, but not extended, lines; often focusing on relationships between father and child or between two lovers, the language frequently shifts from the descriptive and Adamic to the conversational. Many of the poems examine impasses in which Hass finds parallels between the erotic and the artistic, as in the first two lines of "Spring Drawing," which opens the collection: "A man thinks *lilacs against white houses*, having seen them in the farm country south of Tacoma in April, and can't find his way to a sentence, a brush stroke carrying the energy of *brush* and *stroke* / —as if he were stranded on the aureole of the memory of a woman's breast."

In many ways *Human Wishes* is a series of formal variations upon Hass's exploration of the possibilities of human relations. In "Museum," one of the prose pieces, Hass composes a scene of a young man and woman, each of whom is caring for a baby in a museum restaurant: "All around them are faces Käthe Kollwitz carved in wood of people with no talent or capacity for suffering who are suffering the numbest kinds of pain: hunger, helpless terror. But this young couple is reading the Sunday paper in the sun, the baby is sleeping, the green has begun to emerge from the rind of the cantaloupe, and everything seems possible." Hass negotiates the space between misery and pleasure—often noting the ways we fail to register suffering, whether it is presented in art or through another's experience. In some way, to be engrossed with the daily acts of living—holding a child, reading the newspaper, eating—protects us and allows for possibility.

In the prose work that bears the title of *Human Wishes*, Hass's opening is typical: a scene is set and a proposition is offered that will be subsequently explored—"This morning the sun rose over the garden wall and a rare blue sky leaped from east to west. Man is altogether desire, say the Upanishads." Through the daily transactions of writing, of seeking a back to an antique Welsh cupboard, or of conversations, Hass builds layers of meditations on desire. Hass presents the choices we make, out of desire or suffering, that come to define our presence, as he writes in the beginning of one of the concluding poems, "Thin Air": "What if I did not mention death to get started / or how love fails in our well-meaning hands." In the poems such as "Santa Barbara Road" and "Berkeley Eclogue," Hass accumulates and sifts through the particulars of living—whether conversation, objects, or relationships—to understand the tenuousness of language and desire. It is through the raveling of these questions and conversations that we come to understand ourselves as humans.

Hass's fourth book of poems, *Sun Under Wood* (1996), continues his exploration of the long, inclusive line. Unlike **Whitman**'s lines, which accumulate things, thereby creating vast catalogues of American experience, and which Hass's earlier poetry partakes of to some degree, these poems employ a discursive line, more related to conversation than Adamic naming. Many of the same concerns that marked *Field Guide* and continued through the intervening collections are to be found in *Sun Under Wood*: familial relationships, an engagement with history and nature, and the difficulties of language. What is perhaps new and surprising in this collection is the recollecting of his mother's alcoholism, his brother's drug addiction, and his own unraveling marriage and divorce. Yet these subjects also form a continuum of Hass's exploration of human desires; rather than being strictly autobiographical or sensational, they continue his probing of the transience of pleasure. The opening poem, "Happiness," suggests this tension between living and acute awareness: A pair of red foxes, before returning to eating, "looked up at us with their green eyes / long enough to symbolize the wakefulness of living things." Hass creates a sense of causality in the poem, yet happiness seems to exist either as *cause* or as momentary *result*. In poems like "Happiness," Hass balances "the irreducible mysteriousness of the images themselves" (xiv), as he writes of haiku in *The Essential Haiku*, and the revealing discursiveness of sentences.

Perhaps the most often discussed poem of this collection of twenty poems is the long poem "My Mother's Nipples." Composed in sections of long discursive lines, short disjunctive lines, and autobiography in prose, the poem seeks to find ways to both tell and understand the story of his mother's alcoholism and subsequent confinements in institutions with a probing of "where all displacement begins." Poignant and sad, the poem constellates forms of substitution and displacement of grace and nurture. In "Regalia for a Black Hat Dancer," his brother's addiction and his marriage's end become the poem's autobiographic pivots. However, this long poem, like "My Mother's Nipples," traverses a variety of experiences and images; much like **Larry Levis** in his later poems, Hass creates associations and correspondences rather than recounting a particular, unified story. The nexus of pain and joy dominates as the thematic focus, "we beget joy, we beget suffering."

The collection's final poem, "Interrupted Meditation," draws upon many of Hass's themes: history, personal loss, the possibilities of art and language, and sensory pleasures. Recounting a conversation with a survivor of Nazi occupation, the poem begins with the moral question of having done enough to aid Jews in hiding. To Hass, the speaker states that Miłosz, the Polish Nobel Laureate, believes in the redemptive power of language; however, the speaker contends, "*There is silence at the end, / and it doesn't explain, it doesn't even ask.*" Against these two extremes, the revelatory word and the abysm of silence, Hass posits the possibility of lyricism, that of the naming song, or indeed that of pure song. Against the speaker's belief in the limitation of naming, Hass enumerates and describes. In response to his acute awareness of "Everyone their own devastation," Hass offers the modest grace of song and naming—perhaps not entirely compensatory to the degrees of suffering, Hass would no doubt note, but nonetheless necessary.

Further Reading. *Selected Primary Sources:* Hass, Robert, *Field Guide* (New Haven, CT: Yale University Press, 1973); ———, *Human Wishes* (New York: Ecco, 1989); ———, *Poet's Choice: Poems for Everyday Living*, selected and introduced by Hass (Hopewell, NJ: Ecco, 1998); ———, *Praise* (New York: Ecco, 1981); ———, *Sun Under Wood* (Hopewell, NJ: Ecco, 1996); ———, *Twentieth Century Pleasures: Prose on Poetry* (New York:

Ecco, 1984). ***Selected Secondary Sources:*** Bond, Bruce, "An Abundance of Lack: The Fullness of Desire in the Poetry of Robert Hass" (*Kenyon Review* 12.4 [Summer/Fall 1990]: 46–53); Doody, Terrance, "From Image to Sentence: The Spiritual Development of Robert Hass" (*American Poetry Review* 26.2 [March/April 1997]: 47–56); Hass, Robert, trans., ed., *The Essential Haiku: Versions of Bash, Buson, & Issa* (Hopewell, NJ: Ecco, 1994).

James McCorkle

HAWAI'IAN INTERNMENT CAMP POETRY OF JAPANESE AMERICAN INTERNEES

In 1983, Bamboo Ridge Press in Honolulu published a slim volume of tanka by Japanese American poets from Hawai'i who were interned during World War II. Seven years later, George H.W. Bush signed an official apology to survivors of the camps, who each received $20,000 in reparations. That the publication and the apology followed the internment by so many decades speaks volumes about the silences surrounding the internment of Japanese Americans and also the aftermath of that imprisonment. The poetry written by internees offers crucial witness to the reactions of internees at the time of their confinement in concentration camps from Arkansas to Wyoming and elsewhere.

The Jewish Holocaust is not an exact analogy to the Japanese American internment camps, but when Giorgio Agamben, in his *Remnants of Auschwitz: The Witness and the Archive*, writes that "shame" is the dominant sentiment of survivors, he might have been writing about the Japanese American experience. In her crucial memoir, *Farewell to Manzanar* (1973), co-written with her husband, Jeanne Wakatsuki Houston writes that she could not talk openly about her experience for twenty-five years: "as I came to understand what Manzanar had meant, it gradually filled me with shame for being a person guilty of something enormous enough to deserve that kind of treatment" (133). Add fear to shame: In 1973 a reporter visiting Manzanar's camp cemetery asked, "How many people are buried here?" and got this answer from a former inmate: "A whole generation. A whole generation of Japanese who are now so frightened they will not talk" (quoted in Dolores Hayden, 142).

For many of the camp survivors, silence lasted forty years. Hence, John Tateishi prefaces his oral history *And Justice for All: An Oral History of the Japanese American Detention Camps* (1984) by writing, "Although unfairly stigmatized by accusations of disloyalty, they could not find the voice within themselves to tell others, often even their own children, about what happened to them personally" (vii). The Japanese American Citizens League (JACL) Handbook on Redress, directed by Tateishi, reported that in many cases, children of incarcerated Nisei (second-generation Japanese) parents learned about the imprisonment only later in their college history classes. According to Tetsuden Kashima's introduction to *Personal Justice Denied: Report of the Commission on Wartime Relocation and Internment of Civilians* (1982–1983, 1997), most textbooks did not mention internment until the 1980s. He describes the reaction of former internees as a form of "social amnesia . . . a group phenomenon in which attempts are made to suppress feelings and memories of particular moments or extended time periods" (297). Wendy Ng, who composed a reference guide for Greenwood Press on internment, prefaces her book by noting that she is the daughter of an internee who "never revealed to me any more details of her camp experience" (Preface).

Obviously, much of this silence on the part of internees themselves was due to shame and suffering, a fear that speaking about the events of the past would make those events all-too present; in the words of Ben Ohama, "when I read the summary of the commission on Wartime Relocation and Internment of Civilians, I felt a deeper sense of pain and devastation than at the time of my evacuation" (1984 hearings, 793), or in the words of Floyd Shimomura, "Although our bodies have been liberated from the desert camps, I think our souls and our honor still feel imprisoned. Until we are liberated by this Congress, the incarceration will continue" (601). Dori Laub, a psychiatrist who specializes in Holocaust issues, explains, "the speakers about trauma on some level prefer silence so as to protect themselves from the fear of being listened to—and of listening to themselves. That while silence is defeat, it served them both as a sanctuary and as a place of bondage" (*Testimony*, 58). Although she takes issue with the notion that silence is, of necessity, a problem, Patti Duncan writes, "silence is the prison itself; the internment embodies and enacts the greatest silence of all" (78). But some of the silence, as of the early 1980s, was due to the fact that the history of internment had not been written or published. Harry Kubo testified that he had told his children about his internment, but they had not believed him. He ascribed their doubt to the fact that "it has never been published in the book in the literary form that would be made available to them."

So it might seem logical to think that these later silences, on the part of survivors and historians, had been prefigured by the silences of men and women in internment camps (or what the University of Hawai'i Library still calls "evacuation camps" in its catalogue). One might easily agree with **Lawson Fusao Inada**'s poem at the end of the "Camp" section of *Legends from Camp* (1993), where the poet writes about what his neighbor sings of (love, luck, want) and what he fails to sing about, including the "guard towers, guns" that appear "beyond / the plantation" ("Looking Back at Camp," "Jerome").

Tempting as it is, this notion of a complete silence surrounding the Japanese American experience of the camps is false. There *were* songs from the camps, among them the tanka of Hawai'i internees published in Bamboo Ridge's slim 1983 volume, *Poets Behind Barbed Wire*. Many of these poems had been published privately (in some instances in mimeograph form) soon after the war, but were never widely available to a non-Japanese American audience. Poet and editor Richard Hamasaki notes that poems were made available to people who were "trusted."

It's no surprise that Issei and other Japanese Americans whose native language was Japanese would turn to the tanka as their poetic form; the poem has a long literary history, beginning with Japanese court poetry and continuing into modern times with a greater infusion of political content. But the tanka's brevity accomplished another purpose in the camps. As the Nakanos write of Muin Otokichi Ozaki, one of the poets in their collection, "He managed to write approximately 200 poems per sheet in minute handwriting on thin ricepaper stationery which could easily be carried around without official notice" (5). Furthermore, as the editors note, paper was a scarce commodity, and so "these short poems, being less cumbersome than long diaries, were ideal forms for the internees' expression of their pent-up emotions." As Earl Miner writes in his *Introduction to Japanese Court Poetry* (1968), "Japanese literature emphasizes human feeling and reflection in participation with much that we think is opposed to man—especially nature and the divine. The contrast, if simplified more, is between Western faith in persuasive ideas and Japanese faith in cultivated feeling" (9).

If traditional tanka poems testify to their authors' sadness, loneliness, and the love of nature as antidote, then the internment camp tanka continue this tradition, while locating feeling within a decidedly political, military frame. Sojin Takei, for example, as he reaches San Francisco, writes "Autumn deepens / In the City of Fog," but then his sorrows (in military language) "besiege" him. This poem, with its links between fog and sorrow, autumn and evening, could take its place among traditional tanka. But when other poems are taken into consideration, the themes of military constraint begin to emerge. Thus, Muin Ozaki writes of saying farewell to her sleeping children "As I am taken prisoner / Into the cold night rain." The traditional tanka method of linking weather to feeling is pushed into the background, and the fact of imprisonment becomes the central feature of the poem.

Traditional tanka were often about travel; to quote Miner again, "travel was by definition away from the capital and all it represented. The essential nature of the experience, therefore, came to be expressed poetically as a depression and misery commonly tinged with beauty" (6). Yet, if the traditional tanka expresses nostalgia for the past because it is always being lost, the internment tanka expresses nostalgia for the past because it is being taken away by force. Regret replaces nostalgia, under the force of a larger politics: Ozaki writes of his memory of scolding his son for biting his nails as *he* bites his (30). Worse yet, the present represents only lack, and in a state of deprivation even nature offers no solace; many, if not most, Japanese Americans had been farmers in California before the war, so Susan Schweik has noted that for them, pain can be found in its vegetable form: Because there is no one to kiss, "I devour / One raw onion after another" (Keiho Soga, 56).

One of the 1999 National Poetry Series award winners was Lee Ann Rorpaugh, chosen by Ishmael Reed for her book, *Beyond Heart Mountain*. Publishers Weekly (quoted on amazon.com) reports that "Roripaugh manages to bring a history [of the Heart Mountain camp] she never experienced through her own past, to her present self." One might think it unfortunate that the poetic record of that place belongs now to a young poet who did not experience the camps and who writes in mainstream MFA style rather than in haiku or tanka forms, but Roripaugh's book and her prize were made possible by the earlier poets, and by the publishers—including Bamboo Ridge Press in Honolulu—who opened up to such work in the 1970s and 1980s.

More in the spirit of the internment camp poems, perhaps, if not *about* the camps, is Albert Saijo's work, also published by Bamboo Ridge. In *Outspeaks: A Rhapsody* (1997), Saijo, who was interned as a child and later fought in Italy, writes: "I AM AN ANIMAL IN A CAGE & I AM BARKING TO BE LET OUT" (19). Saijo's "rhapsodies" emerge from an experience of the internment camp that is not stated (except in his biographical note at the end) but that is indeed present in his writing. From the tanka he gets his eerie conjunctions of political and natural events; from his own experience comes a disgust at war, colonialism, and racism. Thus, the first section of his poem, "THE GULF WAR" begins with a description of a clear winter day, with cumulus floating through blue sky but moves quickly to a political, concern: "WHILE BACK AT THE RANCH THIS LAST GASP OF WHITE / COLONIALISM SOUNDS HORRIFICALLY OVER ARABIA DESERTA." The poem ends with the poet contemplating the purchase of a television set, and with this tanka-like conclusion to what is otherwise best described as a "rant": "I GOT CHOPPED UP CHICKEN CORPSE UNFROZEN—THE GREEN / BEANS ARE READY—BRING ON THE WAR."

Unlike Saijo, a Nisei who fought in World War II, Richard Hamasaki is a Sansei (third-generation Japanese), whose mother and grandparents were interned at Topaz, and whose father fought in three American wars. In his poem, "Behind Barbed Wire," from *Spider Bone Diaries*, Hamasaki (who was, in part, responsible for publishing the book *Poets Behind Barbed Wire*) writes of family stories that were written by grandparents "grinding black ink with water / wet brushes touching paper" (68). He follows this scene of (Japanese) writing with a poem composed of five tankas, "Shakuhachi," thus paying homage to the tanka poets without explicitly engaging with the camp content. This poem is, instead, about the demise of the sugar industry in Hawai'i, an industry that brought the first member of Hamasaki's family to the islands in 1896. For Hamasaki, the sugar industry represents the American occupation of Hawai'i, an economic brand of imperialism that is linked to the military in the lines, "Eat of the new shoot / sing with the stem of the root / warrior, home from the war" (69). He joins the lament of the interned Japanese American here with a lament for the loss of Hawai'ian sovereignty, a move that has marked Hamasaki's literary career from the beginning.

In her anthology *Against Forgetting: Twentieth Century Poetry of Witness* (1993), **Carolyn Forché** writes,

[A]s North Americans, we have been fortunate: wars for us . . . are fought elsewhere, in other countries . . . We are also fortunate in that we do not live under martial law; there are nominal restrictions on state censorship; our citizens are not sent into exile. We are legally and juridically free to choose our associates, and to determine our communal lives. (31)

Forché's book, which includes poetry of the Armenian genocide, the Holocaust, and the Civil Rights Movement, among several other historical catastrophes, does not contain any work by Japanese Americans, a fact that perhaps explains her misreading of American history. Japanese Americans *were* exiled, their camp letters *were* censored, and they *did* live under martial law. This information has been available since well before Forché published her anthology in 1993. The fact that many did not know or knew little of this episode in American history is the result of several silences, including the silence of the survivor who is afraid to speak, for fear emotions (including grief, anger) will overwhelm him or her.

Publication of the internment poems played a vital role in making Americans aware of the realities of Japanese American internment camps. One might argue that a poem is not a poem until it is (widely) published, especially when its focus is so directly political. These poems, then, did not exist in a material sense for those outside the circle of internees for decades, before becoming part of the communal act of witnessing that took place before the Commission on Wartime Relocation and the U.S. Congress in the early 1980s. Joan Z. Bernstein, the head of that commission, has written that she did not know about the poetry, but the editors of

Poets Behind Barbed Wire, Jiro and Kay Nakano, were well aware of the more public airing of testimony. In the introduction to their book they write, "Although expressed in just a few lines, each of these tanka is in many respects more explicit and poignant in revealing humiliation, agony, loneliness and despair than the thousands of words spoken at the recent Congressional hearings" (vii). While bearing witness to the Holocaust came, of necessity, after the event, which was in many aspects unwitnessable, bearing witness to internment occurred as the event unfolded. The silence that came out of the camps was a silence of suppression, of continued oppression. That a small press like Bamboo Ridge published *Poets Behind Barbed Wire* was an act of witness, of breaking silence. Silence, which we like to think of as ethereal and spiritual, is also historical and material. This slim volume exists to prove that it can be broken open.

Further Reading. *Selected Primary Sources:* Inada, Lawson Fusao, *Legends from Camp* (Minneapolis, MN: Coffee House, 1993); Nakano, Kay, and Jiro Nakano, *Poets Behind Barbed Wire* (Honolulu: Bamboo Ridge, 1983). ***Selected Secondary Sources:*** Kashima, Tetsuden, *Personal Justice Denied: Report of the Commission on Wartime Relocation and Internment of Civilians* (Seattle: University of Washington Press, 1997); Schweik, Susan, *A Gulf So Deeply Cut: American Women Poets and the Second World War* (Madison: University of Wisconsin Press, 1991); Tateishi, John, *And Justice for All: An Oral History of the Japanese American Detention Camps* (Seattle: University of Washington Press, 1984, 1999).

Susan M. Schultz

HAWTHORNE, NATHANIEL (1804–1864)

Known chiefly for his mastery of prose in both novels and short stories, Nathaniel Hawthorne, like many of the lettered persons of his day, also tried his hand at verse—first as a boy and again in his later years. Neither attempt was particularly memorable. Unlike his friends and contemporaries **Ralph Waldo Emerson**, **Henry Wadsworth Longfellow**, **Margaret Fuller**, and **Henry David Thoreau**, Hawthorne never took his own verse seriously. It has been said that Hawthorne was a great poet, but the praise has been directed at the depth and mood of his prose.

Hawthorne was born the only son of Nathaniel Hathorne Sr. and Elizabeth Clarke-Manning on July 4, 1804. Hawthorne Sr., a ship's captain, died in Surinam of yellow fever; Hawthorne was only four at the time. Left with no estate, Elizabeth, the young Hawthorne, and the two daughters, Elizabeth and Marie Louisa, lived for the next decade in a crowded home with ten of their Manning relatives. In 1816, Hawthorne's uncle, Richard Manning, brought the family to his new home in Maine for the summer, and to everyone's surprise, the then-frail Hawthorne regained his health. Two years later, his uncle enrolled him in Bowdoin College. There he met his lifelong friends Franklin Pierce, the fourteenth president of the United States; Horatio Bridge, biographer; and Longfellow.

As an author, Hawthorne sought always the intrinsic rather than the extrinsic, as was his—and contemporary Transcendentalists'—wont. Hawthorne's love of nature, gained that summer at his uncle's home in Maine, his natural bent toward spiritual seeking, and his mistrust of the conservative Puritan within all caused him to be, for a time, comfortable with Transcendentalism. And he was in good company. Through his wife, Sophia Peabody and her sister Elizabeth, both committed Transcendentalists, Hawthorne ended up in the thick of the movement, spending time with Emerson; and although he always held himself back in social situations, he eventually became a member of the Transcendental Club. Through the Peabody sisters and the club, Hawthorne had the opportunity to meet **Amos Bronson Alcott** and George Ripley, the power behind Brook Farm, an early communal experiment. Hawthorne spent six months at Brook Farm before deciding that it was not the life for him.

Hawthorne was unable to escape his Puritan past—the depth of Puritan spiritual commitment as well as the shadows cast by Puritanism's inherent exclusivity and philosophical contradictions. Hawthorne was familiar with his lineage and was well aware that his great-great-grandfather, John Hathorne, was a magistrate at the Salem witch trials. Hawthorne's inability to come to peace with his past haunted him personally and surfaced again and again in his poems and in his novels—his writing and his affiliation with the transcendentalists were means to cope with his own spiritual, political, and artistic issues. There is speculation that Hawthorne changed his name from his given family name of Hathorne (added a "w") and moved away from Salem to his uncle's home, in order to distance himself, by whatever means necessary, from his family's past.

The majority of Hawthorne's poetry was written while wrestling with the demons of adolescence, and many of those poems were written simply to entertain his family. The poems that appear in his novels are generally longer and are written as serious verse (or are meant to seem that way); the poems that appear in his *Spectator* are short and tend to parody poetic conventions of the time. The poems generally involve death and the ocean—possibly with reference to his father. An early poem, "Thomas," suggests the style and theme:

Then, oh Thomas, rest in glory!
Hallowed be thy silent grave,—
Long thy name in Salem's story
Shall live, and honour o'er it wave.

The Spectator was also the title of a famous English periodical published by Joseph Addison and Richard Steele pointed at educating the new middle class. Even at his young age, Hawthorne was aware of Addison and Steele's periodical and intended a double satire by using the voyeuristic title and by the obvious implication of Hawthorne educating his adult family.

His first poem, "The Ocean," was published in the Salem *Gazette* in 1825—contrary to most timelines that discount his poetry and list his novel *Fanshawe*, published in 1828, as his first publication. Although oceans and death recur as themes throughout his small collection of poetry, especially poignant is "The Snow That Comes When Violets Ought to Bloom," a rather bleak poem co-authored with his daughter Una not long before his death.

Hawthorne also wrote a few lighthearted poems as well as a few limericks. Most of Hawthorne's *Spectator* poems employed rather unambitious forms and rhyme schemes. His early poetry consisted of a single quatrain of rhymed couplets; his later poems varied in length, and used rhyme schemes *ABCBDB* or *ABAAB*. The latter, a quintilla, was a fairly well-known Spanish form. Although it was not necessarily known to Hawthorne, the former rhyme scheme, a *corrido*, was also Spanish and was just coming into vogue about the time Hawthorne was writing. Whether Hawthorne was experimenting with Spanish forms or whether he, more likely, was rearranging contemporary patterns is unknown, but taking the time to consciously experiment with stanzaic patterns would have been out of character; Hawthorne was ambivalent about his poetry, and that he lost poems as well as notebooks seems certain. In fact, he cared so little for his verse that he seldom gave his poems titles. And yet Hawthorne's ambivalence and the possibility of lost works are what provide a glimmer of hope—new works may yet be discovered.

Further Reading. *Selected Primary Sources:* Bridge, Horatio, *Personal Recollections of Nathaniel Hawthorne* (New York: Haskell House, 1968); Hawthorne, Julian, *Nathaniel Hawthorne and His Wife: A Biography*, vols. 1 and 2 (Hamden, CT: Archon Books, 1968); Hawthorne, Nathaniel, *Fanshawe: and Other Pieces* (Boston: Houghton, Mifflin, 1876); Peck, Richard E., ed., *Nathaniel Hawthorne: Poems* (Charlottesville, VA: Bibliographical Society of the University of Virginia, 1967); Woodson, Thomas, Claude M. Simpson, and L. Neal Smith, eds., *Centenary Edition of the Works of Nathaniel Hawthorne*, vol. 23 (Columbus: Ohio State University Press, 1994). ***Selected Secondary Sources:*** Minter, David, "Hawthorne, Nathaniel," in *American National Biography*, vol. 10, ed. John A. Garraty and Mark C. Carnes (New York: Oxford University Press, 1999, 357–363); Elder, Marjorie J.,

Nathaniel Hawthorne: Transcendental Symbolist (Athens: Ohio University Press, 1969); Reynolds, Larry J, ed. *A Historical Guide to Nathaniel Hawthorne* (New York: Oxford University Press, 2001).

Thomas L. Herakovich

HAYDEN, ROBERT (ASA BUNDY SHEFFEY) (1913–1980)

Robert Hayden, following a generation after the **Harlem Renaissance** poets, produced a body of work that addressed two issues. First, can **African American poetry** take its form and inspiration from mainstream **modernism**? And second, should it? Hayden's poetry gave a resounding yes to both questions, though not without meeting resistance. He ultimately came to be known as one of the most skilled craftsmen in American poetry and as one of most important poetic chroniclers of African American history and culture.

Hayden was born on August 4, 1913, in Detroit, Michigan, to Asa and Gladys Sheffey. At birth, he was named after his father, but his parents separated shortly thereafter, and his mother, though she remained an influence in his life, gave him up to foster parents, William and Sue Ellen Hayden. His foster parents changed his name—but not legally, as he was to discover many years later when he applied for a passport and found that no such person as Robert Hayden existed. He was then forced to make the legal name change himself. As a child, his physical activities were limited because of impaired vision, but he could read and so threw himself into that pursuit. He enrolled in Detroit City College (which became Wayne State University) in 1932, and he left in 1936 to work as a researcher for the Federal Writers' Project, which became his first significant immersion in black history. He married composer and pianist Erma Morris in 1940, and he enrolled in the Masters' program at the University of Michigan in 1941, where he studied with **W.H. Auden**. Hayden received his degree in 1942, and taught at Michigan until 1946, when he accepted a position at Fisk University in Nashville, Tennessee. He remained at Fisk until 1969, and then returned to Michigan, where he remained on the faculty until his death in 1980.

Hayden was a member of the Baha'i faith, which teaches that humanity is one single race, and that all previous religions have laid the groundwork for the dramatic change to come, that of the unification of all races and nationalities in one global society. This, in addition to his attitude toward the craft of poetry, led him to insist that he was first and foremost a poet, not a black poet. The conflict between this nonracialism and the racial themes of so much of his poetry—he wrote in his *Collected Prose* that "to be a poet . . . is to care passionately about justice and one's fellow human beings" (11)—led to the creative tension that is a great part of his work's power.

His first poetry collection, *Heart-Shape in the Dust*, was published in 1940 to little notice. A chapbook, *The Lion and the Archer* (with Myron O'Higgins) came out in 1948. Subsequent works were *Figure of Time* (1948), *A Ballad of Remembrance* (1962), *Selected Poems* (1966), *Words in the Mourning Time* (1970), *The Night-Blooming Cereus* (1972), *Angle of Ascent* (1975), and *American Journal* (1978). A posthumous edition of *Collected Poems* came out in 1985. In 1967, Hayden edited *Kaleidoscope: Poems by American Negro Poets*.

He won the Julius and Avery Hopwood Award for Poetry at the University of Michigan in 1938 and 1942 (the latter competition judged by W.H. Auden), the World Festival of Negro Arts grand prize in 1966, and the Michigan Arts Foundation Award in 1977. He received National Book Award nominations in 1971 and 1979. He was a member of the Michigan Arts Council (1975–76), the American Academy of Arts and Letters, PEN, and the American Poetry Society. He was Poetry Consultant to the Library of Congress (the position that later was designated Poet Laureate) from 1976 to 1978. He was a Julius Rosenwald fellow (1947), a Ford Foundation fellow (1954–1955), and an Academy of American Poets fellow (1977).

Hayden's most significant poetic accomplishment was one that he never finished, but which influenced all of his poetry, and provided, in fragments, some of his best-known work. He had been deeply influenced by Stephen Vincent Benet's Civil War epic *John Brown's Body*, particularly a passage in which Benet admits that he is not the man who can write the "black-skinned epic" and says that some day a black poet will rise who can write that "epic with the long black spear." Hayden, recalling that inspiration in an essay later published in his *Collected Prose*, said, "I dared to hope that I might be that poet."

He planned his own Civil War epic, *The Black Spear*, but never finished it, at least not in the form of a book-length poem, although an early draft of it was selected by Auden for Michigan's 1942 Hopwood Prize. Several parts of the manuscript, as separate poems, would later appear in *Selected Poems*, and the concerns of *The Black Spear*—a poetry that would tell the truth about black history and the black experience—were concerns that never left him.

Heart-Shape in the Dust had shown strong influences of the Harlem Renaissance authors, and it was a direction he was not to pursue, especially after his period of study with Auden. Although the work was, and remains, highly thought of in the black community, Hayden came to see it as too "nationalist" and felt it was best left behind. He was set on his own course, one that would blend a lapidary focus on craftsmanship with an African American focus that was at once personal and collective, a vision and new awareness that would show up in poets as different as **Rita Dove** and Curtis Mayfield. This was probably the same reason he never finished *The Black Spear*—he had outgrown the influence, if not the inspiration, of Benet.

His next collection, a tiny chapbook, scarcely more than a pamphlet, shared with the more conventional black poet Myron O'Higgins, won notice from critic Selden Rodman in the *New York Times* for its experimental vigor and its ability to bring the weight of modern poetry to bear on the black experience.

For a poet as accomplished and as recognized for his accomplishments as Robert Hayden, he spent much of his life in obscurity. During his tenure at Fisk, even though he published three books, he was little regarded as more than an obscure English professor on his own campus, teaching a full load of freshman composition and basic literature courses. **Galway Kinnell**, during the "freedom rider" period of the civil rights struggle, came to Fisk and sat in on one of Hayden's classes, not realizing that this was Hayden the poet.

Hayden's first real acclaim came in 1966 for *Selected Poems*. In that volume, he included revised versions of several poems originally written for *The Black Spear*, including one, "The Middle Passage," which drew its inspiration from the "Black Spear" story, but had not been in the original manuscript. "The Middle Passage," a story of the slave trade, has come to be considered Hayden's epic. Although fewer than two hundred lines, the poem's emotional and historic scope is immense. "The Middle Passage" could not have been part of the original *Black Spear*—all influence of Benet is gone from it; its godfather, instead, is **T.S. Eliot**'s "The Waste Land."

In "The Middle Passage," three of Hayden's most powerful motivators come together: his awareness of the centrality of Eliot; the lessons he learned from Auden about the necessity of reshaping the canon to the demands of a new time and one's own awareness; and finally, his sense of himself as the carrier of that black spear of historical and cultural truth. The poet **Michael S. Harper** has described "The Middle Passage" as an answer to Eliot. Hayden moved the concerns of modernism beyond Eliot's examination of the barrenness of society to an exploration of the roots of a rich and powerful culture.

The poem, in three parts, tells the story of the slave trade. Part 1 takes us on board a slave ship, and shows us the chilling inhumanity of a world with no borders or laws but itself. Part 2, in the terrifying voice of an unrepentant slave trader, presents a brotherhood of greed (which is no brotherhood at all) between the slave traders and the African tribal kings with whom they traded in human flesh. Part 3 describes the slave revolt on the *Amistad*, led by Cinquez, who became a symbol both of freedom and of the awful violence that must sometimes be its path. Hayden drew on a nonfiction book by **Muriel Rukeyser** for much of his information about the Amistad.

In 1966, as Hayden traveled to Senegal to receive the grand prize from the World Festival of Negro Arts, organized by Senegal's poet-president, Léopold Sédar Senghor, he was at the same time the subject of attack at home. At Fisk University's First Black Writers' Conference, Hayden was assailed as an "Uncle Tom" for his public refusal to allow himself to be called a "Negro poet." Leading the criticism was Hayden's contemporary **Melvin Tolson**. The participants at the conference endorsed the credo of activist Ron Karenga that the first duty of a black artist is to promote revolution and that any art that does not recognize this is "invalid." Hayden's former student, the author and educator Julius Lester, at the time a radical activist himself, recalls visiting Hayden and finding him explosively unrepentant about his refusal to be labeled. Lester, sympathetic to both sides in the dispute, wrote that blacks are seen by the dominant white culture, and are forced to see themselves, in reference to "the cause" and that both groups will stigmatize a black writer who refuses to be categorized.

In retrospect, it is hard to see how the centrality of the black experience to Hayden's work could have been discounted. In addition to his treatment of black history in "The Middle Passage" and the other *Black Spear* poems, he wrote about ghetto life in Detroit and about such iconic figures as Frederick Douglass, Harriet Tubman, Sojourner Truth, Nat Turner, Malcolm X, Jack Johnson, Jelly Roll Morton, Bessie Smith, Miles Davis, and Billie Holiday.

After leaving Fisk for the University of Michigan, Hayden's output increased. Notable poems in his next volume, *Words in the Mourning Time*, include "The Dream" and "'Mystery Boy' Looks for Kin in Nashville." The former, another poem growing out of *The Black Spear*, contrasts the experiences of an aged slave fearful of her own dream of the future and the experiences of a young black soldier in the Union Army. The latter section, concerned with identity (including but not limited to black identity), ends with these haunting lines: "We'll go and find them. We'll go / and ask them for your name again." Also in this collection, "El-Hajj Malik El-Shabazz" eulogizes Malcolm X, using the Muslim name that the black leader had taken near the end of his life. The poem describes Malcolm as "the scourger of his people," who would "drive them from / the lush ice gardens of their servitude." The image is as lush as it is icily precise; in its metaphoric brilliance and its immersion in and separateness from the black struggle, it becomes itself a metaphor for Robert Hayden.

In *Angle of Ascent*, Hayden continues to find new insights into historical figures like Frederick Douglass,

and he finds the same powerful cultural resonance in his own background, growing up in the misnamed "Paradise Valley" section of Detroit.

During the 1970s, Hayden continued to gain respect and to be virtually ignored at the same time. He received two National Book Award nominations (for *Words in the Mourning Time* and *American Journal*), but never won the award. He was selected as Consultant in Poetry to the Library of Congress in 1976 and again in 1977, before the position had been renamed Poet Laureate, with the added prestige that went with the title; in fact, when Rita Dove was named Poet Laureate in 1993, an article in the *New York Times* identified her as the first black poet to hold that position. And shortly after his Library of Congress appointment, critic Phillip M. Richards recalls attending a reading by Hayden at the University of Chicago, among a tiny audience of a few faculty members and graduate students and a group of black elementary school students. It appeared to Richards that he was the only one there who actually had brought along one of Hayden's books. None of this appeared to surprise Hayden: Richards recounts an observation by the poet that "he had been an outsider so long that he did not know how to behave as an insider did."

Hayden's final volume, *American Journal*, returns powerfully to his childhood in the "Elegies for Paradise Valley" and also includes two prose selections which could not be more different, yet are still quintessential Hayden: a "Letter from Phyllis Wheatley" and the log of a visitor from another planet.

In 1980 Hayden participated in a poetry reading at the White House, where Amy Carter pronounced him her favorite. He died in Ann Arbor, Michigan, not long after this visit. No major American newspapers gave him more than a cursory obituary.

Further Reading. *Selected Primary Sources:* Hayden, Robert, *American Journal* (New York: Liveright, 1982); ———, *Angle of Ascent* (New York: Liveright, 1975); ———, *Collected Poems* (New York: Liveright, 1975); ———, *Collected Prose*, ed. Frederick Glaysher (Ann Arbor: University of Michigan Press, 1984); ———, *Heart-Shape in the Dust* (Detroit, MI: Falcon Press, 1940); ———, *Selected Poems* (New York: October House, 1966); ———, *Words in the Mourning Time* (New York: October House, 1970). ***Selected Secondary Sources:*** Bloom, Harold, *Robert Hayden* (New York: Chelsea House, 2004); Harper, Michael S., "Remembering Robert Hayden" (*Michigan Quarterly Review* 21.1 [Winter 1982]: 182–188); Hatcher, John, *From the Auroral Darkness: the Life and Poetry of Robert Hayden* (Saint Petersburg, FL: George Ronald, 1984); Lester, Julius, Review of *Words in the Mourning Time* (*New York Times Book Review* [28 December 1969]: 1); Pavlic, Edward M., "'something patterned, wild, and free': Robert Hayden's Angles of

Descent and the Democratic Unconscious" (*African American Review* 36.4 [Winter 2002]: 533–555); Richards, Phillip M., "Robert Hayden (1913–1980): An Appreciation" (*Massachusetts Review* 40.4 [Winter 1999/2000]: 599–613); Williams, Pontheolla T., *Robert Hayden: A Critical Analysis of His Poetry* (Urbana: University of Illinois Press, 1987).

Tad Richards

HAYNES, LEMUEL (1753–1833)

A black New Englander, Lemuel Haynes had a distinguished career as a congregational minister. Scholars of eighteenth-century congregationalism know Haynes as a respected and faithful pastor, skilled preacher, and published writer. In the 1980s two manuscripts—a poem, "The Battle of Lexington" (1775), and an essay, "Liberty Further Extended" (1775)—were brought to light by Professor Ruth Bogin. These two works prompted scholarly interest in Haynes, whose writing reveals a somewhat paradoxical philosophy supporting, on the one hand, conservative Calvinism and Washingtonian Federalism, and on the other, the abolition of slavery and the protection of human rights.

Although there is uncertainty about the names of his parents, Haynes's father was probably a black slave or indentured servant and his mother a white woman, possibly a servant or the daughter of a prominent family. Haynes was born in West Hartford, Connecticut, and was indentured at five months old to a religiously pious and supportive family named Rose. Haynes lived with his foster parents on their farm in Middle Granville, Massachusetts. There he learned to read and write, and as a young adult, he composed sermons for household worship. His talent for scriptural interpretation was recognized and Haynes was urged to enter the ministry, studying with local clergymen. At the start of the revolutionary war (1775) he enlisted as a minuteman, serving with the Continental Army at Roxbury and Ticonderoga. Illness brought him home early, and he completed his studies and became a licensed preacher in 1780. In 1783 he married Elizabeth Babbitt, a young white schoolteacher, with whom he had ten children. He served as a preacher in Connecticut and Massachusetts and in 1786 was called to serve the church at Rutland, Vermont, making him the first black pastor of a mainstream white congregation in the United States. Haynes remained in Rutland until 1818 when a racist climate took over the congregation. He then served congregations in Vermont and New York until his death in 1833.

Haynes was not a prolific or highly original poet by any means. "A Poem, Occasioned by the Sudden and Surprising Death of Mr. Asa Burt" (ca. 1774) is a moralistic meditation on sudden death. "The Battle of Lexington," his most important poem, is a "patriotic ballad" composed, Haynes writes in the poem's introduction, shortly after "the inhuman Tragedy perpetrated on the 19th of April 1775 by a number of the British Troops." In this preamble, the poet identifies himself as "Lemuel a young Mollato." The poem laments the British attack on "Liberty," charges that Britain has shown itself "Nearly allied to antient [sic] Rome / That Seat of Popery," and calls for reconciliation with the aggressor before ending with a religious remonstration that "Sin is the Cause of all our Woe." What is most interesting about "The Battle of Lexington" is that Haynes wrote his essay "Liberty Further Extended" shortly after the poem. In her study of these two works, Rita Roberts speculates on the rapid "transition from almost unquestioning patriotism" (579) in the ballad to the political criticism of the essay, "Liberty Further Extended: Or Free thoughts on the illegality of Slave-keeping; . . ." Haynes's assertion of his identity as a patriotic subject in the poem and as a man of color in the essay's subtitle, at a time when slave-keeping was a standard part of colonial life, reveals not only courageous risk-taking but also a keen intellect. The essay's argument is worked out by the placement of the preamble to the Declaration of Independence as the essay's preamble. Haynes employs skillful rhetoric, including scriptural support, to expound his argument that slavery is against the cause of "Liberty." Importantly, except for the essay's title, Haynes wrote the essay without any allusions to being black. He displayed unquestioning confidence in his inalienable right to speak to all citizens for the extension of "Liberty" to people of color. As Roberts emphasizes, Haynes did not place himself among the victims of slavery, but as a member of "the dominant class engaged in the battle against one kind of tyranny." (580). In a similar vein, Richard Newman contends that Haynes's self-perception reveals a duality, or DuBoisian "twoness," and that "The double-meanings of 'America' were clear to him" (Haynes, xiii). The largest portion of writing that Haynes produced over his lifetime is accounted for by his 5,500 sermons. These are perhaps the most valuable works in studying Haynes's development as a writer and a human being. The sermons reveal a person thoroughly engaged in his predominantly white community. His most famous sermon, "Universal Salvation" (1805), which was published in Great Britain and the United States, and which brought him recognition in the international Anglo American Protestant world, was an attack on Universalism. In spite of his acceptance into the international religious scene, Lemuel Haynes was sadly dismissed from the Rutland church that he had so faithfully served. About this dismissal Haynes was reported to comment that his former congregation was so wise that after thirty years, "they found out he was a *nigger*, and so turned him away" (Haynes, xxxiv). Besides revealing Haynes's reported great wit, this remark, made at a time when pro-slavery forces and abolitionists were squaring off for the fight of the nineteenth century, poignantly demonstrates Haynes's refusal to take upon himself the cloak of "otherness" through which outspoken black Americans were being silenced. In fact, Haynes was not to be silenced. Two years after leaving the Rutland church, he preached a sermon, "The Prisoner Released" (1820), and later published a pamphlet, "Mystery Developed" (1820), on the unjust conviction and imprisonment of Stephen and Jesse Boorn, who were accused of murder. The prisoners were exonerated and released. In studying Lemuel Haynes's work, the reader is most engaged by his life. Paradoxical, enigmatic, and complex are the words that scholars use to describe Haynes, the very qualities that compel further study.

Further Reading. ***Selected Primary Sources:*** Haynes, Lemuel, *Black Preacher to White America: The Collected Writings of Lemuel Haynes, 1774–1833*, ed. Richard Newman (Brooklyn, NY: Carlson, 1990). ***Selected Secondary Sources:*** Bogin, Ruth, "'The Battle of Lexington': A Patriotic Ballad by Lemuel Haynes" (*William and Mary Quarterly* 72.4 [October 1985]: 499–509); ———, "'Liberty Further Extended': A 1776 Antislavery Manuscript by Lemuel Haynes" (*William and Mary Quarterly* 40.1 [January 1983]: 85–105); Cooley, Timothy Mather, *Sketches of the life and character of the Rev. Lemuel Haynes, A.M., for many years pastor of a church in Rutland, Vt. And late in Granville, New-York* (New York: J.S. Taylor, 1839); Roberts, Rita, "Patriotism and Political Criticism: The Evolution of Political Consciousness in the Mind of a Black Revolutionary Soldier" (*Eighteenth-Century Studies* 27.4 [Summer 1994]: 569–588); Saillant, John, "'Remarkably Emancipated from Bondage, Slavery, and Death': An African American Retelling of the Puritan Captivity Narrative, 1820" (*Early American Literature* 29.2 [1994]: 122–140).

Jane Hikel

HEALY, ELOISE KLEIN. *SEE* KLEIN-HEALY, ELOISE

HEANEY, SEAMUS JUSTIN (1939–)

Seamus Heaney's poetry and prose, especially in their evocation of regionalism, display the deep influence of American poets such as **Robert Frost** and **Theodore Roethke** and thus suggest an abiding transatlantic dimension to his work. A sense of "in-between-ness" is a hallmark of his poetry and has allowed him to place himself repeatedly in ambiguous and mediating positions—politically, culturally, and religiously. For instance, although he is a self-described constitutional nationalist who desires Northern Ireland to be reunited with the Republic of Ireland, Heaney nonetheless has affirmed his affection for the English language by writing in it and praising its linguistic possibilities in his poetry and prose. Seamus

Justin Heaney grew up literally between a symbol of Northern Irish Protestant hegemony—Moyola Park, an estate owned by James Chichester-Clark, a former Unionist Prime Minister of Great Britain—and the village of Toome on the Bann River, where the young Irish nationalist Roddy McCorley was hanged for the part he played in the 1798 Rebellion that aimed to grant Catholics emancipation.

Heaney was raised as a minority Catholic, attending the local primary school in Anahorish, which had both Catholic and Protestant pupils, a rarity in a province dominated by religious segregation in its schools. In 1951, he won a scholarship to St. Columb's College, Derry, and he began his secondary education there. Another scholarship, to Queen's University, Belfast, in 1957, resulted in a First Class Honours Degree in English Language and Literature in 1961. His study of American poets such as Robert Frost confirmed his desire to write about local subject matter and to capture the rhythms of living speech. Additionally, Frost's approving evocation of hard work influenced Heaney's recurring portrayals of traditional craftsmen in his early volumes of poetry.

Although he was offered a scholarship to Oxford for postgraduate work in English literature, Heaney turned it down out of self-doubt and a desire to stay close to his parents. In the autumn of 1961, he began a teacher-training course at St. Joseph's College of Education; the next year, he started practicing for teaching at St. Thomas Intermediary School in Ballymurphy, where he was mentored by the Northern Irish short story writer Michael McLaverty, a regional writer who helped give Heaney courage to write about Northern Ireland and who introduced him to the work of Irish poet Patrick Kavanagh, who affirmed this desire. Heaney's first volume of poetry, *Death of a Naturalist* (1966), is a tribute to Kavanagh's influence, in its rich evocation of the wonder of ordinary life around Heaney's home ground—Mossbawm, the family farm.

The most profound intellectual and cultural endeavor in which Heaney engaged during the early- to mid-1960s was Philip Hobsbaum's creative writing circle, the "Belfast Group," with which Heaney was involved from 1963 through 1966. Hobsbaum's magnetic personality drew an array of outstanding talent into his intellectually demanding group. With its religious and cultural diversity, the Belfast Group gave Heaney the chance to have close Protestant friends for the first time, leading to the appreciation for cultural differences that becomes thematic in much of his work. Hobsbaum's insistence on the formal aspects of poetry, coupled with extensive critical feedback from the group members, forced Heaney to attend to the craftsmanship of his poems and evince a fidelity to art above all else, an allegiance that would enable him to write nuanced poetry about the fallout from the Northern Irish Troubles in his early to mid-career without propagandizing for the Catholic position.

The publication of Heaney's first full volume of poetry, *Death of a Naturalist*, launched a powerful career. This volume signaled the emergence of a voice attuned to local culture and clearly in love with etymology. Along with his immersion in Kavanagh, Heaney had been reading the American poet Theodore Roethke, particularly his volume *The Far Field*, which features evocations of childhood and expresses both the dangers and delights of nature. Poems from *Death of a Naturalist* such as "Mid-term Break," about the death of the poet's four-year-old brother, and the title poem of the volume, about the young Heaney's discovery of mating frogs, are particularly indebted to Roethke.

The most famous poem from *Death of a Naturalist*, "Digging," is Heaney's poetic manifesto. In it he aligns himself with his father and grandfather, both of whom were known for their digging skills. Although he has "no spade to follow men like them," he concludes the poem by vowing, "Between my finger and my thumb / The squat pen rests. / I'll dig with it." The poem thus enables the poet to affirm the agricultural tradition of his predecessors while staking out his own literary terrain. Many of Heaney's poems like "Digging" are metapoetic; they are poems about the art of writing poetry. Tremendous critical acclaim in Britain and Ireland followed the publication of *Death of a Naturalist* and Heaney quickly became famous.

In 1969 his second volume, *Door into the Dark*, was published. Just as many poems from his first volume had celebrated the declining tradition of native crafts in Northern Ireland, so too did poems from this volume, including "The Forge," in which Heaney approvingly recalls watching a blacksmith at his forge. Crucially, Heaney sees analogs for his own poetry in these rural crafts, recognizing in the craftsmen the necessary qualities for a poet: quietness, contemplation, and rhythm. While poems such as "The Forge" and "Thatcher" perform the work of regional cultural anthropology in their celebration of local crafts, others, such as "Bogland," show an increasing international dimension to Heaney's work, revealing particularly the influence of America. "Bogland" begins, "We have no prairies / to slice a big sun at evening," a reference to American terrain. In the penultimate stanza, the speaker explicitly makes a contrast between American and Irish pioneers: "Our pioneers keep striking / Inwards and downwards." Most of the poem, however, focuses upon the rich, dark soil associated with Irish peat bogs. "Bogland" and subsequent bog poems stemmed from Heaney's reading of *The Bog People*, by the Danish archaeologist P.V. Glob. This work inspired him not only to make historical connections between tribal killings in northern Europe and Northern Ireland, but also to cast his poetry in mythical, subterranean images and to burrow further down into his imagination.

The lure of America was strong, and in autumn of 1970 Heaney took a sabbatical from his teaching position in English literature at Queen's University, Belfast, to teach as a Guest Lecturer at the University of California–Berkeley. The young poet welcomed the chance to leave Northern Ireland, which was quickly sinking into widespread street violence. The radicalized Berkeley students, who were then protesting American involvement in Vietnam, made Heaney realize that his poetry could become a force for change back in Northern Ireland. The still-vibrant African American Civil Rights Movement in America also made him realize that Catholics in Northern Ireland shared many historical affinities with American blacks. Despite his desire to write poetry that could ameliorate the situation in Northern Ireland, Heaney still maintained that his primary allegiance was not to his "tribe," Northern Irish Catholics, but to his poetry. That resolve would be sorely tested by events that followed upon his return to the province.

When Heaney returned to Belfast in September 1971, it had been only a month since internment without trial had been introduced in Northern Ireland, a practice that had understandably infuriated the Catholic minority there, since the process was almost invariably used against them in police sweeps against suspected Irish Republican Army members. *Wintering Out*, the volume that was published the following year, however, largely resists tribal allegiances and seeks to unify the Catholic and Protestant traditions in the province through a common dialect, a move seen in poems such as "Broagh." Other poems from the volume, such as "The Other Side," attempt to view Northern Irish Protestants and their culture sympathetically. One of the volume's major poems is Heaney's second bog poem, "The Tollund Man," which concludes with an explicit comparison of the historical violence of Jutland and the atrocities occurring on the streets of Northern Ireland: "Out there in Jutland / In the old man-killing parishes / I will feel lost, / Unhappy and at home." Heaney's uneasy identification of his home ground with that of Jutland suggests both his rejection of violence and his familiarity with it.

In 1972 Heaney moved to the Irish Republic because of the increasing violence in the province and because it afforded him a tax break from the very high rates in Northern Ireland. The geographical distance allowed him to begin writing poems more explicitly about the Northern Irish situation, which were published in *North* three years later. *North* proved to be a controversial volume: critics such as Conor Cruise O'Brien, the Northern Irish poet Ciaran Carson, and the Northern Irish critic Edna Longley accused Heaney of sympathies with violent Irish republicanism in poems that continued to draw upon parallels between bodies pulled from bogs in northern Europe and victims of political violence in the province. However, despite some righteous indignation at the political status of Northern Irish Catholics, the volume critiques violence across time periods and cultures and finally suggests, in poems such as "North" and "Exposure," that the poet's true north is not his province but his self-exploration. These poems confirm that Heaney's poetic posture is that of listener, not doer. The American poet **T.S. Eliot** confirmed the Irish poet in this regard, as Heaney recalled in his 1988 lecture at Harvard, "Learning from Eliot."

Heaney's 1979 volume *Field Work* suggests his continuing ability to focus on his home ground in Northern Ireland for poetic inspiration, but in works such as the volume's finest, "Casualty," the poet transforms a poem ostensibly about a Catholic victim of a sectarian bombing, a fisherman, into a meditation on poetry itself. This poem, like others from his first two volumes, compares a traditional rural craft—in this case, fishing—with the making of poetry, suggesting that the victim's patience, rhythm, and ability to listen as he pulls in his eel nets are exemplary for the poet. A series of ten lovely sonnets, collectively entitled "Glanmore Sonnets," form the core of the volume and anchor it firmly in County Wicklow in the Republic of Ireland.

Perhaps Heaney's most ambitious volume is *Station Island* (1984). Borrowing its tripartite structure from Dante's *Divine Comedy*, the volume begins with a descent to the underworld, in this case, the London Underground; features a middle, purgatorial section set on St. Patrick's Island in Lough Derg, Country Donegal, site of a famous and continuing Irish pilgrimage; and concludes with an airy flight away from the island. Throughout its middle and titular section, the poet wrestles with the question of how well he has used his poetic gifts. This question acquires great poignancy as Heaney confronts ghosts, ranging from a dead schoolteacher to a cousin killed in a sectarian attack, who accuse him of misusing his talents. But the concluding and twelfth poem of this section features the ghostly appearance of James Joyce, who, priest-like, absolves the poet of any sins he might have committed toward those people from his past and who urges him to strike out on his own, freeing himself from the deathly conditions of his native province. Bird-like, the poet does just this in the concluding section, "Sweeney Redivivus," entering a poetic paradise.

Beginning in 1979, Heaney formalized his academic connections in America. After a term at Harvard teaching poetry as a temporary successor to Robert Lowell, in 1982, Heaney began a five-year appointment there, teaching one semester annually. In 1984, he was elected to Harvard's Boylston Chair of Rhetoric. His friend and colleague at Harvard, the critic Helen Vendler, has consistently promoted his work and contributed to the rise of his reputation in America. He became the Emerson Poet in Residence and continued his affiliation with Harvard, visiting the university in non-teaching status every other autumn for six weeks. The American literary critic Weldon Thornton has facilitated Heaney's relationship with The University of North Carolina at Chapel Hill, and Heaney served as speaker at the university's commencement in 1996. The University of North Carolina houses probably the world's largest collection of Heaney items, some of which are collaborative work with Henry Pearson, an alumnus of the university and artist.

Subsequent volumes such as *The Haw Lantern* (1987), *Seeing Things* (1991), and *The Spirit Level* (1996) further explore Heaney's new sense of the ethereal that began toward the end of *Station Island*. In his Nobel Prize address, *Crediting Poetry* (1995), the poet noted about this period of his career, "I began a few years ago to try to make space in my reckoning and imagining for the marvelous as well as for the murderous." Images of the marvelous abound in these volumes. The center of *The Haw Lantern* is the sonnet sequence "Clearances," in memory of the poet's mother who died in 1984. These sonnets not only display the poet's continuing fascination with form, but also demonstrate how he uses the solidity of such form to convey the airy absence of his mother from his life. In one of the most tender sonnets in the volume, the seventh one, the poet recalls a conversation his father had with his mother shortly before she died. Her death opens up a strange new space for the gathered members of the family: "The space we stood around had been emptied / Into us to keep, it penetrated / Clearances that suddenly stood open. / High cries were felled and a pure change happened." The test is for the poet and his surviving family members to preserve the memory of his mother even as her body has died. This might seem especially hard for a poet who previously had been dedicated to capturing in verse the preserved bog bodies that floated into his mind, but even in the next sonnet of the sequence, he seems ready to meet this challenge. He recalls walking around an empty space where the family chestnut tree had lived. Recalling the tree's growth from its original seed and its eventual death and disappearance, he implicitly compares the space created by its absence to that absence of his mother. Both tree and mother seem to become "a bright nowhere, / A soul ramifying and forever / Silent, beyond silence listened for."

The sequence "Squarings" from *Seeing Things* is especially resonant in its evocation of the interaction of the marvelous with the everyday. In the eighth poem from this sequence, part of the subsequence "Lightenings," the poet imagines a ghost ship that appeared to the monks at the Irish monastery of Clonmacnoise and hooked its anchor on the altar rails. Although a crewman climbs down to try to release the anchor, he is unsuccessful and finally must have help from the monks, suggesting how the mortal world impinges on the immortal world and vice versa, a typically Yeatsian view. In the thirty-fourth poem from this sequence, in the subsequence "Crossings," Heaney again displays his penchant for revenant poetry, recalling a bus ride from "San Francisco into Berkeley" back in 1970 that he shared with one other passenger, a soldier bound for Vietnam, whom the poet sees as a shade of "one of the newly dead come back, // Unsurprisable but still disappointed."

The Spirit Level contains a number of poems that look back to the poet's childhood, such as "A Sofa in the Forties" and "The Swing," both of which suggest the strong imaginary world of his childhood. "The Poet's Chair" meditates both on Heaney's vocation and on his father, who had recently died. The ambitious sequence of five poems comprising "Mycenae Lookout" deals with the Trojan War and its violence. Two of the most evocative poems, "St Kevin and the Blackbird" and "Postscript," deal with the posture of receptivity and how that posture may lead to revelations. In the former poem, the poet recalls the famous saint who, while praying in his narrow cell, stretches his hand out the window and has a blackbird fly into it. Patiently, St. Kevin holds his arm out for weeks as the blackbird builds a nest and lays her eggs. He eventually achieves a position of forgetful transcendence. In "Postscript," the speaker urges us to drive into County Clare in western Ireland between the ocean and a lake with swimming swans. This in-between, liminal position enables the speaker to be "neither here nor there, / A hurry through which known and strange things pass / As big soft buffetings come at the car sideways / And catch the heart off guard."

In Heaney's most recent volume, *Electric Light* (2001), he displays his increasingly wide imaginative compass, as various poems are set in the former Yugoslavia and Greece. Childhood is still a predominant theme, as the aging poet casts back in his memory for stirring scenes from his past. There are a series of short, elegiac glosses in memory of other writers such as Norman MacCaig and Sorley MacLean, which are interspersed with longer elegies, including a Hopkinesque poem in memory of the poet's father, "Seeing the Sick." Once again, there is a sonnet sequence; this one is entitled "Sonnets from Hellas" and focuses upon ancient Greek themes and locales. The volume also contains several poems such as "Perch" and "Lupins" that feature the poet's delight in nature. Heaney's powerful poetic voice; his penchant for realizing the wonder in everyday objects; and his fidelity to the imaginative power of his art ensure he will remain a poet of the highest order.

Further Reading. *Selected Primary Sources:* Heaney, Seamus, *Finders, Keepers: Selected Prose 1971–2001* (New York: Farrar, Straus and Giroux, 2002); ———, *Opened Ground: Selected Poems, 1966–1996* (New York: Farrar, Straus and Giroux, 1998). ***Selected Secondary Sources:*** Buxton, Rachel, *Robert Frost and Northern Irish Poetry* (New York: Oxford University Press, 2004); Morrison, Blake, *Seamus Heaney* (New York: Methuen, 1982); Parker, Michael, *Seamus Heaney: The Making of the Poet* (Iowa City: Iowa University Press, 1993); Russell, Richard Rankin, "Poems without Frontiers: Poetic Reception and Political Possibility in the Work of Seamus Heaney," *New Perspectives on Seamus Heaney*, ed. Bland Crowder and Jason David Hall (Basingstoke, England: Palgrave MacMillan, 2006); Vendler, Helen, *Seamus Heaney* (Cambridge, MA: Harvard University Press, 1998).

Richard Rankin Russell

HECHT, ANTHONY (1923–2004)

Anthony Hecht is one of the most accomplished members of a generation of poets that includes **Richard Wilbur, W.S. Merwin, Anne Sexton,** and **Hayden Carruth,** among others. The year of his birth also saw the births of **Denise Levertov, James Dickey,** Daniel Hoffman, and **Louis Simpson** (Ashton Marantz). But Hecht has long stood apart from the majority of his contemporaries and the many poets who followed for two reasons: his virtuosic and sustained use of rhyme, meter, and poetic form; and his ability to write incisively and decently about human cruelty and the horrors of his time. In his verse, criticism, and long career in academia, Hecht has approached poetry with a certain moral and professional dignity, with a sense of responsibility to the tradition and art itself, but also a conviction that poetry is simultaneously a private and a public, civic art.

Anthony Evan Hecht was born in New York City to second-generation American parents of German Jewish descent. He did not have a happy childhood. He did poorly in school, where he befriended **Jack Kerouac,** and suffered through an erratic family life. On three separate occasions, Melvyn Hecht ran his business completely into the ground, attempting suicide after each bankruptcy. Furthermore, the poet's only sibling, Roger Hecht (who also became a poet), suffered from epilepsy and several other serious health conditions. After the stock market crash in 1929, Hecht vividly remembers seeing the bodies of those ruined businessmen who had leapt from buildings covered over with blankets on the city streets.

In 1940 Hecht attended Bard College, then an experiment of Columbia University. Under the guidance of an inspiring but very unstable literature professor, he was drawn to poetry, specifically to the poetry of **T.S. Eliot** and **W.H. Auden.** But this, the first happy period of his life, was cut short in 1943 when he was drafted into the military. His father had schemed to get him discharged on grounds of mental instability, but Hecht refused to go along with the plot.

In Europe, as part of the 97th Infantry, Hecht saw some of the war's fiercest fighting. The 97th liberated Flossenbürg, an annex to the concentration camp Buchenwald in the Bavarian forest. According to Hecht, at the time of their arrival, five hundred prisoners were dying of typhus each day. Because he spoke both French and German, Hecht was employed translating both prisoners' accounts of the camp and the captured war criminals' explanations and denials. This intimate experience with both the perpetrators and victims of cruelty had a significant and long-lasting effect on him, personally and artistically.

After also serving briefly in occupied Japan, Hecht returned to the Unites States in 1947. He enrolled at Kenyon University under the GI Bill, his degree from Bard having been granted *in abstentia*. He studied at Kenyon for one year, under the poet **John Crowe Ransom**, who would publish Hecht's first poems in the *Kenyon Review*. Hecht returned to New York to study with poet **Allen Tate** at New York University. He later traveled to Europe and, while living briefly on the island of Ischia off the coast of Naples, he befriended the poet W.H. Auden. Despite the destabilizing, post-traumatic emotional effects of war, Hecht earned a master's degree from Columbia in 1950 and was awarded the first Prix de Rome for writing, a fellowship that allowed him to live in Rome for a year at the American Academy.

He soon published his first book, *A Summoning of Stones* (1954). During the 1950s and early 1960s, Hecht established himself as an accomplished poet and professor, and established a number of literary friendships and acquaintances. He taught at both Bard and Smith colleges and went again to Rome in 1954 on a Guggenheim fellowship, where he met Richard Wilbur, who would become a close friend. He also married Patricia Harris, in 1954, and had two sons. The couple separated in 1959 and divorced in 1961, at which time Hecht became severely depressed and was hospitalized for three months. In 1967 he took a professorship at the University of Rochester where he taught until 1985.

Hecht was, by this time, well established as a poet, publishing poems and reviews in the most distinguished little magazines. He waited fourteen years, however, to publish a second collection; *The Hard Hours* (1968) won the Pulitzer Prize, cementing his status.

Hecht remarried in 1971, this time to Helen D'Allessandro, the author of several well-known cookbooks. The next decade saw a series of prestigious visiting professorships at Harvard and Yale, more fellowships, and, slowly, more books of poetry: *Millions of Strange Shadows* (1977) and *The Venetian Vespers* (1979). In 1982, he was named the first consultant in poetry to the Library of Congress, the position now called poet laureate. In 1985

he took a position at Georgetown University, where he remained until his retirement in 1993. Rather than teach **creative writing**, as many of his contemporaries did, however, Hecht always taught literature classes. *Obbligati: Essays in Criticism* (1986), his first book of criticism, displayed his deft and wide-ranging scholarship.

He published both his *Collected Earlier Poems* (1990) and a new collection, *The Transparent Man* (1990), simultaneously. Two more collections, *Flight Among The Tombs* (1996) and *The Darkness and the Light* (2001), as well as a book of criticism, *Melodies Unheard: Essays on the Mysteries of Poetry* (2003), followed, proving that, even while approaching eighty, Anthony Hecht was still at the height of his powers.

Hecht's poetry is infused with rich historic, biblical, and literary allusions. He often writes about World War II, the Holocaust, and other horrors with haunting detachment, using elegant language and verse techniques. These levels of artifice help formulate personal experiences into a larger, public act of poetry. By stretching beyond the strictly personal, Hecht forces the reader, as well as himself, to bear witness to and thereby be implicated in the dreadfulness of the scene being described.

The early and widely anthologized poem "More Light! More Light!" (1968), from *The Hard Hours*, does just this. The poem tells of two executions: the first of an English heretic in the sixteenth century, the second during the Holocaust. When a Polish prisoner refuses to bury two Jewish prisoners alive, an SS guard orders the Jews to bury the Pole. When the task is nearly complete, the guard reverses the arrangement again. This time, the Pole does not refuse to bury the Jews, but, when he has finished, the guard shoots him in the stomach and leaves him to bleed to death.

The guard's inexplicable cruelty undoes even the Pole's initial act of courage. The poem is in rhyming quatrains, the coolness of the form heightening the terror. The Pole dies slowly in the last lines, while nothing "rose up in those hours / which grew to be years." There are no signs of hope whatsoever, and no light. The sixteenth-century heretic is executed for a lack of belief while the Jews are killed *for* their beliefs, suggesting that the "logic" governing and justifying such acts is never fixed. The title of the poem, which quotes the writer Goethe's dying words, transforms the plea of the individual into one on behalf of the entire universe.

Hecht depicts a similar scene in a similar structure more than three decades later in "Sacrifice," in *The Darkness in the Light* (2001). After two sections in which the biblical story of Isaac and Abraham is recounted from the perspective of each, Hecht turns to the French countryside of 1945, with the German army in retreat. A lone German officer attempts to commandeer a family's bicycle and, when the family refuses, holds their son at gunpoint. They still refuse, and the solider ultimately retracts his weapon and leaves—though not, Hecht tells us, out of mercy. In the end, the vileness of the family's inaction reverberates; they are cursed to live out their lives "in agonized, unviolated silence." In both poems, the pairing of a Holocaust story with an older historical or biblical scene asserts that such savagery is not new.

Another poem about the Holocaust, "The Book of Yolek," from *The Transparent Man* (1990), demonstrates how Hecht can also use traditional forms to intensify his themes. The end-words of this sestina move through several contexts; for example, the end-word "to" is first encased in "1942" and later in the "numeral tattoo" with which the Nazis mark the young boy. It is as though these words have been tainted with the memory of Yolek's horrific end, a memory whose inescapability is underscored by Hecht's final series of warnings: "Wherever you are, Yolek will be there, too."

In a cruel world, Hecht recognizes the power of art. Even his careful use of ornate language and strict forms to tell horrible tales is proof of this, according to poet and critic Daniel Hoffman: The poet can enjoy these ornaments even in the midst of moral collapse. Similarly, Hecht frequently enfolds his love for other mediums of art—painting, drama, and music—in his poetry. But Hecht does not claim that the power of art is redemptive. Though the father puts his children to bed with fairy tales of good triumphing over evil in "It Out-Herods Herod; I Pray Thee Avoid It" (*The Hard Hours*, 1968), the lingering truth is that he "could not, at one time / have saved them from the gas." Similarly, the speaker in "Peripipetea" (1977) cannot assuage his loneliness with a performance of Shakespeare. He claims he can manufacture equally enjoyable distractions in his own dreams.

Such incontrovertible bleakness is a foundational aspect of much of Hecht's poetry. Another well-known poem from *The Hard Hours*, "A Hill" (1968), encapsulates this loneliness in a single image—that of "a hill, mole-colored and bare," which appears to the speaker as a vision while walking through a Roman piazza. The hill, which entirely eclipses the nearby palace, thus blots out art and civilization altogether. At the poem's end, the speaker places the hill in his memory; he had seen it as a child and often stood in front of it transfixed. Thus, "A Hill" not only presents a rich symbol for the speaker's—and by extension, the poet's—sense of bleakness, but also illustrates his morbid fascination with it. But, as **J.D. McClatchy** notes, the poem offers us no explanation for the hill and no final wisdom; no clear epiphany emerges from the confrontation.

"The eye, self-satisfied, will be misled" when it tries to understand the world, claims the speaker in "The Transparent Man" (1990). Hecht has written many other fine dramatic monologues, including "Green: An Epistle" (1977), "The Grapes" (1979), and "See Naples and Die" (1990). "The Venetian Vespers" (1979), a roughly 1,000-line monologue spoken by a distraught ex-patriot, similarly echoes this theme: "I look and look / as though I could be saved simply by looking." Here, the lost speaker ultimately resigns himself to the limitations of perception and language. While Hecht is known for effectively merging balances between elevated language and blunt, colloquialisms, "The Venetian Vespers" contains some of his densest, most ornate language. Critic Gregory Dowling shows that Hecht is demonstrating the decay of this high style, mirrored in the decay of the ornate city of Venice.

Despite all this disillusionment, Hecht is also capable of great wit. "The Dover Bitch" (1968) and "The Ghost in the Martini" (1977) are only two examples. He has also had great success with **translation**, mainly from the French, as well as a play of Aeschylus. More recently, he has translated poems by Joseph Brodsky, working with the Russian poet. Although not exactly translations, his re-tellings of Bible stories in *The Darkness and the Light* have risen from a similar spirit.

Anthony Hecht's contributions as a critic have been similarly profound and reflect his sense of poetic duty. "*Obbligati*"—the title of his first book of criticism—refers to the critic's obligations to both the works he considers and to their creators. Hecht writes with equal insight into the work of contemporaries such as Richard Wilbur, **Robert Lowell**, and **Elizabeth Bishop**, and also into the work of Marvell and **Dickinson**. Hecht's study of Auden, *The Hidden Law: The Poetry of W.H. Auden* (1993), illustrates his debt to Auden, evidenced in early pieces such as "La Condition Botanique" (1954) and "The Gardens of the Villa D'Este" (1954), composed in long, metrical but naturalistic sentences.

Although his facility as a formal poet and contributions as a critic have long been commended, only recently have younger critics begun to truly recognize the complexity of his moral vision: the civility and the forthrightness with which his poetry has confronted the ugliness of the modern age. Anthony Hecht died on October 20, 2004, in Washington, D.C.

Further Reading. *Selected Primary Sources:* Hecht, Anthony, *Anthony Hecht in Conversation with Philip Hoy* (London: Between the Lines, 2001); ———, *Collected Earlier Poems* (New York: Alfred A. Knopf, 1990); ———, *Collected Later Poems* (New York: Alfred A. Knopf, 2003); ———, *The Hidden Law: The Poetry of W.H. Auden* (Cambridge, MA: Harvard University Press, 1993); ———, *Melodies Unheard: Essays on the Mysteries of Poetry* (Baltimore: Johns Hopkins University Press, 2003); ———, *Obbligati: Essays in Criticism* (New York: Antheneum, 1986). *Selected Secondary Sources:* German, Norman, *Anthony Hecht* (New York: P. Lang, 1989); Lea, Sydney, ed., *The Burdens of Formality: Essays on the Poetry of Anthony Hecht* (Athens: University of Georgia Press, 1989);

Mason, David, "Anthony Hecht at Eighty" (*Weekly Standard* 9.7 [27 October 2003]); Yezzi, David, "The Morality of Anthony Hecht" (*New Criterion* 22.8 [8 April 2004]).

Jon Mooallem

HEJINIAN, LYN (1941–)

Lyn Hejinian is an experimental poet, essayist, and translator. Her texts focus on the discursive construction of knowledge and subjectivity. As one of the leading representatives of the West Coast branch of the poetic movement known as **Language poetry**, she actively participated in the group's heralding of an anti-mimetic, self-reflexive poetic discourse that is opposed to both speech-based **free verse** lyricism and **New Formalism**. In her collection of critical essays, *The Language of Inquiry* (2000), she expresses one of the main tenets of language writing when she calls poetry "the dynamic process through which poetics, itself a dynamic process, is carried out" (1). What distinguishes her from other leading proponents of the group are, on the one hand, the concentration on poetry's philosophical and, in particular, phenomenological potentials and, on the other hand, the avoidance of any facile claims of poetry's immediate political function. This caution also characterizes her relation to **feminism**. While she is acutely aware of the difference gender makes for those living and writing in America today, she treats the cultural and, more specifically, the poetic roles of femininity (and masculinity) not as separate topics but as part of the general process of the construction of meaning in poetic, theoretical, and social discourses. Her explorations of the interconnection of genre and gender have just begun to be investigated by feminist literary criticism.

Hejinian was born in San Francisco in 1941. She spent her high-school years in New England and studied at Harvard University. She graduated in 1963, the first year that women were eligible to receive Harvard degrees. In the same year, her first poems were published. In 1968 she returned to California where she married jazz musician Larry Ochs and had two children. She teaches at the University of California–Berkeley, is the editor of the *Tuumba* chapbook series, and co-edits *Poetics Journal* with **Barrett Watten**. Translations of her work have been published in France, Spain, Japan, Italy, Russia, Sweden, and Finland.

The Civil Rights, women's, and anti-war movements of the 1960s provided the context for Hejinian's rising awareness of the centrality of language in understanding, criticizing, and reconfiguring social and cultural discourses. Her involvement in West Coast language writing after 1968, as well as discussions and collaboration with poets such as Barrett Watten, **Ron Silliman**, **Bob Perelman**, and **Rae Armantrout**, inspired her understanding of the function of poetry as linguistic exploration and provided her with new ways of handling poetic language.

The redefinition of the "language of poetry . . . as a language of inquiry, not the language of a genre" (*Language of Inquiry*, 3), was the basis for starting a number of textual queries in and demonstrations of the ways in which knowledge is linguistically produced. In 1976 she published *A Thought Is the Bride of What Thinking* as the first title in her own *Tuumba* chapbook series. In 1977 *A Mask of Motion* was published by **Rosmarie** and **Keith Waldrop**'s Burning Deck Press, and in 1978 *Writing Is an Aid to Memory* was published by The Figures. Notwithstanding their common epistemological subject, the texts differ greatly from each other. While, for instance, "repetition with a difference" is the underlying thematic and structural principle of *A Thought Is the Bride of What Thinking*, which consists of quasi-aphoristic prose paragraphs, *Writing Is an Aid to Memory* is based on the multiplication of meanings and employs the whole arsenal of poetic tools: lineation, enjambments, indentation, rhyme, alliteration, and assonance. Yet, whether starting from prose or poetry, all three of these texts playfully investigate the relation between thought, language, genre, and reality.

Hejinian's 1978 experimental text, *Gesualdo*, continues to explore the question of how we know what we know. Taking the life and the work of the Renaissance composer Carlo Gesualdo, Prince of Venosa, Count of Conza (ca. 1561–1613) as her subject, she directs her attention more specifically to the techniques and contexts by which a subject, or rather the knowledge about a subject, is discursively constructed. *Gesualdo* demonstrates how the historic figure of an artist is fashioned through generic conventions, including specific discourses on gender and interpretations of his art. Hejinian uses dictionary entries as well as more extensive scholarly texts on Gesualdo's life and art as foils to deconstruct the underlying generic and ideological assumptions of factuality and objectivity. While the poem's layout imitates a dictionary entry or a scholarly publication (maybe even a Renaissance text with rubrics) by placing short italicized phrases in the margins next to extended textual paragraphs, the biographical information is put into disarray by cutting and splicing the source texts:

Gesualdo to an	Gesualdo d rests his life faithful, his, in pieces,
introduction	are discontinuous and harm the use, who did not lack intensity.

Layout, textual organization, use of abbreviations, general diction, and stylistic register of this "nonsense text" still produce a biographical effect, which indicates that biography has less to do with personality and historic specificity than with linguistic routine and certain cultural assumptions. Among the latter are the roles of women as mates and muses of great men—stereotypes that Hejininian's defamiliarized poetic cutups highlight and undermine when she contrasts, for instance, "his violent temper" with "she on the grounds erring" (paragraph 12). Moreover, in a carefully planned movement from impersonal description—"Gesualdo d rests his life" (paragraph 1)—to personal claim—"Here I am. Be it audacious therefore ever" (last paragraph)—Hejinian both foregrounds and consciously employs the normally suppressed subjective bias of biographical discourse. She unabashedly appropriates quotes that refer originally to Gesualdo's mannerist style as metatextual comments upon her own method of composition: "manipulat[ing] for [her] / own ends forms invented in a different spirit" (paragraph 5).

Another related "form" of subject construction that she "manipulated for [her] own ends" was the genre of autobiography. In 1980, at a time when feminist theory started to turn special attention to the study of women's autobiographies, Hejinian published the first version of *My Life*; a second version followed in 1987, and a third one in 2002. Because it is intensely personal the text fulfills the generic expectations of autobiography. It contains not only references to her family, youth, marriage, reading habits, and the like but the number of paragraphs in each version and the number of sentences in each paragraph equal the poet's age at the time of writing. Yet the latter is a device that intentionally undermines rather than helps to create an autobiographical effect. Life writing typically establishes authenticity by avoiding any indication of the aesthetic and formal elements of the genre. Hejinian, on the other hand, plays with these generic expectations. Sentence by sentence, she calls up major autobiographical "building blocks"—time, story telling, personal point of view, textual links—but then refuses to fabricate a consistent whole out of the apparently ready-to-use material. Thus, she neither supplies the ordered retrospective prose narrative normally expected of autobiography nor simulates the closeness and the emotionalism often expected of women's life writing. Instead, readers are offered a text that shifts rapidly between past, present, and future. Stories are not told but enumerated in the form of one-sentence snapshots, and the point of view shifts from sentence to sentence. Connections are established not by narrative but by assonances, alliterations, repetitions, parallelisms, and leitmotifs. The resulting poetic quality of *My Life* is offset by the prose character of the sentences and the paragraphs of a text that is neither poetry (as thought of as **lyrical** or expressive) nor prose (as defined as **narrative** or descriptive text), but is something in between. *My Life* is anti-mimetic, anti-expressive, and generically hybrid; it is also funny,

entertaining, and stimulating. Although it took more than a decade until the importance of the text was recognized in scholarly and, in particular, in feminist criticism, it has since become both the most critically acclaimed and the most popular of Hejinian's books.

Another record of her life is Hejinian's 1991 poetic travelogue, *Oxota: A Short Russian Novel*, which emulates the form of Alexandr Pushkin's *Eugene Onegin*, a classic Russian novel in verse. The title, *Oxota*, is Russian for "the hunt," and "the hunt" in this long poem primarily refers to Hejinian's experiences during her visits to the Soviet Union. In 1983 the poet first visited Moscow and Leningrad when she accompanied her husband, Larry Ochs, and his saxophone quartet on a concert tour. In 1989 she returned to Leningrad, this time together with **Michael Davidson**, Ron Silliman, and Barrett Watten, to attend an international conference on **avant-garde** writing. As is obvious from the very beginning of *Oxota*, the Russian culture felt strange, if not estranging, to the poet. Yet "Strangeness," as Hejinian has argued in an essay under that title, enables new insights (*The Language of Inquiry*, 135–160). It forces one to confront both the other's and one's own reality (in this case, the cultural and language differences between Russia and the United States), and thereby offers an alternative to established ways of seeing and knowing. Hejinian makes use of the epistemological potential of cultural strangeness in *Oxota* by using concrete observations, episodes, and even jokes she overheard during her journeys to initiate philosophical speculations.

Hejinian's *The Cell* (1992) continues to explore the epistemological effects of strangeness by concentrating on the recording of day-to-day activities and dreams. Again, she employs the genre of life writing. This time the diary structure, a string of entries listed according to their day of writing, offers her a way to arrange formally and situate progressively in time that which, otherwise, is neither ordered nor progressive: the workings of the consciousness and the unconsciousness as they are bound to daily experiences, and the production of knowledge in this process. The book records her self-experiments regarding the linkage between daily experience and language. Psychoanalytical and phenomenological concepts and methods of observation are used to explore the ways of knowing the self and reality in poetic writing. By enacting and discussing them, both theories are employed to enhance the possibilities of literary "defamiliarization," that is, to actively (re)construct and (de)form situations and speculations in poetic writing.

Throughout her career, Hejinian has been interested in collaborating with other writers. Her poetic collaborative projects include *Leningrad* (1991), Hejinian's, Davidson's, Silliman's, and Watten's collaborative account of their conference trip to the Soviet Union); *Wicker: A Collaborative Poem* (1996) and *Sunflower* (2000), two poems written with Jack Collom; as well as *Hearing* (1998) and *Sight* (1999), two letter-writing projects with **Leslie Scalapino**. An extensive correspondence with the Leningrad experimental poet Arkadii Dragomoshchenko, whom she met in 1983, led not only to her two translations from the Russian, *Description* (1990) and *Xenia* (1994) but also to the experimental film *Letters Not About Love* (1998), directed by Jacki Ochs. With the painter Diane Andrews Hall, she created *The Eye of Enduring*, which was exhibited in 1996; and with the painter Emilie Clark, she published the mixed media book *The Traveler and the Hill and the Hill* (1998). With John Zorn she collaborated on the composition "Qûê Trân." She is the co-director, with Travis Ortiz, of the literary project *Atelos*, which commissions and publishes cross-genre work by poets.

The fifteen books of Hejinian's *Border Comedy* (2002) are devoted to the further investigation and transgression of generic and epistemological boundaries, or rather to the celebration of "what's between" (11). While the lineated "comedy" moves from line to line and changes the direction of its "meter making argument" literally "between" the lines, it enacts a poetic philosophy of "Between"—between prose, poetry, and drama; between describing, enacting, and knowing: "There we take on not just visibility but inspection and its proper preposition is *between*" (11). Between poetry and epistemology, between psychoanalytical phenomenology and postmodernist writing, Hejinian does not use language as a transparent means to gain knowledge and truth; rather, she follows language's capacity and opacity to create unlimited, and therefore infinite, knowledges and insights.

Further Reading. *Selected Primary Sources:* Hejinian, Lyn, *The Cold of Poetry* (Los Angeles: Sun and Moon Press, 1994); ———, *The Guard* (Berkeley: Tuumba, 1984); ———, *The Hunt* (Gran Canaria: Zasterle Press, 1991); ———, *The Language of Inquiry* (Berkeley: University of California Press, 2000); ———, *The Little Book of a Thousand Eyes* (Boulder: Smoke-Proof Press, 1996); ———, *Redo* (Vinyard Haven: Salt-Works Press, 1984). ***Selected Secondary Sources:*** Brito, Manuel, "Fragment, Sentence, and Memory of the Self in a Poetic Neo-Narrative" (*Revista Canaria de Estudios Ingeleses* 39 [November 1999]: 191–207); Nicholls, Peter, "Phenomenal Poetics: Reading Lyn Hejinian," in *The Mechanics of the Mirage: Postwar American Poetry*, ed. Michel Delville and Christine Pagnouelle (Liège: University of Liège, 2000, 241–252); Perloff, Marjorie, "How Russian Is It: Lyn Hejinian's *Oxota*," in *Poetry On and Off the Page: Essays for Emergent Occasions* (Evanston, IL: Northwestern University Press, 1998, 222–242); Quartermain, Peter, "Syllable as Music: Writing Is an Aid to Memory" (*Sagetrieb* 11.3 [Winter 1992]: 17–31);

Spahr, Juliana, "Resignifying Autobiography: Lyn Hejinian's *My Life*" (*American Literature* 68.1 [March 1996]: 139–158).

Kornelia Freitag

HELLER, MICHAEL (1937–)

Michael Heller is a member of that community of writers whose work can be characterized as poetry of ideas. He is an intellectual, deeply thoughtful and elegant in his perceptions, yet his poetry is never arid; rather, over decades he has constructed a body of work that is sensuous and personal, as well as ruminative and acutely intelligent. Heller's work can be usefully thought of as falling within the tradition of the **Objectivist poets** such as **George Oppen**, **Charles Reznikoff**, and **Louis Zukofsky**. It is fair to say that he perpetuates the Objectivist impulse to be concise and to "[think] with things as they exist" (to quote Zukofsky in his 1931 essay, "An Objective"); still, Heller has elaborated Objectivist precepts in his own way, for he can be autobiographical and intimate while at the same time considering the impersonal truths of human knowledge and behavior. His work has also been influenced by **William Bronk**, Gershem Scholem, and Walter Benjamin, and by premodern figures like John Donne. Heller's poems tend to be meditations on language, history, and knowledge, and they dwell in the essential uncertainty that marks the human dilemma. Their delicacy ultimately derives from the nuances of thought Heller can glory in, which not only describe but stand for a life lived with the assumption that certitude can be rejected in favor of a wealth of particularities that are truthful, albeit ephemeral.

Heller was born in Brooklyn, New York, to Peter and Martha Rosenthal Heller. His father, the son of a rabbi and writer, was brought as a child to the United States from the Belarussian city of Bialystok, now part of Poland. In 1959 Heller earned a BS in mechanical engineering from Rensselaer Polytechnic Institute. In 1964 he won the Coffey Poetry Prize for his work at the New School for Social Research. In 1967 he joined the faculty of the American Language Institute of New York University, where he taught for many years. In 1967, and again in 1989, he received New York Foundation for the Arts fellowships. In 1986 he earned an MA in English from New York University. In 2003 he received the Fund for Poetry Award. He is currently married to the poet and scholar Jane Augustine. Heller's major collections of poetry are *Accidental Center* (1972), *Knowledge* (1979), *In the Builded Place* (1989), *Wordflow: New and Selected Poems* (1997), and *Exigent Futures: New and Selected Poems* (2003); he has also published a prose memoir, *Living Root* (2000), interspersed with poetry, and *Conviction's Net of Branches*, essays on the Objectivists, which in 1980 won the Alice Fay di Castagnola Award.

In *Accidental Center* (1972), Heller's technological education is evident in his fascination with science and philosophy, as well as his capacity for precise observation and imaginative rendering of the encountered world. These are also evident in subsequent collections. In "Pressure," Heller speaks of "spectral pinpricks"; "excitations" are "given and received" between people in a "pulsar's wavepeak." The visible world is palpable and provocative, and a number of these early poems are meditations on photography and mirrors. In "The Portrait," he refers to "the fact of image / flung in photons."

In *Knowledge*, the tendencies laid out in Heller's earlier work are transmuted into a poetry of delicate observations—a poetry, moreover, that is more disciplined metrically—spoken by a sober and deliberate voice. The poet has become more philosophical. "Florida Letter" considers that "only time itself is the obdurate / Against which the heart leaps." Heller can be imagistic, as in "Mourning by the Sea," when, in contemplating the deaths of loved ones, he notices a "dark harbor water mottled green and blue." In "Interminglings," "finite life" is caught "in the pattern's / Verge and shift, in the hovering dust." The tone and pace of these poems is quiet and patient; observation enters into consciousness with inevitability.

In the Builded Place presents various landscapes, such as the mountains of Colorado, the sea, and the city. Whatever the terrain, Heller is capable of making breathtaking associations, instigated by place, such as when he is looking at the night sky in "With a Telescope in the Sangre de Cristos." The mute "glass" of the instrument discloses "The nebula's thumbprint swirls: / This fine life of bonds and connections." Physical and spiritual worlds come together. Other poems explore Heller's Jewish roots which can be both sources for his poetry and tantalizingly out of reach. "Mamaloshon" begins "at night, dream sentences / That will not write themselves." His grieving for his now dead parents gives rise to simple eloquence. Heller and his sister, in "Born in Water," have scattered the ashes of their mother over their father's grave, and, to hold the ashes down against the wind, they have poured water over them from a pitcher, "and added water from our eyes," the fluid like that which came from his mother's womb when he was born. Heller realizes that his "mother and father, as on the day / I was conceived," are now "mingled together."

The new poems in *Wordflow* reveal a poet who is at the height of his powers. In these poems the precepts of the world are distilled into material for the mind, shown in the act of thinking; the poems can be extraordinarily cerebral and subtle, using imagery as a vehicle for thought. What emerges is a consideration of language through which the mind realizes itself. "At the Muse's Tomb" reaches a crisis when Heller says, as if thinking aloud about how poetry and language join people yet also estrange them, "From the great engarblement, words are lifted out, and, in the / current lexicon, crowd aside columns of pictures, taking one past / new literals for contemplation among metonyms of blank." This book also contains poems of place linking Heller to family or friends, but more particularly to an awareness of history and the traditions being passed on through him. Sitting at a café in "In Paris," Heller notes to himself: "Benjamin was here in the late 1930s, jackboots down the street, / wrote to Scholem of his 'estrangement from everyone he knew.'"

Where Heller has increasingly concerned himself with the philosophy of language, culminating in *Wordflow*, in his latest book, *Exigent Futures*, his thinking leads to a philosophy of and meditation on the mind. His language here is more distilled and, although continuing to be imagistic, is less anchored in the details of daily life. Painting a lyrical cityscape as backdrop for his thoughts, Heller poses a question in "Cyclical": "Love hectored: were we to exist, our *being* a kind of corruscation across the sallow air?" The city has an undeniable vitality, one that is irresistible, but it also threatens, with its pace and noise, to overwhelm the spirit. Thus the spirit turns for sustenance to word and thought, which have become the center of Heller's attention. In "Autobiographia" these elements are brought together. The poem begins with an extended question: "Weren't you given a text? To honor the congregation, the organ dulcet, / the cantor's hum, hymnal of Europe's East, steps of sound made fugal." The answer fulfills a promise found in Heller's early writing; the self is alive through its language, articulated in its awareness of its own sublime thinking.

Further Reading. *Selected Primary Sources:* Heller, Michael, *Accidental Center* (Fremont, MI: Sumac, 1972); ———, *Exigent Futures: New and Selected Poems* (Applecross, Western Australia: Salt, 2003); ———, *In the Builded Place* (Minneapolis, MN: Coffee House, 1989); ———, *Knowledge* (New York: Sun, 1979); ———, *Living Root: A Memoir* (Albany: State University of New York, 2000); ———, *Wordflow: New and Selected Poems* (Jersey City, NJ: Talisman House, 1997); Zukofsky, Louis, "An Objective," in *Prepositions: The Collected Critical Essays of Louis Zukofsky*, expanded ed. (1931; Berkeley: University of California Press, 1981). ***Selected Secondary Sources:*** Finkelstein, Norman, *Not One of Them in Place* (Albany: State University of New York, 2001); Foster, Edward, ed., *Talisman: A Journal of Contemporary Poetry and Poetics* (Michael Heller Issue 11 [Fall 1993]). Kimmelman, Burt, "Michael Heller," in *Dictionary of Literary Biography*, vol. 165, ser. 4, ed. Joseph Conte (Detroit: Bruccoli Clark Layman / Gale Research, 1996, 108–119).

Burt Kimmelman

HERRERA, JUAN FELIPE (1948–)

Juan Felipe Herrera is one of the most challenging and one of the few prolific **Chicano poet**s today, having published fourteen books of poetry and six other books of prose, including short stories, young adult novels, and children's books. Hererra's poetry pushes the definition of verse with his experimentation in form, language, images, and sound. A **postmodernist** in his expression, Herrera's compositions are often challenging and dense, requiring some work on the part of the reader. Herrera writes about urban landscapes and their alienated inhabitants; community, multiculturalism, and marginalization; the indigenous and the spiritual; and social protest, change, and justice. His involvement with theater shows in the oratory nature of his poems. He experiments with dramatic and visual art forms more than any of his contemporaries. Herrera's poetry is indeed complex, but always bold and groundbreaking.

Born the only child to Mexican migrant farmworkers in Fowler, California, on December 27, 1948, Herrera was in constant transition until finally settling down in San Diego at age eight. After graduating from San Diego High School in 1968, he went on to UCLA, where he founded *Teatro Tolteca*, and in subsequent years the *Troka* and the Manikrudo Spoken Word Ensemble. Two years after graduating with a BA in social anthropology in 1972, Herrera published his first book, *Rebozos of Love We Have Woven Sudor de Pueblos on Our Backs* (1974). In 1980 he received his MA in social anthropology from Stanford University. His third book, *Facegames* (1987), was awarded an American Book Award from the Before Columbus Foundation. Despite his existing publications and accolades, he enrolled in the Iowa Writers' Workshop and received his MFA in 1990. Herrera also works as an actor, video artist, photographer, playwright, and literary editor. After spending fifteen years as a professor at California State University–Fresno, in 2005 he became the inaugural Tomás Rivera Endowed Chair of the Creative Writing Department at the University of California–Riverside.

Herrera's *Exiles of Desire* (1985) is best know for its portrayal of Chicanos as "exiles" in their own land because of the alienating nature of urban areas. The first of four sections of the book establishes this theme with such poems as "A Poem-Review of *The Elephant Man*," where the urban experience of the character J.X. is juxtaposed against the social-outcast experiences of the hideously deformed John Merrick, known in Victorian England as the Elephant Man. Another poem in this section, "Your Name is X," is riddled with surrealistic images of urban anxiety. In the second section, "Tripitas" are caricatures, but also quasi-intimate portraits, of urban Chicano dwellers with cartoonish names. These characters find themselves in spaces as diverse as a taqueria, a barrio meeting, or a gay pride march. Each one stands on the verge of accomplishing a goal or fulfilling a desire, only to be sidetracked or suppressed. The third section, "Photo-Poem of the Chicano Moratorium 1980/LA," displays Herrera's amalgamation of the visual art form of photography with verse experimentation. Herrera uses fragmented sentences throughout this sequence to replicate a camera's shutter and give the poems a photo essay-like movement. The final section, "Mission Street Manifesto," deals with the shared experience of urban disarray resulting from commercialization and industrialization. Ultimately, the reach of *Exiles of Desire* ranges from the individual to the global.

Herrera revisits the theme of urban disarray in *Love After the Riots* (1996). The book's two lovers, Pinal and Margo, attempt romance against the backdrop of the aftermath of the Los Angeles riots of 1992, fleeing from scene to scene in a TR-3 sports car. Herrera parallels the burning of Los Angeles to the burning of Rome, as he writes, "This is Rome at the end of the century." Aesthetically, the book evokes the mood of a film by Italian director Federico Fellini. The images found in the poems are surrealistic, sometimes disjointed like jump-cuts. The book's narrative thread is also disjointed, mirroring the chaos and confusion of the riots, although the poem titles follow chronological time, such as "8:35 pm," "8:37 pm," and "9:45 pm." The latter technique reflects Herrera's theory that madness and uncertainty need only minutes to be conceived.

Border-Crosser with a Lamborghini Dream (1999) is Herrera's rhythmic spectacle of culture and identity, from the modern Barrio to the ancient Maya. Using popular culture icons such as the black rapper 2Pac, the Tejana singer Selena (who both suffered untimely deaths), Edward Hopper, and Mayan and Aztec cultural figures, the poet complicates the construction of Chicano identity. Individually, the poems' images are disjointed, but the sequences themselves propel the reader from one poem to the next. The book's pace, then, emulates the speed of a Lamborghini (suggesting also a dream of luxury) in a race (both competitive and ethnic); at the finish line (the end of the book) the reader filters the most important and striking images. Life is a blur, Herrera proposes; what the person remembers most—experiences, memories, images—is what creates the person.

Notebooks of a Chile Verde Smuggler (2002) is a peek into a poet's diary in order to understand his makeup. On the one hand, it is a family history and photo album; on the other, it is an autobiography that reveals the makings of a political activist, as reflected in his "June Journals." The sequences "Undelivered Letters to Víctor" and "New York Angelic," provide glimpses into the struggles, frustrations, and desires of a marginalized writer. Considered Herrera's best book to date, *Notebooks of a Chile Verde Smuggler* pushes the limits of poetic form with poems such as "Fuzzy Equations," a presidential critique; "Millennium Omens," which engages in cultural word play; and "Hispanopoly: The Upwardly Mobile Identity Game Show," which is in teleplay form. If Herrera's previous books examine culture and identity, this book attempts to capture subculture and sub-identity. With each new book Herrera publishes, he becomes ever more bold in his poetic experiments.

Further Reading. *Selected Primary Sources:* Herrera, Juan Felipe, *Border-Crosser with a Lamborghini Dream* (Tucson: University of Arizona Press, 1999); ———, *CrashBoomLove* (Albuquerque: University of New Mexico Press, 1999); ———, *Exiles of Desire* (Houston: Arte Publico Press, 1985); ———, *Love After the Riots* (Willimantic, CT: Curbstone Press, 1996); ———, *Notebooks of a Chile Verde Smuggler* (Tucson: University of Arizona Press, 2002). *Selected Secondary Sources:* Lia, Purpura, "Border-Crosser with a Lamborghini Dream" (*Antioch Review* [Summer 2000]); Lomelí, Francisco A., and Donald V. Urioste, *Chicano Perspectives in Literature: A Critical and Annotated Bibliography* (Albuquerque, NM: Pajarito, 1976); Medrano, Michael Luis, "Learning to Not Write: An Interview with Juan Felipe Herrera" (*Dislocate* [Fall 2004]); Olszewski, Lawrence, "Notebooks of a Chile Verde Smuggler" (*Library Journal* [August 2002]).

John O. Espinoza

HEYEN, WILLIAM (1940–)

William Heyen's extraordinary production of poetry, prose, and thematic anthologies is the expression of several aspirations: to face the suffering of both peoples and the creatures of the natural world; to struggle toward understanding; and to extol and celebrate life—in the general sense of life on earth, and in the particular sense of his own existence as it unfolds moment by moment. His attempts to grasp the Holocaust and the pain of its victims resulted in three books, with many of the poems recounting survivors' stories. Other poetry collections have added to the body of eco-literature. In fact, in his memoir, *Long Island Light* (1979), he recalls that the fall of a beloved tree "led me to need words." His absorption with the Lakota chief Crazy Horse, his anguish over the Gulf War, and—curious as it might seem—his fascination with Princess Diana and the complicated feelings regarding her mixed record of success, all gave rise to books. Heyen is recognized as one of the country's relentless poets of conscience, and also as a poet of mystical bent whose method of total immersion can fix upon either the great tragedies of history or the smaller calamities that illuminate the human condition.

Henry Jürgen Heyen and Wilhelmine Auguste Else Wormke immigrated to the United States in 1929 and 1934, respectively, and by the time William Heyen was born in 1940 in Brooklyn, New York, Henry had become a foreman at a Bethlehem Steel plant. His father took pride, Heyen remembers, in selecting crews of carpenters to refit liberty ships into hospital ships to support America's war against the "home countries." Two of Heyen's paternal uncles served in the German army in World War II and were killed in action. One was an apolitical draftee, but the other was an avowed Nazi—for Heyen a troubling familial proximity that would one day fuel his reflections upon the random nature of fate, fortune, and identify.

Heyen and his two brothers grew up in areas around Long Island and finally—most memorably—in Nesconset. In these environs the boy became engaged—one could just as easily say *smitten*—with nature in all forms: flowers and cacti, pond and marine life, birds and animals, wild or farm-raised. *The Chestnut Rain* (1986) offers fond memories of Wexel, the local farmer whose practical-minded yet tender handling of matters pertaining to birth, increase, and death deepened the poet's education.

Heyen graduated from the State University of New York–Brockport in 1961 and two years later married Hannelore Irene Greiner, whose mother had fled Berlin just before the siege of the Russian army. William and Hannelore settled in Brockport and raised two children, Bill and Kristen.

The subject of Heyen's Ph.D. dissertation was **Theodore Roethke**, whose work often describes an ecstatic communion with the wilderness. Heyen was also drawn to the work of **W.S. Merwin** and **William Stafford**. He struck up a correspondence with **Richard Wilbur**, and he admired **Joyce Carol Oates** both personally and professionally.

Heyen's first book, *Depth of Field*, appeared in 1970, and since then he has produced many collections of poetry and prose, as well as edited anthologies. Some of his signature titles, other than those mentioned, are *The Swastika Poems* (1977), *Lord Dragonfly: Five Sequences* (1981), *The Host: Selected Poems* (1965–1990), *Pig Notes and Dumb Music: Prose and Poetry* (1998), the anthology *September 11, 2001: American Writers Respond* (2002), and *Shoah Train: Poems* (2003).

Heyen served as a senior Fulbright lecturer in American literature in Germany (1971–1972); among other awards, he also received a National Endowment for the Arts grant in 1973, a Guggenheim fellowship in 1977, and, for *Crazy Horse in Stillness*, a Lillian Fairchild Memorial Award. In 2001 he retired as professor of English and poet in residence at the State University of New York–Brockport; he still lives in Brockport, writing and publishing regularly.

In spite of the unflagging urge to expose, wonder over, and mourn historical and present day crimes and calamities apparent in his poems, the term "political poet" should not be applied to Heyen without certain qualifications—because for some, the label suggests a rigid or bombastic self-satisfaction. Heyen himself has acknowledged the danger, both artistic and moral, of setting oneself on a pulpit, and generally his poetry disavows snap conclusions and simple solutions. He is fond of an expression of William Stafford's: "Imagine a ghostly question mark behind everything I say" (quoted in Brody 45).

Another of his favorite phrases comes from Roethke: "By long staring, I have come to be." Certainly for Heyen, as probably for Roethke, this "long staring" involves far more than a complacent observation of green and woodsy things. It is compatible in Heyen's cosmology with the Lakota mysticism, his own Zen studies, and the all-embracing spirit of another of his poet models, **Walt Whitman.** These systems and ways of viewing the world support Heyen's feeling that it might be possible to advance—through poetry—an engagement with the subject so intense as to psychically dissolve the membrane between here and there, now and then, I and other. Or if it is not possible, he seems to say, he will nevertheless write as if it were.

At the same time, in a contradiction that seems somehow tenable here, the poems hold that there really is no such dividing membrane; one life streams seamlessly into another —the smaller into the larger—as does one era of history into the next. And, so, if time and place run together, then,in a poem like "L.A. Freeway" in *The Rope* (2004) a freeway might be a river of sorts and Crazy Horse among us still—even during rush hour on the 110.

Further Reading. *Selected Primary Sources:* Heyen, William, *The Chestnut Rain: A Poem* (New York: Ballantine, 1986);———, *Crazy Horse in Stillness: Poems* (Rochester, NY: BOA Editions 1998); ———, *Lord Dragonfly* (New York: Vanguard, 1981); ———, ed., *September 11, 2001: American Writers Respond* (Silver Spring, MD: Etruscan Press, 2002); ———, *Shoah Train: Poems* (Silver Spring, MD: Etruscan Press, 2003); ———, *The Swastika Poems* (New York: Vanguard, 1977). ***Selected Secondary Sources:*** Brady, Philip, "As for Me: A Conversation with William Heyen" (*Artful Dodge* 40.41 [2002]:44–45]); Watson, David, "William Heyen: Heartwood & Witness Power" (*Black Dirt* [n.d.]).

Suzanne Lummis

HIGGINS, DICK (1938–1998)

As an author, poet, composer, publisher, and theorist, Dick Higgins's influence spanned an impressive range of artistic genres and media. A co-founder of the **Fluxus** movement of the 1960s, Higgins was interested in the juxtaposition and fluidity of words, sounds, and visual elements to create what he termed Intermedia or works that "fall between media." His own writing, as well as that published by his Something Else Press, included poetry (**concrete**, **visual**, and **sound**), essays, drama, screenplays, and musical scores.

Richard C. (Dick) Higgins was born in Cambridge, England, on March 15, 1938. He was educated in American boarding schools and later studied at Yale University (1955–1957), Columbia University (1958–1960), the Manhattan School of Printing (1960–1961) and the New School of Social Research (1957–1959). It was at the New School that Higgins met and studied under **avant-garde** musicians **John Cage** and Henry Cowell. Fellow students included Allan Kaprow, Al Hansen, George Brecht, **Jackson Mac Low**, and other artists who would later found the Fluxus movement, an effort to decontextualize words, images, and sounds so as to rearrange them and blur the distinctions between artistic genres. Along with Kaprow, Higgins became an early promoter of "Happenings" during the early 1960s.

Higgins co-founded Fluxus with George Maciunas in 1961, but later broke with Maciunas after a dispute involving delays to a proposed book of Higgins's writings that was to be published by Maciunas's Fluxus Press. The break led to the founding of Something Else Press in 1964 and to the publication of Higgins's *Jefferson's Birthday/Postface.* After moving to California in 1970, Higgins resettled in Vermont the following year. Personal and financial problems forced Higgins to relinquish control of Something Else Press to Jan Herman. However, Higgins soon founded Unpublished Editions because his book *Amigo: A Sexual Oddyssey* (1972) had been rejected by Herman at Something Else.

Higgins entered graduate studies in English at New York University in 1975. His interest in visual and concrete poetry led to his study of earlier forms of visual poetry and resulted in two scholarly works on pattern poetry. In 1981 he moved to Barrytown, New York, and devoted much of his time to writing musical scores, plays, and theoretical works, researching pattern poetry, and publishing works under the Printed Editions (formerly Unpublished Editions) imprint. His last major publication was *Modernism Since Postmodernism: Essays on Intermedia* (1997). Higgins died October 26, 1998, in Quebec City, Canada.

As reflected in his varied interests, Higgins's works encompassed many styles and media. He wrote or contributed to nearly one hundred fifty books, as well as producing musical compositions, films, sound poems, graphics, and other ephemera. His writings appeared in numerous periodicals, including *Asylum, Chelsea Review, Chicago Review, Inkblot, Lost and Found, Performing Arts Journal, Pulpsmith, Semiotext(E), Unmuzzled Ox, West Coast Review,* and *Wormwood Review.*

Higgins's book-length essay entitled *What Are Legends,* was published by Bern Porter in 1960. However, any discussion of his writing, whether poetry or theoretical essays, must touch upon Higgins's role as a publisher, since many of his works from the early 1960s to the mid-1980s were self-published under one of his own imprints

(Something Else Press, Unpublished Editions, Printed Editions). *Jefferson's Birthday/Postface* (1964), the first work from Something Else Press, typified what was to become Higgins's style of blending subjects and genres. As two separate works bound together, the book included all of his writing (performance works, plays, and an essay) over the course of one year from April 1962 to April 1963. The dos-a-dos binding of the two works reflected his interest in the book arts.

Diversity of writing and concern for book design also dominate *foew&ombwhnw* (1969), the title being an acronym for "Freaked Out Electronic Wizards and Other Marvelous Bartenders Who Have No Wings." Disguised as a prayer book, including the imitation leather cloth binding, the pages are divided into four columns across each two-page spread containing theatrical and musical scenarios, drawings and found graphics, poetry and essays. Included is Higgins's "Danger Music" sequence: Danger Music #25 reads in its entirety "decide what you want to do and do it," while Danger Music #38 consists of a single blank line. His famous essay "Intermedia," in which he discusses his definition of the term, is reprinted in this volume from an earlier appearance in Higgins's *Something Else Newsletter* (1966–1973).

A Book About Love & War & Death (1972; Canto One published as Great Bear Pamphlet #2 in 1965) found Higgins experimenting with chance methods to create a prose-verse work using dice to select words from an Indonesian dictionary and construct the five cantos that comprise the book. *Love & War & Death* was written between 1960 and 1970. Two major events in Higgins's life—his early love and marriage to artist Alison Knowles and the death of his brother in Africa—are reflected in the title of the book and in lines such as "all of them had to edit this: we are very weary / The notorious fusty made unconscious pink / breeders" (Canto One, Chapter One). The form of the work was intended by Higgins to be a contrast to the "abstract lyricism" that he felt characterized late 1950s poetry.

For Eugene in Germany (1973) is one of Higgins's least experimental works, both in the form of the individual poems and in the single, unifying theme of the book. Written as a series of what he calls "post poems" for a friend visiting Germany, Higgins states in the preface that "the basic focus was my mind and my environment in [V]ermont"—the first poem, dated April 30, consists of two lines: "an empty room / a postcard on a bed," while the last, dated May 31, reads "you / arrival / sun."

Higgins's interest in visual and concrete poetry dated from his early career as a writer and publisher. In 1967, Something Else Press published Emmett Williams's seminal *Anthology of Concrete Poetry*. After Higgins entered graduate studies at New York University, his interest in tracing the roots of visual poetry led to the publication of *George Herbert's Pattern Poems: In Their Tradition* (1977)

and *Pattern Poetry: Guide to an Unknown Literature* (1987). In the later work, Higgins traces the form back to early Greek and Egyptian designs.

Throughout his career, Higgins consistently expanded and razed the boundaries between writing forms and genres. His experimentation and openness were seen in his own work as well as in the works of those writers he published. Unlike many of the books produced by both **small presses** and publishers of artists' books during the 1960s and 1970s, Something Else Press became known for publishing **experimental** writing that was packaged in more mainstream, trade edition formats. The high-quality and conventional production, as well as Higgins's approach to marketing and distribution, allowed Something Else Press to reach a far broader audience than did most small presses of the time. Over sixty books were produced between 1964 and 1974 by such avant-garde writers as **Gertrude Stein**, John Cage, Brion Gysin, Ian Hamilton Finlay, Alison Knowles, Mashall McLuhan, Emmett Williams, Daniel Spoerri, Al Hansen and Allan Kaprow.

Further Reading. *Selected Primary Sources:* Higgins, Dick, *A Book About Love & War & Death* (New York: Something Else Press, 1972); ——, *foew&ombwhnw* (New York: Something Else Press, 1969); ——, *For Eugene in Germany* (New York: Unpublished Editions, 1973); ——, *Jefferson's Birthday/Postface* (New York: Something Else Press, 1964); ——, *Pattern Poetry: Guide to an Unknown Literature* (Albany: State University of New York Press, 1987). ***Selected Secondary Sources:*** Fox, Hugh, "Dick Higgins: Neo-Dadaist," in *The Living Underground: A Critical Overview* (Troy, NY: Whitston, 1970); Frank, Peter, *Something Else Press: An Annotated Bibliography* (New Paltz, NY: McPherson, 1983); Higgins, Dick, *Dick Higgins: A Bio/Bibliography* (1979; 1986; Barrytown, NY: D. Higgins, 1992).

Christopher Harter

HIGGINSON, THOMAS WENTWORTH (1823–1911)

Although Thomas Wentworth Higginson would publish poems in some of his era's most prestigious periodicals, including *Putnam's*, the *Atlantic Monthly*, the *Century*, and *Scribner's Magazine*, his poetry as a whole never received special notice. Instead, the noted women's rights advocate and abolitionist became a prominent "man of letters" on the basis of his essays and his critical and editorial work. Today, literary critics remember him primarily for corresponding with **Emily Dickinson** during his life and co-editing her poetry after her death. Higginson's reputation as essayist, editor, and literary critic provided him with a much more prominent position in the American poetry community than his own poetic output would suggest.

Higginson was born on December 22, 1823, into a family that placed him in the midst of the Boston area's vibrant literary and intellectual community. Raised in Cambridge, Massachusetts, primarily by his mother and aunt (his father died when he was ten), Higginson was the youngest in his Harvard College class. While in Cambridge and at Harvard, Higginson circulated with some of the century's key intellectual and literary figures, including Theodore Parker, **James Russell Lowell** and **Maria White Lowell**, and members of the Longfellow family. After postgraduate work at Harvard and a degree from the Harvard Divinity School, Higginson served for many years as a member of the clergy, first for a Unitarian church in Newburyport, Massachusetts, and then at a Free Church in Worcester, Massachusetts. Higginson retired from his Worcester pulpit so he could spend more time on abolitionist activities; from then on, he supported himself with income from writing and lectures. Higginson gained national prominence with his activities as an abolitionist and served during the Civil War as commander of the first regiment of freed slaves, the First South Carolina Volunteers. He left his post after less than two years because of poor health and was commonly known thereafter as "Colonel." After his service in the war, Higginson and his wife, Mary Channing Higginson, moved to Newport, Rhode Island, where she died in 1877. Higginson married again to Mary Thacher in 1879 and had with her one daughter, Margaret, who reached maturity. He died in Cambridge on May 9, 1911.

Higginson's career as a published poet began with some success. His "La Madonna di San Sisto," published in the 1843 journal the *Present*, was selected by **Henry Wadsworth Longfellow** for an anthology, *Estray*. Higginson continued to publish regularly in religious and abolitionist periodicals, and, in 1853, he published several poems in *Putnam's*, a short-lived but critically lauded periodical. Higginson garnered significant attention not for his poetry, however, but for his essays. In 1858 he published his first essay for the relatively new *Atlantic Monthly*, and thus began a relationship with the prestigious periodical that lasted into the twentieth century. The *Atlantic Monthly* was only one of many periodicals that Higginson accessed. Personal essays, profiles on renowned persons, and essays on health, nature, abolitionism, and women's education in a variety of publications established Higginson as a prominent public figure and popular essayist. As someone who counted as friend or acquaintance writers like Louise Chandler Moulton, **Mary Mapes Dodge**, **Julia Ward Howe**, Josiah Gilbert Holland, **Oliver Wendell Holmes**, **Bret Harte**, **William Cullen Bryant**, **Helen Hunt Jackson**, **John Greenleaf Whittier**, the Lowells, and others, Higginson certainly was well poised to comment on and participate in the day's literary activities.

Even early on, Higginson the poet was a significant collaborator and editor as well as author. His older sister, Louisa, with whom he shared an early interest in poetry, reportedly chose Higginson's Harvard commencement address topic, "Poetry in an Unpoetical Age" (1841), and wrote portions of it. In addition, all three of his poetry volumes are to some degree collaborative. The 1853 *Thalatta: A Book for the Seaside* is a poetry collection Higginson co-edited with **Samuel Longfellow** that includes some original verse by the two editors. His second collection, *The Afternoon Landscape*, which did not appear until 1889, included poems by his second wife, Mary Thacher Higginson, and by his sister Louisa (S.L.H.). It was followed four years later by the modestly titled and co-authored *Such as They Are: Poems* (1893), which also featured poems by Mary Thacher Higginson. Although Higginson's poetry appeared in periodicals like *Scribner's Magazine*, the *Century*, and the *Atlantic Monthly* shortly before the publication of *Such as They Are*, the 1893 volume largely signaled the end of his poetic publication. Higginson continued writing until his death but focused his efforts on essays, his memoirs, and the definitive edition of his writings.

The access Higginson enjoyed to his era's best **literary magazines** no doubt speaks in part to his formidable reputation as an essayist and his extensive publishing connections. But his poetry also offers a fair representation of the day's larger poetry culture—it voices popular poetic sentiments in the traditional meter and rhyme schemes often associated with nineteenth-century **genteel** poets. Higginson, who titled his memoir *Cheerful Yesterdays*, infused much of his poetry with optimism. His early interest in Transcendentalism and his appreciation of **Ralph Waldo Emerson**, who "wrote fearlessly even of the humble-bee" ("Ralph Waldo Emerson," *Contemporaries*, 19), aligned with his own choice of poetic subjects. His poems celebrate nature at large for the hope and joy it brings ("Joy Cometh with the Morning"), the butterfly for its beauty and freedom ("Ode to a Butterfly"), and the Baltimore oriole for the cheering power of its song ("The Baltimore Oriole"). In Higginson's poetry, the natural world extends comfort and exhibits order even in the face of human loss: The fall of autumn leaves signifies natural order and purpose to one recovering from grief ("The Lesson of the Leaves"), and the pastoral setting of an infant's violet-covered grave affords "peace" ("Beneath the Violets").

Higginson's 1889 and 1893 poetry collections highlight his various public roles and interests. The collections gather lyrics variously suited for the day's poetry culture, as found in magazines and as performed at public venues. His occasional poems recall his vast network of friends and acquaintances. For example, he commemorates **Helen Hunt Jackson** for her "soul of fire within a woman's clay" ("To the Memory of H.H.")

and Whittier for his "high call" to action ("To John Greenleaf Whittier"). Publicly known for his Civil War experience, Higginson wrote poems for recitation at veterans' events ("Waiting for the Bugle") and Memorial Day ("Memorial Ode"). Higginson also dealt, however, in the sentiment and domesticity often ascribed to women's writing but prevalent in much of nineteenth-century poetry. In war poems like "Decoration," for instance, Higginson explores quieter heroics during war: the speaker passes by publicly recognized soldiers' graves to honor with lilies the grave of "the bravest of the brave," an undecorated woman. Other poems, like "The Baby Sorceress," "Sixty and Six," and "Two Voyagers," notably explore the anxieties and joys of fatherhood. Long interested in writing for children, Higginson's most commercially successful book in fact was his 1875 *Young Folks' History of the United States*, and he contributed to a variety of children's magazines over the course of his career, including the first issue of the prestigious *St. Nicholas* in 1873.

If Higginson's poetry exhibited a lack of originality, his critical and editorial roles made him one of the period's tastemakers. Dickinson, who started a decades-long correspondence with Higginson after his 1862 "Letter to a Young Contributor" in the *Atlantic Monthly*, was moved to respond and apply for his editorial judgment. Higginson's "Letter" emphasized his position as a gatekeeper. As Americans clamored to see their names and work published in the burgeoning periodical market, they often encountered brief editorial responses rejecting (or accepting) their submissions via periodicals' correspondence departments. Higginson's "Letter" turned this common editorial act into a lengthy essay; it was the ultimate editorial response. However, he not only stood guard over American letters but also played sponsor to many a poet, including his second wife, Mary Thacher, Helen Hunt Jackson, and **John Banister Tabb**. With initial reluctance, he also co-edited Dickinson's *Poems* (1890) and *Poems* (1891) after her death.

Higginson exerted much of his critical influence in the periodical market. While his publications included book-length biographies of Whittier and Longfellow, Higginson drew notice especially as a result of his position as an early and longstanding contributor to the *Atlantic Monthly* and other leading periodicals and as the poetry critic for the *Nation* from 1877 to 1904. Higginson, who identified the establishment of American literature with the *Atlantic Monthly*, covered a number of American authors in shorter essays, including Emerson, Whittier, **Walt Whitman**, **Sidney Lanier**, Helen Hunt Jackson, and **Edgar Allan Poe**. Heavily invested in an American literary industry, Higginson's critical attention and editorial efforts helped defend, critique, and shape a national literature narrative. Higginson pointed to Emerson as instrumental in the establishment of a dis-

tinctly American literature, arguing that "in the poems of Emerson, not less than in his prose, the birth of a literature was in progress" ("Ralph Waldo Emerson," *Contemporaries*, 19). He criticized Whitman for his lack of form and hackneyed sentiments and praised Helen Hunt Jackson for her brilliant mind. His defense of and belief in an American literature made him an easy target for critics like Andrew Lang, the British poet and critic dominant in American periodicals, who attacked Higginson's promotion of Dickinson's poetry. As a result, Higginson's attention was significantly directed, as well, to defending a place for American criticism in essays such as "A Contemporaneous Posterity," "The Shadow of Europe," and "A Cosmopolitan Standard."

Higginson's poetry represents a minor contribution, and his critical judgments and editorial acts were and are not without controversy. Still, his career reveals much about how nineteenth-century American poetry was published and distributed. And his role in shaping and defending an American poetry culture make him a central figure with which to contend.

Further Reading. *Selected Primary Sources:* Higginson, Thomas Wentworth, *The Afternoon Landscape: Poems and Translations* (New York: Longmans, Green, and Co., 1889); ———, *Contemporaries* (Boston: Houghton Mifflin/Riverside, 1899; reprint Literature House, 1970); Higginson, Thomas Wentworth, and Mary Thacher Higginson, *Such as They Are: Poems* (Boston: Roberts Bros., 1893); Higginson, Thomas Wentworth, and Samuel Longfellow, eds., *Thalatta* (Boston: Ticknor, Reed, and Fields, 1853). ***Selected Secondary Sources:*** Edelstein, Tilden G., *Strange Enthusiasm: A Life of Thomas Wentworth Higginson* (New Haven, CT: Yale University Press, 1968); Higginson, Mary Thacher, *Thomas Wentworth Higginson: The Story of His Life* (Boston: Houghton Mifflin, 1914); Wells, Anna Mary, *Dear Preceptor: The Life and Times of Thomas Wentworth Higginson* (Cambridge, MA: Riverside Press, 1963).

Ingrid Satelmajer

HILBERT, DONNA (1946–)

Originally from the Red River Valley, Southern California poet Donna Hilbert did not begin writing until after her father's death in 1980. She published poems for ten years in literary journals, and then her work caught the attention of an editor at Event Horizon Press, which printed *Mansions* (1990), the debut collection of her career. Having carved her path to poetry through early marriage and motherhood, Hilbert asserts a literary presence that embodies new possibilities for women. Combining subjects both domestic and other-worldly, Hilbert experiments with lyricism, formal structures, and wordplay to make poems not easily identified with a single school or tradition.

Hilbert was born in Grandfield, Oklahoma, in 1946, to a lower-middle-class Methodist family. In her hometown, she lingered over cherry phosphates at the drugstore and attended movies on Sunday nights. Three bachelor uncles taught her to read by helping her first memorize whole stories. At seven years of age, she moved with her parents to the San Fernando Valley area of Southern California: first to Van Nuys, then Reseda, and finally to Northridge. Her childhood was characterized by a freedom to explore vacant lots and orange groves, ride her bike far away from home, and walk to the local library. Though college and her own writing would not be a defined ambition for more than twenty years, her self-education began with reading such diverse writers as Camus, Freud, Graham Greene, Omar Khayyam, and Grace Metalious. By age eighteen, Hilbert married into an upper-middle-class Catholic family, and within five years she was the mother of three sons.

She earned an undergraduate degree in political science from Cal State University–Long Beach in 1978. There, she met poet **Gerald Locklin** and shortly after began to write and publish poems in such journals as *Rosebud, Pearl, Chiron Review,* and *Poetry LA.* Connections followed with **Edward Field** and **Billy Collins**, both of whom encouraged and promoted Hilbert's work. In addition to writing, she completed a master's degree in psychotherapy from the California Family Study Center in 1987 and began teaching poetry workshops both in the United Kingdom and the United States. Her first short story collection, *Women Who Make Money and the Men Who Love Them* (1994), was published by Staple First Editions in England. In 1998, her husband of thirty-three years was killed in a bicycle accident, and two subsequent collections addressed this tragedy: *Transforming Matter* (2000) and *Traveler in Paradise: New and Selected Poems* (2004).

Themes of transition and transformation—whether desired or dreaded—resonate throughout Hilbert's poetry, originating in *Mansions* (1990). "In the Garden Beyond Ourselves" begins as "an **elegy** of desire," contrasting the daily struggles of a married couple with the romantic indulgences of a painter, but finally articulating a connection: "I would wish us all in Arles: Van Gogh, Gaugin, / you and me, our blanket spread, picnicking under plum trees." However, in "This Gun Is Real," she affirms that darkness lingers in memories not easily erased by adulthood or aesthetic expression. In "May," Hilbert traces a sequence of sixteen dreamscape images in a haiku-like rosary, concluding with lines which serve as an epigraph for all her work: "From this deep well I am pulling / a woman."

The idea of poet-witness as midwife develops further in *Deep Red* (1993), both literally, through transformation of mother and self ("Gravity," "Mother in Satin"),

and metaphorically, by discovering identity in reading and expression ("Vocabulary Builders," "The Pursuit of Knowledge"). "Mother Tongue" expresses ownership of the poet's newborn voice with tight, whimsical phrasing and dark puns: "My slick red sticky mother tongue / can lick any little pistol." *Feathers and Dust* (1996) extends motifs of domestic discord through a retrospective persona who asserts literature as vital to sanity. In "At Thirteen I Meet Holden," for example, she recalls her own parent troubles as she hears a girlfriend screaming at her mother. The protective literary imagination serves as a counterpoint to the father who does not attend his young daughter's marriage in "Green Wedding" ("too pissed or too cheap / to make the trip") or who works by day on a telephone pole and then returns home, in "Friday Nights," intimating unpredictable violence as "[he sits] in his chair / like a storm sits on the horizon."

In *Transforming Matter* (2000), Hilbert's poems of grief combine lyric yearning with the discipline of linguistic play. In "Lesson," she addresses her dead beloved: "the transformation of matter, / transforming what matters." Her examinations of nature become increasingly reminiscent of **Mary Oliver** ("February, Los Angeles," and "Peninsula"). Subtexts of social class and gender roles in "Rank" and "Consciousness Raising" prefigure the surreal explorations of the subsequent **prose poem** sequence *Barbie X 3* (2004), which constructs a sardonic allegory reminiscent of **Margaret Atwood**. Responding to the remark that it wasn't fair for Barbie to have "magnificent breasts, but no vagina" Midge points out, "what with / Ken and [G.I.] Joe's obvious deficits, what would she *do* with one anyway?"

Hilbert's *Traveler in Paradise* (2004) invokes the spirit of **Jane Kenyon** in its patient images of dailiness and loss, as expressed in "Fall." The speaker can see the throb of her own pulse, "visible proof that sap / still rises in my limbs," but around her "old life withers / drops away." In the final three poems, Hilbert renews retrospective motifs. The finale, a sonnet framed as apostrophe to the departed spouse, calls out for the mercy of recognition from across time—though finally stating a haunting and inevitable resolve: "I must forbear. / The dead are even colder than we know."

Further Reading. *Selected Primary Sources:* Hilbert, Donna, *Deep Red* (Desert Hot Springs, CA: Event Horizon Press, 1993); ———, *Feathers and Dust* (Desert Hot Springs, CA: Event Horizon Press, 1996); ———, *Greatest Hits 1989–2000* (Johnstown, OH: Pudding House Press, 2001); ———, *Mansions* (Desert Hot Springs: Event Horizon Press, 1990); ———, *Transforming Matter* (Long Beach, CA: Pearl Editions, 2000); ———, *Traveler in Paradise: New and Selected Poems* (Long Beach, CA: Pearl Editions, 2004); ———, *Women*

Who Make Money and the Men Who Love Them (Derbyshire, UK: Staple First Editions, 1994).

Jo Scott-Coe

HILLMAN, BRENDA (1951–)

Brenda Hillman—ambitious, prolific, nervy, and innovative—is widely regarded as one of the most interesting and accomplished contemporary American poets. Known for her agile, groundbreaking, and often demanding approach, Hillman's work ranges from an evocative classical lyricism to disjunctive, acute, and penetrating experimental treatments of temporality, spirituality, and ontology. Though her poetics, more radical with each book, has been often the focus of criticism, Hillman has always been, like **Dickinson** before her, a poet of "the unknown where / the inexhaustible plays against form" ("Cascadia"). Ever concerned with the voice of the subtlest self in an often chaotic and meaningless world, Hillman has fashioned, in the words of Calvin Bedient, some of the most "direct, frank, and original" poetry of her generation (24).

Brenda Hillman was born in Tucson, Arizona, and spent her childhood there, in Brazil, and in Washington D.C. After receiving her BA magna cum laude from Pomona College in 1973, she attended the University of Iowa Writers' Workshop, where she took an MFA. in 1976. Hillman later moved to northern California, where she worked in a bookstore for ten years while raising a family and writing. Since 1984, Hillman has taught at St. Mary's College in Moraga, California. She has also taught at a number of other universities, including the University of Iowa. Since 1998, she has served as a series editor for the New California Poetry Series at the University of California Press. Hillman currently lives in the San Francisco Bay Area and is married to poet **Robert Hass**; she has one daughter and five stepchildren.

Hillman is the author of six collections of poetry: *White Dress* (1985), *Fortress* (1989), *Death Tractates* (1992), *Bright Existence* (1993), *Loose Sugar* (1997), and *Cascadia* (2001). She has also published three chapbooks: *Coffee, 3 AM* (1982), *Autumn Sojourn* (1995), and *The Firecage* (2000). She edited the collection, *The Poetry of Emily Dickinson* (1995) and, with Patricia Dienstfrey, co-edited *The Grand Permission: New Writings on Motherhood and Poetics* (2003).

Among other prizes and awards, Hillman received a National Endowment for the Arts fellowship in 1984 and a Guggenheim fellowship in poetry in 1994. Her fourth book, *Bright Existence*, was a finalist for the Pulitzer Prize in 1993, and *Loose Sugar*, her fifth book, was a finalist for the National Book Critic's Circle Award in 1998.

Hillman established a national reputation with her first four books. While edgy and thematically innovative, they are largely grounded in "traditional" lyrical **narrative** strategies that mix the spare metaphysics of Emily Dickinson with the extremity of **Sylvia Plath** and the desolated sense of self found in **T.S. Eliot**. The writing is vivid yet systematic, trenchant yet architectural, and often brilliantly figurative. Heavily concerned with themes of identity, relationship, alienation, and the liminal, these early works puzzle through modern physics, **feminist poetics**, Gnosticism, and the emblems of the natural world to explore and delineate the "wounds of a true self."

The culmination of Hillman's earlier work came in *Death Tractates* and *Bright Existence*, companion books heavily rooted in personal loss and readings in Gnostic literature, particularly that of the Nag Hammadi library. In both books, Hillman works against the grain of her classically beautiful and lucid lines with erasures, equivocations, pauses, and a wildly original sense of punctuation to prevent easy closure, or often, any closure at all. *Death Tractates*, which Calvin Bedient has called a feminist version of the **epic** vision-quest and "a work of perfect concentration . . . ever in essential movement" (24–25), uses the occasions and amplitudes of the author's grief over the sudden death of a principal mentor as the vehicle for a metaphysical essaying of great depth and subtlety. *Bright Existence*, started before the "interruption" of *Tractates*, and finished after, is organized around deft, often searing, examinations of the "splits" between feminine and masculine, subject and object, thought and its particulars, and both the touching beauty of the world and the need to reject it in order to regain the "dark existence" of spiritual origin. Hillman's later books, *Loose Sugar* (1997) and *Cascadia* (2001), explore some of the same alchemical and psychological terrain she first scouted in her earlier work, but also display an extended thematic range and increasing willingness on Hillman's part to center her poems in the fragmentary and the disjunctive. *Loose Sugar*, an explicitly dialectical, even programmatic book structurally, develops a "post-avant" approach to both anecdotal and deeply meditative material, and often succeeds brilliantly in juxtaposing an experimental approach to language with a deep concern for memory, temporality, sexuality, and spirituality. Writing in the *Kenyon Review*, David Wojhan notes that in *Loose Sugar*, Hillman "sets a standard which very few of her peers can match" (180). *Cascadia*, Hillman's most technically innovative book, mixes short, elegant lyrics and longer, highly metaphorical poems to explore the figurative and spiritual significance of "Cascadia," the prehistoric landmass that eventually became California. Combining poetic fragment with both scientific and vernacular language, the book proves the value of Hillman's oft-quoted assertion that "neither complete fragment nor complete discontinuity is accurate. Only both are accurate" ("Energizing the Reading Process," 3).

In 2003 Hillman published *The Grand Permission: New Writings on Poetics and Motherhood*, co-edited with Patricia Dientsfrey. This anthology of critical essays explores the complex links between the experience of motherhood and the vagaries of literary achievement. Including essays by **Toi Derricotte**, **Carolyn Forché**, **Fanny Howe**, **Maxine Kumin**, and many others, the anthology aims to illustrate that, as the editors put it, "the contemporary woman is no longer isolated in domestic space but is instead accompanied by a rich set of poetic traditions not available to women writing just half a century ago" (xxiv–xxv). Perhaps more important, *The Grand Permission* demonstrates that the poem itself no longer need be the constraining focus of literary thinking, for a supple and useful poetics can be built from socially and personally important life experiences such as motherhood.

Further Reading. *Selected Primary Sources:* Dientsfrey, Patricia, and Brenda Hillman, eds., *The Grand Permission: New Writings on Poetics and Motherhood* (Middletown, CT: Wesleyan University Press, 2003); Hillman, Brenda, *Bright Existence* (Middletown, CT: Wesleyan University Press, 1993); ——, *Cascadia* (Hanover, NH: Wesleyan University Press, 2001); ——, *Death Tractates* (Hanover, NH: Wesleyan University Press, 1993); ——, "Energizing the Reading Process: Juliana Spahr's New Nest" (*How2* I [February 2000]: 3, http://www.departments.bucknell.edu/stadler_center/how2). *Selected Secondary Sources:* Arnold, Kevin, "The Only Constant is the Page Number: Brenda Hillman's *Cascadia*" (*Valparaiso Poetry Review* 4.2 [Spring/Summer 2003]); Bedient, Calvin, "The Reluctant Gnostic" (*Threepenny Review* 14.2 [Summer 1993]: 24–25); Wojahn, David, "Survivalist Selves" (*Kenyon Review* 20.314 [Summer/Fall 1998]: 180).

Joe Ahearn

HIRSCH, EDWARD (1950–)

Edward Hirsch has built his literary reputation on the basis of his award-winning, stately, and neo-Romantic poetry. Hirsch's poetics, and his implicit defense of them in his 1999 collection of essays, *Responsive Reading*, and the best-selling *How to Read a Poem and Fall in Love with Poetry*, argue on behalf of the **lyric** mode as a permanent, indelible force in literary history. Hirsch's unabashed celebration of the passionate and intuitive has resonated with many readers of American poetry.

Born in a suburb of Chicago in 1950, Hirsch was educated at Grinnell College and the University of Pennsylvania. His first book of poems, *For the Sleepwalkers* (1981), received the Lavan Younger Poets Award from the Academy of American Poets and the Delmore Schwartz Memorial Award from New York University. His second book, *Wild Gratitude* (1986), received the National Book Critics Circle Award. His third and

fourth books, *The Night Parade* (1989) and *Earthly Measures* (1994), were listed as notable books of the year in the *New York Times Book Review*. His first book of the twenty-first century, *Lay Back the Darkness* (2003), garnered early strong reviews. In addition, Hirsch has received numerous awards and grants, including the Prix de Rome, a Guggenheim fellowship, a National Endowment for the Arts award and, in 1998, the American Academy of Arts & Letters Award for Literature. Hirsch also received a MacArthur fellowship in 2000.

In an interview with Tod Marshall for the *Kenyon Review* (Spring 2000), Hirsch discussed his attraction to the twentieth-century **East European poets** in general, and to the Polish poets in particular, citing their desire to both escape and embrace the world. Hirsch attributes this vacillation to the historical pressures under which so many Eastern European poets wrote during the twentieth century, lending their poetry an urgency and immediacy lacking in most American poetry. This lack may be even more apparent in the work of poets who come from relatively privileged backgrounds. For Hirsch, his privileged upbringing was tempered by his ethnicity, providing a foundation for what he called his "democratic ethos." Hirsch's narrators are never seriously tempted by the "transcendental" world of traditional religions or utopian politics (in the same interview Hirsch acknowledged his distrust of "didactic" political solutions to the problem of injustice), but they are drawn to the timeless permanence art seems to offer. This tendency to see art as immortal is as old as the creative process. What is new—and American—in Hirsch is how he weds this desire for aesthetic permanence to democratic values. His poems, particularly those from the first three books, shift back and forth between artistic lives and the ordinary lives of working people. This movement parallels the poems' internal vacillations, saying yes and no to the world, saying yes and no to "art," even as they dream of their own permanence.

The dream of permanence haunts all of Hirsch's poetry, but it manifests itself in the first two collections, *For the Sleepwalkers* and *Wild Gratitude*, as a psychosomatic illness, a form of anxiety: insomnia. However, this affliction becomes a useful malady, a way for the poet to live out the democratic ethos. To embrace America means, for Hirsch, embracing nocturnal existence: "For all the insomniacs in the world I want to build a new kind of machine / For flying out of the body at night" ("I Need Help," *Wild Gratitude*). Indeed, Hirsch's first two books of poetry make much of their desire to sing for the night, for those Americans who may be "invisible" to mainstream society. They pay homage to a seamstress ("The Sweatshop Poem"), a waitress ("At Kresge's Diner in Stonefalls, Arkansas"), and a garbage man ("Garbage"). They honor "Poets, Children, Soldiers" and sing "For The Sleepwalkers" whose bodies have "so much faith in the invisible / arrow carved into the carpet." As these lines indicate, the night stands not only for the wayward or marginal but also for the will to live. It is this obstinate desire to exist that, for example, keeps a parking lot attendant at his job even as he half-resents, half-admires, a former classmate who has achieved success and fame ("In the Underground Garage," *The Night Parade*). For Hirsch, the insomniac is a conduit of impulses and drives, giving himself over to rapture and despair, like the poet. In short, the night-walker, like the artist, always risks melodrama for the sake of drama.

Melodrama is a generic hazard of the lyric mode of poetry, but it is a hazard Edward Hirsch's poetry has insisted upon from his first book. Hirsch privileges the lyric as a model of poetry because its emotion counters the dead cold of non-existence. As he writes in "Memorandums," the opening poem of *The Night Parade*, the poet puts "down these memorandums of [his] affections / To stave off the absolute." Art, like family, is a buffer against oblivion and mortality.

Edward Hirsch's last two collections of poems in the twentieth century, *Earthly Measures* and *On Love*, suggest a reorientation, or shift in emphasis, from the lyric to dramatic monologue and philosophical argument. In his first three books of poetry, both modes of poetry are present, but the lyric is clearly privileged. However, 1994's *Earthly Measures* is akin to 1981's *For the Sleepwalkers*, inasmuch as both concern the fate of art and artists struggling against mutability and mortality. Overseeing them all is the figure of Orpheus, haunting the alleys, roads, and streets of the American Midwest as often as the galleries and museums of London, Paris, and Rome. *On Love* (1998) marks another step beyond the autobiographical self of the narrator. The bulk of the book consists of dramatic monologues spoken by philosophers, painters, and writers, ranging from Denis Diderot and Colette to **Margaret Fuller** and Zora Neale Hurston. In the fifteen monologues, some dramatic, some odes, the narrator imagines, considers, and defends the various types, forms, and values of love. Given the nature of many of these odes and monologues, it is not a great leap of faith to imagine them being recited, or sung, in the voice of an Orpheus, still haunting the voice of the poet even in *Lay Back the Darkness*.

Further Reading. *Selected Primary Sources:* Hirsch, Edward, *The Demon and the Angel: Searching for the Source of Artistic Inspiration* (Orlando, FL: Harcourt, 2003); ———, *Earthly Measures* (New York: Knopf, 1994); ———, *For the Sleepwalkers* (New York: Knopf, 1981); ———, *How to Read a Poem and Fall in Love with Poetry* (Orlando: Harcourt, 1999); ———, *Lay Back the Darkness* (New York: Knopf, 2003); ———, *The Night Parade* (New York: Knopf, 1989); ———, *On Love* (New York: Knopf, 2000); ———, *Responsive Reading* (Ann Arbor: University of Michigan, 1999); ———, *Wild Gratitude* (New York: Knopf, 1986). ***Selected Secondary Sources:*** Ferguson, Suzanne, "'Spots of Time': Representation of Narrative in Modern Poems and Paintings" (*Word & Image* 4.1 [1988]: 186–194); Longenbach, James, "Poetry in Review—Edward Hirsch: Eating the World" (*Yale Review* 86.3 [1998]: 160–173); Marshall, Tod, "The Question of Affirmation and Despair: Interview with Edward Hirsch" (*Kenyon Review* 22.2 [2000]: 54–69).

Tyrone Williams

HIRSHFIELD, JANE (1953–)

Jane Hirshfield writes with the precise, attentive, and concentrated style of a **lyric poet** who believes, as she states in her introduction to *Nine Gates: Entering the Mind of Poetry* (1997), that "poetry's work is the clarification and magnification of being" (vii). She combines the techniques of the Western lyric with the attentiveness of a devoted student of Eastern poetry and, particularly, Zen Buddhism. Her poems frequently describe moments of beauty or appearances of the extraordinary in everyday, commonplace events. Through epiphanies, she examines the relationship between the inner self and the outer world, between subjectivity and objectivity.

Hirshfield was born in New York City in 1953, and wanted to be a writer from the time she was in grade school. As a Princeton undergraduate, she pursued a double major in creative writing and literature in translation. After graduating in 1973, she studied Zen Buddhism in an eight-year monastic practice. Upon completing this training, Hirshfield began to publish her collections of poetry: *Alaya* (1982) and *Of Gravity and Angels* (1988). Her work began to receive national attention. She was awarded both Guggenheim and Rockefeller fellowships. She has published three other books of poetry, *The October Palace* (1994), *The Lives of the Heart* (1997), and *Given Sugar, Given Salt* (2001), as well as a collection of essays on poetry, *Nine Gates: Entering the Mind of Poetry*. Additionally, she is an award-winning translator of Japanese poetry.

Alaya, the poet's first volume, begins Hirshfield's investigations into themes that continue to remain with her. The book's opening poem, "How to Give," suggests that living begins with "this daily life" and its "ordinariness." Paying attention to what is ordinary in our lives constitutes an act that Hirshfield describes as "the habit of care." Through such care, we find replacements for things of greater magnitude; our everyday experiences can stand in for historical events. Underlying all of Hirshfield's poems is a sense of her relationship to everything in the world around her.

In later volumes, Hirshfield's poetry tends toward a larger scope, toward more of the world, and toward greater abstractions. In her second volume, *Of Gravity and Angels*, she examines the relationship between the outer self, the "gravity" of the title, and the inner self, the "angels" that represent such ineffable characteristics as beauty and transcendence. For example, in "After Work," a poem influenced by **James Wright**, Hirshfield describes an encounter with two horses. This meeting presents a moment of communion between the inner and outer worlds, as the "mares' eyes shine, reflecting stars, / the entire, outer light of the world here." *Of Gravity and Angels* earned Hirshfield the Commonwealth Club of California's Poetry Medal, as did her next collection, *The October Palace*. The latter volume continues to address the theme of transcendence and its relationship to everyday life, a relationship that rarely appears in moments of grandeur, as we can see in the short poem "Floor." The nails rise from the floor but are "pounded down again, for what we've declared / the beautiful to be." The nails do the work of holding the floor together, but we ironically call the floor beautiful. In her perceptiveness, the poet recognizes that the nails are also beautiful. Thus the poet not only notices the often-neglected beauty of the world but also looks for transcendence through that beauty.

In *The October Palace*, Hirshfield engages a larger frame of reference than herself and her own attentiveness. While her earlier works often dealt with nature on personal, intimate terms, these poems also include references to Greek history and mythology, the painter Bonnard, the Gulf War, and Indira Gandhi's funeral. In these poems, Hirshfield seems to present a view of a world in balance. "Narcissus: Tel Aviv, Baghdad, San Francisco; February 1991," for instance, draws a parallel between the blooming of flowers in California and Israel, and bombs being dropped on Iraq, since the flowers have "stems rising like green-flaring missiles." The world seems balanced between beauty and destruction: The narcissus opens to blossom because it must and, when bombs fall on it, the earth "opened because it was asked," and the bombs "could not be refused." The sense of balance also appears in "The Weighing" in the same volume, where a "few grains of happiness" balance "all the dark." Although this is an imperfect and dark world, the poet reminds us that moments of beauty and happiness still occur, as if to keep the darkness and sadness from overpowering us.

Hirshfield's attention to the connection between darkness or death and beauty shows the influence of **Wallace Stevens** on her work. She has commented on other influences, including practitioners of **modernism** such as **T.S. Eliot**, Anna Akhmatova, C.P. Cavafy, and Pablo Neruda, as well as classical Chinese and Japanese poets. In her two most recent books, the influence of writers such as Akhmatova and Neruda is most apparent in the poems' intimate emotional quality. *The Lives of the Heart* reads like a daybook, with titles of individual poems suggesting the range of emotions she covers: "Secretive Heart," "Mule Heart," "Salt Heart," "Abun-dant Heart," and "Unnameable Heart," to mention a few. The poems each present a speaker undergoing a change or rebirth, as in the last poem in the volume, "Three Times My Life Has Opened," a response to another of Hirshfield's influences, **Emily Dickinson**.

In addition to her own poetry, Hirshfield has received acclaim as an editor and translator, particularly for *The Ink Dark Moon: Poems by Komachi & Shikibu, Women of the Ancient Court of Japan* (1990) and *Women in Praise of the Sacred: 43 Centuries of Spiritual Poetry by Women* (1994). Her own poetry exhibits an attention to images, especially images of nature, similar to that found in classical Japanese poems, as well as a voice in praise of what is sacred, including beauty, transcendence, and the dual nature of life and death.

Further Reading. *Selected Primary Sources:* Hirshfield, Jane, *Alaya* (Princeton, NJ: Quarterly Review of Literature Poetry Series, 1982); ———, *Given Sugar, Given Salt* (New York: HarperCollins, 2001); ———, *The Lives of the Heart* (New York: HarperCollins, 1997); ———, *Nine Gates: Entering the Mind of Poetry* (New York: HarperCollins, 1997);———, *The October Palace* (New York: HarperCollins, 1994); ———, *Of Gravity and Angels* (Middletown, CT: Wesleyan University Press, 1988). *Selected Secondary Sources:* Elkins, Andrew, "California as the World in the Poetry of Jane Hirshfield," in *Another Place: An Ecocritical Study of Selected Western Poets* (Forth Worth: Texas Christian University Press, 2002, 245–290); Harris, Peter, "About Jane Hirshfield" (*Ploughshares* 24.1 [Spring 1998]: 199–205); Suarez, Ernest, "Jane Hirshfield" (*Five Points: A Journal of Literature and Art* 4.3 [Summer 2000]: 54–80).

Gary Leising

HIRSCHMAN, JACK (1933–)

Working in the tradition of **Kenneth Rexroth** and Pablo Neruda, poet and translator Jack Hirschman has created a body of work firmly rooted in his political and personal beliefs. Hirschman has for years considered himself to be an agitprop writer of what he calls "proletarian poetry." His overt blending of his communist and revolutionist ideals with his writing may account for his lack of recognition in mainstream American literary circles. However, Hirschman's political interests have also led to his translation into English of a number of international authors.

Jack Hirschman was born December 13, 1933, in New York, New York. His family was of Russian Jewish descent. Hirschman attended City College in New York, receiving his BA in 1955. He began writing poetry after hearing Dylan Thomas give what was to be his last public poetry reading at City College in 1953. Hirschman has cited the **lyricism** of Thomas's work as an influence on his early poems, particularly those in *A Correspondence* *of Americans* (1960). While a student at Indiana University, where he received his MA (1957) and Ph.D. (1961), Hirschman became aware of the writing coming out of the **Black Mountain School**, particularly that of **Charles Olson**, **Paul Blackburn**, and **Robert Creeley**.

After receiving his Ph.D., Hirschman taught at Dartmouth College (1959–1961) and at UCLA (1961–1966), from which he was fired from his teaching position because of anti-war activities during the Vietnam War. He lived in Venice, California, from 1967 to 1971, but chose not to continue an academic career. Instead, Hirschman concentrated on his writing and translating and began to collaborate with a number of **avant**-garde writers in the United States and Europe.

After the end of his marriage to Ruth Epstein, Hirschman moved to San Francisco, where he became a major figure in North Beach literary circles, along with **Bob Kaufman**, Jack Micheline, Neeli Cherkovski, A.D. Winans, and others. A number of small collections of Hirschman's poetry were published by **small presses** during the 1970s, most notably *Cantillations* (Capra Press, 1974) and *Lyripol* (City Lights Books, 1976). It was during this time that Hirschman began working on his series of long poems, which he calls "Arcanes."

During the 1980s and 1990s, Hirschman devoted much of his time to his activities as a political and cultural activist. He was a member of the Communist Labor Party from 1980 until its dissolution in 1992. Between 1976 and 1989, Hirschman estimates that he disseminated over 100,000 handmade works of propaganda as part of his activism, and he has continued to address homelessness, police brutality, globalization, and working-class issues in his writing, much of which is self-published or issued by small presses. In 2002, City Lights Books published Hirschman's *Front Lines: Selected Poems, 1952–2001.*

Much of the critical analysis of Hirschman's writing centers on his political views and their presence in his poetry. While political and revolutionary themes are prevalent in Hirschman's work, however, they are by no means the only ones. Lyricism and wordplay mark Hirschman's early work. In his introduction to *A Correspondence of Americans*, Karl Shapiro called Hirschman an inventor of "his own particular version of the language." Lines such as "with lobster-shell and breadcrust / We map a chessgame of our future" ("Impressions in the Present-Perfect") may seem crowded with imagery on first reading, but such lines flow easily throughout the collection. Hirschman's ear for language is showcased in *Black Alephs*, a collection of lyrical poems written between 1960 and 1968. The seventh untitled poem in the "Roots" section of the book finds Hirschman resting "in nature" and playing with his children "who fell with the laughter waterfalls make when they hit / green grass."

Hirschman's interest in the kabala began in the 1950s and grew as a result of his associations with California writers Wallace Berman and David Meltzer. Asa Benveniste, who published Trigram Books in London, was another influence. Hirschman's first book to be centered on kabalistic themes, *Yod*, was published by Trigram in 1966. A number of Hirschman's kabalistic translations appeared in Meltzer's literary magazine, *Tree*, between 1970 and 1974.

Political activism became central to Hirschman's life beginning in the 1980s; however, traces of his interest in communism are seen in his work of a decade earlier, most notably in *Lyripol* (1976). In his introduction, Hirschman states that the book is not his, but that the poems were written by "innumerable comrades." This community of the proletariat is repeated throughout the book, as in the poem "The Sleep of the Betrayed," in which such long-sought rest is "the fulfillment / of my red cause." Similarly, in "Kinalchemy," Hirschman is "the worker and poet" who is "climbing the steps / where your birth is dawning" before the poem ends in a single word—"Proletarian."

As evidenced by the birth image, Hirschman seems to believe that the revolution will eventually be won. This hope in the face of struggle is an underappreciated theme in his work. In the title poem from *A Correspondence*, Hirschman compares his and a friend's images to ice "Left in once drunkenly lifted cups." However, the narrator of the poem goes on to say "one by one we'll topple down the ghosts," as he and his friend lean on each other for support. In *The Xibalba Arcane* (1994), a later work in his Arcane series, Hirschman again ends on a hopeful note—"we will no longer subsist on stones," and once the "buying and selling of the heart" ends, the world will be "fresh and new."

Hirschman began his work on the Arcane series in 1972, and over ten books in the series have been published since 1977. Hirschman refers to the Arcanes as a work in progress, and together they act as a serial poem similar to **William Carlos Williams**'s *Paterson* and **Thomas McGrath**'s *Letter to an Imaginary Friend*. Originally inspired by the figure of Le Comte de St. Germain, Hirschman has described the series as an attempt to "bring the spiritual meaning of dialectical thought and feeling forward in a personal/political sense." This is evident in the last poem of *The Jonestown Arcane* (1979), where he writes, "We saw as we rose the governments were falling / in love."

Hirschman first traveled in Europe in 1964, and his frequent trips have helped him make contact with a number of writers from various countries and have led to much of his work as a translator. Beginning with his co-translation of Vladimir Mayakovsky (*Electric Iron*, 1970), Hirschman has **translated** over twenty-five books from the German, French, Spanish, Russian,

738 Hoagland, Anthony Dey (Tony) (1953–)

Albanian, Greek and Haitian Creole, including works by Antonin Artaud, Rene Depestre, Stephane Mallarme, Pablo Neruda, Alexander Kohav, and others. This interest in collaboration and the exchange of poetry and politics have been hallmarks of Hirschman's career.

Further Reading. *Selected Primary Sources:* Hirschman, Jack, *Black Alephs: Poems, 1960–1968* (New York: Phoenix Book Shop, 1968); ———, *A Correspondence of Americans* (Bloomington: Indiana University Press, 1960); ———, *Front Lines: Selected Poems, 1952–2001* (San Francisco: City Lights Books, 2002); ———, *Lyripol* (San Francisco: City Lights Books, 1976);———, *Yod* (London: Trigram Press, 1966); The Xibalba Arcane (Washington, DC: Azul Editions, 1994). ***Selected Secondary Sources:*** Meltzer, David, *San Francisco Beat: Talking with the Poets* (San Francisco: City Lights Books, 2001); Nieli, Marco, "Jack Hirschman's *Arcanes*: Interview with Jack Hirschman" (*Left Curve* 25 [March 2001]: 33–39).

Christopher Harter

HISPANIC POETRY IN THE UNITED STATES. *SEE* LATINO POETRY IN THE UNITED STATES

HOAGLAND, ANTHONY DEY (TONY) (1953–)

Tony Hoagland wields verse as a rock star wields his guitar—making it sing and then smashing it before your eyes in a gorgeous spectacle. He writes about and from the emotional crises of the age through a wise-cracking, tough-talking posture that covers a sensitive core. His poems do not propose solutions but strive to get the specifics of the problem right, whether that problem is desire, masculinity, racism, American consumer culture, or self-involvement. To do this, Hoagland employs keen wit, a tragicomic tone, disarming vulnerability, startling images, multiple levels of diction, a dash of meanness, and, increasingly, a multitude of voices. He self-consciously positions his speaker as a straight, white, middle-class male writing to other men like him, a strategy that allows readers to see the cracks in that construct.

Music—from rap to Cole Porter—is present in much of Hoagland's work, and feminist musician Ani DiFranco has been known to read Hoagland's poems during her performances, illustrating the cultural divide Hoagland straddles. Hoagland's work is in keeping with neo-populist poetics that strive to take poetry out of the ivory tower and into the supermarket, and he is embraced by bloggers and critics alike. **Billy Collins** features Hoagland's poem "Grammar" in his Library of Congress–sponsored "Poetry 180: A Poem a Day for American High Schools," and Hoagland was a featured reader at the 2004 Aldeburgh Poetry Festival, England's leading annual celebration of contemporary poetry.

Born in 1953 in Fort Bragg, North Carolina, Tony Hoagland says he was a "screwed-up teenager" who turned to poetry. He was educated at the University of Iowa and the University of Arizona, and has taught at Warren Wilson College, Colby College in Maine, the University of Pittsburgh, and most recently at the University of Houston. His honors include two grants from the National Endowment for the Arts and a 1985 fellowship at the Fine Arts Work Center in Provincetown.

Hoagland's first three chapbooks were gathered into *Sweet Ruin* (1992), which won the Brittingham Prize in poetry. *Donkey Gospel* (1998) was selected by the Academy of American Poets for the James Laughlin Award. The poems of these early books are, for the most part, **confessional**, hunting out personal, dramatic moments that grapple with selfhood, family loyalty, cultural identity, desire, or masculinity: "When I think of what I know about America, / I think of kissing my best friend's wife," Hoagland writes in *Sweet Ruin*. One can see the influence of **Frank O'Hara** in Hoagland's breezy irony, sly social commentary, inclusion of popular culture, and gleeful over-the-topness.

In *What Narcissism Means to Me* (2003), Hoagland moves from the confessional and toward a more social voice, both in subject—the book opens with a section entitled "America" and overtly asks questions about American culture and bigotries—and in his technique of peopling poems with the voices of friends, lovers, and students. The poems also open up on the page, moving away from the medium-line-length, three-to-five-line stanzas of his first two books, and toward long lines, uneven stanzas, and unpredictable white space, all of which add to the poems' powerful, dissonant effect.

One of Hoagland's accomplishments is in the clarity of his poems. The syntax is not confusing, the narrative never clouded. Rich sound and internal rhyme add speed and unexpected connections to the poems, as in the line "more alarming than going down Niagara on Viagra" from "Rap Music." The language is interesting but not obscure, so the poems move quickly and brightly through images to an understanding that implicates both the speaker and the reader.

Hoagland is a prolific and astute critic as well as a poet, and a book of his essays on poetry, *Real Sofistikashun*, is forthcoming. Although his critical prose reveals a mind receptive to and respectful of varied aesthetics, Hoagland argues with the contemporary **avant-garde**, asking of it in "Appetite for a Dream" some questions his own poetry seeks to answer: "Isn't it possible to have both beauty and subversion? To be self-conscious but not anorectically intellectual? To entertain as well as harass the reader? . . . To problematize the act of reading and writing in ways that aren't so specialized, and elitist?" (29). Hoagland believes that in poetry that matters, to use a phrase from **Dana Gioia**'s essay, poems should speak clearly and viscerally to any reader who picks up a book.

The poems of *What Narcissism Means to Me* mirror what Hoagland discusses in his essays, particularly "Negative Capability or, How to Talk Mean and Influence People" and "On Disproportion." In "Negative Capability," Hoagland advocates for the judicious use of meanness as seen in **William Carlos Williams**'s starkness. He urges poets to stop trying to make themselves likable, and instead work toward shocking the reader. "When a poem becomes aggressive," Hoagland writes, "it rouses an excitement in us, in part because we see that someone has broken their social shackles. We feel intoxicated by that outlaw freedom. . . . We also alertly intuit that we ourselves might be next on the hit list" (33). In *What Narcissism Means to Me*, he writes that "there's something democratic / about being the occasional asshole."

"On Disproportion" is Hoagland's call to arms for poets to abandon moderation and allow themselves to leap, cavort, and rave, as **Wallace Stevens** does in his wilder poems. *What Narcissim Means to Me* embraces that advice in lines like "sometimes I like to sit and soak / in the Jacuzzi of my hate," not necessarily surreal but deliberately headed toward excess. However, for all of Hoagland's hard-hitting attitude, he yearns as well as blusters, playing his own good cop/bad cop, presenting himself as someone who longs for the world's beauty to win out. He ends *What Narcissism Means to Me* with a section titled "Luck" that celebrates the rare, dumbfounding beauty of the flawed world: "What a great journey this is, / this ordinary life of ants and sandwich wrappers." Hoagland's rigorous intelligence devoid of academic stuffiness, his earnest wit and energetic language, make him a vital and distinctly American contemporary voice.

Further Reading. *Selected Primary Sources:* Hoagland, Tony, "Appetite for Dream" (*American Poetry Review* 30.5 [September/October 2001]); ———, *Donkey Gospel* (Saint Paul, MN: Graywolf Press, 1998); ———, "Negative Capability: How to Talk Mean and Influence People" (*American Poetry Review* 32.2 [March/April 2003]); ———, "On Disproportion" (*Parnassus: Poetry in Review* 19.2 [1994]); ———, *Sweet Ruin* (Madison: University of Wisconsin Press, 1992); ———, *What Narcissism Means to Me* (Saint Paul, MN: Graywolf Press, 2003). ***Selected Secondary Sources:*** Blevins, Adrian, "Critical Essay on 'Social Life,'" in *Poetry for Students*, vol.19 (Detroit: Gale, 2004); Hatlen, Burton, "Tony Hoagland," in *Contemporary Poets*, 7th ed. (Chicago: St. James Press, 2001).

Elizabeth Bradfield

HOFFMAN, CHARLES FENNO (1806–1884)

Poet, writer of fiction, and editor of a handful of important periodicals in the 1830s and 1840s, Charles Fenno Hoffman holds a secure place among the New York literati of the nineteenth century. He counted among his contemporaries such luminaries as **William Cullen Bryant**, **Fitz-Greene Halleck**, Rufus W. Griswold, Evert and George Duyckinck, and **Walt Whitman**. As a poet, Hoffman received more attention and praise than most of his peers in Griswold's *The Poets and Poetry of America* (1842), a fact that **Edgar Allan Poe** lamented as unmerited in an otherwise largely positive sketch of Hoffman's abilities as a writer of prose and verse.

Charles Fenno Hoffman was born in New York on February 7, 1806, joining a family with a long and distinguished history in the city. When Hoffman was eleven years old, a severe accident required that one of the boy's legs be amputated just above the knee. A quick recovery and a cork prosthesis allowed him to attend Columbia College at the age of fifteen, but he left after his sophomore year to study law in Albany, New York. Once admitted to the state bar, he began to practice law with his father, Josiah Ogden Hoffman, in New York City. Much like his career at Columbia, however, Hoffman's life as a lawyer lasted only a short while before giving way to his literary interests. He began to contribute various pieces to New York magazines, and in 1832 took up the editorship of a new magazine called the *Knickebacker* (later changed to the *Knickerbocker*), which was destined to become an influential publication in the history of American periodicals.

After a brief but successful association with the *Knickerbacker*, Hoffman traveled to the West in order to improve his health. While away, he wrote letters that documented his travels for the *New-York American*; after their periodical publication, these letters became *A Winter in the West* (1835), Hoffman's first book and a success in both the United States and England. Other prose works followed: a book of American sketches entitled *Wild Scenes in the Forest and the Prairie* (1839) and the novel *Greyslaer: A Romance of the Mohawk* (1840). The books that Hoffman produced after these focused on poetry: *The Vigil of Faith, and Other Poems* (1842), *The Echo, or, Borrowed Notes for Home Circulation* (1844), and *Love's Calendar, Lays of the Hudson, and Other Poems* (1847). Edward Fenno Hoffman, the poet's nephew, collected and edited *The Poems of Charles Fenno Hoffman* (1873) while the poet was confined to the Harrisburg State Hospital because of chronic mental illness.

Hoffman is often identified as a writer of song, lyrical pieces that are rhythmic and musical in their use of meter, rhyme and repetition. One of the most well known, his ballad "Monterey," attempts to re-create the experience of the Battle of Monterey, which took place in northern Mexico during the Mexican-American War.

Although the form is not traditional ballad stanza, the poem's narrative quality and its use of "Monterey" as a refrain place it solidly in the ballad genre. The poem's content suggests another element that often characterizes Hoffman's poetry: he is a patriot-poet. He views the war in terms that glorify the cause, writing in praise of the American agenda, which in turn furthers the emergence of the new nation.

Hoffman's "Sparkling and Bright" is one of his best-remembered pieces. Its lines have that lilting quality that his readers seem to have valued highly. The subject of the poem's light verse is a rather civil form of drinking. Here, the drinking of wine is akin to a kiss from a lover or a friend. The piece is musical in its rhythm and would certainly be easily sung. The internal rhymes work to aid the memory of the singer, and the last lines—"As bubbles that swim on the beaker's brim, / And break on the lips while meeting"—serve as the refrain for all three stanzas.

Hoffman's poetic output during the course of his somewhat truncated career ranged widely beyond these examples of song. Stylistically, he maintained in his poetry a strong sense of rhythm and rhyme and varying degrees of narrative. Although at times his language becomes overly sentimental and unconsciously mock-heroic, it is often rich in both syntax and imagery, well fitted to a host of literary subjects that include romantic love, the American landscape, Old World characters (knights and the like), patriotism, war, heroes and Native Americans.

The poetic career of Charles Fenno Hoffman was cut short by mental illness. Within two years of the 1847 publication of *Love's Calendar, Lays of the Hudson, and Other Poems*, his mental and physical health collapsed. A series of recoveries and relapses took place over the next couple of years, eventually leading to permanent confinement at the Harrisburg State Hospital, where his precarious condition effectively put an end to his creative life and where, after being institutionalized for over thirty years, he died on June 7, 1884.

Further Reading. ***Selected Primary Sources:*** Hoffman, Charles Fenno, *The Echo, or, Borrowed Notes for Home Circulation* (Philadelphia: Lindsay & Blakiston, 1844); ———, *Love's Calendar, Lays of the Hudson, and Other Poems* (New York: D. Appleton, 1847); ———, *The Poems of Charles Fenno Hoffman*, ed. Edward Fenno Hoffman (Philadelphia: Porter & Coates, 1873); ———, *The Vigil of Faith, and Other Poems* (New York: S. Coleman, 1842). ***Selected Secondary Sources:*** Barnes, Homer F., *Charles Fenno Hoffman* (New York: Columbia University Press, 1930); Poe, Edgar Allan, "The Literati," in *The Complete Works of Edgar Allan Poe*, vol. 15, ed. James A. Harrison (New York: AMS Press, 1965).

Michael Cody

HOGAN, LINDA (1947–)

Linda Hogan began her career as a poet, publishing five books of poetry before her first novel, *Mean Spirit*, appeared in 1990. Like many Native American writers who emerged during the 1970s and 1980s, Hogan has published in a variety of genres, writing plays, screenplays, nonfiction prose, memoirs, and short fiction, as well as novels and poetry. And yet, her work is often praised specifically for its poetic qualities, such as her unique use of imagery and language. Her recurring themes of the problems of cultural identity, the destruction of the environment, and the role of women as caretakers and purveyors of values make her an important figure, not only of **Native American poetry**, but also of **feminist poetics**, especially the newly emerging ecofeminist movement. Her most recent volume of poetry, *The Book of Medicines* (1993), a National Book Critics Circle Award finalist and winner of the Colorado Book Award, focuses almost exclusively on the continuing need for the healing of cultural wounds and the establishing of new political and spiritual sensibilities.

Hogan was born Linda Henderson on July 16, 1947, in Denver, Colorado, to Cleona Bower Henderson, a non-Native Nebraskan, and Charles Henderson, a Chickasaw from Oklahoma. Because Charles Henderson was in the military, the family moved a good deal, living in various locations in Oklahoma and Colorado, making frequent visits to southern Oklahoma where the extended Henderson family still resided on Chickasaw allotment land. When Hogan was fifteen, her father ended his military career and the family settled in Colorado Springs, Colorado. After working a variety of odd jobs for a number of years, Hogan began attending college, finally receiving her BA degree from the University of Colorado–Colorado Springs in 1976 and an MA degree in creative writing from the University of Colorado–Boulder in 1978.

While working on her degree, Hogan completed her first book of poetry, *Calling Myself Home* (1979), followed two years later by another collection of poems, *Daughters, I Love You*, and by the play *A Piece of Moon*, produced at the University of Oklahoma, which won the Five Civilized Tribes Playwriting Award. In 1983, she published her third book of poetry, *Eclipse*, followed by two others, *Seeing Through the Sun* (1985) and *Savings* (1988). Also during these years, Hogan taught at a number of schools, including Colorado Women's College and the University of Minnesota before returning to the University of Colorado–Boulder in 1989 as an associate professor in their **creative writing program**.

In 1990, Hogan published her first novel, *Mean Spirit*, which won the Oklahoma Book Award and was nominated for a Pulitzer Prize. In 1991 she published a collection of poems and short fiction, *Red Clay*. Her acclaimed collection *The Book of Medicines* was published in 1993.

The novel *Solar Storms* and a collection of essays *Dwellings: A Spiritual History of the Living World* were both published in 1995. In 1998 she published her third novel, *Power.*

In recent years, Hogan has been increasingly interested in feminist critical theory, the relationship of women to the natural world, and the struggle to introduce Native American and feminist values into mainstream political and environmental discussions. She has collaborated on four projects with the novelist and nature writer Brenda Peterson—*Intimate Nature: The Bond Between Women and Animals* (1998), *The Sweet Breathing of Plants: Women and the Green World* (2000), *Sightings: The Gray Whales' Mysterious Journey* (2002), and *Face to Face: Women Writers on Faith, Mysticism, and Awakenings* (2004).

Hogan's first four volumes of poetry are essentially autobiographical. Many of her poems explore issues related to her mixed-blood heritage and her ongoing search for cultural identity. The cultural labels by which we are known—the racial distinctions, the class and socioeconomic identifiers—seem to her particularly inadequate when searching for a meaningful sense of identity and spirituality. In many of these early poems, the divisions between Native American and white seem almost irreconcilable. In her poem "The Truth Is," from *Seeing Through the Sun* (1985), she describes her mixed blood status making her feel "taped together."

And yet, her earlier poems are also about the power of language and stories to heal cultural wounds. In "Houses" from *Eclipse* (1983), she writes that nothing belongs to us except the search for words, "to say again what has been said / and not heard." Later, in "To Light" from *Seeing Through the Sun* (1985), she emphasizes the power and possibilities of Native American storytelling when she says, "We have stories / as old as the great seas." In her latest collection, *The Book of Medicines* (1993), Hogan embraces a Native American sense of identity and values. She begins with a single long poem, "The History of Red," in which she celebrates the relationship of Native Americans to the land from antiquity to the present. In the middle section, called "Hunger," she recounts the historic atrocities, the destruction of the environment, and the loss of culture and language. But in the third section, "The Book of Medicines," Hogan reconciles this history and offers solace to the "forsaken world" of the middle section. In her poem, "Tear," she uses the image of Chickasaw tear dresses—made in Oklahoma after the Trail of Tears by tearing pieces of cloth because the soldiers didn't trust the women with scissors or knives—to piece together the disparate parts of herself and, by extension, society as a whole. She writes in this poem of the connection between these women and her "unborn children" and, by extension, about the connection between the past and the future: "I am the tear between them / and both sides live."

Further Reading. ***Selected Primary Sources:*** Hogan, Linda, *The Book of Medicines* (Minneapolis, MN: Coffee House Press, 1993); ———, *Calling Myself Home* (Greenfield Center, NY: Greenfield Review Press, 1979); ———, *Daughters, I Love You* (Denver: Laretto Heights College Research Center on Women, 1981); ———, *Eclipse* (Los Angeles: American Indian Studies Center UCLA, 1983); ———, *Savings* (Minneapolis, MN: Coffee House Press, 1988); ———, *Seeing Through the Sun* (Amherst: University of Massachusetts Press, 1985). ***Selected Secondary Sources:*** Allen, Paula Gunn, *The Sacred Hoop: Recovering the Feminine in American Indian Traditions* (Boston: Beacon Press, 1986); Bell, Betty Louise, "Linda Hogan's Lessons in Making-Do" (*Studies in American Indian Literatures* 6:3–6 [Fall 1994]); St. Clair, Janet, "Uneasy Ethnocentrism: Recent Works of Allen, Silko, and Hogan" (*Studies in American Indian Literatures* 6 [Fall 1994]: 82–98).

Edward Huffstetler

HOLLANDER, JOHN (1929–)

Regarded as one of the most formidable American poets of the last half of the twentieth century, both for the quantity and for the difficulty of his work, John Hollander has written eighteen books of original verse and seven books of critical prose; he has also edited over twenty collections of poetry, written several children's books, and collaborated on musical works. Although he is primarily a formalist, Hollander eschews affiliation with any poetic school, especially groups like the **Language poets** and the **New Formalists** that, he feels, politicize their craft. Hollander's prolific output has allowed him to experiment with a variety of formal approaches: he is adept at fixed forms such as the villanelle, the sonnet, and the Sapphic stanza, but he also writes in **free verse**, although his free-verse poems are usually undergirded by structure, if only in the sense of a syllabic line. Most typically, Hollander's poetry fluctuates between two stylistic modes: the surface polish of neoclassical wit and the lush, oracular sublimity of Romantic vision. His poems' surfaces—their verbal complexity and richness—exalt language as a subject unto itself. So where immediate experience (the literal) fails to provide meaning for Hollander, imagination (the figurative) succeeds. For him, the experiences of writing and reading poetry transcend the empirical world's limitations and thus fulfill the Keatsian vision of a poetic synthesis between truth and beauty.

John Hollander was born in New York City in 1929. In 1950 and 1952, respectively, he earned his AB. and MA degrees from Columbia University.

There, Hollander studied with **Allen Ginsburg** and **Richard Howard**, two poets whose work informs Hollander's own: the former for his vatic ambitions, the latter for his formal elegance and his reverence for the masters. While at Columbia, Hollander also studied under Mark van Doren, a poet and critic whom Hollander remembers admiring for his ability to support both creative and critical pursuits, a skill Hollander has emulated in his own career. In 1959, Hollander received his Ph.D. from Indiana University, where he wrote his dissertation on the musicality of sixteenth- and seventeenth-century English poetry. He then went on to teach at several universities and is now the Sterling Professor of English Emeritus at Yale University. Hollander has also won many of the poetry world's most prestigious prizes, including the Yale Series of Younger Poets Award for his first book, *A Crackling of Thorns* (1958); the Levinson Prize from *Poetry* magazine in 1974; and the Bollingen Prize (with **Anthony Hecht**) and the MLA Shaughnessy Award, both in 1983.

In addition to his primary stylistic modes, neoclassical and Romantic, Hollander has developed a group of thematic concerns that can be traced through his many books. The poet is centrally preoccupied with how to transcend the powers of darkness (troped recurrently as night, death, and simply "the dark") that threaten to squelch the powers of light, or poetic vision. Hollander typically poses this problem as a paradox, however, for light, too, contains its own darkness in the form of shadow, another recurring trope in the poet's work. So while poetry is Hollander's "light" means of transcending the dark, it is also the "dark" end of that transcendent journey; to him, the poet's task is to recognize darkness as an inexorable force that, when yielded to, can produce rather than preclude the light of vision.

This Shakespearean notion of poetry as both self-nourishing and self-extinguishing may well be part of the reason that critics like Richard Howard, an aficionado of Hollander's work, early on labeled Hollander's poetry as being "shapely to the point of a glassy impenetrability" (240); the very complexity that illuminates the poet's verse can make it seem opaque. Over the course of his career, however, Hollander has proven to be more than a mere stylist, and his concerns with poetry's ability to provide light amid darkness have shone through as the foundation of a modern visionary's poetic program.

Hollander's first book, *A Crackling of Thorns*, is representative of the poet's neoclassical mode, particularly the volume's first section, which contains many songs, some of which are explicitly written for plays in the manner of sixteenth- and seventeenth-century writers (e.g., "The Lady's-Maid's Song" and "The Bawd's Song," written for *The Man of Mode*). Some of these songs, like "Fragments of a Picaresque Romance," which features two characters named Dick Dongworth and Rose-

blush, also evince the poet's Marvellian affection for bawdiness ("She'll be the bee, and I'll be hornet") mixed with gravitas ("Pitting knowledge and / Despair against each other"). The poet's Miltonic strains also shine through in poems like "Icarus before Knossos," in which a single, enjambed, hypotactic sentence often constitutes the whole of an intricately rhymed stanza.

In his introduction to *Crackling*, which he selected for the Yale Series of Younger Poets Award, **W.H. Auden** admires Hollander's poetry for its "physical diversity" (xiii), by which he means the poet's range of forms, subjects, and dialects. To Auden, this diversity endows poetry with its artistic and "extra-artistic moral value" (viii), as the complexity of the neoclassical style resists the homogenizing aims of public discourse. Auden's affinity for the book is telling, for Hollander's verse here has much in common with Auden's formal virtuosity and demonstrates what Hollander admits to having learned from Auden: a sense of "aesthetic morality" (Suarez, 51). "The Fear of Trembling," from the book's third and most meditative section, reveals this moral obligation to poetic virtuosity, as the speaker enjoins the reader not to fear fear, which may be the product of unsettling ideas or, indeed, unusual language. To him, being afraid allows us "to know that our knowledge of what is true / Of the world casts doubt on what we thought we knew," not only about the world but about ourselves.

In his second book, *Movie-Going and Other Poems* (1962), Hollander expands his sense of moral virtuosity by integrating a vernacular idiom into his established, elevated style. In the book's title poem, for instance, which opens with the prosaic "drive-ins are out, to start with," Hollander depicts the ostensibly pedestrian activity of movie-going as a sublime, imaginative endeavor. Comparing celebrities to mythological characters, the poet suggests that movie-going is an attempt "to keep the gleam / Alive of something rather serious." Like poetry, movies have little pragmatic value in the everyday world; instead, they teach us "how to love, how not to live." The poem, like much of the book, is ultimately an **elegy** for "the colors of our inner life," which are fueled by the imagination but which reality—including death—threatens to destroy. The speaker thus enjoins the reader to "honor them all," for movie-houses, like poetry and love, "fade. All fade, Let us honor them with our own fading sight." The literal world is thus a productively antagonistic force against which Hollander writes: Because he recognizes that his sight fades—that his life and his imagination will end in a dark reality—the poet produces the monument of poetry in the face of "waiting for night / To end or, much the same, to begin" ("Digging It Out").

Hollander has said that with his third book, *Visions from the Ramble* (1965), he began to write "real poetry," an important designation since the book is the poet's first bonafide foray into the Romantic style of the visionary. In the volume's "Proem," the speaker, in Central Park with a girl, invokes his Muse—at once the girl and the dialectic relation between darkness and light—and yearns for light to illuminate the night. What covers this past, the reality of recollection and "fact," is a "band-aid, shockingly white." But the band-aid of poetry must be removed for new poetry to spring forth from the darkness, the past. As always in Hollander, dark and light carry both positive and negative connotations, and the poems that flow from the speaker's tearing off his band-aid evoke the girl's "frowning in scorn, or smiling." The speaker here invokes the tropes that will guide him throughout the volume's visions of childhood, a newly personal foray for Hollander, who until this work had remained wary of autobiographical content.

In many of *Vision*'s poems, fireworks serve as a salient, synecdochic figure of Hollander's dark/light tropology. In "Waiting," for instance, the speaker reveals his patience for revelation and his understanding that, like fireworks, what "flare[s] up into significance" is, like any vision, only temporary. This notion is most clearly expressed in "Fireworks:" "No light can outlast darkness. But light / Is all we have to live by." In "The Ninth of July," Hollander's speaker admits to language as being that light: "To imagine a language means to imagine a form of life." As with all life, however, language, too—"the poem of the world that emerges from shadows"—is subject to an end. For this reason, Hollander affirms visionary language—the white band-aid that must be recognized as a temporary salve for mortality—as the poet's moral obligation: "With night coming on like a death, a ruby of blood is a treasure" ("Helicon"). Here, Hollander resolves his uncertain regard for the literal as evidenced in his first two books: Rather than disdain the world for its darkness, he praises it for revealing that beauty and love are ephemeral. The poet thus realizes that "opening up at all is harder than meeting a measure" ("Helicon"). Poetry, that measured production of life, must now for Hollander contain an imaginative vision that arises from, not in spite of, "a readiness of the heart to accept such fine / Gifts of phenomena" ("From the Ramble").

In 1969, Hollander published a seemingly anomalous collection of shaped verse entitled *Types of Shape* (reprinted in 1999), poems that evoke his affinity for working with forms as catalysts for the imagination. As the speaker of "Skeleton Key" notes, forms permit the poet to "row beyond" the self. Moreover, as Hollander observes in his introduction to the book, such poems allow him to "hid[e] at the appropriate point on the surface" both rhythm and rhyme, as in "The Shape of Time," which contains a "hidden" sonnet (xv). In *Types*, then, we see the beginnings of Hollander's determination to formalize ostensibly free verse, evidenced in the syllabic prosody that dominates the work of his middle career.

Between 1971 and 1975, Hollander returned to his visionary project in three books: *The Night Mirror* (1971), *The Head of the Bed* (1974), and *Tales Told of the Fathers* (1975). In *Night*—of the three, perhaps the most representative of Hollander's vision—the title poem encapsulates the poet's burgeoning interest in the relationship between images and objects as well as his formal interest in syllabics. There, a child sees reflected in what may be either a literal or figurative "night mirror" (in the latter case, a dream or vision) the world's image. Here reality and vision are confused to the point of conflation, and the child chooses "to reject / Freedom of wakeful seeing" found in the literal world "for peace and the bondage of horrors" found in dream, "the pillow's dark side." Where imagination, the image of reality (imagination's object), terrifies the child, so too does the lack of imagination, which brings that "horrible bit of movement / At the edge of knowledge" that the child, and the poet Hollander, cannot resist.

On the lighter side of this somewhat dark, visionary stance, in "Adam's Task" Hollander envisions a world where "work, half-measuring, half-humming, / Would be as serious as play." This notion of serious play exemplifies Hollander's affection for, one might say, "dark light verse," which the poet pursues on a book-length scale in *Town and Country Matters* (1972), a lively collection of erotic and satiric formalist poems, some of which feature the reappearance of Dongworth and Roseblush from *Crackling*. As in that book, the poems in *Town* are formally virtuosic; but as in *Night*, *Head*, and *Fathers*, Hollander maintains in *Town* his qualified defense of poetry's transcendent properties, as "Making something up out of nothing's never / Happy or easy" ("Making It").

In 1976, Hollander published *Reflections on Espionage* (reissued in 1999), a long, allegorical poem in which the poet posits spying as a trope for writing poetry, and the poet as a seeker, not a seer; a receiver, not an originator. The book is composed of a series of syllabic transmissions from a spy named Cupcake (Hollander) to his muse and recruiter, Lyrebird, and his closest spy-friend, Image (**James Merrill**). The poem's other spies are many of Hollander's friends and contemporary poetic influences; they include Muroz (**Robert Frost**), Steampump (Auden), Gland (**Adrienne Rich**), Lake (**Elizabeth Bishop**), Lac (**Robert Lowell**), and Ember (**John Ashbery**). Although the poem contains no definite plot, it does chart the poet's preparation for "Project Lamplight," a paradigmatic work that will contain dream fragments "like shards / Of mirror, each of them reflecting the whole." In a seeming rebuke of *Ramble*'s autobiographical components, "Lamplight" will not contain mere "histories / Of intelligence," or mere reality, which Cupcake condemns Lac for having done in his later confessional work.

In 1978 Hollander completed the projected "Project Lamplight" with *Spectral Emanations* (1978), a book whose title poem represents the apex of the poet's preoccupation with darkness and light. That poem features seven syllabic verse meditations on the seven colors of the spectrum; each poem is followed by prose sections that tangentially describe or expand each poem's themes as well as the long poem's plot, in which the speaker quests for a menorah mentioned in Nathaniel Hawthorne's *The Marble Faun*. According to the Hawthorne story, when each branch of the candle is lit, the white light of truth will shine. Hollander converts this story into a mythic depiction of the poet's quest for vision, which, as always, is fleeting in Hollander's work. As he says in the sequence's final poem, "Violet," "truth is one letter away from death"; so instead of seeking the nugatory end of visionary truth, Hollander's speaker praises the *process* of seeking vision and the quest that will be passed to future seekers: "When we have been stamped out and burned not to lie in the ashes of our dust, it will be to grow."

Perhaps more than his *Selected Poems*, published together with *Spectral Emanations* in 1978, *Powers of Thirteen* (1983), a collection of new verse, serves as a summary review of Hollander's predominant themes, tropes, and styles. Admittedly self-referential, almost to the point of onanism ("Thirteen" contains an acrostic stanza with the poet's own name, and "The Abandoned Task" compares writing poetry to masturbation), *Powers* is composed of 169 (thirteen times thirteen) quasi-sonnets written in thirteen lines with thirteen syllables each. The volume is in this way both formally traditional and experimental, classical and visionary. In terms of content, the book's guiding trope—the number thirteen—offers, when divided into a six-one-six form, a figure of the poet's recurring dichotomies balanced by a fulcrum (a notion the poet develops more literally in "See-Saw" from *Tesserae*). In "Today's Date," the poet defines such a state of thirteen-ness as the place where poetry is conceived, a place outside of time and space where reality is transformed and "where it is always 13/13/13."

Hollander's later books return to his earlier neoclassical style (especially *Picture Window* in 2003) and are concerned predominantly with poetry's efforts to harness and counteract mortality's forces. In *Blue Wine* (1979), a collection of formal lyric verse, Hollander has anticipated this later work's concerns, especially in poems like the Atropos section of "Three of the Fates" and "Piano Interlude" ("*Song is not born in rooms emptied by fulfillment, / But only in long, cold halls, hollow with desire*"). In the long title poem from *Tesserae* (1993), another collection of Audenesque formal verse, the speaker describes his song as a "nocturne" and an imitation of Omar Khayyam's *Rubaiyat*. It is a poem characteristically

caught between dualities—youth/age, life/death, reality/vision—but one that also deconstructs them, for no "future lies in formulae that treat . . . 'Life' as a metaphor for Everything, / And 'Death' for Nothing." So where life is composed of "double-dealings / With ourselves" ("Fire!" from 1999's *Figurehead*), as always for Hollander, poetry can both complicate and reconcile those dualities. In this sense, despite their formally neoclassical aspirations, Hollander's later work aspires like much of his mid-career work to "stabs at transcendence in the evening sky" ("Kinneret" from 1988's *Harp Lake*).

Further Reading. *Selected Primary Sources:* Hollander, John, *Blue Wine and Other Poems* (Baltimore: Johns Hopkins University Press, 1979); ———, *A Crackling of Thorns* (New Haven, CT: Yale University Press, 1958); ———, *The Figurehead* (New York: Knopf, 1999); ———, *Harp Lake* (New York: Knopf, 1988); ———, *The Head of the Bed* (Boston: Godine, 1974); ———, *In Time and Place* (Baltimore: Johns Hopkins University Press, 1986); ———, *Movie-Going and Other Poems* (New York: Atheneum, 1962); ———, *The Night Mirror* (New York: Atheneum, 1971); ———, *Picture Window* (New York: Knopf, 2003); ———, *Powers of Thirteen* (New York: Atheneum, 1983); ———, *Reflections on Espionage: The Question of Cupcake* (New York: Atheneum, 1976); ———, *Spectral Emanations: New and Selected Poems* (New York: Atheneum, 1978); ———, *Tales Told of the Fathers* (New York: Atheneum, 1975); ———, *Tesserae & Other Poems* (New York: Knopf, 1993); ———, *Town and Country Matters: Erotica and Satirica* (Boston: Godine, 1972); ———, *Types of Shape* (New York: Atheneum, 1969); ———, *Visions from the Ramble* (New York: Atheneum, 1965). ***Selected Secondary Sources:*** Bromwich, David, "Self-Deception and Self-Knowledge in John Hollander's Poetry" (*Southwest Review* 86.2–3 [2001]: 246–253); Gross, Kenneth, "John Hollander's Game of Patience" (*Raritan: A Quarterly Review* 20.2 [Fall 2000]: 25–43); Howard, Richard, *Alone with America: Essays on the Art of Poetry in the United States Since 1950* (New York: Atheneum, 1980, 239–275); Suarez, Ernest, "John Hollander" (*Five Points: A Journal of Literature and Art* 6.1 [2001]: 48–68).

Samuel R. See

HOLLO, ANSELM (1934–)

Finnish by birth and long a resident of the United States, Anselm Hollo is far more an international poet than one with an immediate national identity. His poetics reflect many aspects of the **ethnopoetics** developed by **Jerome Rothenberg**; much of the exuberance of the **New York School**'s second generation, most notably **Ted Berrigan**; the concision of line and language found in **Robert Creeley**'s poetry; and the concern with the daily events that provide an opening for meditation, as in much of **Beat** poetry and as in **Philip Whalen**'s work. Publishing exclusively with **small presses**, Hollo has published over thirty collections of poetry. Hollo is also known for his remarkable **translations** of Finnish, Swedish, and Russian poetry as well as for his almost encyclopedic knowledge of poetry. His poetry is improvisational and often full of wit; it affirms life, friends, and the possibilities of reading, as well as being deeply critical of the politics and culture of greed and oppression.

Born on April 12, 1934, in Helsinki, Finland, Hollo's father was a professor of philosophy and his mother a translator and teacher of music. Hollo has lived for the past thirty years in the United States, after being educated in Finland and the United States as a teenager and then living in Germany, Austria, and London, where he worked for the BBC from 1958–1967. During this period, his earliest translations appeared. These included translations of **Gregory Corso**'s work into German and **Allen Ginsberg**'s into German and Finnish, as well as the poetry of Paul Klee, Bertolt Brecht, Penti Saarikoski, Yevgeny Yevtushenko, Andrei Voznesensky, and Semyon Kirsanov into English. In Vienna in 1957, Hollo married the German poet Josephine Wirkus, whose pen name is Josephine Clare. Married until 1974, Clare and Hollo had three children: Hannes, Kaarina and Tamsin. With Clare, Hollo translated **William Carlos Williams**'s *Paterson*; his translations continued with translations of works by authors as diverse as Rosa Luxemburg, Jean Genet, Tomaz Salamun, and François Truffaut. Translations, as Hollo has said, provided an early livelihood, but they also inform Hollo's own poetry as well as reflecting **Ezra Pound**'s *logopoeia*.

In 1967, Robert Creeley invited Hollo to teach at the State University of New York–Buffalo. Since coming to the United States, he has taught at a variety of colleges and universities, including the University of Iowa, Hobart and William Smith colleges, Sweet Briar College, the New College in San Francisco, and the University of Colorado. He is currently associate professor in the Graduate Writing and Poetics Department at the Naropa Institute and makes his home in Boulder, Colorado, with his wife, the painter, Jane Dalrymple-Hollo. Hollo has received many awards for his work as both poet and translator, including a National Endowment for the Arts fellowship for poetry (1979), the P.E.N./American-Scandinavian Foundation Award for Poetry in Translation (1981), the American-Scandinavian Foundation Award for Poetry in Translation (1989), the Finnish Government Prize for Translations of Finnish Literature (1996), the Gertrude Stein Award in Innovative American Poetry (1996), and the Academy of American Poetry's Harold Morton Landon Translation Award (2004).

Like others involved in experimental poetry, Hollo has always had his work published through small presses. Books made by small presses arguably move closest to the poet's own conception of the poem. The small press book also counters the ever-growing consolidation of trade publishers, who are themselves reflective of a conformative consumer culture. Much of Hollo's work can be found in his two volumes of selected poems. These provide access to his work that may otherwise prove difficult to locate, but they also present some minor difficulties. *Sojourner Microcosms: New and Selected Poems 1959–1977* places over half-a-dozen small press book publications primarily from the 1960s into Hollo's early collected work, *Maya: Works 1959–1969*. Hollo's second volume of selected poems, *Notes on the Possibilities and Attractions of Existence*, groups poems by their original place of publication; however, there are minor changes in the texts. For example, Hollo has replaced the use of ampersands in *heavy jars* with "and," thus regularizing and delaying the immediacy of such poems as "Helsinki, 1940."

It may be instructive to consider Hollo's poetry as a sustained and interconnected meditation on the process of living, and on being as fully conscious in duration as in the isolated moment. In that sense, his poetry—and one could include translations both into English and into Finnish—is one unfolding poem. Indeed, Hollo has commented in the introductory note to his collection *Soujourner Microcosms*, that "more & more i begin to see it all as one continuous poem, whether it is a *redimiculum metellarum* (bunting), or an 'annotated topography of chance' (spoerri), or both" (17). Hollo's poems typically move through space, using the page as a field for composition, very much in the tradition of **open form** and the **projectivist** poetics of **Charles Olson**. The poems, however, seldom exert a sense of disruption or interruption; rather, the spaces, gaps, and cantilevered lines create modulations of sound and of refocusing of attentiveness, as exemplified in his early poem "The Coherences," from his 1968 collection *The Coherences*. In this poem the gap between the words *flawless* and *flaws* suggests the poet's apprehension of the coincidence of these two states. The dropped line consisting of the single neologism *leaftime* suggests that slippage of language, allowing us to see that compositional mistakes are uncannily revelatory. The simultaneous slippage of text and sound suggests less the arbitrariness of language than the coherence between word and world. Continuity or the ever-insistent creative process defines Hollo's vision. The everyday and the poetic process are always converging, as suggested in "two for josephine clare," from the 1980 collection *Finite Continued*, where the sound of the children playing and the typewriter merge as "the reassuring / beat of creation."

If the project is a continuous poem, then there is less a sense of defining styles or themes marking periods of Hollo's work. Very generally, however, one can see a stronger predilection for the familial and lyrical in the earlier poems. "Air, to Dream in," from his 1965 collection *& It Is a Song*, is a **lyric** of profound beauty, drawing together the natural world, the world of the poem, the reader, and the ephemeral condition of reading, where the poet's voice is heard only by the solitary reader or listener: "there in the dark / treetops of the sea." While Hollo does not dispose of such lyricism, it increasingly becomes a discrete element, often used as a moment of unfolding or of juxtaposition. Perhaps Hollo's "Buffalo–Isle of Wight Power Cable," from *The Coherences*, marks his movement away from the strictly lyrical as it also marks Hollo's permanent move to the United States. The new world indicated here is alienating and life threatening: "the radiation / you opened the door and it hit you." As the natural world recedes, Hollo develops a critical as well as irreverent voice; and as he does so, American popular culture, paradoxically deployed, becomes more prominent.

Humor pervades Hollo's work: His is a poetry that explores the possibilities of the darkly comic through aphorism, image, juxtaposition, and commentary. Part of Hollo's humor finds parallels in the work of **Frank O'Hara** and Ted Berrigan, both of whom used a notational style to record the minutiae of daily living, finding a redemptive and human dimension in what O'Hara has called his "I do this, I do that" poetics. Hollo will incorporate speech patterns to create a sonic performative space composed of balanced, vernacular phrasing, as in "Info" in his *Lingering Tangos* (1977): "I didn't know it was info / sure it's info hell you know it's info." Hollo plays with compression, vernacular speech, and elements of surprise. In the two-line epigrammatic poem "for instance," from *Finite Continued*, Hollo writes, "death, for instance, is a terrible mistake: / it should only happen to the agreeably edible."

The comedic also becomes an insurgency directed against the seemingly insular poetry world—as in the opening lines from "Home on the Shelf," "Yet another / Collected Poems by a friend," from his 1991 collection, *Space Baltic*—or against the culture's consumeristic conformity—"oh blast this doglike devotion to the US of A / get ready for MacCommunism," from "Arcana Gardens" in *Outlying Districts* (1990). Translations, puns, transcriptions of slang, non sequiturs, and neologisms are found throughout Hollo's work, as are references to figures of popular culture such as Johnny Cash, Davy Crockett, John Lennon, Donald Duck, and John Coltrane. Juxtaposition is perhaps Hollo's most pervasive device and is especially useful in creating comic play. One finds this in the situation described in the very title "Johnny Cash Writes a Letter to Santa Claus," from his *AHOE 2* (1998); however, the poem quickly becomes a meditation on poetry and the role of art, "lyrics to the grand abstruse song / so singular they are." The poem "Blue Ceiling," from *Corvus* (1995), illustrates Hollo's de-familiarizing use of parataxis, as in the opening monostitch lines: "raccoon sees Cat go in and out Small Door / the mental beanie rotor turns." The comic—whether through processes of de-familiarizing or word-play—serves to emancipate, to suggest, as in Zen practice, that there is no master.

While Hollo eschews the notion of master or of canon, as they are forms of ideological structure that control identities, he nonetheless draws upon writers as guides. Vallejo, Rilke, Reverdy, **Edgar Allen Poe**, Kafka, and, especially, Ted Berrigan appear throughout his poetry. Reading, Hollo implies, is an act of rejuvenation and a means by which one can re-enter the human community of both the moment and of millennia. Because he draws upon the deep millennial poetries, Hollo should be seen as a bardic poet as much as a poet of the sardonic, surreal, or irreverent. Throughout his poetry, but particularly the earlier poetry, Hollo evokes the figure of the goddess, whether it is Demeter, Gaia, Kore, or an anonymous northern figure from one of the Finnish or Scandinavian sagas. The early poem "Out of the 'Kalevala,'" collected in both *Maya* and *Soujourner Microcosms*, evokes the potentiality of language, "forget not the spells: / oak spell snake spell," and the generative figure of the goddess, "see her turn / golden / below the charred beams." The *Kalevala*, the Finnish saga, fuses for Hollo the sensate world, the world of song, and the world of the goddess, who "they say she was / the one who sang" the world into being. Access to this regenerative world, the world of the goddess, as Hollo writes in "On the Occasion of Becoming an Echo" remains possible: "The goddess stands in front of the cave / waves me into the drawing."

Whether invoking elemental forces such as Gaia, animals, or mythological figures, Hollo returns us to the world of minute sensations that correspond to the cosmos, as in "Helsinki, 1940" from his 1977 collection, *heavy jars*. Set in his childhood of wartime Europe, Hollo's poem evokes the memory of taking refuge in a bomb shelter, yet it also evokes the chthonic desire of being "in the earth," that is, belonging to the most elemental of life forces, as well as the communal desire that is fundamental, but increasingly eroded, to humans.

Very much part of a number of overlapping poetic movements, Hollo's work has not received the critical attention it demands. Reviewing *Sojourner Microcosms* in *New Letters*, James Hall wrote that "Hollo's work is one of the few verbal extensions of the 50s & 60s revolutions in the fine arts." **Louis Zukofsky** wrote, in his 1950 "A Statement for Poetry," that "the practice of poetry" probes "the possibilities and attractions of existence"—this became the title of Hollo's collection of selected poems as well as a concise description of Hollo's poetry.

Further Readings. ***Selected Primary Sources:*** Hollo, Anselm, *Caws & Causeries: Around Poetry and Poets* (Albuquerque, NM: La Alameda Press, 1999); ———, *Finite Continued* (Berkeley, CA: Blue Wind Press, 1980); ———, *Maya: Works 1959–1969* (London: Cape Goliard, 1970); ———, *Notes on the Possibilities and Attractions of Existence* (Minneapolis, MN: Coffee House Press, 2001); ———, *Outlying Districts* (Minneapolis, MN: Coffee House Press, 1990); ———, *Sojourner Microcosms, New and Selected Poems 1959–1977* (Berkeley, CA: Blue Wind Press, 1977). ***Selected Secondary Sources:*** Foster, Edward, "Interview: Anselm Hollo on Translation," in *Postmodern Poetry: The Talisman Interviews* (Hoboken, NJ: Talisman, 1994).

James McCorkle

HOLMAN, BOB (1948–)

Bob Holman is best known for his pioneering work in **slam poetry** or **performance poetry**, which became prominent in the late twentieth century. Throughout his career, his clear mission has been to bring poetry to a larger public beyond the confines of academia and highbrow culture. Holman has worked as a poetry activist, working to promote an inclusive vision of poetry. Fulfilling many roles as poetry impresario and poet, performer, recording artist, director, and producer, he has engineered the presentation of spoken word to listeners worldwide through live performances and recordings.

Holman was born in 1948 in Tennessee and raised in New Richmond, Ohio, a small river town near Cincinnati. On a boat trip to Holland after high school, he met **Thomas McGrath**, who gave the younger man an impromptu lecture on contemporary American poetry. In 1966 Holman entered Columbia College, where he studied with **Kenneth Koch**. During this time Holman became involved in radical politics, joining the Students for a Democratic Society (SDS). He also became interested in the underground poetry reading scene, and published his first poem in *Rolling Stone* magazine. In 1969 he was accepted into the Cummington Community of the Arts, where he discovered the work of **Ted Berrigan**, **Ron Padgett**, and **Robert Creeley**. After earning his AB in English in 1970, Holman moved to Chicago, where he met Berrigan, who urged him to "live a poetry life."

Continually seeking intersections of "high" and "low" culture, Holman was equally inspired by **Beat poetry** and the **New York School**; by American comedians Ernie Kovacs, Spike Jones, and Lenny Bruce; and by rock musicians such as Jimi Hendrix, Janis Joplin, the Fugs, Frank Zappa, and Captain Beefheart. From 1974 to 1978 he studied with Ted Berrigan, **Alice Notley**, and **Bernadette Mayer** at the St. Mark's Poetry Project and became involved in the frequent readings. As a result of this work with the New York School poets he discovered

Dada and surrealism, which underscored for him poetry's connections to theater and performance. He soon began directing and writing plays at St. Mark's and other venues in the city. In 1977 he started to publish the *New York Poetry Calendar* and was employed through the Comprehensive Employment and Training Act, a federally sponsored artists' program. From 1978 to 1984 he served as coordinator of the Poetry Project, the first of a series of positions he held as organizer, host, and performer in New York City poetry series.

Throughout this period he worked to bring poets of color to a wider audience. Btween 1988 to 1996 he served as co-director, with founder Miguel Algarin, of the Nuyorican Poets' Café, where the performances combined hip-hop, rap, theater, and music. Holman's own poetry became influenced by these various genres, and he recorded his poems for compact discs, radio, and other media throughout the 1980s and 1990s. His strategies for bringing poetry to a larger public included television programs, such as the PBS series *The United States of Poetry* (1996), films, videos, and audio recordings. In the early 1990s he formed NuYo Records, which released a rock radio hit, "No More Mister Nice Girl," by writer/performance artist Maggie Estep. In 1996 Holman and poet Sekou Sundiata founded Mouth Almighty Records, in partnership with Mercury Records. This imprint released a solo recording of Holman's work *In with the Out Crowd* in 1998. He also became involved in new media, publishing his work on a personal website and working as a poetry guide for the informational website About.com starting in 1995. In the late 1990s Holman began a series of visiting professorships in writing at such institutions as Columbia University and Bard College, and in 2001 he founded the Bowery Poetry Club, a venue for spoken word, poetry slams, and other types of performance.

By his own admission Holman has focused more on performing and recording his poetry, and promoting the work of others, than publishing his work. His early poems were printed in chapbook form by **small, avant-garde publishers**; a selection of work he had published or performed during the 1980s and early 1990s was culled for *The Collect Call of the Wild* (1995). In subject matter, style, and structure, the poems owe a great deal to popular culture, American rock and hip-hop music, and the visual arts. The short lyrics show the influence of Creeley in their wit and brevity, as well as in their use of concrete images from daily urban and family life. The influence of the New York School is evident in the variant or absent punctuation, the frequent references to friends and figures from popular culture, and the fragmented syntax. His performance-oriented pieces include monologues written for stage personae, such as "Panic DJ" and "Pasta Mon," which Holman performed in a reggae- and rap-influenced style. His poems range from two lines to several pages in length; the longer pieces often take on a prose-like rhythm, or employ a style reminiscent of the fluid American lyrics of **Allen Ginsberg** and **Walt Whitman**.

Later work includes collaborations with visual artists, such as his wife, painter Elizabeth Murray, and Chuck Close, for whose portraits Holman wrote brief texts, published as *A Couple of Ways of Doing Something* (2003). And, like other poets of political conviction, Holman has responded to the events of his time in poetry. In "Cement Cloud," published in the Winter 2003 issue of the *Literary Review*, the 2001 terrorist attack on the World Trade Center is commemorated in a twenty-line poem and a prose-poem "letter." The first section presents images of the speaker's experience in New York City on the day of the attacks, ending with a statement of grief. The prose section recounts the speaker's individual experience in the wake of the tragedy. Echoing his wife—who "looked me in the eye and said, Do not withdraw!"—he concludes, "Don't withdraw. Use words." Indeed, these last lines could be taken as Holman's poetic manifesto—his insistence on engaging the difficult issues of his day with written, and more often spoken, words.

Further Reading. *Selected Primary Sources:* Holman, Bob, *The Collect Call of the Wild* (New York: Henry Holt, 1995); ———, *Cupid's Cashbox* (New York: Jordan Davies, 1990); ———, *Panic*DJ: Performance Text* (Imperial Beach, CA: VRI Theater Library, 1982); Holman, Bob, and Chuck Close, *A Couple of Ways of Doing Something* (New York: Art of This Century/Pace Editions, 2003). ***Selected Secondary Sources:*** Berold, Robert, "An Interview with Bob Holman" (*New Coin Poetry* [June 2003]: n.p.); Holman, Bob, "The Place of American Poetry" (*What's American Q & A* [Poetry Society of America] [1999], http://www.poetrysociety .org/holman.html); Miller, Stephen Paul, "Ted Berrigan's Legacy: Sparrow, Eileen Myles, and Bob Holman" (*Talisman: A Journal of Contemporary Poetry and Poetics* [2001–2002]: 23–26, 217–223); Smith, Marc, and Mark Eleveld, eds., *The Spoken Word Revolution: Slam, Hip Hop and the Poetry of a New Generation* (Naperville, IL: Sourcebooks, 2003).

Amy Lemmon

HOLMES, OLIVER WENDELL (1809–1894)

Oliver Wendell Holmes was a much-beloved figure who made his mark on the nineteenth-century literary landscape through his often witty and engaging poetry. It is his identification as one of the famed New England **Fireside Poets**— along with **William Cullen Bryant**, **Henry Wadsworth Longfellow**, **Robert Lowell**, and **John Greenleaf Whittier**—for which Holmes is best remembered today.

The author of nearly four hundred published poems, Holmes was born in Cambridge, Massachusetts, on August 29, 1809. His father, the Reverend Abiel Holmes, was a historian and Congregationalist minister, and his mother, Sarah Wendell, was a descendent of the Puritan poet **Anne Bradstreet**. Despite the fact that Holmes's father was harshly dogmatic in his religious views, he was, by all accounts, a good father. By the time Holmes enrolled in Harvard at the age of sixteen, however, he had rejected his father's religious conservatism and pursued a degree in science rather than religion. For a short time after graduating from Harvard in 1829, Holmes pursued law, but he soon enrolled in Harvard Medical School, where he studied for three years.

During his years at Harvard Medical School, Holmes began publishing poetry, primarily in newspapers. Several of his works, including "The Height of the Ridiculous" (1830), "Old Ironsides" (1830), "My Aunt" (1831), and "The Last Leaf" (1831), were well received. He viewed his poetry writing as a hobby for idle hours, however, rather than a serious endeavor. In 1836, he received his MD from Harvard, opened a private practice in Boston, and published his first book, titled *Poems*.

In 1840 Holmes married Amelia Lee Jackson, the daughter of a Boston judge. Together they parented three children: Oliver Wendell, Jr. (a future Supreme Court justice), Amelia Jackson Holmes, and Edward Jackson Holmes. From 1840 to 1847, Holmes continued to practice medicine but also found time to lecture and publish. In 1847 he accepted an appointment as the Parkman professor of anatomy and physiology at Harvard Medical School, a post he held until he retired in 1882. His passion in the classroom made him an effective and popular teacher. He also enjoyed participating in one of Boston's proudest traditions—the dinners of the Saturday Club, Boston's leading literary and intellectual organization, which met the last Saturday of each month at the Parker House and boasted among its members such luminaries as **Ralph Waldo Emerson**, Longfellow, Whittier, and Lowell.

Throughout Holmes's medical career, and following his retirement, he continued to write poetry and prose. The *Atlantic Monthly* published his series of witty essays titled "The Autocrat of the Breakfast-Table" (1858), in which Holmes discoursed on topics including New Englanders, human behavior, faulty logic, and religion. This sequence was followed in 1860 by "The Professor at the Breakfast-Table," and in 1872 by "The Poet at the Breakfast-Table." In the interim, Holmes produced three novels: *Elsie Venner* (1861), *The Guardian Angel* (1867), and *A Moral Antipathy* (1885). In 1885, his biography of Emerson appeared.

In 1886 Holmes traveled to Europe, where he received honorary doctorates from Cambridge, Edinburgh, and Oxford universities. Upon his return, he published an account of his travels, *Our Hundred Days in Europe* (1887). His wife Amelia died the following year. Holmes himself succumbed suddenly on October 7, 1894, at his home in Boston. The funeral service, held at King's Chapel, was conducted by the Reverend Edward Everett Hale. Holmes was eighty-five years old.

As a writer, Holmes was both prolific and versatile, not only a poet but also a humorist, medical essayist, fiction writer, and a biographer. His topics ranged from the dangers of homeopathy in "Homeopathy and Its Kindred Delusions" (1842) to the philosophical reflections inspired by observing "The Chambered Nautilus" (1858), a rare sea mollusk. Holmes's first book-length volume of poetry, titled *Poems* (1836), was a collection of previously published works. The edition featured occasional poetry, **elegies**, and witty verse, along with his most famous poem, "Old Ironsides," a protest against the U.S. Navy's plan to dismantle the frigate *Constitution*, perhaps the nation's most renowned Navy vessel. The poem won Holmes national acclaim when it was published in 1830, and the publicity it generated was instrumental in saving the ship from destruction.

Also noteworthy among Holmes's early poems is "The Last Leaf," originally published in 1831. A blend of humor and pathos, "The Last Leaf" was inspired by the unorthodox appearance of Major Thomas Melville (**Herman Melville**'s grandfather), whom Holmes had observed on the streets of Boston, and earned the praise of **Edgar Allen Poe** and **Abraham Lincoln**. Another popular satirical poem, "My Aunt," was originally published in 1831 and is still occasionally anthologized today. Also significant is the 1846 work *Urania: A Rhymed Lesson*, a didactic yet satirical rejection of Calvinist doctrine.

Among Holmes's prose works, *The Autocrat of the Breakfast-Table* won him immediate popularity. Based on a simple premise—residents of a boarding house discussing various matters at the breakfast table—the series showcases Holmes's gift as a witty and spirited conversationalist who relished verbal sparring. The work depicts the urbane and genial banter of a group of Boston intellectuals, including such characters as the Autocrat, the Professor, the Landlady, the Schoolmistress, and the Divinity Student. The topics included New Englanders, human behavior, faulty logic, and religion. Two sequels followed: *The Professor at the Breakfast-Table* in 1860 and *The Poet at the Breakfast-Table* in 1872. Holmes also published three novels: *Elsie Venner*, the best known of the three, appeared in 1861 and was followed by *The Guardian Angel* in 1867 and *A Mortal Antipathy* in 1885. The three novels are loosely connected by their pre-Freudian examination of various psychiatric conditions.

Today, Holmes is a casualty of the ongoing movement to revise the literary canon. Despite his enormous popularity in the nineteenth century, his writings are the least likely of those of the Fireside Poets to find their way into American literature anthologies.

Further Reading. *Selected Primary Sources:* Holmes, Oliver Wendell, *The Complete Poetical Works of Oliver Wendell Holmes*, ed. H. E. Scudder (Boston: Houghton Mifflin, 1895); ———, *The Writings of Oliver Wendell Holmes*, 13 vols. (Boston: Houghton Mifflin, 1891). ***Selected Secondary Sources:*** Hoyt, Edwin P., *The Improper Bostonian: Dr. Oliver Wendell Holmes* (New York: Morrow, 1979); Small, Miriam Rossiter, *Oliver Wendell Holmes* (New York: Twayne, 1962); Tilton, Eleanor M., *Amiable Autocrat: A Biography of Dr. Oliver Wendell Holmes* (New York: Schuman, 1947).

Denise D. Knight

HONGO, GARRETT (1951–)

An influential figure within the field of **Asian American literature**, Garrett Hongo is well known for his poetry, his prose memoir *Volcano* (1995), and his championing of Asian American literature through his editorial work, including a widely disseminated anthology of Asian American poetry, *The Open Boat* (1993); a book of essays, *Under Western Eyes: Personal Essays from Asian America* (1995); and a volume of selected prose and dramatic works by Wakako Yamauchi, *Songs My Mother Taught Me* (1994).

Hongo was born May 30, 1951, near what is now Volcanoes National Park, Hawai'i. The family soon moved to the north shore of Oahu, where his father, a veteran of World War II, found work as a field hand. In 1957 the family resettled in the Los Angeles area, where Hongo became increasingly aware of racial, ethnic, cultural, and economic diversities as simultaneous forms of harmony and conflict. He was particularly struck by the silence he encountered in the textbooks and among his fellow Japanese Americans regarding the World War II internment. During this period, he also was inspired by a maternal grandfather's injunction to tell the stories and give the testimony of the past that might otherwise be lost.

After completing his BA at Pomona College in 1973, where his commitment to issues of equality and social justice came to maturity, Hongo resided in Japan during 1973–1974, where he strove to forge deeper connections with its rich cultural heritage. After returning to the United States and attending the University of Michigan (1974–1975), where he won a Hopwood Poetry Prize, he moved to Seattle, where he founded a theater group called Asian Exclusion Act. Eventually he enrolled in the MFA program at the University of California–Irvine, graduating in 1980. He has held numerous teaching positions, including those at the University of California–Irvine, the University of Southern California, the University of Missouri, and the University of Houston. Currently, he is Distinguished Professor of Arts and Sciences at the University of Oregon.

In 1978 he collaborated with Alan Chong Lau and Lawson Fusao Inada in a **small press** book entitled *The Buddha Bandits Down Highway 99*. The title paid homage both to the old eastern highway route connecting northern and Southern California and to the various communities and towns along the way, each containing overlooked or forgotten histories. The title also made irreverent reference to the culture of resistance expressed as lawlessness both in Asian traditions and in America's Wild West. This collection sought to defy prevailing literary practices by introducing a subject matter and a style at that time largely unseen and scarcely authorized in conventional publishing circles. Hongo's contribution, a lengthy nine-part poem entitled "Cruising 99," later to be included in his first single-authored volume of poetry, is a striking pastiche of changing rhythms and images. It combines jazzy improvisations with **Whitman**-like catalogues, quotidian details with sacramental imagery. The shifting rhythms of the poem emulate the aimless, shifting patterns of movement associated with youthful cruising, here kept in check through a ceremonial progression toward the actual California town of Paradise. The poem is a daring, complex achievement that strives to join elements of Japanese folklore and Buddhist spirituality to the ephemerae of American youth culture. Evident throughout are the yearnings for connection and recovery that are among the hallmarks of Hongo's poetry.

In 1980 Hongo was selected as a winner in the Discovery/*Nation* poetry contest. By the time Wesleyan University Press published his first solo-authored book, *Yellow Light*, in 1982, his poems had appeared in a variety of venerable journals, including the *New Yorker*, *Antaeus*, *Harvard Magazine*, *Poetry Northwest*, and *Missouri Review*, as well as in numerous ethnic literature outlets, such as *Amerasia Journal*, *Bamboo Ridge*, the *Journal of Ethnic Studies*, and *Hawai'i Review*. Eventually, such crossing over was to prove a point of contention for Hongo. But in the meantime, *Yellow Light* proved highly significant for at least two important reasons. The first was that it heralded a decade in which numerous poets described as Asian American were to receive mainstream literary awards, whether or not their writing took issue with the very concept of the mainstream. The book was also significant because it, along with various other titles to be published in the following years, challenged prevailing assumptions about the content and tone of contemporary American poetry. The majority of its well-crafted poems were stylistically in concert with reigning ideas of poetry in the university **creative writing programs**. But the accents of loss and sorrow, while familiar, were also inflected with

a ritualism Hongo had encountered at first hand in Japan and which he had progressively developed through his writing career. Similarly, while a poetry of or about the working class was scarcely new to American poetry—or new in Asian American poetry—*Yellow Light* succeeded in directing the reading public's attention toward a minority America experiencing ferment, bitter memories, and unrealized potential rather than stability, steady progress, and assimilation.

His next poetry book, *The River of Heaven* (1988), received the Lamont Award given annually for a distinguished second volume of poetry. In 1989 it was nominated for the Pulitzer Prize in poetry. Divided into two sections, the book begins as an effort to reclaim the poet's Hawai'ian birthplace and to commemorate the past. Marked by pain and mourning, the poems constitute acts of personal and cultural reconstruction, often focusing on the lives of family ancestors and now-departed father figures. The book is noteworthy for its lush imagery, the shadings of its rich, lyrical voice, and its ceremonial rhythms that conjure a unity of spirit, even when the fragments of experience prohibit its actual realization. Keenly attuned to racial and class differentials, the second half of the book explores the lives of people, some privileged and some not, situated in a variety of urban enclaves in Southern California. Its underlying motive is to raise the ordinary to the level of legend or myth.

Hongo's other literary ventures are significant as well. His prose memoir *Volcano* is an intriguing meditation on his relationship to a place of sacred origins and stunning natural phenomena. Virtually a **prose poem**, it required research into ecology and geology and altered his relationship to language itself. Along with his poetic achievements, Hongo also has had an important career as an editor. He edited a special Asian American literature issue of the *Greenfield Review* (1977) and served as unofficial editorial advisor to the **Joseph Bruchac**-edited *Breaking Silence: An Anthology of Contemporary Asian American Poets* (1983). His engaging, at times polemical, introduction to *The Open Boat: Poems from Asian America* (1993) sparked debate over the role that identity politics and activist agendas should play in determining the canon of Asian American poetry. Today, he continues to be recognized as a poet and pioneer in the field of Asian American literature.

Further Reading. *Selected Secondary Sources:* Filipelli, Laurie, *Garrett Hongo* (Boise, ID: Boise State University Press, 1957); Sato, Gayle K., "Cultural Recuperation in Garrett Hongo's *The River of Heaven*" (*Studies in American Literature* [Kyoto, Japan] 37 [2001]: 57–74); Slowik, Mary, "Beyond Lot's Wife: The Immigration Poems of Marilyn Chin, Garrett Hongo, Li-Young Lee, and David Mura" (*MELUS* 25.3–4 [2000]: 221–242); Tabios, Eileen,

"Garrett Hongo: *Feeling* Knowing, Knowing *Feeling*" (*Asian Pacific American Journal* 5.1 [1996]: 139–171).

George Uba

HONIG, EDWIN (1919–)

Widely known as a translator and critic, Edwin Honig is important to American letters because of his poetry, best represented by the compilation of his twelve previously published books, *Time and Again: Poems 1940–1997* (2000). The early poetry in the collection suggests an expansiveness, the "roving magnitude" reflected in Honig's often anthologized tree-shaped poem saluting **Walt Whitman**'s determination to continue "quixotically alive against / the hoax of sin & dying." Toward the end of the volume, however, Honig speaks of a darker persistence as he hovers between natural and man-made space. In a late poem, "Chapter in the Life Of," he depicts himself ironically as perched comfortably "on the ledge unready as ever / for the blunt-edged bang of things to come." The progression in those lines from the "comfy perch" through the internal rhymes that connect "ledge" to "edge" suggests that the physical lassitude derives from a metaphysical anxiety, an "edginess" that results in immobility. No longer projecting himself as flowing seamlessly into a Whitmanesque nature, the poet hangs on even as he hangs back because "things to come" are haunted by the memory of things gone by: the "blunt-edged" century of violence he has witnessed.

Born on the day the Versailles Treaty ended World War I in September 1919, Honig came of age in the Great Depression of the 1930s. Drafted into the army infantry, he served on the battlefields of Europe from 1943–1946, endured the disquietude that most intellectuals felt during the McCarthy inquisitions and the Vietnam War, and is still living in the aftermath, and writing about, the Cold War period. He was Briggs-Copeland Professor at Harvard and, from 1957 until he retired in 1982, taught at Brown University, where he formed the **creative writing program** and founded Copper Beech Press.

Twice a recipient of a Guggenheim fellowship and awards from the National Endowment for the Arts and Humanities, Honig traveled extensively, particularly through Spain and Portugal. Perhaps the greatest influence on his own writing was his immersion, facilitated by those voyages, in the work of poets—unknown to English-speaking audiences until he made them available—from the Iberian Peninsula. The first to have translated the **modernist** Portuguese poet, Fernando Pessoa (1971), Honig also wrote the first critical study of Federico García Lorca (1944). His **translations** of six Calderón plays (1994) and, jointly with Alan Trueblood, Lope de Vega's *Dorotea* (1985) are considered the definitive English texts of those Spanish Renaissance

writers. Additionally, he has rendered English versions of the poetry of Miguel Hernández (1990), García Lorca (1990), and of Cervantes's *Interludes* (1964). As a practitioner of the art, Honig published a series of interviews with fellow translators, *The Poet's Other Voice* (1986). For his translations, Honig was knighted by the president of Portugal in 1986 and similarly by the king of Spain in 1996.

Like García Lorca and Pessoa, who were drawn to (and wrote about) Whitman's quest to become the "body's prime / reunionist," Honig anticipates the recoveries celebrated at the end of the first section of his own long poem in four parts, the 1972 *Four Springs*: "High noon. It's time to get up—jump into my pants, / Run out and dance." The expectations of *reculer pour mieux sauter* infuse his early and mid-career poems. The desire to attach—to grandparents, parents, wives, selves, even houses—is part of the Whitmanesque pattern of his poems, what he calls "the body's unthinking lunge towards survival." But, also like García Lorca and Pessoa, Honig steadily questions whether the unifying project ("all men himself alone") Whitman proclaimed in naming his poem "Song of Myself" could withstand the disintegrative pressures of twentieth-century experience.

Although the collection begins with a poem commemorating the pleasure of diurnal return—the magnificent squibs of sunset in New Mexico ("a horse turning turquoise in twilight")—and ends with one expressing the hopeful dawning of "full light . . . for the life that lifts awakened," the sense of déjà vu in the title, "*Time and Again*," typifies Honig's ambivalence. The repetitions inherent to rhythmic timing underscore an original separation anxiety: "it has happened before." Often his poems are organized around fractures: the migrations from Spain and Israel of his father's family before the wars; the traumatic death (for which he was blamed) of his three-year-old brother under the wheels of a Mac truck when Honig was five; the divorce of his parents; the death of his first wife, Charlotte Gilchrist; and his subsequent marriage to and divorce from Margot Dennes. On a geopolitical scale, the sense of a more frightening pattern of inevitable recurrence in "*and again*" comes from a feeling that one catastrophic historical event simply laid the groundwork for another. In that sense his work is postmodernist, casting a previous poetic generation's angst as the outcome of long-ago planted cultural and societal seeds.

The presumption of temporal instability prods the formation of a slippery self: "I wished that I could be . . . so firm a thing as Me or Mine, something / I'd never be." Those disconnections stem from the seemingly endless multiplication of personae, a habit parallel to Pessoa's use of heteronyms. The speaker refers to the "photographing" of the self and compares it to Mathew Brady's photographing of soldiers during the Civil War, "the tired grim lounging dying, / Blue and Gray." The Civil War simile itself is problematic, recording the equivocations of the divided self even as the objectively accurate photograph reflects an emptiness, a doubling at the core that exposes a disinclination for the connections fostering emotional ties: The "possibility to continue detached / is probably almost infinite."

How does the "I" who seems never quite present—always "between himself now / and himself to come"—function poetically? Honig's sense of betrayal by the past—mythically in terms of recognizing the destructive influence of his cultural heritage, psychologically in terms of having to write out of the permutations of loss, and creatively in terms of a fundamental distrust of his own impulses ("alone with my spoofer . . . demanding hopefulness")—leaves him dependent on a new source of invention. "Reborn of inklings," Honig's indeterminate self derives from the variability of the poet's own inscriptions. The intimations of life in "inklings" suggest that he supplies the medium of his own evolution as he casts himself in a series of Rorschach blots which even he has trouble deciphering. Each of the books in the collection is prefaced by one of Honig's puzzling line drawings, impromptu squiggles—still other "inklings"—that shift among animal, human, and imaginary shapes as the viewer scrutinizes them from differing perspectives. But even in the **long poems** of the 1980s, the ink sometimes dries out as Honig begins to doubt his capacity to enact the transformations he craves. In "Gifts of Light," nature pulls the writer out of his sluggishness: "When the sleeper . . . Cannot find himself / the light finds him." In "Near the Pacific: Earth Dreams," the elusive self is met by diminishing returns from the natural world. At the end, the poet is stared down by a mountain lion. The creature intrudes and then "melts in the thickets," suggesting the unreliability of external sources for sustained inspiration: "Where plenty is found / there it is lost."

Honig's recent work reveals his discomfort about living in the wake of the twentieth century and beyond the death of his friends. The trimmed lines reflect the reduced prospects of surviving past eighty. Rather than glorying in high noon, the poet feels acutely subject to time's repetitive determination. "Inklings" decline into "inching[s]." No longer feeling that "the song [automatically] wells up again," Honig writes of the attenuated power of words, a hesitance to "say / What's true," a phrase reminiscent of **Robert Lowell**'s "why not say what happened" in the concluding poem of the 1978 *Day by Day*. Honig's "what's true" is, however, different from Lowell's "what happened." While Lowell's question grants him license to open his private life to public scrutiny, Honig's reluctance even "to say" reflects the simultaneous inadequacy and redundancy of words. Against

the confessional flood (and even therefore against the impulse of his own longer poems), the poet lingers longingly in the hope of lesser "inklings." Nevertheless, his expectation in the *waiting*—"a primed hesitance"—implies a preparedness, like Hamlet's "the readiness is all," for the blank spaces ahead. In contrast to Hamlet's certainty that "the rest is silence," Honig's quiet is pregnant with possibility. Urging himself to build from the feared blankness, he writes, "You've got a clean page / To start with."

Further Reading. *Selected Primary Sources:* Honig, Edwin, *Time and Again: Poems 1940–1997* (New York: Xlibris, 2000); *Translations:* Honig, Edwin, *Calderón: Six Plays* (New York: Iasta, 1994); ———, *Miguel Hernández: The Unending Lightening* (New York: Sheep Meadow Press, 1990); ———, *Federico García Lorca: Four Puppet Plays* (New York: Sheep Meadow Press, 1990); ———, *Divan and Other Poems; Prose Poems and Dramatic Pieces, Play Without Title* (New York: Sheep Meadow Press, 1990); ———, *Fernando Pessoa: Always Astonished* (San Francisco: City Lights Books, 1988); ———, *Fernando Pessoa: Selected Poems* (Chicago: Swallow Press, 1971); ———, with Alan Trueblood *Lope de Vega: La Dorotea* (Cambridge: Harvard University Press, 1985). *Criticism:* Honig, Edwin, *Calderón and the Seizures of Honor* (Cambridge, MA: Harvard University Press, 1972); ———, *Dark Conceit: The Making of Allegory* (Evanston, IL: Northwestern University Press, 1959); ———, *García Lorca* (New York: New Directions, 1944). ***Selected Secondary Sources:*** Brown, Susan, Thomas Epstein, and Henry Gould, eds., *A Glass of Green Tea with Honig* (New York: Fordham University Press, 1994); Hughes, Daniel J., "Edwin Honig," in *The Dictionary of Literary Biography: American Poets Since WW2*, vol. 1 (Detroit: Gale Research, 1980, 347–357); White, J. Clair, and James Chicetto, "Interview with Edwin Honig" (*Connecticut Poetry Review* 7. 1 [1988] 1–12).

Barbara L. Estrin

HOPKINS, LEMUEL (1750–1801)

Lemuel Hopkins was one of the Connecticut (or Hartford) Wits, an often collaborative group of Connecticut elites and professionals led by **John Trumbull**, **Timothy Dwight**, **David Humphreys**, and **Joel Barlow**. Following Annie Russell Marble, critics have viewed Hopkins as a "minor wit" of the circle for the smaller volume of his writing. He collaborated in the writing of *The Anarchiad: A Poem on the Restoration of Chaos and Substantial Night* (1786); *The Echo*, a serial satirical production that appeared between 1791 and 1805; and *The Political Greenhouse for the Year 1798* (1799). Among these works, Hopkins was almost certainly the author of *The Echo* No. XVIII, later published as *The Democratiad, a Poem in Retaliation for the "Philadelphia Jockey Club."* He also authored *The Guillotina: or, A Democratic Dirge* (1796) and some shorter poems, including "Epitaph on a Patient Killed by a Cancer Quack," "The Hypocrite's Hope," and "On General Ethan Allen."

Born in Westbury, Connecticut, in 1750, Hopkins was the son of a prominent farmer. He studied medicine under two local doctors, and in 1776 began to practice in Litchfield. After briefly serving in the American Revolution, he devoted his energies to medicine and, to a lesser extent, writing. He earned an honorary MA from Yale in 1784, the same year he relocated to Hartford. His medical experiments were largely focused on tuberculosis, from which he had suffered as a child, and he became a founder of the Medical Society of Connecticut.

"Epitaph" narrates the tale of a man afflicted by a pimple, whose quack doctor applies bogus cures until "out flew the patient's tortured soul" (*Poetry of the Minor Connecticut Wits*). Significantly, the patient seeks his cure with the aid of "a hand-bill in the weekly news": the quack is not simply an inferior practitioner but a representative of a commercially-driven "advertising" culture. The poem attacking Ethan Allen, whose "one hand is clench'd to batter noses, / While t'other scrawls 'gainst Paul and Moses," decries the Vermont "seer of Antichrist" as a nationally dangerous propagandist who seeks to "teach the Pennsylvania quaker / High blasphemies against his maker." Both poems provide insights into Hopkins's sense of the poetic vocation: The poet was firmly allied with the professional classes—was in fact the voice of conservative tradition for these educated elites—against the vulgar, commercial common folk and the demagogic prose of skeptics and free-thinkers.

This understanding of poetry as an oppositional bulwark against the rise of commercial democracy, informs Hopkins's more elaborate poetic productions. *The Democratiad*, for instance, addresses the debate between Federalists and Democratic-Republicans in the Senate deliberations over the Jay Treaty. Hopkins's most immediate target is Benjamin Franklin Bache, grandson of Benjamin Franklin and editor of the aggressively anti-Federalist *American Aurora*, though he goes on to satirize ten anti-Federalist senators and a number of state political leaders and journalists. The poem follows Senate deliberations in a fascinating way, and in decrying a factionalism "designed to light the Democratic fire" and "call the public spirit into play," Hopkins is less making a simple statement of political opposition than outlining the increasing role of political journals, newspapers, government transcripts, and public demonstrations in the transformation of the American public sphere.

The Guillotina is a similarly situational series of annual productions, with the first reflecting on political conflicts of 1795, including allusions to the French Reign of Terror and radical Irish immigration as well as to the Jay Treaty controversy. The poem also celebrates Federalist leaders: "From themes like these indignant Muse, / Turns, and th'applausive strain pursues," singling out for special praise such aloof patriots as George Washington, Oliver Wolcott, Jr., and Alexander Hamilton.

Hopkins's longer satirical productions have much in common with such longer works of the Connecticut Wits as *The Anarchiad*. While conventional in meter (typically iambic tetrameter or pentameter), the poems are perhaps most innovative in two respects. First, the irony of the poems is not consistent but moves fluidly between satire and parody as if to intensify the described political conflicts. The narrative voices of the forces of anarchy are frequently more rhetorically effective and entertaining than the nonironic voice of Federalist order. Relatedly, the verse of these productions is typically accompanied with a mock textual apparatus and/or heavy prose annotation. *The Democratiad*, for example, contains a preface, a letter from the opposition, and twenty-six explanatory notes.

Together, Hopkins's poetic productions offer a fascinating map of the tenuous position of poetry in Federalist New England. Most obviously, poetry provided a crucial regulative function against the perceived threats of democratic prose and oratory. Poetry's tasks were regulative: it had a duty to deflate rhetoric, challenge emergent, more populist media forms, maintain the standards of a culture confined to the educated elite, and provide an Olympian overview of American society. As Hopkins put it in *The Guillotina* of 1796, "spread Knowledge then; *this only hope, / Can make each eye a telescope*," the purpose of which is to "scan the hypocritic heart" and "keep Faction under." Ironically, the unrelentingly cynical assessment of the Democratic-Republicans was more in keeping with the political discourse of that very party. The critique of new media forms was reliant upon an innovative use of some of these forms, while the poetic project was reliant upon prose for clarification. Assertions of high culture were so entwined with situational discussions of political conflicts as to imply the inseparability of the two. And the synthesizing and quasi-conspiratorial insistence on coordinated actions against "order" likely contributed to the Federalists' sense of the growing irrelevance of political poetry in the new republic. If Hopkins's poetic practice betrays an ambivalence about the power of poetry to influence politics, his overall rhetorical stance affirms a view of poetry as a defensive realm of elites.

Further Reading. *Selected Primary Sources:* Bottorff, William, ed., *The Anarchiad: A New England Poem* (Gainesville, FL, Scholars' Fascimiles and Reprints, 1969); Franklin, Benjamin V., ed., *Poetry of the Minor Connecticut Wits* (Gainesville, FL: Scholars' Facsimiles and Reprints, 1970); Hopkins, Lemuel, *The Democratiad*

(Philadelphia, 1795); ——, *The Guillotina, or a Democratic Dirge* (Philadelphia, 1796). **Selected Secondary Sources:** Arner, Robert D., "The Connecticut Wits," in *American Literature, 1764–1789*, ed. Everett Emerson (Madison: University Wisconsin Press, 1977); Howard, Leon, *The Connecticut Wits* (Chicago, University of Chicago Press, 1943).

Ed White

HORTON, GEORGE MOSES (CA. 1797–CA. 1883)

George Moses Horton's poetry grew out of slavery into something haunting and poignant. Called the "slave bard of North Carolina," he was "the first negro professional man of letters in America and one of the most professional writers of any race in the South" (Carroll, 233). Horton was also the first Southern African American to publish a book of poetry and the only African American man to publish as a slave. While growing up, Horton learned to read but did not learn how to write until 1832, after his first volume was published.

Horton was born a slave on a tobacco farm in Northampton County, North Carolina. William Horton was his master. Since the birth of a slave was rarely recorded, his actual birth date is still unknown, although it is believed to have been around 1797. In his autobiography, *The Black Poet*, Horton claimed he was the oldest of five children from his mother's second marriage. Following slave tradition, his last name was his master's not his father's. In 1800, William Horton moved his farming operation about one hundred miles away to Bynum in Chatham County, which was a short distance from the town of Chapel Hill, the home of the University of North Carolina. Horton and his mother moved with their master, leaving his father behind.

Between 1814 and 1820, Horton participated in a regular Sunday ritual. On Sundays, the traditional day off for a slave, he and other slaves were fruit vendors on the Chapel Hill campus. Horton's poetic career started and flourished through entertaining his customers. Since he could not write at that time, collegians transcribed his poems. Soon, he sold about twelve poems a week. Specializing in acrostics, he took orders and eventually sold personalized original verses and love letters ranging in prices from twenty-five cents to seventy-five cents per order. Besides money, his customers gave him books that influenced his poetry, clothes, and corn whiskey. In the early 1830s, Horton earned so much money that he hired time away from his master, at that time James Horton, for twenty-five cents a week and moved to Chapel Hill. In the 1830s or 1840s, Horton married a slave woman owned by Franklin Snipes, who also lived in Chatham County. They had a boy and a girl who, like their mother, also took the last name of their master. Apparently, his marriage was not a happy one because of the difficulty of living apart while still slaves.

Soon after he started writing poems, Horton became very popular, so much so that he was able to garner support to publish his poetry and to help obtain his freedom. A poet and a novelist from Lancaster Massachusetts, Caroline Lee Hentz, helped him improve his poetry, transcribed some of his poems, and helped him publish his first two poems, "Slavery" and "Liberty and Slavery," in the *Lancaster Gazette* in 1828. Hentz, other prominent people of North Carolina, and abolitionists twice tried and failed to help Horton gain his freedom. In the first attempt, Horton's unyielding master was offered one hundred dollars. The second campaign involved publishing Horton's first volume of poetry, *The Hope of Liberty*, in 1829. Although Hentz left in 1830, Horton fortunately had other supporters who continued these efforts. In 1845 his second volume, *The Poetical Works of George M. Horton, The Colored Bard of North Carolina*, was published. His last book of poetry, *Naked Genius*, was published in 1865. Collectively, the three books contained over one hundred and fifty poems. These do not include the extant unpublished poems. Although his volumes were popular in anti-slavery circles, none of his books sold very well. He was never able to buy his freedom, but Horton was eventually freed with other slaves in 1865. In 1866 he moved to Philadelphia, where he disappeared into obscurity. He is believed to have died in 1883.

Influenced by poets such as Lord Byron, John Milton, and William Shakespeare, and Homer and Virgil in translation, Horton used highly stylized forms in his poems, often writing in rhyming iambic pentameter couplets that blended emotional potency and delicacy. Besides anti-slavery poems, Horton's other themes included religion, love, and nature. One anti-slavery poem, "Slavery," discusses his struggle to reconcile his condition: "Why was the dawning of my birth / Upon this vile accursed earth / Which is but pain to me?" Horton's condition as a slave did not allow for personal freedom or power, but he constantly challenged the institution of slavery through his poetry.

Although some scholars believed his work to be uneven at times, Horton's important contributions to **African American poetry** and to the anti-slavery movement cannot be denied. His struggle, as detailed in his verse, exemplifies the persistence of artistry in the face of adversity.

Further Reading. *Selected Primary Sources:* Sherman, Joan R., ed., *The Black Bard of North Carolina: George Moses Horton and his Poetry* (Chapel Hill: University of North Carolina Press, 1997); Walser, Richard, *The Black Poet: Being the Remarkable Story (partly told by himself) of George Moses Horton, a North Carolina Slave* (New York: Philosophical Library, 1966). ***Selected Secondary***

Sources: Carroll, William, "George Moses Horton, " in *Dictionary of Literary Biography*, vol. 50, ed. Trudier Harris and Thadious M. Davis (Detroit: Bruccoli Clark, 1986); Sherman, Joan R., "George Moses Horton, " in *The Oxford Companion to African American Literature*, ed. William L. Andrews, Frances Smith Foster, and Trudier Harris (New York: Oxford University Press, 1997).

Devona Mallory

HOWARD, RICHARD (1929–)

A prolific poet, translator, and critic, Richard Howard is regarded as a somewhat anomalous twentieth-century figure for his total devotion to a life of letters. He has written twelve books of poetry, translated over one hundred and fifty books into English, and written one of the most valued books of twentieth-century literary criticism, *Alone with America: Essays on the Art of Poetry Since 1950* (1979). Although adept at many verse forms, Howard is best known for his dramatic monologues and dialogues, so much so that some deem him the heir of Robert Browning. With its high diction and frequently period subject matter, Howard's dramatic verse often reads like **elegy**. He has said that he wants to bring to poetry the energy of fiction and drama. In his criticism, Howard eschews affiliation with any poetic school, preferring instead, like his mentor **W.H. Auden**, to celebrate the eclecticism that pervades contemporary American poetry. Howard's devotion to the vitality of literature in America, whether through his own poetry or through his translations and criticism, is unrivaled among his peers and has reinvigorated a reverence for the high art of poetics.

Richard Howard was born in Cleveland, Ohio, in 1929, and was a self-described precocious boy, reading by age two and a half and writing poetry at age four. An adopted child, Howard spent much of his childhood in his grandfather's library and found what he calls his real homes in history and high culture. Howard's exposure to both "homes" was exceptional, for, in addition to reading extensively, he traveled to Europe each year and learned French from his cousin at age five. Howard moved to New York City to study at Columbia, where he earned his BA in 1951 and his MA in 1952. During his time there, Howard studied under Lionel Trilling and Mark Van Doren, and alongside **John Hollander** and **Allen Ginsberg**. Howard then studied for a year at the Sorbonne, and he credits his time in Paris with giving him a sense of stylization, an integral component of his poetic practice. His acquaintance there with writers such as Roland Barthes and Jean Genet also reinforced his literary acquaintance with French luminaries Marcel Proust and Charles Baudelaire, two writers whose work resounds throughout Howard's poetry. After leaving Paris, Howard worked as a lexicographer for two years in Cleveland and two more years in New York. He has

since taught at several universities and is now a professor of practice in the writing division of Columbia's School of Arts and serves as poetry editor of the *Paris Review*.

Many critics have noted that Howard's distinguished work as a translator and a literary critic often overshadows his own poetry. Howard's voluminous and well-received **translations**, especially, lead many scholars to regard him foremost as a translator, a fate sealed when Howard won the National Book Award for his version of Baudelaire's *Les Fleurs du Mal* (*The Flowers of Evil*, 1982). Howard's critical work, too, has earned great esteem, especially *Alone with America*, which was published in an expanded edition in 1980. Far from being eclipsed by this work, however, Howard's poetry is informed by his translations and criticism. In the former case, one sees the mark of Howard's distinction as a poet of multifarious, impersonal (i.e., non-autobiographical) voices, and in the latter, Howard's reverence for master makers and his predilection for elegy and praise.

In his first books of poems, *Quantities* (1962) and *The Damages* (1967), Howard reveals his ability to write intricate formal verse. Permeated with Auden's influence, both books contain poems crafted with Howard's characteristic syllabics, slant rhymes, and witticisms, all of which contribute to an architectural prosody that the poet later refines in the syllabic model of **Marianne Moore**. The books are also distinguished by a variety of forms and tones; unlike his later verse, however, the poems are often autobiographical. Still, these books foretell Howard's later skills as an elegist and dramatic monologist. In "The Old Men Playing Boccie on Leroy Street" from *Quantities*, for example, Howard notes that the cry of the aged is "I appreciate pain." Similarly, in "Intimations of Mortality" from *The Damages*, the poet asks, "How else do we know what we are / Save by tokens of what we have ruined?" With these early books Howard established his concern with mortality, memory, selfhood, and their interrelation. He also reveals his affections for the dramatic monologue and for assuming other voices, rare qualities in twentieth-century poetics so dominated by the lyric, autobiographical "I." Howard suggests this technique in "Intimations" when he says that the "little boy I was / Collected other lives." In "Private Drive: Memorial for a Childhood Playmate" from *The Damages*, this other life is a female childhood playmate with whom Howard's speaker experimented sexually. The speaker's memorial establishes Howard's elegiac technique, as he notes that the girl will never be replaced, "save in that past I don't suffer / But create, in a ritual," the ritual of remembering as an imaginative act.

In his third book of verse, *Untitled Subjects* (1979), Howard demonstrates his burgeoning mastery of the dramatic monologue. The book won the Pulitzer Prize, and the form became characteristic of Howard's work thereafter. Created as a series of fifteen monologues from historical figures like Sir Walter Scott, John Ruskin, and Mrs. William Morris, the poems in *Untitled* are titled only by their dates, ranging between 1801 and 1915. While Howard had written historical monologues in his previous books, this total emphasis on historical characters marks the poet's shift away from the explicitly autobiographical toward a poetics of impersonality related to but distinct from **Eliot**'s doctrine of impersonality. For where Eliot would have the poet escape his own personality through poetry, Howard as poet finds his personality by abandoning it for others'. And while many of his poems contain speakers or characters named Richard, Howard's "Richard" is never a self-contained entity but one reflected in and constructed by others around him. This quandary of selfhood—is the self contained or dispersed, self or other?—is a particularly American poetic problem, and Howard's distinctive solution has marked him as a singular voice—or agglomeration of voices—in American poetry.

In the dedication to *Untitled*, Howard establishes this poetic principle of selfhood, hoping to reap "the rewards of an interest in other people," which he will do if he can "tell my state as though 'twere none of mine." This latter phrase, invoked from another poet, suggests that for Howard every interpersonal relationship is a process of figuration, of simile, between its subjects. One tells of oneself through the pretense of telling of others because, as Howard has Walter Scott say in "1825," one can be "at once another and / The same." *Untitled* also introduces Howard's belief that the overlooked details in everyday life hold divine secrets that one otherwise ignores in the search for transcendence. In "1851," John Ruskin says that those searching for divinity might more successfully find it "by way of bedcovers and / Boa constrictors." This principle of withholding ideas and conveying meaning through details is one Howard has said he recognizes as the defining feature of dramatic verse, and one that he has developed in his later work. He recapitulates it in "For Mona Van Duyn, Going On" from his eleventh book, *Trappings* (1999), wherein the speaker says that most poets "spoil our poems (our lives) because we have / ideas." To the speaker, **Van Duyn**'s skill as a poet was that she renounced "the possession of wisdom / in favor of the power to observe."

For Howard, the wisdom of ideas—or static knowledge—is secondary to the wisdom of observation. What is most extraordinary to him about historical figures is not their fame or their public lives but their private, even unremarkable humanity; this provides a common thread for each of Howard's subjects. In "1825," for example, Scott tells of meeting a sixteen-year-old Charles Darwin, who "seems dull enough, / No match at the tea for Audubon." Darwin's ordinary appearance deceives Scott into

believing that the young man, who would later revolutionize nineteenth-century science and philosophy, is unremarkable, for he has "no dash or glimmer about him." Similarly, in "Even in Paris" from *No Traveller* (1989), a series of letters from two men who think they have seen Wallace Stevens in Paris, Stevens is described by skeptical Ivo as "absolutely unremarkable," for "he might have had anybody's / face." But, like Howard, Stevens revels in the particular as a means to the infinite, and his physical appearance belies his transcendent insights. For, as the speaker from "Oracles" (*Trappings*) says, "Meanings hide / in surfaces, that much I know." And since "a life—is more than a list," as Lady Trevelyan says in "1876," one must examine the voice and overlooked details of a person to uncover those meanings.

In his fifth book of poems, *Two-Part Inventions* (1974), Howard arranges these voices into dramatic dialogues. Comprised of six dialogues about art, *Inventions* develops a preoccupation with the masters that Howard initiated in *Untitled* and features figures such as **Walt Whitman** and Oscar Wilde in "Wildflowers," Rodin in "Contra Naturam," and Alessandro Fiore in "A Natural Death." As epitomized in "The Lesson of the Master," a dialogue between **Edith Wharton** and Gerald Roseman, who both vied for the affection of Gerald Mackenzie, Howard examines the art of creation throughout *Inventions*. As he later explains in "Compulsive Qualifications" from *Fellow Feelings* (1976), a two-part invention is a process of discovery, where two parties "exchange our parts / So we can be found by each other." Such is the case with Wharton and Roseman, who discover that their pursuits of Mackenzie permit them to fashion themselves—Wharton as one who knows desire, and Roseman as one who knows affection. Between them, Roseman says, is the source of their inventions: love. For Howard, this love of the Master—whether lover, artistic mentor, or death—is the source of self-creation. In later volumes, the poet expands his study of the masters of **ekphrasis**, most notably in "Homage to Nadar," a sequence of poems about the French photographer Nadar's subjects that extends across *Misgivings* (1979) and *Lining Up* (1984). In a similar way, *Trappings* features five poems about five different paintings of John Milton dictating *Paradise Lost* to his daughters.

In all of his studies of the masters, Howard has developed his reputation as an elegist. Like the vicar of Boulge's description of Seneca in "1852" from *Untitled*— "Death was his great resource"—Howard's primary subjects are mortality and the dead. For him, as for Liszt in "1882," "*all art is but / elegy.*" As an elegist, Howard's tone is consistently reverential and reflective. While the dramatic nature of his poems gives him the opportunity to be witty and even downright crude, the end effect of most of Howard's poems is somber and honorific. Howard believes in a poetry of praise, a perspective he even attributes to Andre Breton in "The Job Interview" from *Trappings*, who, despite his homophobia, is revered for maintaining that "*criticism will be love, or will not be.*"

Breton's statement also suggests Howard's preoccupation with nothingness, a subject he develops most extensively in his fourth book, *Findings* (1971). For Howard, nothingness is a problem that arises from solitude, a state always linked to solicitude and silence, as in "Lapsus Linguae." But, as he says in "Waiting for Ada," the solution for the solicitude of silence, solitude, and nothingness—all inextricably bound up with mortality—is to create art in homage to the past, what we can never "truly possess save in the form we give" it. With art, one might achieve "illusion without deceit, solitude without / loneliness," as he says in "A Beatification" (*Like Most Revelations*, 1994).

Continuing in these elegiac and dramatic modes, Howard's latest books are most remarkable for their elegies to those who have died of AIDS. With these poems, like "'Man Who Beat Up Homosexuals Reported to Have AIDS Virus'" in *Like Most Revelations*, Howard contemporizes two of his prominent subjects: homosexuality and death. He also shifts his study of the masters from historical figures to his friends. Still, as with those earlier figures, Howard's friends teach him about himself and about the invention of love. Like Mrs. William Morris from "1915" (*Untitled*), Howard's dead are essential to his own identity, and he relies upon the permanence of art to secure his and their lives against nothingness: "These are mine. Save them. / I have nothing save them." With the dead and the past saved, Howard suggests, "memory is endless, life very long, / and you—you are immortal after all" ("At 65," *Trappings*).

Further Reading. ***Selected Primary Sources:*** Baudelaire, Charles, *Les Fleurs Du Mal: The Complete Text of The Flowers of Evil*, trans. Richard Howard (Boston: D.R. Godine, 1982); Howard, Richard, *Alone with America: Essays on the Art of Poetry in the United States Since 1950* (New York: Atheneum, 1969); ———, *The Damages* (Middletown, CT: Wesleyan University Press, 1967); ———, *Fellow Feelings* (New York: Atheneum, 1976); ———, *Like Most Revelations* (New York: Pantheon Books, 1994); ———, *Lining Up* (New York: Atheneum, 1984); ———, *Misgivings* (New York: Atheneum, 1979); ———, *No Traveller* (New York: Knopf, 1989); ———, *Quantities* (Middletown, CT: Wesleyan University Press, 1962); ———, *Talking Cures* (New York: Turtle Point Press, 2002); ———, *Trappings* (New York: Turtle Point Press, 1999); ———, *Two-Part Inventions* (New York: Atheneum, 1974); ———, *Untitled Subjects* (New York: Atheneum, 1969). ***Selected Secondary Sources:*** Bergman, David, *Gaiety Transfigured* (Madison: University of Wisconsin Press, 1991); Longenbach, James, "Richard Howard's Modern World" (*Salmagundi* 108 [Fall 1995]:

140–163); Maxwell, Mary, "Richard Howard's *Trappings*" (*Raritan* 20.4 [Spring 2001]:139–147); McClatchy, J.D., "The Art of Poetry LXXXVI, Interview with Richard Howard" (*Paris Review* 46.169 [Spring 2004]:174–201).

Samuel R. See

HOWE, FANNY (1940–)

Called "the closest thing to **Emily Dickinson** since Dickinson herself," by literary scholar Albert Gelpi, Fanny Howe remains difficult to classify in American poetry. Howe's powerful and original serial poems, composed of brief lyrics, share some concerns with the **Language poets**, including her sister, poet **Susan Howe**, to articulate "voices that are anonymous, slighted—inarticulate." Like many vanguard contemporary poets, her writing is formally innovative, politically committed, and concerned with the materiality of language. Still, Howe's **poetics** remain distinctive in two major areas: they are more informed by precepts of *negative theology* than by post-structural linguistics; and there is in the writing a sense of the spiritual, of the "intense stations of belief," or what Howe calls "bewilderment," a concept that resonates with numerous meanings for her. She is the author of more than twenty books of poetry, fiction, and an important collection of literary essays titled *The Wedding Dress: Meditations on Word and Life* (2003). Her most significant collection to date is her award-winning *Selected Poems* (2000).

The central question of Howe's writing may be, how does art take place in the life of a woman and artist; in a life associated with childhood, children, and (the lowly station of) being a child; in a life that is seemingly or literally imprisoned, exiled, or erased? Not surprisingly, and often most strikingly, Howe's writing articulates the pathways of strength in fragility. Her question is also significant in terms of a handful of figures whose lives and writing are ever-present in Howe's work, including Simone Weil, Edith Stein, Saint Teresa, Samuel Beckett, Edmond Jabes, and Lady Wilde. At times mischievous, musical, and marvelous, Howe's writing arises from language as it is articulated through her life as well as the lives of her privately cultivated theology.

Howe was born in Buffalo, New York, but grew up in Boston. She lived much of her adult life in California, and raised three children on her own. She taught at the University of California–San Diego, among several other places, including the New School. She was the recipient of the 2001 Lenore Marshall Poetry Prize for her *Selected Poems*. Howe has also won awards from the National Endowment for the Arts, the National Poetry Foundation, the California Council for the Arts, and the *Village Voice*, as well as fellowships from the Bunting Institute, the MacDowell Colony, and Annaghmakerrig in Ireland.

Settings for her work often include Ireland, the birthplace of Howe's mother, and the geographic home for her magnificent series of poems *O'Clock* (1995), whose subject is, in part, the spirit articulated in her blunt lyricism. Howe's book *Gone* (2003) is noteworthy for two main sections: the lyrical essay "Doubt," which explores her various influences as noted above, and "The Passion," which is at once a visceral and philosophical retelling of the passion of Christ, where Christ is all but absent. Although Howe's reputation rests chiefly on her poetry, her novel *Indivisible* may be an overlooked masterpiece.

Formally, Howe's main mode is the serial poem—individual sections that form a larger associative aggregate poem. In the essay "Bewilderment," she writes that "to me, the serial poem is a spiral poem." She adds: "In this poetry circling can take form as sublimations, inversion, echolalia, digression, glossolalia, and rhymes." Howe's impulse to investigate the spiritual is also vexed and enriched by her embrace of "negative theology," which posits that all we can know is what God is not, never what God really is: only the negative attributes of the Divine, never its positive ones. In the essay "Immanence," Howe's provides her own formulation of negative theology: "Writing the name 'God' poses a problem since an image of God, as one knows and understands God, can only be empty, negative, *not* sayable." Negative theology reverberates throughout Howe's poetics. In the essay "Bewilderment," she writes, "One definition of the lyric might be that it is a method of searching for something that can't be found. It is an air that blows and buoys and settles. It says, "Not this, not this," instead of, "I have it.'"

Howe explores the theme of imprisonment in its numerous guises. Her investigation of imprisonment is also a complex study of how one might respond to being imprisoned, even if one doesn't realize one is imprisoned. For example, in her essay "Immanence," Howe discusses Edith Stein, the canonized Carmelite nun who converted to Catholicism from Judaism and was killed at Auschwitz. Howe writes, "If a person makes the decision to be the thing that history and chance are already making them be, this decision switches the mechanisms away from the fated into a zone of freedom. This is one definition of a religious act, as it is also of a selfless political act." Imprisonment connected to survival and the knowledge that one is in fact imprisoned is a reoccurring concern for Howe. In the essay "White Lines," she writes, "The prisoner of a jail or hospital has to enter into a radical self-examination or be at the mercy of clocks and routines."

Throughout Howe's work the act of asking questions plays a sustaining role. For her, questions go to the heart of a poetics defined by a state of bewilderment. Howe describes bewilderment as "weakness, fluidity, concealment and solitude." She writes, "The human heart . . . in a state of bewilderment, doesn't want to answer questions as much as to lengthen the resonance of those questions." So, questions operate "to lengthen" their own "resonance." In a seemingly emphatic section of *O'Clock*, she writes, "And no answers, please, to any of my questions."

Not surprisingly, Howe's questions span the range of her concerns artistically, spiritually, and politically. Among other things, she asks: "How does a change in vocabulary save your life?"; "Can you call 'doubt' 'bewilderment' and suddenly be relieved?"; "What does it mean to finish writing a book?"; "Human nature: what is it?"; "If you are turned away by someone inscrutable whom you nonetheless love, what do you learn?"; "How can you be where you never were?/ And how did you find the way?"

Despite her commitment to social justice, Howe's writing does not aspire to transform human nature to conform to a more ideal system. Confronted with perplexing realities, Howe does not seek to extinguish them, but instead embraces bewilderment. The result is that while Howe acknowledges bewilderment as an inescapable quality of life, she necessarily endorses it throughout her writing as an act of artistic, political, and spiritual agency, which may be the central achievement of her most affecting work.

Further Reading. ***Selected Primary Sources:*** Howe, Fanny, "Artobiography," in *Writing/Talks*, ed. Bob Perelman (Carbondale: Southern Illinois University Press, 1985, 68–75); ———, *Economics* (Chicago: Flood Editions, 2002); ———, *Gone* (Berkeley: University of California Press, 2003); ———, *Indivisible* (Los Angeles: Semiotex(e)-Native Agents, 2000); ———, *On the Ground* (Saint Paul, MN: Graywolf Press, 2004); ———, *One Crossed Out* (n.p, 1998); ———, *Selected Poems* (Berkeley: University of California Press, 2000); ———, *The Wedding Dress: Meditations on Word and Life* (Berkeley: University of California Press, 2003). ***Selected Secondary Source:*** Kane, Daniel, *What Is Poetry: Conversations with the American Avant-Garde* (Teachers & Writers Books, 2003).

Thomas Devaney

HOWE, JULIA WARD (1819–1910)

While best known for penning "The Battle Hymn of the Republic," Julia Ward Howe wrote many poems and articles in her lifetime on a wide array of topics, including domesticity, women's rights, anti-slavery, and creativity. Moreover, her work as an abolitionist and suffragette greatly contributed to her popularity as a speaker and writer in the nineteenth century.

Howe, born in 1819 in New York City, had five siblings, two sisters and three brothers. When Howe was only five, her mother died from puerperal fever, a complication that occurred soon after she gave birth for the seventh time. Without her mother to shape her identity, Howe relied on her father for education and affection. Samuel Ward, Howe's father, was a devout Christian and a very successful New York banker. He ruled his household with strict Calvinist doctrine, especially after the death of his wife. Although Howe was not allowed to see operas and theatrical performances in her youth, music and languages were her favorite subjects of study. This interest paid off for Howe when she began to publish her literary criticism, poetry, plays, and other prose.

After the death of her father, Howe became a Unitarian, finding this denomination's doctrine to be less confining. Her new commitment to Unitarianism and her eager devotion to intellectual life led her to meet many important transcendental writers such as **Margaret Fuller** and **Ralph Waldo Emerson**. She met and married Samuel Howe in April of 1843. Her husband, also known as "Chev," was a reputable doctor and philanthropist who threw himself into his work as the director of the Perkins Institute for the Blind. The couple lived in Europe for a time, visiting Rome where Howe's sisters lived. Howe returned to Rome again in 1850, accompanied by the two youngest of her four children. She was eager to participate in the artistic, intellectual society she found there. Chev visited Europe for three months; Howe stayed in Rome for a year, estranged from her husband and her two oldest children. According to Gary Williams's *Hungry Heart* (1999), from this time period sprang her first book of poetry, *Passion Flowers* (1854), which was published anonymously when Howe returned to the United States.

Around the 1850s, Howe became involved in the antislavery movement, a cause her husband championed by editing *The Commonwealth*. In 1853, Howe assisted her husband with editing the free soil publication. After the Civil War, Howe became heavily involved in the foundations of the women's suffrage movement. Along with Lucy Stone, she helped found the American Woman Suffrage Association in 1869, which split off from the more radical national association. Moreover, in 1873 she resurrected the Mothers' Peace Day after writing *An Appeal to Womanhood Throughout the World*, a pamphlet encouraging Christian women to rise up against war and advocate peace.

Passion Flowers was reviewed very favorably. Despite his acknowledgment of her talent, Chev did not approve of her writing and publishing poetry. One reason may have been the subject matter of the poems, which hinted at Howe's unhappiness in her marriage. However, the success of *Passion Flowers* encouraged Howe to write and publish more of her works, such as *Later Lyrics* (1860) and *Lenora, or The World's Own* (1917), a melodrama. *Later Lyrics* did not receive the same enthusiastic reviews or publicity that *Passion Flowers* had. *The World's Own* was produced for a short time in New York and Boston.

Traveling to Washington in 1861, the Howes found themselves in the middle of a Confederate attack. After the battle, Howe heard the retreating soldiers singing "John Brown's Body," a favorite patriotic song. Their singing inspired her to write "The Battle Hymn of the Republic," which was published in the *Atlantic* in 1862. Howe's verses quickly became an unofficial Northern anthem for the Civil War. In response to slavery, Howe's "Battle Hymn of the Republic" proclaims, "As he [Christ] died to make men holy, let us die to make men free, / While God is marching on." This patriotic poem furthered the public's respect for Howe's work, and she began, in turn, to take on the responsibility of voicing her concerns regarding women's rights and peace.

In the 1870s, as Howe involved herself extensively in the American Woman Suffrage Association, she became a contributing editor of the *Woman's Journal*. She also edited *Sex and Education* (1874), a collection of essays that refuted theories of women's educational inferiority put forth in Clarke's *Sex in Education*.

Howe spent the latter years of her life writing poetry and biographical works. Along with writing a biography of Margaret Fuller, she also wrote an autobiographical work, *Reminiscences* (1899). In *At Sunset* (1910) Howe included many poems of tribute to her contemporaries and inspirers, including Margaret Fuller, **Wordsworth**, **Holmes**, and **Whittier**. Her writings and social work left an abiding legacy.

Further Reading: ***Selected Primary Sources:*** Howe, Julia Ward, *At Sunset* (Boston: Houghton Mifflin, 1910); ———, *From Sunset Ridge: Poems Old and New* (Boston: Houghton Mifflin, 1899); ———, *Later Lyrics* (Boston: J.E. Tilton, 1866); ———, *Leonora or The World's Own* (Boston: Ticknor & Fields, 1917); ———, *Margaret Fuller* (reprint Westport, CT: Greenwood Press, 1970); ———, *Passion Flowers* (Boston: Ticknor & Fields, 1854); ———, *Reminiscences* (Boston: Houghton Mifflin, 1899); ———, ed., *Sex and Education* (Boston: Roberts Bros, 1874); ———, *The Hermaphrodite*, ed. Gary Williams (Lincoln: University of Nebraska Press, 2004). ***Selected Secondary Sources:*** Clifford, Deborah Pickman, *Mine Eyes Have Seen the Glory* (Boston: Atlantic–Little, Brown, 1979); Grant, Mary, *Private Woman, Public Person: An Account of the Life of Julia Ward Howe from 1819 to 1868* (Brooklyn, NY: Carlson, 1994); Hall, Florence Howe, *The Story of The Battle Hymn of the Republic* (Freeport: Books for Libraries Press, 1971); Howe, Maud Elliott, *The Eleventh Hour in the Life of Julia Ward Howe* (Boston: Little, Brown, 1911); Tharp, Louise Hall, *Three Saints and a Sinner* (Boston: Little, Brown, 1956); Williams, Gary, *Hungry Heart: The Literary Emergence of Julia Ward Howe* (Amherst: University of Massachusetts Press, 1999).

Allison Kellar

HOWE, SUSAN (1937–)

In interviews and in her autobiographical writings, Susan Howe has noted that her father believed she and her sister could succeed in any endeavor they chose with only two exceptions: "law and history." Consequently, it is not surprising that Howe's initial interest in and training as a visual artist, along with her idiosyncratic readings of eighteenth-century American literature, facilitated her explorations of the relationships between law, history, and geography in the context of pre- and post-revolutionary New England.

Born in Boston, Massachusetts, in 1937, Susan Howe graduated from the Boston Museum School of Art in 1961 and began creating artist books that incorporated collages made from, in part, quotations from other artists. Her sister, the writer **Fanny Howe**, introduced her to the work of **Charles Olson**, and, as she herself has remarked, she saw an instant connection between Olson's interest in archaeology and the artist-theorist Robert Smithson's interest in architectural principles. Reading Olson, **Robert Duncan**, and others inspired Howe's interest in Calvinism and the Puritans, particularly their religious and philosophical ideas of spatiality, mapping, and exploration. Like Olson, Howe is not only interested in the roads not taken by New Englanders and their descendants, but she is also interested in the political, cultural, and philosophical consequences of road building—those metaphysical underpinnings of "New England."

Howe's books of poetry and criticism include *Hinge* (1974), *Chanting at the Crystal Sea* (1975), *The Western Borders* (1976), *Secret History of the Dividing Line* (1978), *Cabbage Gardens* (1979), *Pythagorean Silence* (1982), *Defenestration of Prague* (1983), *My Emily Dickinson* (1985), *Articulation of Sound Forms in Time* (1989), *The Europe of Trusts: Selected Poems* (1990), *Singularities* (1990), *The Nonconformist's Memorial* (1993), *The Birth-mark* (1993), *Frame Structures: Early Poems 1974–1979* (1996), *Pierce-Arrow* (1999), and *The Midnight* (2003). These works can be divided into roughly three periods: early poems that, although already marked by her unique graphic and aural sensibility, nonetheless reward normative reading habits and interpretive procedures; the more challenging "middle" poems; and, finally, the unique blend of scholarly and aesthetic genres in both her criticism and her later collections of poetry.

In all of her work, Susan Howe attempts to write through, as well as write about, private and public histories and their intersections in the field or grid of an official iconography and historiography. In short, Howe is interested in the relationships between print and manuscript cultures—primarily of the seventeenth and eighteenth centuries—at the moment they vie with one another for authority and legitimacy in a nascent secular culture. Howe's interest in the relationship between handwritten and typeset manuscripts may be related to

her background in the visual arts. As an art school major, Howe, from the very beginning of her turn to poetry, treats the page as a miniature canvas. Thus Howe valorizes the spatial and visual, almost as though the letters and words she deploys were the black paint of a monochromatic palette. At the same time, Howe's singular interest in seriality, in extended verse forms, works against her interest in the iconic, thus tempering the spatial effects of her writing by valorizing the temporal dimensions of language.

As a number of critics and artists have long pointed out, the spatial and temporal dimensions of human experience are always in force together, even when one is merely gazing at a painting or listening to a piece of music. Howe drives this point home by pushing her work to the extreme margins of the visual and the aural, using techniques associated with both **concrete poetry** and **ethnopoetics**. In particular, Howe uses these techniques to re-imagine seventeenth- and eighteenth-century American, English and Irish histories, when the struggle between aristocratic and democratic impulses was being played out in a contest over verbal language and visual spectacle. In the geographical context, this struggle has its physical analogues in the exploration, conquest, and partitioning of land, in the conversion of "wilderness" into "nature." In the political and cultural context, the struggle has its analogue in the wars between colonizers (English and American) and the colonized (Irish and Native American). For Howe, the moment the colonists confront the apparent "wilderness" is linked to the moment English grammar and syntax confronts an alien linguistic system in Native American and Irish languages.

For all its difficulty and concern with language, space, geography, history, and marginal figures (especially, though not exclusively, women), Howe's work, as a number of critics have established, is driven by autobiographical history and concerns. In interviews with critics and poets Ed Foster, Lynn Keller, and Tom Beckett, Howe has acknowledged the relationship between her poetry and her family history. In a prose preface to *Frame Structures*, written especially for this selection of her early work, Howe situates her philosophical and poetic meditations on war, patriarchy, and colonialism in relation to her father, who left the family to fight in World War II. Thus, the acquisition of property by the "father of Buffalo," Joseph Ellicott, is played out and against the nomadic existence the Howe sisters lived in the absence of their father. The tense play between personal loss (her father) and public gain (land), between family history and New England history, drives Howe's poetic projects from her earliest work up to and including *The Nonconformist's Memorial.*

In *Hinge Picture*, Howe's first book, a number of the metaphors allude to biblical figures, especially Joseph,

Herod, and the Magi, as Howe explores questions of power, economics, and conquest. In her second and third books, *Chanting at the Crystal Sea* and *Cabbage Gardens*, Howe pursues these themes through the lens of myth and archetype. The problem of the complicity of language and poetry with imperialism and colonialism surfaces most insistently in *Cabbage Gardens*. These issues and concerns culminate in the fourth and last book collected in *Frame Structures*, *Secret History of the Dividing Line*. Here, Howe links issues of family history, colonialism and language to geography, a chain that she will explore in her later poetry and criticism. Dedicated to her father and son, both named "Mark," *Secret History* takes its name from an account of a 1728 surveying expedition by a Virginian aristocrat, William Byrd. Byrd's assignment was to resolve a border dispute between the states of Virginia and North Carolina. Byrd wrote an official account of his findings but he also kept a private journal of his work, full of satire and caricatures of the people he interviewed and came across in his study. Howe's poem initiates a discussion of "borders" and partitions in general—between states (North Carolina and Virginia), between culture and nature ("Wild and tame / are born"), between writing genres (Byrd's official survey and his private journal), between the aural and the visual (quoting Samuel Beckett, she begins the poem "in its first dumb form / language was gesture"), and of course, between the "mark" of her father's death (the "second" time she loses him) and the "mark" (across the stomach) of her son's birth.

The mark of the father, like the mark of the son, is indelible, and Howe pursues its significance into her next collection of poetry, *Pythagorean Silence* (1982), a book that begins her "middle" period. Howe's use of short, nonlinear phrases and words, traditional stanza forms, non-traditional spacing, neologisms, and heterodox syntactical/grammatical constructions reaches its apex in this book and the next three collections of poetry. The title of this collection refers to the five-year vow of silence the disciples of the Greek philosopher and mathematician Pythagoras were required to take. In addition, it names the five years Howe's father was away at war. As in her early work, the three poems that comprise *Pythagorean Silence* explicitly refer to the Second World War (the first poem is entitled "Pearl Harbor") and, beyond that, to the effects of violence and displacement on mothers and children. A third allusion of the title may be to **Nathaniel Hawthorne**'s classic novel, *The Scarlet Letter*. Hester Prynne's daughter out of wedlock, Pearl, is an emblem of uncultivated innocence and naiveté that Hawthorne explicitly links to the natural world. As "Pearl Harbor" is marked by absent fathers, by inconsolable mothers, and by wayward children, Howe reads war as a paradoxical desire for the end of desire, a relentless march toward unending stillness. Per-

haps because she was trained as a visual artist, Howe is sensitive to the possibility that her own aesthetics may reify the page as an icon. Consequently, she types over words, types words diagonally and upside down, forcing the reader to manipulate the book, to turn it, flip it. These procedures can be found in all of her poetry collections from *Pythagorean Silence* on.

In her next collection of poetry, *Defenestration of Prague* (1983), Howe inaugurates a controversial theme she will later explore in more depth in her first book that would be considered as belonging to the genre of scholarship, *My Emily Dickinson* (1985). Howe's theme is oblivion and silence as it relates to women and other figures at the margins of history. On the one hand, Howe's work is recognizably **feminist** in that she wants to "rescue" those voices, those women, almost lost to oblivion, almost "outside" history. At the same time, Howe sees silence and oblivion as desirable states, especially given the damage that language, speech, does to existence in general. Here, Olson's **projective verse** is unveiled as an openly phallocentric stance toward existence, the analogue of encroachment, annexation, and colonization. At least one critic (Schultz, 1994) has criticized this aspect of Howe's project, especially Howe's suggestion that **Emily Dickinson**, for one, chose silence, risked oblivion, not because it was more ethical to do so but simply because she desired to do so.

Defenestration of Prague refers to the apparently unique form of Czech regicide and political assassination in general—throwing enemies out of windows. The first defenestration in Czech history occurred in 1419 and was committed by Hussites. The second, the one that may be more pertinent for Howe's purposes, occurred in 1618 and initiated the Thirty Years War. Howe abstracts from both incidents at the start of the poem that opens *Defenestration*, "Tuning the Sky": "oblivious window of Quiet / closing." The opening page ends with these two lines: "soundless parable possible Quiet to flame / hay." Following Samuel Beckett, Howe implies that the price of speech and language is a "soundless parable possible," now suppressed and stigmatized as "dumb gesture." Moreover, the "hay" refers explicitly to the garbage that the two vice-regents of the Austrian monarchy allegedly fell on when they were defenestrated in 1618. They were thus "saved." In Howe's poem, these vice-regents are speech, are language, projected out of the "mouth" of "Quiet." That Howe intends this section of her book—entitled "Defenestration of Prague"—to be a "history" of language's annexation of silence is verified by the titles of the poems that comprise this part: "Tuning the Sky," "Speeches at the Barriers" and "Bride's Day." And as the invocation of nature ("Sky") and gender ("Bride") suggests, the subjugation of "wilderness" and "women" into compartments and roles is part and parcel of language. This prepares us for the next section of the book, ironically and factually entitled "The Liberties."

The factual reference is to an older, poorer, section of Dublin, Ireland, located in the southwest part of the city. As Back (2002) points out in her critical study, Howe began writing "The Liberties" when she was visiting her sick mother, who was hospitalized in Dublin. The poem concerns Hester Johnson (aka "Stella"), the dutiful, platonic companion of Jonathan Swift from age eight until her death at age forty-seven, and Cordelia, one of the daughters of King Lear. The staged encounter between a historical figure and a character from a play underscores one of Howe's central assumptions: At the margins of history, political or literary, the distinctions between fact and fiction, real and unreal, begin to blur. The section on Stella is entitled "THEIR Book of Stella" while the section on Cordelia is entitled "WHITE FOOLSCAP: The Book of Cordelia." Framing these two sections are "Fragments of a Liquidation" and "God's Spies." "Fragments" is a prosaic biographical sketch of Stella. The title refers explicitly to Swift's burning of her letters to him but his preservation of his letters to her. So all we know of Hester Johnson is through the "history" provided by Swift's letters. "God's Spies" is a dramatized dialogue between Stella and Cordelia, modeled on Vladimir and Estragon in Samuel Beckett's *Waiting for Godot*. In many respects, *Defenestration of Prague* remains Howe's most challenging and most explicitly feminist collection of poetry. It is hardly surprising that her first book of scholarship, *My Emily Dickinson* (1985), would extend Howe's investigations into the question and problem of not merely recovering marginal "voices" but, more important, respecting the very forms of those voices.

In *My Emily Dickinson*, Howe argues that Dickinson was a more radical American poet than either feminist critics (particularly Hélène Cixous, Susan Gubar, and Susan Gilbert) or traditional critics have recognized. Rejecting Dickinson as either the proverbial madwoman in the attic or a frigid and frustrated spinster, Howe emphasizes over and over again Dickinson's freedom of choice. For Howe, what is most important about Dickinson are her willful silences, her deliberate refusals to succumb to the wishes of her primary literary correspondent, **Thomas Higginson**, who pressured her to organize her idiosyncratic syntax and grammar according to the prosodic traditions of a **genteel** literary tradition. In general, the significance of Susan Howe's interrogation of Dickinson's **poetics** can be summed up in one question, whose convoluted structure underscores the complexity and uncertainty of Howe's project: To what extent must Dickinson not only be *read* as an innovative disrupter of nineteenth-century poetic convention—up and through the sedimentation of literary history—but also be *viewed* as a visual artist who

sought to excavate the hieroglyphic remnants of expression per se, in which language would only be a subset? This question concerns the divide between language and other systems of expression, and the relation of this divide to the history of the division of labor. That is, it concerns the history of publishing and its institutions, the book as art object, the book as commodity, the construction of authorship, the relationship between the author and the editor, and the problem of property, both intellectual and cultural.

About the history of publication, we know that Dickinson had a great deal to say (one of her poems begins "Publication Is the Auction of the Mind of Man"). But all these issues surface in her unsettled arguments with the Divine since, for Dickinson, the trappings of Divine transcendence belong to—and indeed, inaugurate—the marketplace. For Dickinson, there are no gifts in scripture, only hard bargaining with ruthless Providence. As noted above regarding the publishing history of some of her work, these issues concern Susan Howe as much as they did Emily Dickinson. And they concern, for Dickinson as for Howe, the question of form. These issues—of publication, of form, of editing—are pursued and displayed by Howe in her next two books.

Articulation of Sound Forms in Time (1987) and *Singularities* (1990) must be discussed in tandem since the books are almost mirror images of one another. Put another way, one could say that *Singularities* is a refraction of *Articulation of Sound Forms in Time*, an amended version of its predecessor. Were one to merely glance at the table of contents in *Singularities*, one would presume that the three titles—"Articulation of Sound Forms in Time," "Thorow" and "Scattering As Behavior Toward Risk"— indicate that the 1987 book has been simply folded into the 1990 book. However, the 1990 version of *Articulation* reveals a change in page format and in content. Whereas the 1987 book's opening poem, "Hope Atherton's Wanderings," spreads out its individual stanzas over as many pages (with one exception), the 1990 reprint is compressed into approximately two stanzas per page. Indeed, the 1990 version points back to the 1987 version by separating the stanzas with a short, solid line, indicating, without reproducing, the original formatting of each page. Moreover, Howe has added a foreword, a brief prose history of Hope Atherton. All of these changes can be accounted for, by noting the two publishers of the two books. *Articulation of Sound Forms in Time* was published in 1987 by Awede, a now-defunct, small independent press. The original book is approximately 9¾ inches by 7¾ inches in size. *Singularities* was published by Wesleyan University Press in a more standard size, 5½ inches by 9 inches. This difference highlights the consonance between the publishing history of *Articulation* and its primary themes. Its two poems, "Hope Atherton's Wanderings" and "Taking the Forest," move from wilderness to civilization, from nature to culture, even as they recover what is lost in the process and, significantly, point to the persistence of the wilderness, of nature, in civilization and culture. Indeed, *Articulation*, as the opening "book" of *Singularities*, is a microcosm of that book. We move from the partitioning and regularity of "articulation" and "sound forms" to "thorow" (Hawthorne's spelling of **Thoreau**'s name) and then finally to "Scattering as Behavior Towards Risk." This last poem is a "found" poem in part, a re-arranging of **Herman Melville**'s description of Billy Budd's execution. Not insignificantly, Billy Budd is described by Melville as "almost illiterate," a stutterer. In short, he is someone almost silent, aphasic, and he dies in the story. It is as though Howe is commenting on the risk she is taking by scattering her words, by stuttering, instead of speaking or writing in "normal," pre-formatted patterns.

Herman Melville certainly understood the risks of breaking out of generic forms, and the failure of his magnum opus, *Moby-Dick*, was already forecast in his short fiction, particularly the short stories "Billy Budd" and "Bartleby the Scrivener." Here are two men who, somehow, did not signify manhood, men who, in the famous words of Bartleby, "prefer not to." In "Melville's Marginalia," the concluding "poem" of Howe's most ambitious and complicated book, *The Nonconformist's Memorial* (1993), Howe deploys chronicle, biography, history, experimental prose, narrative prose, and poetry to examine the place and function of the "feminine" in males, specifically in the little-known Irish poet James Clarence Mangan, seen by Howe as the "model" for Melville's Billy Budd. Still, the bulk of *The Nonconformist's Memorial* concerns the suppression of the feminine in Christian history and doctrine. Insofar as its twin themes—American Christianity and literary history—also underscore Howe's scholarly treatise, *The Birth-mark: Unsettling the Wilderness in American Literary History*, also published in 1993, these two books may also be read as refractions of one another. In *The Birth-mark*, Howe links Emily Dickinson's refusals (of marriage, of publication, of Christian conformity), catalogued in the last section of the book, to her predecessors, an entire history of American suppression. From the antinomian Calvinist Anne Hutchinson, and the doubting minister Thomas Shepard, to the (repressed) homosexual critic F.O. Matthiesen, the notorious "author" of an equally notorious "captivity" narrative, Mary Rowlandson, and the poet **Anne Bradstreet**, Howe excavates and examines the uncertainty, doubt, and contradiction that had to be suppressed at the founding of the American republic. Unlike her approach in *My Emily Dickinson*, Howe here links the choice to be silent, to flirt with oblivion, with the suppression of those who did try to articulate their voices. That link is tied to form, how one is "supposed" to write and speak. In *The Nonconformist's Memorial*, Howe articu-

lates the dividing line between "choice" and "suppression," between "will" and "determinism," by dividing the book into two sections: "Turning" and "Conversion." Etymologically related but significantly different, these terms of change are founded on their implicit active and passive modes. "Turning" is comprised of two poems, "The Nonconformist's Memorial," and "Silence Wager Stories." The first poem concerns, in part, the suppression of the role of women in the Gospels, even though a woman, Mary Magdalene, was the first person to see Christ after his conversion, his resurrection from death. The second poem, in its very title, articulates Howe's struggle: The decision to remain silent or to risk a story is always a gamble. Alluding to the Stephen Dedalus of James Joyce's *Portrait of the Artist as a Young Man*, a young artist who chooses "silence, cunning and exile" rather than the Scylla and Charybdis of Irish nationalism or British colonialism, Howe explores those gaps in secular and sacred history where the voice of the antinomian (e.g., The Song of Solomon), or at least its echo, may be heard.

"Conversion," on the other hand, consists of "A Bibliography of the King's Book Or, Eikon Basilike," published separately by Paradigm Press in 1989, and the aforementioned "Melville's Marginalia." In both poems Howe explores the problem of authorship and originality. "The Bibliography" concerns the memoirs of Charles I, reputedly written while he was in prison. Howe notes that several historians have questioned the authenticity of the memoirs since there is evidence that other individuals revised, edited, and perhaps authored portions of the work. Howe's "poetics of the palimpsest" functions here to excavate and explore the relationship of the individual parts of the "Bibliography." Moreover, Charles I's refusals to answer his interrogators links him to the antinomian Anne Hutchinson who also refused to answer her persecutors. For Howe, the examples of Charles I and Anne Hutchinson suggest that the antinomian refusal crosses—or blurs—class, gender, and political lines.

In her later work, *Pierce-Arrow* (1999) and *The Midnight* (2003), Howe blends prosaic scholarly investigations with her typical non-linear poetic forms. *Pierce-Arrow* is Howe's meditation in prose (the bulk of "Arisbe") and poetry (the last few pages of "Arisbe," "The Leisure of the Theory Class" and "Rückenfigur") on the philosophy of Charles S. Peirce, the father of American pragmatism. Characteristically, Howe is most interested in the interplay between biography and aesthetics. Howe explores Peirce's marriage to a mysterious European woman who eventually finds herself in the role of an editor, assembling her late husband's papers. Content aside, these handwritten, scrawled over, manuscripts represent, for Howe, aesthetic objects prior to their "reduction" as philosophical treatises. Thus, as in *My*

Emily Dickinson, Howe argues for the priority of original manuscripts, not on the basis of mere "originality," but on the basis that the handwritten constitutes the wedding of the visual and the verbal. Thus, in "Leisure of the Theory Class," Howe's fascination with the pens that George Meredith and Charles Swinburne collected is also related to her valorization of the handwritten over the typeset. Finally, Peirce's inability to conform to academia's mold makes him, like Dickinson, an antinomian figure.

Howe's interest in iconoclasm in general takes a markedly different turn in *The Midnight*. Here, Howe explores the function of the interleaf, that pre-modern piece of tissue paper placed between a book's frontispiece and text to avoid one page "bleeding" into another. The relation between frontispiece and text serves, of course, as another example of the division between the visual and verbal. Howe links this division to that between "scare quotes" and "bed hangings," the functional and the decorative. Four sections, entitled either "Scare Quotes" or "Bed Hangings," constitute the "body" of Howe's book. Framing these main texts are an untitled, opening prose section on the frontispiece, the interleaf, and the text, and a concluding poem on Mary Manning, Howe's mother, entitled "Kidnapped." What interests Howe in the two sections "Bed Hangings I" and "Bed Hangings II" is "the weave not the material itself." No longer merely decorative, bed hangings are art objects in themselves, and the same applies to "Scare Quotes" (I and II). In these prosaic ruminations, Howe discusses Fredrick Olmsted, the famous landscaper and architect of the urban park, which Howe links to the sanctification of the book, exemplified by her discomfit when she goes to Harvard's Houghton Library to examine the manuscripts of Emily Dickinson. And this sanctification is also linked to the Anglicization of American speech, the valorization of "standards," exemplified by Henry James who linked the "falling standards" of American speech and writing to the mass influx of European immigrants in the latter half of the nineteenth century. Howe contrasts these models of conformity with the "slovenly" speech, writing, and dress of her own Irish family, as well as with the way books were often recycled, indicating their multi-functionality. Yet, typically, Howe acknowledges her own attraction to the book as art object, to eloquence: "During the nineteenth century old books were often sold to tailors for measures, and to bookbinders for covers. Well I don't buy it" (57). Howe's deification of the book is no doubt a direct result of her interest in blurring the genres of the visual and the verbal. It indicates that Howe thinks of her books as art objects in and of themselves, and, like all the plastic arts, they still retain that auratic value Walter Benjamin saw vanishing with the advent of modernity.

Further Reading. ***Selected Primary Sources:*** Howe, Susan, *Articulation of Sound Forms in Time* (Windsor, VT: Awede, 1987); ———, *Bed Hangings* (New York: Granary, 2001); ———, *A Bibliography of the King's Book or, Eikon Basilike* (Providence, RI: Paradigm Press, 1989); ———, *The Birthmark: Unsettling the Wilderness in American Literary History* (Hanover, NH: Wesleyan University Press, 1993); ———, *Defenestration of Prague* (New York: Kulchur Foundation, 1983); ———, *The Europe of Trusts: Selected Poems* (Los Angeles: Sun and Moon, 1990); ———, *Frame Structures: Early Poems 1974–1979* (New York: New Directions, 1996); ———, *The Midnight* (New York: New Directions, 2003); ———, *My Emily Dickinson* (Berkeley, CA: North Atlantic Books, 1985); ———, *The Nonconformist's Memorial* (New York: New Directions, 1993); ———, *Pierce-Arrow* (New York: New Directions, 1999); ———, *Singularities* (Hanover, NH: Wesleyan University Press, 1990). ***Selected Secondary Sources:*** Back, Rachel Tzvia, *Led By Language: The Poetry and Poetics of Susan Howe* (Tuscaloosa: University of Alabama Press, 2002); Golding, Alan, "Drawing with Words: Susan Howe's Visual Poetics," in *We Who Love to Be Astonished: Experimental Women's Writing and Performance Poetics*, ed. Laura Hinton and Cynthia Hogue (Tuscaloosa: University of Alabama Press, 2002, 152–164); Hersey, Susan, "'Space Is a Frame We Map Ourselves In': The Feminist Geographies of Susan Howe's *Frame Structures*," in *The Greening of Literary Scholarship: Literature, Theory, and the Environment*, ed. Steven Rosendale (Iowa City: University of Iowa Press, 2002, 131–148); McCorkle, James, "Prophecy and the Figure of the Reader in Susan Howe's *Articulation of Sound Forms in Time*" (*Postmodern Culture* 9.3 [May 1999]); Nicholls, Peter, "The Pastness of Landscape: Susan Howe's *Pierce-Arrow*" (*Contemporary Literature* 43.3 [Fall 2002]: 441–460); Quartermain, Peter, *Disjunctive Poetics: From Gertrude Stein and Louis Zukofsky to Susan Howe* (Cambridge: Cambridge University Press, 1992); Schultz, Susan, "Exaggerated History" (*Postmodern Culture* 4.2 [January 1994]).

Tyrone Williams

HOWELLS, WILLIAM DEAN (1837–1920)

One of the most prolific writers in the history of American letters, William Dean Howells helped shape the course of American literature from the mid-1860s to the early 1900s through his dual roles as a fiercely talented novelist and esteemed literary editor. In his own writing, Howells's rare gift for melding the lyrical and the realistic, the classical and the modern, the spiritual and the psychological, broadened the stylistic scope of American literature, as did the work of his close friends Mark Twain and Henry James. In addition to Howells's groundbreaking novels, such as *The Rise of Silas Lapham* (1884) and *A Hazard of New Fortunes* (1890), his tenure as editor in chief of the renowned *Atlantic Monthly* (1871–1881), and his "Editor's Study" (1886–1892) and "Editor's Essay Chair" (1899–1909) columns in *Harper's Monthly* allowed him to further influence the direction of American writing. His championing of writers as diverse as **Hamlin Garland**, **Stephen Crane**, **Charlotte Perkins Gilman**, **Paul Lawrence Dunbar**, and Frank Norris caused the often elitist Eastern literary establishment to broaden its publishing practices to include a variety of American writers who were exploring fresh, groundbreaking narrative terrain in their work, which helped lead to the **modernist** explosion in the early twentieth century. Simply put, William Dean Howells was as important a literary figure as this country has ever produced.

Given the enduring influence of Howells's novels and travel books, it is ironic that he began his literary career as a poet. Howells's earliest publishing credits were in esteemed magazines, thus giving him the needed confidence to dedicate himself to becoming a professional author. It is fitting that Howells's early poems clearly align themselves with European Romanticism. As a largely self-educated young man, he was enamored with writers across the sea, such as Alexander Pope, John Keats, and Lord Byron. Thus, the verses he wrote during the 1860s and early 1870s are marked with a deeply lyrical sensibility. An overriding naturalist impulse runs through his metered verses with a dirge-like pathos; it is only through Howells's topical referencing of hot-button American issues (slavery, most notably) that it is evident these stanzas are written by an American hand. Poems as intensely allegorical as "The Movers" and "Through the Meadow" (both included in Howells's 1873 collection, *Poems*), owe more to the writings of Keats and William Wordsworth than they do to any specific American poet, while poems such as "The Poet" (also from *Poems*) showcase Howells's gift at employing the heroic couplet, a form with which he had become enamored through his extensive reading of Pope. When taken as a whole, Howells's early poems are striking for two reasons: First, they represent a young writer with a limitless ability to breathe fresh life into classical literary forms, and, second, they speak to Howells's chameleonic talents as a writer. It is impressive that the man who wrote the pastoral "The Mulberries" (1871) was the same writer who would later create such realist masterpieces as *A Modern Instance* (1882) and *The Rise of Silas Lapham*.

Howells's early success as a poet resulted in his being accepted into the Boston literary establishment, which was a thriving cultural epicenter in late nineteenth-century America. Howells's ascension into the American literary pantheon began in earnest when **James Russell Lowell**, the respected editor of the *Atlantic Monthly*, having been impressed by Howells's poems, adopted How-

ells as an unofficial surrogate son. Aside from Lowell's consistent publishing of Howells's work, Lowell gave the young writer letters of introduction to established literary giants such as **Nathaniel Hawthorne** and **Ralph Waldo Emerson**. Howells's ability to discuss literary matters with such unquestioned talents was a key stepping-stone for his rapidly developing career. With such vital literary connections established, Howells took a position as the U.S. consul in Venice in 1861, which not only provided him with the needed cultural and experiential capital a writer of Howells's ambitions required, but also was a post that assured him of ample time to devote to writing. Upon his return from Venice in 1865, Howells published his first book, a travel monograph called *Venetian Life* (1866), which sold respectably. From there, he embarked on a feverish decade of prose writing that, in addition to novels and travel books, also included plays and essays. With Howells's ever-increasing success as a prose writer, he abandoned poetry altogether for a number of years. Critics are divided as to why he did so. While many believe Howells used his early poetry as a type of narrative exercise in order to develop his skills as a writer, others believe Howells ceased writing poems because he realized that he would never reach true greatness as a poet. Although reviews of Howells's poetry were always respectful, they were hardly the enthusiastic notices that would establish him as a poet of genius. Howells's close friends, however, could always be counted on to send their heartiest congratulations on his verse; William James was a particular fan of Howells's poetry. But, with the death of his beloved daughter, Winifred (1863–1889), Howells's poetic inspiration (fueled by his unmitigated despair) returned in full force, and he published a large number of poems over the next several years. This later poetry has an impressively contemporary feel, free of the classicist strains that informed his earlier verse.

The American poetic landscape had changed considerably in the years that had passed since Howells's first verses were published; during the 1890s and early 1900s, writers like **Edwin Arlington Robinson**, **Carl Sandburg**, and **Robert Frost**, had helped to spur a fresh movement in American poetry. Therefore, it is no surprise that his later poems reflect this changing tide in American verse, as Howells once again found himself to be playing an integral role during another profound shift in American literature. Where Howells's earlier poetry had not been critically embraced because of its over-reliance on established methods, his later poetry was never wholly accepted because of the despair at the core of many of the poems. Clearly, these were verses written by a man in the throes of an immense sadness, and, although the poems were often fresh (the elegiac "November-Impression" [1891], the philosophical "The Mother" [1902], the prophetic "Black Cross Farm"

[1904]), they failed to reach a wide audience. What is evident in all of Howells's poems, however, is a noble and intense humanity that is as invigorating today as it was when he was alive. Whether it be the scathingly anti-slavery "The Pilot's Story" (1860), or the haunting "The Materials of a Story" (1892), it is clear that Howells believed that art, if it was to be important, must demonstrate a social conscience. Thus, the man who publicly protested the death sentences of the Haymarket Anarchists in 1887, who was one of the earliest sponsors of the NAACP (1909), and who was a devout supporter of women's suffrage, brought the same passion to his poetry which, although not as celebrated as his fiction, is no less a part of Howells's honorable artistic and social legacy.

Further Reading. *Selected Primary Sources:* Howells, William Dean, *Pebbles, Monochromes, and Other Modern Poems, 1891–1916,* ed. Edwin H. Cady (Athens: Ohio University Press, 2000); ———, *Poems* (Boston: Houghton Mifflin, 1873). *Selected Secondary Sources:* Cady, Edwin H., *William Dean Howells as Critic* (Boston: Routledge and Kegan Paul, 1973); Howells, William Dean, *Selected Literary Criticism: 1859–1885* (Bloomington: Indiana University Press, 1993); Lowell, James Russell, *The Function of the Poet and Other Essays* (New York: Kennikat Press, 1920); Lynn, Kenneth S., *William Dean Howells: An American Life* (New York: Harcourt Brace Jovanovich, 1970).

Paul Tayyar

HUDGINS, ANDREW (1951–)

Andrew Hudgins has developed a reputation for storytelling in a public and accessible style. He employs humor and a colloquial, contemporary diction to create **narrative** and autobiographical poetry regularly based on four- and five-beat lines. As a Southern poet in the tradition of **Robert Penn Warren**, **James Dickey**, and **Rodney Jones**, Hudgins relates his experiences of the South in examinations of adolescent longing, family and social life, and encounters with evangelical faith. References to Christian tradition appear throughout his work, often in conjunction with the depiction of his own failure of belief.

Hudgins was born in Texas in 1951. His family moved frequently before settling in Montgomery, Alabama, where he attended high school and college. The trips his family took to visit relatives in Georgia had a formative impact on his geographical identification with the South, an identification recounted in his collection of essays *The Glass Anvil* (1997). Hudgins received his MFA. from the University of Iowa Writers' Workshop in 1983, and received broad acclaim with his first book, *Saints and Strangers* (1985), a finalist for the Pulitzer Prize. He has gone on to publish five more volumes of poetry, while teaching at various universities. The highly-regarded *After the Lost War* appeared in 1988, portraying the life of the Georgian poet and Civil War veteran **Sidney Lanier** (1842–1881). Hudgins convincingly developed the voice of an adolescent boy in the autobiographical *The Glass Hammer: A Southern Childhood* (1994). His most recent collection is *Ecstatic in the Poison* (2003), which draws its title from the childhood experience of playing in the fog generated by a DDT truck.

Hudgins revels in telling the stories of a variety of characters. *Saints and Strangers* is populated by the likes of John Jay Audubon, Holofernes, and one of Solomon's concubines, and raises questions about the kinds of obligation and attachment that develop when one observes others. A sense of attachment informs "Claims," as the decomposing bodies of two murdered women are discovered in the woods. The onlooker notices the care with which the authorities remove the bodies, since "the flesh dissolves at a careless touch / as if to say, *You have no claim on me.*" The observer's experience of helplessness before such an atrocity produces a feeling of connection, even love, for the dead girls. Encounters with violence are frequent in Hudgins's work, playing a central role in the narrative *After the Lost War.* In the voice of Sidney Lanier, Hudgins explores the after-effects of having witnessed acts of savagery. In "Postcards of the Hanging," Lanier mails picture postcards of a lynching to his brother. In the series of messages Lanier seems unaffected by the hanging, until, almost in an aside, he tells of polishing his boots: "When I was through, my hands were black / as the dead man's hands. Even my face was smudged." The following postcard reports his bewilderment afterwards; he walks home barefoot, only to find when he arrives that his "feet [are] sticking to the ground with blood." Guilt asserts itself almost unnoticed.

Flowers appear in Hudgins's poetry as a symbol of strength and persistence, breaking through frozen ground to return year after year. In "The Cult of the Lost Cause," Lanier wants his death to take the form of an impossible blooming. The bright colors of autumn trees lead him to think "*that's how I'd like to die: / that flowering of something that can't flower.*" Hudgins's next volume, *The Never-Ending* (1991), is rife with gardens. "The Ugly Flowers" focuses attention on malodorous plants. Although they bloom "rank as rotten meat," the poet harks back to them when prettier flowers are abundant, desiring to show "the unloved loved, / the death-plant beautiful." Humor often appears alongside suffering. In "Hunting with My Brother," laughter resolves a fistfight between siblings who are dangerously close to becoming a latter-day Cain and Abel. "Praying Drunk" embraces comedy through references to cartoon characters and the strange places elephants will put their trunks. Among the childhood poems of *The Glass Hammer,* "The

Needs of the Joke Teller" relates an entire series of jokes, providing an imaginative look at the sociology of humor. Jokes offer a way of confronting the legacy of racism in the South, as punch lines upend taboos, "knock them to the dirt, / sit on their chests and tickle them." Jokes serve as a form of power, jarring the mind. Hudgins takes pleasure in "the suspended moment as the brain / slips on its cogs and freewheels" when reaching for understanding.

Uncertainty about the power of poetry enters Hudgins's work in interesting ways. He is keenly aware that autobiographical narratives can harm loved ones, and he recognizes poetry's hold over him as an impulse to speak to fill the silence. In *Babylon in a Jar* (1998), "We Were Simply Talking" presents the silent clarity of the moment when his car swerves into the path of oncoming traffic. In that suspended moment between life and death, he "loved / every molecule of breath I wasn't taking." This insight results in the query "why do we always, always have to speak?" Hudgins turns to consider the nature of his commitment to writing poems. "Purple" addresses this commitment in terms of a pull toward metaphor, which the poet experiences as a kind of compulsion. Shasta lilies are "so free of meaning," yet he "can't let them be just blue / or purple," and so he turns them into signs of "royalty." *Ecstatic in the Poison* (2003) indulges in this self-reflexive turn, with such titles as "A Joke Walks into a Bar," "Workshop," and "The Poet Asserteth Nothing." In that volume, metaphor and simile enable the poet to move beyond the controversy that dominates the reception of Andres Serrano's "Piss Christ," yielding a more authentic view of the photo. In his poem of that name, Hudgins makes a case for the beauty of Serrano's image, in which "blood and urine burn like a halo." Hudgins's particular skill is the ability to find wonder in such mixtures of life and death, filth and otherworldliness, waste and exaltation.

Further Reading. *Selected Primary Sources:* Hudgins, Andrew, *After the Lost War: A Narrative* (Boston: Houghton Mifflin, 1988); ———, *Babylon in a Jar* (Boston: Houghton Mifflin, 1998); ———, *The Never-Ending* (Boston: Houghton Mifflin, 1991). *Selected Secondary Sources:* Reynolds, Clay, "Crossing the Line of Poetic Biography: Andrew Hudgins' Narrative of the Life of Sidney Lanier" (*Journal of the American Studies Association of Texas* 20 [1989]: 27–40); Jarman, Mark, "A Conversation with Andrew Hudgins" (*Image: A Journal of the Arts and Religion* 38 [2003]: 91–103).

Jeffrey Galbraith

HUGHES, LANGSTON (1902–1967)

Prolific poet, novelist, essayist, autobiographer, children's book writer, playwright, and lecturer James Mercer Langston Hughes revolutionized the world of American poetry with lyrical writings that overflowed with honesty, beauty, and passion. Hughes was the author of sixteen books of poetry, three collections of short stories, two novels, twenty plays, three autobiographies, four volumes of documentary and editorial fiction, seven anthologies, children's poetry, operas, musicals, numerous critical essays in periodicals, and television scripts. His literary work, which epitomized the complexities and dualities of American and African American experience, was influenced by and was a result of the nineteenth-century literary tradition of American verse, the **Harlem Renaissance** in the 1920s, the Great Depression in the 1930s, and the social and political climate of the 1940–1960 postwar years.

Hughes was born on February 1, 1902, in Joplin, Missouri, to Carrie Mercer Langston, a teacher, and James Nathaniel Hughes, a lawyer. Soon after his birth, Langston's parents separated: His mother was writing verse and searching for a performing career, and his businessman father lived in self-imposed exile in Mexico. Langston grew up primarily in Lawrence, Missouri, with his maternal grandmother, Mary Langston, whose first husband, Sheridan Leary, participated in and died during a federal arsenal raid under the leadership of John Brown who, himself, was hanged for the raid's orchestration. Mary Langston's second husband—Langston Hughes's maternal grandfather—Charles Langston, was also active in the militant abolitionist movement. Charles's brother, John Mercer Langston, was one of the first African Americans to be elected to a public office (1855); he became a well-known and highly respected African American of the nineteenth century. With the history of abolitionist work in his lineage, Langston Hughes sought to reveal the struggles and beauties of black life in America. To do this, and to fill the loneliness caused by the absence of his parents, he turned to the written word. Soon, he fell in love with books, artistic freedom, black music, writing, and politics.

When he was thirteen, Hughes moved in with his mother and her new husband in Lincoln, Illinois. They eventually moved to Cleveland, Ohio, but not before Hughes began writing poetry. His interest in writing was further nurtured while he was a student at a white, cosmopolitan high school in Cleveland, Ohio. There Hughes discovered the works of **Walt Whitman** (*Leaves of Grass*, 1855) and **Carl Sandburg** (*Jazz Fantasies*, 1919), and they came to serve as his literary inspirations. He soon learned to appreciate standard verse, black dialect, and **lyric poetry** by studying the writings of **Paul Lawrence Dunbar** and **Claude McKay**. Through their writings, Hughes was able to discover and rehearse his own authentic voice, as well as explore American language, African American sensibilities, and democratic beliefs. However, Hughes did not immediately immerse himself into the world of writing.

Following high school graduation (1920), Hughes spent a year in Mexico with his father, who tried to discourage him from pursuing a writing career. Hughes's writing career, however, had already been launched with the 1921 publication of "The Negro Speaks of Rivers," in the *Crisis*, edited by **W.E.B. DuBois**. At the advice of his father, Hughes did not commit himself full time to writing; instead, he enrolled in Columbia University in New York City to study engineering.

In 1922, he left Columbia University and worked menial jobs for the next three years: he worked as a busboy, an assistant cook, a launderer, and a seaman/steward on a freighter that traveled to Africa and Europe. As Hughes saw and experienced the world, he became even more dedicated to writing: His frequent visits to clubs to listen to **jazz** and **blues** music and to write poetry. In 1924, he returned to the United States, moved to Washington, D.C., and soon began work on his first two books of poetry, *The Weary Blues* (1926) and *Fine Clothes to the Jews* (1927). *The Weary Blues*, supported by the efforts of white novelist Carl Van Vechten, portrayed themes of racial pride and patriotism; *Fine Clothes to the Jews* reflected the simplicity and sincerity of people. During this time, Hughes published poems in *Vanity Fair* and became acquainted with other black writers of the emerging Harlem Renaissance: Alain Locke, editor of *The New Negro* (1925), Wallace Thurman, **Arna Bontemps**, and Zora Neale Hurston.

In 1926, one of Hughes's finest essays, "The Negro Artist and the Racial Mountain," appeared in the *Nation*. In it, Hughes articulated the necessity of the black poet to be himself and to rejoice in the reality of his dark skin without feeling shame or guilt. Following these writings, a much-anticipated first novel was expected, but was not published until 1930 because Hughes had enrolled in the historically black Lincoln University in Pennsylvania; he completed his undergraduate studies in 1929. At the advice of Charlotte Mason, his financial patron known as "Godmother," Hughes finished his first novel, *Not Without Laughter* (1930), which received excellent reviews and won the year's Harmon Gold Medal for Literature.

The initial success of Hughes's writing career and the unexpected break from Mrs. Mason (and his subsequent breaks from Hurston and Locke, who were still being supported by Mason), inspired him to go on lecture tours. In the 1930s, he spent a lot of time in Haiti (1931), the Soviet Union (1932–1933), Japan (1933), and Mexico (1934) writing radical verse, experimenting with leftist literature, producing essays on capitalism, and translating short stories by Mexican writers. Hughes' collection of short stories on radical politics, race relations, and realism, *The Ways of White Folks* (1934), was published after he was expelled from Japan and while he lived in Carmel, California. Shortly after this volume was published to critical

praise, Hughes left California because of labor unrest and rumored threats of violence against him. In November 1934, he went to Mexico, where his father had recently died. The following June, he retreated to his mother's Oberlin, Ohio, home before traveling to New York City for the Broadway premiere of his play on miscegenation, *Mulatto* (1930), which received mixed reviews. In the same year, he wrote his highly acclaimed poem "Let America Be America Again."

Leading up to World War II, Hughes wrote moderately successful plays: *Little Ham* (1936), *Emperor of Haiti* (1936), *Troubled Island* (1936), *Joy to My Soul* (1937), and *Don't You Want to Be Free?* (1938). In 1938, his mother died of breast cancer. In order to pay for his mother's funeral and to get out of debt, Hughes traveled to Carmel and Los Angeles, California, where he wrote the screenplay for the film *Way Down South* (1939). He also **translated** poetry by Chilean educator and Latin American Nobel poet laureate Gabriela Mistral, and Spanish dramatist and poet Federico García Lorca. The next year, Hughes's autobiography, *The Big Sea* (1940), was published a few months after Richard Wright's book *Native Son* was released to much success. Two years later, Hughes wrote *Shakespeare in Harlem* (1942), in the spirit of the 1920s lyrical blues; he then wrote *Jim Crow's Last Stand* (1943) in order to protest racial segregation in America. Years later, he wrote *I Wonder As I Wander* (1956), a second autobiography that encapsulated the years 1931–1938.

In November 1943, Hughes began writing a column for the *Chicago Defender* newspaper. It was in his "Here to Yonder" weekly column that he introduced readers to the fictional Harlem everyday everyman, Jesse B. Semple, or "Simple." His passionately engaging, eloquently sophisticated columns spoke to the realities of race and racism in America from the perspective of an African American city dweller. Simple represented universal problems, including issues of socioeconomic status or class differences, attitudes toward standard, dialectical, and/or vernacular languages, and racial segregation. Hughes presented such issues, and others, to the reading audience for over twenty years in the *Chicago Defender*. Simon and Schuster published the first edited collection of Simple sketches, *Simple Speaks His Mind* (1950), to outstanding reviews. Following its publication, a critical essay on Hughes, "Tomorrow in the Writings of Langston Hughes" by John Parker, was published in the *College English* journal. The sketches of Jesse B. Semple contributed to Hughes's literary achievement and reputation.

The newspaper sketches and the subsequent books that followed on Simple eventually resulted in *Simply Heaven* (1957), a successful off-Broadway (May 1957) and on-Broadway (August 1957) musical. The following year, the *Langston Hughes Reader* (1958), *Selected Poems of*

Gabriela Mistral (1958), *Famous Negro Heroes of America* (1981), *Tambourines of Glory* (1958), and *The Book of Negro Folklore,* with Arna Bontemps (1958), were released. Hughes's writing career continued to soar, even as he was questioned and criticized by right-wing forces, by Senator Joseph McCarthy, by young black militants during the years of the Civil Rights Movement, and others. Hughes responded to his critics with his *Black Nativity* (1961) Christmas musical play, his *The Prodigal Son* (1961) gospel musical, and his *Jericho-Jim Crow* (1964) gospel play about the Civil Rights Movement.

Indeed, Hughes entered the 1960s with as much energy and passion for writing as he had displayed during his career's earlier years. His history book, *Fight for Freedom: The Story of the NAACP* (1962), was published, and it was followed by the publication of *Something in Common and Other Stories* (1963), *Five Plays by Langston Hughes* (1963), *Poems from Black Africa, Ethiopia, and Other Countries* (1963), the 1963 Broadway production of *Tambourines to Glory* (1958), and *The Book of Negro Humor* (1966). In 1964, he was officially honored at the Poetry Society of America's annual dinner, and in the same year, he participated in the Berlin Folk Festival at the University of Hamburg and then returned to New York City to attend the funeral services of Carl Van Vechten.

While Hughes' career heavily benefited from his political writings, poetic verses, musicals, lectures, and public performances, it also benefited from his children's fiction and his commitment to reveal the beauty and complexities of black life in America.

Popo and Fifina: Children of Haiti (1932) marked the beginning of Hughes's interests in writing for children. With Arna Bontemps, Hughes chronicled the story and adventures of two young children who moved from the countryside of Haiti to a town near the sea. Hughes's *Scottsboro Limited* (1932), illustrated by Prentiss Taylor, used verse to dramatize the tragedy of nine young black men who were falsely accused of raping white, Alabama women. Soon after, Hughes's collection of verse for young readers, *The Dream Keeper and Other Poems* (1932), was published. Beginning with *Famous American Negroes* (1954), Hughes produced a series of biographies on famous people for young readers. In total, Hughes published a dozen books for children and young adults, demonstrating his ability to captivate various audiences while capturing, through powerful writings, the nuances of black life, black experiences, and black culture.

All of Hughes's writings, in one way or another, are connected to his own political beliefs. Hughes had a strong affinity for leftist politics. He never admitted to being a member of the Communist Party, but his longtime defense of communist politics was not an uncommon practice for many black people in the early- to mid-1900s, including W.E.B. DuBois and Paul Robeson. They questioned the reality of equal opportunity, fair treatment, and civil and political rights for black people in America in light of continuing oppressive conditions. Hughes criticized the oppression that black people were subjected to before and after World War II. Publicly, Hughes was criticized for not condemning Joseph Stalin's economic plans and murderous excesses in the Soviet Union. (Neither DuBois nor Robeson, both of whom had received the Stalin Peace Prize, condemed Stalin either.) Even with such criticism, Hughes did not compromise his literary visions and talents.

An idealist, civil rights advocate, radical democrat, and creative artist, Hughes wrote a wealth of radical poems and, in the 1930s, published many of his verses in *New Masses*, a communist-controlled journal. He also founded the Harlem Suitcase Theater in 1938. Such activities brought Hughes under scrutiny. At the height of the McCarthy era, he was forced to appear and testify (1953) in Washington, D.C., about his radical writings and political affiliations with the Communist Party. He denied ever being a member of the party but admitted to the radicalism of many of his verses. Hughes's literary work, while at times receiving unfavorable literary critiques and coming under governmental scrutiny, remained accessible to his intended audiences: black people, the average reader, and the interested public.

During his lifetime, Hughes held visiting teaching positions at Atlanta University (1947) and the University of Chicago (1949). He received an honorary doctorate degree from his alma mater, Lincoln University (1943), participated in a nationally broadcasted radio debate on segregation for the program "America's Town Meeting of the Air" (1944), and collaborated with Mercer Cook, a Howard University professor, on a translation of Haitian author Jacques Roumain's novel, *Gouverneurs de la rosée*. Before his later publications, Hughes had already been dubbed (by 1926) as the poet laureate of black America. More recently, Hughes was honored with the official Langston Hughes United States postage stamp (2002).

Hughes's many notable honors included the Witter Bynner Prize for excellence in poetry (1926), a Guggenheim fellowship (1936), a Rosenwald fellowship (1941), the Anisfield-Wolf Award (1953), an American Academy of Arts and Letters award (1946), and the NAACP Springarn Medal (1960) for contributions to the progress of black people. Hughes was inducted into the National Institute of Arts and Letters (1961). As a delegate from the League of American Writers, Hughes traveled to Paris (1938) to participate in the leftist International Association of Writers Conference; to Nigeria (1960) to attend the inauguration of Nnamdi Azikiwe as governor general of independent Nigeria; and again to Nigeria (1961) with a group of performers organized by the American Society of African Culture.

Hughes died May 22, 1967, in New York City from complications following his prostate surgery. His funeral services were held at Benta's Funeral Home on St. Nicholas Street, Harlem, New York, and his body was later cremated. Several years after his death, the New York City Preservation Commission officially declared Hughes's Harlem residence, at 20 East 127th Street in New York City, as a landmark site; the entire 127th block was renamed "Langston Hughes Place." In 1969, the Langston Hughes Community Library and Cultural Center opened in Queens, New York; the Schomberg Center for Research in Black Culture in New York City houses the Langston Hughes Auditorium (352 seats) and the Langston Hughes Atrium (250 guests).

Two volumes of writing were published in the year of his death: *Black Magic: A Pictorial History of the Negro in American Entertainment* (with Milton Meltzer), and *The Panther and the Lash: Poems of Our Times.* Among his notable works that have been reprinted are *Five Plays by Langston Hughes, Good Morning Revolution: Uncollected Writings of Social Protest,* and *The Sweet Flypaper of Life with Roy DeCarava.* Langston Hughes has a place of his own among America's greatest poets and writers. His work stirred the homogeneity of American art as dominated by white artists and writers and complicated the terrains of race and literature, art and politics, jazz and blues music with traditional verse. His commitment to race pride, his admiration of black people, and his dedication to artistic freedom signify a man and an artist, whose life epitomizes the American intellectual, and the African American writer.

Further Reading. *Selected Primary Sources:* Hughes, Langston, *Ask Your Mama* (New York: Knopf, 1961); ———, *The Best of Simple* (New York: Hill & Wang, 1961); ———, *The Big Sea: An Autobiography* (New York: Hill & Wang, 1940); ———, *New Negro Poets: U.S.A.* (Bloomington: Indiana University Press, 1964); ———, *Montage of a Dream* (New York: Henry Holt, 1951); ———, *Not Without Laughter* (New York, Random House, 1930); ———, *Simple Speaks His Mind* (New York: Simon and Schuster, 1950); ———, *The Ways of White Folks* (New York: Random House, 1934). ***Selected Secondary Sources:*** Bernard, Emily, ed., *Remember Me to Harlem: The Letters of Langston Hughes and Carl Van Vechten* (New York: Vintage Books, 2002); Gates, Henry Louis, *Langston Hughes: Critical Perspectives Past and Present* (Amistad, 1993); Meltzer, Milton, *Langston Hughes: A Biography,* (New York: Crowell, 1968); Rampersad, Arnold, *The Life of Langston Hughes, 1902–1941,* 2nd ed. (Oxford: Oxford University Press, 2001); ———, *The Life of Langston Hughes: I Dream A World, 1941–1967,* 2nd ed. (Oxford: Oxford University Press, 2001); Rampersad, Arnold and David Roessel, eds., *The Collected Poems of Langston Hughes* (New York: Vintage, 1995); Wintz, Cary D.,

"Langston Hughes: A Kansas Poet in the Harlem Renaissance" (*Kansas Quarterly,* 7.3 [Summer 1975]: 58–71).

Valerie Felita Kinloch

HUGO, RICHARD (1923–1982)

Richard Hugo is one of America's most important landscape poets. Unfortunately, this has often led critics to see him as a merely regional poet, associated solely with the Seattle landscape of his youth. This is far from accurate, however, as Hugo renders the landscapes of Italy, Scotland, and Montana as fully as those of Washington. To define Hugo as merely a landscape poet also tends to obscure his insights into human character; the landscapes he writes about are always both external and interior, both natural and human. The natural world becomes an emblem of the imagination, a haven against the dark realities of the world. Hugo's poetry is clearly in the Romantic tradition as he follows William Wordsworth, not only in his affinity with natural landscapes but also in his desire to be the voice of a common man. His poems are colloquial, staunchly anti-academic, and always embrace the losers of the world: the dispossessed, the impoverished, the neglected.

Richard Hugo was born Richard Hogan on December 21, 1923, in White Center, Washington, a small suburb of Seattle. His father abandoned the family shortly after Richard's birth, and his mother subsequently left him to be raised by her parents. Because his grandparents' household was strict, Hugo grew up a lonely child. His lifelong passions of fishing and baseball were developed in this increasingly isolated boyhood. In 1942 he legally changed his name to Hugo after his stepfather. He played semipro baseball before entering the service in World War II. During the war, he served as a bombardier stationed in the Mediterranean. He was discharged in June of 1945 and went on to college, studying creative writing (working most notably with Theodore Roethke at the University of Washington). He received a BA in 1948 and an MA in 1952, the same year he married Barbara Williams and began working as a technical writer with Boeing. After his first book was published in 1961, he went on to teach at the University of Montana, where he eventually directed the **creative writing program**. His years there were marked by a self-acknowledged alcohol problem and periods of psychological instability. He divorced in 1964, but in 1974 he married Ripley Schemm Hansen and raised her children, a family life which proved to be a happy one until his death. In 1977 he became the director of the Yale Younger Poet Series. Despite his difficult childhood and the many challenges he faced as an adult, Hugo persevered and became one of America's most prolific poets. On October 22, 1982, Hugo died at the age of fifty-eight after a brief bout with leukemia.

Richard Hugo's first published poem, "West Marginal Way," clearly announced the themes and style that would mark his work throughout his life. The poem, titled after a street in his childhood neighborhood and included in his first collection, *A Run of Jacks* (1961) re-examines the landscape of his hometown in memory. As he says in one of the poem's finest lines, "some places are forever afternoon," suggesting the obsessive nature of memory and the ways in which he was haunted by place. The town, a bleak mixture of empty lots, sawmills, and gravel pits, is nonetheless rendered in evocative, beautiful language: "A dim wind blows the roses where they please." This line, with its slant rhymes and assonance, its pattern of long o's and w's, is both stylistically and thematically characteristic of Hugo: A lush lyricism is pitted against the harsh realities of the world.

The poem also points toward Hugo's obsession with rivers. The poem ends with a description of a nearby river "split and yellow / and this far down affected by the tide." Rivers, for Hugo, become emblematic of the imagination and, in the same way that the river reaches out toward something larger, the imagination opens itself to greater forces. Waters, poetry, and the imagination become fused in his poetry. This points, however, to one of the central paradoxes of Hugo's work: He is simultaneously realist *and* impressionist. The natural world is written about in realistic terms at the same time as creating an impressionistic, interior experience. In the same collection, for instance, his poem "Trout" marks this insistence on allowing the world to stand as it is and on maintaining the power of the imagination to transform that world. The trout is important on its own terms but can just as easily be seen as a reflection of Hugo's interior existence: "Swirls always looked one way / until he carved the water into many / kinds of current." His poems, then, are both impersonal and deeply personal.

The river as **elegy** continues into his next collection, *Death of the Kapowsin Tavern* (1965). The first section of the book focuses on specific rivers, the Duwamish, Skagit, and Hoh—all Northwest rivers Hugo knew well. Again, he is mining the relationship between rivers and imagination. In "Duwamish Head" he says "to know is to be alien to rivers." Repeatedly Hugo insists on the power of living in states of unknowing, fluid states in which the imagination can take hold. The collection also opens itself more fully, though, to the lives within the landscapes he describes: Indians living in poverty, a squatter being kicked off the land, and, in "Pike Place Market," the fishermen and hawkers who are losing their livelihood in the face of an expanding suburbia with "those militants who hate / the old and odd, and dream of homes where lawns / are uniformly green." Hugo constantly allies himself with the "old and odd" over the uniform, and gives voice to those who are left behind in the wake of "progress"—the women, for instance, who at the end of the poem, are "poking in the garbage for a meal."

The poems, then, become elegies of both the human lives and the natural landscapes being lost in the modern world, a way to hold on to what is passing. In the title poem he suggests that "nothing dies as slowly as a scene" as he reminisces on the burnt remains of the Kapowsin Tavern. The poems prolong the lives in memory, even as he knows "in time the lakes will send / wind black enough to blow it all away." As it was for one of his models, **Wallace Stevens**, memory and imagination are always acts of redemption for Hugo.

His next book, *Good Luck in Cracked Italian* (1969), is more fully about specific memories as he returns to the Italian landscapes where he served in World War II. He renders the scenes as fully and evocatively as he did the Northwest of his first two collections, but here he has come to literally walk among the ruins, the land where, as he says in "Tiberio's Cliff," "war hostages and inept clowns / fell clawing for a wing. Tide has taken." The scenery serves more insistently as a form of emotional landscaping here as he attempts to "stare this cruelty away," visiting G.I. graves and bombed-out villages. Several words and images—wind, women, war, wine, stone, and sea—are interwoven obsessively through the collection in the way that rivers were through the first two collections, elemental nouns that will not let Hugo out of their grasp.

This collection also marks a turn toward an increasing self-consciousness, considering always how this trip relates to his life as a writer. A long sequence, "Last Words from Maratea," insists on the question "Why did you come?"—to which he is never able to offer an adequate answer. The question becomes a driving force of the book as a whole, suggesting a confused relationship that Hugo develops with his own imagination and desires. He is struggling to find the essence or meaning in memory but is unable. He becomes a man divided against himself, a reality that will increasingly occupy his life and work.

"Degrees of Gray in Philipsburg" from his next collection, *The Lady in Kicking Horse Reservoir* (1973), begins "you might come here Sunday on a whim." The poem, one of his most famous, contains one of his trademarks: a second-person narrative that enacts the mind of a divided self. The book as a whole reflects years marked by alcoholism and increasing emotional instability, and this poem, verging on the parodic, encapsulates this state of mind. Just as the speaker constructs a mythology for Philipsburg—"the 1907 boom, eight going silver minds, / a dance floor built on springs"—so, too, he builds a self-mythology. This is the town the self returns to when it hits bottom: "Isn't this your life?" But this gesture points toward a confusion of identity: Is this question directed toward the self or toward the reader, implicating everyone in this broken-down reality? Even as the speaker constructs this mythology of a world of "towering blondes, good jazz and booze," the "you" becomes lost in the contortions of a mind attempting to understand itself: "You're talking to yourself." The poem bears witness to Hugo's increasingly complex tone and his growing ability to render complicated psychological states.

What Thou Lovest Well Remains American (1975) continues to mine this problem of the divided self. Another of his most famous poems, "Goodbye, Iowa," uses the same second-person narrative, beginning "once more you've degraded yourself on the road." In this poem it is, perhaps, clearer that the speaker is speaking to himself: "Then you remembered what / the doctor said: really a hatred of self." The second-person point of view has become increasingly fashionable in American poetry but, more often than not, the point of view fails—a mechanical gesture meant to create aesthetic distance. For Hugo, however, it is more than appropriate. What he has accomplished is a highly self-conscious poetry about characters that remain self-divided and, thus, unable to change. Written in third person, the poem would not allow the reader access into the speaker's true mental state; written in first person, the poem would suggest a level of self-awareness which would indicate that the character should be able to change. Rather than simply following a fashion in American poetry, Hugo has turned the second-person poem into an inventive approach to human psychology.

In 1978 he published *31 Letters and 13 Dreams*, a book that almost singlehandedly began a new American form, the "letter poem." The thirty-one letters are all written to his friends and peers such as **Marvin Bell**, **William Stafford**, **Carolyn Kizer**, **James Wright**, and **Gary Snyder**. As is appropriate for Hugo, the letters are all written from a specific place so that a typical title ran as "Letter to Kizer, from Seattle." The voice is highly colloquial and intimate. As the poems are written to other poets, they naturally discuss Hugo's beliefs about poetry. For instance, in a poem/letter to **Denise Levertov**, he says that he can only populate the landscape "with surrogate suffering, with lame men crippled by more than disease, and create finally / a simple grief I can deal with." The poems, then, continue the self-reflection of his previous two books but in a much more straightforward way than the second-person, convoluted narratives. The poems read like sincere confessions interspersed with feelings of gratitude for the friends who have helped him survive all his trials. The form has been emulated by many after Hugo, but to modest success at best. The thirteen dreams of the book offer a different perspective on these same issues, rendered not as literal dreams or psychoanalytic tools but as a combination of memory and daydream. The dreams function rhetorically to suggest that we are still reading the innermost Hugo, not as autobiography but rather as an intimate, impressionist portrait of memory and desire.

Following another collection that returns to Hugo's childhood town (*White Center*, 1980), Hugo went on to use the landscapes, rivers, and villages of Scotland in *The Right Madness on Skye* (1980). In many respects, the book returns to Hugo's earlier sensibilities, focusing primarily on external landscapes as emblems for his interior life. The title poem, though, follows the speaker's own procession to the grave in what becomes an elegy for Hugo's own life. The poem suggests the speaker has moved away from this nothingness into the lush acceptance of a world he loves, and ends with a tone of gratitude—"Take my word. It's been fun." For one who has devoted his life to poetry, the phrase "take my word" is especially weighted: We can trust him, but we should also read him. For Hugo, in his efforts at honesty in his work, the two necessarily go together. In its truthful, intimate voice, his work reveals an individual attempting to understand his place in the world. As Hugo saw it, this was more than a way of writing: It was his ethical responsibility.

Further Reading. *Selected Primary Sources:* Hugo, Richard, *Death of the Kapowsin Tavern* (New York: Harcourt, Brace and World, 1965); ———, *Good Luck in Cracked Italian* (New York: World Publishing Company, 1969); ———, *The Lady in Kicking Horse Reservoir* (New York: W.W. Norton, 1973); ———, *Making Certain It Goes On: The Collected Poems of Richard Hugo* (New York: W.W. Norton, 1984); ———, *The Right Madness on Skye* (New York: W.W. Norton, 1980); ———, *A Run of Jacks* (Minneapolis: University of Minnesota Press, 1961); ———, *31 Letters and 13 Dreams* (New York: W.W. Norton, 1978); ———, *What Thou Lovest Well Remains American* (New York: W.W. Norton, 1975). ***Selected Secondary Sources:*** Allen, Michael S., *We Are Called Human: The Poetry of Richard Hugo* (Fayetteville: University of Arkansas Press, 1982); Holden, Jonathan, *Landscapes of the Self: The Development of Richard Hugo's Poetry* (Gaithersburg, MD: Associated Faculty Press); Hugo, Richard, *The Real West Marginal Way: A Poet's Autobiography* (New York: W.W. Norton, 1992); ———, *The Triggering Town: Lectures and Essays on Poetry and Writing* (New York: W.W. Norton, 1979); Myers, Jack and Marvin Bell, *A Trout in the Milk: A Composite Portrait of Richard Hugo* (Lewiston, ID: Confluence Press, 1982).

Glenn J. Freeman

HUMPHREYS, DAVID (1752–1818)

With **Timothy Dwight**, **John Trumbull**, and **Joel Barlow**, David Humphreys was one of the group of poets and satirists known as the Connecticut Wits. He is best known for his collaboration with Barlow and Trumbull on *The*

Anarchiad (1786–1787), a mock-heroic **epic**. Humphreys also wrote a number of sonnets, primarily on civic themes; prose works, including *An Essay on the Life of the Honourable Major-General Israel Putnam* and a *Dissertation on the Merino Sheep*; and two plays, *The Widow of Malabar; or The Tyranny of Custom* (1790), and *The Yankey in England* (1815).

Born in Derby, Connecticut, David Humphreys was the son of the Reverend Daniel Humphreys, a Congregational clergyman, and Sarah Riggs Bowers Humphreys. He attended Yale University, earning bachelor of arts (1771) and master of arts (1774) degrees. With the outbreak of the Revolution, Humphreys joined a New York militia regiment in 1776, becoming an aide to General George Washington from June 1780 until the end of hostilities. Humphreys accompanied Washington constantly, acting in effect as his private secretary. He developed a close relationship with Washington and became part of the small, trusted circle that included Alexander Hamilton and the Marquis de Lafayette. Appointed by Congress in 1784 as secretary of the committee designated to negotiate commercial treaties in Europe, Humphreys traveled to Paris and London, returning to the United States in 1786. He was elected that year as representative from Derby to the Connecticut General Assembly. During the late 1780s and 1790s, Humphreys wrote or co-authored his best known poems, including *The Anarchiad.*

Humphreys was made colonel of a United States detachment to suppress Shays's Rebellion, an uprising of poor farmers in western Massachusetts, in 1787. He served as the first United States minister to Portugal (1791) and minister to Spain (1796–1802). In his final act of military service, Humphreys was commissioned a brigadier general in the Connecticut militia in reaction to the War of 1812. In 1797, he married Ann Francis Bulkeley. In his later years, Humphreys raised Merino sheep and was the owner of successful woolen and cotton mills. Humphreys also became a member of the British Royal Society.

Humphreys was one of the primary members of the Connecticut Wits (or Hartford Wits, or the Connecticut Triumvirate), a group that also included lesser writers Mason Fitch Cogswell, Richard Alsop, **Theodore Dwight**, Elihu Hubbard Smith, Noah Webster, and **Lemuel Hopkins**. Humphreys's best-known work, *The Anarchiad*, was written in collaboration with fellow Wits Barlow and Trumbull. It is, as its title suggests, an extended allusion to Pope's *The Dunciad. The Anarchiad*, like most poetry of this period, is imitative of the high Augustan or neo-classical style typical of the social and political satire of English writers Alexander Pope, Jonathan Swift, and John Gay. Humphreys's use of the rigid, neo-classical style (characterized by regular meter—iambic pentameter or hexameter—and heroic couplets) was not only an expression of admiration for Pope; the regular Augustan style reinforces the poem's call for order and stability in the midst of national social, political, and economic uncertainty.

With the glaring exception of Barlow (whose later open support of the French Revolution and other radical positions earned him the particular ire of his fellow Wit Timothy Dwight) the Wits were politically conservative (Federalist), self-conscious "gentlemen," horrified by the threats posed to the new Republic by incidents such as Shays's Rebellion. Protesting the scarcity of money and the burden of taxation, the farmers called for suspension of civil actions against debt. Three hundred men, led by Daniel Shays, marched on the town of Springfield to prevent the sitting of the county courts. Humphreys, with his hero George Washington and the other Wits, deplored Shays and his cohorts for their disruption of civil order. Shays's Rebellion, in addition to various economic crises of the period, was serious enough to prompt the Philadelphia Convention of May–September 1787, and the drafting of the United States Constitution.

In addition to military action, Humphreys and his *Anarchiad* co-authors used all the popular forms of the day—among them epic verse, satire, doggerel, and odes—to condemn the ravages of anarchy in their poem. *The Anarchiad* claimed to be an ancient epic recently discovered in the Ohio Territory. The speaker of the poem, so the writers of the first number claimed, had experienced a vision while standing on an American mountain peak, a vision that enabled "the years of futurity to pass before him." The vision depicted an empire of "Chaos and substantial Night" in North America. The finished text appeared in twelve installments in the *New-Haven Gazette* between October 1786 and September 1787. *The Anarchiad* earned Humphreys and his fellow Wits such a degree of national attention that no printed copies were available for Humphreys to send to George Washington (Silverman, 513).

While serving abroad as secretary to a commission charged with negotiating commercial treaties with European powers (headed by Adams, Franklin, and Jefferson), Humphreys published a *Poem, on the Happiness of America; Addressed to the Citizens of the United States.* Humphreys's poem emerged from his distress over his perception (shared by many British and European observers) that America was teetering on the brink of chaos. As a counter-vision, the fifty-one page poem, published in London in 1786, celebrates an America marked by a kind of middling comfort—peaceful, agrarian, bountiful (but not luxurious), and stable. Similarly, *A Poem on Industry, Addressed to the United States of America* (1794) extols the virtues of agrarian labor (which is what Humphreys means by the "industry" of the title) by imagining America as a reborn Roman republic. From 1776 to 1799 Humphreys also composed twelve, fourteen-line sonnets, among them occasional poems on topics such as the death of General Washington.

Further Reading. ***Selected Primary Sources:*** Humphreys, David, Timothy Dwight, John Trumbull, and Joel Barlow, *The Anarchiad: A New England Poem*, ed. Luther G. Riggs (Gainesville, FL: Scholars' Facsimiles and Reprints, 1967); ———, *The Miscellaneous Works of David Humphreys*, ed. William K. Bottorff (1804; reprint Gainesville, FL: Scholars' Facsimiles and Reprints, 1968). ***Selected Secondary Sources:*** Cifelli, Edward M. *David Humphreys* (Boston: Twayne, 1982); Humphreys, Frank Landon, *Life and Times of David Humphreys: Soldier-Statesman-Poet, "Belov'd of Washington,"* 2 vols. (1917; reprint St. Clair Shores, MI: Scholarly Press, 1971); Silverman, Kenneth, *A Cultural History of the American Revolution* (New York: Columbia University Press, 1976).

Ann M. Brunjes

I

IDEOGRAM

An ideogram (from the Greek [*idea*], "idea," and [*gra-pho*], "to write") is a single graphic form—written with one or several strokes—that represents an object or concept. While ideograms have been used in many languages, including Sumerian, Egyptian, and Mesopotamian, the form is most commonly associated with Chinese. A Chinese ideogram—or "character"—generally combines independent elements (such as "sun" and "moon") to represent a discrete idea ("bright"). The ideogram played an important role in American and European poetry during much of the twentieth century. The best-known practitioner of so-called ideogrammic poetry in North America is **Ezra Pound**, who was one of the first to understand its possibilities. Rebelling against poetic diffuseness, which he associated with "cosmic poetry," Pound elaborated a series of principles around 1913 that became the cornerstone of **Imagism**. Heavily influenced by the scholar **Ernest Fenollosa**, whose treatise on the Chinese written character had recently fallen into his hands, Pound developed an "ideogrammic method" of composition that retained traditional verse forms but intensified their imagery.

Although Pound and his Imagist colleagues were profoundly influenced by the ideogram, they initially saw no reason to modify the appearance of their texts. The effects they hoped to achieve were dependent not on visual perception but on the reader's imagination. In this context, Pound sought to divorce imagery in general from its visual origins. An image, he claimed, is "that which presents an intellectual and emotional complex in an instant of time" and is concerned with the "unification of disparate ideas." Although scholars differ about the value of the ideogrammic method, as well as its derivation, its consequences for Pound's work were both immediate and far reaching. The ideogrammic method was destined to become one of his most important legacies, influencing **Objectivists** such as **Louis Zukofsky**, proponents of **projective verse** such as **Charles Olson**, and **Beat poets** such as **Gary Snyder** and **Allen Ginsberg**. Pound would eventually employ actual Chinese characters in *The Cantos*, the work that was to occupy most of his life.

Surprisingly, Pound's theory of the ideogram encountered resistance almost from the beginning. Although other poets found his remarks fascinating, sinologists protested that they were based on several misunderstandings of the ideogram as a form. In their opinion, Pound's ideas bore little relation to the Chinese system of writing. Like Fenollosa, Pound was convinced that Chinese ideograms still bore traces of their pictographic origins. Not only is their etymology constantly visible, Fenollosa insisted, but they retain more of their original poetic value than any phonetic language. In response, critics have objected that Chinese readers are unaware of each ideogram's etymology or its status as a pictorial object. For all practical purposes, these critics add, Chinese has become a phonetic language. The modern ideogram consists of two signs: a radical, which specifies the class it belongs to, and a second element, indicating how to pronounce it. Although the debate persists to the present day, it has lost much of its original relevance. As Fenollosa noted, "such a pictorial method, whether the Chinese exemplified it or not, would be the ideal language of the world."

Interestingly, Pound and Fenollosa were not the only ones who believed Chinese writing was pictographic. Contemporary documents reveal that this belief was widespread. In France it can be traced back to the publication of Jean Pierre Abel Rémusat's *Recherches sur l'origine et la formation de l'écriture chinoise* (*Research into the Origin and the Formation of Chinese Writing*) in 1827. Intrigued by the pictographic theory, a number of writers and artists modeled their works on the Chinese ideogram as well. The French poet Guillaume Apollinaire called his visual experiments *idéogrammes lyriques* at first because they consisted of a series of pictures. During World War I the Italian Futurist Gino Severini created a number of paintings inspired by the Chinese written character. In an article titled "The Cinematographic Principle and the Ideogram" (1929), the Russian filmmaker Sergei Eisenstein compared the principle of montage to the ideogrammic method.

Further Reading. Bohn, Willard, *Modern Visual Poetry* (Newark: University of Delaware Press, 2001); Fenollosa, Ernest, *The Chinese Written Character as a Medium for Poetry*, ed. Ezra Pound (San Francisco: City Lights, 1936); Géfin, Lazlo, *Ideogram: History of a Poetic Method* (Austin: University of Texas Press, 1982).

Willard Bohn

IGNATOW, DAVID (1914–1997)

In the conclusion to *Open Between Us* (1980), a collection of his interviews and essays, David Ignatow explains that the Great Depression "set the climate for profound, lasting change in literature" (291), which affected him deeply. Graduating from high school in 1932 and already intent on a career in writing, he was influenced by **William Carlos Williams** and **Charles Reznikoff**, who had contributed to a special **"Objectivists"** issue of *Poetry* magazine in 1931, edited by **Louis Zukofsky**. Like the Objectivist poetry he admired, Ignatow's early work brings the **free verse** poetics typical of Anglo-American high **modernism** to bear on social concerns informed by a progressive political sensibility.

With acerbic wit, Ignatow often suggests that even the mundane occurrences of big business in the United States have an undercurrent of violence. Publishing over the course of seven decades, he employed a variety of styles, ranging from Imagist **lyrics** to **prose poems**. As a result, his oeuvre defies classification with any particular school or period, but at every point his work reflects both his early conviction that social conditions shape consciousness and his persistent belief that poetry can serve to illuminate how the particular conditions of modern life can mislead people of every class to identify happiness with acquisitions.

Ignatow was born in Brooklyn in 1914 to first-generation Jewish immigrants from Russia. With the exception of brief teaching stints in Kentucky and Kansas, he lived his entire life in and around New York City. He married Rose Graubart, a writer and painter, in 1937. Later that year they had a son, David, and in 1956 they had a daughter, Yaedi, who edited her father's posthumous *Living Is What I Wanted: Last Poems* (1999). From 1934 to 1939 he was a reporter for the Works Progress Administration (WPA) newspaper project. During the next fifteen years, he worked a variety of jobs, published in several journals, and released a first book, *Poems* (1948), which Williams reviewed enthusiastically in the *New York Times Review of Books*. From 1954 to 1962 Ignatow worked as an executive in his father's bindery, eventually serving as president before selling the business in 1962. His second volume of poetry, *The Gentle Weight Lifter* (1955), received less attention than his first. But in the 1960s a succession of three volumes—*Say Pardon* (1961), *Figures of the Human* (1964), and *Rescue the Dead* (1968)—earned him critical acclaim and enabled him to secure university teaching positions for the rest of his career, including a permanent appointment at York College, a branch of the City University of New York, from which he retired as Professor Emeritus in 1984. He served as an editor for the *Nation* (1962–1963), *Chelsea*, and the *American Poetry Review* (1972–1976). From 1980 to 1984 he was president of the Poetry Society of America. He won Guggenheim fellowships in 1965 and 1973, a Rockefeller Foundation grant in 1968, and a National Endowment for the Arts Award for *Poems 1934–1969* (1970). In 1977 Ignatow received the Bollingen Prize.

One of Ignatow's best-known poems, "Get the Gasworks," from *Poems* (1948) exemplifies the Objectivist technique of attending to concrete details, in this case for the sake of studying the effect of a community's physical and social surroundings. The poem argues that if an author were to incorporate the gasworks, its smokestacks, the nearby tenement buildings, the grimy kids from the neighborhood, and particular elements of the gasworks' river locale, then the poem would represent "the kind of living / that makes the kind of thinking we do: / gaswork smokestack whistle tooting wisecracks." Having introduced the correspondence between the setting of the gasworks and the thoughts of the working people who live in proximity to it, Ignatow dedicates the second half of the poem to a tragic event that results from the periodic incompatibility of the activities of the gasworks and those of the people living in the neighboring streets: A boy chasing a ball is run over and killed by a truck delivering coal for the gasworks. After the funeral the children resume playing ball in the streets, the police continue to chase them, their mothers keep reprimanding them, and in the last two lines, "papa flings his newspaper outward, / in disgust with discipline." Presumably, the flung newspaper reports the child's death, but the singular "papa" could be disgusted either with the failure of the children to be disciplined about safety in the streets or with the unrelenting, disciplined operation of the gasworks, an entity that provides heat and electricity for the residents of the neighborhood and a rhythm for their existence. A child who dashes heedlessly into the street is breaking from the routine of the gasworks, but he cannot impede the progress of the truck or supersede the priorities of the power plant.

In the title poem from his most recognized volume, *Rescue the Dead* (1968), Ignatow concludes with another ambiguous last line. Like "Get the Gasworks," the poem deals with a conflict between the artifice of urban living and the need for human spontaneity. Using the counter-intuitive opposition of those who live and those who love, he describes the former as people who sign their names, carry wallets, and shake hands. To love, by contrast, is to be taken "into a forest where the secret grave / is dug, singing, praising darkness." The final stanza ends with an ironic plea, in which the poet appeals to those who, not subject to love, are free, pleading with them to "rescue the dead." The implication of this peculiar request is that those liberated from love are hardly in a condition to rescue anyone.

The opposition of "life" and "death" becomes increasingly important in Ignatow's later work. He uses abstract terms but renders them concrete by realizing mortality as a defining human experience. In *Living Is What I Wanted* he refuses to complain about the brevity of life, saying, "I am, and that makes me much like everyone else. / Follow Adam, the leader, into the ground."

Further Reading. *Selected Primary Sources:* Ignatow, David, *Against the Evidence: Selected Poems, 1934–1994* (Hanover, NH: Wesleyan University Press, 1993); ———, *Figures of the Human* (Middleton, CT: Wesleyan University Press, 1964); ———, *The Gentle Weight Lifter* (New York: Morris Gallery, 1955); ———, *Living Is What I Wanted: Last Poems*, ed. Yaedi Ignatow (Rochester, NY: Boa Editions, 1999); ———, *Open Between Us*, ed. Ralph Mills (Ann Arbor: University of Michigan Press, 1980); ———, *Poems* (Prairie City, IL: Decker Press, 1948); ———, *Rescue the Dead* (1968); ———, *Say Pardon* (Middleton, CT: Wesleyan University Press, 1961). *Selected Secondary Source:* Terris, Virginia, ed., *Meaningful Differences: The Poetry and Prose of David Ignatow* (Tuscaloosa: University of Alabama Press, 1998).

Jim Zeigler

IMAGISM

One of the most significant single movements of early twentieth-century American and English literature, Imagism has exerted a lasting influence on American **modernist** and **postmodernist** poetry. This "School of Images" (**Ezra Pound**) has been considered by many as the "starting point of modern poetry" (**T.S. Eliot**). What began as a London-based gathering of a dozen or so American and English poets turned into a movement that trained generations of poets, mostly American, in modern writing techniques. By the time it was over, Imagism's revolutionary poetic principles had become widely accepted tools that shaped the mature writing of most of the major poets of the century.

Imagism rejected the "tyranny of the symbolic" (**William Carlos Williams**) and emphasized instead objectivity and directness; clarity, brevity, and hardness of outline; and freedom from metrical laws. Making use of diverse poetic and visual models, Imagism found inspiration in Chinese, Japanese, Greek, and Hebrew poetry, Provençal songs, French anti-symbolist writing, and contemporary visual art forms. Members of the original group included American poets Pound, **H.D.** (Hilda Doolittle), **Amy Lowell**, and John Gould Fletcher, as well as English poets Richard Aldington, F.S. Flint, T.E. Hulme, Ford Madox Hueffer (later Ford), and D.H. Lawrence. Several other poets were influenced by Imagism, including Williams, Eliot, **Wallace Stevens**, **Archibald MacLeish**, James Joyce, **Carl Sandburg**, **Marianne Moore**, and **e.e. cummings**.

The key date for Imagism is 1912. In this year Pound, the chief organizer of the group at the time, sent H.D.'s poems to **Harriet Monroe** with the comment that they were "modern . . . in the laconic speech of the Imagistes" and therefore should appear in January 1913 in her newly launched journal *Poetry* (Chicago) with the byline "H.D., *Imagiste*." This was also the year in which Pound formulated his "A Few Don'ts by an Imagiste," later to be known as the First Manifesto; it appeared in the March 1913 issue of *Poetry*.

It was in his Prefatory Note to "The Complete Poetical Works of T.E. Hulme," published at the end of his *Ripostes* (1913) that Pound first referred to Imagism as a school ("School of Images"). The Imagist movement actually went back a few years earlier. After Pound arrived in London in 1908, he attended Hulme's weekly gatherings in Soho, called "Poets' Club," where he was joined by H.D., Aldington, and other members. During these meetings the group primarily discussed issues of poetic technique, foreign verse forms, and the possibilities of "absolutely accurate presentation" (Hulme). By 1913 Pound speaks of the Imagists as a "live literary group in London," determined to bring about changes in poetry comparable to those in the visual arts, music, ballet, or psychology. For this is the time—"In or about December 1910"—when, as Virginia Woolf famously put it in "Mr. Bennet and Mrs. Brown," "human nature changed." These changes seemed to coincide with other epoch-making events marking the emergence of the new and the modern: the U.S. lecture tour of Freud and Jung in 1909; the Postimpressionist Exhibition in London in 1910; Diaghilev's Russian Ballet and Stravinsky's music in 1911; the 1913 English publication of Freud's *The Interpretation of Dreams*; the publication of James Frazer's monumental work of comparative religion, *The Golden Bough*, which appeared between 1907 and 1915; and the 1913 Armory Show in New York. In these years ideas of the "new" included the search for abstract structures behind visible phenomena as well as the search for the irrational and subconscious beneath the conscious. During the years preceding World War I, Imagism emerged with the aggressive dynamism of the new century as part of the first wave of modernism to break down all that was considered archaic and stale. Modern poetry, like modern art, Hulme insisted in "A Lecture on Modern Poetry," "deals with expression and communication of momentary phases in the poet's mind," and the momentary impressions that form experience would come in images to be captured in **free verse**. After 1917 Imagism ceased to be a movement; its principles, however, have survived.

Imagism was one of the first self-conscious literary movements to craft its own manifesto. Several essays contain statements of Imagist principles, among them Pound's "A Few Dont's by an Imagiste," Flint's "Imagisme," and Aldington's "Modern Poetry and the Imagists." Several years later, in 1918, Pound rephrased these principles in "A Retrospect," narrowing them down to three points:

1. Direct treatment of the "thing," whether subjective or objective
2. To use absolutely no word that does not contribute to the presentation
3. As regarding rhythm: to compose in the sequence of the musical phrase, not in sequence of a metronome (*Literary Essays*, 4)

To these he added a "certain doctrine of the image":

An "Image" is that which presents an intellectual and emotional complex in an instant of time. . . . It is the presentation of such a "complex" instantaneously which gives that sense of sudden liberation; that sense of freedom from time limits and space limits; that sense

of sudden growth, which we experience in the presence of the greatest works of art. (*Literary Essays*, 5)

Of the principles of Imagism, the "direct treatment of the 'thing'" is most significant for it is the basis of Imagism's anti-symbolic stance. The Imagist poet believes the object should be valued for itself and not for the symbolic or metaphorical meanings it might convey. The work of art ceases to be a riddle to be solved, or a code to be decoded, when the physical stands for the metaphysical. Words do not stand for something else but are themselves: tactile, tangible, audible, objective things. Imagism refuses the reading of meanings into phenomena. Assuming that value is immanent rather than transcendent, Imagism treats objects as meaningful in themselves, without human mediation, without the creative meaning making of the poet, as the Romantic-Symbolist tradition would insist. Objects, such as the wheelbarrow in Williams's "The Red Wheelbarrow," will not be taken to mediate and represent human values; instead, ordinary objects will be presented in their objecthood, as beautiful in and of themselves. As Pound stated in "A Retrospect,"

the proper and perfect symbol is the natural object, that if a man use "symbols" he must so use them that their symbolic function does not obtrude; so that a sense, and the poetic quality of the passage, is not lost to those who do not understand the symbol as such, to whom, for instance, a hawk is a hawk. (*Literary Essays*, 9)

In typical Imagist poems, such as Lowell's "A Decade" or Pound's "A Girl," emotions are neither evoked by a symbol nor confessed openly; instead, they are conveyed by the object, the "thing"—red wine, honey, and morning bread in the first case, a tree growing into a woman in the second—directly and precisely treated. As Aldington puts it in "Modern Poetry and the Imagists,"

We convey an emotion by presenting the object and circumstance of that emotion without comment. For example, we do not say "O how I admire that exquisite, that beautiful, that—25 more adjectives woman, you are cosmic, let us spoon forever," but we present that woman, we make an "Image" of her, we make the scene convey the emotion. (quoted in Pratt, 13)

The second principle of Imagism demands language economy: Language is to be taken seriously, leaving no room for redundancy. In one poem, "The Jewel Stairs' Grievance," Pound demonstrates this economy of words by adding notes to his somewhat liberal translation of the poem by Chinese poet Rihaku (Li Po).

The jeweled steps are already quite white with dew,
It is so late that the dew soaks my gauze stockings

(By Rihaku)

NOTE: *Jewel stairs, therefore a palace. Grievance, therefore there is something to complain of. Gauze stockings, therefore a court lady, not a servant who complains. Also she has come early, for the dew has not merely whitened the stairs, but has soaked her stockings. The poem is especially prized because she utters no direct reproach.*

The reader used to late-Victorian verbosity is given a playful exercise in perception here: The note elaborates on what is otherwise contained—but not necessarily noticed—in the poem. Indeed, once the poet uses the exact word, the note becomes redundant.

The emphasis on the *mot juste* also implies that no superfluous word is allowed for mere decoration or ornament. No preexisting form or symmetrical pattern is allowed without being demanded by the actual emotion. In line with this thinking, free verse becomes a fundamental part of Imagism's poetic program, as elaborated in the third principle. By "absolute rhythm" Pound is referring to a rhythm representative of emotion where rhythm is subordinated to meaning and evolves simultaneously with the treatment of the poetic object. Pound's "musical phrase" ("A Retrospect") or Hulme's "fitting of the rhythm to the idea" ("Lecture on Modern Poetry") is poetic form that responds to the inner control of impression or image. This is contrasted with the outer control of a preestablished pattern of accent and rhyme, "rhythm of the metronome" (Pound), or "the comforting and easy arms of the old, regular metre" (Hulme). The poet writing in "absolute rhythm" will rarely, if at all, use regular meter; most often the object treated will demand free verse form.

As its name suggests, the doctrine of the image plays a central role in Imagist writing. "The point of Imagisme is that it does not use images as *ornaments*. The image is itself the speech," Pound writes in his 1914 essay "Vorticism." The function of image in poetry is seen in the de-automatization process: in preventing us from getting too accustomed to what we perceive and helping us to see things as if for the first time. "Poetry endeavors to arrest you, and to make you continuously see a physical thing, to prevent you gliding through an abstract process," Hulme insists in his essay "Romanticism and Classicism." H.D.'s "Priapus" ["Orchard"], together with "In a Station of the Metro" and "Pagani's, November 8" by Pound, present the perfect image in the way they break conventional modes of perception while rendering particulars and exercising attention and alertness. They capture moments of recognition and discovery—the first pear falling, faces lining up in a metro station as if they were petals on a bough, the coalescence of two pairs of eyes exhibiting both similarity and difference in passion—when presupposed dualisms, such as the outer and the inner, the objective and the subjective, suddenly disappear.

This conception of art as determined by perception rather than production coincides with the idea of defamiliarization of the Russian formalists, especially Viktor Shklovsky, and is shared by **avant-garde** artists such as Marcel Duchamp, whose *Bicycle Wheel* (1913) and *Fountain* (1917) turn the mass-produced object into art by the gesture of perception and exhibition.

Further Reading. ***Selected Primary Sources:*** *Des Imagistes: An Anthology* (New York: Albert & Charles Boni, 1914); *Some Imagist Poets*, 3 vols. (Boston: Houghton Mifflin, 1915, 1916, 1917); Pound, Ezra, *Literary Essays*, ed. T.S. Eliot (London: Faber, 1954). ***Selected Secondary Sources:*** Fauchereau, Serge, *Lecture de la poésie américaine* (Paris: Les Éditions de Minuit, 1968, chap. 1); Gage, John T., *In the Arresting Eye: The Rhetoric of Imagism* (Baton Rouge: Louisiana State University Press, 1981); Goodwin, K.L., *The Influence of Ezra Pound* (London: Oxford University Press, 1966, chap. 1); Hughes, Glenn, *Imagism and the Imagists: A Study in Modern Poetry* (London: Bowes and Bowes, 1960); Jones, Peter, *Imagist Poetry* (Harmondsworth: Penguin, 1972); Kenner, Hugh, "Imagism," in *The Pound Era* (Berkeley: University of California Press, 1971, 173–191); Perkins, David, "Imagism," in *A History of Modern Poetry*, vol. 1 (Cambridge, MA: Harvard University Press, 1976, 329–347); Pondrom, Cyrena N., "H.D. and the Origins of Imagism" in *Signets. Reading H.D.*, ed. Susan Stanford Friedman and Rachel Blau DuPlessis (Madison: University of Wisconsin Press, 1990, 85–109); Pratt, William, ed., *The Imagist Poem* (New York: E.P. Dutton, 1963).

Enikő Bollobás

INADA, LAWSON FUSAO (1938–)

Author of three volumes of poetry, many co-authored works, countless poems, and several edited works, Lawson Fusao Inada has infused **Asian American literature** and American literature in general with music, and a spirit of fraternity and equality. Inada's poems frequently demonstrate his ability to imagine himself in someone else's shoes or a situation from someone else's perspective. Inada's contribution to American literature extends beyond his own writings. His biographer, Shawn Holliday, notes, "Even if he had never written a single line of poetry, Lawson Inada's importance to minority literature and Ethnic Studies would be firmly established with his editorial work" (34).

Born May 26, 1938, in Fresno, California, a sansei, Inada was one of the youngest "enemy aliens" to be interned by the U.S. government during World War II. He and his family were sent first to the Fresno Assembly

Center for four months, then to Jerome Camp in Arkansas for two years, and finally to Amache Camp in Colorado for a final year. Because he spent three of his formative years in the camps, much of Inada's poetry is an attempt to understand what internment meant. As Gayle Sato observes, "While almost every writer read or taught under the rubric of Japanese American literature has penned something on the internment, none has made it more central to artistic creativity than Inada, for whom 'writing relocation' has been a lifetime occupation and vehicle for the development of poetic vision and craft" (139). The title poem of Inada's 1997 book *Drawing the Line* tells the story of a boy named Yosh who tries to "draw the line" of Heart Mountain in Wyoming but somehow fails to "include the posts and wire." Inada, as all camp internees must do, draws the line on what he will forgive and forget and what he will not. In "Picking Up Stones," "Nyogen Senzaki, the erstwhile Zen teacher" writes Japanese words with ink and brush on stones that he has gathered and returned throughout the camp. Several residents while away the time in search of these stones, these words, "an Eastern eggless hunt." Inada focuses on camp experience not out of bitterness or misery but because he finds an impetus for poetry there, as he writes in "Children of the Camp": "There was no poetry in camp. / But the people made it so." His most recent contribution to the ongoing pursuit of insight into the internment experience is *Only What We Could Carry: The Japanese American Interment Experience* (2000), an edited collection of writing and pictures from and about the camps.

After their time in the camps Inada's family returned to Fresno where his father slowly rebuilt his dental practice and his mother worked as an elementary school teacher. Inada helped his maternal grandparents at the Fresno Fish Market, the only market of its kind, which his grandparents had established in 1912 (it had been entrusted to friends during the internment). Inada became so close to a neighboring family, the Palominos, that they gave him a Spanish version of his name, Lasano, and a nickname, Chano. They also put his picture above the mantel with those of the five other children in the family. A key juncture in Inada's personal and artistic growth came in the form of his friendship with Sam Jones, the son of an African American preacher; in the Jones household Inada learned the joy of music—gospel and the **blues** from the father, and **jazz** from Sam's older brother. Profoundly influenced by jazz, Inada views himself as a jazz musician playing poetry, integrating beats, phrasings, cross-rhythms, and riffs. In fact, as a sophomore, Inada transferred to University of California–Berkeley, where he had the opportunity to see many of the legends of jazz performing at the Blackhawk Club. In a section of *Legends from Camp* (1992) called "Jazz," Inada relates that one night during

intermission he found Billie Holiday outside behind the club and asked for her autograph. She wrote, "*For Lawson / Sincerely / Billie Holiday* And before he knew it, he was writing poetry" (59).

In 1959 Inada earned his BA from Fresno State University, studying poetry under **Philip Levine**. He then spent some time at the Iowa Writers Workshop, where he met his future wife Janet. After teaching at the University of New Hampshire for a few years, he returned to the West Coast, earning his MFA from the University of Oregon in 1966. Shortly thereafter, he took a position at Southern Oregon University (then Southern Oregon State College), where he continues to teach writing and literature and write poetry. Acccording to Holliday, "In Ashland, he not only helped his wife raise two sons, Miles and Lowell—named after jazz trumpeter Miles Davis and poet **Robert Lowell**—but he has also forged a name for himself as the central poet, historian, and scholar of the Japanese-American internment experience" (17). Inada's critical work has been instrumental in helping to form the Asian American literary canon. His first book, *Before the War: Poems as They Happened* (1971), was also the first book-length volume of Asian American poetry to be published by a major New York publishing house. In 1974 he helped collect and publish the first anthology of Asian American writers, *Aiiieeeee!* He has also edited and written introductions for reprints of work by John Okada and Toshio Mori.

With his poetry, Lawson Fusao Inada demonstrates that the sights and sounds of the internment are as much a part of the American scene as is jazz. His blending of personal accounts and observation with a jazz- and blues-influenced style produces a unique and rich experience for readers, not just of poetry but of history and culture as well.

Further Reading. Selected Primary Sources: Inada, Lawson Fusao, *Before the War: Poems as They Happened* (New York: Morrow, 1971); ———, *Drawing the Line* (Minneapolis, MN: Coffee House, 1997); ———, *Legends from Camp* (Minneapolis, MN: Coffee House, 1992); *Only What We Could Carry: The Japanese American Interment Experience* (Berkeley, CA: Heyday Books, 2000); Inada, Lawson Fusao, with Chin et al., *Aiiieeeee! An Anthology of Asian-American Writers* (Washington, DC: Howard University Press, 1974). **Selected Secondary Sources:** Holliday, Shawn, *Lawson Fusao Inada* (Boise, ID: Boise State University, 2003); Salisbury, Ralph, "Dialogue with Lawson Fusao Inada" (*Northwest Review* 20.2–3 [1982]: 60–75); Sato, Gayle K., "Lawson Inada's Poetics of Relocation: Weathering, Nesting, Leaving the Bough" (*Amerasia Journal* 26.3 [2000–2001]: 139–161).

Carol N. Moe

INDEPENDENCE POEM.
SEE LITERARY INDEPENDENCE POEM

INTENTIONAL FALLACY

Coined by American literary critics and theorists W.K. Wimsatt (1907–1975) and Monroe C. Beardsley (1915–1985) in a co-authored article that was first published in the *Sewanee Review* in 1946, the "intentional fallacy" is one of two fallacies they suggested are responsible for drawing attention away from the text itself in the critical study of poetry. According to their formulation, it is fundamentally wrong to propose that an author's intentions—deduced from biographical or contextual sources—can explain a poem's meaning. At the same time, they believed it is ultimately misguided to suggest that the impact (or "affect") a poem has upon a reader or audience is related to its meaning. To assess the value of a literary work in terms of the (emotional) response of the reader, they claim, is to commit the "affective fallacy" in critical reading.

Wimsatt and Beardsley's ideas may be read in terms of the development of Anglo-American formalist criticism and theory during the first half of the twentieth century, and as part of the advancement of the **New Criticism** in particular. In their essay on the intentional fallacy, they cite several examples of the kind of approach to poetry they sought to dismantle, including John Livingstone Lowes' study of Samuel Taylor Coleridge's "Kubla Khan" (*The Road to Xanadu*) and Charles M. Coffin's study of John Donne (*John Donne and the New Philosophy*), both published in 1927. In these studies Wimsatt and Beardsley saw examples of critics who foregrounded what they presumed to know about authorial intention instead of focusing on evidence encountered in the primary texts themselves. As they put it in their examination of Lowes's study, "There is a gross body of life, of sensory and mental experience, which lies behind and in some sense causes every poem, *but it can never be and need not be known in the verbal and hence intellectual composition which is the poem*" (Wimsatt, 12; emphasis added). Focusing critical attention on the text itself by ruling out biographical and other information about an author, the intentional fallacy became a central tool in the development of New Critical analysis, as exemplified in the 1930s and 1940s by the writings of such figures as **John Crowe Ransom** (1888–1974), **Allen Tate** (1899–1979), and other members of the **Agrarian School**.

In essence, these and other critics, in repudiating the intentional fallacy, encourage readers to consider the poem as a self-contained artifact instead, a "verbal icon," as Wimsatt put it, in which the reader can find all of the information needed to discuss a poem's meaning. This approach raises difficult questions about the evasion of context in New Critical (and Agrarian) discourse, however, and the sense of the poem as a hermetically sealed container unrelated to any of its contexts (biographical, historical, political, cultural) is very difficult to maintain beyond a certain point in literary study. Having said that, the ideas about intention and affect raised by Wimsatt and Beardsley are encountered wherever poetry is read, and they remain useful in redirecting attention toward the text both in the classroom and in the advanced (critical) study of poetry. In recent years, moreover, a number of critics have used Wimsatt and Beardsley's ideas as a basis from which to explore the relationship between autobiography and literary production, as well as the problem of evaluating the extent to which an individual reader or audience creates the meaning of a literary work. The concept of the intentional fallacy has stimulated a great deal of debate since it was first elaborated in the 1940s. As Stephen Matterson and Darryl Jones observe, "the ideal of free-standing autonomy for the poem is an important ideal. But the act of interpretive reading necessarily, and rightly, disrupts any sense of the poem as an object" (90).

Further Reading. *Selected Primary Source:* Wimsatt, W.K., *The Verbal Icon: Studies in the Meaning of Poetry* (1954; Lexington: University of Kentucky Press, 1967). *Selected Secondary Sources:* Lang, Berel, "The Intentional Fallacy Revisited" (*British Journal of Aesthetics* 14 [1974]: 306–314); Matterson, Stephen, and Darryl Jones, *Studying Poetry* (New York: Oxford University Press, 2000); Tung, Chung-Hsuan, "'The Intentional Fallacy' Reconsidered" (*Tamkang Review* 21.4 [Summer 1991]: 377–389).

Philip Coleman

IRISH POETRY

The relationship of Irish poetry to American poetry is complex: a straightforward lineage from poet to poet in some cases, while in others it is more a mirroring of two literary traditions developing under their own unique influences. Common themes, such as the search for an authentic local voice or regional identity, can be identified in both traditions with no particular evidence that one swayed the other, as can the more global themes of war, loss and death, and love and human relationships. The masses of Irish immigrants to the United States over the centuries have certainly exerted an influence on the American voice, and American poetry movements have been interpreted by various Irish writers and reframed within their own experience. The poet **Eavan Boland** has suggested that the primary distinction between Irish writing and American is that the American poet quintessentially views himself as isolated, whereas the Irish poet has a fierce connection to a communal, oral past. However, the Irish and American verse traditions have each influenced the other, and within American poetry some subgroups certainly share a significant Irish heritage or traits.

The earliest-known Irish poems date to the fifth century, as Christian missionaries arrived, bringing with them not only Christian themes and images but also bookmaking. In monasteries all over Ireland, monks and scribes captured the previously orally based verses of the Irish people, even as new, Christian concepts infiltrated the work of the poets of that time. Strongly vernacular in character, early Irish verse is full of short, musical lyrics, often on religious subjects or musings on nature. However, early Irish verse is probably most famous for lengthy sagas, such as the Fenian cycle and the Táin Bó Cúailnge, and the tale of Cuchullain, an Irish Achilles figure.

Ireland had a system of Bardic verse that lasted through the seventeenth century. Bards were a caste of men, not unlike modern-day journalists, who chronicled the deeds of heroes and the histories of peoples and places, using what became a fairly strict rulebook with regard to formal convention, phrasing, alliteration, and the like. Satirists, historians, celebrants, and hurlers of invective, bards held places of honor in Irish society. Bardic verses were often written for a single occasion and recited once to the accompaniment of a lyre or harp, never to be written down. This fundamentally oral nature is arguably responsible for the strong musicality of Irish writing, and its social stature as a "folk" poetry of local people and places was foundational to the later notion of "poetry of place." Its most lingering contribution to the body of Irish literature is probably the Metrical Dindshenchas, a body of place-lore poems that commemorate local myths and naming legends of many significant places in Ireland.

Irish verses written in English appeared around the fourteenth century, and for several hundred years the two traditions moved forward side by side with relatively little cross-pollination. Over time social and political changes had an almost devastating impact on the Irish language, and Anglo Irish writers came to dominate poetry writing. Bardic poetry began to disappear as its original patrons in the Celtic aristocracy were stripped of their power. Irish became the language of the outcast both in literature and in society.

In the late nineteenth century, however, a Celtic revival produced an important fusion of English language with Irish themes, forms, and folklore. The primary force behind this movement was William Butler Yeats. Though he never spoke Irish, his early poetry draws heavily on Celtic images, folk legends, and the Fenian cycle. One of the most influential poets of the late Romantic period and into the Modern era, Yeats was deeply interested in French Symbolism, as well as in theater and in politics (he served the Irish Free State as a senator). Also a devoted occultist, he was influenced by his study of Blake and Emmanuel Swedenborg and by his associations with Theosophist Helena Blavatsky and Golden Dawn founder MacGregor Mathers.

Yeats exerted a strong influence over the work of two of the most influential poets in American history, **Ezra Pound** and **T.S. Eliot** (as well as the Irish poet and novelist James Joyce). Both Eliot and Pound considered Yeats to be the greatest living poet of their time, and both they and Joyce were motivated, in some part, by the desire to compete with Yeats. The influence was reciprocal; Yeats's work after 1910 certainly displays the influence of Pound, who had served as Yeats's personal secretary for a time. Pound introduced Yeats to the work of many prominent modernist poets, and from his 1916 book *Responsibilities and Other Poems* onward, Yeats's work evinces a strong modernist influence.

Although Irish modernism was ultimately to be guided more by Joyce's work than by Yeats's, his earlier, Celtic mode proved extremely influential to the next generation of Irish writers, including Padric Collum, Brian Coffey, and Austin Clarke, and to several groups of American writers in the twentieth century.

Yeats was a key figure for poets of the American "middle generation." For **Robert Lowell** and **John Berryman**, he provided an exciting model for a poetry that embraced traditional forms and rhythms but had a modern flavor. For **Theodore Roethke**, Yeats's sense of the poet as a visionary was foundational, and he explicitly saw Yeats as his personal literary ancestor. Yeats's sense of poetry as revelatory and exalted, his flair for the dramatic, and his embrace of the occult made him a critical precursor for **James Merrill**'s masterpiece *The Changing Light at Sandover*. The lyrical Yeatsian influence is also discernible in the early poems of **Sylvia Plath** and of **W.S. Merwin**.

Yeats's book *A Vision*, concerning his and his wife's spiritualistic experiences, helped to engender a new sense of a poetry of the unconscious that would prove seminal for **Deep Image** poets, such as **Robery Bly**, **James Wright**, and **Mark Strand** (who also drew heavily on the work of Federico Garcia Lorca). The energy Yeats found in French Symbolism, which had also been important for Eliot, carried over to the Deep Image writers and fed the "leaping" quality sought by Bly.

American poets have certainly influenced their counterparts in Ireland as well. Patrick Pearce drew on the work of **Walt Whitman**. Geoffrey Squires was influenced by **Charles Olson**. Eoghan O Tuairisc/Eugene Watters (1919–1982) wrote *The Weekend of Dermot and Grace* (1964), which has a clear antecedent in T.S. Eliot's *The Waste Land*. Thomas Kinsella, whose early work was more influenced by **W.H. Auden**, exhibits the influence of Pound in his later poems, with their looser metrical structure and use of imagery.

Aside from the large number of American poets who specifically owe a debt to Yeats, there are other groups of American poets whose work harks back to pre-Yeatsian Irish poetry conventions, specifically, to the bardic system. Eavan Boland has remarked on the similarities between the Irish bards and the poets of the **Harlem Renaissance**; for instance, **Langston Hughes** shared the bardic interest in musicality, in chronicling the experiences of local people and places. Whitman, **Hart Crane**, and **William Carlos Williams** are all commonly referred to as having a "bardic" voice, and their epic poems carry the Irish echoes of breath-based meter, an exalted tone, and thechronicling of a local "hero."

The Beat generation writers, as well as other "rebel" poet groups of the 1950s, very often referred to themselves as "bardic." Their version of bardic verse, which drew more directly from Pound, Whitman, and Williams, was, like the writing of the Harlem Renaissance, poetry of an explicitly and uniquely American voice and experience and had little to do with the specific images, phrasings, foundational mythologies, or forms of the Celtic version. However, there are distinct, if not always explicitly intended, echoes of those forms. **Beat poetry** shared the vernacular, oral, performance-oriented quality of the original bardic poets, and Beat writers such as **Jack Spicer** and **Richard Brautigan** often composed extemporaneously to the accompaniment of jazz combos in place of the harp and lyre. **Allen Ginsberg** composed according to what he called the Hebraic-bardic breath.

In the 1960s and coincident with the rise of the Troubles in Northern Ireland, a group of Ulster poets began to receive critical and public attention. Prominent among these were Michael Longley (born in 1939), **Seamus Heaney** (born in 1939), and **Paul Muldoon** (born in 1951). Longley and Heaney share a formal conservatism and a willingness to engage with the difficult political situation in Northern Ireland. Robert Lowell deemed Heaney "the most important Irish poet since Yeats," and he is quite probably the most popular poet writing in English today. His earliest influences, **Robert Frost** and Ted Hughes, can be seen throughout his work, which has the commemorative, elegiac, and regional qualities that define so much of Irish writing. Heaney is also known for his influential essays that often meditate upon the intersection of poetry, landscape, and politics. Heaney was awarded the Nobel Prize in 1995 and currently lectures at Harvard. Muldoon, in whose wry humor one can likewise see echoes of Robert Frost, has also been a celebrated and influential poet in the United States and was awarded a Pulitzer Prize (2003) for *Moy Sand and Gravel*, a Guggenheim fellowship, and other distinctions.

He teaches at Princeton University. His work is far more formally experimental than that of Heaney or Boland, combining conventional poetic forms, popular culture, history, and playful but cunning wit.

Eavan Boland, born in Dublin in 1944, has been the most significant woman poet to emerge from Ireland in the second half of the twentieth century. A feminist, though, as she is quick to point out, not a feminist poet, she has nonetheless written on the difficulties faced by women writers in a male-dominated literary world. Boland currently teaches at Stanford University. Her work shows an abiding interest in Irish rhetoric and overstatement blended with an eagerness to find the "naked experience" that is the hallmark of a good lyric poem. She has commented incisively on the differences and similarities between Irish and American poetry and stands as an interesting example of a "hybrid" poet, who draws feely and extensively on her Irish roots but also opens herself to American modes of expression. Poets such as Boland, Muldoon, Kinsella, and Heaney, who all teach in American universities, are probably the most appreciable current link between the Irish verse tradition and verse writing in the United States.

Although, on the whole, American poetry has been far more experimental than Irish (Boland has commented that Ireland could never have produced a **Wallace Stevens**), Ireland's own commitment to its heritage and traditions has provided models for poetry writing that Americans of various regions and generations have used to frame their own contributions to the ongoing dialogue with the past in which all poetry is involved.

Further Reading. Bauer, Mark, *This Composite Voice: The Role of W.B. Yeats in James Merrill's Poetry* (New York: Routledge, 2003); Buxton, Rachel, *Robert Frost and Northern Irish Poetry* (Oxford: Oxford University Press, 2004); Curtis, Tony, *The Art of Seamus Heaney* (Bridgend, Wales: Seren Books, 2001); Hagen, Patricia, *Eavan Boland and the History of the Ordinary* (Bethesda, MD:Academica Press, 2004); Kinsella, Thomas, ed., *The New Oxford Book of Irish Verse* (Oxford: Oxford University Press, 2001); Matthews, Steven, *Yeats as Precursor: Readings in Irish, British, and American Poetry* (New York: St. Martin's Press, 2000); Trumpener, Katie, *Bardic Nationalism* (Princeton, NJ: Princeton University Press, 1997).

Amy Glynn Graecen

J

JACKSON, HELEN HUNT (1830–1885)

Although Helen Hunt Jackson's writing was widely known among American readers of her time, and indeed was admired and promoted by **Ralph Waldo Emerson**, other late nineteenth-century writers such as **Emily Dickinson** and **Walt Whitman** eventually eclipsed Jackson's work, particularly for twentieth-century readers. In addition to poetry, Jackson wrote stories for children, articles for periodicals, and novels. Toward the end of her life, Jackson became a strong advocate for the improved treatment of Native Americans by the government. For this cause, she wrote *A Century of Dishonor* (1881), a book that she sent to every member of Congress, admonishing them to look at their hands, "stained with the blood of their relations." Unfortunately, the impact of the book was negligible. Jackson's most influential book was *Ramona*, a regional novel about a young woman of mixed heritage. As a Native American, Ramona becomes a target for prejudice and mistreatment in mid- to late-nineteenth-century California. *Ramona* was adapted to film four times before 1930, and the novel's influence upon American culture persists into the twenty-first century.

Born Helen Maria Fiske in Amherst, Massachusetts, Jackson was the child of Nathan and Deborah Fiske. Both parents were orthodox Calvinists; both were writers; and Nathan was a professor of Latin and Greek at Amherst College. So it is in Jackson's childhood that one can see two influences that will persist throughout her life: the ancient classics and spirituality.

The normalcy of Jackson's childhood was altered by the death of her parents when she was a teenager. Personal tragedy continued to haunt Jackson after she married Edward Hunt in 1852. One of their sons died in his infancy. Jackson's husband was killed in an accident while conducting research in naval weaponry, and the Hunts' surviving son died two years later. Helen M. Bannan argues that Jackson "turned to writing poetry as an outlet for her grief" (Adamson, 373).

Although Emily Dickinson was a lifelong friend of Jackson, it was **Thomas Wentworth Higginson** who brought recognition to her poetry and acted as a mentor to her. Ralph Waldo Emerson helped in spreading Jackson's fame, by reciting some of her poems in his public readings and selecting five of them for publication in his anthology *Parnassus*. Among those five poems was "Ariadne's Farewell."

In the first two quatrains of the Shakespearean sonnet "Ariadne's Farewell," the persona (Ariadne) voices her distress over the naiveté that allowed her to believe the deceitful promises of Theseus, with whom she had fallen in love. According to Greek mythology, Theseus had promised to marry Ariadne in return for her supplying him with a ball of thread, by which he escaped the labyrinth of King Minos and the dreaded Minotaur. After his escape, Theseus abandons Ariadne.

In the third quatrain of the sonnet, the tone changes as Ariadne bids Theseus, "Go free, if scorn can yield / Thee freedom!" amid the imagery of a bright sun breaking its golden lances on the sea's blue shield. This imagery evokes the hopelessness of Ariadne's love but also two gods: Poseidon, god of the sea and father of Theseus, and Athena, virgin goddess of war. The closing couplet suggests not mere grief but a noble death for Ariadne—suicide.

In Jackson's posthumously published *Poems*, the thirteen-line poem "*Emigravit*" (he has departed) stands out for the peculiarity of its form and its New World theme. The iambic pentameter and rhyme scheme of the opening quatrain of this poem would suggest a sonnet, but where one expects the second quatrain, there is only a three-line stanza, leaving the poem one line short of a standard sonnet and foreshadowing the *this-story-is-unfinished* theme of the poem. Using the imagery of ships, sails, the weighing of an anchor, and "glad farewells," the vision evoked by this first quatrain and the three lines that follow is one of emigration to America as the promised land. In the sestet, the poem conflates America with a spiritual destination, ending with the couplet, "Oh, write of me, not 'Died in bitter pains,' / But 'Emigrated to another star!'"

"*Emigravit*" also stands out because of its intertextuality. Two lines in **Henry Wadsworth Longfellow**'s "Nuremburg" echo the closing sentiment and some of the language of Jackson's "*Emigravit.*" Longfellow's lines refer to "*Emigravit*" as the inscription on a tomb-stone, indicating that he who lies within is not dead but departed, since the "artist never dies." Interestingly, Jackson's first novel *Mercy Philbrick's Choice* (1876) ends with the poem "*Emigravit*" being carved on Mercy's tombstone. Finally, Kate Phillips reports that Jackson herself "left instructions to have the word '*Emigravit*' engraved on her tombstone" (112).

Jackson (going by the name "Hunt" prior to this point) was remarried in 1875 to William Sharpless Jackson. A financier, William Jackson had worked in the railroad industry before starting the El Paso County Bank. William and Helen would be married for almost ten years, during which time Helen would become an advocate and activist for the better treatment of Native Americans.

In 1879 Jackson met Susette "Bright Eyes" LaFlesche, a teacher, translator, and member of the Omaha tribe. LaFlesche was to kindle a passion for the reform of government policy toward Native Americans in the heart of Jackson. Dissatisfied with the progress made toward bringing about positive change for Native Americans by two works of nonfiction she had published, Jackson

changed her approach and wrote *Ramona*, which was first serialized in 1884 and later published as a novel. In the year of Jackson's death, *Ramona* reached best-seller status. *Ramona* remains the brightest gem in the literary legacy of Helen Hunt Jackson, if only because it has been regularly reprinted during the 115 years since its initial publication.

Jackson died of cancer in 1885.

Though lacking the unconventional genius of Walt Whitman or Emily Dickinson, Jackson became a literary darling of late-nineteenth-century America. In a nation repairing itself from the ravages of the Civil War, much of her poetry and fiction resonated with a large segment of the American public. Today, the pageants and other cultural events spawned by *Ramona* stand as a testament to the character of Helen Hunt Jackson and to her place in history as a writer.

Further Reading. *Selected Primary Sources:* Jackson, Helen, *Bits of Travel at Home by H.H.* (Boston: Roberts Brothers, 1878); ———, *A Century of Dishonor: A Sketch of the United States Government's Dealings with Some of the Indian Tribes* (Norman: University of Oklahoma Press, 1995); ———, *Poems* (Boston: Roberts Brothers, 1895); ———, *Ramona: A Story* (Boston: Little, Brown, 1939); ———, *Saxe Holm's Stories* (Freeport, NY: Books for Libraries Press, 1971). ***Selected Secondary Sources:*** Bannan, Helen M., "Helen Maria Fiske Hunt Jackson," in *American Women Writers: A Critical Reference Guide from Colonial Times to the Present*, vol. 2., ed. Lina Mainiero (New York: Frederick Unger, 1980); Odell, Ruth, *Helen Hunt Jackson (H.H.)* (New York: Appleton-Century, 1939); Phillips, Kate, *Helen Hunt Jackson: A Literary Life* (Berkeley: University of California Press, 2003).

Bruce A. Erickson

JACKSON, LAURA [RIDING]. *SEE* RIDING [JACKSON], LAURA

JACKSON, RICHARD (1946–)

Richard Jackson is a poet, editor, translator, and critic whose work demonstrates a philosophical and historical consciousness applied to a Romantic vision of the contemporary world. This world is presented in his poetry by a focus upon a significant moment or memory. Highly acclaimed among his contemporaries, Jackson's passionate, intelligent, and humanist voice has, for over thirty years, enriched American poetry. Richard Jackson was born in Lawrence, Massachusetts, in 1946. After obtaining a BA from Merrimack College (1969) and an MA from Middlebury College (1972), he taught high school English for a few years. In 1976 he received a Ph.D. in English from Yale and in the same year joined the English faculty of the University of Tennessee at

Chattanooga. He is currently a U.C. Foundation Professor of English there teaching creative writing and the literature of Western civilization. Married for the second time, he lives in Chattanooga. Jackson has received many research fellowships and awards for his poetry, criticism, and teaching. An active defender of human rights in the Balkan region, Jackson received the Order of Freedom Award from the president of Slovenia in 2000.

Jackson published his first book of poetry, *Part of the Story,* in 1983. The poems of this volume deal with communication and its philosophical resonance in the contemporary world. Among his themes are the human inability to make any conclusive statement about anything, even in intimate situations, and the elusive nature of language as a medium for emotion. Although poststructuralism is clearly a major philosophical influence, the poet also portrays the post-confessional self in its problematic relationship to the real and imagined other. In 1987 Jackson published a second book of poetry, *Worlds Apart,* in which his preoccupation with language as an imperfect medium remains evident. In "How Far the Light Travels," the speaker and his lover meet "between / two words barely holding / the night together." The inevitable misrepresentation of feeling is compounded by Jackson's sense of a personal history beyond retrieval, when the speaker asks how far light travels across "the salt hay, across the spaces / we invent as we name our pasts." In the title poem, "Worlds Apart," the solitary speaker tearfully registers the motherly instincts of the killdeer and the love offered by human strangers to a beggar on the street. Such love is problematic, however, for it estranges the giver. He suggests that there is no "love that doesn't lead us, sometimes / deftly, further from ourselves."

Although a sense of human imperfection and inability to communicate pervades Jackson's poetry, his voice is anything but sentimental—it affirms existence, emotion, and history in the very act of exposing their precariousness. In his third collection, *Alive All Day* (1992), Jackson's poetic line gets longer and the poems more discursive and generous, accommodating the poet's broadening sense of private and public history that slips through his fingers. In "The Angels of 1912 and 1972," a gallery of deceased family members, friends, and poets is presented through the epiphany of an expanded moment. Painful memories are, by the poem's end, transmuted into a passionate rhetoric that celebrates human ability to love and remember. Such an act of remembrance is finally likened to angelic flying. In the final poem of the book, "Acknowledgements," Jackson acknowledges once again inevitable incompleteness, thanking the chaotic neurons of our brains for their capacity to "respond to stimuli flexibly and so to create / an order for what we never understand."

Jackson has long been interested in translating Italian and Slovene poetry. In 2000 he published a chapbook of Petrarchan adaptations, *Heart's Bridge: Poems Based on Petrarch.* In the same year, he published the book of poems *Heartwall,* for which he won the Juniper Prize. The collection, titled after a poem by Paul Celan, is both elegiac and hopeful. It combines satirical, lyrical, and surrealist approaches to reality. The thematic scope is broadened to include the war in Yugoslavia of the early 1990s. In "No Turn on Red," a deceptively simple traffic sign of a title hides a large poem that incorporates twentieth-century war, suffering, and forgiveness for all parties concerned; the poem compares our lives to dumpsters that "are filling with more mistakes / than we could ever measure." Through all this history of evil, nevertheless, truth "leaves its fingerprints on everything we do."

In 2003 Jackson published a volume of selected and new poems, *Unauthorized Autobiography,* which constitutes a powerful testament to the author's thematic range and control as well as a monumental celebration of the human heart. In "Read Everything Before Doing Anything," the poet contemplates time and mortality: "the moon no longer breathes in my pockets. / The soul's ravens gather on my phone lines." In "Rift," he is reminded that "our internal organs, / the heart included, operate entirely in the dark." It is this clumsy groping in the dark for truth, love, and memory that makes the world, according to these poems, so much worth inhabiting.

Jackson is also a critic and an accomplished editor of poetry **translations**. In 1983 he published *Acts of Mind: Conversations with Contemporary Poets,* a volume collecting his interviews that had mostly appeared in *Poetry Miscellany*—a journal he founded in the 1970s and has edited ever since. Many of the poets note the interviewer's brilliant questions that made them think about their work in new and unexpected ways. Jackson himself admits that as an interviewer, he tries to synthesize the self and other of the language of poetry and criticism. The resulting interviews shed light on both the work of the individual poets and the paths of the creative process. In 1988 a volume on the phenomenology of the epiphanic moment in several American poets, *The Dismantling of Time in Contemporary Poetry,* was published.

Further Reading. *Selected Primary Sources:* Jackson, Richard, *Acts of Mind: Conversations with Contemporary Poets* (Tuscaloosa: University of Alabama Press, 1983); ———, *Alive All Day* (Cleveland: Cleveland State University Press, 1992);———, *The Dismantling of Time in Contemporary Poetry* (Tuscaloosa: University of Alabama Press, 1988); ———, *Half Lives* (Montpelier, VT: Invisible Cities Press, 2002); ———, *Heart's Bridge: Poems Based on Petrarch* (Toledo, OH: Aureole Press, 2000); ———, *Heartwall* (Amherst: University of

Massachusetts Press, 2000); ———, *Part of the Story* (New York: Grove Press, 1983); ———, *Selected Poems* (Ljubljana, Slovenia: Slovene Writers' Union, 2001); ———, *Unauthorized Autobiography: New and Selected Poems* (Ashland, OR: Ashland Poetry Press, 2003); ———, *Worlds Apart* (Tuscaloosa: University of Alabama Press, 1987). *Selected Secondary Source:* Uschuk, Pamela, "Vitality and Vulnerability" (*Tucson Weekly Online* [3 January 2002]).

Jiri Flajsar

JACOBSEN, JOSEPHINE (1908–2003)

Josephine Jacobsen did not achieve widespread recognition for her poetry until she was in her sixties and seventies. During her lifetime, Jacobsen published nine books of poetry, two books of criticism, and four collections of short fiction. She did not teach or become involved extensively in the literary world until 1971, at the age of sixty-three, when she was named Consultant in Poetry to the Library of Congress.

Jacobsen was born Josephine Winder Boylan in Cobourg, Ontario, Canada, on August 19, 1908. Her family moved to the United States three months later. She was educated privately and then graduated in 1926 from Roland Park Country School in Baltimore, which ended her formal education. Jacobsen began writing at an early age and had her first poem published in *St. Nicholas*, a children's magazine, when she was eleven. The idea of loss, which runs through many of Jacobsen's poems, can likely be traced to the death of her father when she was five. In 1932, at the age of twenty-four, she married Eric Jacobsen, a tea importer. The couple lived in Baltimore, but spent half of each year in New Hampshire. They had one son, Eric, who survives along with several grandchildren.

Jacobsen gained critical attention with *Let Each Man Remember* (1940), her first publication, which consisted of fifteen love sonnets and metaphysical love poems. She followed this book with the intensely personal verses of *The Human Climate: New Poems* (1953) and *The Animal Inside* (1966). Jacobsen's early poems adhered to a strict and conventional metrical form; she later wrote according to the unique demands of the individual poem using very free forms but always imbuing the poems with structure and rhythm. Jacobsen's poetry is stark and **minimalist**. Her spare diction unites the passionate commitment of **Louise Bogan** with the precision and compactness of **Elizabeth Bishop** and **Marianne Moore**. Jacobsen uses a subtle, meticulous style in her early poems, which conceals her debts to many major poets. Jacobsen reported being nourished and influenced by **W.H. Auden**, W.B. Yeats, and **A.R. Ammons**. Her use of humor and irony, characteristics she admired in Auden's work, surface in poems such as "Pondicherry Blues" from *In the Crevice of Time: New and Collected Poems* (1995).

Jacobsen received much critical praise and long overdue recognition during the last thirty years of her life following her appointment as Consultant in Poetry. The pinnacle of her success occurred when she was awarded the Lenore Marshall Prize for *The Sisters: New and Selected Poems*, which was cited as the outstanding book of poems published in the United States by an American in 1987. Jacobsen explores the relation of self-consciousness and representation in her poem "In the Crevice of Time" from this book. The poem—reminiscent of Bishop's work in its depiction not only of the object world but also of the subjectivity perceiving it—has a hunter priest looking at his cave painting of the hunt. What he sees is not the "shank or horn or hide" of the animal, the supposed object of his effort, but rather "an arrangement of these by him, and he himself / there with them, watched by himself inside."

Jacobsen's skill in metaphor is evidenced in *The Chinese Insomniacs* (1981), a previous runner up for the Lenore Marshall Prize. In one of the poems, "Bush," the speaker sees the ribbed "drum of the zebra's body /. . . lined with red sunrise," after the lions have fed on it. Jacobsen relates the zebra's blood to the cosmic source of the sunrise rather than to the lion's ravaging of the corpse.

The other, less prominent aspect of Jacobsen's life as a writer relates to her short stories and her criticism. Her second collection of short stories, *On the Island: New and Selected Short Stories* (1989), was one of five nominees for the PEN/Faulkner Award for Fiction. Like her poetry, Jacobsen's stories are subdued and minimalist, dealing with chaos, riot, and murder but in a quiet voice. Several of the stories are set in the Caribbean island of Boudina and show the tragedies that arise when two cultures clash.

In her two books of criticism, *Ionesco and Genet: Playwrights of Silence* and *The Testament of Samuel Beckett*, which were co-authored by William Randolph Mueller, Jacobsen uses her poetic insight to focus on Beckett, Ionesco, and Genet as poets working within the theater of the absurd. It is Jacobsen's appreciation for what she views as Beckett's poetic achievement in his novels that brings her to explore the very different ways in which these three writers use the grimness of the humor and language.

Jacobsen held many important positions in addition to serving as Consultant in Poetry from 1971 to 1973. She served as honorary consultant in American letters from 1973 to 1979 and worked with the Library of Congress in Washington, D.C., from 1973 to 1979. She was the vice president of the Poetry Society of America in 1979 and a member of the literary panel for the National Endowment for the Arts from 1979 to 1983. Among the many awards and honors Jacobsen received are the Borestone Mountain Award (1961, 1964, 1968, and

1972); the MacDowell Colony grant (1973, 1974, 1976, 1978, 1981, and 1983); the Prairie Schooner Award for fiction (1974 and 1986); the Yaddo grant (1975, 1977, 1980, 1982, and 1984); the American Academy Award (1982 and 1984); the Academy of American Poets fellowship (1987); the Shelley Memorial Award for lifetime service to literature from the Poetry Society of America (1992); and induction into the American Academy of Arts and Letters (1994). Jacobsen was also awarded honorary doctorates in Humane Letters from Goucher College (1974), the College of Notre Dame in Maryland (1974), Towson State University (1983), and Johns Hopkins University (1993). She was also awarded a Master of Divinity degree from St. Mary's Seminary College in 1988.

Josephine Jacobsen received the majority of her acclaim in the last third of her life and has yet to achieve canonical status; however, her short stories, criticism, and, particularly, poetry continue to be appreciated and valued. Whether or not her work is included in the chief anthologies, the accessibility of Jacobsen's minimalist style and the warmth and nuance of her poems will assure her a place within the world of American poetry.

Further Reading. *Selected Primary Sources:* Jacobsen, Josephine, *The Chinese Insomniacs* (Philadelphia: University of Pennsylvania Press, 1981); ———, *In the Crevice of Time: New and Collected Poems* (Baltimore: Johns Hopkins University Press, 1995); ———, *On the Island* (Princeton, NJ: Ontario Review Press, 1989); ———, *The Sisters: New and Selected Poems* (Columbia, SC: Bench Press, 1987); Jacobsen, Josephine, and William Randolph Mueller, *Ionesco and Genet: Playwrights of Silence* (New York: Hill and Wang, 1968); ———, *The Testament of Samuel Beckett* (New York: Hill and Wang, 1964). ***Selected Secondary Sources:*** Christie, A.V., "A Conversation with Josephine Jacobsen" (*Image: A Journal of the Arts & Religion* 23 [1999]: 45–61); ———, *The Instant of Knowing* (Washington, DC: Library of Congress, 1974).

Alisa M. Smith-Riel

JAPANESE POETRY

The word "influence" denotes an act of flowing in or inflowing, literally the path of one river flowing into another. Therefore, in order to trace the influences of Japanese culture, poetry, and aesthetics as they move into American letters, one must locate the textual tributaries and estuaries through which these waters meet and infuse one another. While these meeting points stretch back to periods before the nineteenth century, it was not until the beginning of the twentieth century that the flowering of these influences resulted in a distinct and continuous impact on American poetry. From early twentieth-century **Imagism** to the mid-century **Beats**, to the contemporary poetry of Norman Fischer and **Kimiko**

Hahn, Japanese poetic and cultural forms have enriched American poetic content and forms. One can trace these poetic inflows from Japan to three distinct yet often interrelated tributaries: early *japonaiserie* or exoticized Japanese content, translation and adoption of aesthetic forms, and the integration of Japanese epistemological elements. Although these three tributaries basically follow a linear progression (content, form, epistemological integration), it is important to note that all three occur, to greater and lesser degrees, in each of the periods discussed here.

In the mid- to late- nineteenth century, after Commodore Perry forcibly opened Japan for trade in 1854, American interest in things Japanese began to increase as trans-Pacific interactions between the two nations became more frequent. Yet most of the Japanese influences in the nineteenth century were limited to poetic descriptions or treatments of Japanese themes and or images. Many of the most prominent American poets writing in the mid- to late nineteenth century wrote poems on Japanese themes forming a small but important poetic precedent for early-twentieth-century *japonaiserie*. **Walt Whitman**'s "A Broadway Pageant" (1860) describes the first diplomatic envoy from Japan within an American landscape:

Over the western sea, hither from Niphon come,
Courteous, the swart-cheek'd two-sworded envoys,
Leaning back in their open barouches, bare-headed, impassive,
Ride to-day through Manhattan.

Henry Wadsworth Longfellow enriches his pastoral poetics with a Japanese landscape in "Keramos" (1877):

Cradled and rocked in Eastern sea,
The islands of the Japanese
Beneath me lie; o'er lake and plain
The stork, the heron, and the crane.

At the century's end, the art historian and poet **Ernest Fenollosa**, whose posthumously published essay "The Chinese Written Character as a Medium for Poetry" was one of the primary vehicles of Chinese influence on American letters (*see* **Chinese Poetry**), also wrote poems, such as "Sonnet: Fuji at Sunrise" (1893), set within a Japanese landscape:

Startling the cool gray depths of morning air
She throws aside her counterpane of clouds,
And stands half folded in her silken shrouds
With calm white breast and snowy shoulder bare.

Yet arguably the most important turn-of-the-century tributary comes through the work of Lafcadio Hearn. Hearn's influence can be traced to the cumulative effect on Western readers of his many works about Japan, from his well-known *Glimpses of Unfamiliar Japan* (1894) to his posthumous *Japan: An Attempt at Interpretation* (1904). Hearn's work offered American poets a textual stream through which such "glimpses" of Japan began to accumulate and diffuse into the widening subgenre referred to as *japonaiserie.*

Although japonaiserie was a common feature in early-twentieth-century poetry, poets such as Amy Lowell, in her Imagist phase, brought this subgenre to perhaps its most refined level. One of Lowell's early poems, "A Japanese Wood-Carving," included in her first book of poetry, *A Dome of Many-Coloured Glass* (1912), attempts to transport the reader to a peaceful far-off land just as the woodblock served as a cultural portal to the East for Lowell as a child. The woodblock literally hangs over the open door of a "quiet, firelit room," promising "the freedom of earth's vast solitudes."

Japanese themes and landscapes continued to populate Lowell's work, through her *Lacquer Prints and Pictures of the Floating World* to the posthumous publication of *What's O'Clock. What's O'Clock* includes two poems, "Twenty-four Hokku on a Modern Theme" and "The Anniversary," which were constructed in the haiku form of five-seven-five syllable count, yet both poems move away from the themes and scenery of her earlier *japonaiserie* poetry as represented in "Twenty-four Hokku on a Modern Theme" (1921):

XVI
Last night it rained.
Now, in the desolate dawn,
Crying of blue jays. (442)

Over the last century, most Americans have become familiar with Japanese haiku. The haiku's popularity can be seen in its ubiquitous presence from elementary school classrooms to advertisements and online jokes. The appeal stems from its apparently simple form, which belies its complex dimensions and varied history. Historically, haiku were derived from the *haikai* or *renga* (a linked-verse poem), which was composed by a group of poets as a long series of short stanzas. The first short stanza was called a *hokku* ("starting verse"), which bore the responsibility of setting the tone for the whole poem. A *hokku* set this tone by referring to a specific season or place. Many poets wrote *hokku*, which led over time to a new genre by the seventeenth century but did not gain the name "haiku" until the mid-1890s. Bound as they were to this specific history, haiku required that the poet be familiar with its key components: *kigo* (season words), *kidai* (seasonal topics), and a "cutting word"

(often the word *ya),* which works as a punctuation point denoting the break in lines even when the lines are not formally broken on the page. Amy Lowell's use of the syllable count, therefore, does not represent traditional haiku but a hybrid poetic form imbuing short English verse with elements of Japanese prosody.

Although many of the nuances within haiku are not often strictly observed within English poetry, the more general characteristics of haiku played a very important role in the establishment of modern poetry and aesthetics. Many of the key modernist figures fell under the influence of the haiku aesthetic. **Ezra Pound**, the founder of the short-lived Imagist school, became the central tributary of East Asian influence in twentieth-century American poetry. In Pound's case, though his interest in Japanese poetry predates these contacts, one must mention his reading in 1911 of the work of **Yone Noguchi**, including haiku and writing on Japan, and his reading of the translations of Ernest Fenollosa, whose widow had sent Pound her husband's manuscript in 1913. In *Gaudier-Brzeska* (1916), Pound recounts the compositional process that led to one of his most famous Imagistic poems, "Station at the Metro" (1913). Pound describes how he wrote a thirty-line poem but destroyed it because he thought that it was a work "of second intensity." He then recalls that six months later he made a poem half as long and a year later wrote the "*hokku*-like sentence": "The apparition of these faces in the crowd: Petals, on a wet, black bough" (89). Pound further reveals the direct influence of Japanese poetic form on his work when, in the same work, he states, "The Japanese have had the sense of exploration. They have understood the beauty of this sort of knowing" (88). Pound describes how the Japanese *hokku* was, in fact, a shorter form of Chinese poetry, which itself represented a highly condensed and economical form. Pound cites the following haiku to compare to his own: "The fallen blossom flies back to its branch: A butterfly" (88).

Like this haiku, Pound's "Station at the Metro," imposes two distinct images ("faces in a crowd" and "petals on a wet, black bough") to reveal a single complex image, playing off the multidirectional ambiguity inherent in the word *apparition,* which connotes something seen, yet ghostly, something present, yet not fully real. Pound would later describe this technique as the *ideogrammic method,* which creates images through the combination of different images to create dense, complex ideas in a way similar to Fenollosa's discussion of Chinese **ideograms**.

Although most Imagist poetry did not employ formal Japanese poetic forms, many poems followed Pound's use of juxtaposed images as well as his dictum to present only the "things in themselves," resulting in an economic and concise language different from the Victorian verse forms still dominating mainstream verse culture.

Pound, **William Carlos Williams**, and others drew upon Asian verse forms as an alternative literary authority capable of contesting conventional versification in the West. Yet the Imagists are by no means the only tributary through which Japanese poetic forms have entered American letters. The move away from Victorian formalism to free verse, the move away from verbose **pastoral** poetry to a poetics of the everyday, and the emphasis on unexpected even jarring combinations all remain key ingredients to American poetry as a whole. This inheritance is apparent in the work of later poets such as **Larry Eigner**, whose work bears the qualities of Imagism and the later **Objectivists** as well as the detached observational quality of a generalized haiku aesthetic.

The haiku form continues to play a central role in American literary culture from the historically significant "Japanese internment camp Haiku," a collection of haiku written by Japanese Americans while imprisoned in World War II internment camps, to the ubiquitous creative writing assignment. More recently, poets from **Anne Waldman** to Kimiko Hahn have published English poems in other Japanese forms such as the *hai bun*, a hybrid form of prose and verse used by Bash in his *Narrow Road to the Interior.*

The last, yet equally important tributary of Japanese poetic influence arrives through the inflow of religious and philosophical migrations. By the mid-nineteenth century, Buddhist elements were already evident in American letters through the work of **Emerson, Thoreau**, and Whitman, but by the turn of the century, poets such as Fenollosa and Hearn were introducing Japanese Buddhism to Americans with far greater clarity than the Transcendentalists. Nevertheless, it was not until the English publications and missionary work of Japanese Buddhists, such as D.T. and Shunryo Suzuki, that American poets, en masse, would become familiar with Japanese Buddhism. By the mid-twentieth century, these tributaries had clearly begun to alter the mainstream of American poetry. In 1955 the Six Gallery reading in San Francisco officiated by **Kenneth Rexroth** included **Alan Ginsberg, Michael McClure, Phillip Whalen**, and **Gary Snyder**, with **Jack Kerouac** yelling "yeses" and "wows" from the sidelines. These poets, who would become known as the "Beats," integrated Buddhism into their poetry, their poetics, and their views of the self and the world.

Kenneth Rexroth served as a mentor to many of the poets at this reading and introduced a number of Americans to Japanese poetry and Buddhism, serving as an early link in the postwar crossroads between San Francisco and Kyoto. Ever since the publication of *One Hundred Poems from the Japanese* (1955), his work has been widely read. Over his long career Rexroth translated several volumes of poetry from Japanese, including a couple of hundred *tanka* (a short Japanese verse form generally of five lines), and attempted to write his own *tanka* in English. In fact, one can see many Japanese Buddhist references, images, and syntactic elements running through Rexroth's poems. One of the most dramatic instances of translation's transposition, however, occurs in his last major work, *The Love Poems of Marichiko*. Rexroth used the guise of **translation** to write through the voice of a Japanese woman what some have called a work of Buddhist sexual esoterica, personifying abstract ideas, such as desire, and embodying internal and external alchemical processes; other critics have argued that these imagined translations evoke a deplorable stereotype of hypersexualized Asian women. Most can agree, however, that the book represents a return to a "Buddhist flavored" *japonaiserie*. "The moon sinks into the far off hills. / Dew drenches the bamboo grass. . . . At midnight the temple bells ring" (*Marichiko*, XLIII).

Gary Snyder, who studied Buddhism in Japan for twelve years, continually infuses his poems with references to Zen terms, explanations of Buddhist concepts ("No Matter Never Mind"), and use of Buddhist notions of immanence to articulate his ecological politics ("No Nature"). Yet Snyder's integration of Buddhism also serves as a criterion for which poets he chooses to translate, leading to the popularity of Buddhist poets, such as Han Shan, in the United States who are considered less important in Asia. Snyder's own verse often resembles his translations by foregrounding visual elements and distrusting abstract, prosaic features, a reflection of Zen's general distaste for conceptual language as a medium of higher truths. Although similar to that of the Imagists, Snyder's emphasis on visual images is unique in that he continually links this aesthetic to Buddhist metaphysics by emphasizing the enlightening potential of everyday minutiae when foregrounded in the consciousness.

Phillip Whalen, who studied Buddhism in Japan before becoming an ordained monk in the Soto school of Zen and later the abbot of San Francisco Zen Monastery, also works Buddhist concepts, terms, and landscapes into his poetry. Whalen's notion that his poetry is a "picture or graph of a mind moving" (50) reflects a meditative, detached practice of mindfulness characteristic of Zen practice. Notice how he records the activity of his mind in his poem "April Showers Bring Rain?" as it comically moves from detailed, "zen like" observations to the banal interruption of everyday thoughts:

foot / feet
rain / tulip
    move the garbage
    away from the window. (120)

The Buddhist tributary moves beyond the boundaries of the "Beats" to include the chance operations of **John Cage** and **Jackson Mac Low**, the Buddhist ethnographic details of **Lucien Stryk**, **Garrett Hongo**, and Sam Hamill, and the language experimentation of **Leslie Scalapino** and Norman Fischer, among many others. In each of these cases, Buddhist cultural and epistemological practices lead to important developments within American poetry, a national poetry traditionally linked to the Judeo-Christian–based transatlantic canons rather than its more contemporary transpacific association. Even though few religions can claim to have the high profile Zen has enjoyed among American poets over the last century, their poetry is in no way homogeneous but, in fact, demonstrates a surprisingly diverse array of aesthetic and epistemological characteristics. Each poet draws upon the three cultural streams—content, form, and epistemology—in different ways, so while it is helpful to discuss them as distinct phenomena, one can easily see how each often includes elements of the other. What is certain is that Japanese influences have increasingly enriched and changed the shape and texture of American letters and will likely continue to do so for some time to come.

Further Reading. *Selected Primary Sources:* Cortazzi, Huge, and George Webb, *Kipling's Japan* (London: Athlone, 1988); Bash, Matsuo, *Narrow Road to the Interior*, trans. Sam Hamill (Boston: Shambhala, 1991); Eigner, Larry, *Selected Poems*, ed. Samuel Charters (Berkeley, CA: Oyez, 1972); Fenollosa, Ernest, "Fuji at Sunrise," in *The Discovery of America and Other Poems* (New York: Crowell, 1893); Hamill, Sam, *The Essential Bash* (Boston: Shambhala, 1999); Longfellow, Henry, *The Complete Poetical Works of Henry Wadsworth Longfellow* (New York: Buccaneer Books, 1993); Miner, Earl, *The Japanese Tradition in British and American Literature* (Princeton, NJ: Princeton University Press, 1958; rev. ed. 1966; reprint Westport, CT: Greenwood, 1976); Noguchi, Yone, *Japanese Hokkus* (Boston: Four Seas Company, 1920); Pound, Ezra, *Gaudier-Brzeska: A Memoir* (London: John Lane, 1916); Rexroth, Kenneth, *The Love Poems of Marichicko* (Santa Barbara, CA: Christopher's Books, 1978); ———, *One Hundred Poems from the Japanese* (New York: New Directions, 1955); Snyder, Gary, *The Gary Snyder Reader: Prose, Poetry, and Translations* (Washington, DC: Counterpoint, 1999); Whalen, Phillip, *Overtime: Selected Poems* (New York: Penguin Books, 1999); Whitman, Walt, *Complete Poetry and Selected Prose*, ed. James E. Miller (Boston: Houghton Mifflin, 1959); Qian, Zhaoming, *Orientalism and Modernism: The Legacy of China in Pound and Williams* (Durham, NC: Duke University Press, 1995).

Jonathan Stalling

JARRELL, RANDALL (1914–1965)

Randall Jarrell is remembered not only for his finely crafted poetry but also for his role as a public intellectual whose acerbic wit and critical acumen played no small part in establishing the **canon** of American poetry. A masterful stylist in both poetry and prose, Jarrell is best known for his war poems, which concern—as **James Dickey** writes—the hopes and fears of "the small man, the man 'things are done to.'" "The Death of the Ball Turret Gunner" is undoubtedly the most famous of them, ending as it does with the arresting and macabre phrase "When I died they washed me out of the turret with a hose." Unfortunately, Jarrell's war poems overshadow much of his other work, whether poetry or prose. This other work includes his wickedly comic novel *Pictures from an Institution* (1954); his sensitive translations of Goethe, the Grimm Brothers, Chekhov, and Rilke; his many fine essays; and—written in the final years of his life—four complex and touching children's books: *The Gingerbread Rabbit* (1964), *The Bat-Poet* (1964), *The Animal Family* (1965), and the posthumously published *Fly by Night* (1976).

Jarrell was born in Nashville, Tennessee, on May 6, 1914, to the young couple Owen and Anna Campbell Jarrell, twenty-four and twenty years old respectively. Immortalized long before he began writing poetry, Randall posed, when just a boy, for the figure of Ganymede in Nashville's Parthenon. However, his personal life was much less stable than that city monument. His parents' youth and financial troubles led them to separate repeatedly before their final breakup in 1926. Movement was the norm: Jarrell's mother relied on the financial assistance of relatives, which meant moving often from home to home. Considered a prodigy, young Randall read constantly, perhaps to provide some stability to this constantly fluctuating life.

Jarrell would tap his childhood and fashion it into art throughout his life. Indeed, one of his last books, *The Bat-Poet*, features a young bat who becomes a poet only after refusing to relocate with his family: "'What do you want to sleep in the barn for?' [the bat] asked them. 'We don't know,' the others said. 'What do you want to sleep on the porch for?' 'It's where we always sleep,' he said. 'If I slept in the barn I'd be homesick.'" As Richard Flynn has pointed out, over a third of the work in Jarrell's *Complete Poems* directly concerns childhood or children. Moreover, his last book, *The Lost World* (1965), involves the one childhood move that Randall did not regret: his year-long stay in Hollywood with his grandparents, whom he called Mama and Pop. This visit, from 1925 to 1926, ended abruptly with his parents' divorce. He begged his grandparents to allow him to stay, but, of course, they could not, leaving him with such feelings of betrayal that he refused future contact with them. He broke his silence on this matter in his final book, particularly in his three-part poem "The Lost World," in which he writes of his remorse at the pain he caused his grandparents by not writing to them. The title of this book refers both to childhood and to Harry O. Hoyt's silent picture of the same name. Hollywood no doubt seemed like a fairy tale world to young Randall, a world in which one might see dinosaurs and pterodactyls with "[p]apier-mâché smiles, look[ing] over the fence / Of *The Lost World.*"

After his parents' divorce, Randall was summoned back to Nashville, where he stayed with his mother and younger brother, Charles. As a senior in high school, Jarrell was already immensely well read and proving himself to be a capable writer. In 1931 after a fire destroyed his books, young Randall prepared a list of the destroyed or damaged books for an insurance claim. The list is impressive for its quality and diversity, containing such notable titles as Marcel Proust's *Swann's Way*; Lewis Carroll's *Alice's Adventures in Wonderland* and *Collected Verse*; Friedrich Nietzsche's *Thus Spake Zarathustra*; Mark Twain's *Adventures of Huckleberry Finn*; Jean Cocteau's *Enfants Terrible*; **T.S. Eliot**'s *Poems*; and Omar Khayyames *Rubaiyat*. During this time he was writing reviews for the Hume-Fogg High School yearbook, *Echo*, which showed budding wit and critical discernment, two qualities that would characterize his adult criticism.

Hoping that Jarrell would work for the family candy company, his Uncle Howell Campbell sent Jarrell to a commercial school to study accounting, despite Jarrell's interest in literature and drama. So serious was his dislike for business that Jarrell became ill, spending his recovery studying philosophy and writing verse. Campbell ultimately decided to send Jarrell to Vanderbilt, where he met poets **John Crowe Ransom** and **Robert Penn Warren**. Quickly establishing himself as an *enfant terrible*, Jarrell took a degree in psychology. Nevertheless, he studied literature with a growing passion and placed several of his poems in the *American Review* before graduating. The poems were selected by **Allen Tate** to open a special poetry supplement that featured writers such as Warren, Ransom, **Janet Lewis**, and Mark van Doren. During his senior year at Vanderbilt Jarrell was already sending poems to Warren, who had begun to edit the *Southern Review* along with Cleanth Brooks.

After two years as a graduate student at Vanderbilt, Jarrell followed Ransom to Kenyon College. At Kenyon he met **Robert Lowell**, who along with Peter Taylor, roomed with Jarrell in Ransom's home. Both became Jarrell's lifelong friends. Jarrell's early career is marked by fortuitous friendships. Ransom, for instance, soon founded the *Kenyon Review*, in which Jarrell's poems commonly appeared. Likewise Tate encouraged **James Laughlin** at New Directions to include Jarrell's twenty-poem sequence "Rage for the Lost Penny" in *Five American*

Poets (1940), where he would appear beside another life-long friend, **John Berryman**. Tate also became an advocate for Jarrell's first book, *Blood for a Stranger* (1942), sending the manuscript to his own publishing house, Scribner's, and, finally, to Harcourt Brace, where the manuscript was published. *Blood for a Stranger* proved a solid debut, with poems such as "90 North" suggesting the powerfully personal poems of his last years.

In 1939 Jarrell began teaching at the University of Texas at Austin, where he met Mackie Langham, a colleague in the English Department who became his first wife. In 1942 Jarrell enlisted in the U.S. Army Air Force, where he would stay until February 1946. Although he never saw combat, his experiences in the service as both a teacher and flight navigator affected his writing profoundly. The poems written during this period culminated in *Little Friend, Little Friend*, which appeared in 1945, and comprised a large percentage of *Losses* (1948). Poems such as "Eighth Air Force" and "Absent with Official Leave" demonstrate a departure from his earlier, more abstract, and Audenesque style. "Absent with Official Leave," in particular, is, as Jarrell writes, "a quiet poem" comprised of subtle yet resonant images: "He covers his ears with his pillow, and begins to drift / (Like the plumes the barracks trail into the sky)." Similarly, "Eighth Air Force" paints a morally ambiguous yet ultimately sympathetic portrait of "murderers," that is, soldiers, at rest, awaiting their next bombing run. Though a puppy laps water from a flower can while a sergeant whistles an aria, "shall I say that man / Is not as men have said: a wolf to man?"

During the early 1940s, Jarrell also developed and articulated a fairly elaborate theory of poetry, a theory first sketched in "A Note on Poetry," which appeared as a preface to the poems in *Five American Poets* (1940) and was later developed into "The End of the Line" (1942), first appearing in the *Nation*, a magazine for which he would later serve as literary editor. In the recently rediscovered and posthumously published talk "Levels and Opposites: Structure in Poetry," Jarrell expands on the theories suggested by these previous essays, outlining a dialectical theory, one that makes the startlingly **postmodern** claim that "there are no things in a poem, only processes," and that a poem is a dynamic function that hinges upon opposition, that it is as "static as an explosion." Thought to be lost, "Levels and Opposites" was a *Mesures* lecture given by Jarrell at Princeton in April 1942 at the request of Allen Tate. The essay was rediscovered among Jarrell's papers by Thomas Travisano and was subsequently published in the Winter 1996 issue of the *Georgia Review*.

Jarrell was awarded a Guggenheim fellowship in poetry in 1946 (which he did not accept until 1948) and then moved to New York. Here he worked as literary editor for the *Nation* and cultivated a lasting friendship with Hannah Arendt and B.H. Haggin, who encouraged Jarrell's interest in the ballet. For Lowell, Jarrell played the role of his **Ezra Pound**, offering detailed comments about his forthcoming *Lord Weary's Castle* (1946), helping him both before the poems were finished and after the book was published, championing his friend's work tirelessly and honestly. Shortly thereafter, Jarrell moved to Greensboro, North Carolina, and began teaching at Woman's College of the University of North Carolina, where he would stay until his death in 1965. Jarrell's poetry of the time was loosening up considerably, much like the bat's poetic development in *The Bat-Poet*, moving from stricter forms to an openness inspired by Williams. As he writes in **John Ciardi**'s *Mid-Century American Poetry* (1950), "Rhyme as an automatic structural device, automatically attended to, is attractive to me, but I like it best irregular, live, and heard." The poems that would comprise his next collection, *Seven League Crutches* (1951), exemplify this loosening style, especially the volume's best pieces, such as "A Quilt Pattern," "The Night Before the Night Before Christmas," and "Seele im Raum," the book's finale, which begins with irregular—yet heard—rhythms and rhymes: "It sat between my husband and my children. / A place was set for it—a plate of greens. / It had been there: I had seen it / But not somehow . . . / Not seen it so that I knew I saw it."

Promising as it was, however, *Seven League Crutches* would be the last volume of new verse Jarrell would publish for nine years. The 1950s would see the end of Jarrell's marriage to Mackie Langham and the beginning of his relationship and eventual marriage to Mary von Schrader, whom he met at the July 1951 Boulder, Colorado, Writers' Conference. But a poetic aridness came with the happiness that life with Mary afforded him, a dry spell that lasted the whole decade. However, in those ten years he produced an impressive amount of prose, a writing streak initiated by his excellent and still relevant essay "The Obscurity of the Poet," which he presented at Harvard during the summer of 1950. Published in *Partisan* soon thereafter, it would find its way into *Poetry and the Age* (1953), Jarrell's first book of criticism and a testament to the insightful prose he produced during those first years of the 1950s. This work includes essays and reviews that shaped the canon of American poetry and that inform our appraisal of poets such as **Robert Frost**, Robert Lowell, **Marianne Moore**, **Wallace Stevens**, **Walt Whitman**, **Richard Wilbur**, and **William Carlos Williams**. *Poetry and the Age* was followed a year later by his only novel, *Pictures from an Institution*, a best seller, and then, in 1955, by an appointment to the prestigious position of poetry critic for the *Yale Review*, which he held until 1957. An American Horkheimer and Adorno (and many of his essays were contemporaneous with Horkheimer and Adorno's

indictment of the culture industry), Jarrell lamented in his prose what he thought was a deepening fissure between the poet and the public. As he would write in "Poets, Critics, and Readers," "The public has an unusual relationship to the poet: it doesn't even know that he is there." Nevertheless, Jarrell had by this time become a public intellectual of great importance, his renown affirmed by his appointment to the office of the U.S. Poetry Consultant to the Library of Congress in 1956, the office that would, in 1985, become the U.S. Poet Laureate. However, his appointment to the consultantship did not increase his poetic output, and, despite his many accomplishments during the Eisenhower years, Jarrell remained unhappy with his meager production of poetry, joking to Mary, "Help! Help! A wicked fairy has turned me into a prose writer!"

While Poetry Consultant (he held the office until 1958), Jarrell lived in Washington, D.C., where he was to keep office hours at the Library of Congress for four hours a day. During this period, Jarrell's primary poetic outlet was his intermittent translating of Goethe's *Faust*, written on the blank pages of the huge appointment calendar given to him by the Library of Congress. At this time, Jarrell also worked on translations of Rilke, translations that would comprise half of his book of poetry, *The Woman at the Washington Zoo* (1960). Although *The Woman at the Washington Zoo* won him the National Book Award, the fact that only half the book was original verse made him feel, according to Mary, only half a poet.

Doubtlessly, Jarrell's disaffection with America during what Lowell calls "the tranquilized *Fifties*" in "Memories of West Street and Lepke," had much to do with his turn from poetry. Lowell himself spent the 1950s struggling off and on with his autobiography and lost himself, too, in translating verse, turning to Racine's *Phèdra* and "imitating" (which is how he characterized a rather loose form of translation) a hodgepodge of European poems that would be released under the title *Imitations* in 1961. Similarly, Berryman rang in the markedly antipoetic Eisenhower years with the publication of his critical biography of **Stephen Crane** (1950). And, to round out Jarrell's circle of friends (whom Travisano calls "the mid-century quartet"), **Elizabeth Bishop** also was writing prose, hers in the form of short stories for the *New Yorker*. Jarrell's own translation of Goethe perhaps sums up his estrangement from the times: "Who is there nowadays that wants to read / A book of even the least intelligence?" Or, as Jarrell writes in "The End of the Rainbow," figuring the closing down of creativity and perception in technological terms, "The doors shut themselves / Not helped by any human hand, mailboxes / Pull down their flags, the finest feelers / Of the television sets withdraw."

At the end of his stint as Consultant in Poetry, Jarrell and Mary returned to Greensboro, North Carolina. In February 1962, Jarrell was hospitalized for hepatitis and related complications. Hospitalization did not lend itself to poem making. Although he did manage one poem, "The X-Ray Waiting Room in the Hospital," his dry spell continued. However, Michael di Capua, a children's book editor for Macmillan, suggested that the recovering poet translate several fairy tales by Jacob and Wilhelm Grimm, a task Jarrell took up with relish. Jarrell found his work on the Grimms' translations therapeutic, and once he regained his health, di Capua invited him and his wife to New York to discuss further projects. It was at this meeting that Jarrell the children's book author was born.

The Gingerbread Rabbit and *The Bat-Poet*, his first two children's books, were both published in 1964. Illustrated by Garth Williams, *The Gingerbread Rabbit* was only moderately successful. It and the unpublished (and unfinished) "Reginald," a story about a chipmunk whose father and mother get gobbled up, were largely practice runs, neither as aesthetically satisfying as his later work. However, Jarrell proved a fast learner, for *The Bat-Poet* is a complex fairy tale that treats his two favorite subjects—childhood and poetry—with sophistication and without condescending to his child audience. As Flynn notes in *Randall Jarrell and the Lost World of Childhood*, *The Bat-Poet* involves a unique, talented child (bat though he may be) who simultaneously wants to be exceptional and accepted. Flynn argues that Jarrell, who never had a stable family of his own, develops a consistent theme in his children's books: Our need for happy—yet "improbable"—families is so great that we must invent them. Like *The Lost World* (1965), his last—and, according to Lowell, his best—book of poetry, *The Bat-Poet* and *The Animal Family*, both illustrated by Maurice Sendak, deal profoundly with growing up and facing the moral ambiguities of family and desire. However, it was *The Bat-Poet*'s duel treatment of childhood *and* **poetics** that, Mary claims, "triggered" *The Lost World* and broke the writer's block that kept him from making poetry. Indeed, *The Lost World* features three of the poems found in *The Bat-Poet*.

The central poem in *The Lost World* is marked by the tenderness and sensitivity with which Jarrell can handle the viewpoints of other people—young, old, male, female—even as it showcases his technical prowess as a poet. This poem, the eponymous "The Lost World," is written in *terza rima*, a form Jarrell returns to in his last and only posthumously published children's book, *Fly by Night*. "The Lost World"—the poem and the book—is ripe with emotional intensity, humor, and perception. Unfortunately, early reviewers failed to notice the precision with which the poems were crafted and mistook his complicated rendering of childhood and, no doubt, femininity (the first poem in the collection, "Next Day," has

a female speaker) for **sentimentality**. His declining mental health, exacerbated by inconsistent and ineffectual medicinal therapies, led to a suicide attempt several days after Jarrell read Joseph Bennett's infamously cruel review of *The Lost World*.

Jarrell recovered well and resumed teaching in the fall of 1965. Tragically, after a brief hospital stay involving his injured wrist, he was struck by a car and killed on the twilit evening of October 14, 1965. His death prompted friends and acquaintances to produce a memorial volume of essays and remembrances, *Randall Jarrell, 1914–1965*. Edited by Robert Lowell, Peter Taylor, and Robert Penn Warren, *Randall Jarrell* speaks to the power and lasting influence of this brilliant critic and poet.

Further Reading. *Selected Primary Sources:* Jarrell, Randall, *The Animal Family* (New York: Pantheon Books, 1965); ———, *The Bat-Poet* (New York: Macmillan, 1964); ———, *Complete Poems* (New York: Farrar, Straus and Giroux, 1969); ———, *Faust, Part One* (New York: Farrar, Straus and Giroux, 1976); ———, *No Other Book* (New York: HarperCollins, 1999). *Selected Secondary Sources:* Burt, Stephen, *Randall Jarrell and His Age* (New York: Columbia University Press, 2002); Ferguson, Suzanne, ed., *Critical Essays on Randall Jarrell* (Boston: G.K. Hall, 1983); ———, *Jarrell, Bishop, Lowell, & Co.* (Knoxville: University of Tennessee Press, 2003); ———, *The Poetry of Randall Jarrell* (Baton Rouge: Louisiana State University Press, 1971); Flynn, Richard, *Randall Jarrell and the Lost World of Childhood* (Athens: University of Georgia Press, 1990); Griswold, Jerome, *The Children's Books of Randall Jarrell* (Athens: University of Georgia Press, 1988); Jarrell, Mary, *Remembering Randall: A Memoir of Poet, Critic, and Teacher* (New York: HarperCollins, 1999); Pritchard, William H., *Randall Jarrell: A Literary Life* (New York: Farrar, Straus and Giroux, 1990); Thomas, Joseph T., Jr., "'Levels and Opposites' in Randall Jarrell's *The Bat-Poet*" (*Children's Literature Association Quarterly* 27.1 [2002]: 16–26).

Joseph T. Thomas, Jr.

JAZZ

The pecking order of jazz and American poetry completely reversed itself over the course of the twentieth century. Jazz began as the primitive handmaiden to the high-art **sublimity** of poetry; later, poetry was the supplicant art, jazz the altar. To the poet, at the beginning, the jazz musician was the anonymous Negro, an occasion for poetry more than its real subject. Ultimately, the musician would become the reverently addressed Bird, or Lady, or Mingus, or "dear John, dear Coltrane," to quote the title of a book by Michael Harper.

It is hard to say that the reverence was misplaced. Jazz- and blues-based music are America's art forms, the cultural exports that have won worldwide respect. It is equally pointless to criticize the sensibility of an earlier era for being the sensibility of an earlier era. Still, the white culture of the 1920s, the "Jazz Age" youth chronicled by F. Scott Fitzgerald, knew little about jazz and less about the black culture that created it. New York contained some exceptions to this pattern, as white intellectuals such as Carl Van Vechten sponsored black artists from **James Weldon Johnson** to Bessie Smith, and New Yorkers George and Ira Gershwin created *Porgy and Bess*. But the American arts establishment, caught in the heady rush of **modernism**, failed to notice America's foremost modernist without portfolio, who also may have been America's greatest artist: Louis Armstrong. Armstrong was creating a new artistic vocabulary to catch the temper of the times—and unlike many of the other modernists—he was doing it in the language of the people.

But for the early white poets, jazz was background or metaphor. **Mina Loy** used jazz as a setting for urban dramas of love and sexuality—and, of course, race: "The white flesh quakes to the negro soul, Chicago! Chicago!" (from "The Widow's Jazz").

Other poets of the 1920s sought formal inspiration from the music. **Vachel Lindsay** and **Hart Crane**, in very different ways, set out to write poetry to the rhythms of jazz. They succeeded in being the first to prove what later poets, many of them more sophisticated in the study of jazz, would only prove over and over again: that one cannot write poetry to the rhythms of jazz. Nonetheless, the music left its mark on Lindsay's rhythmic drive (though Lindsay would both accept and angrily reject his designation as a "jazz poet") and Crane's jarring complexity.

Contemporary British critics such as Clive Bell and Wyndham Lewis claimed to see the rhythms of jazz as the basis for **T.S.** **Eliot**'s "The Waste Land," which suggests, more than anything else, the conflation of "jazz" and "American" in the minds of many in the 1920s. Eliot's reference to "that Shakespeherian rag" may connect to his youth in Missouri, birthplace of ragtime, but he appears to be using it in the same way that Loy used black music—as a metaphor for primitive spontaneity. In "The Waste Land," Eliot has a lovely woman putting a record on the gramophone—jazz? But Eliot does not know what jazz is. His other American musical reference in the poem, to the moon shining bright on Mrs. Porter, is to a square dance tune, and perhaps his most famous song lyric quotation, the bamboo tree of "Sweeney Agonistes," comes from a **minstrel** show.

Among white poets of the 1920s, only **Carl Sandburg** really wrote about the experience of listening to jazz. Sandburg was a folklorist and a lover of Americana, and his "Jazz Fantasia" shows an understanding of what jazz musicians actually do and the range of emotions they can summon. So already in the 1920s, the

principal ways in which poets were to use jazz had been established: jazz as metaphor, jazz as rhythmic base, and poetry as voice to the jazz musician

As jazz came from African Americans, its most eloquent poet in the 1920s was **Langston Hughes**, who managed all three approaches, frequently in the same poem. "Weary Blues" is a classic example. The poet hears an old blues singer in a Harlem club. He is moved by the music; he reports on the lyric; finally, by a kind of osmosis, he enters into the old blues singer. Yet even in a masterpiece of understanding such as "Weary Blues," the old jazzman is anonymous—"a Negro" heard in some not-quite-remembered joint on Lenox Avenue on some not-quite-remembered night. Hughes used the blues form often in his poetry. One does not actually have to go to a literary sophisticate such as Hughes for great poetry in the blues form—Robert Johnson or Chuck Berry will fill that order quite well—but Hughes provides a powerful bridge.

Jazz and poetry drifted apart in the 1930s and 1940s. For the reasons why, consider Eileen Simpson's anecdote in *Poets in Their Youth* about a time when **Robert Lowell** caught **Delmore Schwartz** listening to a Bessie Smith record and castigated him for his philistinism. Poetry belonged to the academy in those days, and jazz was a long way from achieving acceptance by the academy. As late as 1965, the Pulitzer Prize committee, faced with the prospect of awarding a prize to Duke Ellington for *Such Sweet Thunder*, his tribute to Shakespeare, chose to give no prize at all in music that year.

But by the 1950s, jazz and poetry, in some spheres, had reunited. This was the era of the culture wars between the academics and the **Beats**, and the Beats embraced jazz as their music. Jazz as a rhythmic base and as an inspiration for poetry became a central tenet of the Beats' theoretical connection to their music of choice—curiously, in one sense, because if the danceable rhythms of traditional jazz had proved to be too subtle for poets of an earlier generation, what was to be made of the complexities of Charlie Parker and the beboppers?

Jazz and jazz musicians were actually more important to the Beats as metaphor. As Norman Mailer explained in his 1957 essay "The White Negro," black Americans, and particularly black jazz musicians, were seen by white hipsters as outlaws by the circumstance of racism, having no choice but to be subversive and therefore a role model for the white rebel who chose to oppose the system. **Allen Ginsberg**, in *Howl*, referred to jazz as a subject for contemplation by "angel-headed hipsters"—a symbol of outlaw spirituality. But Ginsberg himself had no strong commitment to jazz. When he became the *eminence grise* of the hippie movement of the 1960s, he switched his allegiance to Bob Dylan and the protest folk-rockers. In an interview not long before his death,

Ginsberg described the desire of the Beats to free themselves from the metronomic cadences of formal verse and to find new cadences based on bebop. This is similar to Hart Crane's assertion to his patron Otto Kahn that he wrote in the rhythms of jazz, when in fact, for Crane, jazz served more as metaphor and inspiration than as music.

Other Beats had a closer connection to jazz. **Jack Kerouac** is often dismissed by jazz aficionados for describing George Shearing, who by then had become a commercial cocktail pianist, as God, but Kerouac actually had a history as a jazz buff. Kerouac described his writing style as "spontaneous bop prosody," but bop was no more spontaneous than it was unheeding of the metronome. Kerouac's volume of poetry, *Mexico City Blues*, is better remembered for its having been written by the author of *On the Road* than for its poetic merit.

Of the Beats, the poet most steeped in jazz may have been Ted Joans, himself a musician. In a 1981 essay, Joans distinguished between the real jazz aficionados and the fellow travelers. The most sophisticated jazz listeners, however, are not necessarily the best poets; the best poets, even the most rhythmically challenging ones, are not necessarily the real jazz mavens. Interestingly, Joans includes the early Leroi Jones in the list of jazz neophytes, although Jones, later known as **Amiri Baraka**, came to be a considerable authority: His nonfiction book *Blues People* is considered one of the classics in its field, and he has written extensively about jazz. He was not one of the most prominent figures on the Beat jazz and poetry **performance** scene, although in later years he did serious work combining poetry, drama, and jazz, including collaborations with musicians such as Max Roach.

Jazz and poetry became a joint performance item in the Beat era. This was not a new idea. Both Langston Hughes and **Kenneth Rexroth** had performed poetry to jazz in earlier times, but it became a phenomenon in the 1950s. **Kenneth Patchen**, a Beat precursor, was one of the first to record his poetry with a jazz group, and perhaps the most dedicated to the hybrid art. Reading poetry to jazz quickly became a staple of the San Francisco club scene. Rexroth, Philip Lamantia, **Lawrence Ferlinghetti**, and others participated in the movement. In his introduction to *A Coney Island of the Mind*, Ferlinghetti states that the poems are written for oral presentation to jazz accompaniment, not for the printed page.

Composer and performer David Amram recalls participating in New York's first poetry-and-jazz performance in 1957 with Kerouac, Lamantia, and Howard Hart. Amram, more an orchestral and chamber composer than a jazzman, also provided the improvised score for Robert Frank's film *Pull My Daisy*.

The notoriety of the Beats helped to turn poetry and jazz into something of a fad, and more ambitious performances were put together. Patchen performed with Charles Mingus and Ferlinghetti with Stan Getz. Probably the best-selling commercial collaboration was between Kerouac and Steve Allen. During this same time period, performers who came from the jazz and entertainment world rather than the literary world were doing similar work. Lord Buckley and Ken Nordine incorporated doggerel, performance poetry, and word improvisations against a jazz background. Buckley died in 1960; Nordine continued to perform "Word Jazz" into the twenty-first century.

Poetry and jazz was a fad, and it died out when the media lost its fascination with the Beats. Patchen, the poet most seriously committed to the form, might have carried it on longer but for his crippling ill health.

The most artistically successful marriage of poetry to the rhythms of jazz was created by the Last Poets, a collective that arose during the Black Power phase of the 1960s Civil Rights Era. Although a number of people were associated with this group, Jalal Nuriddin, Abiodun Oyewole, and Umar Bin Hassan, who wrote and performed the material on the group's first album, are considered the key members. The Last Poets are often described as the first rappers, but their best work, like Hassan's "Niggers Are Scared of Revolution," will bear comparison with the **canon** of twentieth-century poetry.

In the 1960s **Frank O'Hara**'s poem "The Day Lady Died" was more about O'Hara than it was about Billie Holiday, but it did use an individual jazz icon as metaphor—in this case, her death as metaphor for an irreparable rent in the cultural fabric of New York.

Perhaps most powerful during this era were the jazz poems of **Robert Hayden**, which formed a part of his epic mosaic of black history and culture in America. When Hayden wrote about an artist such as Bessie Smith, he was not writing about how she made him feel or using her as metaphor; he was painting a portrait of Bessie herself, with her artistry and regal stage presence.

In 1970 **Michael S. Harper**, with *Dear John, Dear Coltrane*, became the first poet to give jazz and jazz musicians a real centrality in his work. Harper wrote poems about, or addressed to, Coltrane, Billie Holiday, Miles Davis, Elvin Jones, Bud Powell, and Paul Chambers—these were the jazz poems of a poet whose subject was jazz itself. One could write about Billie Holiday as metaphor and expect an audience of general cultural literacy to understand, just as one could expect a general audience to follow the reference to a Negro in a bar on Lenox Avenue. Harper demanded that his audience know jazz.

Hayden, like Hughes before him, had used poetry to celebrate jazz as an expression of black consciousness. Harper had traveled the complete distance from Loy and Lindsay and used poetry to celebrate the artistry of jazz and its performers.

By the end of the twentieth century, jazz was significant enough as a subject for poetry that a successful and respected small magazine, *Brilliant Corners*, edited by Sascha Feinstein, was devoted entirely to jazz literature. **Yusef Komunyakaa** and Feinstein edited two anthologies of jazz poetry. Jazz has been a favorite subject in the poetry of Komunyakaa and **William Matthews**, and poets such as Quincy Troupe, **Billy Collins**, **Wanda Coleman**, **Hayden Carruth**, **Dana Gioia**, **Etheridge Knight**, and **Philip Levine** have paid tribute in their work to jazz music and jazz artists.

The relationship of jazz to modernism is an interesting one. The development of jazz was so rapid and so revolutionary that many critics think of Charlie Parker's music as a repudiation of Louis Armstrong's—the earlier music is called "traditional" jazz and the later "modern." But Armstrong and Parker were not so different aesthetically—both were moderns. The mainstream artistic and cultural community, including the poetry community, tended for a long time to see jazz as something other than the major art form that it is. Jazz, to the mainstream modernists of the 1920s and 1930s, symbolized the unsentimental truth and honesty that they espoused, but they also sentimentalized it, in much the same way that Kerouac would later, seeing jazz as spontaneous and primitive.

The jazz poets of the 1980s and 1990s had a greater understanding of the artistry of jazz. They had no problem understanding what was wrong with a critic like Clive Bell—or even Eliot himself—calling Eliot's minstrel-show reference "jazz."

Perhaps a contemporary, **postmodernist** assessment might be more tolerant of Eliot's paternalistic take on the minstrel-show rhythms of his St. Louis boyhood. The "Zip Coon" aspect of black vaudeville reflects a painful chapter in the history of American racism, but the artists who created it, from Bert Williams and Bill "Bojangles" Robinson to unknown dancers and banjo players, were artists who played an important role in developing the rhythms of American life, speech, and poetry.

Further Reading. ***Selected Primary Sources:*** Baraka, Amiri, *Selected Poetry of Amiri Baraka/LeRoi Jones* (New York: William Morrow, 1978); Crane, Hart, *The Bridge* (New York: Liveright, 1930); Feinstein, Sascha, and Yusef Komunyakaa, eds., *The Jazz Poetry Anthology* (Bloomington: Indiana University Press, 1991); Harper, Michael S., *Dear John, Dear Coltrane* (Pittsburgh: University of Pittsburgh Press, 1970); Hayden, Robert, *Selected Poems* (New York: October House, 1966); Hughes, Langston, *The Weary Blues* (New York: Alfred A. Knopf, 1926); Komunyakaa, Yusef, *Pleasure Dome* (Middletown, CT: Wesleyan University Press, 2001); Lange, Art, and Nathan Mackey, *Moment's Notice: Jazz in Poetry and Prose* (Minneapolis, MN: Coffee House Press, 1993); Lindsay, Vachel, *The Congo and Other Poems* (New York: Macmillan, 1914); Loy, Mina, *Lunar Baedeker & Time Tables* (Highlands, NC: Jonathan Williams, 1958); Sandburg, Carl, *Smoke and Steel* (New York: Harcourt Brace, 1920). ***Selected Audio Sources:*** Baraka, Amiri, *New Music New Poetry* (India Navigation, 1992); Hughes, Langston, *The Poetry of Langston Hughes* (Caedmon, 1969); Kerouac, Jack, *The Jack Kerouac Collection* (Rhino, 1995); The Last Poets, *The Last Poets* (Douglas, 1970); Patchen, Kenneth, *Kenneth Patchen Reads with Jazz in Canada* (Folkways, 1960).

Tad Richards

JEFFERS, ROBINSON (1887–1962)

Robinson Jeffers, poet and stonemason, lived and worked in the Big Sur–Carmel–Monterey region of California, an area forever after identified as "Jeffers country." A pacifist, naturalist, and religious visionary, Jeffers offered a sustained critique of modern life that both angered and inspired his contemporaries. He is widely credited with reviving, indirectly, the environmental movement in America and with providing the intellectual, spiritual, and artistic foundation for deep ecology.

John Robinson Jeffers was born January 10, 1887, in Sewickley, Pennsylvania, His father, Dr. William Hamilton Jeffers, was a Presbyterian seminary professor who taught ancient languages, biblical theology, and church history. His mother, Annie Tuttle Jeffers, was a genteel homemaker. A younger brother, Hamilton (who became a noted professional astronomer), completed the family. Hoping to secure the best education for his eldest son, Dr. Jeffers instructed him in Greek and Latin and then enrolled him in a series of private schools in Switzerland, where courses focusing on the classics were taught in French and German. Accordingly, Jeffers was fluent in five languages by the time he was twelve years old. He began college at the University of Pittsburgh, and then, when the family moved to California, he enrolled at Occidental College in Los Angeles, where he graduated at age eighteen. In 1906 he pursued graduate studies in languages and literature first at the University of Southern California and then at the University of Zurich, Switzerland. After a semester abroad, Jeffers returned with an interest in medicine (resulting from a job translating German medical papers for a family physician) and entered the Medical School of the University of Southern California. He was the top student in his class, but he abandoned medical studies after three years and moved to Seattle, where he took graduate courses in forestry at the University of Washington.

Jeffers's personal life at this time was as fluid as his academic life. Handsome, well dressed, intelligent, athletic, he lived wildly—writing poetry, courting women, and carousing with friends. One woman, Una Call Kuster, soon became the focus of his attention. He met her in a class on German poetry at the University of Southern California, where, after completing her undergraduate studies, she earned a master's degree in philosophy. Despite her marriage to a prominent attorney, Edward Kuster, Robinson and Una engaged in a passionate, illicit romance that began in 1909 and ended—with Kuster's discovery of the affair—in 1912. After a sixth-month solitary sojourn in Europe, designed to give everyone a chance to think things through, Una returned to California. Knowing the marriage was doomed, Kuster initiated divorce proceedings. At the same time, Una and Robinson reaffirmed their commitment to each other. They were married August 2, 1913, the day after Una's divorce became final.

Soon thereafter, the couple moved to Carmel, California. They had intended to live in Lyme Regis on the south coast of England, but the outbreak of World War I forced them to change their plans—fortuitously, it seems, for, as Jeffers says, "when the stagecoach topped the hill from Monterey and we looked down through pines and sea-fogs on Carmel Bay, it was evident that we had come without knowing it to our inevitable place" (Powell, 13–14).

Carmel had already acquired a reputation as a bohemian artists' colony, including such residents as **George Sterling**, **Mary Austin**, Jack London, Sinclair Lewis, Upton Sinclair, Nora May French, William Rose Benét, Van Wyck Brooks, and many other freethinking writers, painters, and musicians. There the couple surrendered to the charms of a nonconformist life based on reading, writing, and exploring the seacoast.

Jeffers's first book of poetry, published at his own expense in 1912, was called *Flagons and Apples*. Composed, for the most part, of derivative love poems, it showed promise, at best. In Carmel, however, he turned his attention to **narrative poetry** and composed several **long poems** about people who lived nearby. A collection of these poems, still largely derivative but displaying signs of incipient strength and originality, appeared as *Californians*; it was published by Macmillan in 1916. Although the book was well received, Jeffers himself was dissatisfied, and he continued his search for a voice that was his own. His unrest was exacerbated at this time by many factors, including the death of his first child in 1914 (a daughter, Maeve, who lived only a day), the death of his father in the same year, the violence of World War I, and the responsibilities occasioned by the birth of twin sons, Garth and Donnan, in 1916.

In 1919 Robinson and Una bought property on a desolate, windblown point of land south of the village of Carmel—and there, facing the Pacific Ocean, they built a small cottage out of local granite boulders, which they called Tor House. Jeffers joined the construction crew and learned the craft of stonemasonry. This experience transformed his inner life. Una captures the moment in a letter to an inquiring scholar: "As he helped the masons shift and place the wind and wave-worn granite I think he realized some kinship with it and became aware of strengths in himself unknown before. Thus at the age of thirty-one there came to him a kind of awakening such as adolescents and religious converts are said to experience" (Powell, 16–17).

After Tor House was completed, Jeffers began work on a garage (which eventually became a kitchen and pantry), a low wall around Una's garden courtyard, and a massive four-story structure named Hawk Tower. At the same time, he began writing poems of exceptional power. Among the first of these was a long narrative titled *Tamar*, which he published at his own expense in 1924. The title character of the poem is a young woman who lives with her troubled family in an isolated seacoast farmhouse. Incest, madness, and supernatural forces draw Tamar and everyone around her into a frenzied dance of death. Since Jeffers had no way to market the book, a crate of unsold copies was stored in the attic. Soon thereafter, he sent gift volumes to George Sterling and James Rorty—co-editors, along with **Genevieve Taggard**, of a new anthology of California verse, *Continent's End* (1925), titled after a poem contributed by Jeffers. Stunned by what they read, they shared *Tamar* with influential friends. Exuberant praise in New York led to a contract with Boni & Liveright. *Roan Stallion, Tamar and Other Poems*, Jeffers's first major book, appeared in 1925—and he became famous overnight.

Jeffers was a modern artist but not a **modernist**. Living in an isolated cottage without electricity or telephone on a low hill beside the sea, away from the rush and excitement of London, Paris, Dublin, or New York, he sought to conserve tradition as he transcended it. His poetry did not involve the ambiguity, irony, language play, and private symbolism of the modernists. The house he built—constructed of undressed boulders hauled up from the shore—was timeless in material and design; a peasant in the Middle Ages, finding such a house abandoned from centuries before, would have moved right in, understanding the structure perfectly. The poetry Jeffers composed was equally timeless in genre, subject matter, and form. As he says in "Point Joe," declaring a guiding principle, "Permanent things are what is needful in a poem, things temporally / Of great dimension, things continually renewed or always present"—like the sea, mountains, wildflowers, and human passion.

Indeed, Jeffers was perhaps the only American poet of the modern age who worked continuously and successfully in traditional narrative, **lyric**, and dramatic modes. Some of his narratives are relatively short, like the classic "Roan Stallion," but many are of **epic** length. Principal titles include, in addition to *Tamar* (1925), *The Women at Point Sur* (1927), *Cawdor* (1928), *Thurso's Landing* (1932), *Give Your Heart to the Hawks* (1933), *Such Counsels You Gave to Me* (1937), *Be Angry at the Sun* (1941), *The Double Axe* (1948), and *Hungerfield* (1954). The poems in addition to the title poems were lyric—some idylls, odes, and sonnets (such as "Fauna," "Night," and "Return"), but mostly forms of his own devising. Noteworthy examples of the latter include "Shine, Perishing Republic," "Hurt Hawks," and "Oh, Lovely Rock." Jeffers also wrote dramatic verse. Some plays explored Christian or medieval themes—*Dear Judas* and *At the Birth of an Age*, for example. Others were Greek in origin, such as *The Tower Beyond Tragedy*, *The Cretan Woman*, and *Medea* (inspired by Aeschylus's *Oresteia*, and Euripides' *Hippolytus* and *Medea*, respectively). *Medea*, performed on Broadway in 1947 by Judith Anderson and John Gielgud, was considered a landmark of the modern stage.

In his youth, Jeffers worked skillfully in established metrical forms and rhyme schemes. As he matured, however, and especially after the transformation that occurred when he was building Tor House, he abandoned rhyme, lengthened his line, and invented his own rhythms. In an early statement describing some of his technical concerns, Jeffers said,

> I want it rhythmic and not rhymed, moulded more closely to the subject than older English poetry is, but formed as alcaics if that were possible too. The event is of course a compromise but I like to avoid arbitrary form and capricious lack or disruption of form. My feeling is for the number of beats to the line. There is a quantitative element too in which the unstressed syllables have part. The rhythm comes from many sources—physics, biology, beat of blood, the tidal environments of life, desire for singing emphasis that prose does not have. (Powell, 116)

Subject matter for Jeffers was rooted in his own personal experience. Indeed, a portion of his work from the beginning to the end of his career deals with immediate concerns: Una; his sons; Tor House and Hawk Tower; the craft of writing; the everyday challenges, wonders, and torments of existence. Beyond his own life, though—which, in truth, he regarded as insignificant— Jeffers was interested in other people, especially in their capacity to inflict and endure pain. His narratives, all tragic, tell stories of men and women pushed to extremes by inner pathology and outer circumstance: Reverend Barclay in *The Women at Point Sur* abandons his wife, rapes his daughter, and goes mad; Lance Fraser in *Give Your Heart to the Hawks* slowly breaks down and then commits suicide after murdering his brother in a

jealous, drunken rage; and the archetypal Medea kills her sons to punish her husband for leaving her. Jeffers's sense of the tragic, informed by literary tradition and a deep knowledge of myth and history, was also conditioned by current events, namely the horrors unleashed in the twentieth century by population growth, consumerism, and, above all, world war. With the vehemence and conviction of a biblical prophet, Jeffers decried civilization and denounced the ignorance, avarice, and cruelty of people and their leaders. Although his denunciations were harsh, they were part of a comprehensive philosophy of life Jeffers called "Inhumanism," which led him away from a preoccupation with his own life, away, even, from what he saw in others as a blinding fixation with humankind, toward an identification with nature and the larger world. Jeffers summarizes this aspect of his philosophy in a preface to *The Double Axe*. Inhumanism, he says, involves

> a shifting of emphasis and significance from man to not-man; the rejection of human solipsism and recognition of the transhuman magnificence. It seems time that our race began to think as an adult does, rather than as an egocentric baby or insane person. This manner of thought and feeling is neither misanthropic nor pessimist, though two or three people have said so and may again. It involves no falsehoods, and is a means of maintaining sanity in slippery times; it has objective truth and human value. It offers a reasonable detachment as a rule of conduct, instead of love, hate and envy. It neutralizes fanaticism and wild hopes; but it provides magnificence for the religious instinct, and satisfies our need to admire greatness and rejoice in beauty. (*Collected Poetry* IV, 428)

The centrifugal force of this worldview runs counter to the centripetal movement of much twentieth-century poetry (where the self is the center of artistic concerns, and human experience is paramount). With the informed mindset of a scientist, Jeffers saw life from a materialist, Darwinian point of view. As a religious visionary, however, he added the perspective of a pantheist. As he said in a letter to Sister Mary James Power,

> I believe that the universe is one being, all its parts are different expressions of the same energy, and they are all in communication with each other, influencing each other, therefore parts of one organic whole. (This is physics, I believe, as well as religion.) The parts change and pass, or die, people and races and rocks and stars; none of them seems to me important in itself, but only the whole. This whole is in all its parts so beautiful, and is felt by me to be so intensely in earnest, that I am compelled to love it, and to think of it as divine. It seems to me that this whole alone is worthy

of the deeper sort of love; and that there is peace, free-dom, I might say a kind of salvation, in turning one's affections outward toward this one God, rather than inward on one's self, or on humanity, or on human imagination and abstractions—the world of spirits. (Karman, 105)

It is important to add here that God, for Jeffers, is not loving or just or human-like. "God is a hawk gliding among the stars," he says in *The Double Axe.* "He has a bloody beak and harsh talons, he pounces and tears." One fierce life is all there is.

Critical reaction to Jeffers waxed and waned through the years. In the 1920s and early 1930s, he was regarded as one of America's greatest poets. In April 1932 his portrait was featured on the cover of *Time* magazine. In 1933, after the bankruptcy of Boni & Liveright, over a dozen major publishers sought to represent him. Random House, Bennett Cerf's new firm, won the contract and, in signing Jeffers and Eugene O'Neill at the same time, acquired immediate literary distinction. As the 1930s wore on, however, some readers tired of Jeffers's darkness and pessimism. This trend persisted through the early 1940s, when Jeffers' bitter denunciation of World War II spared no one, including Americans. Left-ist critics lauded Jeffers's critique of civilization but faulted his unwillingness to join the movement for social change. Humanist and Christian critics disapproved of his perceived misanthropy and faithlessness. **New Crit-ics** saw little value in his long narratives. Nevertheless, Jeffers's broad-based general readership remained loyal, and the production of his *Medea* in 1947 was a major popular success.

After his wife died in 1950, Jeffers published one more book, *Hungerfield and Other Poems* (1954)—and then there was silence, until he himself died. He continued to write during his last years but mostly devoted himself to stonework, improving and enlarging his beloved home. In "Post Mortem," Jeffers imagines a distant future in which someone would encounter his presence in a poem; but, he remarks, "The ghost would not care but be here, long sunset shadow in the seams of the granite, and forgotten / The flesh, a spirit for the stone."

Further Reading. Selected Primary Sources: Jeffers, Robinson, *The Collected Poetry of Robinson Jeffers*, 5 vols., ed. Tim Hunt (Stanford, CA: Stanford University Press, 1988–2001); ———, *The Selected Poetry of Robinson Jeffers*, ed. Tim Hunt (Stanford, CA: Stanford University Press, 2001); ———, *The Wild God of the World: An Anthology of Robinson Jeffers*, ed. Albert Gelpi (Stanford, CA: Stanford University Press, 2003). **Selected Secondary Sources:** Brophy, Robert, *Robinson Jeffers: Myth, Ritual, and Symbol in His Narrative Poems* (Hamden, CT: Shoe String Press, 1976); Everson, William, *The Excesses of God: Robinson Jeffers as a Religious Figure* (Stanford, CA: Stanford University Press, 1988); Karman, James, *Robinson Jeffers: Poet of California* (Ashland, OR: Story Line Press, 1995); Zaller, Robert, *The Cliffs of Solitude: A Reading of Robinson Jeffers* (Cambridge: Cambridge University Press, 1983).

James Karman

JEWETT, SARAH ORNE (1849–1909)

Sarah Orne Jewett, better known as a writer of short stories and regional sketches than as a poet, nevertheless published at least thirty-five poems. Although Jewett herself rightly believed that her prose was stronger and more viable than her poetry, her poetry is part of main-stream nineteenth-century American women's poetry. It deals with domestic and religious topics, often exalts the inspirational qualities of nature, and occasionally pre-sents a moral lesson. Her poetry is also heavily influ-enced by contemporary trends of thought. It has a strong Christian bias and is permeated by the omnipres-ence of a warm, loving Deity; moreover, Philophilus Parsons's version of theologian Emanuel Swedenborg's New Church tenets pervades much of her writing. Although by no means a Swedenborgian, Jewett assimi-lated Parsons's version of Swedenborg's tenets, includ-ing making the best use of her God-given talents for the benefit of humanity. In addition, Jewett grew up reading the works of **Ralph Waldo Emerson**, and, Paula Blan-chard explains, Transcendentalism became "a pervasive, divinely infused continuum embracing all forms of life and reaching across barriers of time and death" (102).

But underlying all other influences was her observa-tion of the gradual decay of the once vital farms and sea-ports of New England. As its rural inhabitants migrated west and to the cities and factories, the remaining resi-dents found it more and more difficult to maintain their former way of life. Thus, Jewett's perspective of New England, its people and its culture, is mediated by her religious principles, respect for the past, compassion, and recognition of humanity's interconnectedness with nature. Such poetry had a large, probably predomi-nantly female, audience as a result of the growing num-ber of periodicals and their increasing circulation.

Jewett, born September 3, 1849, in South Berwick, Maine, grew up in a privileged household. However, she suffered from rheumatoid arthritis, which severely curtailed her formal schooling. She did attend a small day school, then Berwick Academy from 1861 to 1865, but her attendance was frequently interrupted by ill-ness; most of her education came from the books she read in English and American literature and from her close friendship with her father, Dr. Theodore Herman Jewett, whom she accompanied on his physician's rounds throughout Berwick and its environs. Her inter-est in and intimate knowledge of the rural New England character, the flora and fauna of the countryside, and its socioeconomic conditions, subjects that form the foundation of her writings, arose from this period.

Jewett also traveled extensively, especially around New England, and spent a great deal of time in Boston, where she was well known on the Boston literary scene. Although she had become acquainted with her mentors, **William Dean Howells** and **James T. Fields**, at the start of her career, only when she published her first book, *Deephaven* (1877), did she gain serious recognition and expand her friendships with literary personages, including **John Greenleaf Whittier**, **James Russell Lowell**, Harriet Beecher Stowe, **Celia Thaxter**, Henry James, and, later, **Willa Cather**. Perhaps more important, however, was her intense friendship with **Annie T. Fields**, with whom, after Fields's husband's death in 1881, Jewett traveled to Europe and spent part of each summer and winter. Jewett never married, and their friendship has been described as a "Boston marriage." Although Jewett's unpublished love poems describe the intensity of her feelings for Fields and several other women friends, Paula Blanchard argues that no direct evidence of a lesbian relationship exists and describes it as a "romantic friendship" (54). Nevertheless, Jewett and Fields were leading personalities in Boston literary circles. During this period, Jewett published seventeen of her twenty books, including *The Country of the Pointed Firs* (1896), perhaps the acme of her career. Her achievements were honored by Bowdoin College in 1901 when it awarded her the first honorary Doctor of Letters the school ever granted a woman. Sadly, Jewett virtually ceased writing for publication in September 1902, when she sustained severe spinal injuries in a carriage accident. She died from a cerebral hemorrhage on June 24, 1909, in her South Berwick home.

Jewett's writing career began when she was eighteen. In 1868, under the pseudonym of "Alice Eliot," she published her first short story, "Jenny Garrow's Lovers," in *The Flag of Our Union*, and her first poem, "The Baby-House Famine," in the juvenile magazine *Our Young Folks*. All told, Jewett published thirty-five or thirty-six poems, almost all before 1884, in the *Atlantic Monthly*, the *Christian Union*, *Harper's Monthly*, the *Independent, Our Young Folks, Riverside Magazine, St. Nicholas, Scribner's Magazine*, and other periodicals (Weber and Weber). Her most widely available poetry is *Verses* (1916, published posthumously), containing nineteen poems, ten of which were published in periodicals. This privately printed collection, collected by Mark A. DeWolfe Howe at Jewett's sister Mary's request, was "Printed for Her Friends." A number of complete poems and some fragments also exist in manuscript, most held by the Houghton Library, Harvard University (Donovan, 116, note 2). Furthermore, extracts of thirty unpublished love poems are discussed in Josephine Donovan's essay "The Unpublished Love Poems of Sarah Orne Jewett."

Jewett's poems commonly employ simple diction, images, and structure. Her earliest poems were directed at children; only later did she write for adults. Her first published poem, "The Baby-House Famine," was soon followed by other poems addressed to youthful audiences, including "The Spendthrift Doll" (*Murray's Museum*, 1871) and "The Little Doll That Lied" (*St. Nicholas* 1874; *Verses*), both using the homely image of a doll to teach a moral lesson. The children's poems' maternal tone, simple rhyme scheme, and almost singsong rhythm suited their audience. Her later poems, also using uncomplicated language and clear images, take up themes found in her prose, including the decline of New England's once prosperous rural areas, companionship and female bonding, social usefulness, nature, and religion. Rarely are these poems as didactic as the poems for young people; nevertheless, they are sometimes marred by infelicitous rhythm and rhyme.

Noteworthy later poems include those mourning the death of her father in 1878, especially two sonnets, "To My Father, I and II" (*Verses*). Other poems alluding to death, including "Missing" (*Harper's*, 1882) and "Assurance" (*Verses*), emphasize the connectedness between the dead and the living. Particularly revealing of Jewett's religious views is "At Home from Church" (*Verses*), in which the narrator feels "shut out" from communication with God in a conventional church and so turns to nature "Again to catch the tune that brings / No thought of temple or of priest, / But only of a voice that sings." Another poem, "The Gloucester Mother," published in *McClure's Magazine* (1908) and one of her best known, laments the deaths of those lost at sea, yet ends with the hope that "If they must sleep in restless waves, / God make them dream they are ashore / With grass above their graves" (*Verses*).

Other poems develop themes commonly associated with Jewett's prose. For example, an adaptation of a Swedenborgian principle, to make the most of one's talents, is expressed in a number of poems, including "Discontent" (*Verses*) and "A Four-Leaved Clover" (*Verses*). Women's isolation and need for companionship finds expression in several other poems, including "Caged Bird" (*Verses*) and "The Widow's House" (*Verses*). Additional poems are paeans to nature emphasizing the connectedness between man and nature, including "Flowers in the Dark" (*Verses*), "A Night in June" (*The Christian Union*, 1880), "Boat Song," (*Verses*), and "A Wild Rose" (*Chicago Times-Herald*, 1895). A lament for the decline of New England, "On Star Island," reiterates the importance of the past and mourns the decline of Gosport, Massachusetts; thus, Jewett's narrator "rang the knell for Gosport town" (*Harper's Magazine*, 1881, and a different version in *Verses*). "A Farmer's Sorrow" (*Manhattan Magazine*, March 1884; *Exeter Letter*, April 1884) is especially eloquent on this theme. In a poignant dramatic monologue, the old farmer mourns his son's rejection of the ancestral farm in pursuit of an education. As a result, the overeducated heir is unable to run the farm. Sadly, the old farmer declares, "'Twas him [Dan, the son] that should have had the place; 'twas father's 'fore 'twas mine. / I'd like to kep' it in the name; but I ain't goin' to whine." Although the rhythm is sometimes awkward, the tone, avoiding excess **sentimentality**, is moving, and Jewett's use of dialect is nonobtrusive and appropriate to the character.

Despite occasional infelicities, Jewett's poetry had wide appeal. It is accessible: Its images, structure, and language are clear, vivid, and appropriate. Furthermore, her combination of nature and domestic topics, as well as contemporary religious movements and regional color, contributed to its appeal. Although not as prolific a poet as many of her contemporaries, Jewett published in most of the major periodicals that circulated primarily in New England and along the eastern seaboard. She is also one of the few nineteenth-century American women writers who, although having a family inheritance, comfortably supported herself by her pen, both through her poetry and prose.

Further Reading. *Selected Primary Sources:* Jewett, Sarah Orne, *Sarah Orne Jewett Letters*, ed. Richard Cary (Waterville, ME: Colby College Press, 1958); ———, *Verses*, ed. M.A. De Wolfe Howe (Merrymount Press, 1916); Sarah Orne Jewett Text Project, www.public.coe.edu/~theller/soj/ess/donovan1.html. ***Selected Secondary Sources:*** Blanchard, Paula, *Sarah Orne Jewett: Her World and Her Work* (Radcliff Biography Series) (Reading, MA: Addison-Wesley, 1994); Cary, Richard, *Sarah Orne Jewett* (New York: Twayne, 1962); Donovan, Josephine, "The Unpublished Love Poems of Sarah Orne Jewett," in *Critical Essays on Sarah Orne Jewett*, ed. Gwen L. Nagel (Boston: G.K. Hall, 1984, 107–117); Weber, Clara Carter, and Carl J. Weber, *A Bibliography of the Published Writings of Sarah Orne Jewett* (Waterville, ME: Colby College Press, 1949).

Mary Rose Kasraie

JOHNSON, EDWARD (1598–1672)

The author of the first published history of New England, *Wonder-Working Providence of Sions Saviour* (1654), Edward Johnson composed sixty-seven poems for the book, most of them memorializing first-generation founders of New England.

Edward Johnson was born in 1698, the son of a parish clerk in Canterbury, England, trained as a joiner and married around 1618. In 1630 Johnson migrated to Boston, where he began to establish himself (becoming a freeman in 1631 and obtaining license to trade with Indians). After a short time in England, Johnson returned with his family to New England in 1636, in the midst of the Antinomian Controversy, the most consequential dispute over theological issues in the early colony. Johnson was soon convinced by the arguments of Thomas Shepard and others who represented the emergent "New England Way," and became a lifelong advocate of that orthodoxy. Though of relatively humble background, Johnson became well known as a leading citizen and founder.

A polemical history, Johnson's *Wonder-Working Providence* is most commonly characterized as "bombastic." The book had long been considered both poor historiography and erratic writing until scholars began to identify Johnson's "typological" reading of history. *Wonder-Working Providence* works more as an extended argument about the special status of New England as an elect nation than as a factually driven narrative of early times. Earlier critics tended to dismiss Johnson's poetry along with his prose. Although Harold Janz describes the "some 67 sets of verses" that are interspersed throughout the narrative as "most of them mediocre to poor, a few showing flashes of poetic mastery," he nevertheless praises Johnson's "sure sense of what constitutes the truly epic, namely the elevation of a set of local events into the universal under the span of a great unifying vision" (12). Janz further notes that Johnson makes "a successful transfer of Homeric dactylic rhythms into English, a feat that will appear all the more remarkable if we consider the clumsy attempts to do so in England before his time and failure to do anything comparable for two centuries after his time" (13).

Jesper Rosenmeier defines an **epic** quality of Johnson's work in terms of biblical models, citing his "wailing muse" of lamentation and his use of Canticles as a literary model that is simultaneously typological and poetic. Rosenmeier finds Johnson's poems "significant because they show us that a century after Luther, the principle of finding Christ's presence in biblical realities—the types—had now been extended to make even contemporary, historical presences into prophetic, type-like figures" and calls Johnson "the first historian and poet in New England who sought to create a past by converting the dead among the first generation Puritans into memories that could support the living generations on their march to the New Jerusalem" (170). On the most basic level, Johnson's poems to New England's first-generation leaders are meant to be exemplary—verse hagiographies and "living elegies" written to guide the current generation. More complexly, the poems grant first-generation leaders' typological status—fulfillment of biblical precedent inviting millennialist identification of New England as an elect nation.

Most critics focus on Johnson's typological artistry rather than his formal skill. Often the same characteristics of Johnson's verse are described, variously, in admiring or condemning terms. What is "bombastic" according to one judgment is shrewdly "typological" according to another; the same features that reveal a failure of poetic skill in one context prove to be epic or baroque elsewhere. Some critics argue that specific formal idiosyncrasies of Johnson's verse advance his typological, millennialist agenda. Rosenmeier, for example, identifies a multi-voiced persona "whose voice is simultaneously that of the dead ancestors, of the eternal Christ, and of the living poet," noting, "This multi-voiced persona often strikes the reader as hopelessly confused. Johnson seems not to have known or cared enough about the craft of poetry to have made clear who is saying what in his memory poems. Yet the reader's confusion may well have been the effect that Johnson deliberately set out to create" (171). Jeffrey A. Hammond sees Johnson's almost formulaic elegy as effacing the differences between the living and dead, suggesting, "Such historiographic dismissal of any significant difference between dead saints and living saints illustrates an axiom central to elegy in early New England" (148).

Harrison T. Meserole attributes to Johnson all the verse in a short, anonymous book entitled *Good News from New England* (1648), although no definitive evidence has emerged to prove or disprove the authorship. In addition to poems that bear some resemblance to those in *Wonder-Working Providence*, there are verse descriptions of the natural environment of New England. The intended audience for *Good News* seems to be English, and the poems cataloguing natural resources might usefully be read in comparison to the verse in **William Wood**'s promotional tract *New England's Prospect*.

Though not always praised for literary merit, the prose and poetry of Johnson's *Wonder-Working Providence* worked together to forge a distinctive sense of history and memory that was a living, guiding force to its seventeenth-century audience and to early American literary imagination.

Further Reading. Selected Primary Sources: *American Poetry of the Seventeenth Century*, ed. Harrison T. Meserole (University Park: Pennsylvania State University Press, 1985); Johnson, Edward, *Wonder-Working Providence of Sions Saviour in New-England (1654) and Good News from New England (1648)*, ed. Edward J. Gallagher (Del Mar, NY: Scholars' Facsimiles & Reprints, 1974). **Selected Secondary Sources:** Hammond, Jeffrey A., "The American Puritan Elegy," in *A Literary and Cultural Study* (Cambridge: Cambridge University Press, 2000); Jantz, Harold, "American Baroque: Three Representative Poets," in *Discoveries & Considerations: Essays on Early American Literature & Aesthetics Presented to Harold Jantz*, ed. Calvin Israel (Albany: State University of New York Press, 1976, 3–23); Rosenmeier, Jesper, "To Keep in Memory: The Poetry of Edward Johnson," in *Puritan Poets and Poetics: Seventeenth-Century American Poetry in Theory and Practice*, ed. Peter White (University Park: Pennsylvania State University Press, 1985, 158–174).

Meredith Neuman

JOHNSON, FENTON (1888–1958)

Though paid little attention in recent years, Fenton Johnson was an energetic contributor to the New Poetry Movement in the era of World War I. As a poet, Johnson was gifted with a sense of lyrical balance and the ability to capture vernacular speech with impressive accuracy. He authored some memorable poems, and the continuing presence in anthologies of a few of Johnson's most controversial works offers a model of the **prose poem** form. His work also set a pattern for later African American writers who wanted to explore the urban experience or express militant political views.

Born on May 7, 1888, in Chicago, Fenton Johnson was the only son of Elijah and Jessie Taylor Johnson. The family enjoyed moderate affluence, and after graduating from public schools, Johnson was able to attend the University of Chicago and Northwestern University. He taught for a year at Kentucky State University in Louisville and later spent a year studying at Columbia University's School of Journalism in New York.

While in New York he was active in local politics. In 1916 he returned to Chicago and, with support from businessman Jesse Binga, launched a journal titled the *Champion Magazine*. Focused on literary matters, culture, and political issues, the magazine was an intellectual success but failed as a business venture. Johnson tried again with the *Favorite Magazine*, which lasted from 1917 to 1921 but never achieved the quality of the earlier project. The failure of the *Favorite* led to Johnson's withdrawal from the literary scene, although in the 1930s he worked on the staff of the Federal Writers Project of the Works Progress Administration (WPA). When that project ended, however, Johnson returned to obscurity. He died on September 17, 1958.

Johnson began writing in his teen years and had short plays produced at Chicago's Pekin Theater. *A Little Dreaming* (1913), his first collection of poems, emulates the popular literature of the period. Like most **African American poets** in that era, Johnson followed the lead of Paul Laurence Dunbar (1872–1906), writing poems in traditional English-language stanza forms and poems in what was then known as "Negro dialect." These dialect poems were generally exercises in humor and nostalgia that, in the hands of a gifted writer, could also accurately record regional vernacular idiom. The standard English poems generally presented themes inspired by the Romantic poets. Johnson was good at both approaches but was particularly interested in examining racial themes. His interest in capturing the power of vernacular expression is the force that leads Johnson away from the standardized clichés of literary dialect and generates his best writing. Some of this work is collected in *Visions of the Dusk* (1915) and *Songs of the Soil* (1916). Anticipating the use that **Langston Hughes** (1902–1967) and **Sterling A. Brown** (1901–1989) would make of blues music, Johnson studied the spirituals and attempted to adapt them for literary use. "Who Is That A-walking in the Corn" and "The Lonely Mother (A Negro Spiritual)" (1916) are among the best of these poems.

Johnson's spirituals are not adaptations of songs that were copied down by **Thomas Wentworth Higginson** or popularized by Fisk University's Jubilee Singers after the Civil War; these are new compositions artfully utilizing the idiom and customary allusions of authentic folk forms created by the former slaves. "Song of the Whirlwind" (1915), for example, powerfully connects biblical images with the hope of the downtrodden for redemption:

> Oh, my soul is in the whirlwind
> And my bones are in the valley;
> At her spinning wheel is Mary
> Spinning raiment of the lilies.

The meter resembles that of the choral music that inspired Johnson, while a playful but apposite allusion to Matthew 6:28 and domesticity in the reference to Mary resembles the sermonic style of the black church in which biblical events are often spoken of as if they were contemporary happenings. Similarly, using subtle near rhyme, "My God in Heaven Said to Me" (1915) offers the modern metaphor, of a train ("gospel train") for an ancient yearning to meet God.

Other poems express Johnson's political position. "Children of the Sun" is an anthem reflecting militant black nationalism and the emerging diasporic consciousness that energized **W.E.B. DuBois**'s international pan-African conferences and Marcus Garvey's Universal Negro Improvement Association (UNIA). Here the poet volunteers to awaken the passions of "the star-dust folk, striving folk! / Sorrow songs have lulled to rest." He would remind them of the power of redemption by reconstructing an ethnic history framed in both religious and political terms. Thus, the people he addresses—descendants of enslaved Africans—are, in fact, "Children of the Nazarene, / Children who shall ever sing / Liberty! Fraternity!" Using a similar thematic approach, a poem entitled "The New Day" (1919) employs elevated poetic diction and biblical allusions to describe the contribution made by African American soldiers in World War I.

James Weldon Johnson, looking back to that era in *The Book of American Negro Poetry* (1931), considered Fenton Johnson to be "a young poet of the ultra-modern school," a technically skilled experimentalist who also "voiced the disillusionment and bitterness of feeling the Negro race was then experiencing." The intensity of Fenton Johnson's expression, wrote the editor, "went further than protests against wrong or the moral challenges that the wronged always fling against the wrong-doer; he sounded the note of fatalistic despair" (140). This judgment was triggered by the shocking outburst in the prose poem "Tired" (1919): "Throw the children into the river; civilization has given us too many. It is better to die than it is to grow up and find out that you are colored." Eugene B. Redmond argued that "critics were unprepared for [Johnson's] irony and poetic assimilation of themes and feelings previously glossed over by Christianity and other anesthetics" (167).

Written as part of a sequence titled "African Nights," the prose poems Johnson published in **literary magazines** in 1918 and 1919 constitute his last truly active participation in literary circles. Under the banner of the *Favorite Magazine*, Johnson published *Tales of Darkest America* (1920), a small book of stories and vignettes, and *For the Highest Good* (1920), a collection of editorial essays, but these received little notice and vanished into the mists of literary history with the magazine itself.

Further Reading. *Selected Primary Sources:* Redmond, Eugene B., *Drumvoices: The Mission of Afro-American Poetry* (Garden City, NY: Anchor Books, 1976); Thomas, Lorenzo, *Extraordinary Measures: Afrocentric Modernism and 20th Century American Poetry* (Tuscaloosa: University of Alabama Press, 2000).

Lorenzo Thomas

JOHNSON, GEORGIA DOUGLAS (1880–1966)

Georgia Douglas Johnson, the "lady poet" of the **Harlem Renaissance**, was a significant contributor to the movement as a poet and playwright. She also participated in and fostered conversations about black artistic production through her poetry, publishing three volumes between 1918 and 1928, and through the informal literary salons that she hosted in her Washington, D.C., home. The black literati and intelligentsia, including **Jean Toomer**, **Countee Cullen**, Jessie Fauset, **Langston Hughes**, Zora Neale Hurston, **W.E.B. DuBois**, **Alice Dunbar-Nelson**, Alain Locke, **James Weldon Johnson**, **Angelina Grimké**, and **William Stanley Braithwaite**, met at these gatherings. Johnson's significance in American literature arises from her contributions to the Harlem Renaissance and also to her place as the best-known female poet of the New Negro Renaissance.

Johnson, born to biracial parents Laura Douglas (black and Native American) and George Camp (black and white), grew up in Rome, Georgia. She taught for ten years after graduating from Atlanta University's Normal School, studied at Oberlin Conservatory of Music in 1902, and then served as an assistant principal in Atlanta. While in Atlanta, Johnson met and married Henry Lincoln Johnson, an attorney. In 1910 the

Johnsons moved to Washington, D.C. Henry died in 1925, leaving his wife to raise their two sons, a task that left her with little time to write, but write she did. Three years after her husband's death, Johnson published her third book of poetry, *An Autumn Love Cycle* (1928), and several award-winning plays. *The Heart of a Woman* (1918) and *Bronze* (1922) preceded *An Autumn Love Cycle*. Johnson's fourth volume, *Share My World*, appeared in 1964. Georgia Douglas Johnson died on May 14, 1966.

In both *Heart* and *Love Cycle*, Johnson writes **lyric poetry** using traditional forms to investigate issues of love, disappointment, death, and sadness, and she develops themes of spiritual triumph and strength—more often than not, the strength of women to triumph over disappointment and disillusionment. A tension arises throughout Johnson's first two volumes between an overt Victorian feminine gentility and a covert critique of patriarchy. Poems such as "The Heart of a Woman," "Gossamer," "Peace," "Dreams of the Dreamer," and "My Little Dreams" from *Heart* expose the limitations that patriarchal mandates impose on women's talents and aspirations.

The gentleness of "The Heart of a Woman," for example, shatters in the poem's imagery of violence and constraint: "alien cage," "plight," "breaks, breaks, breaks," and "sheltering bars." If this poem reveals "the secrets of woman's nature" as Braithwaite claims in his introduction to the volume, then frustration and resentment mark that nature. In these poems, Johnson relegates women's ambitions, imagination, and creativity to the heart; yet in so doing, she casts the "sheltering bars" of domesticity as dream-stifling restraints. The persona in "My Little Dreams" may indeed pray to forget their existence and force them "within [her] heart," but the poem reveals the price women pay by such sublimation.

Bronze furthers Johnson's thematic concerns of love, sorrow, and disappointment, but as the poet herself expresses in the author's note to the volume, "This book is the child of a bitter earth-wound. . . . I know that God's sun shall one day shine upon a perfected and unhampered people" (81). Writing in the introduction to *Bronze*, DuBois claims that the poems demonstrate "what it means to be a colored women" (7). Claudia Tate states that *Bronze* "was probably Johnson's most commercially successful book because it was packaged as work of strong racial awareness" (iii). In this volume Johnson evokes the 1920s New Negro language of racial uplift. The nine sections of the book bear titles such as "Exhortation," "Supplication," "Shadow," "Motherhood," and "Exaltation," emphasizing the uplift rhetoric, and the titles of individual poems highlight the racial themes: "Sonnet to the Mantled," "Prejudice," "The Passing of the Ex-Slave," "The Octoroon," "Black Woman," and "Shall I Say, 'My Son You're Branded?'" Johnson, however, seems to have found the mandates of

the New Negro Movement just as limiting as those of patriarchy, admitting to fellow poet **Arna Bontemps** "that she did not enjoy 'writing racially'" (Hull, 18). Critic Gloria T. Hull identifies *Bronze* as Johnson's "weakest book [which] reads like obligatory race poetry" (160).

Whereas men such as Locke, DuBois, and Braithwaite, in their introductions to her volumes, lauded her "delicate" touch, "rhapsodic" tone, "ardent sincerity of emotion," and "naïve and sophisticated style" and described her poetry as "intensely feminine," "simple, sometimes trite," and "sincere and true," recent scholars (Hull, Tate, and Stetson) read against the grain, identifying a biting irony in many of Johnson's poems. These critics argue that rather than reinforce the prevailing social conditions, Johnson offered a veiled critique of "racial and gender oppression" (Tate, xviii). These inquiries into Johnson's work suggest the complications of categorizing a poet as they trouble Johnson's designation as "lady poet" of the Harlem Renaissance. Georgia Douglas Johnson's poetry reveals how race and gender intersect within several literary traditions of America: nineteenth-century Euro-American literary tradition, black American tradition, a tradition of female poetry, and American literary history.

Further Reading. ***Selected Primary Sources:*** Johnson, Georgia Douglas, *An Autumn Love Cycle* (New York: Vinal, 1928); ———, *Bronze: A Book of Verse* (Boston: Brimmer, 1922); ———, *The Heart of a Woman* (Boston: Cornhill, 1918); ———, *The Selected Works of Georgia Douglas Johnson* (New York: G.K. Hall, 1997). ***Selected Secondary Sources:*** Hull, Gloria T., *Color, Sex and Poetry: Three Women Writers from the Harlem Renaissance* (Bloomington: University of Indiana Press, 1987, 115–211); Stetson, Erlene, "Rediscovering the Harlem Renaissance: Georgia Douglas Johnson, 'The New Negro Poet'" (*Obsidian* 5 [1979]: 26–34); Tate, Claudia, Introduction, in *The Selected Works of Georgia Douglas Johnson* (New York: G.K. Hall, 1997, xvii–lxx).

Catherine Cucinella

JOHNSON, HELENE (1906–1995)

Helene Johnson was an important early poet of the **Harlem Renaissance**. Her work defies conventions of female writers of the early-twentieth century and reflects the political, racial, and aesthetic conflicts of the 1920s. She helped to establish Harlem as a literary center and the Harlem Renaissance as a valid cultural movement. Her first poem was published in 1924, and three poems were selected by **James Weldon Johnson** and **Robert Frost** for prizes in a 1926 competition. Frost called Johnson's poem "The Road" the "finest" poem submitted. Her last published poem, "Let Me Sing My Song" appeared in 1935 in *Challenge*, a journal established by her cousin Dorothy West. Her work abandoned romantic themes and poetic conventions and is characterized by an expression of hopeful desire for the future and an unsentimental view of ghetto life and the suffering of the past. Her work contains an almost contemporary sense of lyricism, humor, pathos, and a dedication to the idea of overcoming physical, social, or imaginary boundaries. Johnson's poems, "Chromatic words / Seraphic symphonies," are some of the most respected of the Harlem Renaissance.

Johnson was born Helen (without the final *e*) Johnson on July 7, 1906, in Boston, Massachusetts, and raised in Brookline and in Oak Bluffs, Massachusetts. Her parents were Ella Benson Johnson of Camden, South Carolina, and George William Johnson of Nashville, Tennessee. She was an only child. Her mother's parents had been born as slaves in South Carolina. She attended the Boston Girls' Latin School and took writing courses at Boston University and Columbia University. Her early influences were **Whitman**, Tennyson, Shelley, and **Sandburg**. At the end of 1924, Johnson submitted a poem, "Trees at Night," to the Urban League's official magazine, *Opportunity*, which won an honorable mention at their first annual literary awards ceremony in May 1925. Encouraged by her success, she moved to New York City in January 1927. With the encouragement of Zora Neale Hurston, she quickly became one of the youngest writers of the literary and cultural renaissance happening in Harlem. In the late 1920s and early 1930s, she published frequently in well-known **literary magazines** and newspapers of Harlem, including *Opportunity*, the *Messenger, Fire, Challenge*, and *Vanity Fair*, but did not publish a book in her lifetime. Johnson married William Hubbell, a motorman, in 1933, and they had one daughter, Abigail McGrath. Although she continued to write for herself, her work was published less and less frequently in subsequent years, when she worked inside the home and as civil service correspondent for the Consumers Union in Mount Vernon, New York. Her work appeared in **Arna Bontemps**'s anthology *American Negro Poetry* in 1963. She was intensely guarded and shy about her personal life and declined to read publicly as late as February 1987, when she was eighty. When asked by the scholar Cheryl A. Wall in 1987 if she was surprised by the continuing interest in the Harlem Renaissance, she answered, "[I am] never surprised by repetition." From the early 1960s until the early 1980s, she lived in Greenwich Village near Washington Square Park. Her health began to decline in the late 1980s from osteoporosis. She died on July 6, 1995, the day before her eighty-ninth birthday. Most of her known poetry and selected letters spanning the period 1927–1948 have been collected in the volume *This Waiting for Love*, published in 2000 by the University of Massachusetts Press.

Johnson's poems are generally **free-verse lyric poems**; several are rhymed or in black vernacular, and several are iambically regular Shakespearean sonnets. Her subject matter sometimes concerns the natural world or **pastoral** themes. One of the most important and best-known poems, "Magula," appeared in anthologies in 1927 and 1989. It tells the story of the romantic longings of an African American woman who is lured away from a clergyman by a poet. The poem ends with an apparent indictment of the church: "Would you sell the colors of your sunset and the fragrance / Of your flowers, and the passionate wonder of your forest / For a creed that will not let you dance?"

Her political poems take up the most shameful violations of civil rights. Her November 1926 poem "A Southern Road" concerns a lynching and anticipates Billie Holiday's haunting song "Strange Fruit" by more than a decade. The poem describes a "blue-fruited black gum" tree, from which dangles a figure, "Swinging alone, / A solemn, tortured shadow in the air."

Many of Johnson's poems are set on Harlem's streets and focus on everyday life there in the 1920s. "Bottled" considers a teenager "darkly dressed fit to kill" who "stopped to hear an / Organ grinder grind out some jazz." Her "Sonnet to a Negro in Harlem" reflects the unsentimental quality of most of her verse: "Your perfect body and your pompous gait, / Your dark eyes flashing solemnly with hate, / Small wonder that you are incompetent / To imitate those whom you so despise." This critical stance is balanced by an empathy for the poor and the working class, as in "Rootbound": "Heavy shovels / Boiling soapsuds / Opening cab doors / Washing cuspidors / Running numbers / Selling 'hot goods' / Dodging cops."

Johnson's views on race, neither **sentimental** nor unsympathetic, maintain an informed authority. Her brief **Dickinson**-like quatrain "I Am Not Proud" has implications for her status both as African American and as female: "I am not proud that I am bold / Or proud that I am black. / Color was given me as a gage / And boldness came with that." Johnson's spirited imagination and her vital and original talent as a poet have continued to bolster her importance as a Harlem Renaissance figure, although she remains under-appreciated.

Further Reading. *Selected Primary Source:* Johnson, Helene, *This Waiting for Love*, ed. Verner D. Mitchell (Amherst: University of Massachusetts Press, 2000). ***Selected Secondary Source:*** Pace, Eric, "Helene Johnson, Poet of Harlem, 89, Dies" (*New York Times* [11 July 1995]: B14).

Sean Singer

JOHNSON, JAMES WELDON (1871–1938)

James Weldon Johnson worked as a lawyer, teacher, songwriter, lobbyist, and diplomat, but he is best known for his work as a poet, critic, civil rights activist, and as the first African American general secretary of the NAACP. He has had a long-lasting influence on the field of African American literature.

Johnson's early life was free from many of the hardships experienced by African Americans at the turn of the century: His father was a successful waiter at a resort in Florida, and his mother, a schoolteacher, came from an established family in the Bahamas and received a formal education in New York City. As the son of a middle-class family, then, Johnson was spared much of the abject poverty and racism that marked the lives of many African Americans in the Southern United States after the Civil War. Johnson was educated throughout his childhood and earned a bachelor's degree from Atlanta University in 1894. During his college years, Johnson spent his summers teaching African American children who were otherwise unable to attend school. This experience helped prepare him for his first profession as a teacher and principal of Stanton School in Jacksonville, Florida. Although his early life may have been privileged compared with those of many African American young men, even then Johnson was demonstrating a commitment to the education and economic betterment of African Americans who were struggling under Jim Crow.

After working as an educator, Johnson established a short-lived newspaper in Jacksonville, the *Daily American*. He studied law on his own and became the first African American admitted to the Florida bar. His career in law was short, and he soon turned to an old hobby of his, poetry. He began composing songs with his younger brother, Rosamond, and studied writing at Columbia University. Johnson, his brother, and songwriter Bob Cole became an immensely popular songwriting trio on Tin Pan Alley, releasing over two hundred songs, including a campaign song for Teddy Roosevelt. During this period, many of Johnson's lyrics used African American dialect in the style of the **minstrel** shows of the day.

In 1900 the Johnson brothers wrote "Lift Every Voice and Sing," to be sung by children for Lincoln's birthday. This song, like some of Johnson's other work, has been criticized for its politics, since it does not express real outrage toward white racism. Nonetheless, it became so popular among African Americans that twenty years later it was adopted by the NAACP as the Negro National Anthem.

In 1907 Johnson's career took another turn, and he became a U.S. diplomat first in Venezuela and then in Nicaragua. In 1914 his diplomatic career ended when the Wilson administration pulled back from earlier strides in the appointment of African Americans to important political positions.

Johnson completed his first major literary project during his years as a diplomat: *The Autobiography of an Ex-Colored Man*, which he published anonymously in 1912 with little success, and again under his name in 1927. The fictional biography is loosely based on events from his own life and that of his friend Judson Douglass Wetmore. Wetmore, like the *Autobiography*'s protagonist, passed for white for part of his life, and Johnson used this as a way for his protagonist to view life as an African American from many perspectives. The novel was important not primarily for its aesthetic merits but for the commentary on race in the United States, which Johnson interspersed throughout the novel. The book laid out a complaint central to Johnson's thinking—that African Americans were forced to define themselves first and foremost as African Americans—and "not from the view-point of a citizen, or a man, or even a human being." He claimed that this caused African Americans to live according to racist stereotypes around whites and that it overshadowed the accomplishments of African Americans who were considered successful only in terms of their race.

In the years following the first publication of the *Autobiography*, Johnson focused his literary efforts on poetry and published several volumes of his own verse and edited three important anthologies of African American poetry. His first major poetic accomplishment was "Fifty Years," published in 1913 in the *New York Times* to mark the fiftieth anniversary of the Emancipation Proclamation. He republished it in a book of his poetry in 1917, which included poems on many subjects and explored different narrative styles, including dialect. After the publication of *Fifty Years*, Johnson rejected dialect in his poems, believing it perpetuated racist stereotypes and was an insufficient voice for **African American poetry**. In 1927 he published *God's Trombones*, a dramatized sermon, in which he tried to capture a distinctive African American style without using dialect. Johnson's other literary achievements include *Black Manhattan* (1930), a dramatization of African American life in Harlem; *St. Peter Relates an Incident* (1930), a satirical poem depicting the resurrected Unknown Soldier as a black man; *Along This Way* (1933), his autobiography; *Negro Americans, What Now?* (1934), a collection of lectures; and several essays in periodicals.

During Johnson's prolific poetic career, he also served as secretary of the NAACP and actively lobbied for civil rights, especially anti-lynching laws. Johnson became a significant and highly respected leader in the **Harlem Renaissance** in the 1920s and was involved in many activities ranging from his NAACP work to important literary criticism that helped propel the movement. Two years after resigning from the NAACP, Johnson accepted a position teaching creative literature at Fisk University. He taught there for six short but productive years before he was killed in a car accident in 1938.

Further Reading. *Selected Primary Sources:* Johnson, James Weldon, *The Autobiography of an Ex-Colored Man* (New York: Alfred A. Knopf, 1927; reprint New York: Vintage, 1989); ———, *Complete Poems*, ed. Sondra Kathryn Wilson (New York: Penguin, 2000). *Selected Secondary Sources:* Bronz, Stephen H., *Roots of Negro Racial Consciousness: The 1920's: Three Harlem Renaissance Authors* (New York: Libra, 1964); Fleming, Robert, *James Weldon Johnson* (Boston: Twayne, 1987); Price, Kenneth M., and Lawrence J. Oliver, eds., *Critical Essays on James Weldon Johnson* (New York: G.K. Hall, 1997).

Amanda Gailey

JOHNSON, RONALD (1935–1998)

One way to characterize Ronald Johnson's visionary poetry is to coin a word: *optidelic*, or vision manifesting. To say the poetry is visionary is to place it in a tradition whose antecedents are **Whitman**, Blake, Smart, and Milton as well as, more recently, **Charles Olson** and **Robert Duncan**. Johnson's transformation of acoustic and visual imagery into lyric and epic presences takes on redemptive properties. While it would be misleading to see Johnson as a Christian poet like Blake, Smart, or Milton, he was, nonetheless, a *vates*, a poet-seer. The purpose of poetry for Johnson was *seeing*.

In BEAM 4 of his epic poem, *ARK*, Johnson writes, "Pressure on the surface of an eye makes vision, though what these same pressures focus to the radial inwardness of a dragonfly in flight is unimaginable. Through pressure also, the head-over-heels is crossed right-side-up, in eye as camera." The dragonfly's composite eye is an emblem for the pressure of poetic thought on the poet's desire to see, using the poem as both a magnifying and a telescopic lens. Johnson concludes BEAM 4 by pronouncing, "After a long time of light, there began to be eyes, and light began looking with itself." Poetry is Johnson's focusing energy, the optical science that transforms light into vision. In the third part of *Radi os*, Johnson enjoins the light, which he hails as "bright effluence of bright essence," to "shine inward" and

> there plant eyes
> that I may see and tell
> Of things invisible

Johnson wants us to "simply see as much as possible, to be sentinel for incidence" ("Hurrah," 26).

In 1977 Ronald Johnson published a book unique to his oeuvre but exemplary of his visionary ideals. *Radi os*, his rewriting-through-excision of Milton's *Paradise Lost*, can be seen as a hinge on which Johnson's work swings. Johnson was forty-two years old and had already begun, seven years earlier, to devote himself to the work that would make up *ARK: The Foundations*, the first part of his long poem, *ARK*. If his earlier work, as found in such collections as *The Book of the Green Man* (1967) and *The Valley of the Many-Colored Grasses* (1969), can be described as visionary collage, then the work on *ARK* begun in 1970, of which *Radi os* was conceived to be an integral part, might be usefully considered as **epic**, Transcendentalist bricolage. (He confessed, "I spent years reading in the two huge volumes of the Dover Edition of **Thoreau**'s *Journal* to sharpen my eye and how it intersects with text. I learned how Henry David could set down the miniscules, then slip right into the unconscious, speculating about snakes in his stomach or eating a red raw muskrat" ["Hurrah," 25].) In the early 1970s the scale of Johnson's work shifted, concerning itself more explicitly with cosmology and cosmogony. *Radi os* is the work that marks that shift.

The idea of *Radi os* is as ingenious as it is enviable—which perhaps explains its cultish appeal to poets: to cut away from Milton's poem, as if it were a block of marble, in order to find his own poem within it, as if it were a sculptural form hidden there. In this sense, there is something **postmodern** about *Radi os*. The poem begins by equating the primordial Tree of Knowledge with a cosmic Adam, the "Man." Johnson uses *Paradise Lost* as a historic telescope to see through to the beginning of creation, where he finds resplendent light waiting to be turned into "luster." He concludes the poem with the injunction

> For proof look up,
> And read
> Where thou art

Johnson's early work in poetry took the form of lyrical collage of quotations, history, and mythology in the 1960s, and **concrete poetry** in the 1970s. Practice in both of these modes prepared him for the great work of *ARK* that he began in 1970. Johnson came to poetry when he started college at the University of Kansas in 1953. However, he dropped out in order to enlist in the Army, to take advantage of the GI Bill, which allowed him later to attend Columbia University, from which he received a bachelor's degree in English literature in 1960. In New York City, his real education in poetry began when he became **Jonathan Williams**'s companion. Williams had recently come from **Black Mountain** College, where he had been a student and had begun to issue publications of some of the poets associated with that institution from his imprint, eventually known as the Jargon Society. Indeed, many of the artists and poets at Black Mountain, students and teachers alike, relocated to New York City, especially in Greenwich Village, in the late 1950s. Thus, with Williams as a guide, Johnson made contacts with many of the luminaries of experimental American poetry at mid-century, including Duncan, Olson, and **Louis Zukofsky** (who would become one of his principal poetic models), as well as **Allen Ginsberg**, **Denise Levertov**, and **Robert Creeley**. And under Williams's guidance, he began to write poetry.

These early poems, written in 1959 and 1960, exhibit a curiosity for the ways language can be layered with meaning by combining elements of "local knowledge"— in Johnson's case about his native west Kansas plains (he was born in Ashland, Kansas, in 1935)—with the formal innovations typified in Olson's "**projective verse**." To these Johnson added a lyric sensitivity toward the placement of words as they generate motion, as in "Quivera," which begins by asking whether Coronado saw "an horizon of dark funnels tapering / toward the earth," and clouds "drawn like lightning toward the funnels" from which his men fled to hide in the grass. For a boy from Kansas, the memory of bison is as mythic as Coronado is historic or as tornadoes are terrifying. The complex associations and unusual patterns of Johnson's poems prompted Guy Davenport to write, "If the finely textured geometry of words Ronald Johnson builds on his pages is not what we ordinarily call a poem, it is indisputably poetry" (191).

In the early 1960s Johnson and Williams walked the length of the Appalachian Trail, and conducted two walking tours of Britain and parts of Europe. On these tours the poets camped along the way, staying with poets and artists whenever possible. It was in England that Johnson imagined his first foray into the **long poem**, *The Book of the Green Man* (1967). Conceived as a seasonal poem to invoke the eponymous, autochthonous figure of British legend, Johnson used this project to expand his sense of poetic expression while refining his visionary instinct.

Johnson became interested in concrete poetry through his friendship with Scottish poet Ian Hamilton Finlay. Johnson published regularly in Finlay's periodical *Poor. Old. Tired. Horse*, as well as issuing several publications through John Furnival's Finial Press in Urbana, Illinois, among them *Balloons for Moonless Nights*, which contains perhaps his best-known concretion, the poem that reads in its entirety "o / moon," such that the "o" of the first line appears to be rising out of the word "moon," emblem of the goddess Diana. (This concretion, like many of Johnson's others, reappears in *ARK*, "BEAM 5.") Johnson claimed his volume of concrete poems based on Mahler's Ninth Symphony, *Songs of the Earth*, to be among his favorite works. Subtitled "twelve squarings of the circle," the book begins with one of his most ingenious poems, "earthearthearth" repeated on seven lines (thus forming a square). Written so, the word "earth" yields its subtle music; one finds "hear the earth," with "ear the art," as well as "hearth" nestled against "ear" and "heart." Johnson would put the lessons learned from concrete poetry, as well as those from the

visionary collage he practiced in his early verses, to stunning, original use when he incorporated these techniques and others in the composition of *ARK*, his masterpiece.

Although begun, as already noted, in 1970, and issued in partial publications in 1980 and 1984 (*ARK: The Foundations* and *ARK 50*, respectively), *ARK* is a major long poem of the American **modernist** tradition that has yet to be absorbed into the creative imagination of our literary past. This situation is most likely the result of the relatively recent publication of the entire work, which did not appear until 1996. Hopefully, this situation will change as Johnson's readership continues to expand. *ARK*, with its creative ebullience and vocalic concision, deserves as broad an audience as possible; though consciously modeled after modernist epic poems such as **Ezra Pound**'s *Cantos*, Zukofsky's "*A*," and Olson's *Maximus Poems*, *ARK* is unlike any of these. It stands out also against the background of other visionary epics, such as *The Temple*, *Paradise Lost*, *Jubilate Agno*, or Blake's *Milton*. **Thom Gunn** once remarked, "In fifty years, we will wake up and realize that Dante was living among us, *ARK* is that good."

ARK—whose composition corresponds with the years Johnson lived in San Francisco, roughly from the end of the 1960s until the early 1990s—is an integrally structured poem, composed in ninety-nine parts, with thirty-three "Foundations," which he calls "Beams," ascending with thirty-three "Spires," and completed with thirty-three "Ramparts," which he also calls "Arches," such that they join the horizontal and vertical elements of the previous parts of the poem into a visual and sonic unity. Johnson's non-poetic models for *ARK* helpfully orient readers in understanding its overall shape and intent. For the jacket copy of *ARK: The Foundations*, Johnson wrote, "Inside these covers is a model for a monument, to be dedicated *Bison bison bison* (imagine it so carved), at its base." Other architectural models guided the poet, especially the work of so-called naive artists, such as Simon Rodia's Watts Towers, the Facteur Cheval's *Palais Ideal* in Hautrives, and Raymond Isidore's *Petit Pique-Assiete* in Chartres. In the works of these bricolage masters, Johnson discovered a technique he could apply toward assembling his own poem, captured in a phrase he translated from Isidore's writings as "Slowly, a man / makes / *(a mosaic / of earth and sky)* / his house" (*Spirit*). Johnson's other non-literary model was musical, specifically the notes written by Charles Ives for his Fifth Symphony, which the composer called "The Universe" but in fact never completed. This astonishing composition, intended for two or more orchestras working at cross purposes, was imagined in three parts: Part 1, "Past: Formation of the waters and mountains"; Part 2, "Present: Earth, evolution in nature and humanity"; and Part 3, "Future: Heaven, the rise of all to the Spiritual." Ives wrote of this symphony that it "is a striving to . . . trace with tonal imprints the vastness, the evolution of all life . . . from the great roots of life to the spiritual eternities, from the great inknown to the great unknown," a statement that could serve very well as a credo for Johnson's poem.

ARK's essential plasticity, its piece-by-piece constructedness, yields an incredible variety of poetic forms—too many, in fact, to be easily summarized. A look at the opening of "BEAM 30, The Garden" serves to demonstrate some of the characteristic properties of this poem. Dedicated to Patricia Anderson, one of Johnson's sponsors who had been diagnosed with cancer and had undergone radiation therapy, Johnson uses this beam as an opportunity to peer into the cosmology of the body, exploring its cellular structure with a microscopic, lyric eye, all the while casting his glance heavenward, where he sees a grand, Ptolemaic procession of planets and stars. The poem begins "'To do as Adam did,'" a quotation from Thomas Traherne that announces the poet's intention to begin by naming what he sees, followed by the lines about the planets Mercury ("through the twilight's fluoride glare Mercury in perihelion") and Pluto ("to Pluto foot tilt up the slide at either plane / and build a garden of the brain"). He then describes the cortices of the brain ("Internetted eternities, interspersed / with cypresses") A few lines later, he complements this vision of the inner workings of the brain with a couplet of Dantescan compression, "Fixed stars / with fireflies jam the lilac," followed by this statement: "The Lord is a delicate hammerer." If Johnson's poetry can be said to provide a theology, these three lines may sum it up.

Upon completing *ARK* in the early 1990s, Johnson turned his mind toward smaller poetic projects, including "Blocks to Be Arranged in a Pyramid, *in Memoriam AIDS*," a poem made up of sixty-six quatrains, and "psalm of the soul." In the final years of his life, he added poems to his last, posthumously published collection, *The Shrubberies*, written while he worked as a gardener in an historic park in Topeka, Kansas. These are pastoral poems for the end of a life, from simple observations—"A homing of hummingbirds / to a singular blossom"—to an apocalyptic finale:

on the screen
the primal scene
a scream of out

In 1998 Johnson died from the complications of a stroke resulting from a brain tumor. Since his death, his work has continued to garner attention from enthusiastic new readers, determined to carry on his legacy. *Enthusiasm*, as Johnson liked to remind us, is to be filled with a god; in the case of Johnson's work, enthusiasm is to be filled with the mysterious structural unities of the cosmos itself.

Further Reading. *Selected Primary Sources:* Johnson, Ronald, *ARK* (Albuquerque: Living Batch, 1996); ———, *The Book of the Green Man* (New York: Norton, 1967); ———, "Hurrah for Euphony" (*Chicago Review* 42:1 [1996]: 25–31); ———, "Interview with Peter O'Leary" (*Chicago Review* 42:1 [1996]: 32–53); ———, *Radi os* (Berkeley, CA: Sand Dollar, 1977); ———, *The Shrubberies* (Chicago: Flood Editions, 2001); ———, *Songs of the Earth* (San Francisco: Grabhorn-Hoyem, 1970); ———, *Valley of the Many-Colored Grasses* (New York: Norton, 1969). ***Selected Secondary Sources:*** Bettridge, Joel, and Eric Murphy Selinger, eds., *Ronald Johnson: Life & Work* (Orono, ME: National Poetry Foundation, 2005); Davenport, Guy, "Ronald Johnson," in *The Geography of the Imagination* (San Francisco: North Point Press, 1981).

Peter O'Leary

JONES, LEROI. *SEE BARAKA, AMIRI*

JONES, RODNEY (1950–)

Rodney Jones's poetry combines wit and humor with philosophical musings about the value of language and the poet's transcription of life's moments into forms of lasting aesthetic significance. His interest in the ephemera of life is supported by observations from his own experiences in his native Alabama and other areas as disparate as the American Midwest and El Salvador. His poems often show an uneasy joining of characters—the mechanic, the farmer, the religious grandmother, the cows—with his own perspective as the poet. This juxtaposition creates a narrative stance in which the persona straddles two worlds—that of the artistic poet who is, nonetheless, clothed in the jeans and blue collar of the working class. Though he is often compared to **Robert Penn Warren** and other Southern **narrative poets**, Jones also has the kind of objective voice one might find in **Elizabeth Bishop**. His well-crafted language transforms the ordinary into something beautiful, typically through the use of inventive metaphor. Jones is able to take a lowly subject and make it grand, often creating odes to the unexpected beauty inherent in that once thought of as ugly.

Rodney Jones was born on February 11, 1950, to Lavon and Wilda Owens Jones in Falkville, a town of a few thousand in northern Alabama. He received a BA in English from the University of Alabama at Tuscaloosa in 1971 and an MFA from the University of North Carolina at Greensboro in 1973. Since then he has taught at Virginia Intermont College (1978–1984) and at Southern Illinois University since 1984. Jones married his first wife, Virginia Kremza, in 1972; they have one daughter, Alexis. He and his present wife, Gloria Nixon de

Zepeda Jones, a native of El Salvador, whom he married in 1981, have one son, Samuel.

Rodney Jones has written seven volumes of poetry and garnered many awards, including the Jean Stein Prize in Poetry from the American Academy and Institute of Arts and Letters (1989), the National Book Critics Circle Award (1990), and in 2003 the Harper Lee Award, given annually by the Alabama Writers' Forum to a living, nationally recognized Alabama writer. In addition, his book *Elegy for the Southern Drawl* (1999) was a Pulitzer Prize nominee in 2000. In 2003 he was one of two finalists for the Illinois Poet Laureate position.

Although Rodney Jones's poetic voice and themes deepen as he grows more self-assured as a poet, many of the characteristics of his poetry can be found in both earlier and later books. Jones's reliance on natural influences as a catalyst for his work, as well as his interest in the value of poetry as a method for understanding the human condition, can be found throughout his oeuvre. In his first book, *The Story They Told Us of Light* (1980), he uses personal memory and the landscapes of his native Alabama to arrive at truths about the nature of memory and loss. These poems tend to use sharp contrasts, such as order and disorder and darkness and light, as the work attempts to reconcile the disparities of human experience.

Jones's second book, *The Unborn* (1985), although reliant on many of the same natural subjects, has a more assured poetic voice. Jones's commonplace subject matter—tomatoes, mosquitoes, laundromats—becomes the linchpin for more complicated moral and philosophic debates, as Jones contemplates such things in "Edisonesque" as "The soul of a possum [as] an empty wallet / tossed into a trash bin by thieves." Often the grotesquerie of an idea or image becomes Jones's method for finding the sublimity in such objects. In addition, Jones meditates on the use of memory and imagination and its relevance for interpreting experience. This theme can be seen in many poems, from the narrator's imaginatively rendering a house fire backward in "Remembering Fire" to the use of personal history recalled as the narrator washes clothes in "The Laundromat at the Bay Station."

Jones's third book, *Transparent Gestures* (1989), makes use of many of the dynamics of his earlier work. Here, however, his narrators ponder the lives of politicians and academics while trying to value the uniqueness within such incongruent experiences. Jones also examines situations and objects from his childhood as they represent ideas such as mercy ("Burnt Oil and Hawk") or resurrection ("Mimosa"). The last section of the book, "The Weepers," includes poems that attempt to reconcile cynicism with genuine feeling. The title poem of this section, for example, begins with the narrator imagining

typical scenarios that might provoke sadness, and how easily these topics serve those who desire a chance to weep. Yet the narrator who has so brutally chastised those who weep learns about the value of tears when he grieves.

Apocalyptic Narrative and Other Poems (1993) further explores Jones's strong affinity for natural subjects, as well as man's plight within that natural world. He returns to real landscapes—sometimes from memory, sometimes, as in "Meditation at Home," from his present—to suggest the value of memory and its ties to that landscape. Often these memories are tinged with the narrator's realizations about aging and death, although, as the title poem suggests, the poet must continue to write in spite of life's inevitable cataclysms. In most cases, the poet's interpretation is only one person's word for any given event, feeling, or truth, but one that must be valued. In "A Story of the South Pacific," for example, Jones suggests that even if "the story" is not true, sometimes having a story is better than having nothing: "It is not much. It is only one whisper / In a gallery of whispers, but you have / To take somebody's word for the world."

In *Things That Happen Once* (1996) and *Elegy for the Southern Drawl* (1999), Jones returns to an examination of familiar but often unusual topics. The poems within *Things That Happen Once*, for example, scrutinize historical events from the perspective of a narrator both curious and jaded about the experiences. There poems are more narrative in tone, although Jones also tackles the perennial topic of the poet's place in examining the world. "The Consolations of Poetry," for example, describes the inadequacy of language to express grief or to speak about the human condition.

In *Elegy for the Southern Drawl*, Jones recounts the wider arc of history and its effect on the individual, a theme that resonates in the **elegiac** tone of many of the poems, including poems honoring the lives of those now dead, such as "Plea for Forgiveness," concerning **William Carlos Williams**. This tone continues in other poems, such as "Elegy for the Southern Drawl," which laments, even as it applauds, the passing of language, attitude, and time, as well as the narrator's acceptance of the ephemeral nature of these things.

Jones's seventh collection, *The Kingdom of the Instant* (2002), takes the influence of history and religion and the author's experience in the South to display the relevance of the moment on one's life, as well as the long-lasting effects of those influences on future experiences. As in *Things That Happen Once*, Jones returns to the exploration of the minutiae of the moment and its ramifications on the narrator's present and future.

In all, Jones's work establishes the value of using the known world in all its forms—from the grotesque to the **sublime**—

812   Jordan, June Millicent (1936–2002)

to extrapolate some possibilities for understanding the self and the value of the individual experience. Although Jones persistently interrogates the poet's ability to reveal and transcend that experience, his poems suggest the necessity of such examination.

Further Reading. ***Selected Primary Sources:*** Jones, Rodney, *Apocalyptic Narrative and Other Poems* (Boston: Houghton Mifflin, 1993); ——, *Elegy for the Southern Drawl* (Boston: Houghton Mifflin, 1999); ——, *The Kingdom of the Instant* (Boston: Houghton Mifflin, 2002); ——, *The Story They Told Us of Light* (Tuscaloosa: University of Alabama Press, 1980); ——, *Things That Happen Once* (Boston: Houghton Mifflin, 1996); ——, *Transparent Gestures* (Boston: Houghton Mifflin, 1989); ——, *The Unborn* (Atlantic Monthly Press, 1985). ***Selected Secondary Source:*** Tarleton, Adam, Review of *The Kingdom of the Instant* (*Carolina Quarterly* 55 [Summer 2003]: 83–84).

Rebecca Flannagan

JORDAN, JUNE MILLICENT (1936–2002)

Educator, activist, essayist, poet, novelist, and playwright June Jordan is one of the most published African American writers in America. From 1969 to 2002, she authored twenty-eight books of poetry, political essays, and children's fiction; over four librettos and discographies; more than four poetic recordings; and numerous critical commentaries on the politicization of language, democratic relations, and the universal sufferings and oppressions of disenfranchised people. In addition to her voluminous repertoire of politically charged writings, she is known for her distinguished career as a university professor and a social activist. Her popular recognition, as evident from her writings, teachings, and activist efforts, can be associated with the rise of black consciousness during the 1960s and 1970s "second renaissance" of **Black Arts** and with the development of an anti-racist feminist movement in "a democratic state."

The only child of West Indian immigrant parents Granville Ivanhoe Jordan and Mildred Maud Fisher Jordan, June Jordan was born on July 9, 1936, in Harlem, New York. In 1942 her parents moved from Harlem to Brooklyn's Bedford-Stuyvesant community. As a teenager, Jordan was the only black student at Milwood High School, a New York City prep school. After one year, her parents enrolled her in Northfield School for Girls, a Massachusetts prep school that proved to be even more hostile to Jordan's racial and cultural identities than Milwood High. However, it was at Northfield School for Girls that Jordan's love for language and words was cultivated. She would later foster this love affair in her undergraduate studies, publications, speaking engagements, and international activist efforts.

In 1953 Jordan enrolled at Barnard College in New York City (1953–1955), searching for "the connection between the apparently unrelated worlds of white and Black" (*Civil Wars*, 98). Although not introduced to this connection at Barnard College, Jordan became unrelentingly active in the college's student publication before officially dropping out some years, and numerous experiences, later. While an eighteen-year-old student at Barnard College, Jordan became acquainted with Michael Meyer, a twenty-four-year-old white student enrolled in Columbia University, during an anti-McCarthy petition signing. They married in 1955, although Jordan and Meyer's parents utterly opposed their union. They moved to Chicago, Illinois, where Meyer studied anthropology at the University of Chicago and where Jordan enrolled (1955–1956) before leaving for New York City. Upon her return to New York, she reentered, albeit briefly, Barnard College (1956 to 1957) and became involved in the Civil Rights Movement and in urban planning. She would eventually collaborate with R. Buckminster Fuller on an architectural redesign of Harlem, New York (1964). In 1958 she gave birth to and eventually accepted full responsibility for her only child, Christopher Meyer. In 1963 Jordan became an assistant to the producer for *The Cool World*, a Shirley Clarke film adaptation of Warren Miller's novel about Harlem. Then, in 1965, after ten and a half years of marriage, Jordan and Meyer divorced.

During the 1960s, Jordan (under the name of June Meyer) began writing poems and stories for such publications as the *New York Times*, the *New York Times Magazine*, *Black Creation*, *Partisan Review*, *Essence*, the *Urban Review*, *Village Voice*, the *Nation*, *Black World*, *Evergreen*, and *Esquire*. In 1969 Crowell published *Who Look at Me*, Jordan's first book of poetry. In this book, Jordan depicts the strength and beauty of African American lives, identities, and experiences by poetically telling the stories of the twenty-seven paintings included. After the publication of *Who Look at Me*, Jordan published other books in various genres, including *Some Changes* (1971), *Fannie Lou Hamer* (1972), *Dry Victories* (1972), *New Days: Poems of Exile and Return* (1973), *Things That I Do in The Dark: Selected Poetry* (1977), *Passion: New Poems 1977–1980* (1980), *Civil Wars: Selected Essays 1963–1980* (1981), *Kimako's Story* (1981), *Civil Wars* (1981), *On Call: New Political Essays 1981–1985* (1985), *Living Room: New Poems 1980–1984* (1985), *Lyrical Campaigns* (1989), *Naming Our Destiny* (1989), *Technical Difficulties: African-American Notes on the State of the Union* (1992), *Poetry for the People: A Blueprint for the Revolution* (1995), *Affirmative Acts: Political Essays* (1998), *Soldier: A Poet's Childhood* (2000), and *Some of Us Did Not Die* (2002). In addition to these texts, Jordan authored several plays, including *In the Spirit of Sojourner Truth* (May 1979, Public Theater, New York City) and *For the Arrow That Flies by Day* (April 1981,

Shakespeare Festival, New York City). She was lyricist and librettist of "Bang Bang uber Alles" (1985) and "I Was Looking at the Ceiling and Then I Saw the Sky" (1995). In all of her works, Jordan sought to make available the beauty and freedom of language measured by truth, honesty, sound, and rhythm.

Jordan's beauty and freedom of language are powerfully exemplified in her landmark young adult novel, *His Own Where* (1971), nominated for the year's National Book Award. *His Own Where* makes use of black English, or African American spoken English, to discuss environmental conditions (and urban redesign efforts) affecting black life and love. Her essay "White English/Black English: The Politics of Translation" (1989) further alludes to the beauty and freedom of language unencumbered by codes of power and issues of white privilege, mandates, and standards. Both her essay and her young adult novel encourage people—through honest, provocative language—to "join forces to cherish and protect our various, multifoliate lives against pacification, homogenization, the silence of terror" (*Moving Towards Home*, 38).

In addition to pursuing a writing career, Jordan was a research associate and writer for the Technical Housing Department of Mobilization for Youth in New York (1965–1966) and a poet-in-residence for Teachers and Writers Collaborative in New York City (1966). From 1967 to 1978, she taught English and Literature at the City College of New York, Yale University, Sarah Lawrence College, and Connecticut College. Jordan became a tenured professor at the State University of New York, Stony Brook, and until her death in 2002 was a professor of African Studies and director of Poetry for the People Collective at the University of California–Berkeley.

Jordan's many honors include a Rockefeller Foundation grant (1969–1970) for creative writing, a Prix de Rome Award in Environmental Design (1970–1971), a Nancy Bloch Award (1971) for her book *The Voice of the Children*, a Yaddo fellowship (1979), a National Endowment for the Arts fellowship (1982), and a Achievement Award for International Reporting from the National Association of Black Journalists (1984). Jordan received the Ground Breakers–Dream Makers Award from the Women's Foundation (1984); she also received the Lila Wallace Reader's Digest Award (1995–1998). Since 1984 Jordan has been included in the *Who's Who in America* publication; she was also honored with the PEN Center USA West Freedom to Write Award (1991).

Further Reading. *Selected Primary Sources:* Jordan, June, *Civil Wars: Observations from the Front Lines of America* (New York: Simon & Schuster, 1981); ———, *His Own Where* (New York: Crowell, 1971); ———, *Moving Towards Home: Political Essays* (London: Virago,

1989); ———, *Who Look at Me* (New York: Crowell, 1969). ***Selected Secondary Sources:*** Brogan, Jacqueline Vaught, "From Warrior to Womanist: The Development of June Jordan's Poetry," in *Speaking the Other Self: American Women Writers*, ed. Jeanne C. Reesman (Athens: University of Georgia Press, 1997, 198–209); Erickson, Peter, "The Love Poetry of June Jordan" (*Callaloo* 9.1 [Winter 1986]: 221–234); Kinloch, Valerie, "June Jordan and the Linguistic Register: A Statement about Our Rights," in *Still Seeking an Attitude: Critical Reflections on the Work of June Jordan*, ed. Valerie Kinloch and Margret Grebowicz (Lanham, MD: Lexington Books, 2004).

Valerie Felita Kinloch

JORIS, PIERRE (1946–)

Pierre Joris is renowned for his versatility as a poet, translator, theorist, and anthologist of the avant-garde. Since the publication of his first book of poems, *The Fifth Season* (1971), he has written over twenty books of poetry, translated over fifteen books of poetry and prose, and edited several anthologies. Joris, who has lived in Europe, North Africa, and the United States, practices the poetic nomadism that he outlines in *A Nomad Poetics* (2003), an ars poetica that champions a process-oriented **poetics** and posits movement as a primary goal of poetry.

Pierre Joris was born in Luxembourg in 1946. His early life was informed by three languages: Lëtzebuergesch, French, and German. As a result, numerous European authors influenced Joris's later work, and Joris would eventually translate many of these writers into English, including Tristan Tzara and Paul Celan. A formative moment came for Joris at the age of fifteen, when a poem by Paul Celan was read aloud at school. After this reading, Joris began actively seeking out other poetry. During his teenage years, Joris discovered another of his later influences—the American **Beats**. Joris would later translate work by many Beat writers into French, including books by **Jack Kerouac**, Carl Solomon, and **Gregory Corso**. Most important, the multilingual environment of Luxembourg awakened in Joris a view that, as he would later say in his "Nomad Manifesto" (1994), "all languages are foreign"; it is impossible for any language to exist as a transparent, frictionless medium.

Despite a childhood predilection for literature, Joris departed from Luxembourg to study medicine at the Faculté de Médecine de Paris in 1965. After a year and a half, however, Joris withdrew from the medical program, ultimately crossing the Atlantic to earn a BA from Bard College in 1969. Here Joris was exposed to a number of American writers who would influence his later work: **Robert Duncan**, **Robert Creeley**, and **Robert Kelly**. After earning his degree from Bard,

Joris re-crossed the Atlantic to study in England. While in England Joris first studied under the influential Eric Mottram at the Institute of United States Studies, and then under **Ted Berrigan** at Essex University, where he ultimately earned an MA in **translation** in 1975. During this period, Joris began to publish seriously as a poet and translator. In 1972 he published his second book of poems, *Trance/Mutations,* and his third, *A Single-Minded Bestiary,* followed in 1974. Joris's translation work in the 1970s was predominantly from English to French, and began with the Beat figure Carl Solomon.

Citing his "deep disgust" with English political decline, Joris spent 1976 to 1979 teaching at the University of Constantine in Algeria. These three years were especially productive, as Joris published six volumes of poetry and continued translating the American Beats and the **modernist** European avant-garde: Tristan Tzara's *Negro Poems* (1976), Jack Kerouac's *Mexico City Blues* (1977), and Gregory Corso's *Sentiments Elegiaques Americains* (*Elegiac Feelings American*) (1977). Joris would later translate many writers from the Francophone Maghreb, including Habib Tengour and Abdellatif Laâbi. Returning to Europe, Joris spent the early 1980s as a freelance writer, and he also published several books of poetry, including *Tracing* (1982), *The Book of Luap Nalec* (1982), and *Net/Work* (1983). Joris then returned to the United States to earn a Ph.D. from SUNY–Binghamton in 1987. In 1992 he joined the faculty at SUNY–Albany. Since then he has published two collected volumes of his work: *Poasis: Selected Poems 1986–1999* and *A Nomad Poetics: Essays* (2003). Along with **Jerome Rothenberg**, Joris co-edited a two-volume anthology, *Poems for the Millennium* (1995 and 1998). This transnational anthology focuses on the global avant-garde, including poems in Inuit, Kannada, and Nahuatl (Aztec).

Joris's early poems are marked by a recursive and roaming **lyric** voice that posits speech as the primary force of poetry. For example, in *Hearth-Work* (1974) Joris portrays the potential of language as small sparks, "seed & syllables . . . fire particles," that swarm in a metaphoric hearth. These sparks spring from the quotidian: "hearth work is heap . . . the slag / of the daily life." Joris's early work also focuses on the migratory subject. In *Tracing* (1975), he declares that "there is no such / thing as west" and insists that the poet must abandon him- or herself to movement.

In the 1980s and early 1990s, Joris's poetry began to focus more overtly on the concept of nomadism and its two primary components: movement and mindfulness. Drawing on the conceptual nomadism outlined by the French philosophers Giles Deleuze and Felix Guattari, Joris composed a number of essays that explore the poetic potential of the nomad, many of which are collected in *A Nomad Poetics*. These essays complement much of his later poetry. For example, the title of his second collected volume of poems, *Poasis: Selected Poems 1986–1999* (2001), a portmanteau word combining "poem" and "oasis," is indicative of Joris's nomadic attitude toward the writing process. Dotting the nomad's uncertain landscapes are stops, respites to write; within these "poases," the "poem" collides with the "oasis." In an earlier book of poems, *The Irritation Ditch* (1991), Joris describes the necessary yet seductive nature of "the oasis problem": "a place to come to & and go from / never to be in, caught there." To rest too long at the oasis would cause the poet to lose the mindfulness that is acquired through constant movement and to become sedentary. For Joris, poetry must move to remain vibrant. Recently, Joris has produced what he refers to as "voco-visual performances." One example, *SUMERICABACH*, which Joris performs in collaboration with Nicole Peyraffite, is presented along with a digital video projection and background music.

Further Reading. ***Selected Primary Sources:*** Joris, Pierre, *Breccia: Selected Poems, 1972–1986* (Echternach, Luxembourg: Editions Phi; Montreal: Guernica, 1987); ———, *A Nomad Poetics: Essays* (Middletown, CT: Wesleyan University Press, 2003); ———, *Poasis: Selected Poems 1986–1999* (Middletown, CT: Wesleyan University Press, 2001); ———, *Poems for the Millennium: The University of California Book of Modern & Postmodern Poetry*, ed. Jerome Rothenberg and Pierre Joris (Berkeley: University of California Press, 1995). ***Selected Secondary Sources:*** Cohen-Cheminet, Geneviève, "Poems for the Millennium: Jerome Rothenberg et Pierre Joris lisent Charles Reznikoff," in *Collage/Montage/Assemblage, Poésie Anglaise et Américaine*, ed. Paul Volsik (Paris: Cahiers Charles V, Université Paris VII Denis Diderot, 2003, 119–135); Glenn, Jerry, "Paul Celan 2000" (*Shofar: An Interdisciplinary Journal of Jewish Studies* 20.2 [2002]: 122–128).

Gordon Hadfield

JOSEPH, ALLISON (1967–)

The poetry of Allison Joseph evokes a culturally diverse girlhood in the Bronx, highlighting the cultural complications experienced by young women of color growing up in mainstream America in the 1970s and 1980s. Employing narrative **free verse** with some instances of blank verse and sonnet forms, Joseph's **concrete**, descriptive poems re-create scenes depicting the ways in which a child, a young woman, and eventually a mature adult negotiate a tricky territory governed in part by race and gender, and by the legacy of her immigrant parents.

Joseph was born in London to parents of Caribbean background and raised in the Bronx, New York. She graduated from Bronx High School of Science in 1984 and then studied literature and writing as one of only a few nonwhite students at Kenyon College, publishing a poem in the *Kenyon Review* while still an undergraduate. During Joseph's sophomore year of college, her mother's death from lung cancer prompted many of the poems in what would become her first book. After graduating in 1989, she earned an MFA in creative writing and poetry in 1992 from Indiana University, where she studied with **Yusef Komunyakaa**, who became her thesis advisor. Joseph met and married poet Jon Tribble during her time in graduate school. Her thesis manuscript, *What Keeps Us Here*, won the Ampersand Press Women Poets Series Prize and was published in 1992, and was then awarded the John C. Zacharis First Book Prize from Emerson College and *Ploughshares*. From 1992 to 1994 she taught at the University of Arkansas at Little Rock, moving to Southern Illinois University at Carbondale in 1994, where she joined **Rodney Jones** and **Lucia Perillo** as part of the poetry faculty. In 1995 she founded and began editing *Crab Orchard Review*, which also began publishing books through the Southern Illinois University Press in the late 1990s.

In 1997 two collections of her poems were published: *Soul Train* and *In Every Seam*. Unfortunately, Joseph also lost her father in December of that year, inspiring some of the poems in her next book, *Imitation of Life*, which appeared in 2003. In 2004 her fifth collection, *Worldly Pleasures*, was published by Word Press. Throughout her career she has received a number of fellowships and awards from the Illinois Arts Council, the Bread Loaf and Sewanee Writers' Conferences, and other organizations.

Joseph was only twenty-five when her first collection, *What Keeps Us Here* (1992), appeared and, as might be expected, the work focuses a great deal on childhood experiences. Like **Gwendolyn Brooks**, an early role model, Joseph evokes an urban neighborhood in painstaking detail—the street corners, shops, school, subway, and buses, as well as the people of her childhood home. A number of the poems commemorate her mother's life and then-recent death, presenting images of her both as a young nursing student in London and as a chemotherapy patient. The poet's father is also imagined as a young man in Grenada, dreaming of American prosperity.

In Every Seam (1997) further mines the subject of youth, with vignettes from school encounters and other growing-up experiences. In several of the poems, the poet creates portraits of her father in the cultural context of his life, defining her relationship with him. "My Father's Heroes" lists the cultural icons to which her father paid homage—not political figures but rather athletes and musicians—many African American but some white, a fact that the speaker finds compelling. She presents the experience of a black student on a white college campus in "Higher Education" and satirizes the academic attitude toward African American writers in "Academic Instructions" ("Don't write / about being black"). "The White People Next Door" describes the

neighbors' reaction to the speaker's interracial marriage; other poems wax lyrical on the physical side of love. The book's title appears in the last line of the poem "Plenty," set in a fabric store, tying the collection together with a metaphorical thread.

Soul Train, also released in 1997, focuses more on the social aspects of adolescence—from high school dances to "hanging out" and negotiating friendships and the complicated expectations society holds for young women. In this collection Joseph also introduces a series of gutsy monologues, scattered throughout this and subsequent books, in which the speaker refers to herself as "Home Girl" ("Home Girl Talks Girlhood," "Home Girl Steps Out," "Home Girl Dreams a Dance Partner"). The narrative arc of the book takes the speaker through young adulthood to the point where she glimpses a more mature state. The closing sequence, "Genealogy," pays tribute to Joseph's parents, their youthful meeting, the growth of their relationship over time, and their effects on her own life.

In her fourth book, *Imitation of Life* (2003), Joseph continued to explore African American girlhood, presenting personal and cultural identity through narrative poems of lyric intensity. Poems in this book are often in stanzas using roughly four- or five-beat lines; the voice continues to be accessible, witnessing the girl's experience with clear, specific details of setting ("Remember the market beneath the el, / the wooden stalls that shook each time / a train rumbled overhead?") and revealing details of the speaker's self. Poems of childhood include images of hair straightening ("Frying Hair") and leaving for college ("Numbers"). Other poems use adult subjects to reveals the larger implications of the childhood memories and echo earlier references to music, education, and language. Using concrete, descriptive language, the poems recall the speaker's childhood experience, almost as if in response to her blue-collar father's admonition to "write it properly, / . . . and write / it plainly, so I can read it" ("Translating My Parents").

Worldly Pleasures takes Joseph's traditional childhood material into a more mythic mode, showing a greater distance from the experience while remaining specific and detailed. A series of poems present schoolgirl archetypes ("The Jealous Girl," "The Shy Girl," "The Dangerous Girl," "The Dreamer," "The Gossip," etc.), giving insight into the motivation of each titular character. The title poem, an evocative description of sensual love, is followed by "A Sermon," which marries the sensual to the spiritual. As in her previous dealings with love, the subject inspires Joseph's most musical language, short lines spilling easily into each other. The poet, always attentive to story and the senses, shows in this collection a mature vision integrating the vividness of childhood memories with the immediacy of adult experience.

Further Reading. ***Selected Primary Sources:*** Joseph, Allison, *In Every Seam* (Pittsburgh: University of Pittsburgh Press, 1997); ———, *Imitation of Life* (Pittsburgh: Carnegie Mellon University Press, 2003); ———, *Soul Train* (Pittsburgh: Carnegie Mellon University Press, 1997); ———, *What Keeps Us Here* (Port Townsend, WA: Ampersand Press, 1992); ———, *Worldly Pleasures* (Cincinnati, OH: Word Press, 2004). ***Selected Secondary Sources:*** Johnson, Judith E., "New Works: *In Every Seam*" (*Women's Review of Books* 14.10–11 [July 1997]: 28–30); Pardlo, Gregory, "Review of *Imitation of Life: Poems*" (*Black Issues Book Review* 5.3 [May–June 2003]: 59); Stanton, Maura, "Review of *What Keeps Us Here*" (*Ploughshares* 18.4 [Winter 1992]: 237–239).

Amy Lemmon

JOSEPH, LAWRENCE (1948–)

Something of a lone wolf in the contemporary poetry scene, Lawrence Joseph remains aloof from the poetry world by virtue of his other career as a law professor and scholar. His legal knowledge, often present in the poetry, came to the fore with his prose work *Lawyerland: What Lawyers Talk About When They Talk About Law* (1997). Having quietly built his reputation as a poet over the past twenty years, Joseph created a wider audience for all his work with the tough-minded mix of fact and fiction in *Lawyerland*. Although not a **Language poet** by any means, Joseph's obsession with breaking apart speech and his interest in (among others) **Gertrude Stein** and **Louis Zukofsky** suggest a similar background in a distinctly American poetic tradition. He continues to publish both poems and prose in a wide variety of legal and literary publications, and critics—especially those from the recent Law and Literature school of scholarship—have reevaluated his poetry in light of his two careers.

Born in Detroit, Michigan, to the children of immigrant Lebanese and Syrian parents in 1948, Joseph, a Maronite Catholic, attended parochial school in the parish of the famous radio priest Charles Coughlin. After Jesuit high school, he graduated from the University of Michigan, where he received a Hopwood Award. He earned his second BA in English from Cambridge University before returning to the University of Michigan for his law degree. After clerking for a Michigan Supreme Court judge, he taught law and also worked for a major New York City law firm. He eventually settled in Manhattan with his wife, the painter Nancy Van Goethem, and has taught primarily tort and employment law for years at St. John's University School of Law in Queens. Joseph's debut collection, *Shouting at No One* (1983), won the Agnes Lynch Starrett Poetry Prize for a first book; it was published by the University of Pittsburgh Press, which also published Joseph's second book,

Curriculum Vitae (1988). Both volumes were enthusiastically reviewed in literary journals and celebrated for their singular voice: at once intensely personal yet objective, rooted in the facts of his life but also discursive and abstract. Joseph's third book of poems, *Before Our Eyes* (1993), though less rant than the earlier work, is equally indignant. An urban wanderer and "cosmopolitan talker" (as **James Merrill** put it) to the core, the poet here exercises his conscience against a world-political background.

In *Shouting at No One*, Joseph declares himself "the poet of my city," which is, of course, Detroit, a city everywhere in decline. He travels its gritty streets, which provide many of his images: the factories, the smoke stacks, the slums. His "howling" voice ("Then") rehearses the facts of his history: the family market looted in a riot, his father shot by a thief, and his own time on the assembly line. Joseph's poems in this volume rely on his sense of ethnicity (Lebanese), class (working), and religion (Catholic). In poems such as "The Phoenix Has Come to a Mountain in Lebanon," he imagines and reenacts the drama of diaspora. As he tells us in "Not Yet," "there is so much / anger in my heart," but this does not stop him (in other poems) from crying, singing, and praying. An envoi ("*I was appointed the poet of heaven*") announces that the "I" of these poems (not always the poet Joseph) would be "*pulled from a womb / into a city*," and one of Joseph's strongest poem in the volume, "There Is a God Who Hates Us So Much," echoes this very line. Joseph's first book pulses with the beat of Marvin Gaye and the cadences of the Latin Mass—both quoted in its longer poems.

The divided self reflected in *Shouting at No One* is more apparent in *Curriculum Vitae*, and the overall intensity diminishes somewhat, as Joseph announces straight away that he intends "to speak more softly" ("In the Age of Postcapitalism"). In fleshier, longer lines, he returns to familiar subjects: his parents and grandparents, factory rats, and Detroit in ruins. And as the title poem makes clear, the connection between Beirut and the Motor City still obtains—Joseph mines his roots for a number of poems that bear witness to his ethnic heritage, most notably "Sand Nigger" and "Rubaiyat." His Catholicism, especially his concern with sexual desire, continues to shape his sentiments, and his diction can be anxious as well: "I confess / too much" he tells us in "Let Us Pray." But Joseph also expands his worldview. The law, economics, and finance begin to exert their influence, less for their subject matter than for their unique languages (see, for example, "Any and All"). Being a moral man in the modern world here becomes more complex here: The self is "an abstraction" ("Stop Me If I've Told You"), and the poet lives merely "in words" ("I Pay the Price"). No matter how much Joseph struggles toward a more impersonal aesthetic, he remains, by the end of the collection (in the last poem, "There I Am Again"), "the grocer's son / angry, ashamed, and proud as the poor with whom he deals."

With *Before Our Eyes*, Joseph achieves the kind of urbanity he celebrates in two poets he greatly admires (and about whom he has written essays): James Schuyler and **Frederick Seidel**. Like Schuyler (and **William Carlos Williams**), Joseph simply records "what's before our eyes," as the title poem has it. But Joseph is also a trenchant observer of the sociopolitical scene, like Seidel, and given to metaphysical musings in the manner of **Wallace Stevens**. In short, he wants "to see everything simultaneously" ("Some Sort of Chronicler I Am"). In less simple terms, the poet hopes "to bring / depths to the surface, to elevate / sensuous experience into speech / and the social contract" ("Before Our Eyes"). Although Detroit and family continue to surface in these more abstract poems, Joseph draws much of his street-smart imagery from New York City, with its dramatic mix of wealth and poverty. Everything he observes in the world of global politics and corporate finance convinces him that anarchy reigns in the public square and that the greatest "refuge" is "in observation" ("Just That"). Consciously avoiding an intensely personal voice ("never use the word 'I' unless you have to"), Joseph nevertheless finds solace in the heart and the soul, both of which continue to be shaped by Catholic theology and the urban funk of rhythm and blues.

Further Reading. *Selected Primary Sources:* Joseph, Lawrence, *Before Our Eyes* (New York: Farrar, Straus and Giroux, 1993); ———, *Curriculum Vitae* (Pittsburgh: University of Pittsburgh Press, 1988); ———, *Lawyerland* (New York, Farrar, Straus and Giroux, 1997); ———, *Shouting at No One* (Pittsburgh: University of Pittsburgh Press, 1983). *Selected Secondary Sources:* Schlag, Pierre, et al., Special section on Lawrence Joseph (*Columbia Law Review* 101.7 [November 2001]: 1730); Skeel, David A., "Practicing Poetry, Teaching Law" (*Michigan Law Review* 92.6 [May 1994]: 1754).

Thomas DePietro

JOSSELYN, JOHN (CA. 1608–1700?)

The known contribution of John Josselyn to American poetry consists of three short poems that appeared in his two travel promotional narratives. *New-Englands Rarities Discovered* (1672) and *An Account of Two Voyages to New-England* (1674), both reveal a lively and inquisitive mind at work in the New England environment and presage the development of common American genres, such as the tall tale, the ghost story, and the nature essay. His writing is at once gullible, perceptive, sharp-edged, and good-humored, a combination that is generally appealing.

Biographical information on Josselyn is spotty and much of it conjectural. However, it is known that the Josselyn family was an established one, with branches in Essex, Hertfordshire, and Kent, all descended from Gilbertus Josselinus, who accompanied William the Conqueror to England. The date and location of John Josselyn's birth is "probably 1608" at Torrell's Hall, Willingale Doe, Essex (Lindholdt, xiv). He was one of two sons of Sir Thomas Josselyn, an impoverished member of the gentry who received his knighthood from James I in 1603. Nothing is known of Josselyn's education, though a pronounced interest in the medicinal powers of New England plants that is evidenced in both books strongly suggests an extensive background in medicine and a probable training as a physician. Josselyn twice traveled to New England, his first visit lasting from 1638 to 1639 and the second from 1663 to 1671. On both occasions Josselyn lived with his brother, Henry, on the Maine coast in what is now known as Scarborough. The visits accorded Josselyn opportunities to explore the New England countryside and to discover and carefully describe its flora and fauna. In fact, Josselyn's careful observations of New England plants and wildlife recorded in his first book earned him a three-page notice in the *Philosophical Transactions* of the Royal Society in 1672. He also found the time during his visits to collect a variety of tall tales and "stretchers" from the English settlers, to become well acquainted with Native American culture, and to run afoul of the governing Puritans.

Josselyn's poetic production reveals a sensibility more acute than might be suggested by the size of output, and it gives a clear indication of the powerful effect that the physical realities of New England had upon the English imagination. Even his shortest poem, a four-line verse meditation on a New England spring appearing in *Two Voyages* (1674), shows the wonder the land instilled in its European settlers. Although only a humble mountain spring, "Swift is't in pace, light poiz'd, to look in clear / And quick in boiling." It has all the qualities without which "no water could be good" (33–34). A small outlet of mountain water has the power to capture the attention. Josselyn's most famous poetic effort is included at the end of *Rarities* (1672) almost as an afterthought in a section titled "A Description of an Indian Squa" (101–102) and is intended as a "Divertisement, or Recreation" (99) for readers who have preserved through his natural observations. In the introduction to his poem, Josselyn dismisses Native American men as "somewhat Horse Faced," but he notes that the women "have very good Features; seldom without a *Come to me*, or *Cos Amoris*, in their Countenance" (99–100). The poem itself is a challenge to the reader to decide "Whether White or Black be best," as the reader is invited to put the "Senses to the quest." The narrator of the poem is captivated by the

"Black ones'" soft and smooth skin and ready wit and observes that "Nor can ought so please the tast [*sic*] / As what's brown and lovely drest." The speaker concludes that in spite of what may be said in favor of "White and Red" that "darkness was before the Day." In the end, "such perfection here appears / It neither Wind nor Sunshine fears." Whatever else may be said of the beauty of the Native American woman, hers is a beauty best seen out of doors and in contact with nature, and it will not be shut away. For all its objectification, Josselyn's verse expresses yet another example of the impact nearly every part of the New World had upon the Europeans. And Josselyn's poetry and detailed physicality stand in striking contrast to the more spiritual verse commonly associated with the period.

However, Josselyn's most deft verse is his description of a storm encountered during his first voyage from England to America, an event recounted in *Two Voyages* (1674). Near the end of the account, Josselyn tells of "a little black cloud" that appeared at three in the afternoon. Within two hours, the wind had become "boisterous," the sea had "grown huge," and the day turned "pitchie dark" (25). As "the Seas rage" and "the sad clouds sink in showers," sky and sea dissolve into one another, as if "the high-swoln-seas" had reached up and "Heaven to Seas descended." In a few able lines, Josselyn invokes a world turned nearly upside down: "the Sea with lightning Burns." The storm so disturbs the normal order that "the Pilot" does not know which way to turn: "Art stood amaz'd in Ambiguity." The striking last line suggests something of the magnitude, mystery, and wonder of nature in the New World, and the possible effects it could have upon those new to the experience.

Besides the writing of his two books, nothing is known of Josselyn's activities after his return to England in 1671. Even the year of his death remains unclear. Most authorities simply date his death as post-1692. However, Lindholdt cites one authority as having connected the traveler with a tombstone in Willingale Doe that gives 1700 as the date of his death (xxiii).

Further Reading. ***Selected Primary Sources:*** Josselyn, John, *New-Englands Rarities Discovered* (Bedford, MA: Applewood Books, n.d.); ———, *John Josselyn, Colonial Traveler. A Critical Edition of Two Voyages to New England,* ed. Paul J. Lindholdt (Hanover, NH: University Press of New England, 1988). ***Selected Secondary Sources:*** Gura, Philip F., "Thoreau and John Josselyn" (*New England Quarterly* 48 [1975]: 505–518); Lindholdt, Paul J., "Introduction," in *John Josselyn, Colonial Traveler. A Critical Edition of Two Voyages to New England,* by John Josselyn (Hanover, NH: University Press of New England, 1988); Wardenaar, Leslie A., "Humor in the Colonial Promotional Tract: Topics and Techniques" (*Early American Literature* 9 [1975]: 286–300).

Walt Nott

JUANA INÉS DE LA CRUZ, SOR (1648/1651–1695)

Sor Juana Inés de la Cruz is arguably the most significant American poet of the seventeenth century. The baroque poetry and drama of this nun, whose likeness now adorns the Mexican 200-peso note, was among the best produced by writers of the Spanish Golden Age, regardless of gender or place of birth. Of course, her being a woman and an American contributes to our understanding of her fame then and now. In her writings, Sor Juana demonstrates a wide-ranging intellect that places her in the midst of European letters. She also mounts defenses of women and portrays Mexican cultures in ways that contribute to the decentering of a European cultural core.

Juana Ramírez de Asbaje was born in San Miguel Nepantla, outside of Mexico City, in 1648 or 1651, the illegitimate child of Doña Isabel Ramírez de Santillana and Pedro Manuel de Asbaje y Vargas Machuca. Her mother was a *criollo*, born in New Spain to parents who immigrated from Andalusia, and her father was reportedly a Basque nobleman. Young Juana achieved a remarkable level of education with the help of the teachers at a school for girls and her grandfather's library. Sometime between the ages of eight and thirteen, she went to live with her wealthy aunt and uncle in Mexico City before entering the service of Doña Leonor Carreto, Marquesa de Mancera, wife of the newly arrived viceroy, when she was fifteen. For the next five years, Juana was active at court (save for a brief sojourn in the convent of the exceptionally austere Carmelites) until entering the convent of San Jerónimo in 1669 at the age of twenty.

Her earliest surviving work is a *loa* to the Holy Sacrament written in 1658, but her best-known works were written after she professed as a nun. Sor Juana was a baroque writer, and as such her poetry hinges on elaborate conceits, word play, and antitheses as well as an impressive pansophism, a quality evident in the works of many other writers of her time, both men and women, but rarely accomplished with such mastery. In 1668 Juana passed an examination by leading intellectuals at the viceregal court in Mexico City, solidifying her position as a prodigy and an oddity. The title page of her first published collection of poetry, *Inundación Castálida* (1689), perpetuates this by referring to her as *la musa dezima*, or the Tenth Muse (a title given to numerous learned women of the early modern period, including another early American poet who strove to demonstrate her knowledge in many intellectual areas, **Anne Bradstreet**). Her wide-ranging learning reflects her brilliance and her immersion in baroque cultural values, but ironically it is often cited as a way to *extract* her from her culture and set her apart as an exception and as a muse, not someone with the agency of a writer.

Her works include religious and secular lyrics and dramas in many forms and a prose theological treatise, published by the Bishop of Puebla, Don Manuel Fernández de Santa Cruz y Sahagún, as *La Carta Atenagorica*, or *Letter Worthy of Athena*. This latter work led to one of her best-known and most frequently translated pieces, *La Respuesta a Sor Filotea* (*Answer to Sister Filotea*), as well as her ultimate silencing. Having published *La Carta Atenagorica*, the Bishop of Puebla then wrote an open letter to Sor Juana taking her to task for writing and pursuing learning in a manner inappropriate for a woman and nun. He wrote in the guise of a fellow nun, Sor Filotea, and Sor Juana's reply is a well-argued autobiographical defense of her intellectual activities and those of other learned women. It is an instructive compendium of common arguments and rhetorical devices used in pro-woman arguments of the time as well as one of the best sources for information about Sor Juana's life.

Sor Juana wrote **lyric poetry** in many metrical forms common to Spain's literary Golden Age, including romances, *endechas*, *redondillas*, *décimas*, sonnets, *liras*, and *silvas*. Although some of these poems treat religious subjects, many are secular. In them she defends her literary and intellectual activities, mocks sexist hypocrisy, praises patrons, engages in the banter of court, and, of course, writes of love. Among her love poems are lyrics addressed to Laura (Doña Leonor Carreto) and Lysis (María Luisa Manrique de Lara y Gonzaga, Condesa de Paredes, and Marquesa de la Laguna). These poems engage the conventions of Renaissance love lyrics and in doing so treat the nature of love and its contradictions, the endurance and limits of poetry, and the speaker's deep feelings for the beloved. They speak to Sor Juana's facility with the conventions of an important lyric form as well as the strength of her personal relationships. The balance between personal and conventional expression inevitably sparks debate. Whatever the nature of Sor Juana's personal relationships, it is useful to recognize that other female poets of the seventeenth-century, such as Katherine Philips, wrote love poems to women and that their engagement of the Petrarchan tradition in poems describing love of both men and women serves as an important comment on the use of women as objects of desire and inspiration in that tradition.

The poem that many judge to be her masterpiece and that Sor Juana herself claimed was the only work she wrote purely for her own pleasure is *Primero Sueño* (*First Dream*). In this dream poem, she chronicles the trajectory of both body and soul during a night's sleep. While lungs breathe, heart beats, and stomach churns, the soul rises through successive levels of human learning, aspiring to and almost achieving total, divine knowledge, only to awaken. Notably, it is not until the final line of this poem that we learn that the dreamer and speaker is female. Like other dream poems, *Primero Sueño* explores the limits of human knowledge as well as transgressions committed in pursuit of that knowledge. But unlike her models, Sor Juana's dreamer does not have a guide. Whether reflecting her **modernism**, skepticism, feminism, or some other -ism, this device allows Sor Juana to emphasize the dreamer's solitary quest as well as the futility of that quest. It also enables her to develop a radically syncretic understanding of areas of thought more fully than would be possible if a guide representing a particular worldview provided an authorizing framework.

Although she wrote numerous lyrics meant to be read or circulated informally, at least a third of Sor Juana's poetic output was written for **performance**. Among her dramas are three *autos sacramental* (one-act plays celebrating the Eucharist), two comedies, thirty-two *loas* (short one-act plays intended as prefatory pieces for longer works), and several *saintes* or farces. She also wrote numerous songs, especially *villancicos*, a form of carol or peasant song. Both religious and secular works were written primarily for court audiences, not public performance, though in 1680 she prepared a triumphal arch at the cathedral in Mexico City in honor of the newly appointed viceroy and vicereine, the Marquis and Marquesa de la Laguna, along with a description and explication of this arch in prose and verse entitled *Neptuno alegorico* (*Allegorical Neptune*).

Although much of her work was written with Spanish audiences in mind and seems rather isolated from more "American" topics, the *loa* to *The Divine Narcissus* is noteworthy for its portrayal of Aztecs and the conflict between Spanish Christianity and native beliefs and peoples. She also wrote two *villancicos* entitled "*Ensaladilla*" in which she represents the voices of blacks and Indians (the latter in Nahuatl *tocotines*, one entirely in Nahuatl, the other in Nahuatl and Spanish). The dominant culture of New Spain was highly attuned to racial differences and hierarchies. Sor Juana's representation of Indian culture and languages demonstrates knowledge and sensitivity that has led some to praise her as an early critic of colonialism, but it also betrays a condescending and exoticizing Eurocentric perspective.

Two years after writing *La Respuesta a Sor Filotea*, Sor Juana renounced secular letters and got rid of most of her books and musical instruments (at one point she is believed to have owned over 3,000 books). In 1694 she signed documents abjuring her learned activities. She died on April 17, 1695, at the age of forty-six, having fallen ill from nursing victims of an epidemic. In addition to *Inundación castálida*, published in Spain in 1689 with the help of the Condesa de Paredes, the second and third volumes of her collected works, *Segundo volumen* and *Fama y Obras póstumas*, were published in Spain in 1692 and 1700, respectively.

Further Reading. ***Selected Primary Sources:*** Cruz, Sor Juana Inés de la, *Fama y obras póstumas* (Madrid, 1700); ———, *Inundación Castálida de la unica poetisa, musa dezima, Soror Juana Inés de la Cruz* (Madrid, 1689); ———, *Obras completas*, 4 vols., ed. Alfonso Méndez Plancarte and Alberto G. Salceda (Mexico: Fondo de Cultura Económica, 1951–1957); ———, *Poems, Protest, and a Dream: Selected Writings*, trans. Margaret Sayers Peden (New York: Penguin, 1997); ———, *Segundo volumen* (Sevilla, 1692). ***Selected Secondary Sources:*** Merrim, Stephanie, *Early Modern Women's Writing and Sor Juana Inés de la Cruz* (Nashville, TN: Vanderbilt University Press, 1999); Merrim, Stephanie, ed., *Feminist Perspectives on Sor Juana Inés de la Cruz* (Detroit: Wayne State University Press, 1991); Paz, Octavio, *Sor Juana* (Cambridge, MA: Harvard University Press, 1988); Villar, Luis M., *The Sor Juana Inés de la Cruz Project*, http://www.dartmouth.edu/~sorjuana/.

Tamara Harvey

JUSTICE, DONALD (1925–2004)

The poetry of Donald Justice is wrapped in the cloak of his reputation as a theorist and essayist and, most significantly, his reputation as a teacher. Associated with several writing programs, he is best known for his role in the development of the University of Iowa Writers' Workshop. Justice was a famously nonprolific poet, a fact that also plays a part in the perception of him as something *besides* a poet.

This is all likely to change over time. History will note his reputation as a teacher, but as those directly affected by him as students pass into that same history, the poetry is what will remain. And over time, the lack of prolific output becomes less important, as a poet comes to be known primarily for a representative group of anthologized pieces. In fact, a smaller output may well mean that a larger percentage of the artist's work is remembered. Robert Johnson wrote fewer than two dozen songs; fully a quarter of them are recognized as masterpieces. In the future, Donald Justice is likely to be remembered as a poet who gave his age a quiet but compelling insight into loss and distance and who set a standard for craftsmanship, attention to detail, and subtleties of rhythm.

Justice was born August 12, 1925, in Miami, Florida, and raised in the South. His father was a carpenter, and the lives of working men of his father's generation became one of the recurring themes of his poetry, even though he is more associated with themes of art, music, and aesthetics. He graduated from the University of Miami in 1945. Although he was always interested in writing poetry—his early letters include a group of poems sent to the Mississippi poet George Marion O'Donnell in 1943, asking for a critique—his original major in college was in musical composition, and he studied with composer Carl Ruggles, who encouraged his talent. Ultimately, however, he took his BA in English from 1942 to 1945. He received an MA from the University of North Carolina in 1947, where he met his wife, the writer Jean Ross. He then headed north and west to Stanford University, where he studied for two years (1947–1948) but was frustrated in his desire to be allowed to work with poet and critic and champion of formal verse **Yvor Winters**, although he did audit Winters's classes. It is interesting to speculate what the effect of a closer relationship with Winters, who believed in a highly focused—some say narrow and arbitrary—definition of perfection in poetry, might have had on the young Justice. In any case, he left Stanford and came to continue his studies at the University of Iowa, where he worked with Paul Engle, **Robert Lowell**, and **John Berryman** and earned his Ph.D. in 1954. After a stay in Europe as a Rockefeller Foundation fellow and short teaching stints at the University of Missouri–Columbia and Hamline University in St. Paul, Minnesota, he returned to Iowa in 1957—first as a replacement for Paul Engle, who was on sabbatical leave, and then, after Engle's return, as a full-time faculty member. Justice remained at Iowa through 1966. For many, Justice came to personify the Iowa Workshop approach to the teaching of poetry, both by those criticized what they perceived as its timidity and rejection of bold innovation, and by those who appreciated his generous yet persistent urging to his students that they hold themselves to their highest standards. As his student and later colleague **Marvin Bell** said in a eulogy, "As a teacher, Don chose always to be on the side of the poem, defending it from half-baked attacks by students anxious to defend their own turf. While he had firm preferences in private, as a teacher Don defended all turfs. He had little use for poetic theory."

He taught at Syracuse University from 1963 to 1970, at the University of California at Irvine from 1970 to 1971, at Iowa again from 1971 to 1982, and finally at the University of Florida in Gainesville from 1982 until his retirement in 1992. He also held visiting professorships at Princeton (1976) and the University of Virginia at Charlotte (1980). After his retirement, he returned to live in Iowa City.

His first collection of poems, *The Summer Anniversaries*, published in 1960, was the Lamont Poetry Selection of the Academy of American Poets for 1959. *Departures*, published in 1973, was nominated for the National Book Award, and *Selected Poems,* published in 1979, won the Pulitzer Prize for poetry in 1980. Other collections included *Night Light* (1967), *The Sunset Maker* (1987), *Collected Poems* (2004), and several chapbooks from small presses. Justice edited the collected poems of two admired contemporaries, **Weldon Kees** (1960) and **Henri Coulette** (1990, with **Robert Mezey**). *A Donald Justice Reader* (1992) included poetry, short stories, a memoir, and a collection of critical essays; *Oblivion* (1998) contained more criticism and miscellaneous prose pieces. He wrote the libretti for Edward Miller's opera *The Young God—A Vaudeville* (1969) and Edwin London's opera *The Death of Lincoln* (1976).

He was awarded the Inez Boulton Prize by *Poetry* magazine in 1960; a Ford Foundation fellowship in 1964–1965; National Endowment for the Arts grants in 1967, 1973, 1980, and 1989; a Guggenheim fellowship in 1976–1977; the Harriet Monroe Award from the University of Chicago in 1984; an Academy of American Poets fellowship in 1988; the Bollingen Prize for poetry in 1991; and the Lannen Literary Award for Poetry in 1996. In 1997 he was elected a chancellor of the Academy of American Poets. He died August 6, 2004, after a long illness, which had rendered him unable to accept the position of Poet Laureate of the United States for 2004.

"Great Leo roared at my birth," Justice began "The Summer Anniversaries," which was to become the title poem for his first collection. But that ironic glance at grandiosity, with its allusion to Hotspur's dismissal of Owen Glendower's bombast in *Henry IV, Part I*, proved to be a dodgy issue for Justice, and the entire stanza was omitted from the poem as included in *New and Selected Poems*. In that collection, the poem begins with what had been the second stanza. The speaker is ten years old, and the ironic self-aggrandizement is more painful: "I was wheeled superb in a chair / Past vacant lots in bloom / . . . In secret proud of the scar / dividing me from life." But in his final book, *Collected Poems*, the stanza is restored—perhaps, as many would theorize, because it was simply too good to be left out, but more likely because Justice heard some nuanced variation on his theme that left a vacancy with its absence, in spite of his famous credo that all the best revision was cutting out extraneous material. In this public instance of major revision, we get a sense of what he meant when he told an interviewer for the *Iowa Review*, "I have a sort of Platonic notion that somewhere exists ideally the poem I'm trying to write, if only I can find it." Justice gently mocked his own sparse output and endless revision toward the ideal in "The Thin Man" (from *Night Light*), where he admits he indulges himself "In rich refusals" and that "Nothing suffices."

Justice's work abounds in the fixing of moments in the treacherous pages of time. "The Poet at Seven" flies a paper airplane and spins around in circles, leaving the reader to find the hint of the nascent poet in the little boy. "The Summer Anniversaries" takes a young man from age ten through seventeen, twenty, and thirty. One of his best-known poems, "Men at Forty" (from *Night Light*) notes that men at this age "Learn to close slowly / The doors to rooms they will not be / Coming back to." In *The Sunset Maker*, "Tremayne," the alter ego of Justice's late years, "as usual, misquotes / Recalling adolescence

and old trees / In whose shade he once memorized that verse."

Time, fixed and fleeing, is of concern to Justice outside of his autobiographical verse as well. In "On the Death of Friends in Childhood" he imagines dead friends in a twilit schoolyard "[f]orming a ring, perhaps, or joining hands / In games whose very names we have forgotten" (*The Summer Anniversaries*). He stops time in the reconstructed past in "Young Girls Growing Up (1911)" to re-create a long-past courtship ritual that captures timeless longing. In the remembered past, he is occasionally sociopolitical ("Cinema and Ballad of the Great Depression") but more often aesthetic and personal, as in the series of tributes to his first piano teachers (all the above from *The Sunset Maker*).

Music played a recurring role in the poetry of the one-time student of composition, although he himself rejected this notion. He told **Dana Gioia** in an interview,

> I can't think of any effect at all [of the study of music on his poetry]. None . . . I don't happen to think that poetry is—or can be—very "musical." It's a figure of speech, basically. My God, how I've heard the term misused and abused! That may be how the study of music affected me—to make me less tolerant of the kind of nonsense uttered on this score. Some even go so far as to speak of the melody of poetry. But the fact is that poetry has no melody, which involves pitch . . . "Musical" when applied to poetry seems to mean approximately what "poetic" means when applied to music.

Nevertheless, critics and readers have felt the forms of music in Justice's poems structured around themes and variations and in his "Sonatina in Green" and "Sonatina in Yellow." With characteristic understatement, Justice chose to title these poems after a musical form considered to be technically less demanding than the sonata. Musicians, composers, teachers of music, and overheard strains of music all occur prominently in his work.

Known as brilliant technician, Justice showed his command of received forms most frequently in his early poems. *The Summer Anniversaries* is a virtuoso display of forms, particularly the sestina. In "A Dream Sestina," which recalls Dante, Justice writes that he "woke by first light in a wood" and saw a circle of faces around him, some of them those of friends: "I knew that I had lost my way." At the same time in its repetition of words, this sestina creates an echo of Dante's *terza rima*, as well as his circles of hell. "Sestina on Six Words by Weldon Kees" pays tribute to a poet whose work in the form deeply influenced the young Justice. Regarding "Here in Katmandu," the modest poet took credit in an interview for technical innovation: "All the sestinas that had been written in English before, all I had read, anyway, were in iambic pentamenter, or at least what I would call a casual pentameter. . . . But I consciously shortened the lines; I varied the length of the lines. Nowadays anyone may do that. The Katmandu sestina has a small place in the history of the form, I think."

The six end words in the "Kees" sestina are "others / voyage /silence / away / burden / harm"—hardly distinctive enough, some would say, to warrant acknowledgment. But acknowledgments were always an important issue for Justice. His poem titles are full of them: the Kees poem, "Last Days of Prospero," "After a Phrase Abandoned by Wallace Stevens," and "Variations on a Text by Vallejo." His later collections, from *Departures* on, end with "Notes" in which Justice discloses the minutest of debts to others.

In his later work, he moved further in the direction of **free verse**, but always carefully modulated and always with what has been called "the ghost of meter." In *Departures*, particularly, he worked with experimental forms, most notably the poems that took their genesis from the chance dealing out of "vocabulary" and "syntax" cards, a concept he said occurred to him after playing poker with **John Cage**. But the formal verse was always there, and in *The Sunset Maker* he returned in several poems to rhyme and meter and to received forms, including the pantoum and villanelle.

Because of Justice's close identification with the Iowa Writers' Workshop, his formal brilliance, and his rejection of ego, even in his autobiographical poems (in a telling revision, the line "How fashionably sad my early poems are!" in *Night Light* becomes "How fashionably sad those early poems are!" in *New and Selected Poems*, and the revision remains in *Collected Poems*) made Justice something of a lightning rod for criticism in certain cir-

cles. His poetry has been criticized as lacking vitality, afflicted with weary passivity, focusing on trivialities, concerned only with literature, and not very interesting literature at that. But for others, Justice himself was the Platonic ideal he spoke of aspiring to. Critic David Yezzi described Justice's poems as "compos[ing] a body of work that, though inimitable, younger writers would do well to study for its fluent musicality and gently blooming, almost ineffable melancholy." Others have similarly cited his work for its suitability for imitation. His former student **Charles Wright**, in an article on Donald Justice, put it this way: "Poets are like restaurants—as soon as they are successful, they are imitated. Really good poets are like really good restaurants—they are inimitable, though one is continually nourished there."

Further Reading. *Selected Primary Sources:* Justice, Donald, *Collected Poems* (New York: Alfred A. Knopf, 2004); ———, *Departures* (New York: Atheneum, 1973); ———, *A Donald Justice Reader* (Hanover, NH: Middlebury College Press, 1991); ———, *New and Selected Poems* (New York: Alfred A. Knopf, 1995); ———, *Night Light* (Middletown, CT: Wesleyan University Press, 1960); ———, *The Summer Anniversaries* (Middletown, CT: Wesleyan University Press, 1960); ———, *The Sunset Maker* (New York: Atheneum, 1987). *Selected Secondary Sources:* Gioia, Dana, Interview (*American Poetry Review* 25.1 [January–February 1996]: 37–46); Interview (*Iowa Review* 11.2–3 [Spring–Summer 1980]: 1–21); Wright, Charles, "Homage to the Thin Man" (*Southern Review* 30.4 [Autumn 1994]: 741–744); Yezzi, David. "The Memory of Donald Justice" (*New Criterion* 23.3 [November 2004]: 21–25).

Tad Richards

K

KAMAKA'EHA, LYDIA. *SEE* LILI'UOKALANI, QUEEN

KAUFMAN, BOB (1925–1986)

Bob Kaufman (Robert Garnell Kaufman) was born in New Orleans, Louisiana, on April 18, 1925, into a Catholic African American family. Along with fellow poets **LeRoi Jones/Amiri Baraka** and Ted Joans, Kaufman has become best known as an African American or black **Beat poet** due primarily to his association with **Jack Kerouac** and **Allen Ginsberg** as well as with the **San Francisco Renaissance**.

While occupying a marginal status in terms of the Beat generation, Kaufman's breadth of style, form, and innovation enriches the definition of Beat poetics and extends a Beat aesthetic into the **African American poetry** tradition. Kaufman's poetry effectively merges **jazz** poetry inspired by **Langston Hughes**, surrealism in the traditions of Guillaume Apollinaire and Aimé Césaire, Beat/hipster street poetry, and adaptations of bebop formal and tonal qualities. Among his influences he counted the poets **Hart Crane**, Federico Garcia Lorca, Arthur Rimbaud, Charles Baudelaire, and **Walt Whitman** as well as the jazz musicians King Pleasure and Charlie Parker.

Perhaps mythologized more than that of any other Beat poet, Kaufman's life became folklore among the North Beach and Greenwich Village artist/poetry communities of the 1950s through the 1970s. Apocryphal stories arose from his public visibility as a radical street poet and renowned drifter, despite the poet's stated desire for anonymity. For example, he is said to have joined the Merchant Marines at age thirteen and survived four shipwrecks (he enlisted at eighteen and became a leading organizer in the National Maritime Union), and his grandmother was purportedly a voodoo practitioner and his father a German Orthodox Jew (Kaufman had an extensive knowledge of New Orleans culture, and his great-grandfather may have been Jewish). In fact, many of the stories were fabricated by Kaufman himself as an extension of his street poetry performances. Harassed by police, incarcerated and institutionalized on numerous occasions, his public vulnerability defined the dangers of being both a vocal Beat and a socially critical African American at a time of heightened sociopolitical tension and defensive white supremacy.

The double marginality Kaufman experienced informs many of his poems, especially in regard to the theme of abnegation of identity. In "Jail Poems," from his first published collection, *Solitudes Crowded with Loneliness* (1965), the anonymity of being a prisoner issues from the anonymous postscript "Written in San Francisco City Prison Cell 3, 1959." With identity reductively defined by the intersection of space and time, the line of the poem "Someone whom I am is no one" makes the poet visible through and despite his invisibility as a prisoner while simultaneously abnegating his identity. Furthermore, "I am not me" contradicts the subject/object relationship of identity with a presence and absence that clarifies Kaufman's ambivalence regarding anonymity. This poetics of presence and absence echoes the sociocultural marginality of being both a Beat outsider and an African American, a double marginality that Kaufman responded to by choosing anonymity and silence rather than submitting to their sociocultural enforcement.

The poetic intersection of solitary imprisonment, artistic alienation, and cultural isolation in poems such as "Jail Poems" also expresses the brutality and ostracism Kaufman experienced as a street poet. The impact of these experiences coupled with the San Francisco poetic establishment's lack of seriousness toward him led Kaufman in the early 1960s to take a vow of silence that lasted nearly until the end of the Vietnam War. Although stories about this vow reached legendary proportions and suspicion grew concerning the extent of the silence, he neither wrote nor performed during this period. Moreover, the intention behind this vow of silence, to stand in solidarity with the world's silenced and anonymous poor by becoming silent and anonymous, reflects the poetic response in many of his poems.

In 1959 Kaufman co-founded *Beatitude* magazine, in which his major work, the "Abomunist" sequence, first appeared. Published as a broadside in 1959 by City Lights and also in *Solitudes Crowded with Loneliness,* "Abomunist Manifesto" exemplifies Kaufman's jazz and bebop poetics, **Dadaist**-surrealist style, and Beat "rejectionary philosophy." Operating mainly as satire, the "Abomunist" poems often employ a linguistic play that improvises phrasing and sound, reminiscent of Langston Hughes's jazz poetry. Additionally, this play functions along a fragmentation that not only deconstructs meaning in an anti-authoritarian gesture but also reclaims minoritarian expression from dominant cultural suppression, echoing the **negritude** of Aimé Césaire.

First, the term "Abomunism" itself entails abbreviations, compressions, and glidings that challenge and extend rather than subsume and limit possibilities of meaning (*a*tom *bom*b, *abom*ination, com*munism*, -*isms*, etc.). Second, Kaufman signed the poems "by Bomkauf," which in part reflects the collapse of identity he faced in his daily life as a multi-marginalized outsider. However, "Bomkauf" also represents resistance and challenge to sociocultural oppression—for example, African American reclamation of surname and the power to determine one's own identity—and demonstrates Kaufman's declaration "I want to be anonymous. . . . My ambition is to be completely forgotten" (*Ancient Rain,* ix).

The overall humor and linguistic play of "Abomunist Manifesto" flows musically, with short phrasings of lines and improvisation of word-sounds such as

"Abomunist Rational Anthem" (also appearing in his second book, *Golden Sardine* [1967], as "Crootey Sango"): "DEE BEETSRAWISIT, WAPAGO, LOCORO, LO. / VOOMETEYEREEPETIOP, BOP, BOP, BOP, WHIPOLAT." While the syllabic sounds and combinations can be deciphered into various meanings, the rhythms and tonal qualities relate more to scat technique and reflect the bebop liberation of free-form improvisation from imposed structure. The sound pattern also reminds us that Kaufman primarily performed his poems aloud without recitation of the written word.

The poems in *Solitudes Crowded with Loneliness,* written in the late 1950s through the early 1960s, were transcribed from oral form, compiled, and edited by Eileen Kaufman, his wife, before being published by New Directions. Besides addressing and referencing the poet's inspirers (including Billie Holiday, Charles Mingus, Charlie Parker, Hart Crane, and Albert Camus), many of the poems allude to or directly name fellow Beats. Furthermore, they describe Beat geographies and the sometimes desperate, often devastating existence of a cultural outsider. For instance, in the poem "Bagel Shop Jazz," "Shadow people" make a desperate attempt at a culturally integrative ethos outside of the strict sociocultural conformity of Cold War America. Against the politics of integration, marked by cultural appropriation and assimilation, the "Shadow people," "Hoping the beat is really the truth," approach their own appropriation of black cultural forms such as jazz more as a quest for subjective survival.

Aesthetically, Kaufman also demonstrates an integrative approach in his harmonizing of African American jazz with European-based surrealism. Composed of surrealist word juxtapositions and rich contrasting imagery, many of the poems detail a distinctly visual relationship of the outsider's body with its devastation by drugs, exploitation, and general street life. However, the damage and even death of the body continually retains the possibility of spiritual and physical resurrection. While the pores of the poet's skin in "Dolorous Echo" serve as "Millions of little / Secret graves" for emotions that refuse to stay dead, his life, too, moves in this echo so that, as the final line states, after death he will not remain dead. Of further significance, the poem describes dead birds not remaining dead in the millions of trees that are the poet's hair, "Bird" being a nickname for Charlie Parker. Thus beyond the surrealistic resurrection of the physical body, not remaining dead is analogous to the tumultuous history of African American cultural forms and the death by cultural appropriation jazz faces but yet triumphs over. Ultimately, physical, spiritual, and cultural survival is one and the same and depends on the poet's body where it makes itself felt.

Kaufman continued the harmony of jazz with surrealism in his second book, *Golden Sardine* (1967), the title of which comes from a phrase he wrote on a scrap of paper. Although the poems feel more rushed in their composition compared with *Solitudes Crowded with Loneliness*, they possess the same energy and rich expression as the first collection. The opening poem, "Carl Chessman Interviews the PTA from his Swank Gas Chamber," is a surrealistic **narrative poem** based on an innocent victim of capital punishment. The poet, himself often a victim of wrongful arrest and imprisonment, interweaves absurdist descriptions of an unjust American judicial system, religion, history, and California popular culture, evoking a tone that is at once bitter, compassionate, and satirical.

The presence of simultaneous tones constitutes a major characteristic of Kaufman's poetic critique of the American sociocultural landscape. The conflation of sorrow, anger, solitude, and humor in the poem "On" as much defines the outsider's voice of the poem as does the fact that the poem contains no grammatical subject. Formally, "On" follows the structure of the first line: "On yardbird corners of embryonic hopes, drowned in a heroin tear," with the poet subsequently replacing the word "yardbird" (after the second line) and following the preposition "of" with a pair of objects. Besides the lyrical quality rendered by this form, the nominative ellipses clearly establish a sense of detachment from the middle-class Anglo images listed in each line. The evocation of Charlie Parker in the first two lines signifies an outsider artistic allegiance between the bebop innovator and the African American Beat poet, while the disdain expressed toward the conformist, middle-class landscape, all objects of prepositions, aligns the poet with a community of Beat outsiders. Humorously, the corners that contain the images (and cause "parkerflights") bring to mind the corners of squares, a common epithet for conformists in jazz and Beat parlance.

While jazz elements and inspirations exist in most of Kaufman's poetry, certain poems address jazz directly in their titles and content. Of the jazz poems in *Golden Sardine*, "'Round About Midnight" is one of the most well known. The title comes from the Thelonious Monk composition "'Round Midnight," which also became the Miles Davis standard "'Round About Midnight." The poem differs from many of Kaufman's other jazz poems in that the form is structured with a regular, steady rhythm, rhyme, and repetition of the title line. The function of jazz in this poem is purely contextual. Here the poet and a "jazz type chick" listen to jazz and feel its effects, such as "Stirring up laughter, dying tears" and eventually inducing sex.

The jazz poem "O-Jazz-O," on the other hand, uses short, uneven lines to produce a jazz rhythm. Initially playing off the polysemy of the word "string," the poem engages jazz images (string, notes, needle, musical tears, drumsticks) that detail a fragmented African American cultural history. However, jazz "strings" the images into

cohesiveness and implicitly demonstrates history as a continuous process of reclamation. The poem represents this process through a metaphoric relation of jazz elements and images to birth, origin, religion, loss, diaspora, and emotion, a relation drawing on song more than written narrative to reconnect history with ancestry.

The history of Kaufman's own poetry echoes the process of historical reclamations through jazz, specifically, the re-collecting of diasporic songs and stories. Indeed, many of his oral poems survive only due to Eileen Kaufman's transcriptions. Such is the case with much of the poetry in *The Ancient Rain: Poems 1956–1978* (1981), which brackets Kaufman's vow of silence with previously uncollected poems from 1956 through 1963 and newer poems from 1973 through 1978, many transcribed from tape recordings.

Included in the earlier poems of *The Ancient Rain* is "War Memoir: Jazz, Don't Listen to It at Your Own Risk," in which the poet uses the pronoun "we" to speak simultaneously from and against a culture that has grown indifferent and become lost in avarice and warfare. When taking a rest from murder, "we" finally take time to listen to jazz whose persistence pays off. "We" are restored to life. Even though the poem uses the plural pronoun, the voice still imparts a solitude, still sounds as if it comes from an outsider who refuses to deny or ignore that which fuels his flight. The outsider returns in the "secret jazz," carries the secret of jazz. Secrecy coincides with moments of compassion "[w]hen guilty we crawl back in time, reaching away from ourselves," and it is only then that we listen, "feel / And live."

When Kaufman publicly ended his vow of silence in February 1973, he recited his poem "(All those ships that never sailed)." The poem's theme, a return of the unaccomplished now accomplished forever, correlates with Kaufman's return to poetry while also revealing the physical toll of his absence: his body, once beautiful, "is now a museum of betrayal." Like the representations of fragmented history in his earlier poems, his body now appears fragmented, each part remembered only through past sensual human contact.

The theme of return in this collection gets its most comprehensive depiction in the concluding poem, "The Ancient Rain." In this long narrative poem, the refrain "Ancient Rain" pulls together historical and prophetic images as it signals an eternal return of revolution and war. Because the Ancient Rain "is the source of all things" and "knows all secrets," it can function as both destroyer and redeemer, obliterating hegemonic historical discourses so that an inclusive history can be rewritten. For this task the poet evokes Garcia Lorca's surrealist work *The Poet in New York*, and attempts to remove Lorca from the non–African American intellectuals who misinterpret him, situating him instead within the history of racial struggle along with the likes of Crispus Attucks.

This gesture signifies Kaufman's poetics as well as his politics, both speaking with an integrative transformation and both never finding the appreciation they deserve. Here his spoken desire for anonymity becomes more poignant than ironic when one considers the precarious survival of his work during his equally precarious life. Bob Kaufman died of emphysema and cirrhosis on January 12, 1986, in San Francisco.

Further Reading. *Selected Primary Sources:* Kaufman, Bob, *The Ancient Rain: Poems 1956–1978*, ed. Raymond Foye (New York: New Directions, 1981); ———, *Cranial Guitar: Selected Poems*, ed. Gerald Nicosia (Minneapolis: Coffee House Press, 1996); ———, *Golden Sardine* (San Francisco: City Lights, 1967); ———, *Solitudes Crowded with Loneliness* (New York: New Directions, 1965). *Selected Secondary Sources:* Damon, Maria, ed., "Bob Kaufman: A Special Section" (*Callaloo* 25.1 [Winter 2002]: 105–231); ———, "'Unmeaning Jargon'/ Uncanonized Beatitude: Bob Kaufman, Poet," in *The Dark End of the Street: Margins in American Vanguard Poetry* (Minneapolis: University of Minnesota Press, 1993, 32–76); Lee, A. Robert, "Black Beats: The Signifying Poetry of LeRoi Jones/Amiri Baraka, Ted Joans, and Bob Kaufman," in *Beat Down to Your Soul: What Was the Beat Generation?*, ed. Ann Charters (New York: Penguin, 2001, 303–327).

Jeffrey B. Falla

KEES, WELDON (1914–1955?)

Weldon Kees was a poet, critic, novelist, abstract expressionist painter, **jazz pianist**, and filmmaker. He performed and published along with the best-known **modernist** poets, including **Robert Lowell, Elizabeth Bishop, Kenneth Rexroth,** and **John Berryman.** Kees created multimedia expression fifty years before the rest of the world—experimenting with film, music, visual art, collage, and the written word. Although he enjoyed some success in all the arts he practiced, he never achieved the fame of most of his contemporaries. His elusive and troubled life ended mysteriously with his disappearance in 1955. At the time of his death, there was little critical interest in his work, but he now holds cult status.

Harry Weldon Kees was born on February 24, 1914, in Beatrice, Nebraska, to John and Sarah Kees, who owned a hardware store and were prominent members of Beatrice society. From childhood, Kees was interested in writing, music, and art. At the University of Nebraska, from which he graduated in 1935, he became part of a literary circle surrounding Lowry Charles Wimberly, the editor of *Prairie Schooner.* Editors had little interest in his first novels, but more than forty of Kees's short stories were published between 1934 and 1945. His first book of poems, *The Last Man,* was published in 1943. He began working for the

Federal Writers' Project in Lincoln and reviewed books for *Prairie Schooner,* where he became acquainted with many editors, critics, and poets. He met and married Ann Swan, and they remained in Denver until 1943, when they moved to New York. By this time, Kees was writing frequently for *New Directions,* the *Partisan Review, New Republic, Time,* the *New York Times, Poetry,* and Paramount's newsreel services. Around the end of World War II, Kees abandoned fiction and started painting in the Abstract Expressionist style, exhibiting his work alongside that of Hans Hoffman and Willem de Kooning. His second book of poems, *The Fall of the Magicians,* was published in 1947. Around 1948, Kees succeeded Clement Greenberg as the art critic for the *Nation.* The Keeses moved to San Francisco in 1950, at the cusp of the literary renaissance there. He continued publishing poems in literary magazines and exhibited his paintings, and also became interested in New Orleans–style jazz. He composed song lyrics and jazz tunes and began experimenting in photography and film, including collaborations on behavioral science films with the anthropologist Gregory Bateson. His last book of poems, *Poems 1947–1954,* appeared in 1954 and included poems published in *Partisan Review,* the *New Yorker,* and *Harper's.* In June and July 1955, Kees suffered from depression, and told friends he thought of resettling in Mexico because **Hart Crane** had escaped the pressures of America there. On July 18, 1955, Kees's car was found on the north end of the Golden Gate Bridge. Neither a suicide note nor a body was found, but he was never seen again. In 1960 **Donald Justice** rediscovered Kees's poems and made them available in a new collected edition.

Kees romanticized darkness and sadness. In some ways a contradictory figure, he found the values of his contemporary generation insipid and preferred the styles of an earlier generation of writers (such as Crane), but he also was an aesthete whose poems embodied the cutting edge sensibilities of his era. Most of Kees's poems are experimental in terms of mixing prose styles with the laws of metered and free verse. These experiments often resulted in a quiet, contained lyricism tempered by formal qualities.

Rexroth described Kees as living in a "permanent and hopeless apocalypse." His well-known poem, *1926,* demonstrates a nostalgia for an imagined, lost past: "The porchlight coming on again, / Early November . . . A phonograph is playing *Ja-Da.*" His third-person persona, Robinson, appears in several poems and is a transparent mask though which Kees's sentimentality toward psychological darkness could be expressed: "The mirror from Mexico, stuck to the wall, / Reflects nothing at all. . . . Robinson alone provides the image Robinsonian."

Kees saw the pleasures of existence as a subterfuge masking an extraordinary gloominess that he saw everywhere and that contributed to the fog in which he lived.

Generally the tone of his poems is pensive and tinged with regret or sorrow. In "Early Winter" he says, "the room is cold, the words in the books are cold." Another poem, "Poem Instead of a Letter," closes with the image of winds blowing through the mind, "and every syllable is false, and dry."

Many of Kees's poems express an alienation from the world; which is almost solipsistic, but in a way that sets him apart from his contemporaries Robert Lowell and John Berryman, for example. In his revised introduction to the 1960 edition of *The Collected Poems of Weldon Kees,* Justice attributes the most tasteful and moving qualities of Kees's verse to his cumulative body of work rather than isolated moments of brilliance. Justice also praises Kees's satiric eye, particularly in the Robinson poems in which scorn is mixed with pity. The inventiveness and imaginative leaps in his poems have demanded the interest of many contemporary poets, especially since his interest and restlessness reflected in his exploration of other arts fueled his poems, the art for which he is most admired.

Further Reading. ***Selected Primary Sources:*** Kees, Weldon, *The Collected Poems of Weldon Kees,* ed. Donald Justice (Lincoln: University of Nebraska Press, 2003); ———, *Selected Short Stories of Weldon Kees,* ed. Dana Gioia (Lincoln: University of Nebraska Press, 2002); ———, *Weldon Kees and the Midcentury Generation: Letters 1935–1955,* ed. Robert E. Knoll (Lincoln: University of Nebraska Press, 2003). ***Selected Secondary Sources:*** Reidel, James, *Vanished Act: The Life and Art of Weldon Kees* (Lincoln: University of Nebraska Press, 2003); Siedell, Daniel A., ed., *Weldon Kees and the Arts at Midcentury* (Lincoln: University of Nebraska Press, 2003).

Sean Singer

KELLY, ROBERT (1935–)

The poetry of Robert Kelly resists summary not only because of the vastness of his published oeuvre and the range of forms he has so thoroughly explored, but also because of the scope of his interests and devotions. His work to date constitutes a fascinating, sustained, and unusually variegated celebration of the "written" life. In well over fifty books of poetry, four collections of short fiction, and a novel (the published volumes representing but a fraction of his daily writing practice), Kelly has so succeeded in faithfully yet imaginatively transcribing the activity of conscious experience, in all of its various registers, that an editor might, from this vast archive, assemble several disparate *Selected Poems,* each one characterized by a different set of compositional strategies, yet each as focused, committed, and singularly musical as the next. From traditional **lyric** to the collage-oriented, fragmentary texts associated with **Charles Olson**, from book-length poems to the three-line "lune" (his own invention),

Kelly has always striven to integrate a metaphorical and musical density with the ancient bardic ideal that poetry remain competent to tell the tale of the tribe. After the examples of Dante, Coleridge, and **Ezra Pound**, he envisions the poet's vocation in the most comprehensive of terms—as "a scientist of the whole" (*In Time,* 25) as much as a careful musician of emotional and sexual intimacy.

Born in Brooklyn in 1935, Kelly attended the City University of New York and carried on graduate studies in medieval literature at Columbia University. He was a lecturer in English at Wagner College from 1960 to 1961. In 1961 he began to teach at Bard College in the Hudson Valley, where he has remained ever since (he currently holds the Asher B. Edelman Chair of Languages and Literature). He has, in addition, served as co-director of the writing program at the Milton Avery Graduate School of the Arts (an affiliate of Bard College) and has held visiting appointments at several other universities. In 1980 he received the Los Angeles Times First Annual Book Award for *Kill the Messenger Who Brings Bad News* and in 1991 the American Book Award (from the Before Columbus Foundation) for *In Time,* as well as the Award for Distinction from the National Academy and Institute of Arts and Letters.

Early but enduring associations with such writers as **Jerome Rothenberg, David Antin, Gerrit Lansing, Paul Blackburn, Diane Wakoski,** and **Clayton Eshleman** reveal both a formative experimentalism derived from the **Black Mountain School** and a thoroughly internationalist perspective, though his range has proved to be more catholic and unpredictable compared with most of his peers. What he does explicitly share with these poets is the powerful tutelary influence of Olson (and, by extension, Pound), an interest in composition by field, and the conviction that a poem could represent a legible record of the *work* or *process* by which the author was led to its proposals (*see also* **Open Form**). As an exponent of such a processual aesthetic, Kelly's talent for eliciting very traditional delights—those of lyricism and figurative invention—remain a unique contribution to **postmodern** American literature. It was also in the 1960s that he was most active as an editor of magazines, having established *Chelsea* (with **George Economou**), *Trobar,* and *Matter* during these years.

Kelly was associated in his early career with the provisional and never doctrinaire poetics of **Deep Image** (a phrase he coined in 1961). This loosely defined program served as a locus of intention for many of the poets mentioned above, and as a convenient means of identifying them as members of a common "movement," though the phrase later came to be associated most strongly with **Robert Bly**. An interest in coordinating depth-psychological researches into myth and unconsciousness resources (including surrealism, Jungian analysis, and shamanism) with a gathering interest in body awareness, informed much of this Deep Image work (*see also* **Ethnopoetics**). Indeed, some of Kelly's memorable early poems manage to capture the elusive combination of primordial grace and animal immediacy one might associate with a cave image from Lascaux: "who walks out with flowering skull and starfish fingers / and clay runs out of his nostrils" (*Red Actions*).

A massive erudition and remarkable familiarity with the imaginative sciences (alchemy, astrology, and other various "occult" means of investigation) drive a good deal of Kelly's early mature work and reveal his debt to **Robert Duncan**, who insisted, like Olson, that the poet cultivate a holistic awareness. Indeed, certain books of the late 1960s and early 1970s (principal among them *Axon Dendron Tree, Songs I–XXX, Flesh: Dream: Book*, and *The Loom*) fairly spill over with both literary allusion and the minutiae of an *arcana mundi*—alchemical, historical, metaphysico-theological, and linguistic. Yet a warmth of tone coupled with a line of extraordinarily acute balance and swiftness often rescue even the more difficult among these texts from the presentational aridity one might associate with Pound or Olson. The important theoretical statement *In Time* (1971) provides an unusually persuasive condensation of his "total poetics," a document sufficiently ambitious to embrace the cosmic orientation of ancient cities, a universal grammar of history, the place of dream interpretation in the psychic economy, and matters of diet and traditional medicine. And lest one come to the mistaken conclusion that he is addicted to gigantism, it should be noted that Kelly has also frequently worked on a far smaller scale: The "Spels" in *Thor's Thrush* (1962), *Lunes* (1964), *The Flowers of Unceasing Coincidence* (1988), and the more recent *Runes* (1999) all demonstrate, for a writer so given to plenitudes and summits, a remarkable talent for the miniature.

"Ode 16," a characteristic lyric, boldly announces Kelly's larger ambitions, beginning "That I came to know it all—." As with a majority of his poems, it would be difficult to assign to these eighteen lines a conventionally univocal subject. The diction, though—which in places can only be described as ripe, almost plummy, full of vegetable imagery and closely coordinated assonances reminiscent of Keats's "To Autumn"—might serve as a thematic caution against the claims of barren epistemologies that would posit an objective reality aloof from the immediacy of articulation, of the physical act of speaking: "real is intimate, hard to find, / locked & released at once in thought" (*Red Actions*).

Such combinations of thematic scope and intimate register are hallmarks of Kelly's best work. The musical cadence of his lines, governed as much by sudden and bold shifts in statement as by continuity of sound ("Ode 16" serves as an excellent example), would persuade the reader to resist easy paraphrase or closed interpretation, to give over to an unceasing "melody" of perceptual

awareness, of which the poem can serve as both instrument and record. The "consolations" of syntax and "poignant imagery," in "Ode 16," must in the end be accounted "deceitful resurrections" for such a processual poetics (*Red Actions*). The musical moment, despite apparent repetition, never sounds the same, nor should one, ideally, ever cease to reframe his or her experience according to the flux of circumstance and context. With this in mind, Kelly can be read as a philosophical poet, but one whose reason, inseparable from the demands of the body and fed by a deeply erotic engagement with language, will not be satisfied with the convenience of traditional argument but rather, through incessant activity (and the metabolism of an intellectual omnivore), will boldly attempt to approximate Being itself, to "spell incessantly the sum of all" (*Spiritual Exercises*).

As early as 1965, Kelly writes in his postscript to the important anthology (co-edited with Paris Leary) *A Controversy of Poets*, "In general, the new poetry is the product of those poets who believe in the word, who believe in the word's strength, who do not say: *the words failed me*, but who may confess: *I failed the words*" (565). This conviction, voiced again and again in his work in almost every conceivable formulation, amounts to a kind of theological linguistics: We must, paradoxically, not presume to use language voluntarily, according to the dictates of a supralinguistic will; rather, language speaks through, contains, us. *It* is the vital center, the locus of genius and redemption, not the individual, and only through observance of this reversal will one accomplish anything like a transformation or transcendence. At the close of the fourteenth section of *The Loom* (subtitled, "Pain: Dream of the Burnt Heart"), in the process of exorting the reader to "Be the other thing," Kelly unwinds a litany of upwards to eighty "other things" the reader might "be," among them "a broken sword," "the lawless seed," "the process," and finally, at the end of the list, "The god." Thus, only through the word, in the most literal sense, can one achieve apotheosis.

The middle 1970s and 1980s proved to be extraordinarily fertile. Some of Kelly's most cohesive, powerful books—among them *Kill the Messenger* (1979), *Book of Persephone* (1978), *Spiritual Exercises* (1981), and *Under Words* (1983)—date from this period. His explorations into what he has referred to as "polysyntax," in such longer poems as "Sentence," "The Emptying," and "Mercury," prefigure the linguistic indeterminacy of the succeeding generation of **Gertrude Stein**-inspired avant-gardists, though with the difference that he does not feel bound to a complete abandonment of normative syntax and meaning making. As suspicious as the **Language poets** might claim to have been of the subjective "high lyrical," Kelly has proven to be just as suspicious of the "low aleatoric." However disjunctive the associational combinations or harsh the parataxis in, for example, "Sentence" in *Spiritual Exercises*—a book-length sequence of unpunctuated quatrains—he rarely, if ever, is willing to relinquish the syntactic coherence of the line to strenuously willed deformations. "Syntax is a faculty of soul," Valery claimed, and though recondite in reference, Kelly's language nonetheless remains grounded in the speech act and, as such, rooted in the *polis*: "this camarilla of discourse that never stops / Thursdaying its motives to the city to the world."

Since the late 1980s and 1990s, Kelly's books (though, again, one generalizes at one's peril) have taken on an even warmer, occasionally almost demotic accessibility, but with no sacrifice of powers. Important among these collections are *Not This Island Music* (1987), *A Strange Market* (1992), and *The Time of Voice* (1998). This trend accompanies a growing interest in short prose fiction, in which the laying in of connective narrative tissue provides a spacious antiphon to the compacted statement and metaphor of the poetry. Several comparatively recent long poems, such as "Man Sleeping," and the book-length *Mont Blanc* (1994) generously demonstrate his willingness to "tolerate his own inclinations" toward associative permissiveness—more fearlessly than in even the much longer *The Loom*. *Mont Blanc*, in particular, an "expansion" of the Percy Shelley original, in which Kelly "inscribes" additional material in "the spaces" of the parent text (a practice similar to cabalistic *notarikon*, where each letter of a word is used to generate yet another word), could be construed as a kind of "Anatomie of the World" (though this might be said of many of his poems). Written while he was vacationing in the Chamonix region, the poem nearly accomplishes, in its thirty-four wildly veering cantos, Kelly's oft-avowed intention to say everything, all at once; it is both a grand act of homage and a glorious scandal of unfettered interpolation. To read the poem through in one sitting can produce in the reader the effect of fortuitously tuning in to a universal radio frequency through which the world has momentarily chosen to channel the totality of utterances, both casual and momentous: a single but vast river of images—of "large codes" and "ancient tongues"—that, in Shelley's words, "ceaselessly bursts and raves." *Mont Blanc* represents Kelly at the height of his powers; as but a mere forty-five–page segment of a veritable Okeanos, streaming with poems, stories, and novels, it amply illustrates the dimension of this poet's extraordinary achievement.

Further Reading. ***Selected Primary Sources:*** Kelly, Robert, *The Alchemist to Mercury*, ed. Jed Rasula (Richmond, CA: North Atlantic, 1981); ———, *The Book of Persephone* (New Paltz, NY: Treacle, 1978); ———, *The Common Shore* (Los Angeles: Black Sparrow, 1969); ———, *The Convections* (Santa Barbara, CA: Black Sparrow, 1978); ———, *Doctor of Silence: Fictions* (Kingston, NY: McPherson and Co.,

1988); ———, *Finding the Measure* (Los Angeles: Black Sparrow, 1968); ———, *Flesh: Dream: Book* (Los Angeles: Black Sparrow, 1971); ———, *The Flowers of Unceasing Coincidence* (Barrytown, NY: Station Hill, 1988); ———, *In Time* (West Newberry, MA: Frontier, 1971); ———, *Kill the Messenger Who Brings Bad News* (Santa Barbara, CA: Black Sparrow, 1979); ———, *The Loom* (Los Angeles: Black Sparrow, 1975); ———, *The Mill of Particulars* (Los Angeles: Black Sparrow, 1973); ———, *Mont Blanc* (Ann Arbor, MI: OtherWind, 1994); ———, *Not This Island Music* (Santa Rosa, CA: Black Sparrow, 1987); ———, *Red Actions: Selected Poems 1960–1993* (Santa Rosa, CA: Black Sparrow, 1995); ———, *The Scorpions* (Garden City, NY: Doubleday, 1967; reprint Barrytown, NY: Station Hill, 1985); ———, *Songs I–XXX* (Cambridge: Pym-Randall, 1968); ———, *Spiritual Exercises* (Santa Barbara: Black Sparrow, 1981); ———, *A Strange Market* (Santa Rosa, CA: Black Sparrow, 1992); ———, *The Time of Voice* (Santa Rosa, CA: Black Sparrow, 1998); ———, *A Transparent Tree: Fictions* (Kingston, NY: McPherson and Co., 1985); ———, *Under Words* (Santa Barbara, CA: Black Sparrow, 1983). ***Secondary Sources:*** "The Blade of Seth and the Peacock's Tale: Towards a Poetics of Alchemy in Robert Kelly" (*Boxkite* 1 [1998]); "An Interview with Bradford Morrow" (*Conjunctions* 13 [1989]: 137–166); "'Mirroring an Altogether Different Set of Lights': Silence and Redemption in Robert Kelly's Polysyntaxis" (*Notus* 13.1 [1993]); Robert Kelly Issue (*Vort* 5 [1974]); Schelb, Edward, "The Charred Heart of Polyphemus: Tantric Ecstasy and Shamanic Violence in Robert Kelly's *The Loom*" (*Contemporary Literature* 36.2 [1995]: 317–339); ———, *The Traffic of Names: On the Poetry of Robert Kelly* (Wollongong, Australia: University of Wollongong Press, 2003); "Slain Agamemnon and the Harmony of the Spheres: On Robert Kelly's Axon Dendron Tree" (*Notus* 12.1 [1993]: 89–111).

Michael Ives

KEMBLE, FANNY (FRANCES ANNE) (1809–1893)

Fanny Kemble was a dynamic woman whose life spanned nearly the entire nineteenth century. Hers is a name synonymous with such significant social movements as the abolition of slavery. Although she was most often recognized for her journals, Kemble's poetry is also an important aspect of her writing.

Born in London in 1809, Kemble fulfilled her family's stage legacy early on when, at age nineteen, she played Juliet in Shakespeare's *Romeo and Juliet* at Covent Gardens to rave reviews. Her extraordinary talent led to a tour of American stages (reluctantly undertaken in 1832 in an attempt to help alleviate the family's financial woes), during which Kemble penned her first published journal, *Journal of Frances Anne Kemble* (1835). The tour further proved to be an important event in Kemble's life: While in Philadelphia, Kemble met Pierce Butler, heir to landholdings of Major Butler, then U.S. senator from South Carolina. Kemble and Butler wed in 1834. Kemble, outspoken about her anti-slavery sentiments, later claimed not to know the source of Butler's family fortune.

By 1838 she and Butler had become parents to Sarah ("Sally") and Frances Anne ("Fan"); Butler had also inherited Major Butler's two Georgia plantations. The pivotal point of their turbulent marriage came during a visit to one of the plantations in Georgia. Her firsthand experience with her husband's slaveholdings strengthened Kemble's abolitionist convictions and provided her with material for future memoirs. Kemble's views created a rift with her husband, and the couple returned to Philadelphia estranged. The state of their marriage continued to decline, largely due to Butler's extramarital affairs. Miserable, Kemble left Philadelphia and gave up the rights to her children, returning to England in 1844; it was during this year that she published her first volume of poetry, *Poems*. Kemble continued to write during this period, and after traveling to Italy, she sold *Year of Consolation* (1847), the only journal she wrote deliberately for publication. Further financial troubles prompted Kemble's brief return to the stage, after which she became a Shakespearean reader. Butler sued for divorce, and, charged with desertion, Kemble returned to Philadelphia in 1848.

After divorce proceedings were made final in 1849, Kemble returned to England to escape an increasingly acrimonious relationship with Butler, and for the next several years she toured and lectured. Her daughters' differing loyalties caused a further split in the family. While Sally married into a Yankee family, Fan remained loyal to Butler and opposed the publication of one of Kemble's most compelling works, *Journal of Residence on a Georgian Plantation* (1863), which revealed the harsh and cruel conditions suffered by slaves on Butler's plantations. Fanny's relationship with daughter Fan became increasingly strained. Interestingly enough, this anger led Fan to publish her own memoir of Southern life in 1883, which garnered little critical attention and was quickly forgotten.

In later life, Kemble mended the relationship with daughter Fan and continued to publish autobiographical works, including a memoir serialized in 1875 in *Atlantic Monthly*, which developed into *Records of a Girlhood* (1878). She continued to travel, visiting with her daughters and friends both in America and Europe, composing *Records of Later Life* (1882) and *Notes of Some of Shakespeare's Plays* (1882). A revised volume of poetry, *Poems*, was published in 1883. Her first and only work of fiction, *Far Away and Long Ago* (1889), was admired by friend Henry James. Her final publication was *Further Records*, released in America in 1891. Kemble died in 1893.

Knowledge of Kemble's life is necessary to appreciate the social and cultural currents that influenced her most significant compositions. Today her journals receive the lion's share of criticism (though they are not all equally regarded), but her poetry is equally deserving of attention. *Poems* (1844) marks Kemble's first published foray into poetry. This volume of ninety-four poems, whose style largely reflects the author's lifelong commitment to literary classics, furthered the public's estimation of Kemble's writing. These poems demonstrate the influence of Romanticism, emphasizing her personal relationship with her subjects and her individual interpretation of the natural world. Her voice is clear and uncluttered in these autobiographical poems; at times it even rings with masculinity, which was odd during a period that often emphasized lyricism and effeminate poetry. Kemble skillfully used the Shakespearean sonnet, and also employed combinations of quatrains and couplets and formal syntax to articulate the hopelessness with which she viewed society. Frequently melancholy, many of these poems formally address the universal struggle of humanity despairing against predestined fate or the universal nature of love and loss.

A revised edition of *Poems* was released in 1883; this work contains pieces published earlier as well as twenty-five new works, including several **lyrics** regarding the Civil War. She trumpets the fall of Richmond and the surrender of Lee, but curiously does not address the topic of slavery except by rare mention. Kemble addresses the fall of Richmond by rejoicing in the fall of "power decrepit" and celebrating the future, personifying it as "that hopeful Star" that redeems all who look upon it.

Kemble's journals, in comparison, reflect the writer's candid and at times biting observations of American manners and society. Nineteenth-century readers were often surprised and sometimes insulted by the sharp wit of the actress they'd come to adore. Among her early chronicles are suggestions of her stance against discrimination, a theme Kemble picks up in *Journal of a Residence on a Georgia Plantation*. Received with great critical acclaim, its publication was intended to sway British and European sympathies away from the Confederate South. Here Kemble firmly establishes herself as an abolitionist, frankly chronicling the cruelties and injustice suffered by slaves during the months she spent on Butler's plantation. She bluntly details the inhumane floggings (and lack of justification thereof) and notes especially the physical conditions suffered by female slaves. Most notable about this work is the vividness of her writing, regardless of topic; passages about the brutal living conditions of slaves and the hypocrisy surrounding the slaveholders' ideology are juxtaposed with numerous lyrical nature passages. This style, showcased in the journals published throughout her life, reflects the lively, unpretentious flair that first attracted audiences.

The striking contrast between Kemble's poetry and journals exemplifies her dexterity as a writer, poet, journalist, actress, Shakespearean scholar, and abolitionist. She is rightly credited with influencing American society on many fronts. She was a writer whose work is inextricably tied to the events of the nineteenth century; as poet, avid letter writer, and devoted journalist, Kemble kept powerful records of changing social trends, and her work continues to be studied today as a historical record of the abolitionist movement.

Further Reading. ***Selected Primary Sources****:* Kemble, Frances Anne, *Journal* (Philadelphia: Carey, Lea & Blanchard, 1835); ———, *Journal of a Residence on a Georgian Plantation in 1838–1839* (New York: Harper & Brothers, 1863); ———, *Poems* (Philadelphia: John Penington, 1844); ———, *Poems* (London: Richard Bentley & Son, 1883); ———, *Records of a Girlhood,* 2nd ed. (New York: Henry Holt and Co., 1879); ———, *Records of Later Life* (New York: Henry Holt and Co., 1882); ———, *Year of Consolation* (Hartford: Silas Andrus & Son, 1851). ***Selected Secondary Sources:*** Clinton, Catherine, *Fanny Kemble's Civil Wars* (New York: Simon & Schuster, 2000); Marshall, Dorothy, *Fanny Kemble* (New York: St. Martin's Press, 1978); Wright, Constance, *Fanny Kemble and the Lovely Land* (New York: Dodd, Mead, 1972).

Elisabeth C. Aiken

KENNEDY, X.J. (1929–)

X.J. Kennedy has described himself as a dinosaur, as he has always written in rhyme and meter. Certainly, some critics have been inclined to take him seriously on this count; whereas **Richard Wilbur** and **Anthony Hecht** were treated at least with grudging respect, Kennedy was often a target for opponents of formal verse. Part of the reason for this is that he combines a formal structure with demotic speech; to some critics, this combines the worst of both worlds. However, Kennedy's first collection of poetry, *Nude Descending a Staircase,* and his two most recent volumes, *Dark Horses* and *The Lords of Misrule,* have received much more favorable critical reaction. Part of the reason for this is that poetry in rhyme and meter are generally more acceptable post-1985 than in the 1960s and 1970s, but it is also true that the two recent collections are the strongest since his first. Regardless of the harsh critical reaction at times, it is not unreasonable to claim that, through his collections of poetry for both adults and children as well as his anthologies for both age groups, his colorful readings and, most influentially, his textbooks, X.J. Kennedy may have introduced more people to poetry than anyone else on the current poetry scene.

X.J. Kennedy was born Joseph Kennedy in Dover, New Jersey, shortly before the crash of the stock market, as he likes to point out. When he was twelve he published his own science fiction magazine, *Terrifying Test Tube Tales.* Kennedy graduated from Seton Hall in 1950 and earned his MA from Columbia in 1951. He joined the Navy for four years as an enlisted journalist, studied at the Sorbonne for a year upon leaving the service, and then spent six years at the University of Michigan, where he did not complete his doctorate but did meet his wife Dorothy, who also in time became his collaborator on textbooks and other projects. Because of his name, Kennedy was called "Ambassador" during his youth, and then in the navy was stationed on the SS *Joseph Kennedy.* Tired of the jokes, when he sent out his first poems, on a whim he stuck an X on the front of his name. The poems were published, and X.J. Kennedy was born. Kennedy has also taught at the Women's College at the University of North Carolina (now known as UNC Greensboro), and then for fifteen years at Tufts. In 1978 Kennedy left academe and became a freelance writer, often in collaboration with his wife, and published composition and literary textbooks. Kennedy's *Introduction to Literature* became the best-selling text of its kind, and his genre texts have become standards as well. Many of these editions have now been handed on by Kennedy to **Dana Gioia**. Kennedy also published the poetry magazine *Counter-Measures* for a number of years to provide an outlet for poetry in traditional measures that had become increasingly difficult to place in mainline publications. He has also written many children's books and children's anthologies, as well as anthologies of poems for adults, such as *Pegasus Descending* (compiled with James Camp and **Keith Waldrop**), a collection of bad verse, and *Tygers of Wrath: Poems of Hate, Anger, and Invective.*

Kennedy's first collection, *Nude Descending a Staircase,* won the 1961 Lamont Award of the Academy of American Poets and includes several signature Kennedy poems. "First Confession"—also the first poem in the book—evidences many characteristics that are unique to Kennedy's voice. The speaker remembers when, as a youth who seems to have much to confess, he approaches the "telltale booth." The diction can range from referring to the priest as the "robed repositor of truth" to the money filched from the funds meant for the collection plate "[w]ith which I'd bribed my girl to pee." The boy is filled with religious awe and the light of forgiveness, for a while, but the narrator is older and more jaded who describes the boy's next communion: "[I] stuck my tongue out at the priest: / A fresh roost for the Holy Ghost." The volume also contained such central poems to the Kennedy canon as "On a Child Who Lived One Minute," "Little Elegy," "In a Prominent Bar in Secaucus One Day," "Ars Poetica," and the title poem. The book also puts on display most of the forms that would interest the poet: *Nude Descending a Staircase* includes **lyric** and **narrative** poems, songs, epigrams, **translations**, **light verse**, and **children's poetry**. Some critics found such a range of tones in a moderate-size volume disconcerting. One might better say that it represented Kennedy's range and appeal to different audiences.

Kennedy's next few volumes are no longer available; however, selections from them (as well as from *Nude*) are housed in *Cross Ties: Selected Poems*, which was published in 1985 and promptly won the Los Angeles Times Book Award for Poetry. The book gathers much fresh light and children's verse; however, the bulk of "serious" work is not up to his first collection. There still are notable works, such as the title poem and "Hangover Mass." "Poets" is an interesting poem, but one can see why certain quarters might have difficulties with it. Poets are first described as generally inept, then are compared to swans ("Birds of their quill: so beautiful, so dumb") who stand vacant-mindedly as their feet become encased in ice. The poem ends with the rescue workers who are "enduring all their crap."

It is in Kennedy's two most recent collections that one sees the promise of his first book thoroughly realized. *Dark Horses: New Poems* was published in 1992 and featured consistently exceptional work. Particularly noteworthy are "The Arm," "Separated Banks," "Rat," "On the Square," and "The Waterbury Cross." Some combine seriousness and humor in Kennedy's typical manner, while others are as bleak as anything he has written. There are also some very lyrical, gentle works; the poem "Woman in Rain" discusses the un–self-conscious beauty of a woman, ending "But then, what planet knows its name?"

Published in 2002, *The Lords of Misrule: Poems, 1992–2001* is one of Kennedy's most sustained books, and also branches out in some new directions. Certainly, Kennedy's voice—the formal structure, the demotic speech—is readily apparent, as, for example, in "Invocation," which appeals to the Muses of form to "Regulate the revels / Of these half-crocked lines." It is hard to imagine another poet who would choose to introduce a collection of his verse (especially since it's his first collection of "adult" verse in a decade) in such a way. "The Purpose of Time Is to Prevent Everything from Happening at Once" is funny yet sad, ending "Time takes its time unraveling. But, still, / You'll wonder when your life ends: Huh? What happened?" There are several poems of remembrance of things past from childhood to early adulthood; an elegy for **Allen Ginsberg** written in trochaic tetrameter lines; poems of travel; "A Curse on a Thief," which keeps the Irish curse tradition alive and kicking; and a narrative poem, "The Ballad of Fenimore Woolson and Henry James," which is an interesting departure from anything the poet had written before.

The Lords of Misrule concludes with "September 12th, 2001," which addresses the 9/11 disaster with indirection. The lovers jumping to their deaths from the 82nd floor "aren't us." The speaker wakes with his love to "the incredible joy of coffee / and the morning light." Yet the time given them is still "pitiful," and the image of the "joy of coffee" is moderated by a comparison of the couple to "bubbles rising and bursting / in a boiling pot." In his elder years, X.J. Kennedy appears to be in full control of his powers.

Further Reading. *Selected Primary Sources:* Kennedy, X.J., *Cross Ties: Selected Poems* (Athens: University of Georgia Press, 1985); ——, *Dark Horses: New Poems* (Baltimore: Johns Hopkins University Press, 1992); ——, *The Lords of Misrule* (Baltimore: Johns Hopkins University Press, 2002). ***Selected Secondary Sources:*** Morris, Bernard E., *Taking Measure: The Poetry and Prose of X.J. Kennedy* (Selinsgrove, PA: Susquehanna University Press, 2003).

Robert Darling

KENYON, JANE (1947–1995)

Jane Kenyon's poetry is notable for a number of reasons, not the least of which are her attention to the "luminous particular," as the poet **Donald Hall** has phrased it, and her control over **lyric** forms. Kenyon's attention to "luminous particulars" makes her poetry, which addresses such matters as religious faith, sexuality, depression, and personal responsibility, unusually accessible to readers. A poet who paid rigorous attention both to the sounds of words and to the anecdotes and images she employed, Kenyon rewards multiple, attentive readings, during which the precision of a word, or an artfully hidden internal rhyme scheme, may suddenly reveal itself. Richly allusive to the work of Anton Chekov, **Robert Frost,** Vladimir Nabokov, John Keats, and **Emily Dickinson**, to name only a few authors, Kenyon's poetry is quiet, direct, and self-aware without being hermetic or self-absorbed.

Kenyon was born in Ann Arbor, Michigan, to a musician father and a seamstress mother. Her only sibling, a brother, was five years older than she. Educated in Ann Arbor's public schools, Kenyon attended the University of Michigan in Ann Arbor, where she began as a French major but switched to English and, in 1969, won the Avery and Jules Hopwood Award for her poetry. Kenyon earned a BA and an MA in English at the University of Michigan. She wed poet **Donald Hall** in 1972, and in 1975 they left Ann Arbor, where Hall had taught, to move to his family home in New Hampshire.

The move to New Hampshire gave rise to Kenyon's well-documented emotional and intellectual journey toward **religious faith**. Poems such as "Let Evening Come" and "Briefly It Enters, and Briefly Speaks" speak most directly of Kenyon's understanding of the divine;

however, such musings appear in many of her poems. While these contemplative poems generally end with reconciliation to a God the poet cannot fathom, they are seldom cloying or facile. Kenyon renders the difficult journey toward faith and acceptance, if not understanding, of a supreme being, in disciplined poetry characterized by attention to concrete physical and emotional detail. Additionally, many of Kenyon's most effective late poems (such as "Pharaoh" and "Afternoon at Mac-Dowell") concern a spouse's efforts to come to grips with her beloved's frailty and probable death; ironically, Kenyon, who tried to steel herself against the possibility of Hall's loss to cancer, died of leukemia shortly before what would have been her forty-eighth birthday. Hall survives her.

Kenyon's most significant volumes of poetry are *The Boat of Quiet Hours* (1986), *Let Evening Come* (1990), and the posthumous work *Otherwise: New and Selected Poems* (1996). Her translations of the work of Russian poet Anna Akhmatova, published in *Twenty Poems of Anna Akhmatova* (1985), have been characterized by poet and critic **Hayden Carruth** as "the best in English." The translation project was undertaken at the suggestion of poet **Robert Bly**, who had pressed Kenyon to take on a poetic "master" in order to more fully develop her own poetic style. That style, highly original, but with overtones of Akhmatova, Emily Dickinson, Dylan Thomas, and John Keats, resulted in such durable poems as "Let Evening Come," which concludes with the reminder that "God does not leave us / comfortless, so let evening come." In "Mud Season," from *The Boat of Quiet Hours*, Kenyon offers a startling variation on Robert Frost's poem "Two Tramps at Mud Time," writing not of human commercial interaction, but of ground scarred by the plow and how "the crocus prepares an exaltation / of purple, but for the moment / holds its tongue."

Jane Kenyon's poetry is also informed by the bipolar disorder (manic depression) that sometimes made it difficult for her to write, as well as by the losses she watched her friends and neighbors endure. When asked, during the course of an interview with David Bradt, to answer the question "What's a poet's job?" Kenyon answered that it is to "tell the whole truth . . . in such a beautiful way that people cannot live without it; to put into words those feelings we all have that are so deep, so important, and yet so difficult to name" (*One Hundred White Daffodils*, 183). In "Having It Out with Melancholy" and "The Sandy Hole," Kenyon does precisely these things, sharing acute observations about how depression "ruined [her] manners toward God" and how, at the burial of a small child, no mourner "dares to come near [the child's father], even to touch his sleeve." In "Reading Aloud to My Father" Kenyon ultimately warns readers that if a dying person should try to pull his or her hand away from the hand of a person trying to

give comfort, "you must honor that desire, / and let them pull it free." In these poems, the paralysis of depression and the stunned helplessness the living feel before implacable death are rendered with the attention to large truths made evident in moments of extreme difficulty.

Kenyon's poetry is inward-looking, but ultimately sidesteps the **confessional** mode characterized by such poets as **Adrienne Rich**, **Sylvia Plath**, **Robert Lowell**, and **Anne Sexton**. Kenyon is more reticent about self-revelation than are the poets named above, but nonetheless mines moments of personal difficulty, or her observation of such moments, as a launching point for her meditations on life, loss, faith, love, and human striving. This willingness to be personal without indulging in narcissism contributes to the ease with which many readers take to her poetry.

Further Reading. *Selected Primary Sources:* Kenyon, Jane, *A Hundred White Daffodils* (St. Paul, MN: Graywolf Press, 1999); ———, *Otherwise: New and Selected Poems* (St. Paul, MN: Graywolf Press, 1996); ———, with Vera Sandomirsky Dunham, *Twenty Poems of Anna Akhmatova* (St. Paul, MN: Nineties Press and Ally Press, 1985). *Selected Secondary Source:* Timmerman, John H., *Jane Kenyon: A Literary Life* (Grand Rapids, MI: William B. Eerdmans, 2002).

Angela M. Salas

KEROUAC, JACK (1922–1969)

Jack Kerouac is known primarily as the author of such novels as *On the Road* (1957) and *The Dharma Bums* (1958), innovative works that established him and the movement he represented most prominently in the public imagination—the **Beat** generation, the "beatniks," as important players in the world of post–World War II literature. Kerouac was also an active and energetic poet, writing several volumes of verse, most of them published after his death.

Kerouac was born in the working-class town of Lowell, Massachusetts, to French-Canadian parents. Although he spoke French as a child and occasionally wrote poetry in French, his spoken English as an adult carried no trace of a French accent. He briefly attended Columbia University in New York on a football scholarship, and spent part of World War II in the Merchant Marine before deciding to become a professional writer. He officially launched this career when his novel *The Town and the City* was published in 1950; he discovered the vocation's challenges when *On the Road* took seven years to find a publisher, and when other novels languished even longer before appearing in print. His fortunes rose after a widely noted poetry reading at the Six Gallery in San Francisco, which made literary stars of participants **Allen Ginsberg** and **Gary Snyder** and attracted new attention to their close friend Kerouac, who attended but stayed on the sidelines. This association gave him membership in the so-called **San Francisco Renaissance** of poetry and poetics, helping him find publishers for many of the manuscripts he had already written. But disparagement from suspicious critics and too much belief in his own "wild beatnik" persona slowed and then stalled his momentum, and he entered a long period intermittently marked by public exhibitionism, ongoing experiments with psychedelic drugs, religious uncertainty, political conservatism, and severe alcoholism that severely shortened his life. He was married twice, briefly both times, and engaged in countless other romantic and sexual relationships. He never stopped writing, however; the novel *Vanity of Duluoz: An Adventurous Education, 1935–1946* was written and published one year before he died. His media appearances made him the most famous figure of the Beat group until his death in 1969 at age forty-seven.

His allegiance to poetry never waned. He wrote his first poems during childhood and adolescence; moved decisively toward fiction as a young adult; and renewed his commitment to poetry in the middle 1950s with the lengthy *Mexico City Blues (242 Choruses)*, published in 1959 by Grove Press, the only major volume of Kerouac verse to reach print during his lifetime. This book was not received with enthusiasm, and as critic James T. Jones has suggested, it might have been utterly overlooked by the popular press were it not for the notoriety of a scornful *New York Times* review by **Kenneth Rexroth**, himself a key forerunner of the Beat sensibility.

Kerouac published verse everywhere, from small **experimental** publications to *Jubilee*, a Roman Catholic magazine, and his poetic oeuvre spans all the decades of his career. The verses collected in *Scattered Poems* (1971) were composed between the middle 1940s and the late 1960s; those in *San Francisco Blues* (1983) date from 1954; *Old Angel Midnight* (1973) was written in 1956; the works in *Heaven & Other Poems* (1977) were penned between 1957 and 1962; *Pomes All Sizes* was compiled in 1960, although not published until 1992; and the ambitious *Book of Blues*—passed over by the Beat-friendly City Lights Publishers because **Lawrence Ferlinghetti**, who had founded the company and its Pocket Poets Series in 1955, found it at variance with his own idea of pure poetry—belatedly appeared in complete form in 1995.

On some levels, Kerouac took a traditional view of poetry and prose as distinct literary forms. In his 1958 novel *The Subterraneans* the character standing in for him acknowledges the "common old distinction between verse and prose," and Kerouac recognized the fact that novels and short stories are expected to have some kind of narrative framework. Yet in deeper ways he appeared willing to accept the idea that "it's all poetry," as the character representing Beat writer **Gregory Corso** says

in *The Subterraneans*, referring to literary art in general (83). "You guys call yourself poets," Kerouac wrote to Ginsberg in the middle 1950s, because you "write little short lines, I'm a poet but I write lines paragraphs and pages and many pages long." As he wrote in his introduction to Kerouac's *Pomes all Sizes*, Ginsberg felt contemporary critical understanding of Kerouac suffered from "the constant problem of falling between two stools, prose and poetry," adding that his colleague "was classified a novelist despite the evidence of 'October in the Railroad Earth' [1952], *Mexico City Blues*, and *Visions of Cody* that the distinction between the two forms was in certain writers artificial—they are inseparable" (1992, i).

Kerouac was attracted to a wide array of **poetic forms**. Calling him a "poet supreme," critic Regina Weinreich notes that he wrote sonnets, odes, psalms, and **blues**, as well as an enormous number of **haiku**, the rigorously formal genre of short Japanese verse. **Haiku** appealed to Kerouac's fascination with the Zen form of Buddhism as well as his often-overlooked proclivity for occasional excursions into a literary genus that he found conducive to the revision and rewriting that his "first thought, best thought" philosophy led him to eschew in his longer-form works. More evidence that Kerouac saw poetry and prose as intimately fused is found in Weinreich's observation that many of his haiku verses were embedded in pages otherwise filled with blocks of prose, scribbled notes, and even street addresses.

Kerouac's writing in all formats was strongly shaped by an array of techniques he devised for spontaneously expressing what he paradoxically called "the unspeakable visions of the individual" on the printed page. These techniques, outlined in his essay "Essentials of Spontaneous Prose" (1958), include "blowing," whereby the writer extemporizes fluid verbal riffs in the manner of an improvising jazz musician; "sketching," whereby the writer views or imagines a subject and then sketches it with words just as a visual artist would draw it with lines; and the all-embracing "spontaneous bop composition," whereby the writer spins out words in a wholly intuitive manner with no allowance for pause during the process or revision after it. Equally conducive to poetry and prose writing, such methods place Kerouac's work about midway between the stream-of-consciousness techniques pioneered by such authors as James Joyce and Virginia Woolf, from whom he drew encouragement, and the **postmodern** pastiches of such stylists as Thomas Pynchon and Beat writer William S. Burroughs, on whom he exerted significant influence.

Like other Beat poets—Corso, Ginsberg, Ferlinghetti, and Snyder among them—Kerouac rooted his work in a Romanticist sensibility, or, in Friedrich Nietzsche's terminology, a Dionysian one. This approach emphasizes values of immediacy, unpredictability, and freedom from sociocultural norms. It is typical of Kerouac's predilection for impulsiveness and "wild form" that in the collection *Trip Trap* (1973) he criticized the "dreary, negative . . . dry rules" that he found in **T.S. Eliot**'s theoretical views even as he pronounced Eliot's poetry "sublime" in itself. His insistence on spontaneity was so unflinching that he criticized Ginsberg for correcting typographical errors in manuscripts he gave Kerouac to read.

Just as he hesitated to draw boundaries between prose and poetry, Kerouac felt that the audible sounds of words are closely intertwined with their meanings. At times sound played a primary role in his writing, as when he described "the charging restless mute unvoiced road keening in a seizure of tarpaulin power" in *On the Road* without knowing at the time, according to Ginsberg, what a tarpaulin actually is. A more extended example is the poem appended to the 1962 novel *Big Sur*, entitled "Sea," throughout which Kerouac attempts to capture sounds of the Pacific Ocean in such onomatopoeic lines as "Kataketa pow! Kek kek kek!" Ginsberg has cited music as different as that of baroque composer Johann Sebastian Bach and **jazz** improviser Thelonious Monk as strong influences on Kerouac's writing, and Kerouac himself named writers ranging from the eighth-century Chinese poet Han Shan to the pre-Romantic British poet William Blake as inspirations for "wham wham the true blue song of man," which was in his eyes the unique poetic contribution of the music-loving San Francisco group. His many public readings and audio recordings, often accompanied by jazz-inflected music, provide additional signs of his commitment to the spoken as well as the written word.

Kerouac's contributions to **modernist** and postmodernist poetics include a radical celebration of spontaneity and autobiographical self-reference; a willingness to seize ideas and inspirations from sources as diverse as canonical literature, mass-media discourse, and everyday conversation; and a sense of spiritual possibilities induced by a personal faith that oscillated between, and often idiosyncratically combined, the Catholic doctrines with which he grew up and the Buddhist concepts that he enthusiastically embraced as a young adult—an aspect of his thought that anticipated the New Age movement and other contemporary manifestations of religious eclecticism. The influence of Kerouac's poems and writing techniques has been traced to many subsequent poets, including such major figures as **Bob Dylan** and **Amiri Baraka**, as well as writers who traveled in Beat circles when the loosely knit group was still extant. His legacy has also been passed along by the Jack Kerouac School of Disembodied Poetics, founded in 1974 by Ginsberg and **Anne Waldman**; now known as the Naropa University Department of Writing and Poetics, it retains a strong commitment to the literary and spiritual values that Kerouac espoused.

Kerouac's seminal *On the Road* was famously dismissed by author Truman Capote as being mere "typing," not authentic "writing." Ironically, however, Kerouac's refusal to recognize solid dividing lines between diverse aspects of literature and its production makes Capote's often-quoted remark seem less a sarcastic criticism than an unwitting testament to the spontaneous bop composition that Kerouac so single-mindedly devised and practiced.

Further Reading. *Selected Primary Sources:* Kerouac, Jack, *Big Sur* (New York: McGraw-Hill, 1981); ———, *Book of Blues* (New York: Penguin Books, 1995); ———, *Book of Haikus*, ed. Regina Weinreich (New York: Penguin Books, 2003); ———, *The Dharma Bums* (New York: Penguin Books, 1976); ———, "Essentials of Spontaneous Prose" (*Evergreen Review* 2:5 [1958]: 72–73); ———, *Heaven & Other Poems* (San Francisco: Grey Fox Press, 1977); ———, *Mexico City Blues (242 Choruses)* (New York: Grove, 1959); ———, "October in the Railroad Earth," in *Evergreen Review Reader 1957–1966* (New York: Blue Moon Books, 1993); ———, *Old Angel Midnight* (San Francisco: Grey Fox Press, 1993); ———, *On the Road* (New York: Penguin Books, 1976); ———, *Pomes All Sizes* (San Francisco: City Lights Books, 1992); ———, *Scattered Poems* (San Francisco: City Lights Books, 1971); ———, *The Subterraneans* (New York: Grove Weidenfeld, 1989); ———, *Visions of Cody* (New York: Penguin Books, 1993). ***Selected Secondary Sources:*** Charters, Ann, ed., *The Portable Beat Reader* (New York: Viking, 1992); Donaldson, Scott, ed., and Jack Kerouac, *On the Road: Text and Criticism* (New York: Penguin Books, 1979); Jones, James T., *A Map of Mexico City Blues: Jack Kerouac as Poet* (Carbondale: Southern Illinois University Press, 1992); Nicosia, Gerald, *Memory Babe: A Critical Biography of Jack Kerouac* (London: Penguin Books, 1986); Saijo, Albert, and Lew Welch, *Trip Trap: Haiku along the Road from San Francisco to New York* (San Francisco: Grey Fox Press, 1998); Weinreich, Regina, *The Spontaneous Poetics of Jack Kerouac: A Study of the Fiction* (New York: Paragon House, 1990).

David Sterritt

KEY, FRANCIS SCOTT (1779–1843)

Despite being a diplomat and a soldier, a slaveholder and a defender of freedom, a celebrity and a relatively private person, a lawyer and a hymnist, Francis Scott Key is best known for writing what were to become the words of the national anthem of the United States of America, "The Star-Spangled Banner." Hence, the Francis Scott Key most U.S. citizens are familiar with is the widely known cultural icon of America, not the poet. Yet a book of his poetry was published posthumously in 1857 under the title *Poems of the Late Francis S. Key, Esq.*, and six of his poems were published in the *Lyra Sacra Americana* in 1868 (Meyer).

Francis Scott Key was born August 1, 1779, to John Ross Key and Anne Phoebe Key on their plantation, Terra Rubra. Key enrolled at St. John's College in Annapolis, graduating as valedictorian before studying law with his uncle. After marrying in 1802, Key moved to Georgetown and practiced law in the District of Columbia.

A deeply religious individual, Key was a low-church Episcopalian who wrote several hymns during his lifetime. Notably, Key held war in disregard, advocating the employment of peaceful means for the resolution of conflicts among nations. Despite his opposition to the War of 1812, Key twice entered military service during the war and also served as a general's aide in the unfortunate Battle of Bladensburg, in which the American forces were routed. This defeat allowed the British to advance unopposed on Washington, D.C., where they set fire to the Capitol and other government buildings.

A few days after the Battle of Bladensburg, British forces seized and imprisoned Dr. William Beanes, a friend of Francis Scott Key. When Key learned of Beanes's imprisonment, he secured the permission of President James Madison to negotiate, along with John S. Skinner, for the physician's release. The negotiation was successful, but the British would not allow the men to return to shore until some time after the British attack on Fort McHenry, just outside of Baltimore, had subsided.

From a boat in the Patapsco River, Key observed the bombardment of Fort McHenry by the British and began writing what would soon become published in Baltimore under the title "The Defence of Fort McHenry." Interestingly, Sam Meyer reports, "The earliest surviving manuscript in Key's own hand shows that he had not troubled to give the poem a title" (78). About a month later, the poem appeared in sheet music form to be sung to the tune of "Anacreon in Heaven." It would take over one hundred years before "The Star-Spangled Banner" would become the national anthem of the United States in 1931, ensuring Francis Scott Key's place in American history.

As a formal poem, "The Defence of Fort McHenry" consists of four stanzas. Each stanza has eight lines and uses the rhyme scheme ABAB–CCDD. While the first three stanzas are primarily concerned with battle for Fort McHenry, the fourth stanza is clearly a paean to God, whom the poem's persona (arguably Key) credits with creating and preserving the nation.

Unlike "The Defence of Fort McHenry," many of Key's poems were written for relatives or friends. Like his hymns, much of Key's poetry was devotional in nature, observes Meyer. Key was noted for being both a private and modest person, so it is not surprising that his poetry was not collected and published until after his death.

After the War of 1812, Key again practiced law and continued to live at his original residence in Georgetown until 1828, when canal construction prompted him to relocate. He also served as the United States Attorney for the District of Columbia from 1833 to 1841. Francis Scott Key died of pleurisy on January 11, 1843.

Nearly two hundred years after they were first written, the words of "The Defence of Fort McHenry" still reflect some significant aspects of the American psyche, including hope in uncertainty, support for a just war, courage in the service of freedom, and, for many, a dependence upon God. Such is the power of poetry—and of poets like Francis Scott Key.

Further Reading. ***Selected Primary Sources:*** Key, Francis Scott, *Poems of the Late Francis Scott Key, Esq.* (New York: Robert Carter and Brothers, 1857); ———, *The Power of Literature and Its Connexion with Religion* (Bristol, CT: Bristol College, 1834). ***Selected Secondary Sources:*** Delaplaine, Edward S., *Francis Scott Key, Life and Times* (Brooklyn, NY: Biography Press, 1937); Meyer, Sam, *Paradoxes of Fame: The Francis Scott Key Story* (Annapolis, MD: Eastwind, 1995); Molotsky, Irvin, *The Flag, the Poet, and the Song: The Story of the Star-Spangled Banner* (New York: Dutton/Penguin, 2001).

Bruce A. Erickson

KILMER, ALFRED JOYCE (1886–1918)

Alfred Joyce Kilmer won wide national acclaim for his poem "Trees" when it was published in *Poetry* magazine (1913). This effort was by no means his first venture into published poetry; however, his first volume, *Summer of Love* (1911), attracted only slight attention. Kilmer claimed the influence of William Butler Yeats and Alfred, Lord Tennyson on his collection of sonnets, ballads, and **lyrics**. Kilmer was a newspaperman, a journalist of little distinction, who wrote much sentimental doggerel and one distinctly excellent poem. Most of his work is marked by a religious enthusiasm; a Roman Catholic convert, Kilmer poured his fervor into his lines, but that quality did not always make his pedestrian rhymes into poetry.

Alfred (the first name was dropped early in his professional career) Joyce Kilmer was born in New Brunswick, New Jersey, of upper-middle-class parents. His father was the chief chemist for Johnson & Johnson; his mother was a minor writer and composer. Kilmer attended Rutgers College (1904–1906) and earned a BA (1908) from Columbia University. He was married after college to Aline Murray, and they had four children. Kilmer first earned a living by teaching Latin at Morristown High School. He gave up teaching for a writing post with a horseman's magazine, but a disagreement with the publisher led to a change. He took a job as a clerk at Charles Scribner's Sons bookstore. Kilmer then landed work as an editorial assistant for the *Standard Dictionary* (1904–1912). Kilmer sent poetry contributions, with some success, to a wide variety of newspapers and magazines. His first volume of poetry, a collection of these contributions, *Summer Love*, was published in 1911. Kilmer was named literary editor of the Episcopal magazine *The Churchman*.

Kilmer was gaining some renown. He was already included in *Who's Who*; he served as Corresponding Secretary of the Poetry Society of America and conducted the poetry section of the *Literary Digest*, a post he held for the last nine years of his life. In 1913 Kilmer joined the magazine and book review section of the *New York Times*. Kilmer led an active professional life; in addition to his newspaper and literary work, he was a popular lecturer who followed the Dickensian tradition; his recitations were theatrical performances.

In the fall of 1913 his daughter, Rose, was afflicted with infantile paralysis; deeply moved, Kilmer became a fervent convert to the Roman Catholic faith. This religious influence permeated his poetry thereafter. The publication of "Trees" in *Poetry: The Magazine of Verse* that same year made Kilmer well known nationwide. (The poem was set to music in 1917 by his mother in her *Whimsical Whimsies* and became endeared to millions.) When the United States entered World War I, Kilmer joined a National Guard officers' training camp. At thirty years old and as the father of four children, he was unlikely to be drafted, but Kilmer wanted to serve. Kilmer quit officers' training after a short time and enlisted as a private in the 7th Regiment of the New York National Guard, but later transferred to the 165th Regiment—the old "Fighting 69th" of legend. Kilmer felt, correctly, that this group would be posted to France faster than the 7th. As a living advocate of the church militant, he was eager to serve in the field. Kilmer was promoted to sergeant after his group reached active duty in France. He also rejected an opportunity to become an officer because he would have had to leave his regiment to do so. Kilmer served as an intelligence clerk, with frequent voluntary missions in the field. The events of his death were reported by his friend and colleague on the *New York Times*, Alexander Woollcott, writing for the *Stars and Stripes*. In July 1918, Kilmer volunteered for a night scouting mission to find a German machine gun nest and was killed by a sniper's bullet. Sergeant Kilmer was awarded the Croix de Guerre, posthumously.

Any topic was apt to find its way into Kilmer's verse. Subjects that Percy Bysshe Shelley or Tennyson would have spurned—a railroad station, a delicatessen—proved inspiring for Kilmer, and he enjoyed the ability to write of the commonplace. Kilmer once observed that he would use any topic three times: once in a poem, once more in an article, and once again, finally, in a lecture. After his conversion to Catholicism, religious

themes emerged and Kilmer developed ties with poets of similar persuasion—Hilaire Belloc and G.K. Chesterton, for example. Kilmer wrote his "The Annunciation" (1917) using a pseudonym, John Langdon. He used this device more than once; in this case, the reason is not known. The poem was an entry in the competition to honor the Virgin Mary conducted by the *Queen's Work*, the national Sodality periodical. Kilmer revealed his identity when he was announced the winner. A typical blending of poetic and religious piety occurs in the last lines of Kilmer's "In Memory," written to honor the memory of nineteenth-century poet-priest and Roman Catholic convert Gerard Manley Hopkins: "You knew within the cypress-darkened hollow / . . . it was Christ that was your own Apollo, / And thorns were in the laurel on your hair."

Kilmer's most enduring poem, "Trees," with its memorable opening line, "I think that I shall never see / A poem lovely as a tree," has delighted millions of readers. Critics might quibble over analogies that described trees with a "hungry mouth" against the "earth's sweet flowing breast" with a "nest of robins in her hair." If readers loved the sentiment then, many find it merely sentimental now. Unquestionably, Kilmer patterned his verse after others, notably George Herbert, Richard Crashaw, A.E. Houseman, and Coventry Patmore. His "To Certain Poets" (1916) mocks contemporary poets, who Kilmer believed were "aesthetic" or "too delicate": "You little poets mincing there / With women's heart's and women's hair!"

Kilmer's unyielding belief in Catholicism and his hard service in France were summarized in "Rouge Bouquet" (1918): "There is on earth no worthier grave / To hold the bodies of the brave" than where, writes Kilmer, "they nobly fought and nobly died." These sentiments convinced his widow to leave Sergeant Kilmer in his wartime grave when the Army offered to have his body sent home to New York for burial. Kilmer was an admirer of Rupert Brooke, who, among the World War I poets, most closely approached Kilmer's own sentiments regarding war. He wrote in "In Memory of Rupert Brooke": "But let no cloud of lamentation be / Where, on a warrior's grave, a lyre is hung." The sentiment, unpalatable to a post–World War I world, is dignified by Kilmer's own enthusiastic military service and its nearly inevitable conclusion.

Kilmer contributed his work to a wide range of publications—from his first, in *Moods* (1909), to his last, "The Peacemaker" (October 1918), in the *Saturday Evening Post*. Newspapers, popular magazines, and the many poetry journals of that day were vehicles for Kilmer's work. Critic H.L. Mencken (whose *Smart Set* published several of Kilmer's poems) described Kilmer (1919) as only a "minor poet" who did "one or two things rather well," a journalist who did "diverse things rather badly," and a lecturer who seems to have done "scarcely anything."

Kilmer was a professional writer as well as a poet. He had no desire to "report" the war. If he had, he would have served as a correspondent, he told friends. But before he embarked with the Rainbow Division for France, he contracted with his publisher to write a book, "Here and There with the Fighting Sixty-Ninth." No copy was sent back to New York. He wrote, reports Robert Cortes Holliday, in one of his last letters, "My days of hack writing are over. . . . The only sort of book I care to write about the war is the sort people will read after the war—a century after it is over!"

The greatest memorial to Kilmer is one that he, especially, would have approved. The Joyce Kilmer Memorial Forest, 3,800 acres of virgin woodland, located in North Carolina, was dedicated in 1936. President Franklin D. Roosevelt wrote, "It is particularly fitting that a poet who will always be remembered for the tribute he embodied in "Trees" should find this living monument."

Further Reading. *Selected Primary Sources:* Kilmer, Joyce, *Main Street and Other Poems* (New York; Doran, 1917); ———, *The Circus and Other Essays and Fugitive Pieces,* ed. Robert Cortes Holliday (New York: Doran, 1921); ———, *Summer of Love* (New York: Baker & Taylor, 1911); ———, *Trees and Other Poems* (New York: Doran, 1914). ***Selected Secondary Sources:*** Cargas, Harry J., *I Lay Down My Life: A Biography of Joyce Kilmer* (Boston: St. Paul Editions, 1964); Kilmer, Annie Kilburn, *Memories of My Son, Sergeant Joyce Kilmer* (New York: Brentano's, 1920); Kilmer, Kenton, *Memories of My Father, Joyce Kilmer* (New Brunswick, NJ: Joyce Kilmer Centennial Commission, 1993).

S. L. Harrison

KIM, MYUNG MI (1957–)

Myung Mi Kim is a Korean American poet whose experimental verse captures the nuances of diasporic existence. Kim's work is preoccupied with both the contemporary condition of ethnic minorities in the United States and the history of U.S. involvement in the Korean peninsula, yet her politics are framed in an aesthetics that refers to a century of American poetic innovation, from the opacity of high **modernism** (her poetry resonates in particular with **Ezra Pound**'s insistence on visibility and the difficulty of **Gertrude Stein**) to the work of another Korean American artist, **Theresa Hak Kyung Cha**, whose experimental epic *Dictée* provided an important backdrop for Kim's adventurous poetry. Kim's compelling juxtapositions have the effect of making simple words seem strange, and this defamiliarization gives her readers a deeply personal taste of the immigrant experience at the same time that it gestures toward an aesthetic renewal of the language.

Born in Seoul, Korea, in 1957, Kim immigrated to the United States with her family at the age of nine. The significance of this relocation is perhaps best described in her own words from her long poem *Dura* (1998), in a chronology numbered from 6.1 to 35.0 in which she recounts her own thirty-five years. At "8.5" her Korean experience is expressed as "Fried meat dumplings and sweet rice cakes," followed by the transition to the United States in "9.8": "One of the first words understood in English: stupid." Her career includes a BA from Oberlin College, an MFA from the University of Iowa, and an MA from Johns Hopkins University.

Kim's first book of poems, *Under Flag* (1991), considers the difficulties and repercussions of crossing the Pacific. "And Sing We," the opening poem, overlays diaspora with oceanic movement: "Depletion replete with barraging / Slurred and taken over / Diaspora." The sound of "Depletion replete" evokes the successive emptying out and filling of waves, which combines with the slur of mingling waters to express the sensation of migration. Like the movement of the surf, memories of the place left behind flow into the new world, and the poem gives us a memory set in Korea, prefaced with "And this breaks through unheralded—." With this memory, Kim asks a crucial question in a child's voice "Once we leave a place is it there," and her poetry tracks the appearance of such unheralded evocations of place.

"Into Such Assembly" expresses this collision between the new place and the old one that refuses to stay behind. The poem describes the naturalization ceremony, in which Kim writes out the authority and banality of the event: "Now tell me, who is the president of the United States? / You will all stand now. Raise your right hands." She balances this opening section with an equally heavy memory of Korea that features recognizably Oriental objects such as "lacquer chests in our slateblue house." These paired evocations are followed by a small line, flanked by white space: "Neither, neither." The poem refuses both official America and Orientalized Korea, and instead asks, "Who is mother tongue, who is father country?" She postulates an evenly split parenthood, but there is no neat answer to the question; instead, the poem goes on to consider different ideas of "over there," from Korea as a degraded battlefield to a repository of childhood delights, finally imagining sweeping waters overtaking the peninsula and closing on oceanic flows as the only certainty of an existence caught between countries and tongues.

Under Flag's title poem shows us the Korean War from several perspectives, imagining the experience of different participants in the war as well as considering the war's aftermath in figures like "an uncle with shrapnel burrowing into shinbone for thirty years." Her poem moves freely through these multiple understandings, and she includes her own position toward these events:

"Not to have seen it yet inheriting it." This vision of war depicts a collective or cultural memory, and the surprise of her inheritance is that it includes the American military perspective, rendered in the individual experience of one "Corporal Leonard H." shot on a hilltop. This depiction stands in dramatic contrast to elderly Koreans "sitting in the warmest part of the house with comforters draped around their shoulders peeling tangerines," but in bringing together such divergent moments, Kim shows us that they have been forced to share the same world. She is describing something more than an ethnic inheritance; in demonstrating the paradox of a Korean American vantage point, she insists on claiming both American and Korean experiences.

Kim's **long poem** *Dura* takes up the American **epic** tradition, in which a personal account of her thirty-five years, previously cited, stands at the heart of a journey toward a refashioned homecoming. "Cosmography," the opening section, elaborates the universe of the text, illustrating the slow dawning of land and language from a primordial ocean. The poem imagines several different journeys across this expanse, and in the following section, entitled "Measure," she juxtaposes Marco Polo's voyage to the Orient against the experience of those living in the fantastic region he seeks to discover. The next section, "Labor," describes the opposite movement: "Due west directly west." *Dura* embarks on the immigrant's westward flight only after establishing this world of discovery; she insists that this later diasporic movement be considered against Polo's heroics, and the startling achievement of casting the Asian immigrant as another in a series of epic discoveries folds what has typically been cast as a very different narrative into a long history of oceanic travel. In the aesthetic daring of Kim's long poem, she suggests that the epic's tale of discovery and homecoming can be extended to a late–twentieth-century plight. *Dura*'s longest section, "Thirty and Five Books," imagines her own story in these terms; in describing both personal and historical convergences, Kim's work interrogates Western incursions into Asia and Asian American experience in the United States by demonstrating a complicated inheritance—one that is both political and aesthetic.

Further Reading. *Selected Primary Sources:* Kim, Myung Mi, *The Bounty* (Minneapolis, MN: Chax Press, 1996); ———, *Commons* (Berkeley: University of California Press, 2002); ———, *Dura* (Los Angeles: Sun & Moon Press, 1998); *Under Flag* (Berkeley: Kelsey St. Press, 1991). ***Selected Secondary Sources:*** Kang, Laura Hyun Yi, "Compositional Struggles," in *Compositional Subjects: Enfiguring Asian/ American Women* (Durham, NC: Duke University Press, 2002, 215–270); Kim, Elaine, "Korean American Literature," in *An Interethnic Companion to Asian American Literature*, ed. King-Kok Cheung (Cambridge: Cambridge

University Press, 1997, 156–191); Lee, James Kyung-Jin, "Myung Mi Kim" (interview), in *Words Matter: Conversations with Asian American Writers*, ed. King-Kok Cheung (Honolulu: University of Hawaii Press, 2000, 92–104).

Josephine Park

KINNELL, GALWAY (1927–)

Galway Kinnell is a poet of great reputation known for ambitious, intensely imagistic, and musical **lyric** and **narrative** poetry. He is also a translator of note, having produced versions of Francois Villon, Yves Bonnefoy, and Rainer Maria Rilke, among others. Kinnell is one of the most prominent members of a generation of poets that turned away from the ironic and symbolic **New Critical** style, championed by writers such as **John Crowe Ransom** and **Richard Wilbur**, to work more intuitively and imaginatively from immediate experience. His highly concentrated **free verse** features a rich and exotic diction, keenly observed particulars, and an often faultless sense both of the integrity of the line and the possibilities of the long, rythmic, and enjambed compound-complex sentence. Working within the major tradition of **Whitman**, Yeats, and **Crane**, Kinnell is a poet of intense feeling whose work can be read, in the simplest sense, as an extended, decades-long meditation on time and mortality. His poetry also often finds its subjects in examinations of the world's brokenness, personal and spiritual emptiness, and in ongoing celebrations of the natural world, creaturely life, erotic love, and children.

Critics have faulted Kinnell for a tendency toward brutality and primitivism, especially in such middle-period poems as "The Bear" and "The Porcupine." He has also sometimes been characterized as a poet aching for transcendence but limited by his refusal to participate in a traditionally religious belief system. Kinnell is perhaps best seen, however, as a "modern Romantic" moralist, privileging the natural world, its creatures, and its ways over a failed technological civilization that has produced death camps and atomic weapons. Kinnell's poetics can be seen as springing from three sources: a search for the depths of self uncorrupted by civilized life; wilderness, wildness, and primitivism; and a poetics of empathy, what Kinnell has called a "tenderness toward existence," that has enabled him to write poetry of great inclusiveness and feeling.

Kinnell, like **Robert Bly**, **W.S. Merwin**, **James Wright**, and **Gary Snyder**, has often been classified as a **Deep Image** poet. While this accounting may help make sense of Kinnell's middle-period poetry, he has always been a poet of great technical range and one who, especially in his later period, has produced work that resists easy categorization. He is perhaps better thought of as a poet who has made good use of what **Denise Levertov** described in her 1965 essay "Some

Notes on Organic Form" as a poetry "based on an intuition of an order, a form beyond forms, [where] creative works are analogies, resemblances, natural allegories. Such a poetry is exploratory" (7). Yet Kinnell is not representative of any school of poetry other than that of his own singular voice.

Kinnell was born February 1, 1927, in Providence, Rhode Island, to first-generation Irish and Scottish immigrants. As a teenager, he studied poetry and met the poet Roger Nye Lincoln at the Wilbraham Academy in Massachusetts before serving in the United States Navy from 1944 to 1946. After spending a summer at **Black Mountain** College, he graduated from Princeton University summa cum laude in 1948. At Princeton, he roomed with the poet W.S. Merwin and studied with the poet Charles G. Bell. In 1949 Kinnell earned an MA at the University of Rochester. Kinnell began his teaching career as an instructor in English at Alfred University in Alfred, New York, where he taught from 1949 to 1951, and then from 1951 to 1955 he worked as the supervisor of a liberal arts program at the downtown campus of the University of Chicago. In the late 1950s, he traveled and taught in France and Iran, where he was a Fulbright lecturer. He published a translation of Rene Hardy's *Bitter Victory* in 1956.

In 1960 Kinnell published his first book of poems, *What a Kingdom It Was*, a collection of imagistic, musical, relatively formal poems that **James Dickey** called "warm, generous, and friendly" (Nelson, 66). Concerned, as are most first books, with finding expression for the isolated depths of the human subject, *Kingdom* includes a compelling series of poems that define a post-Christian, existential sense of sacramental life, death, and rebirth. In the estimation of most readers, *Kingdom*'s most durable artifact is the long, ambitious, and physically vivid poem of city life, "The Avenue Bearing the Initial of Christ into the New World" (1960). "Avenue," which describes Jewish immigrant life in the slums of New York's Lower East Side, exhibits, according to Andrew Taylor, "a Whitmanesque openness to experience, and a ready flow of sympathy, of compassion" (Nelson, 33). The poem, a veritable hymn to the immediacy of particular human life, works, like much of Whitman's poetry, by accumulation of detail, and not by compression. Consequently, the poem brims with exotic city dialects, smells, and sights and contains vivid descriptions of East Village, large-souled meditations on the reeking yet still beautiful East River, and a Villon-like sense of the ruggedness and pathos of ordinary human life.

Kingdom also contains the elegy "Freedom, New Hampshire" (1960), which Kinnell wrote in memory of his brother, Derry, who was killed in a car crash in 1957. A moving, frank examination of the death of a beloved, "Freedom" celebrates the continuity of life but refuses to take comfort in a process that, while on-flowing, ultimately cannot heal our deepest losses: "That was this man. When he is dead the grass / Heals what he suffered, but he remains dead."

During the early 1960s Kinnell worked odd jobs and supported himself with Guggenheim fellowships, translating, and other grants. In 1963 he worked for the Congress of Racial Equality, registering black voters in the South. He was jailed for a week in Plaquemines Parish, Louisiana, for civil rights activism. In 1964 he published his second book, *Flower Herding on Mount Monadnock*. *Monadnock*, a subtle and deceptively simple book, established many of Kinnell's characteristic naturalistic and psychological themes. In "Middle of the Way" (1964), a loose, sometimes nearly diaristic account of hiking the snow-filled mountains of the Pacific Northwest, Kinnell writes, "I lie on the earth the way / Flames lie in the woodpile." Fire imagery, often best understood as a symbol of the intensity of life lived in full consciousness of impending death, figures prominently throughout Kinnell's poetry and is often symbolically counterpoised to darkness. This darkness, for Kinnell is not just the "negative" darkness of death, but also often the "positive" darkness of the pre-conscious and subconscious mind. As Kinnell puts it, at the end of the poem, "I know I live half alive in the world / I know half my life belongs to the wild darkness." *Monadnock*, like much of Kinnell's later work, contains a number of moving meditations on time and mortality. In "Spindrift" (1964), for example, the poet writes that an old man comes to know and accept "a kind of gratefulness / Towards the time that kills him."

In 1965 Kinnell married Inés Delgado de Torres. That year he also participated in the Poets for Peace reading at Town Hall in New York City, the first of many anti-war readings he would undertake. He also published his translation of *The Poems of Francois Villon* (1965) and, in 1966, the novel *Black Light*, which gave imaginative form to his experiences in Iran. In *Black Light* Jamshid, an Iranian rug weaver, flees into exile after killing a man who insults his daughter. The book examines his journey across the desert, into Teheran, where in the red-light district he realizes he may have slept with the daughter for whom he has killed. **Mona Van Duyn** called *Black Light* "a strange, haunting book" with a "flawless" style (Nelson, 73).

In 1968, after the birth of his children (Maud Natasha in 1966, Finn Fergus in 1968), Kinnell published *Body Rags,* which attempted to provide (in the words of the author) a "truth to poetry . . . based on *all* of experience" (emphasis added). For Kinnell, this effort to expand poetry's experiential range extends even to gritty, unflinching, and imaginative examinations of nonhuman life, including bears, porcupines, crows, and flies. *Body Rags* received wide critical acclaim and was given special mention by the judges of the National Book Award for Poetry. Writing in the *Nation*, **John Logan** noted that with the publication of *Body Rags* "we can single out Kinnell as one of the few consummate masters in poetry" (Nelson, 76). *Body Rags* contains the novel and memorable anti-war poem "Vapor Trail Reflected in the Frog Pond" (1968), which was a parody of Whitman's "I Hear America Singing." The poem documents Kinnell's growing despair over both the Vietnam War and the domestic repression that accompanies it in the form of the "crack of deputies' rifles" and the "sput of cattleprod" The final poem, "The Bear" (1968), one of Kinnell's best-known poems, plumbs the roots of primitive consciousness in its account of a hunter who tracks and kills a bear, only to climb inside its carcass for protection from the cold, and then, in dream, to become the bear in death and rebirth. Reborn—as bear, or shaman, or poet—the speaker asks, "what, anyway / was that sticky infusion, that rank flavor of blood, that poetry / by which I lived?"

Also in 1968 Kinnell published his translation of Yves Bonnefoy's *On the Motion and Immobility of Douve*, which won the Cecil Hemley Poetry Prize from Ohio University Press. In 1969 Kinnell, then living in Spain, won the Ingram Merrill Foundation Award, an Amy Lowell traveling fellowship, a National Endowment of the Arts grant, the Brandeis University Creative Arts Award, and the Shelley Prize from the Poetry Society of America.

Throughout the 1970s Kinnell held short teaching appointments and visiting professorships at a large number of colleges and universities, including, among others, Reed, Columbia University, Sarah Lawrence, the University of Iowa, the University of Hawaii at Manoa, and the University of Nice. In 1970 Kinnell published Yvan Goll's *Lackawanna Elegy* and in 1971 *The Book of Nightmares*. *Nightmares*, an autobiographical and **confessional long poem**, finds intense mythic and transcendental correlatives to the primal experiences of birth, death, and parenting. *Nightmares*, widely considered to be "one of the most ambitious works in contemporary poetry" (as Morris Dickstein wrote in the *New York Times*) made Kinnell famous, but also signaled the end of his attempts to write the feverish, perhaps overwrought, post-Romantic poetry he had been writing since the late 1960s. Modeled after Rainer Maria Rilke's *Duino Elegies*, it is composed of ten sections, each in seven parts, that, in turn, describe the terrors of mortality, war, and the manifold varieties of human cruelty. Although the book cherishes bright moments of immediate human significance, it also insists on what M.L. Rosenthal, in his review, calls the "private horror . . . of a meaningless universe" (Nelson, 84).

Although some critics have faulted *Nightmare*'s repetitive diction, lack of irony, and perhaps too-easy existentialism, others have praised its intricate, weblike texture,

elegiac renderings of the ephemeral, and the ways Kinnell consistently finds identities between a visionary poetics and its individual and temporal locus. Kinnell himself perhaps best characterized the book in his remarks on Rilke's poetry in a 1972 interview with Wayne Dodd and Stanley Plumly collected in *Walking Down the Stairs*: He "writes only what for him is a matter of life and death. There's nothing trivial, no bright chatter, no clever commentary. He writes at the limit of his powers" (43). *Nightmares*, with its literary roots in Kinnell's readings of Rilke, Whitman, and **Eliot**'s *Four Quartets*, perhaps works not because of its "literary" underpinnings, but as a new myth of the hero who quests not for valor, but for the soul's deepest groundings in the fundaments of physical being-in-the-world, a metaphorical journey "back" to the unitary consciousness of the child and the primitive.

Kinnell took nine years to write his next book of poems, the much quieter and domestically focused *Mortal Acts, Mortal Words* (1980). Speaking of this book, Harold Bloom said, "Of his contemporaries, only the late James Wright and **Philip Levine** have been able to write with such emotional directness" (Nelson, 104). Compared with *Nightmares*, *Mortal Acts* is a happier ("no matter what fire we invent to destroy us / ours will have been the brightest world ever existing") and perhaps more forgiving ("sometimes it is necessary / to reteach a thing its loveliness") book. Filled with long, musically elaborate sentences, beautiful mouthy old words ("wastreled," "moil," "curvetting") and precise descriptions of the natural world and its creatures, *Mortal Acts* presents, in the words of Hank Lazar, "a passionately moral poetry . . . of a man saying directly, eloquently, and emotionally the things that he knows" (Nelson, 117).

In 1982 Kinnell published his *Selected Poems*, which won both the Pulitzer Prize and the National Book Award in 1983. That same year he organized the Poets Against the End of the World reading, which protested nuclear armament and proliferation. In 1984 he was made a MacArthur Fellow and appointed as Samuel F.B. Morse Professor of Arts and Sciences at New York University, a position he retained until 2005. In 1985 he published *The Past*, which won the National Book Critics Circle Award. *The Past*, which contains a moving series of meditative elegies for a lost marriage (Kinnell and his wife divorced in 1985) and for lost friends (**Richard Hugo**, James Wright), also contains masterful invocations of the creaturely world, including its seas, driftwood, ponds, dragonflies, and geese—all part of the struggling yet beautiful "post-Darwinian" world that Kinnell sees as he reckons his losses.

In 1987 Kinnell published *The Essential Whitman*, notable for its inspired selection of poems from among the many versions Whitman published, revised, and republished throughout his life. Kinnell, who in the introduction calls Whitman "his principal master," even goes so far as to create composite versions of poems built from what Kinnell considers the best parts of several different versions (3). In this sense, as he notes in the introduction, Kinnell manages to produce versions of some Whitman poems that never existed before.

In 1990 Kinnell published *When One Has Lived a Long Time Alone*, which, as the title suggests, takes human loneliness as a major theme. Perhaps the most memorable, and technically inventive, poem in this collection is the title poem, a sequence of eleven 13-line sections, each a complete sentence, and each beginning and ending with the words "when one has lived a long time alone." This poem, which aims to achieve "the halo of being made one," frankly examines the human need for love, or for at least the presence of another creature, even a common garden snake, the speaker's companion throughout much of the poem, for whom he plays Mozart and who becomes both figure and *comerado* as the poem develops. Bernard Dick, writing in *World Literature Today*, called the title poem a "real triumph" and notes that "never has loneliness been so seductive, so strangely inviting, so desirable, and at the same time so horrifying."

Kinnell followed *Long Time Alone* with a new volume, *Imperfect Thirst*, in 1994. This book, perhaps not as consistently strong as *Long Time Alone*, is built of five sections, each containing five poems that deal, in Kinnell's typically lyrical and mournfully celebratory way, with physical love, trees, snakes, flies, and even human excrement ("Holy Shit"). Kinnell also speaks strongly for the primacy of the human imagination, as in "The Deconstruction of Emily Dickinson" (1994), when he imagines flooring "with one wallop" a too-pedantic professor who insists on philology rather than a creative and imaginative understanding of Dickinson's refusal to commercialize her art. The book ends with an elegy, "Neverland" (1994), which describes the author's ongoing meditations during the death of his sister. Showing, even near the close of his career, how the poem can be a place and a vehicle for the mindful, rigorous working through of the conditions of existence, Kinnell attempts to delineate, as always, not only the fullest measure of consciousness, but also the price one pays for it.

In 1999 Kinnell published his translations (co-authored with Hannah Leibmann) of Rilke in *The Essential Rilke*, and in 2000 he published a second, often markedly revised selected collection in *A New Selected Poems*. Kinnell currently lives in New York and Vermont. He served as the Vermont State Poet from 1989 to 1993. He also served as the director of the Squaw Valley Community of Writers from 1979 to 2003.

Further Reading. *Selected Primary Sources:* Kinnell, Galway, *Black Light* (San Francisco: North Point Press, 1980); ———, *Body Rags* (Boston: Houghton Mifflin, 1968); ———, *The Book of Nightmares* (Boston: Houghton Mifflin, 1971); ——— *The Essential Whitman* (Edison, NJ: BBS, 1992); ———, *Flower Herding on Mount Monadnock* (Boston/Cambridge: Houghton Mifflin/Riverside, 1964); ———, *Imperfect Thirst* (Boston: Houghton Mifflin, 1994); ———, *A New Selected Poems* (Boston: Houghton Mifflin, 2000); ———, *The Past* (Boston: Houghton Mifflin, 1985); ———, *Selected Poems* (Boston: Houghton Mifflin, 1982); ———, *Walking Down the Stairs: Selections from Interviews* (Ann Arbor: University of Michigan Press, 1978); ———, *What a Kingdom It Was* (Boston: Houghton Mifflin, 1960); ———, *When One Has Lived a Long Time Alone* (New York: Knopf, 1990). ***Selected Secondary Sources:*** Dick, Bernard F., "A New Selected Poems" (book review) (*World Literature Today* 74.4 [Autumn 2000]: 819); Dickstein, Morris, "Intact and Triumphant" (*New York Times* [19 September 1982]: 369); Harris, Peter, "Varieties of Religious Experience," (*Virginia Quarterly Review* 71.4 [Autumn 1995]: 654); Levertov, Denise, *The Poet in the World* (New York: New Directions, 1973); Nelson, Howard, ed., *On the Poetry of Galway Kinnell: The Wages of Dying* (Ann Arbor: University of Michigan Press, 1987); Zimmerman, Lee, *Intricate and Simple Things: The Poetry of Galway Kinnell* (Urbana: University of Illinois Press, 1987).

Joe Ahearn

KINZIE, MARY (1944–)

Mary Kinzie writes poetry in which observation becomes a lavish act of perception, blending description with the intensification of conscious thought. Kinzie's poems focus on such issues as motherhood and the nature of the moral life, demonstrating an affinity with the work of **Eavan Boland** and the modernist poet **Louise Bogan**. The aesthetic principles that inform Kinzie's work are clear from her prose essays and reviews, in which she critiques the prose qualities that distinguish recent poetry. Kinzie crafts poems whose serious tone and probing intelligence derive from her belief in the responsibility of exploring ethical concerns, which she has modeled on the work of the novelist J.M. Coetzee.

Mary Kinzie was born in Montgomery, Alabama, in 1944. She attended Northwestern University, the Free University in Berlin, and Johns Hopkins University. Since 1979 Kinzie has directed the creative writing program at Northwestern University. Her first collection of poems, *Threshold of the Year* (1981), won the Devins Award. *Masked Women* and *Summers of Vietnam* were published together in 1990. *Autumn Eros* (1991) appeared soon after, followed by *Ghost Ship* (1996) and *Drift* (2003). *Drift* is distinct from previous collections in its use of experimental forms and turn toward abstraction. Kinzie's prose criticism positions her in the tradition of such poet-critics as **Robert Pinsky**. In the prose collections *The Cure of Poetry in an Age of Prose: Moral Essays on the Poet's Calling* (1993) and *The Judge Is Fury: Dislocation and Form in Poetry* (1994), Kinzie takes an unflinching look at contemporary poetry. *A Poet's Guide to Poetry* (1999) assembles her vast knowledge of poetic technique for fledgling poets.

The poems in *Autumn Eros* provide access to Kinzie's method of composition. "Lunar Frost" presents a child speaker riding in the car with her family. Despite her father's idea of education (she has "Learned to iron, and save"), her desire for knowledge exceeds the confines of her gender role. She embraces an unruly desire to capture the "Flicker at the core / Prior to understanding." Kinzie's poetry dwells close to the line separating individual consciousness from the world, where meaning is inchoate. The child delights in this formlessness and uncertainty, deconstructing the reality of her world "Into incompletion." For Kinzie, the knowledge rendered in the act of perception can take the form of a kind of pleasurable nearsightedness, a thickening of focus at the onset of experience. In "Pine" she recounts gazing upon a forest of evergreen trees as a child, when "the whole body grows myopic / Focused on that near infinity." This sense of enjoyable myopia resonates as a metaphor for her verse more generally. Kinzie's strength of vision is checked by the frequency with which she embraces limitations and restrictions. In her use of rhyme, meter, and traditional forms such as the sestina Kinzie productively brings these restrictions on herself.

Sight assumes an important role in *Ghost Ship*, as Kinzie observes how children develop their own ability to view the world. In "Alcaics for My Niece," Kinzie employs a classical syllabic form to describe the growth the infant will experience. Soon she will "start to hum and whir / With sight." The infant will begin to see "The woven world—bright, dark—that unravels in / Faces sewn with the features expressing soul." The constructed quality of the world in her poems serves to intensify the role of the imagination as a generative faculty. A young child demonstrates the ability to "watch the dead to life" in the poem "Only Child." In "Alcaics" Kinzie describes the infant's dreams like the seeds of cottonwood flowers, which on "Warm days will float loose . . . embryonic / Substance of fantasy, spreading forests." The experience of motherhood exists in tension with this creative function, as the mother realizes her unstable position in the child's life. In "Emblems" Kinzie explains that the "child urges me to watch her but the sun pours fuzz / On everything it glances from." The sun obscures the poet's gaze, and in that moment of blindness the poet envisions the child's eventual separation from her. It is a separation in which "I'm included / in a nimbus of indifference like chaff." Many poems reflect on exclusion or separation from others, often in reference to the experience of

aging. Yet the pull toward observation remains inexorable, even when the revelation yields hard truths. In "Baltimore" the body of a horse lies discarded in the street, with one "eye still open on the world he leaves." The open eye is testimony to Kinzie's unyielding attraction to the imperfect world.

Although the visual represents the dominant mode of observation in much of her work, Kinzie employs sound as a way of focusing the poems in *Drift.* "Ropework" offers an extended meditation organized according to the aural dynamics of her environment. A rope hangs from the roof, noisily banging against the side of her building. This sound produces a series of reflections, from the odd metaphysical conceit that the building is "being sped by a quirt to gallop off / through the cool blue days" to more discursive considerations of the relations among sounds and ideas. In "Hour on Hour" the aural helps to initiate the experience of womanhood, as the poet recollects hearing a song of difference, notes of "uncertain" music "like threads / of light." The synesthesia of this image captures the bountiful act of mind in Kinzie's poems, revealing a poet intimately involved in the richness of life lived in human time.

Further Reading. ***Selected Primary Sources:*** Kinzie, Mary, ———, *The Cure of Poetry in an Age of Prose* (Chicago: University of Chicago Press, 1993); ———, *Drift* (New York: Alfred A. Knopf, 2003); ———, *Ghost Ship* (New York: Alfred A. Knopf, 1996).

Jeffrey Galbraith

KIRBY, DAVID (1944–)

In a blurb for David Kirby's *The House of Blue Light*, **Albert Goldbarth** searches for apt comparisons that will illuminate Kirby's talents. He cites a number of figures from literature, popular culture, and stand-up comedy: Spalding Gray, Lenny Bruce, Lily Tomlin, **Kenneth Koch**, Woody Allen, Harry Crews, Eartha Kitt, Rainer Maria Rilke, Dave Barry. That such a list could be put together is remarkable; that it is extremely accurate, even more so. David Kirby's poems combine the narrative features of the best storytelling with the outrageous humor of stand-up comedy while still delivering serious messages of emotional resonance. Though many of Kirby's poems contain moments of laugh-out-loud humor and always present entertaining stories, it would be misleading to present him as merely a practitioner of comic verse or solely a **narrative** poet. Rather, he uses comedy and storytelling to disarm the reader, which increases the emotional impact of the poems' more serious revelations. The complexity of his syntax and the direct quality of his diction also owe a debt to the author's Southern background. In the sprawling sentences and down-home delivery, a reader can hear the cadences of William Faulkner and Mark Twain.

Kirby was born in 1944 in Baton Rouge, Louisiana. At age five he contracted polio, but was treated early enough to prevent the debilitating effects suffered by so many others during that epidemic. He attended Louisiana State University, and after receiving his bachelor's degree, he entered the Ph.D. program of Johns Hopkins University. He received that degree at age twenty-four and was hired by the English Department of Florida State University, where he is still teaching as the Robert O. Lawton Distinguished Professor of English. Kirby's first full-length collection, *Sarah Bernhardt's Leg* (1983), was published by the Cleveland State University Poetry Center, and his second, *Saving the Young Men of Vienna* (1987), won the Brittingham Prize for Poetry and was published by the University of Wisconsin Press. *Big-Leg Music* (1995) initiated Kirby's relationship with Orchises Press, with which he has published several volumes. His next book, also from Orchises, was *My Twentieth Century* (1999), and it is this volume that launched the familiar long-sentence, humorous, narrative poem that has become his trademark. Such poems also dominate *The House of Blue Light* (2000), published in the Southern Messenger Poets series edited by **Dave Smith** for LSU Press. Two more books quickly followed: *The Travelling Library* (2001) from Orchises and *The Ha-Ha* (2003) from LSU (also in the Southern Messenger Poets series). In addition to his books of poems, Kirby has also been a prolific scholar, publishing works of criticism on Herman Melville, Henry James, and **Mark Strand**, as well as a collection of essays, *What Is a Book?* (2002).

The poems of Kirby's first three full-length books display the wit and straightforward voice of his later work, but are not so ambitious or so expansively narrative as the poems of his maturity. For instance, "Saving the Young Men of Vienna" (which first appeared in *Sarah Bernhardt's Leg,* not the subsequent volume that bears the title) demonstrates his good-natured but mildly sardonic sense of humor as the speaker imagines the young men of Freud's Vienna, with their sexual dilemmas and confusion. At the end of the poem, he suggests that Dr. Freud saves these men, allowing them to embrace "at last the common unhappiness." We see in this poem the same blend of humor and serious revelation that characterizes Kirby's later work. We also see formal similarities, as the poem is structured in five 6-line stanzas and composed in three longish sentences. But the humor is not so boisterous, the revelation not so profound, and the syntax neither so complex nor so graceful as the work of his maturity. Also, the poem is entirely meditative, and while this is not a completely absent characteristic in the later work, where it appears there the meditation is usually connected intimately to incident. The poems of *Sarah Bernhardt's Leg, Saving the Young Men of Vienna,* and *Big-Leg Music* have their virtues, but they are also what Kirby himself has referred to—in a prefa-

tory note to a collection of his selected early poems, *I Think I Am Going to Call My Wife Paraguay* (2004)—as his "apprenticeship" and his "early work." In the same note, he refers to one poem from *Big-Leg Music* as "the last poem of the early work and the first of the later." This poem is "The Potato Mash (More Indefinite and More Soluble)" and is indeed the most complete incarnation in any of the first three books of what has become his signature style. It relates the comical and "stupid" adventures of David Kirby as adolescent manager of a rock and roll band, yet it manages to make a sweeping association between these experiences and the work of Debussy, Mallarmé, and Verlaine. Much of Kirby's subsequent works continue to manage just such unlikely connections between high culture and low experience.

Having discovered his true métier, Kirby fully realized its potential in his next book, *My Twentieth Century,* in which he expands the voice of his early work into sprawling narrative poems of varying and complex stanzaic structure. The voice in this book is one of a poet completely at ease with, and in control of, his medium. The comfort level is obvious from the first poem, cheekily titled "Author's Note." Its first line is "As I begin thinking about these new poems," and the speaker proceeds to explain the impulse to write the very poems in the book the reader is holding, as well as listing the work of others to which these poems might be compared. Thus, a completely trustworthy autobiographical speaker is created, but by the end of the poem, this speaker (David Kirby, surely) reminds us of the fact that all real truth exists in art, not the mundane recording of facts: "Because if I write about it, / and you read what I've written, it happened." The expansive nature of Kirby's mature poems is also evident in the sheer length of those in *My Twentieth Century:* There are only twenty-one poems in this 128-page book. The poet's confidence in his voice and in his choice of subject is also reflected in such poems as "The King Is Dead," in which the speaker doubts the value of Elvis Presley's contribution to modern music, and "Mr. Andrews," a poem entirely based upon the author's summer job installing Sears appliances as the assistant to the remarkably taciturn title character.

Kirby followed the stylistic breakthrough of *My Twentieth Century* with a more fully honed exploration of his new mode in the masterwork *The House of Blue Light.* His confidence is again on display in this volume, as he dares to write poems with such titles as "Catholic Teenager from Hell Goes to Italy," "Roman Polanski's Cookies," and "Moderation Kills (Excusez-Moi, Je Suis Sick as a Dog)." That all of these poems contain lines that can elicit belly laughs from a solitary reader and yet still manage to arrive at profound revelations about the human condition is a testament to the singular art of David Kirby. Such achievements are also evident in the subsequent volumes: *The Travelling Library,* which draws extensively on the poet's European travels, and *The Ha-Ha,* an eclectic collection similar in its diversity to *The House of Blue Light.* Kirby seems to be at the height of his powers, having refined a truly original art form out of the unlikely combination of narrative strategy, complex syntax, irreverent humor, profound intellectual and emotional searching, and intricate stanzaic structure. His success with such a formula has made David Kirby an original in American poetry.

Further Reading. *Selected Primary Sources*: Kirby, David, *Big-Leg Music* (Washington, DC: Orchises, 1995); ———, *The Ha-Ha* (Baton Rouge: LSU Press, 2003); ———, *The House of Blue Light* (Baton Rouge: LSU Press, 2000); ———, *My Twentieth Century* (Washington, DC: Orchises, 1999); ———, *Sarah Bernhardt's Leg* (Cleveland: Cleveland State Poetry Center, 1983); ———, *Saving the Young Men of Vienna* (Madison: University of Wisconsin Press, 1987); ———, *The Travelling Library* (Washington: Orchises, 2001); ———, *What Is a Book?* (Athens: University of Georgia Press, 2002). ***Selected Secondary Sources*:** Halliday, Mark, "Gabfest" (*Parnassus: Poetry in Review* 26.2 [2002]: 203–215); Klappert, Peter, "The Invention of the Kirby Poem" (*Southern Review* 36.1 [Winter 2000]: 196–207); MacQueen, Steve, "Sho' Like to Ball: David Kirby Hits 'Em High and Low in a Galloping Career through the Quirky World of Free Verse" (*Florida State University Research in Review* 14 [Winter 2004]: 12–23).

Dan Albergotti

KIYOOKA, ROY (KENZIE) (1926–1994)

Painter, poet, and photographer Roy Kiyooka's influence in both literary and artistic circles extends far beyond the boundaries of his native Canada. His reputation as a "multimedia" artist par excellence has become firmly cemented around works such as *The Fountainebleu Dream Machine,* in which there is a complex interplay between word and image, and *Pear Tree Pome,* in which a spare, intense lyricism plays itself out. More important, these works have made him crucial to both the relatively new field of **Asian American** and Asian Canadian studies and to the introduction of first **Allen Ginsberg**'s and **Philip Whalen**'s Japanese-influenced poetry and later the introduction of new American poets **Charles Olson, Robert Duncan, Robert Creeley,** and **Denise Levertov** to western and later the rest of Canada. Such a contribution to the literary and cultural richness of both the United States and Canada cannot be underestimated.

Kiyooka was born in Moose Jaw, Saskatchewan, in 1926, the third of seven children, to Harry Shigekiyo and Mary Kiyoshi Kiyooka. That Kyoshi's father was a former samurai in the Meiji era reknown for his swordsmanship—"the last great master of the Hasegawa school of Iai" (*Mothertalk,* 15)—remained a vital force in Kyoka's adult attempts to piece together an identity, a historically grounded and linguistic home, a "mother tongue" in a post–Pearl Harbor world. Another crucial impetus was the bombing of Pearl Harbor in 1941 and the subsequent internment of persons classified as "of the Japanese race" along American and Canadian coasts. Despite his living outside of what were then called "protected zones," his sudden awareness of himself as a racialized other gradually transformed itself into a lifelong exploration of the modes of power that operate in and through language. As he writes in *Wheels* (1969–1985), "i learned to speak a good textbook English. . . . i never saw the 'yellow peril' in myself."

Kyoto Airs (1964), however, marks Kiyooka's inaugural attempt to work through and transform an imperialistic English into a self-identified "inglish" that attempts to reveal the triadic power struggle between self, other, and language. This first book of poetry immediately stands as a record of Kiyooka's return to Japan—a record that is only minimally about Japan itself and that concerns itself more with, as he puts it, "origins, kinships, and what you call heritage" (Varley, 3). But it is also, and more significantly, concerned with approaching the language and culture of the Japanese half of his bifurcated identity at the same time as it's concerned with articulating an "i's" gradual acceptance of being perpetually both alienated from and at home in Japanese and English language and culture: He defines himself as linguistically differentiated, for among both English and Japanese he sees himself as "a tongue- / twisted alien." Moreover, these poems speak to how this fraught relationship with language is inevitably bound up with an equally fraught sense of personal and national histories and geographies. At a stylistic level, Kiyooka's engagement with alienation and home comes through in the spare, unhurried, and gently musical rhythms and line breaks of *Kyoto Airs*—a style that manages to produce haiku-like poems that are simultaneously directly influenced both by Japanese literary traditions and by **Snyder's**, Ginsberg's and Whalen's idiosyncratic appropriation of such literary traditions.

Kyoto Airs also begins Kiyooka's lifelong attempts to write a poetry strongly inflected by his training as a painter and a sculptor, which since the mid-1950s, had gained him a reputation as one of Canada's most promising artists. While such a visual sensibility is most evident in "Road to Yase," in which "green" is repeated, steplike, down the page as a visual representation of the "green / on the road / to Yase." *The Fontainebleau Dream Machine: 18 Frames from a Book of Rhetorick* (1977) garnered significant critical attention for its evocative interplay of finely crafted collages and partly autobiographical poems. A serial poem of eighteen parts invites the reader to wander through the Delacroix-inspired "rooms" and reflect on the wide-ranging cultural critique that Kiyooka puts forward. Ultimately, through collages that deconstruct Western art and its claims to originality and through the accompanying poems that are, as Kiyooka puts it, "autobiological" in the sense that all boundaries between "Kiyooka" as author and the artwork have been dissolved or confused, *The Fontainebleau Dream Machine* is remarkable in its ability to simultaneously be and comment on itself as a verbovisual, thoroughly open-ended work of art.

Many argue, however, that *Pear Tree Pomes* (1987), which was nominated for the prestigious Governor General's Award, is not only Kiyooka's most remarkable work but also the crowning achievement in Canadian poetry from the 1980s. Again intertwining text and image—this time with watercolors by David Bolduc—this serial poem ostensibly uses the motif of a pear tree's seasonal transformations to address the transformative power of love and its loss. However, like all of Kiyooka's work, *Pear Tree Pomes* must be simultaneously read as a record of the process of thinking and writing, in turn inseparable from its representation of language, memory, and nature itself as inherently processual—anything but stable, inert and so finally knowable; as he writes early on about the pear tree, "as i sit here writing its virtues down on paper i can see / call it the 'real' pear tree just outside the study window." Clearly drawing on **Wallace Stevens**'s poems of movement and relationality and his awareness of the permeability of subject and object, "such as they are these words bear / a testimonial to all the weather we lived through together."

Further Reading. *Selected Primary Sources:* Kiyooka, Roy K., *The Fontainebleau Dream Machine: 18 Frames from a Book of Rhetorick* (Toronto, ON: Coach House Press, 1977); ———, *Kyoto Airs* (Vancouver, BC: Periwinkle Press, 1964); ———, *Mothertalk: Life Stories of Mary Kiyoshi Kiyooka* (Edmonton, AB: NeWest Press, 1997); ———, *Pacific Windows: Collected Poems of Roy K. Kiyooka*, ed. Roy Miki (Vancouver, BC: Talonbooks, 1997); ———, *Pear Tree Pomes* (Toronto, ON: Coach House Press, 1987); ———, *Stoned Gloves* (Toronto, ON: Coach House Press, 1970). ***Selected Secondary Sources:*** Kröller, Eva-Marie, "Roy Kiyooka's 'The Fontainebleau Dream Machine': A Reading" (*Canadian Literature: A Quarterly of Criticism and Review* [Summer–Fall 1987]: 113–114); Miki, Roy, "Coruscations, Plangencies, and the Syllibant: After Words to Roy Kiyooka's *Pacific Windows*" (Afterword), in *Pacific Windows: Collected Poems of Roy K. Kiyooka*, ed. Roy Miki (Vancouver, BC: Talonbooks, 1997); Varley, Chris, "Intersections" (interview), in *Roy K. Kiyooka: 25 Years: An Exhibition Organized and Circulated by the Vancouver Art Gallery* (Vancouver, BC: Vancouver Art Gallery, 1975).

Lori Emerson

KIZER, CAROLYN (1925–)

Carolyn Kizer is a feminist and a socially active poet whose work and life have demonstrated a passionate commitment as much to justice as to art. In addition to early poems that treat traditional subjects such as nature and later work that is often personal, where family and friends become sources for inspiration, Kizer has consistently written poems about social and political issues. Her artistic concern with society's problems has been mirrored in her personal action. In a characteristic gesture, Kizer, along with poet **Maxine Kumin,** resigned in 1999 from the Board of Chancellors of the Academy of American Poets to protest that organization's neglect of poets of color.

Born in Spokane, Washington, Kizer was the only child of Benjamin H. Kizer, a well-known lawyer active in various liberal causes, and Mabel Ashley Kizer, who earned a Ph.D. in biology from Stanford and was also committed to social justice. In her book of essays, *Proses: On Poems and Poets,* Kizer writes of her childhood and the influences her father and mother had on her development as a writer. The poet married Charles Stimson Bullitt in 1948 and had three children before the union ended in divorce. She married John Marshall Woodbridge in 1975.

Kizer earned a BA degree from Sarah Lawrence College in 1945 and did graduate work at Columbia University and at the University of Washington, where she was a student of **Theodore Roethke**. She co-founded the journal *Poetry Northwest* and was its editor from 1959 to 1965. In addition, Kizer was a State Department visiting artist in Pakistan during 1964–1965 and served as the first Director of Literary Programs for the National Endowment for the Arts. In 1985 Kizer won the Pulitzer Prize in Poetry for *Yin: New Poems;* other honors include the Theodore Roethke Memorial Foundation Poetry Award, the Frost Medal of the Poetry Society of America, and the American Academy and Institute of Arts and Letters Award.

Carolyn Kizer has distinguished herself not only as a poet, but also as teacher, critic, and translator. She has served as poet-in-residence at many universities, as acting director of the graduate writing program at Columbia University, as a lecturer at Barnard College, and as a senior fellow in humanities at Princeton University. Her publications include *The Ungrateful Garden* (1961), *Knock Upon Silence* (1965), *Midnight Was My Cry: New and Selected Poems* (1971), *Yin: New Poems* (1984), *Mermaids in the Basement: Poems for Women* (1984), *The Nearness of You* (1986), *Carrying Over: Poems from the Chinese, Urdu, Macedonian, Yiddish, and French African* (1988), *Proses: On Poems and Poets* (1993), *Picking and Choosing: Essays on Prose* (1996), *Harping On: Poems 1985–1995* (1996), *100 Great Poems by Women* (as editor) (1998), and *Cool, Calm & Collected: Poems 1960–2000* (2001).

In many of the volumes following *The Ungrateful Garden,* Kizer intersperses new poems with those from earlier books. In keeping with this practice, *Cool, Calm & Collected: Poems 1960–2000,* in addition to new work, contains selections from all of the poet's earlier poetry collections and provides a useful overview and compendium of Kizer's development as a writer.

Kizer's volumes often contain snapshot lessons in American history. For example, in "Poem, Small and Delible" (1965), a **lyric** that memorializes the picketing of Woolworth's during the Civil Rights era, the poet writes, "Art and Action, mostly incompatible, / Could support each other now and then," a practice that Kizer's poems take seriously. For instance, in "The Death of a Public Servant" (1961) she mourns the suicide of a Canadian ambassador accused by a United States Senate subcommittee of being a communist. "The First of June Again" (1971) decries both the Vietnam War and the lack of concern for environmental issues in the United States, while "Season of Lovers and Assassins" (1971) concerns Robert Kennedy's assassination. Similarly, in "Fin-de-siècle Blues" (2001) the poet laments the advent of AIDS and the "endless lists of victims" of twentieth-century atrocities.

Feminism is central to the poet's thought, and "Pro Femina," a piece Kizer has worked on for several decades, is perhaps her best-known poem. The first three sections initially appeared in *Knock Upon Silence*; the fourth section, "Fanny," was published in *Yin*; and part 5, "The Erotic Philosophers," was first included in *Cool, Calm & Collected,* a volume that contains all of "Pro Femina." Often satiric, the first three parts of this work consider the role of liberated women, especially writers. Kizer condemns the time when "poetry wasn't a craft but a sickly effluvium" and counsels that women must write tough-minded, real poetry for "we are the custodians of the world's best-kept secret: / Merely the private lives of one-half of humanity." "Fanny" is about Fanny Osbourne Stevenson, wife of Robert Louis Stevenson, who sacrificed her own life to support her husband's creativity, while "The Erotic Philosophers" details Saint Augustine's and Kierkegaard's lives and these two philosophers' attitudes toward women.

Cool, Calm & Collected has two epigraphs, one a line from **W.H. Auden,** "Stagger onward rejoicing," and the other, **Gertrude Stein**'s admonition "Be cool inside the mule." Both suggest Kizer's stoic yet optimistic and often humorous approach to dealing with life's harshest realities. Eschewing sentimentality and self-pity as unworthy of art, Kizer employs instead wit, irony, intelligence, and craft. Her technical gifts are considerable, and especially in earlier work, Kizer often uses intricate forms to contain the chaos of subjects she treats. Whatever her topic or structure, Kizer unfailingly extols the merits of living with courage and passion; her poems are exemplars of art's capacity not merely to represent but to engage, and particularly to engage the most painful problems of history.

Further Reading. *Selected Primary Sources:* Kizer, Carolyn, *Cool, Calm & Collected: Poems 1960–2000* (Port Townsend, WA: Copper Canyon Press, 2001); ———, *Proses: On Poems & Poets* (Port Townsend, WA: Copper Canyon Press, 1993). ***Selected Secondary Sources:*** Finch, Annie, Johanna Keller, and Candace McClelland, eds., *Carolyn Kizer: Perspectives on Her Life and Work* (Fort Lee, NJ: CavanKerry Press, 2001); Rigsbee, David, ed., *An Answering Music: On the Poetry of Carolyn Kizer* (Boston: Ford-Brown & Co., 1990).

Elizabeth B. House

KLEIN-HEALY, ELOISE (1943–)

Eloise Klein-Healy has been an enduring figure in West Coast poetry and education since the late 1970s. Her poetry has influenced the writing of the lesbian, gay and women's communities as well as reaching a wide and diverse American audience (*see also* **Gay and Lesbian Poetry**). Klein-Healy's work is marked by craftsmanship and clarity. Her subject matter spans a broad range of American experiences, such as baseball, commuting, birding, injustice, and casual violence. Her poetry is marked by wit and practical wisdom. Although she returns to the Greeks frequently, she is a thoroughly American poet in her curiosity and optimism in the face of an ever-complex **postmodern** world.

Born on September 4, 1943, in El Paso, Texas, Klein-Healy's early life was marked, like those of many "war babies," by World War II and the absence of her enlisted father, who was stationed in India. She was just over two years old when her father returned and the family moved to Sioux City and then Remsen, Iowa, finally, in 1953, migrating west to North Hollywood, California. Klein-Healy's experience is representative of the postwar migration of veterans and their families to the promise of Southern California.

Klein-Healy's poetry is rooted in the West but retains a Midwestern sensibility for the practical and for the plain but well spoken. It is the landscape of Los Angeles that becomes the foundation for her images, both natural and urban. Klein-Healy as transplanted native writes of a rarely acknowledged or understood Los Angeles, one that is filled with neighborhoods and the ordinary and where the diverse nature of the city unfolds over a vast eclectic landscape. Southern California is the platform she uses effectively in *Packet Beating Like a Heart* (1980), *Artemis in Echo Park* (1991), and *Passing* (2002).

The city again also defines her fourth volume, *Artemis in Echo Park.* Klein-Healy writes, "The city of Los Angeles, especially my lovely Echo Park, provided a living laboratory in which to test my belief in the influence of layers of history beneath our feet." It is the layers of neighborhoods and diverse experiences that stand out in poems such as "From Los Angeles Looking South," "Two Centuries in One Day," "Toltecs," and "Another Island," and to which she speaks directly in "The City Beneath the City," where, among other buried layers, she resurrects the history of the Chinese men who, because their wives were banned from being with them, dug tunnels so that the women "would live / in hiding. Under the cover of night / they spread out the secret earth to dry." What emerge in *Artemis* are the layers of injustice beneath America as a whole. It is in this volume that she takes the local beyond to the global.

Klein-Healy has had a long respected and influential teaching career at several Southern California universities, most notably as founding chair of the MFA in Creative Writing Program at Antioch University, Los Angeles. But it is from her experience as the Coordinator of Women Studies at California State University–Northridge that her fourth volume, *Women's Studies Chronicles*, emerged. Here is a work where the poet's voice is a scream against a landscape filled with landmines of misogyny, homophobia, and violence, and nowhere is that more clear than in poems such as *The Test* and *The Rape Victim's Newest Boyfriend*. In the *Test* Klein-Healy not only takes her students "to the wall / in *The Handmaid's Tale*," she "held in front of them / the photos / of the Triangle Shirt Waist Factory girls" and insists they "touch the concrete before these women / smash against it like bags of groceries / you'd spill going into your house." The experiences she puts her students and the reader through in this volume are relentless chronicles of daily inhumanity with no respite. *Women's Studies Chronicles* is a departure from Klein-Healy's voice and tone, but is of a piece with the rest of her work in its clarity, albeit extended to a graphic hardness.

In *Passing* she returns to many of her earlier themes, but this time they are tempered by not only experience but also an awareness of the ephemeral nature of human love and life. Her love poems are laced with the tenuousness of recovery from illness, the often painful and angry reality of caretaking, and the inevitability of death. This is best illustrated in *Latin from the Mass, My Shoes*, and *Suite for Young Man Dying. Passing* is filled with the life and landscape of Los Angeles and is best illustrated by the fast-paced, long-lined, witty ride through postmodern life in *Los Angeles Is a Virgo. Passing* is an intelligent tapestry of **elegy**, **lyric**, and classical forms. This volume has some of her finest poetry in written form, the strongest being a sestina about the Olympic champion diver, *Louganis*. This poem is good example of her plain and well-spoken style as well as her mastery of craft.

Further Reading. ***Selected Primary Sources:*** Klein-Healy, Eloise, *Artemis in Echo Park* (Ithaca, NY: Firebrand Books, 1991); ———, *Building Some Changes* (Venice, CA: Beyond Baroque Foundation, 1976); ———, *Ordinary Wisdom* (Los Angeles: Paradise Press, 1981); ———, *A Packet Beating Like a Heart* (Los Angeles: Books of a Feather Press, 1980); ———, *Passing* (Granada Hills, CA: Red Hen Press, 2002); ———, *Women's Studies Chronicles* (Laguna Poets Series, no. 99) (Laguna Beach, CA: Inevitable Press, 1998).

Jacqueline De Angelis

KLEINZAHLER, AUGUST (1949–)

The poems of August Kleinzahler, international winner of the prestigious *TLS/Griffin Poetry Prize* in 2004, were described by the judges of that competition as texts that are always "ferociously on the move, between locations, between forms, between registers." Born in Jersey City, New Jersey, but currently living in San Francisco, where he writes a weekly music column for the *San Diego Weekly Reader*, Kleinzahler briefly attended the University of Wisconsin as an East Asian Studies major before dropping out to travel to Canada, where he took a degree in English at the University of Victoria in British Columbia in 1973. There he came under the influence of British expatriate poet Basil Bunting, whose poem *Briggflatts* Kleinzahler has said "was everything [he] wanted in poetry" during the period when he was striving to find his own voice in the 1970s. *A Calendar of Airs*, Kleinzahler's first book, was published in 1978, and it has been followed by seven other collections to date, as well as a collection of prose pieces—by turns autobiographical, critical, and meditative—*Cutty, One Rock: Low Characters and Strange Places, Gently Explained* (2004). He has taught creative writing at Brown University, the University of California–Berkeley, and the Iowa Writers' Workshop, as well as to homeless veterans in San Francisco, but on the whole Kleinzahler is dismissive of "the 28yearoldshitheadsfromstanford.com" as he has described academia in one of his online columns. At various stages in his career he has also worked as a taxi driver, a locksmith, a logger, and a building manager.

Many of Kleinzahler's earlier collections—including *The Sausage Master of Minsk* (1977) (a chapbook), *A Calendar of Airs* (1978), *Storm Over Hackensack* (1985), *On Johnny's Time* (1988), and *Dainties and Viands* (1989)—are now out of print, but a number of the poems contained in these volumes are included in *Live from the Hong Kong Nile Club, Poems 1975–1990*, a collection published by Farrar, Straus and Giroux in 2000. Although Kleinzahler says in a prefatory essay to this collection that "much of what's gathered in [it] now feels remote to [him]," it nonetheless affords a useful introduction to a poet whose most recent collections "go places he has never gone before," as the dust jacket note to the British (Faber and

Faber) edition of *The Strange Hours Travelers Keep* (2004) puts it.

So where do Kleinzahler's poem go? The question does not have a straightforward answer, but the division of *Live from the Hong Kong Nile Club* into two sections, "East" and "West," suggests the geographical, cultural, and historical sweep of his writing. This is not only registered by his poetry's explorations of life on the East and West coasts of the United States of America, but Kleinzahler is also interested in the cultural cartographies of the Eastern Hemisphere and its occidental opposite, a point that is signaled by the epigraphs to *Live from the Hong Kong Nile Club*: One is from *The Confucian Analects*, and the other is provided by Miles Davis. "If you're not nervous, you're not paying attention" the Davis epigraph reads, in turn summarizing the combination of attentiveness and compulsive formal and thematic restlessness that pervades Kleinzahler's poetry.

Critics and reviewers have compared Kleinzahler's poetry to **jazz** music, not only because of explicit references in his poems to jazz musicians—Miles Davis, Bill Evans, Scott Lafaro, and others—but also because of what Peter Campion has called their attempt to "embody individual spaces in time" (37). Connections between Kleinzahler's poetics and early **Imagism** have also been suggested, and various critics have enumerated the wide range of figures—literary (from **William Carlos Williams** to **Thom Gunn**) and non-literary (from Herman E. Johnson to Willem de Kooning)—who have influenced his work. In recent years, however, Kleinzahler has developed a rhythmic and syntactical method that cannot be traced to any single precursor. As Thom Gunn has suggested with regard to the influence of Williams on Kleinzahler's work, "The poetry of Williams is . . . a point of origin from which he moves out" (27). One may discern certain cultural and aesthetic sources or influences in some of his writing, in other words, but in recent years Kleinzahler has forged ahead and created a voice in American poetry that is uniquely his.

In the same way that he has absorbed a wide range of influences in the achievement of a unique style, Kleinzahler is also adept at recording the voices of those he hears around him, of figures such as the schizophrenic Green in the title poem of *Green Sees Things in Waves* or "An Englishman Abroad" in *The Strange Hours Travelers Keep*, among many others. He is an incessant eavesdropper, and he listens to the world like a child "listening to neighbors mow / sniffing summer through the curtains" as he writes in "Staying Home from Work," from *Live from the Hong Kong Nile Club*. Reading Kleinzahler, one encounters a poetic soundscape whose "jaunty skips and riffs solace the ear," as Helen Vendler has put it (404): He might not approve of the term "jaunty," but "skips and riffs" seems about right for a poet whose poems conjure the sounds and words of Tom Waits and Thelonious

Monk as much as they do the divergent rhythmic and syntactic manners of Bunting or **Frank O'Hara**. "I have loved the air outside Shop-Rite Liquor . . . better than the Marin hills at dusk" he writes in "Poetics," summarizing his poetry's desire to apprehend what in the same piece he calls the "Air full of living dust," from *Live from the Hong Kong Nile Club*, a poetry that thrives in an atmosphere of diverse elements and whose contemporaneity is never in doubt.

Further Reading. ***Selected Primary Sources:*** Kleinzahler, August, *Cutty, One Rock: Low Characters and Strange Places, Gently Explained* (New York: Farrar, Straus and Giroux, 2004); ———, *Green Sees Things in Waves* (New York: Farrar, Straus and Giroux, 1998); ———, *Live from the Hong Kong Nile Club: Poems 1975–1980* (New York: Farrar, Straus and Giroux, 2000); ———, *Red Sauce, Whiskey and Snow* (New York: Farrar, Straus and Giroux, 1995); ———, *The Strange Hours Travelers Keep* (New York: Farrar, Straus and Giroux, 2003). ***Selected Secondary Sources:*** Campion, Peter, "August Kleinzahler and the 'Music' of American Poetry" (*PN Review* 28.4 [March–April 2002]: 37–39); Gunn, Thom, "Responsibilities: Contemporary Poetry and August Kleinzahler," in *Shelf Life: Essays, Memoirs, and an Interview* (London: Faber and Faber, 1993, 22–33); Vendler, Helen, "A Dissonant Triad" (*Parnassus: Poetry in Review* 16.2 [1991]: 391–404).

Philip Coleman

KLEPFISZ, IRENA (1941–)

Irena Klepfisz's political activism in the Jewish community and her lesbian and feminist orientations are reflected in the themes of her poetry: lesbian and Jewish identity; memory and forgetting; history and cultural politics; and survival after the holocaust. Klepfisz is also concerned with the preservation of the Yiddish language, "the mother tongue," and *Yidishkayt*, the Yiddish way of life.

Irena Klepfisz was born in Nazi-occupied Warsaw, Poland, in 1941 to secular Jewish parents who belonged to the Jewish Bund, which based its beliefs on the socialist principle that there should be a fair distribution of wealth instead of the economic disparity that existed. Irena's father survived being shot and wounded when he jumped from a train that was taking him to Treblinka. He was later killed during the 1943 Warsaw Ghetto uprising when he threw himself on a Nazi machine gun to protect his friends. Irena's mother, who had blue eyes and blond hair, was able to "pass" as an Aryan. After a period of hiding, Irena and her mother were able to escape to Sweden and later emigrate to the United States in 1949, when Irena was eight years old. In school Irena excelled in math and science but always wanted to be a writer, despite her lack of success in English classes. She went on to receive her BA and MA from City College of New York and later a Ph.D. in English Literature from the University of Chicago.

For Klepfisz writing poetry began as therapy. First, as a teenager, she wrote to deal with the frustration and anger of being dislocated three times and, later, to deal with the suicide of a fellow child survivor. Klepfisz's poetry remained a secret pleasure until graduate school, when a friend convinced her to submit her work to the *American Poetry Review* and the *Chicago Review*, where it was published. In the 1970s Klepfisz began teaching in New York and discovered a new identifiable voice as she transformed her thoughts into print and developed silence as a major theme within her writing. Klepfisz wrote many strong poems focusing on the Holocaust, but she was determined not to cash in on Jewish suffering. She wanted to write about other things as well, although she felt the poems about her own experiences were insignificant in comparison to the horrors of the Holocaust.

While in New York Klepfisz became aware of feminism and gay issues. Her acknowledgment of her sexuality, despite alienating her from her Jewish roots, brought her into an arena where she felt comfortable sharing her poetry through the various alternative presses sponsored by feminist and lesbian groups. World events, including conspicuous anti-Semitism in America, compelled Klepfisz to return to specifically Jewish themes and the subject of the Holocaust, so with a new feminist focus she attempted, poetically, to work out the issues faced by Jews in America.

Keeper of Accounts (1982) is autobiographical in its presentation of Klepfisz's development as a poet, feminist, and Jew. The book's four sections focus on two themes: the negative power of untillable "soil," in the form of either anti-Semitism or the struggle to survive in a hostile environment; and the ability of the human spirit to fight against the contamination at its roots, digging deeper until it finds cleaner soil. The theme of captured life and disrupted bondings is explored in "From the Monkey House and Other Cages." These poems contain the fragmented images of Irena's childhood in the Warsaw Ghetto, "a broken comb / an umbrella handle a piece of blue plastic chipped pocket mirror," when she was often fearful and unsure. "Different Enclosures" explores the tensions that arise when working people realize that their dreams of beauty and freedom do not match the realities of their controlled days and assigned tasks. In the third section, "Contexts," a woman gives an old man the freedom of his past by spending her days translating a text for him, while at the same time her own freedom is slipping away. The context then shifts as she sees other women come and go on their way to work and the empty idleness of those "waiting for something to begin." A mixture of prose and poetry, "Work Sonnets,"

uses office work and its insignificant tasks to explore how having freedom to do something significant must be squeezed into daily routines. This section was inspired by Klepfisz's commitment to feminism and the loss of her teaching job. The impact of Klepfisz's socialist Jewish Bund upbringing, like that of Tillie Olsen and **Judy Grahn**, is reflected in these poems. In "Urban Flowers" Klepfisz explores the theme of life bursting forth from unexpected places. Here there is always energy beneath the earth; no end is final. The book culminates with the section "Inhospitable Soil," where Klepfisz tells the story of the women from her life in "Glimpses from the Outside," "Bashert," and "Solitary Acts." Using everything she had learned from the feminist movement, she applies it to the Jewish experience and the lives of those who tell its history. The end of the poem "Solitary Acts" pays tribute to those who, in their own way, acted courageously and would not give in to the killing.

In 1983, on the fortieth anniversary of the Warsaw Ghetto uprising, Klepfisz returned to Poland with her mother and realized that she had a responsibility for Yiddish culture. In her essay "Secular Jewish Identity: *Yidishkayt* in America," published in *Dream of an Insomniac: Jewish Feminist Essay, Speeches and Diatribes* (1990), Klepfisz speaks of her realization and her determination to introduce **Yiddish** into her poems, but in a way that was neither artificial nor denigrating. Her first poem, *Etlekhe Verter oyf Mame-Loshn / A Few Words in the Mother Tongue*," is meant to be an oral poem. It ends with the repetition of "*zi kholmt*" (she dreams) and is completely in Yiddish. For those who do not know Yiddish, some meaning is lost, which is Klepfisz's point. Although Klepfisz does not expect English to be replaced by Yiddish, she hopes for a movement toward bilingualism to preserve languages spoken by Jews. Klepfisz believes Yiddish is more than a language: It represents a way for the Ashkanazi Jews to define themselves in terms that existed prior to the war, rather than in relation to the Holocaust or Israel.

Klepfisz's work also includes *The Tribe of Dina: A Jewish Women's Anthology*, which she co-edited with Melanie Kay-Kantrowitz. She continues to examine the subjects of women and Yiddish, including topics such as feminism, in *Yidishkayt* and *Found Treasures: Stories by Yiddish Women Writers*. In 1995 she served as conference coordinator and co-editor of the proceedings for *Di Froyen: Women and Yiddish*. She has also been Visiting Professor of Jewish Women's Studies at the universities of California, Wake Forest, and Michigan State. At present, Klepfisz is teaching courses on Jewish women at Barnard College and creative writing at Centre College in Kentucky. Klepfisz's writing will continue to bring notice to the causes and concerns of Jewish women.

Further Reading. ***Selected Primary Sources:*** Klepfisz, Irena, *Different Enclosures: The Poetry and Prose of Irena Klepfisz* (London: Onlywomen Press, 1985); ———, *Dreams of an Insomniac: Jewish Feminist Essays, Speeches, and Diatribes* (Portland, OR: Eighth Mountain Press, 1990); ———, *A Few Words in the Mother Tongue: Poems Selected and New (1971–1990)* (Portland, OR: Eighth Mountain Press: 1990); ———, *Keeper of Accounts* (Watertown, MA: Persephone Press, 1982); Pacernick, Gary, *Meaning & Memory: Interviews with Fourteen Jewish Poets* (Columbus: Ohio State University Press, 2001). ***Selected Secondary Sources:*** Kwinter, Michelle, "Irena Klepfisz," in *Contemporary Lesbian Writers of the United States: A Bio-Bibliographical Critical Sourcebook*, ed. Sandra Pollack and Denise D. Knight (Westport, CT: Greenwood Press, 1993, 287–291); Shreiber, Maeera, "The End of Exile: Jewish Identity and Its Diasporic Poetics" (*PMLA 2* [March 1998]: 113, 273–287).

Alisa M. Smith-Riel

KLOEFKORN, WILLIAM (1932–)

William Kloefkorn, named the Nebraska State Poet in 1982, is a regional poet in the most esteemed sense of that designation. If one takes regional poetry to mean a complex reciprocal relationship between a person and a landscape, a history and a future, an individual perspective and a communal embrace, then Kloefkorn is a thoughtful and dedicated practitioner of that art. A midwesterner by birth and affinity—his only lengthy absence from Kansas and Nebraska came during his service in the armed forces—Kloefkorn's poetry explores the history, culture, and geography of the Midwest. "I like poems that are closely related to place, using imagery and language that I identify as regional," Kloefkorn said in an interview with Rebecca Dinan Schneider (35). His work, both in verse and in prose, revolves around family, memory, the importance of the particular, and the significance of the commonplace.

Kloefkorn was born in Kansas on August 12, 1932, to Ralph and Katie Marie Kloefkorn. He spent his early years in Attica, Kansas, a rural town of less than seven hundred people. His farm-based family was hard-working yet lived on the edge of poverty. Kloefkorn notes in his memoir, *This Death by Drowning* (1997), that although his parents did not attend college (only his mother finished high school), their colorful, metaphor- and simile-filled language fascinated him and sparked his love of words and the music of language.

Kloefkorn received his BS in Education (1954) and his MS in English (1958) from Emporia State University in Emporia, Kansas. He received permission to write a creative thesis, *Cold Pease-Porridge: A Novel of Kansas Life*, which remains unpublished. In 1962 he joined the faculty at Nebraska Wesleyan University, where he taught literature and creative writing until his retirement as pro-

fessor emeritus in 1997. Besides his activities as a college professor, Kloefkorn was instrumental in beginning Nebraska's Poets in the Schools program.

Kloefkorn received the Lincoln Mayor's Arts Award, the Nebraska Governor's Arts Award (1987), and the Mari Sandoz Award (1987). He has been awarded honorary doctorates from Nebraska Wesleyan, Midland Lutheran College, and Ripon College. Kloefkorn is married and the father of four children and grandfather of eleven. He continues to live and write in Lincoln, Nebraska.

Since Kloefkorn began as a writer of prose, not poetry, it is natural that he lists major fiction writers such as **Willa Cather**, Mari Sandoz, Mark Twain, and William Faulkner as influences. However, Kloefkorn also maintains close connections with other midwestern poets, including Dave Etter, **Ted Kooser**, and Victor Contoski. He shares their concern for writing that incorporates intimate details of a specific locale and attempts to provide insight into the universal human condition. In his interview with Schneider, Kloefkorn characterized his language as "distinctive and plausible." He prefers not to use language that is "elitist, fluff, [or] polysyllabic" (36).

Kloefkorn frequently uses a persona or narrator for his book-length collections of **free-verse**, interrelated poems. "I don't have much luck with poems unless they have people in them," Kloefkorn says, calling an uninhabited place "pretty sterile" (Schneider, 35). *Alvin Turner as Farmer* (1974), Kloefkorn's first book publication, which centers on both a speaker and a place, has become the benchmark for collections about farmers and farming and demonstrates Kloefkorn's concern with the individual in a rural setting. In *Ludi Jr* (1976), Kloefkorn speaks through the imaginative and universal antics of a young boy whose name is "the first half of ludicrous." Kloefkorn calls Ludi Jr "half scamp, half prodigy . . . a young fellow trying to tell the truth." Poem titles, such as "even after a long evening's activity, / ludi jr has not yet decided whether to be an archangel," and "ludi jr as the hired hand, / pays dearly for what / he is paid for," can barely be separated from the poems as a whole. Each title encapsulates the mock heroic tone that is Kloefkorn's approach to life's ultimately serious problems.

Platte Valley Homestead (1981) and *Sergeant Patrick Gass, Chief Carpenter: On the Trail with Lewis and Clark* (2002) also feature personae. In *Platte Valley Homestead*, a series of untitled, nonlinear poems, Kloefkorn uses the voice of a homesteader, Jacob, who tells of homesteading on the Platte River with his wife Anna. Kloefkorn wrote *Platte Valley Homestead* while living in an isolated cabin in the same area. In *Sergeant Patrick Gass* Kloefkorn traces the explorations of Lewis and Clark through the perspective of an actual, although less famous, member of the party.

In addition to numerous volumes of poetry, Kloefkorn has published the first two of four projected memoirs: *This Death by Drowning* and *Restoring the Burnt Child* (2003). The symbols and imagery of each volume focus on one of the four classic elements of ancient thought: water, fire, earth, and air. Kloefkorn has also published short stories and a collection of Christmas stories for his grandchildren. Many of his stories recur from collection to collection. In all of his work Kloefkorn may tell and re-tell, fashion and re-fashion events from his past. He brings both humor and compassion to his work and, like Ludi Jr, strives to tell the truth.

Further Reading. *Selected Primary Sources:* Kloefkorn, William, *Ludi Jr* (Milwaukee, WI: Pentagram Press, 1976); ———, *Platte Valley Homestead* (Lincoln, NE: Platte Valley Press, 1985); ———, *This Death by Drowning* (Lincoln: University of Nebraska Press, 1997). ***Selected Secondary Sources:*** Lovett, Steven, "An Absolute and Utter Respect for Language: William Kloefkorn's Poetry" (*Midwest Quarterly* 45.1 [Autumn 2003]: 94–109); Sanders, Mark, ed., *On Common Ground: The Poetry of William Kloefkorn, Ted Kooser, Greg Kuzma, and Don Welch* (Ord, NE.: Sandhills, 1983); Schneider, Rebecca Dinan, "Bringing Poetry to the People: Six State Poets Proclaim Virtues of Verse" (*The Writer* 114.4 [2001]: 34–39).

Diane Warner

KNIGHT, ETHERIDGE (1931–1991)

Etheridge Knight spent eight years in an Indiana prison, where he began his career as a poet. His prison experience informs much of his work, which features themes both of the literal incarceration of prison life and the figurative incarcerations of drug and alcohol addictions, prostitution, poverty, and racism. His early poems, particularly, detail prison life, including "Hard Rock Returns to Prison from the Hospital for the Criminal Insane" and "The Idea of Ancestry." Later poems, such as "A Black Poet Leaps to His Death" (1981), chronicle the hardships of African American life. However, not all of Knight's writing is so grim. Other poems, including "Belly Song" (1971), celebrate the self, love, and sexuality in a manner reminiscent of **Walt Whitman**, while poems like "On the Birth of a Black / Baby / Boy" (1978) glory in the birth of Knight's children. His poetic voice often combines African American oral verse forms, such as the "toast," which incorporates profanity and slang, with formal verse forms, such as haiku. Thus, many of his poems include a combination of street language and disciplined, rigid structure and "literary" voice.

Knight was born in Corinth, Mississippi, on April 19, 1931, one of seven children born to a relatively poor family. He dropped out of school in the eighth grade and joined the Army at the age of sixteen. Working as a medical technician during the Korean War, he suffered a shrapnel wound. After ten years of service, Knight was discharged from the Army. He began committing crimes to support his drug and alcohol addictions, and in 1960 was sentenced to eight years in prison for robbery. In prison Knight began to identify himself as a writer by creating poetry and writing letters for his fellow inmates. During his incarceration, poet **Gwendolyn Brooks** became his mentor and visited him. Shortly before his release from prison, his first book, *Poems from Prison* (1968), was published. He joined other African American poets, including his first wife, **Sonia Sanchez**, in what was eventually known as the **Black Arts Movement**. This artistic movement, seen by its members as a corollary to the Black Power movement in politics, celebrated the importance of community and freedom among African Americans. Knight also began the Free People's Poetry Workshops, readings held in local bars, whose participants ranged from well-known poets, such as Brooks and **Robert Bly**, to local homeless people. Knight was well known for his dynamic poetry readings and was a popular speaker on college campuses and elsewhere. After divorcing Sanchez, Knight married twice more and had three children. He died of lung cancer in 1991 at age fifty-nine.

Even before Knight began publishing his poems, he was reading them aloud to his fellow prisoners. As a result of these beginnings and of the influence of "toasts" on his writing, the oral tradition looms large in Knight's poetry. Knight does not shrink from using scatological and racial epithets to achieve an authentic tone in these early poems, as in "Hard Rock Returns to Prison from the Hospital for the Criminal Insane." This poem, narrated by another prisoner, tells the story of Hard Rock, a tough, scar-covered inmate who receives a lobotomy and electroshock and returns much altered. When insulted now, rather than responding violently, he "Just grinned and looked silly, / His eyes empty like knot holes in a fence." The other inmates, initially unwilling to accept what has happened to Hard Rock, try to convince themselves he is just "being cool," but without really believing it. The prisoners are "crushed" by this alteration, since Hard Rock "had been our Destroyer, the doer of things" they could only dream about. Another early poem, "The Idea of Ancestry," is more personal. It details the "47 pictures" of relatives that decorate the narrator's cell. The narrator asserts his connection to these family members, even as prison separates him from them: "I am all of them, they are all of me." Also in *Poems from Prison* is "For Malcolm, A Year After," a eulogy to Malcolm X written a year after his assassination. Knight writes that he is attempting to control his anger by writing in a disciplined structure of "foot and strict iamb." Knight inverts the common conceit that the poem will be a sort of eternal life for its subject when he writes, "The verse will die—as all men do— / But not the memory of him!" He thus asserts that poetry's life is finite, but not so the memory of a great man.

His second book, *Black Voices from Prison* (1970), is a collection of poems by several writers and includes all of Knight's earlier poems as well as "A WASP Woman Visits a Black Junkie in Prison," in which the two characters, initially wary of and uncomfortable with each other, find a connection when the prisoner asks, "'You got children, Ma'am?'" This "broke the dam," and she begins to talk about her children. Although she does not offer "pills / To cure his many ills" or "compact sermons," her visit is salutary: After she leaves he "for hours used no hot words."

Winner of the 1987 American Book Award, Knight's last major book, *The Essential Etheridge Knight*, contains most major poems from his previous books as well as some new poems. Included in this text are poems celebrating his children's lives, such as "On the Birth of a Black / Baby / Boy," dedicated to his son, Isaac, and "Circling the Daughter," a loving tribute to his daughter, Tandi, at age fourteen. He writes that Tandi's first fourteen years of life "Have brought the moon-blood, the roundness" while the chorus announces, "*Ooouu-baby-I-love-you.*" This combination of stunning imagery and pop-song triteness reflects the mixture of profundity and shallowness that often typifies adolescence.

Etheridge Knight's poems are full of ambivalence. The most prevalent themes are personal freedom and responsibility to community. The prison poems are often hard, while Knight's many poems celebrating the women in his life—wives, daughters, and others—are often remarkably tender. His poetry manages to balance these seemingly conflicting emotions and tones while retaining a distinctive poetic voice.

Further Reading. *Selected Primary Sources:* Knight, Etheridge, *Belly Song and Other Poems* (Detroit: Broadside, 1973); ———, *The Essential Etheridge Knight* (Pittsburgh: University of Pittsburgh Press, 1986); ———, *Poems from Prison* (Detroit, Broadside, 1968); Knight, Etheridge, et al., *Black Voices from Prison* (New York: Pathfinder, 1970). ***Selected Secondary Sources:*** Anaporte-Easton, Jean, "Etheridge Knight: Poet and Prisoner: An Introduction" (*Callaloo* 19.4 [Fall 1996]: 941–946); Joyce, Joyce Ann, "The Poetry of *Etheridge Knight*: A Reflection of an African Philosophical/Aesthetic" (*Worcester Review* 19.1–2 [Spring/Summer 1998]: 105–118).

J. Robin Coffelt

KNIGHT, SARAH KEMBLE (1666–1727)

Although the extant poems by diarist Sarah Kemble Knight are relatively few, they provide important insight into the centrality of poetry as a genre for cultured "amateur" writers in early New England. Moreover, Knight's witty short verses suggest a wide range of tone and subject available to poets from Puritan New England, which is in distinct contrast to the philosophically and theologically serious works of devotional poets such as **Anne Bradstreet** and **Edward Taylor**.

Born in Boston, among the first generation of New Englanders to be born in the New World, Sarah Kemble married Richard Knight in 1689. Sarah Kemble Knight, like many other women in early New England, was an active assistant in her husband's business. She may also have run a school, although claims that she taught writing to Benjamin Franklin seem to be legend rather than fact. In 1704 Knight traveled to New York to help settle the estate of her cousin, a trip that lasted five months, including both travel and negotiations related to the estate. During this journey—unusual for a woman traveling alone—Knight kept the journal for which she has become known, a journal that evidently circulated relatively widely in manuscript. After her husband's death, Knight continued business activities, speculating in land, keeping an inn, and running farms in Connecticut until her own death in 1727.

Embedded within the journal are a series of lyrical or humorous verses commenting on various episodes in Knight's narrative. Addressing the moon as it guides her through a dense forest while on horseback, Knight foregrounds her consciousness of the possible conflicts between Renaissance poetic conventions and Puritan values: "Fair Cynthia, all the Homage that I may / Unto a Creature, unto thee I pay." Here we see Knight taking up a theme common in Bradstreet's poetry (the injunction among Puritans to avoid idolatrous attachment to anyone other than God) in what turns out to be a lighthearted way: After noting the danger of idolatry, Knight goes on to write a conventional paean of thanks to the moon for its guidance during a frightening night journey. Knight's verse is always lighthearted, but sometimes her wit is more pointed, as in "I ask thy Aid, O Potent Rum!" in which she laments that drunken neighbors in a tavern continue to make an uproar rather than passing out. Perhaps Knight's funniest poem was written after a stop at a public house owned by a family named DeVille, where hospitality was scarce. Punning on the family's name, Knight writes a warning to other travelers to avoid the house, for "Here dwells the Devill—surely this's Hell."

One of the most intriguing aspects of Knight's verse is the way in which she introduces it into her narrative and describes her own poetic work. According to Knight, her creation of verse is often spontaneous; she even claims that she uttered one of her poems "on the spot" in an outpouring of emotion upon witnessing a specimen of extreme poverty. In other cases, she says she composed her verses spontaneously but had to wait until getting off her horse to write them down. In the case of her invocation to rum, Knight mentions that she took to verse because it was her "old way of composing my Resentments." All this suggests that for Knight and her audience, writing verse was a commonplace activity, undertaken as part of a literate approach to daily life. Knight's incorporation of verse throughout her journal suggests the commonplace books on which she might have modeled her journal, in which verse and prose mixed regularly. Most important, though, Knight reminds us that the Puritan approach to the world was not always somber and that their literate practices included Renaissance notions of wit.

Further Reading. *Selected Primary Sources:* Andrews, William L., ed., *Journeys in New Worlds: Early American Women's Narratives* (Madison: University of Wisconsin Press, 1990, 67–116). *Selected Secondary Sources:* Derounian-Stodola, Kathryn Zabelle, "The New England Frontier and the Picaresque in Sarah Kemble Knight's Journal," in *Early American Literature and Culture: Essays Honoring Harrison T. Meserole,* ed. Kathryn Zabelle Derounian-Stodola (Newark: University of Delaware Press, 1992, 122–131).

Angela Vietto

KNOTT, BILL (1940–)

Throughout his career, Bill Knott has maintained outsider status in American poetry. This is largely due to the fact that no literary camp can adequately house his prickly nature, let alone his body of work. His efforts on and off the page have often been polarizing, inciting debate on everything from the **canon** to the **avant-garde**. Critical comment on his poetry ranges from vigorous praise of its invention to equally vehement complaint about its unevenness and impenetrability. Still, many agree that Knott is a truly singular poet whose best work is some of the most refreshingly adventurous verse published by an American of the late twentieth century. Knott has embodied, for many, the role of the poet as ecstatic seer, a romantic perception that has been applied to other "American Rimbauds," such as **Bob Kaufman**. Despite the timing and tone of his first book, Knott has outlived his association with the counter-culture of the 1960s as he has outlived the **Beats**, writing with a relevance that easily keeps pace with the times. Yet he remains conspicuously un-anthologized and under-read, self-publishing several volumes of poetry as chapbooks and artist books to preserve a marginal presence between publishing contracts. These books include *Collected Political Poems 1965–1993* (1993) and *Sixty Poems of Love and Homage* (1994).

Little is published about the life of the man who introduced himself provocatively as "a virgin and a suicide." Knott was born William Killborn Knott in Carson City, Michigan. His mother died when he was six years old,

and five years later his father followed. Knott spent several years in an orphanage until he joined the U.S. Army at age sixteen, serving as a medic during the Vietnam War. After his discharge, Knott returned to the Midwest, studying poetry in Chicago alongside **Gwendolyn Brooks** and **John Logan**. He later earned an MFA at Vermont College. Knott has held positions at numerous institutions and, notably, the prestigious Iowa Writers Workshop. His *Selected and Collected Poems* (1977) won the Elliston Prize in 1979. He received a Guggenheim fellowship in 2003. He is an associate professor at Emerson College in Boston, where he has taught since the early 1980s.

Unsettling to absurd, difficult to jocular, socially malcontent to self-deprecating, Knott's relentlessly aware work has, beneath the surface, maintained a fairly steady aesthetic trajectory. His poetry performs its own production, not only with frequent metapoetic tropes but also with consistent public revision and experimentation in process, form, and language. Although the results of his more obvious experiments have led many readers to categorize his work as surrealist—like that of collaborator **James Tate**—Knott is equally influenced by **Deep Image** poets (particularly **Robert Bly**) and by the concentrated immediacy of haiku. His books swing from dense, assonant outpourings of leaping associations to stripped-down, epigrammatic tercets, all in the turn of a few pages.

For his first book, *The Naomi Poems, Book 1: Corpse and Beans* (1968), he famously took the pseudonym "Saint Geraud (1940–1966)." Knott borrowed the name from *La Tartuffe Libertin* (ca. 1700, *The Lascivious Hypocrite*) an eighteenth-century French pornographic novel by an anonymous author in which the protagonist, Geraud, ran a debauched orphanage. The birth and death dates served at least two purposes: The first creates the sensational impression of work published posthumously; and the next was Knott's response to the Vietnam War, of which he claimed to be a casualty. This tension between audacious play with reader expectations and great personal outrage runs through the body of his published work. "Corpse and Beans" in itself alludes playfully to Robert Desnos's *Corps et Biens* (1930, *Bodies and Goods*) with serious intent. Desnos, a noted French surrealist, died in a concentration camp in 1945, and *The Naomi Poems* is a book largely concerned with death (as war) and love. Although these themes suggest traditional poetic ambitions, Knott's use of vernacular undermines grandiloquence. For example, the poem "Nuremberg U.S.A." sets the themes in a pressurized stanza of classical allusion and 1960s military-speak and protest, ending with the lines "If bombing children is preserving peace, then / my fucking you is a war crime."

Against this more discursive style, Knott wrote *Aurealism: A Study* (1969), a chapbook that began to drive his reputation as a surrealist in later volumes. His third book, *The—Poems. Book 2: Auto-Necrophilia* (1971), was published the same year as *Nights of Naomi* (1971), leading some critics to assume that Knott was rushing his poems to press too quickly. As a clear departure from the craft of *The Naomi Poems, Auto-Necrophilia* continued his deliberate exploration of automatic-writing. Bits of familiar lucidity surface for the reader of this work, yet *Auto-Necrophilia* is, as a whole, decidedly more elusive. The title suggests a problematic self-love, and the self-referential quality of the poems proves the title apt. Besides serving as a source for generative strategies, the internal resonance of the works asserted an autotelic quality to his oeuvre—a perception that persists today—together with some critical doubt as to the value or success of these risky poems. *Auto-Necrophilia* chronicled a sort of performance of Knott coming into himself; he dropped the pseudonym—although he kept the dates. If these words were posthumous, the author was more likely a suicide than a casualty of war.

By his fourth book, *Nights of Naomi*, Knott was fully engaged in a level of linguistic investigation and recreation that further marginalized him as a difficult experimental writer. Many readers and critics of the time seemed unwilling to do the work of navigating the chapbook-length volume. The poems—or perhaps, a single poem divided into thirty-two mostly untitled sections—maintain a daunting density in which images explode into surprising associations: "To shatter the teethmarks dangling from rockets/Herding legends through the Rasputin-tenderized echoes." The bulk of the book is written as apostrophes, an approach that frames the emotionally dramatic phrases as overwhelming, or overwhelmed, love poems.

Love Poems to Myself (1974) finds the poet freed from convention—perhaps the result of his dogged experiments—yet seemingly more attentive to the line between innovation and obfuscation. More than ever, his penchants for inventing words ("dottily") and mashing them together ("greatbig") are allowed the space to serve the poems and not simply ornament the already baroque lines. The work is as risky as his previous books, but in the opening stanza from "Breeze Nomadly Coupling / Summer Sounds / Precision Insects Chomping," these risks seem leveraged against more than their own existence. "As much as a person could die in one instant / A lifetime—scoot over a little." Here Knott gracefully interrupts formal syntactic constructions with a vernacular intimacy. This opens up the remainder of the poem up to a palpable reticence and restlessness that resonates with his constant awareness of mortality. Also worth noting at this point, Knott was publishing as "Bill Knott" sans the dates, thus discontinuing the device he had begun with *The Naomi Poems*.

Conversely, *Rome in Rome* (1976) was a return of sorts to the unrest of his first book. Instead of the violence of war, Knott addressed the violence of oppression, in particular the oppression suffered by the poor. Knott's own poverty certainly fueled this biting, often cruel, satirical volume. "Funny Poem" takes Jonathan Swift's modest approach to social comment as Knott writes "death loves rich people" and suggests that we should "GIVE DEATH WHAT IT WANTS."

In the 1980s *Becos* (1983) and *Outremer* (1989) showed a maturing artist honing his craft and again integrating up-to-date anxieties into his work. Having left behind the surrealist explosions, if not the wrought phrasing, Knott began to explore formal poetry with increased rigor, particularly the sonnet. The year 1989 also saw the publication of *New Poems 1963–1988*.

In *The Unsubscriber* (2004), which follows *The Quicken Tree* (1995) and *Laugh at the End of the World: Collected Comic Poems 1969–1999* (2001), Knott continues to vacillate between brief poems that concentrate his acrobatic intelligence and those poems in which a more performative language dizzies the reader with flashes of alliteration, pun, rhyme, and the virtuosity (if not always a virtue) of play. Economy and excess are constantly at war, and Knott presents his epigrammatic poems as "an interlude" between sections of longer poems. The last two sections of the book are heavily footnoted, a feature that feints at letting readers inside his once hermetic lines; however, in true Knott style, many of the notes serve as self-contained glosses or sardonic meta-commentary. Still, this evidence of hyper-awareness is what forces readers to wonder whether Knott is intentionally difficult or simply enthralled by word games. It is also what makes his work so dynamic. From *The Unsubscriber*, in "Poem" he states, "underline my words / after you erase them." Here Knott writes with an awareness of his own marginalized status. It is a typically self-reflexive moment, but one in which his own longing is transformed into a wry plea for further reading.

Further Reading. *Selected Primary Sources:* Knott, Bill, *Love Poems to Myself* (Boston: Barn Dream Press, 1974); ———, *The Naomi Poems, Book 1: Corpse and Beans* (Chicago: Follett, 1968); ———, *Nights of Naomi* (Boston: Barn Dream Press, 1971); ———, *Rome in Rome* (Brooklyn: Release Press, 1976); ———, *The Unsubscriber* (New York: Farrar, Straus and Giroux, 2004); Lux, Thomas, "For Bill Knott in Celebration and Anticipation of His Selected/Collected Poems" (*Ploughshares* 12.04/1 [Fall 1977]: 25–38). ***Selected Secondary Sources:*** Klipschutz, "Bill Knott: No Man Is an Eyelid (A Wandering Fan's Notes)" (*Pith* 2.2 [Summer 2000], www.pith.net/pith5-00/eyelid.htm); O'Rourke, Meghan, "I Have Work to Dream" (*Poetry* 185.5 [February 2005]: 387–391).

Douglas Kearney

KOCH, KENNETH (1925–2002)

Kenneth Koch was the leading exponent of the open, humorously experimental poetry typical of the **New York School** and of much contemporary and **postmodern** poetry today. The first member of the New York School to achieve recognition and success in the 1950s, he achieved that almost impossible mix of simultaneously being an avant-garde poet and a popular, even enjoyable, writer.

His influence on a whole generation of American poets, especially in New York, has been immense, but his reputation abroad has yet to fully develop, perhaps due to a dearth of critical work. As to why most of the original members of the New York School (**John Ashbery**, **Frank O'Hara**, and James Schuyler) have generated a considerable amount of critical work, and Koch has not, may have to do with his reputation as the joker in the pack. His much-cited nickname, Dr. Fun, however, belies one of the great technicians of contemporary poetics as well as one of the most innovative and active minds writing in English in the second half of the twentieth century.

Born in Cincinnati, Ohio, in 1925, Koch began his studies at the University of Cincinnati, where he began training as a meteorologist. When war broke out he served in the U.S. Army in the Pacific before returning to the United States to re-commence his education. He went on to take his first degree at Harvard before being sent on a Fulbright scholarship to Aix-en-Provence. The influence of European writers, especially late-nineteenth-century and early-twentieth-century poets, has remained pronounced throughout his career.

Back in America he received his doctorate from Columbia and remained a resident of New York. Unlike many of his peers, Koch did not then establish a career in the New York arts scene but instead went into education. Before joining Columbia's faculty, Koch taught at Rutgers and the New School for Social Research. His contributions to the theory of teaching creative writing and the use of creative writing as a teaching aid, particularly in the texts *Wishes Lies and Dreams* (1970), *Rose, Where Did You Get That Red* (1973), and *I Never Told Anybody* (1977), have been very influential in the area of pedagogy and education.

In this way he also oversaw the development of a number of second-generation New York poets who attended his creative writing classes. Among his students at the New School, Jordan Davis notes, were **Joseph Ceravolo**, Bill Berkson, Tony Towle, Gerard Malanga, Daniel Krakauer, and Ruth Krauss. At Columbia Koch continued to influence numerous other writers. Davis recalls **Ron Padgett**, **David Shapiro**, **David Lehman**, **Bob Holman**, Hilton Obenzinger, Keith Cohen, Aaron Fogel, Lawrence Wieder, Siri Hustvedt, Michael Friedman, and Steven Hall. An immensely generous and

inspiring teacher, his legacy in the fields of writing and teaching poetry is profound.

While Koch's early works in the 1950s, *Poems*, *Ko; or a Season on Earth*, and *Permanently*, were often met with critical incomprehension, with the appearance of his landmark collection *Thank You*, the qualities often admired in his work became clearly apparent. This collection demonstrates the skills of clarity, lyricism, virtuosity, humor, conceptualism, and innovation which were to mark out the future direction of his poetic career. To summarize Koch's work one needs simply to read carefully this collection. This does not mean that Koch's work has not developed since *Thank You*; however, because he was able to do so much so early, some of his later work is a further exploration and refinement of these poems.

The first thing to note is Koch's infectious and infamous exuberance, which is put at the service of an avant-garde attack on American academic poetry in works such as "Desire for Spring": "I want to turn like a mobile / In a new fresh air! I don't want to hibernate / Between walls, between halls!" These walls and halls can be taken for the corridors of academic life, which Koch and his New York contemporaries rightly saw as having a stultifying influence on American poetry after the war. As avant-garde attacks go, it is one of the most good humored, but such lightness of touch must not be mistaken for a limitation of intention or intensity. Koch was always an extremely ambitious writer and a canny interpreter of his age, as can be seen in the poem "Fresh Air." In this short narrative poem, one of Koch's favored genres, the poet attacks the mythical Poem Society for failing in its duties to the modern age: "Where are young poets in America, . . . they are trembling in publishing houses and universities . . . / gargling out innocuous . . . poems about maple trees and their children."

The collection also demonstrates Koch's uncanny ability to parody or mimic almost any poetic style. In "Variations on a Theme by William Carlos Williams," **Williams**'s everyday aesthetic or ordinariness is not mocked by Koch so much as celebrated in a sly manner. One is never entirely sure with Koch's parodies, such as the use of *Don Juan's terza rima* in *Ko* and "Seasons on Earth," his rewriting of Apollinaire in "A Time Zone" or use of Ovid in "Io," whether his work is a satire, a postmodern exercise in intertextuality, or just an homage. Certainly, interviews with the poet and his own articles on poetry suggest that his enthusiasm for poetry is genuine. However, his sense of poetry as a ready-made entity is central to his aesthetics, so one must conclude that his use of others' texts as a basis for his own is a central part of Koch's postmodern poetic practice.

Another central aspect of Koch's work to be found in *Thank You*, manifested in poems such as "The Artist," "Geography," and "The Circus," is his revival of **narra-**

tive poetry. Although a great deal has been made of postmodern innovations in narratology in the fields of prose and film, critics have failed to recognize that Koch's work represents one of the most challenging reevaluations of narrative of the modern era.

Influenced by the automatic writings of Surrealism, but filtered through mechanistic, predetermined systems, the kind one finds in Raymond Roussel, the work of **John Cage,** and the OuLiPo group, a Koch narrative can be first confounding, then tedious, then amazing, and then confounding once more—all of this in the space of one or two lines. Its narratives are pure play based on simple, clearly defined rules of prosody, motifs, and recurrence. One of the few major articles on Koch's work to date, Jean-Paul Tassoni's study of *Ko* highlights the role of play as a moment of interregnum between old and new systems. The works, he argues, attempt not only to extend this period of interregnum, but also to highlight the extent to which our lives may be co-opted by these systems.

It is certainly valid to locate Koch's narrative poems within the avant-garde and postmodern traditions as well as to consider them key to his poetic practice. However, there is a part of these works that exceeds these terms. One gets the feeling in a poem such as *Ko*, which tells the story of a Japanese baseball poet, a neurotic financier, an unhappy cockney, and an "action poet," that away from the very strong restrictions of the Byronesque *terza rima*, the aim is, as in Byron's *Don Juan* and Ariosto's *Orlando Furioso*, to get a sublime ecstasy of the now as a state of freedom down on paper.

In the later retrospective poem "Seasons on Earth," Koch describes the period of the writing of *Ko*: "I had the thought while I was writing *Ko* / To get into the poem every pleasure / I'd ever had." This is not an immodest ambition, but it also explains the difficulty critics have had coming to terms with Koch's work. It is something of a cliché, but it is true to say that we still do not, in the West, have a theoretical framework to deal well with states of happiness or comedy.

The French theory of *jouissance*, as popularized by Roland Berthes, best describes what Koch's poetry attempts. His work is an erotic celebration not only of life and language but also of ideas and poetics, a celebration that is also transcendent and disruptive. Of all of Koch's **long poems,** the most confrontational is *When the Sun Tries to Go On*, a poem he wrote over an intense, ecstatic period of three months. This forms a part of a triumvirate of early New York School poems of great length, along with Ashbery's "Europe" and O'Hara's *Second Avenue*. These poems, if they can be said to be about anything—O'Hara for example explicitly denies this in relation to *Second Avenue*—are about the process of consciousness as the poets grapple with the idea of poetic language within the medium of poetic language

itself. If Koch's poem owes a debt to Ashbery's "Europe," it is one repaid by Ashbery's seeming effort to copy Koch's formula of an all-engrossing poem in his later, more lucid but less joyously loose, *Flow Chart*.

Thank You contains early examples of two other typical Koch methodologies of composition, which are interrelated versions of what Koch calls "poetry ideas," based on the dream that there might be such a thing as a poetry language. The typical poetry idea is a simple rule, decided in advance, that dictates the composition of the poem. This idea is then repeated throughout the poem, although it may mutate or change in the process. The other side of this might be called the serial poem, or a poem made up of many very small poems all based on a single idea, within which the poet is allowed almost total freedom of expression and execution. In *Thank You*, for example, we have "The Brassiere Factory" with its various, ridiculous versions of the phrase "Arm in arm we fled the brassiere factory." We also have "Collected Poems," made up of a number of micro-poems in which the title is often longer than the poem itself.

These poetry ideas are in their nascent stage in Koch's first collection, but they come to dominance in the later part of his career. These predetermined structures of repetition may be understood as "poetry machines," little, mechanistic modes of controlling the infinite number of things the poet could say (Watkin, "Poetry Machines"). They form a kind of generative grammar of poetry made up of a limited number of rules that can be used to parse up the Koch poem, however surreal, random, and complicated the poem might become. In this view, it is not just that Koch, like many artists, uses a predetermined system to control his ideas, but that Koch's grammar of repetition and variation forms the basic grammar of poetic language in general.

One other innovation Koch puts forward might be called the thesis poem. In this connection, Koch's work may be elucidated through the application of the French literary theorist Julia Kristeva's divisions of poetic language into the semiotic and the thetic (*Revolution in Poetic Language* [1984]). For Kristeva the semiotic is the disruptive possibility of infinite code without meaning which one finds in language and in the human unconscious. In contrast, the thetic is a structure of control used to rein in this infinite free-play so as to generate meaningful discourse. If the semiotic is the explosion of language and ideas such as one typically finds in a long Koch poem, the thetic is the strict control his poetry machines impose on this material. Although within Koch's oeuvre a number of poems, such as *When the Sun Tries to Go On*, are almost totally semiotic, many rational "How to" poems are nearly purely thetic.

These "How to" works are all charming and insightful. In "The Art of Love," the poet explains how to love women, while "Some General Instructions" is full of use-less advice—"Be able to make a mouth and cheeks like a fish"—modulated occasionally by something useful: "Do not be defeated by the / Feeling that there is too much for you to know." Of all of these, "The Art of Poetry" is, as one might imagine, the most suggestive and interesting. As a postmodern version of Pope's "Essay on Criticism," it is not only a comprehensive cat-alogue of one of the most inventive poetry minds of the age but also the only real manifesto of New York School **poetics** that exists (if one accepts that O'Hara's "Person-ism" is more a parody of **Charles Olson** than a system-atic mode of practice).

The tenets set out by "The Art of Poetry" suggest that the revolutionary ethos of New York School poetry first- and second-generation. A few will suggest that they are at once playful, earnest, and persuasive. (1) Schizo-phrenic poetry, although apt for the anxiety of the age, lacks the tightness and discipline necessary for poetry; (2) correcting work is a mistake; (3) a coterie is vital; (4) poetry and day-to-day life are synonymous; (5) poetry never runs out; (6) one should not be an exigent poet ("By exigent I mean extremely careful, wanting each poem to be a conclusion / Of everything he sees, feels and knows"); and (7) the poet must occupy the role of "experiencer and un-experiencer" of life, by which Koch means that the poet should experience and write as much as possible, but one should not write about the experience of writing itself or sacrifice experience for the sake of poetry. Another important possible meaning of this is that the poet's application of language to expe-rience breaks up the accepted codes of day-to-day expe-rience.

These ideas describe a postmodern practice of poetry that Koch and the New York School have excelled in. Rejecting the high seriousness of modernist poetics, they embrace a process-based poetic practice that sees poetry as something one does in day-to- day life, in the same way that one loves, eats, talks to friends, and so on. This bridging of the gap between poetry and life is a central tenet of avant-garde aesthetics and is central to Koch's lifetime of work. However, the poet warns, one should not mistake life for poetry because poetry is made up of heterogeneous matter called poetic language. The medi-ation of experience through this matter, perhaps through the use of poetry machines, has a significant effect of denaturalizing life, what **Charles Bernstein**, in his *A Poetics* (1992), has gone on to call anti-absorptive poetics.

This is a major difference between Koch and Ashbery, the two great conceptual rivals of the New York School. Koch sees writing as part of life but describes it as an expe-rience of a different order, which can be so all-consuming as to actually threaten life experience. In contrast, Ash-bery does not seem to see poetry as different from expe-

rience but rather as just one aspect of the experiential fabric that makes up the ambient zone of consciousness.

This difference in approach can be seen by compar-ing *When the Sun Tries to Go On* with Ashbery's *Flow Chart*. Koch's long poem of poetic consciousness is a time-out from rationality and an exploration of language as material otherness. Ashbery's much later poem, how-ever, depicts the day-to-day vacillations and peregrina-tions of the mind in language, indeed *as* language. Whereas Koch finds jouissance in taking one away from rational consciousness into the semiotic field of linguistic material, Ashbery never knows consciousness; rather, he meditates on the place of consciousness within lin-guistic and poetic fields.

Koch's point about the exigent poet is linked to the truth that poetry is an inexhaustible source and ties in to his final comment in "The Art of Poetry" on poetic clo-sure: "At the end of a poem / One may be tempted to grow too universal. . . . poetry and life are not like that. Now I have said enough." One is tempted to wish that all poets had read these lines and taken them to heart as what they show is a postmodern incredulity toward the most tired and unjustifiable of poetic narratives. The poet is not a craftsperson, slaving away at a jewel, which will teach us a big lesson, whether we like it or not. Instead, the poet is a participant and intervenor in the great adventure of experience, which is the mediation of experience through language, the experience of that mediation, and the writing up of that experience as an experience all its own.

While Koch was a prolific writer, he also collabo-rated with many visual artists, especially the painters Larry Rivers and Alex Katz. Rivers, more often than not, provided the original cover art for Koch's collec-tions, and their close relationship is typical of New York School practices, in general, which took an open, syn-aesthetic attitude toward the arts from the 1950s on. This openness to other genres is shown in Koch's work in a wide variety of literary fields. He wrote numerous off-Broadway plays and closet dramas, which are collected in *Bertha and Other Plays* (1969), *A Change of Hearts* (1973), *One Thousand Avant-Garde Plays* (1988), and *The Gold Standard* (1996), as well as a novel, *The Red Robins* (1975), and a collection of short stories, *Hotel Lambosa* (1993)—all of this, in addition to his pedagogical works and two lengthy collections of poetry theory and criticism, *The Art of Poetry* (1996) and *Making Your Own Days* (1998). The poet even drew and wrote his own poetry idea–inspired comics.

After the invention of his new thetic style in *The Plea-sures of Peace* (1969) and *The Art of Love* (1975), Koch con-tinued to experiment in the many collections that followed: *The Duplications* (1977), *The Burning Mystery of Anna in 1951* (1979), *Days and Nights* (1982), *On the Edge* (1986), *Seasons on Earth* (1987), and *Straits* (1998). His landmark collection *One Train* and his selected poems entitled *On the Great Atlantic Rainway* (both 1994) were awarded the Bollingen Prize. *New Addresses* (2000), a quasi-autobiographical collection of apostrophes, was followed by two posthumous publications in 2003, *A Possible World* and *Sun Out: Poems 1950–1952*.

Many of these collections also contain refinements of early innovations, such as returns to poetry machines in "Study of Time" and "My Olivetti Speaks" and serial poems such as "In Bed," "On Aesthetics," and "Artificial Intelligence." We also see further explorations of narrative poetry in "With Janice" and *Impressions of Africa*, alongside sophisticated and ambiguous parodies of Roussel (*Impressions of Africa*), of Ovid ("Io"), and of Chinese poetry ("The First Step"). We even have the occasional thetic "How to" poem, such as "A New Guide."

In poems such as "The Seasons" in *Straits*, which rewrites Thompson's classic eighteenth-century work of the same name, we find Koch re-inventing blank verse for a contemporary age. We also, as the poem opens, realize this is not a postmodern parody but rather a form of respectful re-appropriation of a found text. Like pop art or contemporary conceptual art, Koch picks up aesthetic material from the collective consciousness and remakes it into something entirely original that is still tinted by the colors and textures of the original. David Spurr has talked of these poems as taking one "beyond irony" into a realm of total innocence.

Along with a complex, post-parodic and post-ironic appropriation of past poets and genres, Koch has also updated the recollection poem, of which Wordsworth is still the great exemplar. Two examples of this are "Seasons on Earth" and "A Time Zone," which are also aesthetic parodies. In these works a delicate and exciting fusion of recollection, narrative, commentary, experimentation, and aesthetic theorizing combines to form a poetic fabric of memory and present-tense process that is unique to Koch. They are a form of lighthearted, postmodern Proust, in which recollection is mediated through language, the now of the poem's constructions. The fluidity of memory of the past is encountered simultaneously as the past, as something happening afresh for the poet for the first time, and as a fact of language and memory. Along the way "Seasons on Earth" and "A Time Zone" are also moving and profound works of autobiography, another genre Koch has re-invented in his work. As such, they are testimony to one of the great poets and minds of the postwar period whose work is still much misunderstood. He is perhaps one of the most significant postmodern writers, at the same time able to make his art totally contemporary while revisiting with great virtuosity the technical history of English **prosody**. Perhaps the last word should go to the ever-loquacious Koch himself, who concludes "A Time Zone" with what is the perfect summation of the true spirit of a great avant-garde writer: "I'm excited I'm writing at my typewriter and it doesn't make too much sense."

Further Reading. *Selected Primary Sources:* Koch, Kenneth, *The Art of Love* (New York: Random House, 1975); ———, *The Art of Poetry: Poems, Parodies, Interviews, Essays, and Other Works* (Ann Arbor: University of Michigan Press, 1996); ———, *The Burning Mystery of Anna in 1951* (New York: Random House, 1979); ———, *Days and Nights* (New York: Random House, 1982); ———, *The Duplications* (New York: Random House, 1977); *The Gold Standard* (New York: Knopf, 1995); ———, *Hotel Lambosa* (New York: Coffee House Press, 1993); ———, *I Never Told Anybody: Teaching Poetry in a Nursing Home* (New York: Random House, 1977); ———, *Ko, or A Season on Earth* (New York: Grove, 1960); ———, *Making Your Own Days: The Pleasures of Reading and Writing Poetry* (New York: Simon & Schuster, 1999); ———, *New Addresses* (New York: Knopf, 2001); ———, *On the Great Atlantic Rainway: Selected Poems 1950–1988* (New York: Knopf, 1994); ———, *One Thousand Avant-Garde Plays* (New York: Knopf, 1988); *One Train* (New York: Knopf, 1994); ———, *A Possible World* (New York: Knopf, 2004); *The Red Robins* (New York: Random House, 1975); ———, *Rose, Where Did You Get That Red: Teaching Great Poetry to Children* (New York: Vintage, 1990); ———, *Seasons on Earth* (New York: Penguin Books, 1987);———, *Sleeping with Women* (Los Angeles: Black Sparron Press, 1969); ———, *Straits* (New York: Knopf, 1998); ———, *Thank You, and Other Poems* (New York: Grove Press, 1962); *When the Sun Tries to Go On* (Los Angeles: Black Sparrow Press, 1969); ———, *Seasons on Earth* (New York: Penguin, 1987); ———; *Selected Poems 1950–1982* (New York: Vintage, 1985); ———, *Sun Out: Selected Poems 1950–1952* (New York: Knopf, 2004); ———, *Talking to the Sun: An Illustrated Anthology of Poems for Young People* (New York: Metropolitan Museum of Art, 1988); ———, *Thank You and Other Poems* (New York: Grove, 1962); ———, *When the Sun Tries to Go On* (Los Angeles: Black Sparrow, 1969); ———, *Wishes, Lies and Dreams: Teaching Children to Write* (New York: Perennial, 2000). ***Selected Secondary Sources:*** Chinitz, David, "'Arm the Paper Arm': Kenneth Koch's Postmodern Comedy," in *The Scene of My Selves: New Work on New York School Poets*, ed. Terrence Diggory and Stephen Paul Miller (Orono, ME: National Poetry Foundation, 2001, 311–326); Davis, Jordan, e-mail correspondence with the author;*Jacket Magazine*, special issue on James Schuyler (http://jacketmagazine.com/15/); Pelton, Theodore, "Kenneth Koch's Poetics of Pleasure," in *The Scene of My Selves: New Work on New York School Poets*, ed. Terrence Diggory and Stephen Paul Miller (Orono, ME: National Poetry Foundation, 2001, 327–344); Spurr, David, "Beyond Irony" (*American Poetry Review* 12.2 [March/April 1983]: 42–43); ———,

"Kenneth Koch's 'Serious Moment,'" in *The Scene of My Selves: New Work on New York School Poets*, ed. Terrence Diggory and Stephen Paul Miller (Orono, ME: National Poetry Foundation, 2001, 345–356); Tassoni, Jean-Paul, "Play and Co-Option in Kenneth Koch's *Ko, or a Season on Earth*: 'Freedom and the Realizable World!'" (*Sagetrieb* 10.2 [1991]: 123–132); Watkin, William, *In the Process of Poetry: The New York School and the Avant-Garde* (Lewisburg, PA.: Bucknell University Press, 2001); ———, "Poetry Machines: Repetition in the Early Poetry of Kenneth Koch" (*EnterText* 1.1 [December 2000]: 83–117).

William Watkin

KOERTGE, RON(ALD) (1940–)

Ron Koertge found social and artistic fellowship among several poets who, like him, migrated to Los Angeles and Long Beach in the 1960s or 1970s. They had academic credentials similar to those of other English and writing teachers of their generation, yet advanced a playful, sometimes scabrous, generally populist approach to poetry. The disposition of this work was sufficiently distinct that Southern Californians who attended to that end of the literary world sometimes referred to "that Long Beach thing," until **Charles Harper Webb** brought forth a trio of anthologies solidifying the term **stand-up poetry** (Red Wind Books, 1990; Statewide Technical Books, 1994; University of Iowa Press, 2002). In a seminal paper he delivered to a Phi Beta Kappa conference in 1988, Webb cited Koertge as one of five poets exemplifying the style.

However, well before his poetry had received this somewhat legitimizing—and somewhat stigmatizing—stamp, Koertge had established an identity, particularly among young male poets looking for alternative models. In the introduction to an early **small-press** offering of Koertge poems, *How to Live on Five Dollars a Week* (1977), editor Ted Simmons declared, "When you see the name *Campbell's* on a can, you know it's soup. When you see the name *Koertge* on a book cover, you know it's humor." But while—by his own admission—his poetry often speaks to the adolescent in the adult, Koertge's greatest practical success has come from his sophisticated, verbally rich Young Adult books, which seem to address the grown-up in the adolescent.

The poet was born in 1940 in an agricultural area of Illinois, where he learned to drive tractors and toss hay. Later he would joke, "Those skills certainly paid off when I moved to the Los Angeles area." As a graduate student at the University of Illinois, Koertge met fellow student **Gerald Locklin**, who would eventually accept a teaching position in the English department at University of California–Long Beach. Locklin showed him a little magazine unlike any he had seen—a stapled, low-budget production called the *Wormwood Review*. The examples therein suggested that poetry could embrace more spontaneous, irreverent forms of expression and a broader range of subject matter than he had supposed. Soon after, he wrote his first poems. In 1965 he moved to South Pasadena to teach at Pasadena City College, a position he would keep until his retirement in 2002.

In the early years Koertge provided poems to virtually any editor who wrote to request some, and two decades later the acknowledgments list in *Making Love to Roget's Wife: New and Selected Poems* (1997) would tell a story about the feverish—if ultimately unsustainable—energies of the fly-by-night publishing world: *Blind Alley, Forehead, Happiness Holding Tank, Purr, Smudge, Squeeze Box, Oink,* and *Truly Fine Press*.

Although their subscriber base was small indeed, these magazines did circulate. One enduring friendship began when a little-known writer, having just arrived in Southern California for his sabbatical, called to say he had encountered Koertge offerings in all sorts of odd quarterlies and occasionals and felt a great affinity for his style. Down the line—little known no longer—that friend, Billy Collins, would write, "Ron Koertge is the wisest, most entertaining wiseguy in American Poetry."

In the meantime Koertge managed to take discouraging responses and glean from them opportunities for enterprise. When a friend wrapped up her impressions of his unpublished adult novel with the comment "Maybe you should write for teenagers," he proceeded on her advice. He reworked the manuscript into *Where the Kissing Never Stops* (1986). He has since published several Young Adult novels, receiving a Kentucky Bluegrass Award for *The Brimstone Journals* (2001) and a PEN Center USA Literary Award for Children's Literature for *Stoner and Spaz* (2002). After a dozen slender poetry books from tiny presses, he found a supporter in Miller Williams, whom Koertge acknowledges to be a great editor as well as an independent-minded publisher. *Life on the Edge of the Continent: Selected Poems* (1982) became the first of his three books with the University of Arkansas Press.

Koertge once described the appeal of another seminal influence, New York City poet **Edward Field**, who, he noticed, "wrote a very easy line, liked a joke and loved movies. And he was always absolutely frank about who he was." Those same qualities course through his own poetry, from his earliest book to the latest. Beyond this summation, a survey of poem titles can prepare the reader for what to expect: "The Manager of the Drive-in Dairy," "Plastic Man Alone in the Luncheonette Reaches Length of the Counter for the Salt," "Admission Requirements for U.S. and Canadian Dental Schools," and "Panty Hose" (*Making Love to Roget's Wife: Poems New and Selected*, 1997).

What Koertge's readers are not likely to guess is the extent to which the anti-lyrical bent in his poetry seems to reverse itself in his Young Adult fiction, especially in the later books, where striking images abound. A teen spotted in a shopping mall parking structure seems a "spectrally thin girl on this corporate darkling plain stacked five stories high." And when one friend takes leave of the other, the speaker observes, "Margaux likes to lean into the mean wind that is Sara. And when she is suddenly on her own, abandoned, left to her own devices, she's all aslant" (*Margaux with an X*, 2004).

Retired from teaching, Ron Koertge lives with his wife, Bianca, in their home of many years near the South Pasadena Library. He maintains a writing schedule almost as exacting as an office employee's. Forthcoming publications include a poetry collection, *Fever*, and a Young Adult book, *Boy Girl Boy*.

Further Reading. *Selected Primary Sources:* Koertge, Ron, *Geography of the Forehead* (Fayetteville: University of Arkansas Press, 2000); ———, *Life on the Edge of the Continent* (Fayetteville: University of Arkansas Press, 1982); ———, *Making Love to Roget's Wife: Poems New and Selected* (Fayetteville: University of Arkansas Press, 1977); *Margaux with an X* (Cambridge, MA: Candlewick Press, 2004). ***Selected Secondary Sources***: Barry, David S., "History Poetry and Suspense" (*Pasadena Star News* [2 March 1997]); Blubaugh, Penny, "Suffering Is for Amateurs" (*YA Attitudes* 4.1 [Fall 2004]); Kowit, Steve, "The Present State of American Poetry" (*New York Quarterly* [Spring 1989]).

Suzanne Lummis

KOMUNYAKAA, YUSEF (1947–)

A native of Bogalusa, Louisiana, Yusef Komunyakaa has contributed to the diversity of contemporary American poetry by drawing on sources in African American culture, classical Greek and Roman mythology, and historical and current events, notably the Vietnam War, in which he served as a journalist. Komunyakaa's literary style and technique reflect the influence of the oral tradition in African American cultural expression. His appropriation of **blues** and **jazz** as the basis for the narrative structure of his poetry as well as his incorporation of the black vernacular reflects the influence of poets such as **Langston Hughes** and **Amiri Baraka**. His poems thus reflect the influence of both the **Harlem Renaissance** and the **Black Arts Movement** in the context of the American poetic tradition.

Born James Willie Brown, Komunyakaa assumed his distinctive surname, as Joyce Pettis writes, "not as a symbolic rite of personal liberation but rather as an assertion of kinship ties. The name belonged to Komunyakaa's great-grandparents who, entering the United States in Florida shortly after 1900, self-protectively took on an American name" (203). Komunyakaa graduated from Central High School around 1965 (Pettis, 203). As the child of a carpenter, Komunyakaa gained experience with precision and measure, which assisted him in developing craft as a writer. In an interview he states "In retrospect, I realize that—since my father was a carpenter, I assisted him early on and his tinkering with things, how he would measure a board and search for precision—I realize that my time with him taught me something about writing as well. The ability to go back and revise; revision for me means to 're-see.' I understand revision as a very important element of writing" (Marshall, 147). After graduating from high school, Komunyakaa enlisted in the military and traveled to Vietnam around 1969. While in Vietnam, he worked as a journalist for the army. The experiences in Vietnam and the activities he witnessed influenced his poetry (Pettis, 203). After serving in Vietnam, Komunyakaa enrolled in a creative class at the University of Colorado in Colorado Springs around 1973 (Marshall, 147). He obtained an undergraduate degree from University of Colorado, and he received graduate degrees from Colorado State University and University of California at Irvine in the 1970s (Pettis, 204). Komunyakaa married Mandy Jane Sayer around 1985, and they had a daughter (Pettis, 204). After his marriage with Sayer ended, Komunyakaa married Reetika Vazirani, and the couple also had a child. In July 2003 Reetika Vazirani killed herself and their child Jehan in a murder-suicide (Hedges). Presently, Komunyakaa serves as a professor in Princeton University's creative writing program.

Komunyakaa's poetry, notable for its diversity, focuses on a variety of themes, including travel, migration, identity, colonialism, popular culture, religion, history, family, sexuality, and war. In *Dedications & Other Darkhorses* (1977), Komunyakaa explores poetry, the relationship between the individual and the landscape, sexuality, urban development, and the Vietnam War. In "Returning the Borrowed Road," the speaker argues that one must obtain distance and learn to relinquish control in order to write a poem. Komunyakaa adopts irony in the poem "Urban Renewal," in which the speaker describes the destruction to the environment or urban landscape to bring about something new. The speaker states, "Perhaps, it's the angle of life these days / Everything melts." The juxtaposition of machinery destroying objects amid pigeons at the end of the poem represents the tension between industrialization and the natural world. The themes of death and loss pervade other poems, such as "The Violinist Returns from War," which describes a person brutally injured in a war.

Lost in the Bonewheel Factory (1979) contains a number of poems that focus on sexuality, power, betrayal, murder, and nature. "S&M," which represents sadism and masochism, focuses on the nexus between sexuality and power. "No Love in This House" also focuses on sexuality and lust. The speaker and the beloved engage in sexual intimacy, but the beloved calls out another man's name. Komunyakaa blends the themes of sex and death in the poem "Reconstruction of a Crime," in which the speaker describes a crime of passion. A husband opens a door and comes upon his wife and her lover, shooting them both. The husband then commits suicide. The matter-of-fact tone belies the tragedy. Both sex and death are represented as inevitable acts in the cycle of life and death.

Copacetic (1984) features poems that explore the human condition. The poem "Soliloquy" Man Talking to a Mirror" focuses on the theme of class, identity, and deferred dreams. "More Girl Than Boy" explores the theme of friendship, music, and language. Death serves as the focal point of "April Fool's Day," in which a fifteen-year-old dead speaker muses on life and death. Race, identity, and ethnicity frame "An African Exchange Student Awaits the Arrival of an African Princess." Komunyakaa tackles the significance of musical artists in the poems "Elegy for Thelonius" and "Copacetic Mingus."

I Apologize for the Eyes in My Head (1986), dedicated to May Jane Sayer, features poems about interpersonal relationships. In "When in Rome-Apologia," the male speaker asks a husband for forgiveness for his attention to the man's wife, which was prompted by music, liquor, and the appearance of the wife's body. The speaker wryly states, "I apologize / for the eyes in my head." Identity functions as a central issue in the poem "The Falling-Down Song," in which the speaker feels alienated, dissipated, and incomplete. Nature, death, heritage, and loss permeate the poem "Landscape of the Disappeared." The speaker notes the presence of the ancestors in the present life; the poem suggests a connection with and an alienation from the ancestors. These poems explore the human condition in its complexity and diversity.

Poems in *Toys in a Field* (1986) also deal with the issue of war. In "Ambush" the speaker describes soldiers in the context of the natural landscape awaiting the time to attack the enemy. A sense of impending death for the soldiers or the enemy pervades the poem. "Monsoon Season" also focuses on the theme of nature. The speaker describes the setting as a jungle environment, with a temporary respite from the rain falling so hard. The speaker notes, "My poncho feels like a body bag," suggesting the death of soldiers brought back in body bags. These poems resemble poems in *Dien Cai Dau* in their exploration of the wartime experience in evocative symbolic language.

Komunyakaa's experiences in Vietnam inform *Dien Cai Dau* (1988), a collection that reflects and extends the tradition of American poets, such as **Walt Whitman**, writing about war. "Camouflaging the Chimera" describes soldiers at war about to ambush the enemy. The themes include identity, nature, war, and death; "Tunnels," examines the plight of a soldier who must climb into tunnels, that may be filled with bombs. The poem focuses on the ever-present possibility of death for those active in war. "You and I Are Disappearing" focuses on the theme of death, nature, and memory. As Angela M. Salas notes, "The poem describes the death of a Vietnamese woman by napalm, and in it Komunyakaa's narrator is like a piece of film, marked forever by what it has captured and been captured by" (39). "Facing It" focuses on the aftermath of the construction of the Vietnam War Veterans Memorial. The "it" refers to the memorial, the past, the legacy of the war, the veterans, and other people affected by the war. The speaker identifies with the memorial and looks at the names on the wall, touching the name of a soldier, which brings back a memory. Later, the speaker sees another veteran with no arm, again making the speaker face the past and the legacy of the war.

In *February in Sydney* (1989), topics of poems range from loneliness and alienation to loss and the connections between individuals. "When Loneliness Is a Man" profiles a man who uses beer to alleviate his solitude. The poem "Boxing Day" recounts a fight between two boxers, using the sport as a symbol of masculine power and aggression. The title poem focuses on racism and the potentiality for music to ease or transcend pain. The poems in this collection reflect Komunyakaa's concern with human life and experience.

Magic City (1992) serves as a collection of poems that connect with Komunyakaa's heritage. As Salas notes, "In *Magic City*, Komunyakaa makes an imaginative return to his childhood home of Bogalusa, Louisiana. Bogalusa, a poor, working-class town, was known as *Magic City* to the Choctaw who had once inhabited the land upon which the town was founded; hence, the ironic title of Komunayakaa's volume" (40). The volume highlights the significance of sense of place in the poet's work. The poem "Glory" which highlights the antics of working-class people playing and watching baseball, uses baseball as a metaphor for life and survival. As Salas writes, "The makeshift field is a field of dreams, in which teenage fathers are heroes to their wives and children" (41). In contrast, "Fleshing-out the Season" tackles the subject of miscegenation in American history between blacks and whites. The poem focuses on a white male with a double life—a white wife and a black mistress and a white and a black son. Both women remember the man, and the legacy of miscegenation lives on in the sons. The popularity of Komunyakaa's poetry generated the compilation *Neon Vernacular: New and Selected Poems*, 1993. The book features previously published poems and a section called "New Poems," with poems such as "Moonshine," which focuses on father-son relationships, and "Salt," which addresses racism, identity, and heritage. The evocative poem "Praising Dark Places" serves as a meditation on race, nature, and fear. This collection features poems from *Dedications & Other Darkhorses, Lost in the Bonewheel Factory, Copacetic, I Apologize for the Eyes in My Head, Toys in a Field, Dien Cai Dau,* and *February in Sydney.*

Thieves of Paradise (1998) features poetry on sexuality, history, memory, parent-child relationships, and nature. For example, "Nude Interrogation" is a **prose poem** in which Angela, a woman who is undressing, asks a war veteran if he killed anyone in the war. "The Deck," another prose poem, also focuses on history and interpersonal relationships. The speaker, the son, builds a deck, which reminds him of his father. The deck is a metaphor for the past. The hammer functions as the symbol of history and the common connection with the father. The poem's content and subject matter connect with Komunyakaa's own family history, as his father worked as a carpenter. "Rhythm Method" represents a play on words, connecting the strong syllabic scheme of the poem with the titular form of birth control. The irony of the poem rests in its celebration of sexuality and reproduction in the animal and human world. Sex represents a natural act contributing to the cyclical pattern of life.

Talking Dirty to Gods: Poems (2000) features the juxtaposition of sexuality and classical Greek and Roman mythology, and popular culture. The collection connects with other poems published by Komunyakaa. As Angela Salas notes, "Like its predecessors, *Talking Dirty to the Gods* takes into consideration the matters of war, betrayal, music, myth, and love, and thus cannot be said to be a total departure from what readers expect of Komunyakaa" (47). In "Infidelity," Komunyakaa dramatizes and explores Zeus, the Greek god, and his propensity for love, sex, and deception, while "August" serves as a mediation on nature, the seasons, and the past. "The God of Variables" focuses on interracial relationships in the context of O.J. Simpson, the ex–football player acquitted of murdering his white wife, and Emmett Till, a black youth murdered for whistling at a white woman in Mississippi. The two figures from history and popular culture represent the nexus of race and sex, that is, the politics of black male and white female sexuality. The poems in *Talking Dirty to the Gods* show Komunyakaa's penchant for using classical allusions and contemporary popular culture references in his explorations of sexuality.

Pleasure Dome: New and Collected Poems (2001) features previously published poetry, and newer poems that focus on identity, migration, and environment. The collection features poems from previous collections, including *Dedications & Other Darkhorses, Lost in the Bonewheel Factory, Copacetic, Toys in a Field, I Apologize for the Eyes in My Head, Dien Cai Dau, February in Sydney, Magic City, Neon Vernacular,* and *Thieves of Paradise.* In "Never Land" Komunyakaa comments on the tension between race,

ethnicity, and identity through the figure of Michael Jackson. Jackson, according to the poem's speaker, loses his identity as a black man. "NJ Transit," in contrast, represents a highly imagistic poem about stops, way stations, and points of transition in life. Nature, travel, migration, and the city frame this poem. Komunyakaa's poem captures snapshots in time, place, and space to illustrate mobility and change in the relationship between the individual and the surrounding world. The "Early Uncollected" section includes poems such as "Langston Hughes," which describes Hughes "as this word weaver" amidst the jazz age, and "Cubism," which celebrates the experimental twentieth-century movement in art and its impact.

Taboo (2004) treats subject matter such as history, identity, race, and sexuality with a focus on the role of blacks in society and culture. In "Lament & Praise Song" Komunyakaa explores the legacy of **Phillis Wheatley**, an early African American poet, while "Monticello" explores the issues of miscegenation in relation to former U.S. president Thomas Jefferson, who is known to have engaged in sexual relations with a female slave. The poem "Captain Amasa Delano's Dilemma" explores the issues of race and identity from the perspective of a character in **Herman Melville**'s short story "Benito Cereno," which is about a slave revolt. These poems, as well as others in this collection, reveal Komunyakaa's penchant for literary and historical allusions in his rendering of identity politics.

Komunyakaa's poetry can be placed within the context of the neorealism movement in African American literature in his exploration of history and its meaning for the present and future lives of individuals. Additionally, his exploration of race, class, and gender links his work with other contemporary **African American poets**, such as Amiri Baraka. While his poetry contains universal themes, his appropriation of jazz and blues connects him with Harlem Renaissance poets such as Langston Hughes, while his use of classical Greek and Roman mythology places him in the tradition of a diverse range of writers, such as **Countee Cullen** and T.S. Eliot. In his role as teacher, poet, essayist, and cultural critic, Yusef Komunyakaa represents an influential figure in contemporary American poetry.

Further Reading. *Selected Primary Sources*: Komunyakaa, Yusef, *Copacetic* (Middletown, CT: Wesleyan University Press, 1984); ———, *Dedications and Other Darkhorses* (R.M.C.A.J. Books, 1977); ———, *Dien Cai Dau* (Middletown, CT: Wesleyan University Press, 1988); ———, *February in Sydney* (Matchbooks, 1989); ———, *I Apologize for the Eyes in My Head* (Middletown, CT: Wesleyan University Press, 1986); ———, *Lost in the Bonewheel Factory* (Amherst, MA: Lynx House Press, 1979); ———, *Magic City* (Hanover, NH: Wesleyan

University Press, 1992); ———, *Neon Vernacular: New and Selected Poems* (Hanover, NH: Wesleyan University Press, 1993); ———, *Pleasure Dome: New and Collected Poems* (Middletown, CT: Wesleyan University Press, 2001); ———, *Taboo* (New York: Farrar, Straus and Giroux, 2004); ———, *Talking Dirty to the Gods* (New York: Farrar, Straus and Giroux, 2000); ———, *Thieves of Paradise* (Hanover, NH: Wesleyan University Press, 1998); ———. *Toys in a Field* (Black River Press, 1986). **Selected Secondary Sources**: Hedges, Chris, "A Poet of Suffering, Endurance, and Healing" (*New York Times*, [8 July 2004]: 2); Marshall, Tod, *Range of the Possible: Conversations with Contemporary Poets* (Spokane, WA: Eastern Washington University Press, 2002); ———, Pettis, Joyce, *African American Poets: Lives, Works, and Sources* (Westport, CT: Greenwood Press, 2002); Salas, Angela M., "Race, Human Empathy, and Negative Capability; The Poetry of Yusef Komunyakaa" (*College Literature* 30.4 [Fall 2003]: 32–53).

Sharon L. Jones

KOOSER, THEODORE (TED) (1939–)

Ted Kooser began establishing a reputation in the 1970s as a regionalist poet and as a poet of clarity. During the last decade of the twentieth century and the beginning of the twenty-first, in a time of increasing backlash (in some circles) against **modernist** obscurity in America art, Kooser came rather swiftly to the forefront of American poetry, culminating in his selection as U.S. Poet Laureate in 2004 and again in 2005.

Kooser was born April 25, 1939, in Ames, Iowa, the son of a merchant. He was raised in the Midwest and says that he has never lived outside of Iowa or Nebraska. He graduated with a BS from Iowa State University in 1962 and received an MA from the University of Nebraska in 1968. He took a teaching assistantship at Nebraska but soon realized that although he was committed to writing poetry, he had no interest in an academic career and went to work as a trainee with an insurance company, Bankers Life Nebraska. He remained in the insurance business for over thirty years, finally retiring as a vice-president of public relations at Lincoln Benefit Life in 1999. His first marriage ended in divorce; he is married to Kathleen Rutledge, editor of the Lincoln *Journal Star*.

Kooser was awarded National Endowment for the Arts fellowships in 1976 and 1984 and has won a number of regional awards: the John H. Vreeland Award for Creative Writing from the University of Nebraska in 1964; the Society of Midland Authors Poetry Prize in 1980, 2004 (with **Jim Harrison**), and 2005; the Governor's Arts Award from the Nebraska Arts Council in 1988; the Mayor's Arts Award from the city of Lincoln in 1989; the Merit Award from the Nebraska Arts Council in 2000; the Mari Sandoz Award from the Nebraska

Library Association in 2000; Nebraska Book Awards for poetry in 2001 (*Winter Morning Walks: One Hundred Postcards to Jim Harrison*) and for nonfiction in 2003 (*Local Wonders*); and the Friends of American Writers Prize in 2003. He received the Pulitzer Prize for poetry in 2005 (*Delights and Shadows*).

Probably the word most closely associated with Kooser and his work is "heartland." When he was selected as Poet Laureate, newspaper headlines described him as a poet from the heartland; to less charitable reviewers, such as Brian Phillips in *Poetry*, "the word 'heartland' seemed to embroider itself in six-inch sampler letters across the covers of his books." Librarian of Congress James H. Billington, in announcing Kooser's appointment as Poet Laureate, described him as "a major poetic voice for rural and small town America" and pointed out that he was the first Laureate to hail from the Great Plains. A predecessor in the office, **Billy Collins**, said of his appointment that "the middle section of the country needed greater poetic representation."

Kooser's attitude toward this geographical summation of his aesthetic appears to have been ambivalent. "If you look at my poems one by one," he told an interviewer from *USA Today* in 2005, "you'll find lots of them that could have been written anywhere, in cities, in empty places." Nevertheless, his subject matter typically stays close to home, and he treats with assurance the cartography of small town rural America and the genealogy of families rooted in that experience. In one poem (from *Delights and Shadows*) he describes the eponymous "Grasshoppers" as the size "of the pencil stub my grandfather kept / to mark off the days since rain," and compares their color to the dust of country roads that lead back into the dust bowl years of the 1930s—reminding us that his family's roots go back to that era when so many left their farms.

As for the issue of accessibility, Kooser has made it clear that this is at the center of his aesthetic. In an interview for *Poets and Writers* he describes trying out poems on his secretary or a co-worker, and going back and reworking it if the reader didn't understand it at first hearing. For his Laureate project, a series of press releases to newspapers featuring a short poem by a contemporary poet and Kooser's own brief commentary, he has emphasized that he wants to present poems that the average newspaper reader will understand.

The issue of accessibility in poetry became a controversial one in the late twentieth century, as the public role of art came under political and aesthetic scrutiny. Offending bourgeois sensibilities has long been a goal of Western art, especially twentieth-century art, but as public arts funding grew more controversial, so did political debates over the subject matter of art. Obscurity tends to be associated with the avant-garde and with the political left; during a time of conservative dominance in American politics, it is probably not surprising that the laureateship went to an anti-obscurantist poet.

One sees relatively little thematic or stylistic development in Kooser's work over time: The subject matter is of family and place; and the observation of nature and individuals is always at the heart of it, as is the sense that there are mysteries beyond our grasp, although perhaps not so elusive if we take the time to contemplate them. In the title poem from his collection *Flying at Night*, he notes and draws a connection, from the vantage point of an airplane, between a dying galaxy and a farmer, "feeling the chill of that distant death," turning on a light in his yard.

But in the late 1990s, after suffering from and being cured of oral cancer, and then retiring from the insurance business, Kooser's focus turned increasingly to mortality. This is especially true of his collection *One Hundred Postcards to Jim Harrison*, written to his friend, the poet and novelist, during morning walks that were part of his recovery from cancer. This sense of a special connection to life's grandeur and minutiae, arising from the contemplation of its end, is also an important theme of his 2004 Pulitzer Prize–winning volume, *Delights and Shadows*.

Further Reading. *Selected Primary Sources:* Kooser, Ted, *The Blizzard Voices* (Minneapolis, MN: Bieler Press, 1986); ———, *A Book of Things* (Lincoln, NE: Lyra Press, 1995); ———, *Braided Creek: A Conversation in Poetry* (with Jim Harrison) (Port Townsend, WA: Copper Canyon, 2003); ———, *A Decade of Ted Kooser Valentines* (Omaha, NE: Penumbra Press, 1996); ———, *Delights and Shadows* (Port Townsend, WA: Copper Canyon Press, 2004); ———, *Flying at Night* (Pittsburgh, PA: University of Pittsburgh Press, 2005); ———, *Hatcher* (Lincoln, NE: Windflower Press, 1978); ———, *A Local Habitation and a Name* (San Luis Obispo, CA: Solo Press, 1974); ———, *Local Wonders: Seasons in the Bohemian Alps* (Lincoln, NE: University of Nebraska Press, 2002); ———, *Official Entry Blank* (Lincoln: University of Nebraska Press, 1969); ———, *One World at a Time* (Pittsburgh, PA: University of Pittsburgh, 1985); ———, *Sure Signs: New and Selected Poems* (Pittsburgh, PA: University of Pittsburgh Press, 1980); ———, *Weather Central* (Pittsburgh, PA: University of Pittsburgh Press, 1994); ———, *Winter Morning Walks: 100 Postcards to Jim Harrison* (Pittsburgh, PA: Carnegie Mellon University Press, 2000). *Secondary Sources:* Interview (*American Libraries* 35:11 [December 2004]: 31); Phillips, Brian, *Delights and Shadows* (review) (*Poetry* 185: 5 [February 2005]: 396); Weeks, Linton: "Nebraska's Ted Kooser Named New Poet Laureate" (*Washington Post* [12 August 2004]: C1).

Tad Richards

KOSTELANETZ, RICHARD (1940–)

The prolific experimental artist Richard Kostelanetz began writing **visual poetry** (or **concrete poetry**) in the 1960s and works in a variety of forms and media, including **minimalist** fiction, **sound poetry**, numerical literature, videotape, holography, and conceptual art. Kostelanetz is also a critic, editor, and publisher, with interests in the work of innovative artists, musicians, and writers. He has edited books on **Gertrude Stein** and **e.e. cummings** as well as on musicians **John Cage**, Philip Glass, and Frank Zappa and artists Moholy-Nagy and Naum Gabo, among others. Kostelanetz's own creative work appears primarily in little magazines and in editions by **small presses**, including his own Future Press and Archae Editions.

Kostelanetz was born in New York in 1940. He was educated at Brown University (BA in 1962) and Columbia (MA in 1966). During 1964 to 1965, he was a Fulbright Scholar at King's College London. Kostelanetz has been the recipient of Pulitzer and Guggenheim fellowships, and numerous grants from the National Endowment of the Arts. His first publications were literary criticism and reviews in the 1960s. In 1970 Kostelanetz published his first collection of poetry, *Visual Language*, and edited an anthology of visual poetry, *Imaged Words and Worded Images*, as well as books on Moholy-Nagy and John Cage. In the same year, Kostelanetz co-founded Assembling Press, which published the series *Assemblings*, collections of avant-garde art and literature submitted in an 8½ × 11–inch format and bound by the editors. By 1970 Kostelanetz had begun working in minimalist modes and experimenting with fiction, and minimalist fiction remains one of his most fruitful creative fields. Kostelanetz co-edited the little magazine *Precisely* from 1977. In the mid-1970s he began exploring the artistic potential of new technologies, working with audio- and videotape and producing his first hologram in 1978. Simon Fraser University held a retrospective exhibition of Kostelanetz's work, *Wordsand: 1967–1978, Art with Words, Numbers and Lines, in Several Media*, in 1978. Kostelanetz has maintained his commitment to formally experimental arts, in wide-ranging critical and editorial efforts and creative ventures, through the end of the twentieth century. He still resides in New York.

Kostelanetz's primary interest is in the formal possibilities of his art, rather than its expressive properties, although a referential element is often crucial to the constructivist design of his work. For example, one of Kostelanetz's best-known concrete poems, "Echo" (1967), creates a visual analogue for the meaning of the title word by manipulating its written characters. The letters appear in white on a black background, curving and gradually increasing in size until the largest of all, the final "O," appears to bounce back into the word from the furthest line of the "H," repeating itself in smaller concentric circles. "After Hawthorne" (1967) makes use of the title, as many minimalist and visual poems do, in order to achieve its full potential. Although the poem itself, which consists of a very large, blocky capital letter "A," appears in black ink in *Imaged Words and Worded Images*, one imagines it in the scarlet version worn by Hester Prynne. "Tributes to Henry Ford" features the letters "A" and "T," representing early model automobiles negotiating traffic patterns. Kostelanetz's "Nymphomania" and "Disintegration" (1968) are among his other much-reprinted visual poems. *Portraits from Memory* (1975) is a collection of intimate, handwritten portraits of women.

The page is the compositional unit in *Fields, Turfs, Pitches, Arenas* (1979), with a seven-inch square space or "field" provided for the presentation of each poem. The first group of poems is made up of four words, such as "memory," "retrieval," "selectivity," and "chronology," arranged along the edges of the page, beginning from each corner. In the second group the number of words increases to eight, and finally to sixteen words per poem, set up in four squares per page. The spatial arrangement is meant to facilitate relationships between the words that would not be possible in a sequential, linear poem. Some of the poems are composed along thematic lines, with subjects such as the city, excessive or inane language use, rituals, spaces, attitudes, and emotions. In other poems the relations between the words are based on verbal similarity, such as a group of words ending in "-ite," starting with "ar-," or including "angl"; in the preface Dan Jaffe says these exhibit the "language process" that he finds prominent in the poems.

The "Solos" in *Solos, Duets, Trios, Choruses* (1991) consist of words partitioned into the smaller words that occur within them; one of the words Kostelanetz finds in "psychotherapist," for example, is "rapist." The "Duets" of the book's title are two capitalized words in large type presented next to one another. The typographical presentation lends itself to the visual relationship Kostelanetz wants us to see between the words in addition to any semantic resonance we may find. There are visual and sonic echoes in pairs, such as "diminish" and "minister," while "blood" coupled with "yeast" and "hirsute" with "pinball" are striking by virtue of contrast. "Trios" is constructed on the same principles but with three elements, while the poems in "Choruses" are made of handwritten words forming a circle. The groupings are organized similarly to those in *Fields, Turfs, Pitches, Arenas*, by theme or partial orthographic similarity.

According to Larry McCaffery, Kostelanetz's experiments are "united by a common concern with discovering what the essence of a genre, form, technological process, or style should be or do" (*Some Other Frequency*, 196–197). Kostelanetz explores these issues by combina-

tion, as in his "intermedia" work, such as video poetry or by minimalist reduction. The latter strategy as well as the former can result in genre confusion. For example, Kostelanetz's *Three Element Stories* appear to be visual poems made of three words. The presence of a full stop on the page marks them out as fiction rather than poetry by indicating an implied sentence and therefore fictional narrative. The distinction is between fiction, which Kostelanetz takes to be a dynamic form involving sequential development (a quality he finds in the sentence), and poetry, which he regards as static and centered on the image.

Further Reading. ***Primary Sources:*** Kostelanetz, Richard, *Fields, Turfs, Pitches, Arenas* (Kansas City, MO: BkMk, 1979); ———, *I Articulations* (New York: Kulchur, 1974); *MoRepartitions* (Port Charlotte, FL: Runaway Spoon, 1994); ———, *Numbers: Poems and Stories* (New York: Assembling, 1976); ———, *Portraits from Memory* (Ann Arbor, MI: Ardis, 1975); ———, *Repartitions IV* (Port Charlotte, FL: Runaway Spoon, 1992); ———, *Solos, Duets, Trios, Choruses* (New York: Future Press, 1991); ———, *Three-Element Stories* (New York: Archae, 1998); ———, *Visual Language* (New York: Assembling, 1970); ———, *Wordworks: Poems New and Selected* (Brockport, NY: Boa, 1993); Kostelanetz, Richard, ed., *Imaged Words and Worded Images* (New York: Outerbridge and Dienstfrey, 1970). ***Secondary Sources:*** Grumman, Bob, "Mnmlst Poetry: Unacclaimed but Flourishing," in *Light and Dust Mobile Anthology of Poetry* (1997), http://www.thing.net/~grist/l&d/grumman/egrumn.htm; Martin, Stephen-Paul, "Media/Countermedia: Visual Writing and Networks of Resistance," in *The World in Time and Space: Towards a History of Innovative American Poetry in Our Time* (*Talisman: A Journal of Contemporary Poetry and Poetics* 23–26 [2001–2002]: 469–497); McCaffery, Larry, and Harry Polkinhorn, "Alternative, Possibility, and Essence: An Interview with Richard Kostelanetz," in *Some Other Frequency: Interviews with Innovative American Authors* (Philadelphia: University of Pennsylvania Press, 1996, 196–218).

Karen Alexander

KOWIT, STEVE (1938–)

After an apprenticeship in New York's Lower East Side coffeehouse poetry scene in the 1960s, two years in San Francisco during its psychedelic heyday, and several years traveling around the United States and Latin America, Steve Kowit emerged as one of Southern California's most significant vernacular poets. In his introduction to Kowit's *Mysteries of the Body* (1994), James Ulmer says, "There is an artlessness to [Kowit's] poems that marks one kind of artistic vision, a seemingly off-hand manner where craft erases its own footprints, a quality one admires, for example, in Li Po or Tu Fu or the best of **William Carlos Williams**." Kowit's casual manner, however, belies a scholarly, philosophical bent. He has published translations of Neruda's political verse, poems by Ernesto Cardenal, several loose versions of the poetry of Catullus, and a volume of adaptations of Sanskrit erotic poetry.

Born in Brooklyn, New York, in 1938, Kowit is the younger of two children whose parents came from immigrant European Jewish families. A tennis star in high school and while at Brooklyn College (he was the captain of the New York Junior Davis Cup squad), Kowit developed a passion for poetry with his discovery of the work of **Hart Crane**. He started publishing his own poetry while at Brooklyn College (*Beloit Poetry Journal* and *New York Times Sunday Book Section Poets Column*), where he was a student of the philosophers John Hospers and Martin Lean. After taking a degree in philosophy, he studied with **Stanley Kunitz** at the 92nd Street YMCA in 1965 and with **Robert Lowell** at the New School for Social Research in 1966.

The most profound influence on his writing, however, came from his involvement with New York's Lower East Side coffeehouse poetry scene at Les Deux Megots and Le Metro during the mid-1960s and the writing of **Robinson Jeffers**, Henry Miller, Louis Ferdinand Céline, **Walt Whitman**, and **Allen Ginsberg**. "'Howl' opened up a territory, at least for me," says Kowit, "that the modernists had spent the first half of the century trying to close off. Since then I've avoided the seductions of modernist fragmentation and hypercomplexity."

After an unpleasant stint with the U.S. Army (1965 to 1967), Kowit took an MA at San Francisco State College, where he studied with **Kay Boyle** and worked in a private weekly poetry group with **Jack Gilbert** and **Linda Gregg**. An anti–Vietnam War political activist, he refused continued Army Reserve service in 1967 to protest the nation's hostile relationship with Cuba and Vietnam, vowing to never again put on a U.S. military uniform. After Army Intelligence interviewed him at length at his Haight-Fillmore apartment and he received orders to report for active duty, he moved to Seattle, where he and Mary Petrangelo were married. To avoid prison, Kowit and his wife left the United States, traveling through Mexico, Guatemala, and Peru for much of the following six years.

He returned to the United States in 1973 and worked as an editor and writer at a small publishing house in Miami, Florida, then taught at community colleges in Idaho and Maryland. In 1978 he moved to San Diego, California, where he and his wife have resided since. Kowit has taught at the University of California–San Diego, San Diego State University, United States International University, San Diego City College, and Southwestern College (where he has been on the faculty for the past sixteen years). He completed an MFA at War-ren Wilson College in 1991, studying with Alan Williamson, **Stephen Dobyns,** and **Heather McHugh**.

In the 1970s he spent two years in the Church of Scientology and in the 1980s three years in the Gurdjieff work. In the late 1980s Kowit was a student of Vipassana at the Los Angeles Meditation Center, spending five years as an active member of both the Zen Center Los Angeles and the Zen Center San Diego. In 1984 he organized and ran the first animal rights group in San Diego and has been committed to the animal rights struggle ever since.

A former editor of *Poetry International* and the current poetry reviewer for the *San Diego Union-Tribune*, Kowit is the recipient of a National Endowment fellowship for Poetry, the Atlanta Review Prize, the Paumonak Prize, a San Diego Book Award, and two Pushcart Prizes. Kowit lives in the backcountry hills near the Tecate, Mexico, border with his wife Mary and several companion animals.

A poet of political fierceness and anguish, Kowit has written of the war hysteria that followed the 9/11 disaster: "What a fog / of feculent speeches! What a ghoulish intoxication!" and has described the American public's reaction as "Ozymandian folk. . . waving their flags / & shrieking for blood!" ("The Equation"). His poetry can be intensely political, funny, and compassionate. In the introduction to an early collection of Kowit's work, *Cutting Our Losses*, **Harold Norse** speaks of the poet's grace, humor, humanity, and colloquial skill, and *CHOICE* has written of his "memorable exhilaration, a singular concentration of language, and a flow of razor-sharp images springing irrepressibly from his humanity." Referring to Kowit's 2000 collection, *The Dumbbell Nebula*, **Thomas Lux** wrote that Kowit "has more energy, more passion, more fire and more humor in his left little finger than most poets have in their whole bodies." This passion is evident in a poem like "Notice," which registers his shock at the death of a friend and colleague. The poet urges the reader to "drop to your knees now & again / . . . & kiss the earth & be joyful."

An influential West Coast teacher since the 1970s, Kowit edited *The Maverick Poets* (1985), the first anthology of contemporary American poets working in accessible modes, and is the author of an influential guide to writing poetry, *In the Palm of Your Hand: The Poet's Portable Workshop* (1995), which **Dorianne Laux** called "a gift from a gifted and inspiring teacher, a way in to a world of poetry, written by an enlightened guide who knows that world and loves it."

Further Reading. *Selected Primary Sources:* Kowit, Steve, *The Dumbbell Nebula* (Berkeley, CA: Roundhouse Press, 2000); ———, *In the Palm of Your Hand: The Poet's Portable Workshop* (Gardiner, ME: Tilbury House, 1995); ———,

Lurid Confessions (Pomeroy, OH: Carpenter Press, 1983); ———, ed., *The Maverick Poets* (Santee, CA: Gorilla Press, 1988). **Selected Secondary Sources**: Marshall, Jack, *Glowing Fire* (Berkeley, CA: Poetry Flash #123, June 1983); Norse, Harold, *Preface to Cutting Our Losses by Steve Kowit* (New York: Contact II Publications, 1982); Ulmer, James, *Foreword to Mysteries of the Body by Steve Kowit* (Houston, TX: Uroboros Books, 1994).

Terry Hertzler

KRAMER, AARON (1921–1997)

Among progressive modern American poets working with social and political themes and using traditional forms, Aaron Kramer may well be the most accomplished. From his first protest poems, written in the mid-1930s when he was barely a teenager, to his pointed critiques of the 1983 war in Grenada and Ronald Reagan's 1985 visit to Nazi graves in Bitburg, what stands out about Kramer's work is the musical character of his acts of political witness. Rhyme, meter, and traditional stanzaic forms in Kramer's poetry contain and direct anger, satire, and anguish about a century of singular violence.

Kramer was born at home in a cold-water flat in Brooklyn, on December 13, 1921. His 1937 poem "The Shoe-Shine Boy," published when he was fifteen years old, is a definitive vignette about class. The speaker reports seeing "a child whose shoes looked old / Shining another's, till they shone like gold." From then on he would question exceptionalist claims about his country. The poem is notably also a deliberately ironic use of heroic couplets. Kramer adopted traditional meters—favoring iambic trimeter, tetrameter, and pentameter—in part to install a radical politics within inherited rhythms. He wanted to radicalize the root and branch of our literary tradition, not to abandon it for alternative forms.

The poems deploying these techniques in time would cluster around recurring themes and historical events. His first poems about exploited labor appeared in 1934; his last was published in 1995. His earliest poems about the suppression of freedoms in the United States date from 1938, and he continued writing them through the 1980s. He is one of perhaps only two American writers to produce a series of poems about McCarthyism, from his satiric "The Soul of Martin Dies (1940) to "Called In" (1980), his poem of outrage against those compelled to testify before the House Un-American Activities Committee. Over four decades he would repeatedly write poems about the Holocaust. Like a number of American poets who came of age in the 1930s, he wrote poems about the Spanish Civil War through much of his life. Finally, he had a continuing interest in and commitment to testifying about African American history.

This last subject occasioned what is perhaps his masterpiece—the twenty-six poems comprising the 1952 sequence "Denmark Vesey," about abortive plans for an 1822 slave revolt in Charleston, South Carolina. Probably the single most ambitious and inventive poem about race ever written by a white American, "Denmark Vesey" is distinguished, in part, by Kramer's skill at negotiating the political relationship between form, sound, diction, and meaning.

The first poem offers a hint of internal rhyme in Kramer's riveting definition of plantation agriculture—"acres rooted by uprooted hands"—and then gives the first full rhymes to slavery, as the founder of the middle passage gets the inspiration to kidnap African men, women, and children, then sees the idea become a thriving business, as "inspiration swiftly turned to gold. / The first shocked screams were muffled in the hold."

In a typical Kramer strategy, the hint of internal rhyme in the first poem is fulfilled in the second: "*The sobs and moans cut through my bones.*" The line is spoken by the one white resident who *does* hear the wife of a slave owner or auctioneer. This poem, "Auction Block," is a brilliantly executed dialogue between her and her husband, with their respective statements differentiated in italic and roman type. The poem reinforces what will be a constant theme in the sequence: White civilization is grounded not only in its indifference to the suffering it imposes on its darker brothers but also in a suppression of its own humanity. This theme builds until the devastating poem "Vesey's Nightmare," Vesey being the freed black who was the leader of the slaves. In his nightmare, delivered in off-rhymed five-beat couplets, white cannibals and vampires feed on black bodies and decorate themselves with human trophies—like ghouls elevated to positions of social prominence: "The lovely brocade their ladies wore / had once been Negro grandmothers' hair."

The poem "Vesey Speaks to the Congregation" gives Vesey's bodily identification with the oppressed slaves in rhymed couplets: "my back is marked by your masters' whips; / and from your wounds my own blood drips." The reaction of the whites to intimations of revolt gets its own distinctive rhythm. In "The Legislators Vote" the relentless, lurching rhythm perfectly instantiates the legislature as an institutionalized lynch mob: "Fine them! Jail them! Bind them! Starve them! Brand them! Flail them!" Vesey finally warns the slaves not to hope for salvation from above; if they do, they will remain slaves until they die. He urges them, instead of crying, to "cry freedom! freedom! and arise." It is a call to African Americans but also a general rallying cry issued in the midst of McCarthyism.

Nearly half a century after composing "Denmark Vesey," while he was hurriedly copyediting the three books that would soon comprise his posthumous publications, Kramer was persuaded that they would soon be forgotten after his death. "Denmark Vesey" was issued in a small, privately published chapbook. It remained unavailable thereafter until the University of Illinois Press issued Kramer's *Wicked Times: Selected Poems*, the first comprehensive collection of his work, in 2004. The only literary scholar who took notice of the poem sequence in the intervening decades was Alan Wald.

If it is true that "Denmark Vesey" is, as some believe, one of the masterpieces of American **modernism**, why has it languished almost unknown for fifty years? It is partly a result of timing. He was drawn to the proletarian poetry movement in the 1930s, but its other members were young adults, born a critical few years earlier. **Langston Hughes** was born in 1902 and **Edwin Rolfe** in 1909. Even **Muriel Rukeyser**, born in 1913, was eight years older than Kramer. So he was effectively but a child proletarian poet, hardly likely to receive critical attention. As he grew older, his use of traditional forms distinguished him from most other poets on the left, who saw **Whitman** as their precursor and free verse as their natural style. In a way, the poets most likely to be sympathetic to his formal choices were those also most likely to be offended by his politics. Kramer's first pamphlet, *The Alarm Clock* (1938), was funded by a local Communist Party chapter. Thereafter, Kramer's poetry was issued by **small presses** or privately printed. He had a following among New York radio audiences and received some prominent reviews in the 1940s, but he never received the further national attention he deserved. He had a variety of minor jobs until obtaining a position teaching English in 1961 at what would later become Dowling College. In addition to his poetry, he published a number of collections of translations, including volumes of Heine, Rilke, **Yiddish poetry**, and poems about the Holocaust. His critical books include *The Prophetic Tradition in American Poetry* (1968) and *Melville's Poetry* (1972).

Yet his major legacy, still not fully recognized, is his poetry. He sought in the music of poetry not only cultural knowledge but also incitement to change. In a series of tributes to other political poets, one hears echoes of his ambitions and his regrets. "The tyrants of Chile are hunting Neruda" is the line that opens his poem to one. He imagines, whimsically, that "not being Yevtushenko has its advantages." And he observes of Paul Celan, "so yours was the breakthrough that should have been mine." But his tribute to Boris Pasternak catches the truth that witness must be its own reward: "over your countrymens' heads, on wings that are splendid, / the swan of your sorrow and theirs is beginning to fly."

Further Reading. *Primary Sources:* Kramer, Aaron, *The Prophetic Tradition in American Poetry, 1835–1900* (Rutherford, NJ: Farleigh Dickinson University Press, 1968); ———, *Wicked Times: Selected Poems*, ed. Cary Nelson and Donald Gilzinger (Urbana: University of Illinois Press, 2004). ***Secondary Sources:*** Gilzinger, Donald, "An Aaron Kramer Bibliography," http://www2.sunysuffolk.edu/gilzind/akbib.htm; Gilzinger, Donald, and Cary Nelson, "Aaron Kramer: American Prophet," in *Wicked Times: Selected Poems* (Urbana: University of Illinois Press, 2004, xvii–lix); Wald, Alan, *Writing from the Left: New Essays on Radical Culture and Politics* (New York: Verso, 1994).

Cary Nelson

KROETSCH, ROBERT (1927–)

Largely responsible for the introduction of such **postmodern** concepts as intertextuality, generic indeterminacy, resistance to closure, and an interrogation of the metaphysics of presence and origins, as well as epistemology and ontology, to Canadian readers, the poetry of Robert Kroetsch exemplifies the theoretical turn of the late twentieth century against **modernism** and of the poet as a unified speaking subject. Although some have questioned his adherence to the tenets of postmodernism in his own practice, his major poetic project, *Field Notes*, as a **long poem** composed of long poems, has become the exemplar of what many believe is the quintessential Canadian form—the discontinuous long poem. It is, therefore, difficult to conceive of contemporary **Canadian poetry** without the presence of Kroetsch.

Born in the mining and agricultural community of Heisler, Alberta, to a family of farmers, Kroetsch was excused from manual labor due to illness and, consequently, spent much of his youth alone—gardening and engaging in intellectual pursuits. Kroetsch studied English and philosophy at the University of Alberta (BA, 1948), followed by several years in which he was employed in the work camps of northern Canada. He returned to academic life in 1954, this time in the United States, where he received a master's degree from Middlebury College in Vermont in 1956. Becoming more interested in creative writing, Kroestch was awarded a Ph.D. for a novel manuscript from the University of Iowa (1961). That same year he began teaching at SUNY–Binghamton, where he met William Spanos, with whom he founded *Boundary 2: A Journal of Postmodern Literature* (1972–). Kroetsch returned to Canada in 1978 to take a teaching position at the University of Manitoba and married literary critic Smaro Kamboureli in 1982. Since his retirement in 1995, Kroetsch has continued to write and is consistently in demand as a guest lecturer, as a contributor to journals, and as a writer in residence.

Kroetsch began his literary career and gained much of his early critical acclaim as a novelist. His third novel, *The Studhorse Man*, for example, received Canada's most prestigious literary honor, the Governor General's Award, in 1969. In fact, Kroetsch did not publish his first poem until he was well into his thirties, and it would be another fifteen years before his first collection of poetry appeared. *The Stone Hammer Poems* (1975) gathers these years of poetic exploration, beginning with Kroetsch's use of Blackfoot orature in "Old Man Stories," and soon moves to a poetic exploration of several legendary Canadian figures, including the painter Tom Thomson and the outlaw Albert Johnson. *The Stone Hammer Poems,* however, is most significant for its inclusion of "Mile Zero," a poem Kroetsch would rewrite in an act of poetic deconstruction ten years later, and for its title composition. A meditation on origins, landscape, language, and epistemology, "Stone Hammer Poem" is not only one of Kroetsch's most anthologized and critically examined poems but also is a prologue for what has become his life's work: *Field Notes.*

The first long section of *Field Notes* to be published discretely is *The Ledger* (1975), which, along with *Seed Catalogue* (1977), initiates Kroetsch's exploration of autobiography through found material, oral storytelling, and list poems. In its use of primary documents and its attention to the importance of the local (in this case the pioneering community of Bruce County, Ontario, where Kroetsch's German ancestors first settled), *The Ledger* is comparable to **Charles Olson**'s efforts in *The Maximus Poems*; yet, in its playfulness and interest in the voices of the common populace, it is perhaps closer to **William Carlos Williams**'s achievement in *Paterson.* Using the structural framework of the ledger of expenses and debts, which his grandfather accrued through his life, Kroetsch typographically constructs his poem in a series of columns, exploring the binaries of loss and gain, which occur through immigration, colonization, and industrial development, in both the familial and social body.

With *Seed Catalogue* Kroetsch turns his poetic gaze west to aestheticize his birthplace of Heisler. In this collection the structural conceit is the use of passages from the sales catalogue of *McKenzie's Seeds,* alongside autobiographical elements and the oral tall tales of the community also found in *The Ledger.* In this case, however, the investigation is not so much one of balancing and loss but the question of absence: how to build a settlement from nothing and—with the horticultural elements and frequent references to Adam and Eve—how to build a new Eden. For the speaker, the fundamental problem is how one can become a poet in the absence of a literary tradition, few peers, and a general ambivalence to the institutions of elite culture. Although the poetic persona of the *Seed Catalogue* has abandoned the community by the poem's conclusion, the sequence does suggest that one can create a vital culture and literature without recourse to ballet, opera, Sartre, the Parthenon, or Heidegger.

Later editions of *Seed Catalogue* also collect various shorter poems, one of which, "How I Joined the Seal Herd" (1979), was eventually included as part of *Field Notes.* In this parody of Romanticism, the poem's speaker shrugs off the trappings of civilization—along with much of his clothing—to frolic and couple with a female seal, hoping, at the poem's conclusion, that their progeny will be a true synthesis of the human and animal, or of culture and nature. In its bawdiness, as well as its utilization of both oral and aural imagery, "How I Joined the Seal Herd" is an appropriate segue between the exploration of genealogy and geography in *The Ledger* and *Seed Catalogue* to the more parodic and experimental poetry of *The Sad Phoenician* (1979).

Based on the principles of syntaxis and parataxis, each line of *The Sad Phoenician* begins with the word "and" or "but," alternating through a series of twenty-six alphabetic poems. Inspired by the idea that the real innovation of the Phoenician alphabet was that each graphic unit could be sounded (rather than pictographically representing a concept), Kroetsch constructs a poem representing this oral exuberance—one that records the voice of *hoi polloi,* consisting of clichés and idioms, bragging and verbal showmanship, sexual innuendo and conquests, and frequent interjections of such non-semantic expressions as "ha" or "ho." Although there is a loose narrative concerning the poet and his various loves, the real pleasure of the poem is found in the play of sound and in the often elusive metaphorical associations Kroetsch makes to each letter of the alphabet. In contrast, this series is followed by "The Silent Poet Sequence," in which the voice of the previous section has now been silenced, or else refuses to speak, in the presence of a powerful figure of aurality/orality, Earache the Red. Although maintaining the and/but structure of the previous poem, "The Silent Poet Sequence" is much more restrained and melancholy, suggesting that the ecstasy of orality cannot be maintained indefinitely.

Having realized that his long poems were now making up a larger enterprise, Kroetsch collected "Stone Hammer Poem," *The Ledger, Seed Catalogue,* "How I Joined the Seal Herd," and *The Sad Phoenician* as *Field Notes* in 1981. Also included in this volume were three new sequences, "Sketches of a Lemon" (1980), "The Winnipeg Zoo" (1981), and "The Criminal Intensities of Love as Paradise" (1981), all of which move from public address to interior monologues and an examination of linguistic signification. "The Winnipeg Zoo" is a more somber revisiting of the themes expressed in "How I Joined the Seal Herd": the interaction between humans and animals, as well as the violence done to poetic subjects as a result of the artistic process. Like **Wallace Stevens**'s "Thirteen Ways of Looking at a Blackbird," Kroetsch's "Sketches of a Lemon" is a twelve-part sequence, both serious and mocking, expressing the phenomenological difficulty of describing a lemon with any assurance. Finally, "The Criminal Intensities of Love as Paradise" returns to the columnar format of *The*

Ledger with passages recounting a pair of lovers camping in a provincial park juxtaposed with poems that are more allusive and nonreferential (what Kroetsch would later call "post-surreal") in an attempt to express the unconscious poetic drives and inner thoughts simultaneously at work in quotidian life.

Kroetsch's next publication, *Advice to My Friends* (1985), is a substantial collection featuring eight long poems, all of which fall within the greater frame of *Field Notes*. Concerned primarily with intertextuality, travel, and domestic relations, *Advice to My Friends* is Kroetsch's most challenging and suggestive work, yet also his most compressed, with potentially expansive ideas relegated to relatively short poetic sequences. The title poem, for example, is a parody of both the sonnet sequence (with few poems featuring the traditional fourteen-line and volta structure) and the epithalamium, where Canadian popular and "high" culture is wedded through mock marital festivities (painter Emily Carr marries Howie Morenz, Montreal Canadiens center), while other "sonnets" refer and respond to the works of respected Canadian poets. Kroetsch's previously Romantic tendencies are deconstructed in "Mile Zero," complete with self-conscious footnotes, and new, more experimental poetic passages being inserted between the stanzas of the earlier poem. As Ann Munton suggests, "Letters to Salonika" reverses *The Odyssey*—here the male poet stays at home fretting about the exploits of his female lover in Greece and questions his own masculinity—while the trilogy of travel poems, "Postcards from China," "Delphi: Commentary," and "The Frankfurt *Hauptbahnhof*," uses respective trips to China, Greece, and Germany to explore poetic notation, influence, origin, and familial relationships. *Advice to My Friends* then culminates in two lyric sequences, "Sounding the Name" and "The Poet's Mother." In these poems Kroetsch, much like Roland Barthes in *Camera Lucida*, meditates upon a photograph of his mother in her youth and, in so doing, creates a moving elegy to a woman Kroetsch lost at the age of fourteen.

Considering the strength of *Advice to My Friends,* the next installment of *Field Notes, Excerpts from the Real World* (1986), is a somewhat disappointing **prose poem**. Divided into ten sections and utilizing a mock journal format, the poem combines elements from "Letters to Salonika" (addresses to an absent lover) with those of *The Sad Phoenician* (word play and clichés derived from country-and-western songs). Although there are a number of arresting images and observations, these are often followed by banal statements, leading one to consider the possibility that *Excerpts from the Real World* is a deliberate attempt to sabotage the sentimental voice and poetic poignancy achieved with "The Poet's Mother."

Three years after the appearance of this collection, Kroetsch published *Completed Field Notes* (1989), adding

two final sections, "Spending the Morning on the Beach" and "After Paradise." The first is a relatively minor poem, which expands upon the travels featured in *Advice to My Friends* to include Fiji, Australia, and New Zealand. "After Paradise," however, is a powerful examination of failure, mutability, and closure, which, like the final sections of **Pound**'s *Cantos*, provides cohesion to a large-scale enterprise, even in its fragmentary structure. Since this publication, no new sections have been added to *Completed Field Notes*, and a more recent edition in 2000 contains only minor revisions to the existing poems.

Having "completed" his *Field Notes* and returned to fiction and criticism for much last decade, it appeared that Kroetsch had concluded his poetic career. Thus, it came as a surprise to many readers to see a new collection from him at the turn of the century, *The Hornbooks of Rita K* (2001). Following in the spirit of Nabokov's *Pale Fire, The Hornbooks of Rita K* is a narrative poem, consisting of over one hundred poetic fragments by the fictional Albertan writer, Rita Kleinhart (who has mysteriously disappeared), with commentary, memoirs, and annotations by Raymond, a former lover and self-proclaimed poet, included in each section. As the poems of Kleinhart are often mere scraps on postcards or on the titular hornbooks, the voice of Raymond dominates the discourse, making him a clear descendant of Kinbote. Readers, however, cannot fail to note that Rita and Raymond share the initials R.K., which are also those of Kroetsch himself—suggesting that this text is as much as response to Kroetsch's own public persona, and a parody of his own frequently masculine poetics, as it is a postmodern mystery. Whether or not *The Hornbooks of Rita K* will remain a parallel text to *Field Notes* or will be eventually subsumed by it, it is a remarkable condensing and refining of Kroetsch's interests in autobiography, textual archeology, and the epistolary form as they have developed over the past forty years.

As well as engaging with postmodernism through the founding of *Boundary 2*, Kroetsch has published many critical essays, several of which have become classic documents in Canadian poetics. Of particular importance are his contributions to theories of the long poem, prairie poetics, postcolonialism, and postmodernity in Canada. Many essays on these subjects are collected in *The Lovely Treachery of Words* (1989), and thoughts on these matters can be found in *Labyrinths of Voice* (1982), a book-length interview with Kroetsch.

Further Reading. *Selected Primary Sources:* Kroetsch, Robert, *Completed Field Notes: The Long Poems of Robert Kroetsch* (Edmonton: University of Alberta Press, 2000); ———, *The Hornbooks of Rita K* (Edmonton: University of Alberta Press, 2001); ———, *The Lovely Treachery of Words: Essays Selected and New* (Toronto: Oxford University Press, 1989); ———, *The Stone Hammer Poems*

(Lantzville, BC: Oolichan, 1975). **Selected Secondary Sources:** Davey, Frank, ed., "Robert Kroetsch: Reflections" (*Open Letter* 5.8/9 [1984]); Munton, Ann, "Robert Kroetsch," in *Canadian Writers and Their Works: Poetry Series*, vol. 10., ed. Robert Lecker et al. (Toronto: ECW, 1992, 67–186); Neuman, Shirley, and Robert Wilson, *Labyrinths of Voice: Conversations with Robert Kroetsch* (Edmonton, AB: NeWest Press, 1982); Rudy, Susan, "Having Written Her Name in His Book" (*Open Letter* 9.5/6 [1996]: 75–92); Thomas, Peter, *Robert Kroetsch* (Vancouver, BC: Douglas & McIntyre, 1980).

Stephen Cain

KUMIN, MAXINE (1925–)

Maxine Kumin is one of the twentieth century's foremost poets of place. Although her body of work spans a range of subject matter, most of her poems reflect life on her farm in rural New Hampshire and the universal lessons to be learned from nurturing animals and crops into life, and later into death. Never pat or sentimental, Kumin's poems map the subconscious forests of the dreaming world, the exquisite details of New England seasonal change, and human life's abundance of joy and grief.

Maxine Kumin was born in Germantown, a neighborhood of Philadelphia, in 1925. Her father was a pawnbroker. She wrote her first poem at the age of eight, on the occasion of the death of a newborn puppy. Also at eight she learned to swim, at a day camp in Ambler, Pennsylvania. Later in life she would draw connections between learning the rules of **prosody** and the ineffable rhythms of the sidestroke and backstroke.

Kumin grew up next door to the convent of the Sisters of St. Joseph and attended the convent school until she switched to a public high school in Philadelphia. Interested in horses from an early age, she rode as often as she could; she also had aspirations of being an Olympic swimmer. At summer camp, swimming long distances, she matched memorized poems to the cadences of the crawl, breathing poems aloud as she swam. At eighteen, Kumin was invited to work at Billy Rose's Aquacade, as part of a unit that performed synchronized swimming, touted as "poetry in motion." Her father forbade it on the grounds that revealing one's body in a bathing suit was immodest and that her childhood swimming fixation was inappropriate for a grown woman. She had wanted to attend Wellesley because of its swimming pool. Instead she earned a BA in history and literature at Radcliffe in 1946 and a MA in 1948. That same year, her first son, Danny, was born. That year Kumin returned to poetry, and over the next few years she published short light poems in such journals as the *Saturday Evening Post* and the *New York Herald Tribune*. In 1957, with three children under the age of ten, she signed up for a poetry workshop taught by John Hughes, which encouraged her to try her hand at more substantive poetry and sealed her love affair with words.

In addition to Hughes, Kumin cites **W.H. Auden**, **Karl Shapiro**, and **Randall Jarrell** as strong poetic influences, noting that these were the poets of her generation surfacing out of World War II. Another major influence was her eighteen-year friendship with **Anne Sexton**, whom Kumin met in Hughes' workshop. The two women became members of the New England Poetry Club together and served as sounding boards for each other's poetry until Sexton's suicide in 1975. When Kumin went to Kentucky in 1973 to be a writer-in-residence at Center College, she and Sexton read poems to each other every night over the phone.

In 1960 Kumin's first children's book, a story in rhyme, was published. Her first collection of poems, *Halfway*, came out in 1961. Her second volume of poetry, *The Privilege,* followed four years later, along with her first novel. Her third book, *The Nightmare Factory*, appeared in 1970. The year 1972 brought Kumin's fourth collection of poems, *Up Country: Poems of New England*, which garnered her the Pulitzer Prize for Poetry in 1973. Her other awards have included an American Academy and Institute of Arts and Letters Award for excellence in literature (1980), as well as six honorary degrees. In 1981 and 1982 she served as poetry consultant to the Library of Congress. In addition to her thirteen (to date) collections of poems, Kumin is the author of a memoir, four novels, a collection of short stories, more than twenty children's books, and four books of essays, most recently *Always Beginning: Essays on a Life in Poetry* (2000).

Kumin's poems and prose are grounded in the details of rural New England life. In 1976 she and her husband moved to a New Hampshire farm, where they breed horses. Kumin admits to some reclusive tendencies, although she has said in interviews that she neither would nor could leave the world behind entirely. The hermit who recurs in *Up Country* can be read as a manifestation of Kumin's love of solitude. The hermit's most prosaic activities take on an otherworldly tinge in Kumin's verse. In "The Hermit Meets the Skunk," he scrubs his dog, musing that if the dog were to be held down, "his four legs held at four corners / and slit open by the enthusiast" the "true nature of Dog" would be revealed. Exquisite language dots "The Hermit Has a Visitor;" we see the hermit lying "curled like a lima bean / still holding back its cotyledon." His visitor, described in a quatrain of resonant images, proves to be a mosquito.

The inanimate world comes alive in Kumin's verse. In "Stones" (1972) she shows how the eponymous lumps "rise up openmouthed into walls and from time / to time imitate oysters or mushrooms." There is a resonance between Kumin's work and **Louise Glück's** *The Wild Iris* (1992). Whereas Glück's flowers and bulbs cry out to their maker in clearly religious language, Kumin's Jacob's Cattle beans and fiddlehead ferns speak without morals or longing. The same can be said of many of the animals she describes, such as the dog catching and releasing frogs in "Custodian" (*Nurture*, 1989). "Nothing is to be said here / of need or desire. No moral arises," she tells us. The dog merely does what it knows how to do, and so, she implies, do we.

Kumin's description of winter horses growing their long fur stockings ("The Horses," *Up Country*) shows the wonder of the natural world in plain but resonant speech. In contrast, in "In Warm Rooms, Before a Blue Light" (*Nurture*) Kumin describes with clinical distance and reserve the egg-warming vigil suffered by male Emperor penguins. It is the distant human viewer in the poem that turns nature's transcendent marvels into subjects of scientific curiosity. Often humans and animals do not interact kindly or well in Kumin's work. The narrator of "Woodchucks" (*Up Country*) tries bombing the title animals with gas and poisoning them with cyanide before shooting the mother and her cubs. By the poem's end, she is vaguely uneasy about the one chuck remaining and her own murderous impulses.

Kumin is not purely a **pastoral** poet. She engages the political world in poems such as "The Poet Visits Egypt and Israel" (*The Long Approach*, 1985), "After the Cleansing of Bosnia" (*Connecting the Dots*, 1996), and "William Remembers the Outbreak of Civil War" (2002), which speaks in the voice of a Sudanese refugee. Poems about her mother and daughter, her family's European history, role models **Marianne Moore** and William Wordsworth, and even the chambermaids at a Marriott hotel show her skill at evoking both interpersonal and historical drama. Most of her poems spring from the natural world, and it is as a poet of the rural and natural life that Kumin will be remembered.

Many of Kumin's poems encode messages about how we should interact with the natural world. Sometimes she masks her anger at humanity's destructiveness with black humor, as in "Thoughts on Saving the Manatee" (*Nurture*, 1989). After an unsentimental recital of the sea creatures' beauty, Kumin advises that we return to the custom of eating them and finish the endangered beasts off. "Let's stop pretending we need them / more than they need us," she writes with noticeable bitterness. In other poems she eschews direct address of the reader, preferring to remind us of our role as stewards of the natural world by showing us, for instance, her awe at the birth of a colt in "Praise Be" (*Looking for Luck*, 1992).

Kumin's reverence for the land and its natural rhythms verges on **Wendell Berry**–like agrarianism. "I believe in living on grateful terms / with the earth," she writes in "Credo" and in "Hay," from the same collection, "Allegiance to the land is tenderness" (*Looking for Luck*). "The Brown Mountain" (*The Long Marriage*, 2002) glorifies her compost pile, its "tomatoes cat-faced or bitten into" and "lettuces . . . revised / as rabbit pellets, holy with nitrogen." To Kumin's farm-honed sensibilities, death and decay are a part of life: the foals that don't make it, the squirrels her cats kill, and even the suicide of her beloved friend. "When you live with the weather of New England, neither winter nor spring stands for finality, and the small births can be allowed to balance the large deaths—though one must always hedge one's bets," observes **Alicia Ostriker** of Kumin's work in "Making the Connection: The Nature Poetry of Maxine Kumin" (*Dancing at the Devil's Party*, 2000).

The figure of the bear, which some critics have called Kumin's totem, recurs throughout her body of work. In "You Are in Bear Country" (*The Long Approach*), the reader is reminded to "Keep clear / of . . . garbage dumps, carcasses." As a last resort, she advises us, play dead; and above all, we should "Cherish / [our] wilderness." The narrator of "In the Park" (1989) turns an encounter with a grizzly bear into a brush with God. "Déja Vu" (1996) spins a love story between a woman and a bear: He feeds her berries and honey, they dally in briars, they bed down for the winter in a pine nest. At the poem's end, the woman has returned home with their cub, knowing a bear prince will lure their daughter back to the wilds someday.

There's wry humor in many of Kumin's poems. In "Of Wings" (*Looking for Luck*), she writes, "Angels subsist on ambrosia. / Eagles mainly on fish." She compares Chicago's O'Hare Airport with medieval visions of heaven. She imagines **Emily Dickinson** in the 1990s, wearing magenta tights and faxing poems to *Thirteenth Moon*. In "An Insider's View of the Garden" (*Connecting the Dots*) she lauds "unquenchable dill" along with "bony and bored red peppers" and announces gaily, "For all of you, whether eaten or extirpated / I plan to spend the rest of my life on my knees."

Kumin's poems preserve a harvest of time. In "Telling the Barn Swallow" (*Looking for Luck*) she tells the eponymous bird that "this hour / must outlast the pies and the jellies, / must stick in my head like a burdock bur."

The outsider status conferred by being a Jew in a Christian world is a theme in Kumin's early work, as seen in poems like "Living with Jesus" (1975), which begins "Can it be / I am the only Jew residing in Danville, Kentucky, / looking for matzoh in the Safeway and the A&P?" Her convent-school experiences make an appearance in poems like "The Nuns of Childhood" (1992), although in her later work religion is a source for metaphors, which spice up otherwise nonreligious poems. Kumin has said that poems' ineffability are a kind of religion for her. Critics have also noted an earth-centered spirituality in her work, which glorifies natural cycles of death and life.

Although she is capable of **free verse**, Kumin has always been most comfortable writing in traditional poetic forms, as evidenced by *Connecting the Dots*, which begins with a crown of sonnets and ends with a skillful sestina. In a 1975 interview Kumin admitted that she enjoys formal poetry because it is hard. "I believe that writing in a rhyme scheme startles you into good metaphor," she said. In her essay "A Rock in the River" Annie Finch observed that Kumin "stands out among poets of her generation in her facility with iambic pentameter . . . [and] because of the strength and eloquence of the passages in triple meter that occur consistently in her work" (*Telling the Barn Swallow*, 23).

In July 1998 Kumin took one of her horses to a carriage-driving clinic. The horse bolted and the carriage fell, breaking Kumin's neck. After her recovery (chronicled in her memoir *Inside the Halo and Beyond*), Kumin returned to themes of illness and mortality in her poems with new poignancy. In "Wagons" (*The Long Marriage*) she shows us women in physical therapy, "learn[ing] to adjust to their newly-replaced hips." Spinal cord injuries, she tells us in "Grand Canyon" (2002), are like snowflakes: no two alike.

Emily Grosholz has noted Kumin's peculiar tendency in her poems to transform people into animals and vice versa. In her essay in *Telling the Barn Swallow* (1997), she reads this as an emotional equivalence ("Kumin cares as sharply about the animals, wild and domestic, that inhabit her New Hampshire farm as she does about her friends and family," 47) and as encapsulation of an important message that "we human beings are animals among animals, and we must not let our temperamental strangeness sever us from our fellows, from the earth."

There is something to be learned from the everyday births and deaths of horses and swallows, tomato plants, and insects: This credo is implicit in Kumin's poems. With her choice to live a rural life and with her writing, which connects the reader with her husband's shoveling sawdust and mares' struggling to foal, Kumin teaches her quiet lesson: The grand cycles of human life and history are cut from the same cloth as the compost pile that lies dormant in winter, always ready for the coming spring.

Further Reading. *Selected Primary Sources:* Kumin, Maxine, *Connecting the Dots* (New York and London: W.W. Norton, 1996); ———, *Halfway* (New York: Holt, Rinehart and Winston, 1961); ———, *House, Bridge, Fountain, Gate* (New York: Viking, 1975); ———, *The Long Approach* (New York: Viking Penguin, 1985); ———, *The Long Marriage* (New York: W.W. Norton, 2002); ———, *Looking for Luck* (New York: W.W. Norton, 1992); ———, *The Nightmare Factory* (New York: Harper & Row, 1972); ———, *Nurture* (New York: Viking Penguin, 1989); ———, *The Privilege* (New York: Harper & Row,

1965); ———, *Up Country: Poems of New England* (New York: Harper & Row, 1972). ***Selected Secondary Sources:*** Grosholz, Emily, *Telling the Barn Swallow: Poets on the Poetry of Maxine Kumin* (Hanover: University of New Hampshire Press, 1997); Norris, Jean, "An Interview with Maxine Kumin" (*Crazy Horse* 16 [Summer 1975]) (reprinted in Kumin, Maxine, *To Make a Prairie* [Ann Arbor: University of Michican Press, 1979]); Ostriker, Alicia, "Making the Connection: The Nature Poetry of Maxine Kumin," in *Dancing at the Devil's Party* (Ann Arbor: University of Michigan Press, 2000).

Rachel Barenblat

KUNITZ, STANLEY (1905–)

Although he came of age in the heyday of **T.S. Eliot** and **Ezra Pound,** Stanley Kunitz took a conservative approach to **modernism,** following more classic models than most twentieth-century poets have done. More liberal, on the other hand, in accepting **free verse** forms than **Robert Frost,** he nevertheless rejected the vogue of the later free-verse **confessional poetry.** Influenced by the writings of Carl Jung, his poetry is often metaphysical and laden with symbols. His early work, strongly classic in both form and content, met with accolades from the publication of his first book, *Intellectual Things,* in 1930. The subsequent three books were published at roughly fourteen-year intervals. When, much later, he began publishing more frequently, he had found a more personal voice and had moved toward a greater acceptance of twentieth-century form, content, and style. **John Ciardi** referred to him as a neglected poet in 1958, but Kunitz has now been widely admired for several decades, for both his technique and his originality.

Kunitz served as Consultant in Poetry to the Library of Congress from 1974 to 1976. His honors include the Pulitzer Prize, the Bollingen Prize, a Ford Foundation grant, a Guggenheim Foundation fellowship, Harvard's Centennial Medal, the Levinson Prize, the Lenore Marshall Poetry Prize, the Harriet Monroe Poetry Award, a National Endowment for the Arts fellowship, and the Shelley Memorial Award. Kunitz served as judge of the Yale Younger Poets Contest from 1969 to 1977, was named State Poet of New York, and is a Chancellor Emeritus of the Academy of American Poets. In 1993 Stanley Kunitz, at age eighty-eight, was awarded the National Medal of the Arts by President Clinton. In October 2000, at age ninety-five, he began serving as Poet Laureate of the United States.

Stanley Kunitz was born in Worcester, Massachusetts, on July 29, 1905, to immigrant Lithuanian parents, Solomon Z. and Yetta Jasspon Kunitz. His father committed suicide six weeks before Stanley was born. His stepfather, Mark Dine, died of a heart attack when Kunitz was fourteen. In 1922 he graduated from Worcester's Classical High School and won a scholarship to

Harvard University. During his college summer vacations, he worked as a cub reporter for the *Worcester Telegram*. With his college degrees, Kunitz sought employment in New York City. He also completed and published his first book of poems.

After a brief marriage to poet Helen Pearce, Kunitz remarried in 1939. From this marriage to Eleanor Evans, his only child, Gretchen, was born. In 1958 he divorced his second wife and married the artist Elise Asher, who died in the spring of 2004.

Throughout the 1920s Kunitz supported himself through freelance writing. In 1927 he became an editor at H.W. Wilson Company, where he edited the *Wilson Bulletin*, which became the *Wilson Library Bulletin*. During World War II he edited a U.S. Army news magazine titled *Ten Minute Break* along with performing duties in the Air Transport Command.

In the 1930s, a young **Theodore Roethke** sought out Kunitz at his home, initiating a friendship that would last until Roethke's death in 1963. In 1946 Roethke requested that Kunitz replace him on the Bennington College faculty. After Bennington College, Kunitz taught in **creative writing programs** at the University of Washington, Queens College, Brandeis University, and Columbia. While at Brandeis in the late 1950s, Kunitz met weekly with **Robert Lowell** in Boston and helped him to shape his groundbreaking volume of poems *Life Studies*.

The poems of Kunitz's first volume, *Intellectual Things*, are, as the title suggests, intellectual. They are also archaic in their development and imagery, their elevated diction, and their artificial style. By the time of his second book, *Passport to the War* (1944), Kunitz had relaxed his concept of poetic imagery to allow more human figures to move in his poems and had shifted his diction to the things of this world, displacing the mythological machinery of the earlier book. In *Stanley Kunitz, An Introduction to the Poetry*, Gregory Orr quotes Kunitz as saying it is his poetic concern "to convert life into legend, to 'find the drama in a nutshell'" (18). Orr writes that Kunitz dramatizes his life and relationships in terms of three primary legends: "the father legend" (6), "the mother/beloved legend," and the "legend of being" (7). Of these themes, the father legend is particularly developed in *Passport to the War*—notably in one of Kunitz's most famous poems, "Father and Son," in which he cries—to father or stepfather?—"Father! . . . Return! You know / the way. I'll wipe the mudstains from your clothes." The mother/beloved legend covers unsure ground as the poet attempts to separate infant mother love from adult loves. Near the conclusion of the book, "Open the Gates" explores his legend of being and points toward past and future growth: "I stand on the terrible threshold, and I see / The end and the beginning in each other's arms."

Kunitz's third poetry book, *Selected Poems, 1928–1958*, won the 1959 Pulitzer Prize. While this book finds the poet even more involved in the things of this world, his intellectualism continues to make demands. The title of "The Class Will Come to Order," for example, begins with epigraphs from Dante's *Vita Nuova* and James Joyce's *Finnegans Wake,* and the second stanza concludes with a reference to Plato: "How wise was he who banned them from his state!"

In 1971 Kunitz published *The Testing-Tree*, which marks a sea change in Kunitz's development. "The Portrait" exposes a sensitive family history that had previously remained closed, introducing the wraith-father image that has haunted so much of Kunitz's poetry. The poem concerns the suicide of his father. It begins, "My mother never forgave my father." Among the sins of fathers are homes broken by unfaithfulness and wrecked by gambling debts or by physical abuse, but in this case the unforgivable sin is that of abandonment through willful death. According to the poem (and to family history), the suicide took place in a public park in springtime, "when I was waiting to be born."

Kunitz's mother refuses to let the father's name be spoken, but the speaker in the poem can hear and feel those silences, which come "thumping" into his mind. He finds his father's pastel portrait in a cabinet in the attic and carries it down to show his mother. She silently rips it to shreds, after which—in a striking dispondee (four stressed words in a row)—she "slapped me hard." While the missing father had been a presence in Kunitz's earlier poetry, in this poem, for the first time, he has brought him out of the cabinet, down from the attic. As the poem's last line reports, at least fifty years after that slap, the speaker still feels his cheek burning.

In painting a portrait, the good artist conceals as well as reveals. With all the detail about place and season, with the description of the father's lips, moustache, and eyes in the portrait, Kunitz does not reveal the method of suicide. Marie Henault reports that when he read at the Worcester Poetry Festival in 1971, Kunitz said he would never "'forget Worcester,' the city of his birth, as it had so 'scarred' him" (88). Perhaps the emotions described and released in the writing of "The Portrait" allowed Kunitz to return to his youth in Worcester, not erasing those emotional scars but sublimating them. Since his "sixty-fourth year" (when he wrote "The Portrait"), he has written some of his best poems evoking that youthful period.

But it is the long title poem of *The Testing-Tree* that is the most famous, not only for its introduction of the spare, lean style of later Kunitz but for its conflation of the personal and the global. Told from the viewpoint of a child, who uses an old oak for target practice, the poem evokes the sorrow of living in "a murderous time" when the heart "lives by breaking." The boy, excluded from local baseball games, roams the ditches and woods looking for throwing-stones, following the steps of Massassoit, the Indian who forged the first treaty with the pilgrims. He comes to a clearing, where he finds the testing-tree. Asking the blessing of his father on his right arm, he pitches his stones against the tree. While the game is only a "test," the boy plays "for keeps," hurling his stones "for love, for poetry / and for eternal life."

In the fourth and final section of "The Testing-Tree," the world of nature and the tree are gone, replaced by the mechanized world of war. It is a modern world that holds no "key" by which a boy might find a path back into the woods. This change is reflected as much by larger world events as it is by the story of a boy's growing out of innocence. In 1968, struggling with the poem's closing, Kunitz saw on television the news of the assassination of Martin Luther King, Jr., and immediately completed the poem. While "The Testing-Tree" does not directly engage the King assassination, the last nine lines, with their reference to "a murderous time," clearly take the poem out of the sphere of the personal and into larger issues of the American past.

The Poems of Stanley Kunitz: 1928–1978 collects a half-century of the poet's work and thus offers numerous and widely varying examples of Kunitz's weaving of the personal and the trans-personal, among them a number of poems that explore the nature of **poetics** itself. "The Catch," a slender, nineteen-line, **imagistic** poem seems to trace a **pastoral** moment in which the action is elemental: Sitting by a pond, a father catches a dragonfly (never named as such) in a net and grants his child's request to see it. But, he warns, the price for seeing it is one the child will pay for—the poem repeats—"all your life." More than half of the short poem is devoted to description of the movement of the flying insect, but the characterization of the insect as a "delicate engine / fired by impulse and glitter" seems equally to describe the poem itself, or what a poem might be. Whatever darts over the pond at sunset, in the first line of the poem, is never named, and is so ephemeral as to be "less image than thought," even thought "come alive." It is following the latter phrase that the net passes deftly through the air, capturing the insect. The poem, while simple, is elusive. Is one to read for moral allegory? If so, are we to think that everything fleeting and beautiful is destined to be owned, viewed, and thus destroyed? And why should the innocent, curious child be compelled to "pay" all his life for the privilege of a single glance at this treasure of nature? This Kunitz, of course, does not answer. The poem consists of a moment of wonder at a delicate and beautiful existence; it is also, itself, an instance of that fleeting existence. The word "catch" does not appear in the poem, yet the catch of "The Catch" is, variously, the dragonfly, the poem, and the reader, who takes the place of the curious child marveling over the "delicate

engine." The poem is, like the insect, a "thought come alive."

Kunitz not only writes from private myths, but he adds private to public. His sixth book of poetry, *Next-to-Last-Things* (1985), contains, among other poems of mythic properties, animal poems such as "The Snakes of September," "Raccoon Journal," and "The Wellfleet Whale," all three of which demonstrate sympathy for the non-human world. In "The Snakes of September," rather than fearing the snakes, the speaker reaches out his "hand and stroke[s] . . . their skins." The loosely structured "Journal"—gathering diary entries made between July 14 and October 31, 1984—develops the idea of man's ecological evils revisited upon him by the raccoon, who, unlike animals on the endangered species list, will never disappear; he has "come to take possession." In "The Wellfleet Whale," a record of several days' events, man is again dwarfed by nature, yet rather than standing in opposition to it, the persona of the poem feels a shudder of affinity with the stranded and dying whale.

Kunitz's next poetry book, published to commemorate his ninetieth birthday, was *Passing Through: The Later Poems, New and Selected* (1995), which won the National Book Award. Kunitz mines his childhood in poems such as "My Mother's Pears" and "Halley's Comet." The latter poem opens in a first-grade classroom as the teacher tells the students there will be no school tomorrow if the comet should crash into the earth. The mixture of humor and horror also characterizes the description of the boy having what he imagines is his "last meal" with his family. The mother is the chiding mother often found in the poems of Kunitz, failing to address the boy's problems and sending him off to bed. As the boy tries unsuccessfully to sleep that night, he calls out, as he has in earlier Kunitz poems, to his missing father. Alone, he moves through the dark, "waiting for the world to end."

Perhaps the greatest irony is that between the real speaker of the poem, ninety (one hundred at this writing) years old, who reads the line "I'm the boy in the white flannel gown . . . searching the starry sky" and the man who indeed waits "for the world to end." This contrast underlines one of Kunitz's "Reflections" that serve as a preamble to *The Collected Poems*: "Years ago I came to the realization that . . . we are living and dying at once" (13).

In an essay in his latest book, *The Wild Braid* (2005), Kunitz writes about trimming a juniper bush he has planted in his garden at his summer home in Provincetown, Masschusetts. Over the years, his pruning operations have taken on the art of *bonsai*. He writes,

> The danger is that you cut away the heart of a poem, and are left only with the most ordered and contained element. A certain degree of sprawl is necessary; it

should feel as though there's room to maneuver, that you're not trapped in a cell. You must be very careful not to deprive the poem of its wild origin. (57)

These sentences sum up Kunitz's poetic development through the twentieth century, from the early, air-tight cells of coded language toward, with each new collection, the "wild braid" of creation. Though always careful of language and form, Kunitz has increasingly invited that vital "sprawl" into his poetry. The major shift occurred between the *Selected Poems* of 1958 and the publishing of *The Testing-Tree* in 1971. Poetry as process is all-important to Kunitz; as he announced in his poem "The Layers" (*The Poems of Stanley Kunitz, 1928–1958*), "I am not done with my changes."

Further Reading. *Selected Primary Sources:* Kunitz, Stanley, *The Collected Poems of Stanley Kunitz* (New York: W.W. Norton, 2000); ———, *Intellectual Things* (New York: Doubleday-Doran, 1930); ———, *Next-to-Last Things: New Poems and Essays* (Boston: Atlantic Monthly Press, 1985); ———, "Openhearted: Stanley Kunitz and Mark Wunderlich in Conversation" (*American Poet* [Fall, 1997]); ———, *Passing Through: The Later Poems, New and Selected* (New York: W.W. Norton, 1995); ———, *Passport to the War* (New York: Holt, 1944); ———, *The Poems of Stanley Kunitz, 1928–1978* (Boston: Little, Brown, 1979); ———, *Selected Poems, 1928–1958* (Boston: Little, Brown, 1958); ———, *The Testing-Tree* (Boston: Little, Brown, 1971). ***Selected Secondary Sources:*** Ciardi, John, "*SR*'s Quarterly Round-Up" (*Saturday Review* [27 September 1958]: 18); Davison, Peter, *The Fading Smile* (New York, W.W. Norton, 1996); Henault, Marie, *Stanley Kunitz* (Boston: Twayne, 1980); Orr, Gregory, *Stanley Kunitz, An Introduction to the Poetry* (New York: Columbia University Press, 1985); Robson, Roy Raymond, *Bless in a Congregation: Holism in Stanley Kunitz' Latest Poetry, "The Layers"* (private printing, Meadville, PA: Allegheny College, 1985).

Carle Johnson

KYGER, JOANNE ELIZABETH (1934–)

Joanne Kyger is a somewhat elusive figure in the history of post–World War II American poetry, in part because she was a young woman in a context that tended to devalue the work of women poets but also because of her thoroughly unique use of poetic materials. Kyger never attached herself to any one school or locale. Instead, she incorporated and modified the New American **poetics** being forged in this period for her own ends. As a result, commonalities between her work and that of a range of major figures and movements, both her modernist predecessors and her contemporaries, are apparent. Despite her claim in "The Pigs for Circe in May," "I think of people *sighing* over poetry,

using it, I / don't know what it's for" (*Places to Go*, 9), Kyger seems to have "used" poetry—not in the creation of a purposeless affect, as she hints at in these lines, but to investigate the phenomenal world.

Kyger's early poems collaged fragments of thought, perception, and description into a larger, epic or historical, design; in this respect, she follows in the lineage of **T.S. Eliot** and **Ezra Pound**. At the same time, her poems attend to speech, the line, and the seemingly mundane; in this, **William Carlos Williams** is an obvious influence. This combination provided a way to work daily female experience into the poetic modes vaunted by her postwar mentors and peers, although in later poems she departs from this mode to reinvent herself poetically. Perhaps Kyger's largest contribution to American poetry is a poetic form derived from a seemingly daily, ritual practice. Individual poems often, but not always, include a date of composition, and they are, for the most part, short, conversational, devotional, and journalistic. They never stand apart from or outside of time and the interactions, both collective and individual, that mark it. Her poems exhibit an elegant formalism that makes them immediately recognizable. Her "vocally sculpted" (Notley, 95) lines are often positioned at slightly different distances from the left-hand margin and appear to levitate cloudlike in the middle of the page. This visual effect contributes to a sense of motion and perceptual immediacy. Kyger's influence is attested in the words of her younger near-contemporary **Alice Notley**, for whom Kyger is "one of the women who's shown me how to speak as myself, to be intelligent in the way I wish and am, rather than suiting the requirements of established intellectuality" (108).

Kyger grew up in Southern California and attended the University of Santa Barbara before moving north and encountering her early mentors, who were members of the **San Francisco Renaissance**. During the brief period in which Kyger first lived in the San Francisco (1957 to 1959), **Robert Duncan**'s mythic consciousness and **Jack Spicer**'s exactitude exerted more influence on her than the jazzy street vernacular of the **Beat** poets who were then coming into prominence. Yet, as witnessed in poems and journals she wrote during her travels in Japan and India with then husband **Gary Snyder** (chronicled in *Strange Big Moon* [2000]), she shares an affinity for Buddhism with the Beats; this translates in her work to an attention to nonlinear thinking and visionary consciousness. It was during this same period that she encountered **Charles Olson**'s essay "**Projective Verse**" and began to develop her own style of "open field" poetics; in this she exhibits an affinity to the **Black Mountain School**. The witty and conversational aspect of her poems reveals her connections to the second-generation **New York School** of poets—Kyger befriended **Anne Waldman**, Lewis Warsh,

Ted Berrigan, Tom Clark, and others in the late 1960s while living in New York. In 1969 she moved to Bolinas, California, where she joined a community of poets who have come to be known as the loosely defined Bolinas School, which has included (at different times) Bill Berkson, Tom Clark, **Robert Creeley**, **Bob Grenier**, **Aram Saroyan**, **Philip Whalen**, and others. In Bolinas she worked to form the "bio-consciousness" that was definitive of the "greening" of certain regions and communities in the United States at the time. "The Mesa" in Bolinas is now her home. Kyger has authored over eighteen books of poetry since *The Tapestry and the Web* was published in 1965.

Despite her "unlocatable" status, location has always been central to her poetics as a source of social, cultural, historical, and geographical investigation. This is evident in works such as *The Wonderful Focus of You* (1979), whose opening section "Out My Window, begins with a poem," characteristically untitled and dated ("April 4"), begins in the pose of wonderment and observation: "The same landscape only changed / by the progression of time"(1). As in many of her poems, material persistence inspires thoughts about the impermanence of human existence and relationships. The next poem, "The Brain Impressed in Its Oddities," contains the line "But how on earth do we *live*" (3). The question of being, of surviving, is particularly relevant in the case of a female poet in an era in which her work would likely be overshadowed by that of her male peers. For example, though Kyger contributed to *A Curriculum of the Soul*—a series of pamphlets brought out beginning in 1972 by the Institute of Further Studies as an homage to Charles Olson—the original twenty-eight–volume lineup consisted of male poets only. Kyger is among three women invited to take over various slots (after the death of an original contributor, for example). Her contribution, *Phenomenological* (1989), in the spirit of Olson, chronicles a 1985 trip to the Yucatan Peninsula. This travel poem, while it accounts for the daily concerns and records details and historical facts, reveals a geopolitical situation that *also* defines her experience of Mayan culture: U.S. teenagers riding "up and down on / history's past conquests" (n.p.), a Tonto poster in an American-cowboy style restaurant, a pair of sunglasses made in Korea encountered on a beach. Kyger muses about the Yucatan Olson observed in his *Mayan Letters* thirty years previous: "so much / emptier" (n.p.).

Such layerings are a consistent, significant feature of her work. Her first book of poems, for example, written both in San Francisco and in Japan (and published shortly after her return to San Francisco), features San Francisco-as-Ithaca in a series of "Penelope" and "Odyssey" poems. *The Tapestry and the Web* (1965) stands beside **H.D.**'s *Helen in Egypt* (1961) as an act of imaginative intervention into epic invention; both poets reconfigure female epic figures, dominant gender ideologies, and transmitted histories such that the epic is made new. Unlike H.D., Kyger makes no pretense of re-narrating events as an alternative, imaginative history. Instead, she treats the page as a canvas and interweaves fragments of the mythic and the daily. As Kyger writes in the third "Tapestry" poem, she chose to work "with the detail / on the fragment" and to search "for bigger & better things" (*Tapestry*, 40). Her nonlinear narrative technique stems from her reading of Homer; a spacious, tapestry-like weaving of thoughts and perceptions is a common structural device in her work, as reflected in other early books constituted in whole or in part by longer (or serial) poems (*Places to Go* and *Desecheo Notebook*, for instance) and in more recent books collecting short poems that address related themes (such as *Some Life* and *Again*).

Kyger's second book, *Places to Go*, marks a turning point in which she critiques the Western, rationalistic mode of thought that her earlier book had attempted to incorporate. "DESCARTES AND THE SPLENDOR OF: *A Real Drama of Everyday Life*" parodies the pursuit of "PURELY EXECUTED REASON" (*Places to Go*, 90) and begins to chip away at notions of perfection and order that are foundational to her inherited epistemology. Although it rejects Cartesianism and empiricist thinking, it preserves the value of knowledge through self-discovery; indeed, travel becomes a mode for this, as exhibited in several books written in Mexico (*Mexico Blondé* [1981], *Phenomenological*, and *Patzcuaro* [1999]). In later books, her approach changes from parody to instruction and contemplation, in the mode of Buddhist thought: "What is this self / I think I will lose if I leave what I know" (*As Ever*, 157); mythic figures of Eastern religion frequently appear in her work, and the mythological as a parallel, living universe to which the individual is linked by the particular action of the poem is often invoked to reconcile fleeting earthly existence. In "Recently," for example, spring flowers are depicted as "Opening flashes to an underworld of historical familiarity," and yet the knowledge of history is not the coup d'etat: "awakening" resides "down under where memory is myth" (*Again*, 166).

At the heart of Kyger's poems is the desire to make "saying" the equivalent of "being." This is reflected in "Ah Phooey," a poem that protests an editor's diagnosis that an essay "on **Eco-Poetics**" is in need of revision; for Kyger her work amplifies "Real notes"—she cites the crickets' chatter "back and forth in their particular rhythmic tone / varying with your thoughts" as an analogy for composition (*Again,* 162). She comments retrospectively on her hybrid poetics in "The Fog Is Halfway over the Mesa": "combining / these strands into a useful cord, a thread / to throw into the dream" to form a clear, if provisional, picture (*As Ever*, 302).

Further Reading. ***Selected Primary Sources:*** Kyger, Joanne, *Again: Poems 1989–2000* (Albuquerque, NM: Alameda, 2001); ———, *As Ever: Selected Poems* (New York: Penguin, 2002); ———, *Desecheo Notebook* (Berkeley, CA: Arif, 1971); ———, *Joanne* (Bolinas, CA: Angel Hair, 1970); ———, *Mexico Blondé* (Bolinas, CA: Evergreen, 1981); ———, *Patzcuaro* (Bolinas, CA: Blue Millennium 1999); ———, *Phenomenological* (Canton, NY: Grove, 1989); ———, *Places to Go* (Los Angeles: Black Sparrow, 1970); ———, *Some Life* (Sausalito, CA: Post-Apollo, 2000); ———, *Strange Big Moon: The Japan and India Journals: 1960–1964* (Berkeley, CA: North Atlantic, 2000); ———, *The Tapestry and the Web* (San Francisco: Four Seasons, 1965); ———, *The Wonderful Focus of You* (Calais, VT: Z Press, 1979). ***Selected Secondary Sources:*** Berkson, Bill, "Joanne Kyger," in *Dictionary of Literary Biography, Vol.16: The Beats: Literary Bohemians in Postwar America* (Detroit, MI: Gale Research, 1983, 324–328); Notly, Alice, "Joanne Kyger's Poetry" (*Arshile: A Magazine of the Arts* 5 [1996]: 95–110); Russo, Linda, "Dealing in Parts and Particulars: Joanne Kyger's Early Epic Poetics," in *Girls Who Wore Black: Women Writing the Beat Generation*, ed. Nancy Grace and Rhonna Johnson (New Brunswick, NJ: Rutgers, 2002); Russo, Linda, ed., *Joanne Kyger Feature* (*Jacket Magazine* 11 [April 2000], http://www.jacketmagazine.com/11/index.html).

Linda Russo

L

LANGUAGE POETRY

A large discrepancy exists between the number of people who hold an opinion about Language poetry and those who have actually read it. As an indicator of this gap, a primer on "The Poetry Pantheon" in the *New York Times Magazine* (19 February 1995) lists Paul Hoover, **Ann Lauterbach**, and **Leslie Scalapino** as the most representative Language poets—a curious choice given that neither Hoover nor Lauterbach appears in any of the defining publications of Language poetry, and that Scalapino, though she came to be associated with Language poetry, is far from a central figure. Only a quarter-century after the phrase was first used, "Language poetry" has come to serve as an umbrella term for any kind of self-consciously **postmodern** poetry or to indicate vague stylistic characteristics—parataxis, dryly apodictic abstractions, elliptical modes of disjunction—even when they appear in works fundamentally opposed to the radical poetics that originally gave such notoriety to the name.

The term "Language poetry" may have first been used by **Bruce Andrews**, in correspondence from the early 1970s, to distinguish poets such as Vito Hannibal Acconci, Carl Andre, **Clark Coolidge**, and **Jackson Mac Low**, whose writing challenged the vatic aspirations of **Deep Image** poetry. In the tradition of **Gertrude Stein** and **Louis Zukofksy**, such poetry found precedents in

only the most anomalous contemporary writing, such as **John Ashbery**'s *The Tennis Court Oath* (1962), **Joseph Ceravolo**'s *Fits of Dawn* (1965), **Aram Saroyan**'s *Cofee Coffe* (1967), or **Jack Kerouac**'s *Old Angel Midnight* (1959/1964). On the one hand, such writing stood in contrast to Deep Image poetry and the anti-intellectual and speech-based **poetics** that characterized the various counter-culture schools—**Beat**, **Black Mountain School**, **New York School**, **San Francisco Renaissance**, and so forth—presented in Donald Allen's *New American Poetry* (1960). On the other hand, such writing also challenged the confessional poetry of the East Coast establishment and the emphasis on "voice" and "craft" in the increasingly ubiquitous creative writing workshop. In both cases, the dominant mode in poetry took personal and emotive expression as its basis. Language poetry, by contrast, valued artifice over nature, writing over speech, metonymy over metaphor, and intellect over sentiment.

In 1973 Bruce Andrews edited a number of the journal *Toothpick, Lisbon, and the Orcas Islands*. Based on the eclectic radicalism of the journal *0 to 9*, which had been edited by Vito Acconci and **Bernadette Mayer** in the late 1960s, Andrews's collection was the first clear indicator of the degree to which the poetic avant-garde of the 1970s would challenge the assumptions of contemporaneous poetry. A more focused, strategic, and self-conscious grouping of the avant-garde mode that would come to be termed "Language poetry" appeared in 1975, when **Ron Silliman** edited a suite of work for the **ethnopoetics** journal *Alcheringa*. His telegraphic headnote to the selections reads

> 9 poets out of the present, average age 28, whose work might be said to "cluster" about such magazines as *This*, *Big Deal*, *Tottel's*, the recent *Doones* supplements, the Andrews-edited issue of *Toothpick*, etc. Called variously "language centered," "minimal," "non-referential formalism," "diminished referentiality," "structuralist." Not a *group*, but a *tendency* in the work of many. (104)

In addition to Silliman himself, those "language centered" writers comprised Bruce Andrews, Barbara Barracks, Clark Coolidge, Lee DeJasu, **Ray DiPalma**, **Robert Grenier**, David Melnick, and **Barrett Watten**. As other writers of "diminished referentiality" came into dialogue with one another, beginning to appear less like a tendency and more like a group, "Language poetry" took on the stability of a proper name. In an essay published in 1977, introducing such work to a Canadian audience, **Steve McCaffery** uses the phrase in this nominal sense, and through an association with the title of the journal *L=A=N=G=U=A=G=E* (edited by Andrews and **Charles Bernstein**), the name stuck.

In 1982 two other magazine collections attempted to present Language poetry to a general poetry audience. The provocatively titled "Realism" appeared in the journal *Ironwood*, again edited by Silliman, with an annotating essay by Kathleen Fraser, and the *Paris Review* presented a "Language Sampler," edited by Charles Bernstein. Two subsequent book anthologies, Silliman's *In the American Tree: Language, Realism, Poetry* (1986) and **Douglas Messerli**'s *"Language" Poetries* (1987), further expanded—and complicated—the landscape of names most associated with Language poets. In addition to Andrews, DiPalma, and Watten, who appear in all five of these collections, the most frequently included writers are Charles Bernstein, Clark Coolidge, Tina Darragh, Alan Davies, **Robert Grenier**, **Carla Harryman**, **Lyn Hejinian**, P. Inman, **Bob Perelman**, Peter Seaton, James Sherry, Ron Silliman, **Diane Ward**, and **Hanna Weiner**. One also finds, with slightly less frequent appearances, **Rae Armantrout**, Alan Bernheimer, Michael Gottlieb, Ted Greenwald, and **Susan Howe**. Although they are not a presence in these particular collections, **Michael Davidson**, **Michael Palmer**, Steve McCaffery, and Tom Raworth have also been closely associated with Language poetry; other writers who worked under its sign include **David Bromige**, Tom Beckett, Steve Benson, Abigail Child, Lynne Dreyer, Erica Hunt, David Melnick, Nick Piombino, Stephen Rodefer, Kit Robinson, and Fiona Templeton.

Unlike many earlier **avant-garde** movements, Language poetry was never defined by an official membership list or shared manifesto; the sense of a cohesive movement came in part from the surprisingly consistent roster of participants in a relatively closed economy of journal and book publishing, reviewing, and readings. Many of the writers, that is, were also creating the very venues in which each other's work appeared by editing journals, publishing small press books and chapbook series, producing radio programs, or curating reading and lecture series. Rather than working within already established institutions of publication and promotion, these writers established parallel sets of institutions. In particular, they put out journals devoted to poetry (including, in rough chronology, *Joglars*, *Tottle's*, *This*, *Hills*, *A Hundred Posters*, *Roof*, and *Miam*) as well as journals more focused on theory, criticism, and reviews (including *L=A=N=G=U=A=G=E*, *The Difficulties*, *Paper Air*, *Temblor*, *Poetics Journal*, and *Jimmy & Lucy's House of "K"*). Moreover, the availability of increasingly affordable print technology in the 1970s permitted individuals to found a number of new presses, including The Figures, Tuumba, Sun & Moon, This, Potes and Poets, Pod, Asylum's, O Press, Awede, and Burning Deck. Additionally, programs such as Lyn Hejinian and Kit Robinson's "In the American Tree" (KPFA), Susan Howe's "Poetry" (WBAI), and Bob Perelman's "Talks Series" provided forums for the further dissemination of the new poetry and poetics.

Indeed, the robust discussions of poetics and the simultaneous production of both poetical and theoretical texts came to be seen as a hallmark of Language poetry. The familiar references to the writings of the Frankfurt School, French deconstruction, and Russian formalism, taken together with the highly visible, lively, and sometimes strident debates over poetics, the conception of poetry as an intellectual art, and the development of hybrid forms of writing that combined poetry and criticism (such as the collage style of review essay showcased in *L=A=N=G=U=A=G=E*), led some detractors to charge that the tail of theory was wagging the dog of poetry. The publication record and correspondence of the poets does not support this premise, but Language poets did set themselves apart by the assumption that poets would articulate their writerly projects in intellectual and theoretically grounded terms.

A further sense of coterie emerged as the personal and social relationships between these writers developed, with communities coalescing in the San Francisco Bay Area, and less visibly in New York City and Washington D.C., where Michael Lally and Doug Lang energized a politicized avant-garde writing scene. However, one of the most striking aspects of the parallel institutions that developed around Language poetry points away from coterie and toward a larger audience of interested readers. In addition to new presses and journals, an unprecedented network of formal distribution was elaborated and established. In addition to Berkeley's Small Press Distribution (which replaced the distribution service that had been run out of Serendipity Books since 1969), New York's Segue Book Distribution (in operation from 1980 to 1993 and associated with Roof Books and *Roof* magazine), and to a lesser extent the Minneapolis-based Bookslinger (which began as Truck Distribution in 1976, and operated until 1993), disseminated the hundreds of **small press** books published by Language poets.

As the wider audience for Language poetry emerged and the social groupings of its participants solidified, the presumption of a collective program, homogeneous style, or shared poetics made many of the writers anxious about the term itself, which for a time was often put in scare quotes and reduced to "so-called 'language' poetry," just as the inclusion or exclusion of equals signs between the letters, in imitation of the journal's name, seemed to require justification by critics and reviewers. As the term eventually came to be more or less grudgingly accepted even by the writers themselves, the nagging question of a defining poetics, accordingly, remained—as did the increasingly obvious fact that any strict or unifying definition would require so many exceptions as to be of little use. Nonetheless, critics have noted various aspects of a family resemblance; and regardless of their applicability to the poetry itself, one can easily trace repeated themes in the discussion about Language poetry.

The comforting fiction of a unified **lyric** subject, for instance, has been a frequent target of Language poetry. As Charles Bernstein summed it up: To take the self as the primary organizing principle of writing would be a mistake. (*Content's Dream*, 408) For many of the language writers, that self was replaced with an Althusserian subject, constructed at the intersection of social institutions, and the poet was understood as an "author function" in Foucauldian terms. Others envisioned a multiple and contradictory subject in the terms proposed by Gilles Deleuze and Félix Guattari; still others picked up on the poetic tradition of Arthur Rimbaud, for whom "*Je* est un autre (The 'I' is an other)." As the force of the authorial "I" was dispersed in these ways, an attendant argument for the empowerment of the reader was proposed. Based on Umberto Eco's model of the "open" text, and encouraged by Roland Barthes's prediction that "the death of the author" would be predicated on the birth of the reader, Language poets frequently invoked the figure of an active reader collaboratively constructing meanings rather than passively receiving the writer's message.

This reconceptualization of the relation between writer and reader was one of the ways that Language poetry pitted itself against a model of language in which communication was imagined as a "conduit," "transom," or "bullet." In that model, a sender was seen to transfer a stable message to a receiver with little flux or interference. By focusing instead on the materiality of the message and the context of its transmission, Language poets continued to modify and reconfigure the communicative model, repeatedly questioning the naturalness of language in the process. Many early works, including *zaum*-like compositions of nonce words, cultivated indeterminacy or organized language in terms of its material properties rather than its discursive message. With a focus on an independent linguistic sign that was not subservient to its referent, these poems foreground their own text rather than being oriented toward any external reference. At the same time, many poems displayed an analogous interest in testing the seemingly natural fit and hierarchical relation between signifier and signified.

In the late 1970s many of the writers associated with Language poetry began to shift their attention to longer prose works and to develop the distinctive mode of radically disjunctive parataxis that Ron Silliman termed "the new sentence." Such writing would characterize much of Language poetry in the 1980s, but even with this new style's tendency toward fewer grammatical disruptions and a greater interest in discursive social speech, the poems continued to emphasize the constructedness and artifice of writing, rather than any kind of natural or unmediated expression. In part, this defamiliarization was inspired by Russian formalism and took the form of estranging colloquial language or laying bare the devices by which literary language achieved its effects. But the sense of linguistic estrangement was also influenced by the Sapir-Whorf hypothesis that language constructs reality rather than describes it, inflecting rather than reflecting our experience. A similar sense of the relation between the social and linguistic provided the ground for the political dimension many Language poets claimed for their writing. Continuing the dream of the twentieth century's avant-gardes, this claim proposed that disruptions in the textual order were analogous to, or could even provoke, disruptions in the social order.

Although those political goals may not have been achieved, Language poetry did succeed in affecting the style of many poets—even those far removed from the history and assumptions of Language poetry—who have acquired a greater tolerance for disjunction, disruption, and abstraction in the wake of Language poetry's more radical example. The phenomenon of Language poetry is still too recent and evolving to permit any definitive conclusions about its ultimate transformation or demise, but if literary history is any guide, two conditions will define the fate of Language poetry's future. First, from any broader perspective on American poetry in general, individual writers will emerge as more or less significant poets, regardless of any group affiliation or activities.

Second, the initial function of Language poetry as an avant-garde challenging dominant poetic modes and established institutions will be taken on not by writing that continues in the Language poetry vein (second- or third-generation Language poetry, or its imitators), but by one of the modes that Language poetry itself refused, repressed, or could not at the time imagine: conceptual, procedural, visual, digital, and so forth.

Further Reading. ***Selected Primary Sources:*** Andrews, Bruce, and Charles Bernstein, eds., *L=A=N=G=U=A=G=E* (selections as *The Language Book*) (Carbondale: Southern Illinois University Press, 1984), www.princeton.edu/eclipse; Andrews, Bruce, Charles Bernstein, Ray DiPalma, Steve McCaffery, and Ron Silliman, *LEGEND* (New York: Language/Segue, 1980); McCaffery, Steve, "The Politics of the Referent" (*Open Letter,* ser. 3, 7 [Summer 1977]); Messerli, Douglas, ed., *"Language" Poetries: An Anthology* (New York: New Directions, 1987); Silliman, Ron, ed., *In the American Tree* (Orono, ME: National Poetry Foundation, 1986). ***Selected Secondary Sources:*** Bernstein, Charles, *Content's Dream: Essays 1975–1984* (Los Angeles: Sun & Moon Press, 1986; reprint Evanston, IL: Northwestern University Press, 2001); Lloyd, David, "Limits of a Language of Desire" (*Poetics* 5 [May 1985]: 159–167); McCaffery, Steve, *North of Intention: Critical Writings 1973–1986* (New York: Roof, 1986); Perloff, Marjorie, "The Word as Such: L=A=N=G=U=A=G=E Poetry in the Eighties," in *The Dance of the Intellect: Studies in the Poetry of the Pound Tradition* (Evanston, IL: Northwestern University Press, 1996, 215–238); Silliman, Ron, *The New Sentence* (New York: Roof, 1987).

Craig Dworkin

LANIER, SIDNEY COPTON (1842–1881)

In the years shortly following the close of the American Civil War, Sidney Lanier seemed literally to embody the fading ideology of the Confederate lost cause. Here irony mixes with pathos, because Lanier was never fired with strong sectional feeling. He came to the war a cavalier, not an ideologue. Yet his wasting body—weakened with the disease he contracted in a Northern prison camp—personified the suffering the South subsequently endured during Reconstruction. In this way, he became not simply a voice but an icon.

This is perhaps best seen in Baltimore sculptor Hans Schuler's bronze and granite monument on the fringes of the Johns Hopkins University campus in Baltimore, Maryland, where Lanier taught briefly before he died. It depicts him in an intensely private moment, not as a vigorous man in a public, civic, or performative role, any of which he would have easily adopted during his lifetime, but as a recumbent figure, sitting with his legs crossed indifferently before him, in an act of composition, pencil in hand, with hat, coat, and flute tossed at his side. It

evokes a mood that is meditative, pensive, and wearied. Less imposing than retiring, it is more of an anti-monument, content in its obscurity. It is a poignant symbol of a waning sensibility that Lanier struggled to shape poetically but which ultimately yielded to an irresistible set of imperatives and realities. This is unfortunate, because it gives only a hint of his true cultural importance, which is that of an intermediary, whose impulses and achievements were as thoroughly social as they were personal, pointing to the future while artfully encoding the past.

The eldest of three children born to Robert Sampson and Mary Jane Anderson Lanier, Sidney Lanier was born in Macon, Georgia, on February 3, 1842. His paternal grandfather, capitalizing on Macon's development as a commercial and transportation center, operated a hotel there. He appears to have been a man of means, which he was not loath to share. He provided the funds for one son to tour Europe and for another, Sidney's father, to pursue his education at Randolph-Macon, a Methodist college in Ashland, Virginia. Although he never achieved distinction in his chosen profession, the law, Robert Sampson Lanier presided over a household that was loving and happy.

Educated in a local academy and then privately, Sidney Lanier entered Oglethorpe University, a Presbyterian school favored by his mother, in January 1857. Its president was Samuel K. Talmadge, who had connections to New Jersey and Princeton. He fostered a Calvinism that was persuasive and, to the impressionable student, formative. Lanier read Carlyle, which, in turn, led him to read the German Romantic writers. He also came under the influence of James Woodrow, whose ideas on evolution would later lead to condemnation at the General Assembly of the Presbyterian Church. (Woodrow's sister was the mother of Woodrow Wilson.) He arranged for Lanier to secure an appointment as tutor at Oglethorpe upon graduation in 1860.

He had begun to write poetry and had become an accomplished, virtually self-taught, flautist. Acceding to his parents' view that music was not a suitable profession for a gentleman, Lanier hoped to prepare for an academic career in Germany at Heidelberg, following Woodrow's example. But war intervened.

Macon was the site of early and strenuous reaction to the result of the election of 1860, declaring its independence the same month that Lincoln was elected. Lanier, whose conception of war, like that of any Southern gallant, was filtered through the Waverly novels and the chronicles of Froissart, later wrote in his novel *Tiger-Lilies,* set during this period, that "the new war-idea" had "arranged the sanctity of a righteous cause in the brilliant trappings of military display, pleasing, so, the devout and the flippant which in various proportions are mixed elements in all men" (Starke, 42). In June 1861, shortly after finishing his work at Oglethorpe, he, along with his brother Clifford, volunteered for military service and immediately proceeded to Virginia, serving at Drury's Bluff when the ironclad *Monitor* fired upon Confederate fortifications there in May 1862. The following month he participated in the Seven Days campaign in which he may have been wounded. In August he joined the Mounted Signal Service. During this period he found time to pursue his study of German poetry, attempting to translate poems of Heine, Goethe, and Schiller. He also composed pieces for the flute, setting to music some of Tennyson's poems.

In 1864 he saw action in Petersburg and was subsequently assigned to blockade duty in Wilmington, North Carolina. He was almost immediately captured and sent in November 1864 to Point Lookout, a Northern prison camp for enlisted men in Maryland, where he was to spend the duration of the war, a tenure that was moderately fruitful but ultimately disastrous.

Conditions in the camp were harsh, unsanitary, and characterized by a cruel instability and injustice. Approximately four thousand men are known to have died during the twenty-two months it was in operation, most from disease. The camp was grossly overcrowded—designed to hold ten thousand prisoners, it held as many as twenty thousand after Union General Ulysses S. Grant stopped prisoner exchanges. Lanier rarely revisited this period in his life, but he bore its effects, having contracted a form of consumption that was, in the end, to prove fatal.

At the camp he met and befriended **John Banister Tabb**, a fellow blockade runner then still in his teens. Tabb would later convert from Anglicanism to Catholicism and receive Holy Orders. Unlike Lanier, Tabb never overcame the affronts of that period in his life. Like Lanier, however, he was drawn to poetry and music, finding some recompense in the joy he experienced in hearing Lanier play the flute. He would later write, "When palsied at the pool of thought / The poet's words were found, / Thy voice the healing angel brought / To touch them into sound." Lanier and Tabb would remain friends after the war. At Point Lookout, Lanier continued his study of German poetry and completed his translations of some lyrics of Heine and Herder.

He was released in February 1865, perhaps by paying a bribe with gold a friend managed to smuggle into the camp, and returned to Macon, securing various jobs in education as well as work as a hotel clerk. Abandoning hope of an academic career, he worked for a brief time in his father's law firm. Conscious of the need for a restoration of Southern letters, he wrote poetry for publication and obtained the assistance of a wealthy cousin, the financier J.F.D. Lanier, to help underwrite the publication in New York of his novel *Tiger-Lilies*. Upon its appearance, reviewers framed it in regional terms and characterized him as a Southern figure to follow. In December 1867, he married Mary Day at Christ Church (Episcopal) in Macon.

The marriage, a happy and fruitful one, would last fourteen years. For much of this time, Lanier traveled in pursuit alternately of a cure and a suitable position. Lanier and Mary engaged in an ardent and richly detailed correspondence that offers considerable insight into Lanier's activities and state of mind. It reveals a man of strong character, formed in the Southern tradition of duty, honor, and civility, but nevertheless unsettled by powerful artistic impulses, which are themselves conflicted between compelling desires to perform on the flute and write lyric poetry. His travels took him to New York on several occasions, where he found the opportunity to hear performances of symphonic music (then something of a novelty in the United States).

In 1872 he went to San Antonio, Texas, which at the time had a substantial German community that promoted musical performance. Lanier performed with several local ensembles. He also wrote and published a group of short essays on Texas history and culture. The move to San Antonio had been taken in the hope of restoring his health. In that respect it was a failure. He became more attuned and reconciled to his inevitable death and, accordingly, determined to spend his remaining years pursuing his musical and literary passions.

In April 1873 he again ventured to New York, determined to seek an orchestral position. En route, he stopped in Baltimore and visited his friend Henry Clay Wysham, a lawyer and amateur musician, who introduced him to Asger Hamerik, the Danish-born, French-trained composer, theorist, and—most crucially for Lanier—conductor. Hamerik, a protégé of Berlioz, had become director of the Academy of Music (later Peabody Conservatory of Music) in 1871 and was making arrangements to form a full-time professional symphony orchestra in Baltimore. After hearing Lanier play some of his own compositions on the flute, Hamerik immediately offered him the position of first flautist in the unorganized orchestra. Although Lanier's sojourn to New York was a critical success, he had not secured an orchestral position when Hamerik contacted him to say that the orchestra had been formed. Lanier returned to Baltimore, where he was to make his home until his death, accepting the position on reduced terms and on a shortened schedule.

At this moment in its history, Baltimore was in a vexed and complicated political state of affairs. Many of its citizens had been strongly sympathetic to the South, and the North staffed the city with what was in essence an occupying force. More than a few members of its professional and political elite were still smarting from rough treatment endured at federal hands during the Civil War. At the same time, the city prospered in the postwar years with the expansion of trade and the manufacture and consumption of goods. It rose in size, wealth, and productive capacity. Despite this, it lacked the cultural institutions of the great European cities. Led by George Peabody, who by this time had set up permanent residence in London while retaining a strong affection for the city where he began to amass his fortune, people of wealth and position initiated a cultural campaign in the fields of art, music, education, and medicine. Baltimore became a major center in these and related fields. Lanier's arrival occurred during its first burgeoning years. He felt that at last he had found his true métier.

In a November 29, 1873, letter to his father, who wrote suggesting that Sidney return to Macon to resume the practice of law, Lanier movingly reveals the stakes he sees for himself as an artist:

> My dear father, think how, for twenty years, through poverty, through pain, through weariness, through the uncongenial atmosphere of a farcical college and of a bare army and then of an exacting business life, through all the discouragement of being wholly unacquainted with literary people and literary ways—I say, think how, in spite of all these depressing circumstances, and of a thousand more which I could enumerate, these two figures of music and of poetry have steadily kept in my heart so that I could not banish them. (Starke, 168)

More than one observer has claimed the reference to "farcical" Oglethorpe to be unfair and overstated. But the letter reveals that the strength of filial ties has yielded to a determination to exercise more freely his mounting creative energies. It also suggests that he conceived of his artistry in performative and social terms, not as an alienated isolé. His art was fundamentally discursive and founded on a thriving geniality. Here he could perform, lecture, and write.

In 1876 he settled his family in Baltimore. He had established himself as a favored performer not only under the baton of Hamerik but with other performing ensembles in the region. His poetry had achieved national renown in 1874 with the publication of "Corn" in *Lippincott's*, a Philadelphia rival to the Boston-based *Atlantic.* In 1876 he worked on a commission for the U.S. Centennial Commission, the words to a cantata composed by Dudley Buck. Writing about the performance thirty years later, the former president of Johns Hopkins University, Daniel Coit Gilman, recalled that "[w]ords and music, voices and instruments, produced an impression as remarkable as the rendering of the Hallelujah Chorus in the nave of Westminster Abbey. It was an opportunity of a lifetime to test upon a grand scale his theory of verse. He came off victorious." (Starke, 244)

The following year J.B. Lippincott published *Poems,* the only volume of Lanier's poetry to appear during his lifetime. He achieved continued success as a public lecturer, and in 1879 Johns Hopkins University invited him to join its faculty. His lectures were collected in *Science of English Verse* (1880), which enjoyed a period of critical influence into the twentieth century.

By 1881 Lanier could no longer lecture on his feet. Seeking—vainly—relief for his deteriorating health in the mountains of North Carolina, Lanier traveled to Asheville, where he joined his brother and family and worked on a number of literary and scientific projects. He continued, however, to weaken, and he died on September 7, 1881. His body was carried to Baltimore, where, after services at the Anglo-Catholic Church of St. Michael and All Angels, he was buried in Greenmount Cemetery in a plot provided by family friends, the Turnbulls.

It is undeniable that Lanier was animated by great ambition, demonstrated in all of his work—as critic and as orator, but chiefly as musician and poet. In this he shares the impulse and aims of the great Romantic poets. He perhaps overemphasized poetic technique at the expense of the imagination—and this is not solely a theoretical issue, since the emphasis affected his poetic practice, especially his metrics. At the same time, he can be seen as the bridge between John Keats and **Wallace Stevens**. That is, the poems are at once seminal, providing as they do an imaginative audacity that anticipates the grandeur of Stevens, and belated, because they hark back to the ebullience of Keats. In any event, the speaker of the poems invariably mediates too much, imposing a sensibility that is frequently redundant. Writing in another dark time, **W. H. Auden** modestly epitomized poetry as a mouth. One cannot help but believe that Lanier, who was temperamentally disposed to agree, would have derived great benefit from this image.

At one time he enjoyed critical respect. Poems such as "Corn," "The Song of the Chattahoochee," "The Marshes of Glynn," and his last poem, "Sunrise," gained him a national audience and serious professional attention. He also benefited from popular interest, and he was extolled as a true Southern bard. But he has been crowded out. Once ranked alongside **Poe** and **Whitman**, he no longer figures so prominently in the **canon**. Today, his reputation is hampered less by disdain than by an intractable indifference.

Further Reading. *Selected Primary Sources:* Lanier, Sidney, *The Centennial Edition of the Works of Sidney Lanier*, 10 vols, ed. Charles R. Anderson (Baltimore: The Johns Hopkins University Press, 1945). ***Selected Secondary Sources:*** DeBellis, Jack, *Sidney Lanier* (New York: Twayne, 1972); ———, *Sidney Lanier, Henry Timrod, and Paul Hamilton Hayne: A Reference Guide*

(Boston: G.K. Hall, 1978); ———, *Sidney Lanier: Poet of the Marshes* (Atlanta: Georgia Humanities Council, 1988); Gabin, Jane S., *A Living Minstrelsy: The Poetry and Music of Sidney Lanier* (Macon, GA: Mercer University Press, 1985); Starke, Aubrey H., *Sidney Lanier: A Biography and Critical Study* (Chapel Hill: University of North Carolina Press, 1933).

John P. Koontz

LANSING, GERRIT (1928–)

Gerrit Lansing is not a member of any school of poetry, and his verse does not resemble that of anyone else. To chart a poetic lineage it is necessary to evoke a host of forebears. Among Lansing's are the American Transcendentalists (particularly **Emerson**, **Thoreau**, and **Frederick Goddard Tuckerman**), the late French **Symbolists**, and the surrealists. Contemporary poets with whom Lansing shares certain affinities include **Robert Duncan**, **Charles Olson**, **Robert Kelly**, Stephen Jonas, **John Wieners**, and **Robin Blaser**. Lansing's greatest debt, however, is to three primary inspirations: the natural world, love, and magic. Magic includes not just what he has discovered in the work of Aleister Crowley but also material in much older esoteric texts, ranging from the Kabbalah to Sufism, and in the hermetic philosophy of Paracelsus and Hermes Trismegistus. In essence, what Lansing has done is to unify all of his learning, associations, and experience, and use it as material for his poetry.

Lansing was born in Illinois and educated at Harvard. After graduating in 1949 he moved to New York, where he enrolled at Columbia, earning an MA in English literature. Subsequently he worked in publishing. At Harvard he knew **John Ashbery** and **Kenward Elmslie**; after the move to New York, his circle enlarged to include, among many other poets, **Frank O'Hara**, **Kenneth Koch**, **Robert Creeley**, **Diane Di Prima**, and **Jonathan Williams**. In 1958 he moved to Gloucester, Massachusetts, the town with which he is most associated. There he became friends with Charles Olson, and with the Boston poets Stephen Jonas and John Weiners. It was in Gloucester that he founded the short-lived but highly influential magazine *Set* (1961–1964). From 1972 until 1982 he lived in Ft. Lauderdale, Florida, and Annapolis, Maryland, with his life partner, Deryk Burton, a yacht captain. In 1982 he returned to Gloucester, where he still resides. His first book of poems, *The Heavenly Tree Grows Downward*, was published by Matter Press in 1966, followed by an expanded volume with the same title in 1977 (North Atlantic Books). In 1995 Talisman House brought out *Heavenly Tree / Soluble Forest*, which includes generous portions of work from the earlier collections, as well as significant new material. (All quotations here are from this edition.) In 2003 Pressed Wafer issued a selection of Lansing's prose and poetry, *A February Sheaf.*

The three principal themes in Lansing's work—nature, love, and magic—are fueled by an intense regard for language and precise diction, employing a wide range of imaginative imagery that frequently brings these three central concerns into a powerful harmony, or, in some cases, exquisite juxtaposition.

To best understand how these elements intertwine in Lansing's **poetics**, it is necessary to examine the concept of the heavenly tree, which provides a title to three of his collections. The image of the inverted tree, with its roots in the ether or heaven and its branches growing downward to the earth, is a symbol found in a range of ancient texts, most notably the Kabbalah. In the Kabbalah, this heaven-rooted tree represents spiritual growth, as well as being symbolic of the human nervous system, in which the "root" is centered in the brain and the "branches" extend throughout the body. For Lansing, this image is profound. It unites the corporeal with the spiritual, the heavenly with the earthly, and esoteric knowledge with lived experience.

These Imagistic and metaphorically rich concepts figure prominently in many of his poems. In "Perianth," for instance, the connection between the body, metaphysics, and nature is explicit. The poem opens with the statement: "By far the best farmers / lovers are / whose bodies glisten in the light they make / and throw so carelessly around them in molten afternoons." As the poem progresses, the imagery becomes more erotic even as it begins to meld with the esoteric: "Perianth is the word I wrote / . . . / to remind me of the floral unity of love / and also how we double on ourselves the world / when our bodies shoot / and the heavens open." Similarly, the concluding lines of his poem "The Dark Grammarian" unite even more succinctly these elements: "Mournful angels spire down his black syntax / To health. Mad and warm as children, they splash / And couple in the joyous sea."

That it is possible to embrace the physicality of the human experience as a natural being while also reaching beyond oneself into more metaphysical strata is not a contradiction. Indeed, for Lansing, as for Emerson and Crowley, the externality of experience always finds its way inside; the inner self always is looking out: "Within the skull the skill / within the winter dream the whirligig / within within / all & everything," he writes in "In Erasmus Darwin's Generous Light." The notion is stated even more emphatically in his **long poem** "Stanzas of Hyparxis": "Outer space and inner space misnomers / when what is meant (nomen, numen) / is rhymed in megalith and microspore / and mirror is parity non-conserved." The poem concludes with this explicit message: "How far out you go / it is within."

For Lansing, this ultimate looping back of outer experience and observation into the "within" is the major (and often magical) subject of poetry itself. Writing is itself an attempt to make something external of the internal. As such, it is an act of transformation, in which words and syntax and grammar are actors who play out their roles as guides to what would otherwise be unknowable. This is not to imply that meaning is fixed, even to the author himself. Writing is simply a guidepost pointing the way to further discovery. What the reader or writer discovers there is of his or her own making. This concept is perhaps best exemplified by these lines from his long poetic sequence *The Soluble Forest*: "A WRIT is a route, a way and the map of a way. It figures and we make of it our figure. I make it of mine. It is mind, and no mind, inner and dinner and outer and doubter."

Further Reading. ***Selected Primary Sources:*** Lansing, Gerrit, *A February Sheaf* (Boston: Pressed Wafer, 2003); ———, *Heavenly Tree / Soluble Forest* (Jersey City, NJ: Talisman House, 1995); ———, *The Heavenly Tree Grows Downward* (New York: Matter Press, 1966). ***Selected Secondary Sources:*** Baker, Robert, "The Metaphysics of Gerrit Lansing" (*Rain Taxi* [Fall 2001]); Foster, Edward, ed., Gerrit Lansing issue (*Talisman: A Journal of Contemporary Poetry and Poetics* [Winter 1995/1996]); Smith, Dale "On Poetry and the Occult" (*Skanky Possum* [August 2003]).

Christopher Sawyer-Lauçanno

LARCOM, LUCY (1824–1893)

Lucy Larcom, poet and essayist, wrote for periodicals and published twenty-five books, most of them poetry, but also an autobiography and several anthologies, the first three in collaboration with **John Greenleaf Whittier**. Although one of the earliest and youngest contributors to the *Lowell Offering*, she composed the bulk of her work after she left the Lowell, Massachusetts, mills. In her later years, she frequented Boston's literary circles, including the women's group that gathered around **Annie Adams Fields**, wife of **James T. Fields**, and editor and partner in Ticknor and Fields. Larcom's prose is graceful and meticulously crafted, but she is best known for her poetry. Overall, it possesses many characteristics representative of the rich, varied, and often overlooked contributions of nineteenth-century women poets.

Larcom, born in Beverly, Massachusetts, was the seventh of eight children. As her modern biographer, Shirley Marchalonis, points out, Larcom's life falls into six distinct periods (1–2). The first, her childhood, introduced her to poetry, particularly hymns, but ended when her father, Benjamin Larcom, died in 1832. Larcom and the younger children accompanied their mother to Lowell, Massachusetts, where she unsuccessfully ran a female mill workers' boarding house; indeed working in the mills from 1835 to 1846 initiated Larcom's literary career. Although mill girls worked long hours, Larcom read voraciously, joined the mill girls' Improvement Circle, and attended Lyceum lectures featuring such speakers as Ralph Waldo Emerson. Most important, her contributions to the mill girls' periodical, the *Lowell Offering*, gained her literary recognition and introduced her to her mentor-to-be, John Greenleaf Whittier. In the next period, 1846–1852, pioneering on the Illinois prairie, she taught in a district school; pursued her education at Monticello Seminary in Godfrey, Illinois; and became more fully qualified to teach. She also contributed poetry and essays to the *New England Offering* (formerly the *Lowell Offering*), the *National Era* (edited by Whittier), and other periodicals.

In 1852, disenchanted with rustic life in the West, Larcom returned to Massachusetts. From 1854 to 1863, she taught at Wheaton Seminary in Massachusetts. Although she resented teaching's demands on her time, her salary gave her financial independence. She also made the years at Wheaton creative and productive, publishing four books and contributing poetry and essays to *Arthur's Home Magazine*, the *Congregationalist*, the *Crayon*, the *Atlantic Monthly*, and other periodicals. The last two periods of Larcom's life were productive and satisfying. She met Annie Fields, became a regular at the Old Corner Bookstore, and, from 1864 to 1870, served as co-editor, then editor, of *Our Young Folks*, a children's magazine. By 1870 when the magazine was sold, Larcom had become physically and emotionally debilitated. She briefly returned to teaching, but soon resigned to concentrate on lecturing, editing, and writing. She died in Boston on April 17, 1893, financially independent and publicly acclaimed for her prose and poetry.

Larcom's poetic oeuvre is diverse, including occasional poetry, children's poetry, religious poetry, and nature meditations. *Poems* (1868), *Wild Roses of Cape Ann and Other Poetry* (1880), and the 1884 Household Edition of *Larcom's Poetical Works* [*Lucy Larcom's Poetry*] consist primarily of previously published material; *Larcom's Poetical Works*, the most complete, includes the previous two books and some new material, mostly nature meditations and religious poetry. *An Idyl of Work* (1875), her unsuccessful blank verse attempt at a novel, is marred by a weak plot; however, it presents many of Larcom's themes and vividly illustrates mill girls' lives and environment, which are also described in her autobiography, *A New England Girlhood* (1889). Her last book, *At the Beautiful Gate* (1892), affirms her religious faith and contains "Withdrawal," a moving meditation on John Greenleaf Whittier's death.

Her poetry is variously autobiographical, topical, and religious; her style varies but is for the most part lyric, narrative, or dramatic. Her best-known poems, such as "Hannah Binding Shoes" (1857) and "The Rose Enthroned" (1861), received great acclaim. "Hannah" vividly and poignantly narrates a woman's patient and helpless waiting for her husband, lost to the treacherous sea, one of Larcom's common themes. "The Rose Enthroned" is one of her most powerful poems; its length, controlled lines, and the religious symbolism of the rose and beauty underlie the parallel she draws between the chaotic formation of the world and mankind's upheaval during the Civil War, at the end of which "the rose can bloom." Other poems, including "A Little Old Girl" (1875), "Sylvia" (1872), and "Watching the Snow" (1869), address women's confinement, loneliness, and lack of autonomy. However, "Unwedded" (1868), a dramatic monologue, suggests that spinsterhood has its advantages for "many a mother, and many a wife, / Draws a lot more lonely, we all know well."

Several poems address the rewards of work, especially teaching; others address faith and death, nature's restorative powers, myth and legend, and the Civil War. "The Trees" (1885) employs one of Larcom's more complex analogies: "Never yet has poet sung a perfect song, / But his life was rooted like a tree's, among / Earth's great feeding forces." "A Loyal Woman's No" (1885), resonantly autobiographical, explains Larcom's broken engagement: "If such as you, when Freedom's ways are rough / Cannot walk in them, learn that women can!" "Weaving" (1885) addresses the Civil War and questions the reliance of Northern industrialism on Southern slavery, especially the work of women slaves, for "how much of your wrong is mine, / . . . / The bread you starve for fills my mouth."

Larcom's poetry explores a variety of verse forms and topics, personal and public, including women's lives, nature, politics, and religion. It was very popular, usually thoughtful, though sometimes **sentimental** and unevenly crafted. Nevertheless, her themes appealed to the public, and, because of the prolixity of periodicals and the increase in American literary publications in the nineteenth century, her verse reached an ever-increasing, largely female reading public. At her death, the *Boston Globe* called her "one of the best of our minor poets" (quoted in Marchalonis, 263).

Further Reading. *Selected Primary Sources:* Larcom, Lucy, *At the Beautiful Gate* (Boston: Houghton, 1892); ———, *An Idyl of Work* (Boston: Osgood, 1875); ———, *Larcom's Poetical Works* [also titled *Lucy Larcom's Poetry*], Household Edition (Boston: Houghton, 1884); ———, *A New England Girlhood* (Boston: Houghton, 1889); ———, *Poems* (Boston: Fields, Osgood, 1868); ———, *Wild Roses of Cape Ann and Other Poetry* (Boston: Houghton, 1880). ***Selected Secondary Sources:*** Addison, Daniel Dulaney, *Lucy Larcom: Life, Letters, and Diary* (Boston: Houghton, 1894). Marchalonis, Shirley, *The Worlds of Lucy Larcom, 1824–1893* (Athens: University of Georgia Press, 1989); Walker, Cheryl, *The Nightingale's Burden:*

Women Poets and American Culture Before 1900 (Bloomington: Indiana University Press, 1982).

Mary Rose Kasraie

LATHROP, ROSE HAWTHORNE (1851–1926)

Rose Hawthorne Lathrop devoted her creative energies to poetry and fiction between 1874 and 1892, hoping to explore a literary talent that she inherited from her famous father, **Nathaniel Hawthorne**, and to find lasting personal fulfillment in her writing. In addition to short stories for children and adults, and a novel serialized in the *Boston Courier*, Lathrop published a volume of verse titled *Along the Shore* (1888), and at least eight other poems appeared in popular magazines such as *Catholic World, Century,* and *Scribner's Magazine.* Such modest success, however, failed to sustain her growing spiritual needs. Consequently, during the mid-1890s she redirected her efforts by writing a few articles and one book, *Memories of Hawthorne* (1897), about her father's literary life; she also began what would become a lifelong spiritual mission—caring for destitute people incurably ill from cancer. Her religious vocation lives on through the Dominican Sisters of Hawthorne, an order of nuns that Lathrop founded, and that operates, hospice facilities across the United States.

Born in 1851 in Lenox, Massachusetts, Rose spent her early years abroad and did not enjoy as much of her parents' time and attention as had her older siblings: Her childhood coincided with her father's demanding position as United States consul to Liverpool and her mother Sophia's weakening health. In 1860 the Hawthornes moved back to Massachusetts, where they lived at the Wayside, Nathaniel's name for the house in Concord where **Louisa May Alcott** and her family once had resided. With Nathaniel's death in 1864 came increasingly pressing financial concerns, which prompted Sophia to move the family to Europe. While abroad, Rose met George Parsons Lathrop, whom she married in 1871, the same year her mother died. The couple moved to New York City and then to Massachusetts as George launched a successful literary and editorial career, and the Lathrops found good friends in literati **Thomas Bailey Aldrich** and **Emma Lazarus**. In November 1876 Rose gave birth to Francis, her only child, but his death from diphtheria in February 1881 plunged the Lathrops into a sadness that the Catholic Church eventually helped to ease. They converted to Catholicism in 1891; yet this spiritual connection could not dispel the marital doubts that had prompted Rose to separate from her husband several times between 1881 and 1895, when she formally left him in order to answer a profound calling to aid the poor.

Between 1896 and 1901 Rose established a hospice service for impoverished, terminally ill cancer patients in New York City's Lower East Side, moving from two cramped rooms to successively larger quarters. In June

1901 she opened the spacious Rosary Hill Home in Sherman Park (later Hawthorne), New York. As part of her religious vocation, Rose created the Dominican order of nuns mentioned above, which she also incorporated as the Servants of Relief for Incurable Cancer. She served as Mother Superior for this order, under the name Mother Mary Alphonsa, until her death in 1926. Rose also composed a variety of spiritual writings, including *A Story of Courage: Annals of the Georgetown Convent of the Visitation of the Blessed Mary* (1894), co-written with her husband, and wrote articles for Catholic venues to raise money for and awareness about her charitable cause. Though she was little known, *Time* included Rose in its 1976 special report *Remarkable American Women: 1776–1976*, and in 2003 she was officially proposed for sainthood in the Catholic Church.

Death proved an indelible influence on Lathrop's personal and poetic life: Her father died the day after she turned thirteen, her mother a few months before she married George Parsons Lathrop. Her son died after just four and one-half years of life, and her husband a half hour before she could reach his hospital bedside in 1898. Grief and despondency proved lasting emotional challenges that Rose wrestled with in verse. *Along the Shore (AS)* resounds with a tension between dark and light impulses that reflects the influences of seventeenth-century and nineteenth-century **poetics**, especially the work of **Edgar Allan Poe** and the pre-Raphaelites. For instance, Poe's "Masque of the Red Death" echoes within "A Youth's Suicide" as the dancing "merry-makers" mock with "pealing laughter" the youth's belated realization that he, like the arrogant revelers, mistakenly undervalues life until it is too late. His disdain in the opening line, "He handed his life a poisoned draught," quickly plummets into shocked awareness that he is complicit in the world's madness. Death also provokes wisdom in "The Fault-Demon," published in March 1884 in *Century*. Here Rose reworks Poe's "The Raven" in a vein both unexpectedly humorous and deeply prophetic. A maiden's tombstone reveals that the demon, embodied as a raven that "only said 'Caw!'," represents an earthbound pride that cannot sustain its fiendish hold in the face of the Church's resonant influence—a poetic ending that unconsciously prefigures Rose's later life as a self-denying caretaker for those close to death. Similarly, "Francie" (*AS*), Rose's **elegy** for her son, unwittingly rehearses in miniature that future self-renunciation in a poem congruent with **Anne Bradstreet**'s and **Edward Taylor**'s elegies for children. Here, however, Rose parallels the grieving parent with "withered petals," thereby inverting the conventional analogy of dead children and faded flowers to highlight the searing grief imprisoning the living. That the parent "shall lie content in the earth" by poem's end because the child "will live in heaven" signals not a suicidal impulse but a complex acceptance of an anguish that makes life itself seem a cof-

fin. Mourning assumes genocidal contours in "The Outgoing" (*AS*), in which Rose contributes to the "vanishing Indian" myth so prevalent at the turn into the twentieth century. Although the poem speaks to WASP anxiety about white supremacy amid darker-skinned people—a concern manifested in the lone male warrior who ends the poem and, by extension, his life and that of his people—it is Native American *mothers* who foresee "no road for the Indian" and therefore "wish for no more daughters," "bow[ing] their heads and their pride" as they dominate three of the poem's four stanzas. Here self-abnegation indeed presages racial abnegation, but placing indigenous women's concerns at the poem's core heralds a feminist concern *in* and *for* a patriarchal world where Native American and white men prize lethal combat over procreation and life. In this respect Rose's interest in women's reform efforts, which she discussed as a speaker at the 1893 Columbian Catholic Congress, infiltrated her poetry as well as her personal life.

Although many poems in *Along the Shore* excoriate the material, fashionable world—especially the poem "Neither!," in which a male persona, à la **T.S. Eliot**'s Prufrock, disparages middle age in tones reminiscent of Ecclesiastes and **modernism**—"The Roads That Meet" reveals Rose's burgeoning awareness that devotion to God incorporates both darkness and light. Each "road"—art, love, charity—reflects Rose's life choices, two of which she relinquished because the third so strongly compelled her. And as the poem's final lines express, though the third choice may indeed be errant, "still God has need of this,— / Even our mistake."

Further Reading. *Selected Primary Sources:* Lathrop, Rose Hawthorne, *Along the Shore* (Boston: Ticknor & Co., 1888); ———, "The Fault-Demon" (*Century* 27.5 [March 1884]: 798); ———, *Memories of Hawthorne* (Boston: Houghton, Mifflin, 1897; new ed. 1923); Lathrop, George Parsons, and Rose Hawthorne Lathrop, *A Story of Courage: Annals of the Georgetown Convent of the Visitation of the Blessed Mary* (Cambridge, MA: Riverside Press, 1894). ***Selected Secondary Sources:*** Judge, Jean, "Rose Hawthorne's Poetry" (*Nathaniel Hawthorne Review* 13.2 [Fall 1987]: 19–20); Valenti, Patricia Dunlavy, *To Myself a Stranger: A Biography of Rose Hawthorne Lathrop* (Baton Rouge: Louisiana State University Press, 1991).

Sandra Burr

LATIN AMERICAN POETRY

Underlying any discussion of the influence and connections between the poetries of Latin America and those of the United States is the idea of a **poetics** of the Americas. The notion of a poetics of the Americas suggests intercontinental connections as an alternative to national literatures that build on the idea of cultural identity as a result of vernacular institutions. A poetics of the Americas involves the attempt to establish a connection between writing practices in different countries or languages, based on those countries' concern for similar issues, among them the newness of America in a continental sense, translation as cultural practice, and the New World's relation to Europe as a point of departure for Americans' own poetic practice. The idea of the Americas cuts across languages and history in a way that complicates the simplicity of clear boundaries between literatures and cultures.

One of the most evident instances (and causes) of the influence of Latin American poetry on the poetry of the United States is the rise of **translation**, especially from the 1960s to the present. Translations from the Spanish of Pablo Neruda, César Vallejo, Octavio Paz, Nicanor Parra, Gabriela Mistral, Roberto Juarroz, and Pablo Cuadra, or from the Portuguese of Carlos Drummond de Andrade, for example, brought to the United States both stylistic innovations and new possibilities for both a fresher, more excitingly surreal and a more politically charged poetry. Many of the translators during this period were prominent poets in the United States, including **Elizabeth Bishop**, **W. S. Merwin**, **Mark Strand**, **Clayton Eshleman**, **Nathanial Tarn,** and Ben Belitt. **Robert Bly,** however, was arguably the most influential of translators; with his journals *The Sixties* and *The Seventies* Bly brought the energy of Latin American poetry to the attention of a wide and otherwise insulated audience.

In a parallel development, the growing Hispanic and Chicano communities within the United States have expanded the idea of "America" and offered points of departure for a better understanding of present cultural affairs. Although the interest in a poetics of the Americas seems widespread in the United States today, it has a much longer tradition in Latin America. By retracing key moments in the history of this literary tradition, many of them originating from within Latin America, we can uncover a cultural critique embedded in the conceptualization of the Americas that questions, among other issues, the hierarchical order of North and South and revisits the relation between experimental writing and politics.

The following examples show how this idea of a poetics of the Americas has been in circulation for some time and has been approached from several points of view.

One of these South-North encounters concerns **José Martí**, whose best-known essay, "Our America," first published in New York in January 1891, was highly influential. Martí was born in Cuba and worked as a journalist during his exile years in the United States. He was one the leading intellectual figures in the Cuban war for independence from Spain. His poetry is some of the first to create a sense of directness and transparency as an effort to distinguish itself from Spanish literature and define what would be known as **modernismo**. In "Our America" Martí's America is for the most part Spanish America, yet his argument calls attention to concerns about the United States' expansive politics. The essay addresses, the conflicted history of the South's connection with the North. From very early on, Spanish America thought of America as one continent politically divided into three segments (North, Central, and South)—despite the linguistic and political differences that characterized the North. Thus, Martí's essay reflects a long-standing conceptualization of America that stresses geographic unity within the continent and explains why in Spanish the term "America" is almost never used in the plural.

The insistence on continental oneness, as well as the critical interest in the United States, has always been a defining factor when thinking of the Americas from a Spanish American perspective. Martí's "Our America," develops the idea that nature is one of the defining characteristics of the land: "This is why in America the imported book has been conquered by the natural man. Natural men have conquered learned and artificial men. The native half-breed has conquered the exotic Creole. The struggle is not between civilization and barbarism, but between false erudition and Nature" (113). Martí's idea of nature, although clearly influenced by Romanticism, carries a strong call for political unity that echoes the pan-Latin Americanism of the 1960s. Informed by his contact with American culture, Martí anticipates U.S. cultural imperialism and also reinforces the idea of pan-Latin Americanism, a concept that had circulated since colonial times. By elaborating on a poetics that distinguishes itself from Europe while defining the vernacular as the fusion of indigenous and European influences, Martí's work became foundational for later Spanish American writers on the subject of the Americas.

As Latin Americans continued developing their poetics, they never completely disregarded the United States; in fact they often looked to the United States, both to find commonalities and to stress differences. In this sense, an important point of intersection between South and North poetics are the writings of Chilean poet Pablo Neruda, who in 1950 published his *Canto general* (General Song), an encompassing series of poems that fuses and intermingles a personal and a collective voice. Neruda's poetics is associated with **Walt Whitman**'s but, as is the case with several of these trans-American intersections, Neruda redefined Whitman's poetics in order to accommodate his commitment to a pan-Latin Americanism, a position that Neruda associated with his own communist ideals. Some critics have indicated that if *General Song* is a Spanish American rewriting of Whitman's *Song of Myself,* it is also a departure from the individual voice to the collective by way of recreating in this poem a continental history from times prior to the Spanish Conquest all the way to his present. In one of the famous sections of *General Song*, "The Heights of Macchu Picchu," Neruda fuses the epic and originality of Spanish America with its indigenous past and offers to give voice to those who cannot speak: "Hasten to my veins and to my mouth // Speak through my words and my blood"(42).

As Martí and Whitman did before him, Neruda provided a sense of identity clearly associated with the Americas as a new territory, distinct from Europe.

What Neruda did in the 1950s for Whitman (and what, in the novel, Gabriel García Márquez would later do for Faulkner), Ernesto Cardenal and José Coronel Urtecho did in the 1960s for **Ezra Pound**. Urtecho and Cardenal, both born in Nicaragua, studied at Columbia University in the 1940s, where they became acquainted with the work of Pound and the **Imagists**. Influenced by the Imagist idea of a direct image, they also adopted Pound's notion of re-creating tradition through translation. They founded *Exteriorismo*, a poetics that was also known in Spanish America as *Coloquialismo*. Urtecho was among the first Spanish American poets to edit and translate into Spanish an encompassing anthology of American poetry, *Panorama y antología de la poesía norteamericana* (Panorama and an Anthology of U.S. Poetry) (1949), which included authors from **Longfellow** to **Emily Dickinson** to **Muriel Rukeyser**. This anthology, although edited only by Urtecho, exemplifies Urtecho's and Cardenal's affinity with the notion of redefining tradition through translation. As was the case with Neruda's reading of Whitman, Cardenal is committed to redefining Spanish American poetic tradition by means of a new literary genealogy. Where Pound looked for his poetic sources among the troubadours and **ideogrammatic** writing, Cardenal turned instead toward primitivism.

Two of *Exteriorismo*'s main characteristics are the erasure of a poetic "I" and, in the particular case of Cardenal, the inclusion of news, documentary references, sentences, or quotes as an integral part of a poem. The erasure of a poetic "I" plus the use of a very direct, colloquial language help to create an effect of transparency. In his *Antología de poesía primitiva* (Anthology of Primitive Poetry) (1979), Cardenal re-creates, with a translation technique that resembles some of Pound's own translations, the poetry of what he calls "primitive," a term that in Cardenal's poetics stands as an antecedent of *Exteriorismo*'s simplicity. Cardenal's and Urtecho's poetics developed in part as an appropriation of Pound's idea of re-appropriating tradition through translation, but in their case the desire to reformulate tradition was at the service of a Spanish American identity. Cardenal, himself a priest, was also deeply influenced by **Thomas Merton**, and although he declares Pound to be his most important literary model, Merton remains one of his strongest religious and spiritual points of reference; Cardenal associates his political activism with the principles of liberation theology.

Although *Exteriorismo* was Cardenal and Urtecho's movement, other Spanish American poets of the 1960s and 1970s shared their interest in colloquialism, among them the Chilean poet Nicanor Parra, who, along with the Guatemalan peot Rafael Arévalo Martínez, was first translated into English by **William Carlos Williams** in the early 1940s. In fact, Williams's collection of essays, *In the American Grain* (1925)—a book that is as much about Montezuma and Ponce de León as it is about Cotton Mather and Benjamin Franklin—put forward a view of the continent that merged South and North, creating a sense of historical continuity throughout the continent.

These encounters have been for the most part unilateral, however—involving Spanish America's gaze at the Anglo American North, as was the case with Cuban poet and editor José Lezama Lima's interest in **Wallace Stevens** and **T.S. Eliot**. It was not until the mid-1990s that an actual dialogue between several poets from both South and North America addressed directly the limits and possibilities of a poetics of the Americas in a continental sense.

In the spring of 1994, *L=A=N=G=U=A=G=E* magazine poets **Charles Bernstein** and James Sherry and translator Molly Weigel, all from the United States, and the editor of *XUL* magazine, Jorge Santiago Perednik from Argentina, and David Huerta from Mexico met in New York to discuss the limits of a poetics of the Americas. The magazine *XUL* appeared for the first time in 1981 and is still being published; *L=A=N=G=U=A=G=E* started in 1978 and ended its publication in 1982. The meeting was preceded by a series of translations into English and Spanish of their works, and it was supported by a sense of commonality based on a shared interest for theoretical thought as well as a strong practice of formal experimentation as political resistance. The *L=A=N=G=U=A=G=E* participants had been influenced by the political debate opposing the Vietnam War, and *XUL*'s poetics was in part a response to Argentina's military dictatorship of the 1980s. For both magazines, poetry implied the possibility of a political praxis that permitted, without the demands of commercial publishing houses, a revision of the criteria around which the community was organized. Whatever the case, whether it was to address the regulations proposed by the Spanish Royal Academy of Language—the appropriation of language that took place during the military government—or the general but pervasive normalization of language, *L=A=N=G=U=A=G=E* and *XUL* proposed an experimental poetics as political resistance. In an essay on the Americas, Charles Bernstein extends a comment made by Jorge Santiago Perednik on the issue of resistance when he writes, "I understand this also to mean that poetry, insofar as it resists reification as culturally sanctioned Poetry, is also impossible—and for that reason takes place. For the sake of this collection, I would like to add America to this list, for America is impossible and for this reason, also, it exists" (113).

Equally substantial to the magazines' exploration was that both were committed to considering the reader an active participant. Jorge Perednik maps Argentina's poetic scene as well as the larger political landscape when he distinguishes between an implosive and explosive poetics: "the explosive, whose movement goes out from the poem, in search of an author or the propagation of a meaning, and the implosive, in which the outside is attracted by a centripetal force, where the reader implodes toward the poem" (XX). Perednik's characterization is a comment on the politics of poetic practice. Both magazines shared the notion that poetic experimentation and political subversion come together to question of the limits of representation. In both cases, $L=A=N=G=U=A=G=E$ as well as *XUL*, it is a matter of bracketing the concept of representation as a natural option and bringing attention to the materiality of the word. This exchange that began in 1994 has extended through translations, anthologies, and public readings in Cuba, Brazil, and Argentina, and it will most likely continue to develop, as evidenced in new anthologies and translation projects throughout the continent.

Further Reading. *Selected Primary Sources:* Bernstein, Charles, *My Way: Speeches and Poem* (Chicago: University of Chicago Press, 1999); Cardenal, Ernesto, ed., *Antología de la poesía primitiva* (Madrid: Alianza Editorial, 1979); Livon-Grosman, Ernesto, ed., *The XUL Reader* (New York: Roof Books, 1997); Martí, José, *Writings on the Americas* (New York: Ocean Press, 1999); Neruda Pablo, *Canto General* (Berkeley: University of California Press, 1991); Urtecho, José Coronel, ed., *Panorama y antología de la poesía norteamericana* (Madrid: Seminario de Problemas Hispanoamericanos, 1949); Williams, William Carlos, *In the American Grain* (New York: A & C Boni, 1925). *Selected Secondary Sources:* Bernstein, Charles, and Bruce Andrews, eds., *The Language Book* (Carbondale: Southern Illinois University Press, 1984); Lezama Lima, José, *Selections* (Berkeley: University of California Press, 2005).

Ernesto Livon-Grosman

LATINO POETRY IN THE UNITED STATES

Latino poetry in the United States is receiving increasing recognition for its vitality, political expressiveness, and stylistic innovations. In part, its boom is driven by those who write primarily in English. Also, much of the Latino poetry written in the United States has emerged from a need for Latinos to document their experiences in their adopted homeland. Many of the voices that resound in the poems confront issues of assimilation, cultural heritage, artistic expression, identity formation, family, and their place in history. For others, this poetry serves as a response to the pressures of the dominant culture of the United States.

As a whole, Latinos have played a pivotal role in what it means to be American. Readers in the United States and scholars of American literature have begun to realize the importance of this transnational group of writers. "Latino poetry" here will refer to poetry produced by Latino authors who were either born or have lived in the United States for a significant amount of time and who choose to write in English, Spanish, or both. Although there have been Latinos writing poetry in the United States since the 1700s and before, particular attention must be given to the explosion of Latino writers in the last half of the twentieth century. A large part of this explosion was the Chicano arts movements of the 1960s and early 1970s. The Mexican American or **Chicano poets** found their voices in the Civil Rights Movement of the 1960s and the grassroots efforts of César Chávez and Dolores Huerta. Poets such as Rodolfo "Corky" Gonzales and Luis Alberto Urista (Alurista) helped set the stage for the literary movement blossoming today. Around the same time, Puerto Rican poets in the New York City area found themselves also inspired by the political pressures of the 1960s, as did the Cuban American poets who fled their island nation in several waves to escape political and economic persecution during the Castro regime. Much of Cuban American poetry has been seriously influenced by the different waves of Cuban exiles over the past half century: those who fled Cuba in the 1960s; another group that left in the early 1980s as part of the *Mariel* boat lift; and the last wave of immigrants in the early 1990s, who made their way in *balsas*, or homemade rafts. In addition, Latino writers who have come to the United States from the Dominican Republic, Chile, and Peru, among other countries, have also contributed and continue to add diversity to this evolving body of work.

The oldest and most established group of Latino poets is the Mexican American or Chicano, with roots in the southwestern United States during the time of the Spanish conquistadores. This early poetry of discovery depicts the expeditions of Spaniards as they made their way down through the Southwest, Mexico, and Central America. Works such as **Gaspar Pérez de Villagra's** *Historia de la Nuevo México* (History of New Mexico) (1610) serve as the first poetic records documenting the travels through this area. Later Mexican Americans developed a peasant or *campesino* tradition that carries strong ties to the land, reflected in the popular tradition of the *corridos*, the popular ballads of the mid-nineteenth century that recount heroic exploits. These *corridos* serve as a foundation for the Chicano poetry of the twentieth century, as the oral and written word are fused to form what is perhaps one of the earliest forms of code switching. During the Civil Rights Movement of the 1960s and the grassroots efforts of movements like that of the United Farm Workers led by César Chávez, the United States experienced an explosion of poetry from Mexican American writers. Among the most renowned poets of the time was Rodolfo "Corky" Gonzales, who grew up in Denver's East Side barrio during the Depression. His father had emigrated from Mexico and instilled in the young Gonzales a sense of pride in his Mexican history. In the mid-1960s Rodolfo founded an urban civil rights and cultural movement called the Crusade for Justice. Corky Gonzales became one of the leaders of the Chicano movement and was a strong proponent of Chicano nationalism. His groundbreaking poem "I Am Joaquin" reflects this: "I am the masses of my people and I refuse to be absorbed. / I am Joaquin / I SHALL ENDURE!" Gonzales's battle cry laments the plight of the Chicanos while at the same time finding inspiration in his Mexican roots.

Other notable poets writing in a similar or related vein include such figures as **Juan Felipe Herrera**, **Ray Gonzalez**, **Ana Castillo**, **Lorna Dee Cervantes**, **Pat Mora**, and **Gary Soto**. Also worth mentioning is **Luis Omar Salinas**, whose contribution to Chicano and Latino poetry includes such works as *Greatest Hits* (2002), *Sometimes Mysteriously* (1997), and "My Father Is a Simple Man." His 1970 rendition of his persona as "Crazy Gypsy" underscores the theme of Tex-Mex border town roots and earned him recognition both as a Chicano poet and as one of the leaders of the Fresno School of poets, which included Gary Soto, Ernesto Trejo, and Leonard Adame, among others. In addition to the more traditional themes, over the last four decades Chicano poetry has taken up such diverse issues as U.S.–Mexico border relations, Catholicism, bilingualism, and the mixed cultural heritage of the U.S. Southwest.

Much of the growth of the Chicano poetry movement is due to the increasing number of Chicana poets on the contemporary literary scene. Fueled by a desire to establish their own voices, to combat the oppressive, machismo-laden literary history of their ancestors, these female poets explore issues of feminism, sexuality, religion, and women's role in history. Gloria Anzaldúa, from south Texas, is a leading figure in the Latina feminist and lesbian movement, and her most influential book, *Borderlands/La Frontera: The New Mestiza* (1987), has served both as feminist analysis and as the seminal study on Latino borderland studies. Lorna Dee Cervantes is one of the first Chicana poets to receive recognition, and early on she founded the literary magazine *Mango* as a way to deliver the Chicana message. Her poetry deals primarily with identity and rootedness, alienation, and the oppression of women and minorities. Her collections include

From the Cables of Genocide: Poems of Love and Hunger (1992) and *Emplumada* (Plumed) (1991).

Probably the most famous of the Chicana authors is Sandra Cisneros, noted particularly for her acclaimed novel *The House on Mango Street* and also as the first Hispanic writer to win the prestigious MacArthur Award (1995). Her stories, essays, and poetry center on her experiences as a Mexican American in the Chicago area, and her work has carried the Chicana movement to the forefront of literary feminism. Another important Chicana figure is Lucha Corpi, also heavily involved in the Chicano civil rights movement. In Corpi's poetry, intimacy and sensuality reign, defined by her bilingual artistry and code switching, a practice that dominates much of the Chicana literature of the time. Some of Corpi's most influential collections are *Variaciones sobre una tempestad* (1990) (Variations on a Storm) and *Palabras de mediodía* (1980) (Noon Words).

Puerto Ricans form the second-largest group of Latino writers contributing to the canon of Hispanic poetry in the United States; theirs also is a literature that emerged from the political turmoil of the 1960s. **Puerto Rican** American poets first began to write with the goal of eliminating their colonial status both in the United States and in Puerto Rico. Most Puerto Ricans moved to the mainland under the duress of economic strife on the island. The urban crisis of black Puerto Rican youth and the sensibilities of women in the barrio dominate many of the poems of this ethnic group. The term "Nuyorican" was first used by Puerto Ricans on the island to denote emigrants who settled mostly in the New York City area, where they created an identifiable body of literature. At the time, the term "Nuyorican" had negative connotations but was later reclaimed by Puerto Rican authors such as Jesus Colón, who is considered the founding father of the Nuyorican movement. The Nuyorican movement continues to be a vital and creative force in the Latino artistic community, and present-day poets include **Miguel Algarín**, Martita Morales, Willie Perdomo, and Sandra María Esteves.

Puerto Rican American poets dominated the Latino literary scene of the northeastern United States for decades. One notable figure, **Martín Espada**, has been called a modern-day **Walt Whitman**; his poems reflect his Puerto Rican heritage and his life's experiences from bouncer to tenant lawyer. He has written *A Mayan Astronomer in Hell's Kitchen: Poems* (2000), *Imagine the Angels of Bread* (1996), *City of Coughing and Dead Radiators* (1993), and *Trumpets from the Islands of Their Eviction* (1987). Espada's poetry explores issues of ethnic pride and the racial tensions of inner-city Puerto Ricans as they attempt to associate with U.S. culture, as evident in his poem "Niggerlips." Another important figure in the Puerto Rican poetic movement is Tato Laviera, who was born in Puerto Rico and has lived in New York City since 1960. Both poet and playwright,

Laviera has been deeply concerned with social and cultural issues facing New York Puerto Ricans. His poetry has been heralded as a celebration of Puerto Rican and Afro-Caribbean cultures. His playful nature and command of both Spanish and English, as well as Spanglish, allows for double readings; indeed, his work has been critical in contemporary studies of bilingual and bicultural issues facing the Puerto Rican community in the United States. His best-known poem pays homage to the great Puerto Rican outfielder Roberto Clemente.

The poetry of **Victor Hernández Cruz** depicts Puerto Ricans culturally torn between maintaining their native language and recognizing the need to speak English in order to function in the United States. He blends Spanish, English, Spanglish, and music; his is a poetry intended for oral delivery. Along with Laviera and Hernández Cruz, Bronx-born Sandra María Esteves has taken ethnic pride as a theme of her poetry. She has been described as a "Puerto Rican-Dominican-Borinqueña-Quisqueyana-TainoAfrican-American." One of the founders of the Nuyorican poetry movement, Esteves has six collections of poetry to her name: *Finding Your Way* (2001), *Contrapunto in the Open Field* (1998), *Undelivered Love Poems* (1997), *Bluestown Mockingbird Mambo* (1990), *Tropical Rain: A Bilingual Downpour* (1984), and *Yerba Buena* (Spearmint) (1981). **Judith Ortiz Cofer** is a Puerto Rican–born poet who has always been isolated from Puerto Ricans but constantly obsessed with the island. The daily life of residents of a Puerto Rican barrio during the 1960s and 1970s is the main theme of many of her collections of poetry, which include *The Latin Deli: Prose and Poetry* (1993), *Terms of Survival* (1989), and *Reaching for the Mainland* (1987). Some critics have claimed that in Cofer's poetry the well-developed voices of marginal characters, with an emphasis on women's issues, are among the best literary depictions of incidents of daily life in Hispanic barrios.

Cuban American poetry has a rich and varied history, just like its Chicano and Puerto Rican American counterparts. As far back as 1823, Cuban writer José María Heredia left Cuba for America to avoid being taken to prison. Heredia's poetry sharply criticized Spanish authoritarian rule. Later in that century, writing in Spanish, **José Martí** fled Cuba for the United States, where he wrote about his homeland and echoed many of the same sentiments as Heredia.

Although Mexican and Puerto Rican poets share a common resistance to American culture, Cuban American poetry develops a sense of nostalgia for Cuba as post-1959 diaspora. Cuban American poetic expression is marked by the frustrations of political exile. Poets such as Carolina Hospital and Archy Obejas recreate a space in which the poetic voice yearns for a lost homeland. Nostalgia appears to be a staple of Cuban American literature, as seen in Pablo Medina's "The Exile."

The speaker's connection to the past and historical events is ever present in the works of poets such as Ricardo Pau-Llosa, Medina, and Hospital. Others, such as Gustavo Pérez Firmat, are identified with the "one-and-a-half" generation of Cuban American poets, those who fall somewhere between the first and second immigrant generations. Pérez Firmat's poetry is dominated by themes of biculturalism, as well as the code switching, bicultural-bilingual double entendres, and playfulness that are often linked to the Cuban *choteo*. Marginalized, these "one-and-a-halfers" never feel completely at ease in either generation, and their poetry expresses this, as in Pérez Firmat's poem "Dedication," where he grapples with the problem of the two seemingly different worlds: "how to explain to you / that I don't belong to English/ though I belong nowhere else, / if not here."

Another important member of the Cuban American canon is Carolina Hospital, who over the years has captured the transition of her community from the status of exile to immigrant to American. In 1988 she compiled the first anthology of Cuban American literature, *Los atrevidos* (The Daring Ones), where she openly embraced English and bilingualism in a literature that was here to stay in the United States. Archy Obejas is a lesbian Cuban American poet who writes primarily in English. Much of her poetry, as well as her novels, explores identity conflict as seen from ethnic, religious, and sexual perspectives. As a gay Latina and a member of the Jewish minority within the Latino community, Obejas challenges the normative aspects of traditional Latino poetry.

Although much of the Cuban American poetry is deeply rooted in the reality of exile, it is still quite diverse. The first wave of Cubans came to the United States (1959–1962, 1965–1968) from the middle or professional class, and they have maintained their cultural differences and have refrained from assimilating linguistically, as seen in the poetry of Heberto Padilla. The second generation of poets, the "one-and-a-halfers" such as Maya Islas, José Kózer, Lourdes Gil, and Emilio Bejel, continue to publish in Spanish as part of a need and a form of resistance. The third group of Cuban poets is represented by the children of the first wave of immigrants. This newer generation tends to write in English and lacks the memories of their parents' Cuba, and for this reason they do not share the nostalgia of the first generation.

Of the lesser-known Latino poetry, that of Dominican Americans represents the new generation of Hispanics in the Unites States. Dominican American poets can be divided into two groups: those who left as exiles during the Rafael Leonides Trujillo dictatorship and those who left as immigrants after his death. The most renowned Dominican American poet, **Julia Alvarez**, was born in New York City in 1950 but lived in the Dominican Republic until she was ten. Alvarez and her family were forced into exile when her country fell under the dictatorship of Trujillo and her father unsuccessfully attempted to overthrow Trujillo's regime. A prolific writer of novels, children's stories, and poetry, her works deal with concerns of women, assimilation, and Dominican politics, to promote women's issues in her exile experience. Her poetry includes *The Woman I Kept to Myself* (2004), *The Other Side/El otro lado* (1995), and *Homecoming* (1984). Another important Dominican poet is Rhina Espaillat, who was born in the Dominican Republic and has lived in the United States since 1939. Writing both in Spanish and English, Espaillat's poetry mirrors her love of family, culture, and diversity. Much of her poetry is centered on bilingualism as an experience that alters perception of language and thought. Her most-recognized works include *Rehearsing Absence* (2001), *Mundo y Palabra/The World and the Word* (2001), *Where Horizons Go* (1998), and *Lapsing to Grace* (1992). Less recognized but equally interesting are the works by Dominican immigrants Sherezada (Chiqui) Vicioso and Alexis Gómez Rosa. Both Dominican poets write in Spanish and share similar concerns of ethnicity, race, uprootedness, and fitting in in New York. Both Vicioso and Gómez Rosa have returned to the Dominican Republic, where they continue to write about their New York/Dominican experiences.

In the last forty years a Latino literary renaissance has occurred in the United States. It is a literature that has evolved out of the economic, social, and cultural oppression of an ethnic group. U.S. Latino poets have created a formidable legacy in a short time, and they are making their way into mainstream American literature. This growing corpus of poets continues to speak to the Latino situation as rooted in their parents' past while constantly reevaluating and challenging many aspects of their adopted culture.

Further Readings. ***Selected Primary Sources:*** Del Rio, Eduardo, *The Prentice Hall Anthology of Latino Literature* (Upper Saddle River, NJ: Prentice Hall, 2002); Kanellos, Nicolás, *Herencia: The Anthology of Hispanic Literature of the United States* (Oxford: Oxford University Press, 2002); ———, *Hispanic Literature of the United States* (Westport, CT: Greenwood Press, 2003); Madsen, Deborah L., *Understanding Contemporary Chicana Literature* (Columbia: University of South Carolina Press, 2000); Olivares, Julián, ed., *Tomás Rivera: The Complete Works* (Houston: Arte Público Press, 1992); Paredes, Américo, *Between Two Worlds* (Houston: Arte Público Press, 1991); Pérez-Torres, Rafael, *Movements in Chicano Poetry: Against Myths, Against Margins* (Cambridge: Cambridge University Press, 1995); Quintana, Alvina E., *Home Girls: Chicana Literary Voices* (Philadelphia: Temple University Press, 1996); Sánchez, Marta Ester, *Contemporary Chicana Poetry: A Critical Approach to an Emerging Literature* (Berkeley: University of California Press, 1985); Suárez, Virgil, and Delia Poey, *Little Havana Blues* (Houston: Arte Público Press, 1996).

Selected Secondary Sources: Borland, Isabel Alvarez, *Cuban-American Literature of Exile: From Person to Persona* (Charlottesville: University of Virginia Press, 1998); Delgado, Richard, and Jean Stefancic, *The Latino/a Condition: A Critical Reader* (New York: New York University Press, 1998); Hernández Cruz, Victor, *Red Beans* (Minneapolis, MN: Coffee House, 1991); Pérez-Torres, Rafael, *Movements in Chicano Poetry: Against Myths, Against Margins* (Cambridge: Cambridge University Press, 1995); Ramos, Juanita, ed., *Compañeras: Latina Lesbians* (New York: Routledge, 1994).

H.J. Manzari

LAUGHLIN, JAMES (1914–1997)

On the advice of **Ezra Pound**, James Laughlin began his publishing business while still in college, storing books in his dorm room and personally selling books to bookstores. His firm, New Directions, grew to become arguably the most important publishing establishment of the twentieth century, bringing into print an amazing number of distinguished authors. Laughlin's goal was to get into print authors whose modern works might not have otherwise been published; profits were never a concern for him. His list of authors includes Pound, **T.S. Eliot, William Carlos Williams, Wallace Stevens, e.e. cummings, Marianne Moore**, Henry Miller, **Gertrude Stein, Elizabeth Bishop, Kenneth Rexroth, Denise Levertov, Lawrence Ferlinghetti**, Hermann Hesse, **Delmore Schwartz, Randall Jarrell**, F. Scott Fitzgerald, William Faulkner, and many more. In addition to his publishing endeavors, Laughlin wrote fiction, essays, literary criticism, articles on skiing, and sixteen volumes of his own poems. The latter have received increasingly favorable recognition since his death.

Laughlin was born James Laughlin IV in Pittsburgh, Pennsylvania, on October 30, 1914. His father was Henry Hughart Laughlin and his mother was Marjory Rea Laughlin. His great-grandfather migrated from Northern Ireland to sell crockery, and he worked his way across Pennsylvania, making enough money to enter the steel business. His company, Jones and Laughlin of Pittsburgh, became the fourth-largest steel mill in the nation. Laughlin was expected to enter this business, but on an early visit to the foundry he thought it resembled a noisy inferno. Rejecting that career, he became interested in literature during his years at private schools in Pittsburgh, Switzerland, Massachusetts, and then the Choate Academy in Wallingford, Connecticut. At Choate one of his teachers was Dudley Fitts, a translator of classical literature and friend of Pound.

Laughlin entered Harvard in 1933 to study Latin, Italian, and English and American literature. His professors were so conservative that one of them would leave the room at any mention of modern poets such as Eliot or Pound. During his sophomore year Laughlin decided to escape Harvard to pursue his interest in modern poetry. Going first to Paris to work as a handyman for Gertrude Stein, he then went, with an introduction from Fitts, to Rapallo, Italy, to attend what Pound called his "Ezuversity." After about six months, Pound announced that Laughlin would never make it as a poet. He suggested that he become a publisher instead. He also urged Laughlin to finish his degree so his father would give him more money. Laughlin went first to ski in Austria, a lifelong passion that would lead one day to a profitable business venture. Then he proceeded to do both of the things Pound recommended.

On his return to Harvard, Laughlin first published modern **experimental poetry** in a section of a social credit magazine called *New Democracy*. When that magazine foundered, Laughlin began to publish on his own. His first book was an anthology titled *New Directions in Prose and Poetry* that included works by then-controversial poets and authors like cummings, W.C.Williams, Moore, Henry Miller, Stein, Bishop, Eliot, Pound, Fitts, and Stevens. It also included poetry by Tasilo Ribschka, described as a night watchman in Saugus, Massachusetts. Ribschka was actually Laughlin, who never accepted Pound's negative judgment of his poetry.

New Directions in Prose and Poetry has been published most years since that time. Laughlin began working out of offices in a stable on his Aunt Leila's estate in Norfolk, Connecticut, where he had come for visits even before college to escape the grimy industrial urban scene in Pittsburgh. He sought authors of great talent without regard for their mass-market appeal. In the preface to his first anthology, Laughlin wrote that he was angry with the big publishers who did not use money from best sellers to help experimental writers find a wider audience. Laughlin was never concerned about profitability but rather about the quality of literature he printed. Consequently, it would be some twenty-three years before his press earned a profit. Since he was on the board of the Harvard *Advocate*, Laughlin took his first anthology to the printer of that journal. For $396 he had seven hundred copies printed, but he forgot to ask the printer to number the pages. Undaunted, he spent weekends and other time off from Harvard driving in his Buick with a trunk full of books, selling copies to sympathetic bookstore owners for a couple of dollars each. He once traveled as far as Nebraska hawking his books.

When Laughlin graduated from Harvard in 1939, he had already published a dozen books. And Pound was right about his father giving him money, for Laughlin received $100,000 upon graduation at a time during the Depression when a family could live quite comfortably on $2,000 a year. Laughlin invested the money so that he could live on the interest, while still relying on his aunt and father to help with the expenses of the publishing business. He did not inherit more of his family's immense

wealth until the 1950s. His Aunt Leila was a great help financially, but she on rare occasions prevented Laughlin from publishing work he knew to be worthy. For example, he passed on Vladimir Nabokov's *Lolita* and Henry Miller's *Tropic of Cancer* and *Tropic of Capricorn* so as not to offend his aunt, but he did help those authors find publishers elsewhere.

In 1941, able after his graduation to channel more energy into publishing, Laughlin started a series of books titled *Poets of the Year*. Then he started another series that he called *New Classics*, devoted to reprinting good books that big presses had allowed to go out of print. This series included works by Henry James, Evelyn Waugh, Faulkner, and Fitzgerald. Another major contribution to American publishing was his printing of books by foreign authors writing in English or translated into English, such as Dylan Thomas, Nabokov, Hesse, Pablo Neruda, Boris Pasternak, and Octavio Paz.

A conspiracy developed among talented experimental authors to help Laughlin succeed. Authors referred other good artists to Laughlin. Pound recommended W.C. Williams and Henry Miller. Williams recommended Rexroth, who led him to Levertov, Ferlinghetti, and **Gary Snyder**. Miller recommended Hesse. Schwartz steered him to Jarrell and **John Berryman**. All of this help brought financial successes. Ferlinghetti's *A Coney Island of the Mind* and Hesse's *Siddhartha* both sold more than a million copies for New Directions. Laughlin then followed his own advice to big publishers and devoted profits to bringing dozens of authors into print.

Although some of his authors were rather difficult people, Laughlin was skilled at maintaining good relations with them. He paid so much attention to them that an immense collection of correspondence accumulated over the years. After Laughlin's death, in fact, 1,298 boxes of material were taken from his home to Harvard, including letters to and from him. The letters exchanged with **Thomas Merton**, for example, numbered 739. From this vast correspondence several volumes of letters have been published by W.W. Norton, including those to and from W.C. Williams, Pound, Rexroth, Henry Miller, and Schwartz. Similar volumes in the future will focus on figures such as Tennessee Williams, whose poetry Laughlin published.

During his first three decades, Laughlin published some five hundred volumes, almost two hundred of poetry. He also kept most of his books in print, unlike more profit-minded publishers. Another curious experiment was his hiring of unemployed poets to help with publishing duties. He was eventually able to move his headquarters from his aunt's stable to New York and employ a professional staff. His home, however, remained in Norfolk for the rest of his life. Ironically, Laughlin had taken his sabbatical from Harvard to pursue modern literature with Pound because the universities were biased against new literature, but New Directions became profitable in part from the orders of university professors who began using the books for their classes. Laughlin once estimated that half of New Direction sales came from university use. He had been instrumental in changing literary tastes.

Laughlin began to publish his own poetry not only in his anthologies of others' work, but also in small, privately printed volumes distributed to friends. He seemed content to keep his own writing in the background, claiming once that poetry is a "divine gift" he did not have. He felt, however, a compulsion to write it, saying poems came to him whole as if from someone else, often at bedtime. He did very little revision of these inspirations. By and large the literary figures who became famous in part due to his publishing company paid little attention to Laughlin's poetry. One exception was Ferlinghetti, who repaid Laughlin's boost to his career with the publication of two volumes of the latter's poetry through his City Lights Books, *In Another Country* (1978), just fifty-eight pages long, and *James Laughlin: Selected Poems, 1935–1985* (1985). Many felt these books were gestures of appreciation by Ferlinghetti, but readers—though not in large numbers, and in spite of the fact that Laughlin humbly described his work as just light and **sentimental** verse with no great thoughts—soon realized he was a good poet.

Selected Poems includes a large number of poems that illustrate Laughlin's innovative arrangement of lines, which one critic calls "typewriter metrics," a technique requiring that lines in a poem be no more than two or three typewriter strokes longer than the lines above or below it. Within this rather difficult structure, Laughlin preferred to use direct and simple American English and little punctuation. In his poem "Some People Think" (1985), he wrote that some prefer complicated, adorned poetry, but he likes "plain speech" and brevity. He was influenced also by the direct styles of classical poets he admired, such as Horace, Catullus, Martial, Propertius, and Ovid. The lack of punctuation, modeled after medieval manuscripts, causes readers to figure out where sentences end and begin, slowing the eye enough to invite more attention to what is being said. Laughlin handles this technique so skillfully that the lack of punctuation is little noticed. Many poems in *Selected Poems* are short, less than a page in length, and quite easy to read.

Like Pound, Laughlin sometimes integrates other languages into his poems, including Latin, Greek, Italian, and French. He took Pound's advice to study modern foreign languages, and seems to have especially liked French, which he uses exclusively in some poems. Unlike Pound, Laughlin often provides translations of foreign-language passages in *The Collected Poems of James Laughlin* (1994). He even provides complete translations of his French poems on facing pages to make them more accessible.

A poem that uses both English and Italian gracefully and that has been widely admired by critics is "In Another Country" (1985). Like many of Laughlin's poems, it is about a romantic adventure. Laughlin, six-foot-five, handsome, and from a wealthy family, apparently had quite a number of these experiences in his time, providing material for many poems. In this case, the young narrator and an Italian girl approach each other at a train crossing. The narrator changes course to walk with the beautiful girl, and they go off swimming in the sea, quickly falling in love. The narrator knew little Italian then, but knows it better when he tells this story, suggesting he has spent years of thinking over what happened, during which time his Italian improved. He quotes the excited young girl, shifting from English to Italian as she takes him to her secret grotto along the shore, where he is invited to touch secret parts of her. He eventually must leave her, but there is a subtle hint of loss on his part about this departure seen from the perspective of a much later time.

Some critics feel that Laughlin's best poetry is his love poetry. Another interesting example is "I Like You" (1985), which provides a glimpse of his travels to sell books in his early days. The narrator makes love in his car to a bookstore clerk he has met. Afterward he moves on, never to see her again. The woman mentions stronger feelings for him than those suggested by quick sex in a car, but perhaps she chose to have what little of him she could. This poem too conveys regret on the man's part, hinting there is a point even in the life of an experienced lover when he might wonder what emotional possibilities were missed if the need for sex had not been so powerful at the moment.

Another love poem is "Love Is Accumulative" (1985), in which the narrator says sex is a sacrament when it is an expression of true affection. Laughlin looks also at love not working well. In "Les Amants" (The Lovers) (1985), one of his "stolen poems" based on art by others, he prints a small version of the René Magritte painting for which the poem is named, depicting a couple kissing with bags over their heads. The poem concerns the way that two can be in love with what they imagine the other person to be, not really knowing who that lover is. *Selected Poems* includes some other experimental poems, like Laughlin's "American" French poems, and poems by his alter ego, named Hiram Handspring. Some poems in *Selected Poems* are inspired by Laughlin's friendships with famous literary people. "Some of Us Come to Live" (1985), for example, is a poem dedicated to Pound in which Pound's *Cantos* are compared to the palace at Versailles, full of rooms where anyone can find a rich intellectual home. In "Tennessee" (1985), Laughlin remembers Tennessee Williams, who had caught the "sudden subway" he called death, and about whom Laughlin had many good memories from Key West,

Italy, and London. The narrator understands that his friend's death hints at his own mortality.

In 1994 *The Collected Poems of James Laughlin*, a rather large volume with more than five hundred pages of poems, was published. One example of his American French poems in this volume is "La luciole" (The Firefly) (1994), a love poem in which the woman is symbolized by a firefly that will not stay cupped in the narrator's hands. He wonders what she's looking for and feels it's not him. Nevertheless, she becomes all the more interesting to him. "The Beautiful Muttering" (1994) is another poem about Pound in which his *Cantos* is praised for a portrayal of a man growing from youth to old age and embodying in graceful phrases all that man learned and experienced.

Other poems in *Collected Poems* are about other literary friends. "So Much Depends" (1994) is an appreciation of W.C. Williams. "The Moths" (1994) is about Nabokov's passion for collecting moths attracted by the lights outside a picture window (a hobby that almost killed both Nabokov and Laughlin once on a trek up a mountain, though that is not discussed in this poem). In "The Shameful Profession" (1994) the profession of the title is writing poetry, which the narrator doesn't want his neighbors to know about, especially the big, burly ones who drive pickup trucks and might see him as unmanly. When exposed as a poet, the narrator decides not to abandon his passion to write, though he suspects folks now look at him oddly.

Some of the most powerful poems in *Collected Poems* are those about personal loss. "Ave Atque Vale" (Hail and Farewell) (1994) is about a man shaking a corpse dressed for his funeral, wanting the eyes to open. The dead man is the narrator's father. "The Empty Room" (1994) is a bright, sunny place that arouses terror in the narrator's mind. It is apparently the place where Laughlin's wife Ann spent her final days, and the bright sun accentuates her absence. Finally, "Experience of Blood" (1994) is about the suicide of Laughlin's son, who had stabbed and slashed himself with a kitchen knife so fiercely the entire bathroom was carpeted in blood. Laughlin had experienced some grim moments before, like identifying the body of Dylan Thomas with its blackened head in the morgue, but what could prepare one to spend four hours mopping up a son's blood? The narrator says he had to clean it up himself "because after all it was my blood too."

More books of poetry were published in the final years of Laughlin's life and after. He seemed to lose his reticence about his own work. Among the books were *The Man in the Wall* (1993), *The Love Poems* (1997), *The Secret Room* (1997), and *Poems New and Selected* (1998). In addition to poetry, Laughlin published *This Is My Blood* (short stories, 1989), *Random Essays* (1989), and *Random Stories* (1990). *Pound as Wuz* (1987) includes Laughlin's

acceptance of a psychiatrist's diagnosis that Pound's anti-Semitism was an expression of mental illness. Laughlin, who never agreed with Pound's support of Mussolini or his anti-Semitism, recalled that Pound was not like that in the earlier days. *Byways* is a long work in verse that includes Laughlin's memories of W.C. Williams, Pound, Eliot, Merton, and others, as well as of his own childhood and other periods of his life.

Among Laughlin's many awards are honorary degrees from Yale, Brown, and other universities. In 1977 he received the Carey Thomas Award for distinguished publishing, and in 1989 he was awarded the Robert Frost Medal from the Poetry Society of America. In 1992 the National Book Foundation presented him with its Distinguished Contribution to American Letters Award, and in 1995 he was inducted into the American Academy of Arts and Letters. That same year the Academy of American Poets created the James Laughlin Award, with an endowment of $5,000 for a poet's second book.

In addition to his impressive publishing accomplishments and his extensive number of poems, Laughlin turned his love for skiing into a successful business in Utah. He helped found the Alta Ski Lift Company, which became one of the most popular ski resorts in the country and sold nearly $13 million in lift tickets during the 1996–1997 season. Laughlin also served for seventeen years (1952–1969) as president of Intercultural Publications, a part of the Ford Foundation that aimed in part to increase European knowledge of American culture. Laughlin was married three times. His first marriage was to Margaret Keyser in 1942, with whom he had two children, Paul and Leila (who was named after the aunt who supported Laughlin's publishing ambitions). This marriage ended in divorce in 1952. In 1957 he married Ann Resor, with whom he had two more children, Robert and Henry. Ann died of cancer in 1989. At the time of his death from a stroke on November 12, 1997, Laughlin was survived by his third wife, Gertrude Huston Laughlin; two of his sons; his daughter; and six grandchildren. Although his poetry has been getting positive responses in recent years as more of it has become available, and it is possible it will become more widely admired in the future, Laughlin is still remembered primarily for his astounding success at bringing so many great literary figures into print. He was one of the most significant publishers of the twentieth century.

Further Reading. *Selected Primary Sources:* Laughlin, James, *Byways* (New York: New Directions, 2005); ———, *Collected Poems* (Wakefield, RI: Moyer Bell, 1993); ———, *A Commonplace Book of Pentastichs* (New York: New Directions, 1998); ———, *The Love Poems* (New York: New Directions, 1997); ———, *Poems New and Selected* (New York: New

Directions, 1998); ———, *Pound as Wuz* (St. Paul, MN: Greywolf, 1987); ———, *Random Essays* (Wakefield, RI: Moyer Bell, 1989); ———, *Random Stories* (Wakefield, RI: Moyer Bell, 1990); ———, *Remembering William Carlos Williams* (New York: New Directions, 1995); ———, *The Secret Room* (New York: New Directions, 1997); ———, *Selected Poems* (San Francisco: City Lights, 1986). **Selected Secondary Sources:** Carruth, Hayden, "Introduction," in *The Collected Poems of James Laughlin* (Wakefield, RI: Moyer Bell, 1994, xv–xxxi); Gussow, Mel, "James Laughlin, Publisher with Bold Taste, Dies at 83" (*New York Times* [14 November, 1997]: D19); Perloff, Marjorie, "James Laughlin (1914–1997)" (*Parnassus: Poetry in Review* 23.1/2 [1998]: 24–32); Leibowitz, Herbert, and Mary Karr, "The Father of Us All" (*Parnassus: Poetry in Review* 23.1/2 [1998]: 8–23); Laughlin, James, "National Book Awards Acceptance Speeches: James Laughlin" (National Book Foundation, 1992, www.national book.org/nbaacceptspeech_jlaughlin .html); Hall, Donald, "James Laughlin of New Directions" (*New York Times* [23 August 1981]: 13); Kuehl, Linda, "Talk with James Laughlin: New and Old Directions" (*New York Times* [25 February 1973]: 46–48).

Alan Kelly

LAUTERBACH, ANN (1942–)

Often compared to the work of **John Ashbery**, Ann Lauterbach's poetry is in the **postmodern** lyric vein, exhibiting an acute sense of narrative's inherent instability and at the same time retaining a post-Romantic attachment to the idea of the engaged, witnessing subject. Lauterbach's early poetry of the 1970s exhibits a tight compositional method and deals overtly with the vicissitudes of human perception as both reflective and constitutive of the material and visual realms; on both of these counts, her work resonates with the poetry of **Wallace Stevens**. Her later work opens up in form, making use of longer disjunctive lines and syntax to allow for silence and reader participation. As in the earlier work, these poems also explore the complexities of intellectual and affective experience, though in more intricately embedded layers that are ultimately resistant to narrative closure. Like **Mei-mei Berssenbrugge** and **Amy Gerstler**, Lauterbach engages frequently with the visual arts in her poetry, and her work appears in museum catalogues and collaborations with contemporary visual and installation artists as well as in anthologies of postmodern poetry. Together with contemporaries **Rae Armantrout**, Berssenbrugge, **Carla Harryman**, **Lyn Hejinian**, **Fanny Howe**, and **Susan Howe**, Lauterbach is often discussed in the context of the innovative or **experimental poetry** movement of American women.

Born in 1942 in Manhattan, Ann Lauterbach grew up in New York City and studied painting at the High School of Music and Art. Upon graduating from high school, she left New York to study literature at the University of Wisconsin–Madison, completing her BA in literature there before going on to graduate work at Columbia University. Lauterbach eventually left graduate school in favor of moving to London, where she worked for seven years variously as editor, teacher, and director of the literature program at the Institute of Contemporary Arts. Returning to New York in the mid-1970s, Lauterbach worked in art galleries until the mid-1980s. Her first collection of poetry, *Many Times, but Then*, was published in 1979 when Lauterbach was thirty-seven years old. In the mid-1980s, Lauterbach began teaching full time in writing programs at several American universities, including Columbia, Princeton, the University of Iowa Writers Workshop, City College of New York, and the Graduate Center at City University, New York. She served as writing director at the Milton Avery Graduate School of Arts at Bard College before becoming the Ruth and David Schwab II Professor of Language and Literature at Bard in the late 1990s. By this time, Lauterbach had been named a Guggenheim Fellow in 1986 and a Fellow of the John D. and Catherine T. MacArthur Foundation in 1993. Her collections *Before Recollection* and *Clamor* were published in 1987 and 1991, respectively. Lauterbach published *And for Example* in 1994 and *On a Stair* in 1996, the latter including a long poem, "A Clown, Some Colors, a Doll, Her Stories, a Song," that was originally published as a book in collaboration with visual artist Ellen Phelan. In 1999 Lauterbach wrote "All View (13 Windows)," a response to Ann Hamilton's installation art piece at the Aldrich Museum, which introduces the installation in the museum catalogue. In addition to having collaborated with numerous visual artists, Lauterbach has written extensively on art and poetics, most recently in a series of influential essays titled "The Night Sky" for the *American Poetry Review*. Her *If in Time: Selected Poems 1975–2000* was published by Penguin in 2001. She continues to teach at Bard College and lives in New York City and Germantown, New York.

Ann Lauterbach's poetry explores the inherently unstable nature of all narrative while revealing the relationships among perception, dialogic engagement with the visual, and the dynamism of intellectual and affective response to the ever-shifting material world. Far from displaying an open-ended relativism, however, Lauterbach's poetry is rooted in a deeply felt attachment to the material and the visual, even as she works to show the role of the engaged subject in ordering and creating the external according to angles of perception, personal feeling, and history. "The Template," which opens *If in Time: Selected Poems 1975–2000*, provides an example of Lauterbach's narrative disruptions via engagement with and overt modulations of visual data. The poem begins with the concrete image of a prostitute described in narrative syntax heavily laden with specific nouns, common adjectives, and prepositions showing definite location. Immediately on introducing the image, however, Lauterbach begins to play with the tools and loci of perception, indicating first a window where "the green light / of a pond" casts an accent light on the tableaux, and then introducing "the male child, nine" as a suddenly visible, previously hidden, witnessing and interrogating figure—an alternative viewer. Thus, the initial promise of a controlled narrative thread is methodically yet delicately undercut by indicators that the narrative is not static but rather is always lit by particular light (which can change, and which also has different meanings for different viewers), told by particular individuals (who may or may not reveal themselves in their entirety), and informed by the intrusion of memory and associative thought processes (which may or may not be obviously "related" to previous content). In the second paragraph of the poem, she writes that "[a] garden is an idea" as much as it is a physical space or visual scene, meaning that we are always looking simultaneously at the history and structure of our own ideas about objects and at the physical objects themselves.

As a lyric poet, Lauterbach habitually employs the trope of the "lyric I," and critics agree that many of the voices overheard in her poetry reflect dialogues or musings in the mind of the poet. But, as in "The Template" and elsewhere, Lauterbach's "I" is most often both physically innocuous and intensely present as an agent of perception. Having presented the image of the prostitute and the young boy in the opening scene of "The Template," Lauterbach's "I" overtly enters the poem at its midpoint to inaugurate a series of digressions into memory and reverie that culminate in a place "where what is is / changed by language." For even as her language engages the object world, altering perception of that world, her "I" serves to both direct our gaze and offer through the very multiplicity of images possibilities for individual readers' unique perceptions. That is, rather than a totalitarian "I" who determines absolutely what the reader will engage, Lauterbach's "I," in concert with her accumulations of images, opens a path for readers to reconsider their own processes of perception; in this way Lauterbach models a method, rather than prescribing a meaning.

Quoting occasionally from **Ralph Waldo Emerson**, Lauterbach layers into her poetry an acute interest in the nineteenth century philosopher's work with the nature of reality and representation. Together with a poem by **modernist** poet **George Oppen**, an epigraph from Emerson opens her recently published selected poems, *If in Time*: "Time dissipates to shining ether the solid angularity of facts. No anchor, no cable, no fences, avail to keep a fact a fact." As an introduction to her body of work thus far, this quote reinforces Lauterbach's prevailing interest in de-naturalizing the material for her read-

ers so they may consider their physical surroundings anew. At the same time, Emerson's statement indirectly alludes to the medium by which facts are presented or undermined as facts: language itself. Lauterbach's "The Same Moon" from the previously uncollected section of *If in Time* echoes Emerson's skepticism about fact while demonstrating Lauterbach's virtuosity in showing humans in perceptual relation to their object world as well as in relation to each other. In this poem, a young woman "graduate" who prefers "what is said / to be said without hindrance / *this is this, that that*" is juxtaposed against the poem's speaker and a companion for whom the aural and visual are part of "the artifice of eternity." This alternative, analytical relationship to the material is subsequently framed in relation to a hermit, emblem of both the mysterious and the solitary, emerging from a casket dressed in "the vocabulary of rags." For Lauterbach, even as we question received relationships among objects, the exchange of ideas with another is equally significant in keeping the object world alive and interesting; the figure of the abject, death-inflected hermit underscores the inherent poverty of a language kept too private. As the poem concludes, all three figures resolve in a perceptual shift as mere players under the "night sky's / ritual exchange— / take this, give that away." Juxtaposed against the false confidence of the young woman's "*this is this, that that,*" these concluding lines undermine the earlier statement of concrete final knowledge while foregrounding the process of an ultimately irresolvable, always inexact exchange inherent in the traffic among people, ideas, objects, and language.

If there is any way to synthesize Ann Lauterbach's interrelated poetic engagements with the visual, intellectual/affective processes of thought, and language as medium, it might best be mapped in relation to the concept of borders or transitional spaces. As "The Template" and "The Same Moon" both explore, it is in the shifts among scenes and the juxtapositions between disparate elements that meaning is suggested. Lauterbach's 1994 collection *And for Example* develops her interest in transitional spaces at the level of material language itself. The collection opens with an epigraph from philosopher and phenomenologist William James, an American scholar known for his interrogations into language as a medium for self-knowledge. Addressing the role of conjunctions and prepositions in mechanically linking ideas and objects at the level of language, James writes, "We ought to say a feeling of *and*, a feeling of *if*, a feeling of *but*, and a feeling of *by*, quite as readily as we say a feeling of *blue* or a feeling of *cold*." Lauterbach extends this idea of the material and sensory significance of otherwise innocuous linking words into the poetry of this collection, playing with syntax to foreground transitions of language in distinct relation to her complex and shifting images. The effect is that of a rigorously denaturalized language that on the surface appears to signify in the usual lyric sequence, resulting in an alternative, somewhat reversed example of Language poetry. In this light, a line in "The Prior" (*And for Example*), "only excess / as a form of boredom," can be read both in its context of its reference to a B movie, and as an invitation to reconsider the relationship between excess and boredom, with the feeling of "as" hovering in a suddenly visible, active state. Similarly, the line "Wanting to say this is not the same / *this* is not the same as *this*" highlights the presence of presumably similar objects in a syntax that foregrounds structures of separateness while concealing revelatory nouns. The line thus concerns the mental act of linking or separating objects, not the objects themselves. In the presence of Lauterbach's preoccupation with perspective and productions of the real, this manipulation of the mechanics of normative language produces another way of experiencing a denaturalized world. When Lauterbach writes in "Stepping Out" (*And for Example*), "From up here in the bleachers / things seem real, but provisional," the emphasis is placed on that liminal space of "seem" and reinforced in the transitional "but." Finally, for Lauterbach, in a world where our faculties of perception have been examined, tested, and re-attuned, one can depend only on the process of exchange and association, not on notions of the real as finite or knowable. As she asserts almost wistfully in "Stepping Out," a poem introduced with a quotation on the nature of reality from Wallace Stevens, master of denaturalized perception, there is "[o]nly the finality of rhythm / on which to insist: rhythm as the example."

Further Reading. *Selected Primary Sources:* Lauterbach, Ann, *And for Example* (New York: Penguin, 1994); ———, *Before Recollection* (Princeton, NJ: Princeton University Press, 1987); ———, *Clamor* (New York: Penguin, 1991); ———, *If in Time: Selected Poems 1975–2000* (New York: Penguin, 2001); ———, *Many Times, but Then* (Austin: Texas University Press, 1979). *Selected Secondary Sources:* Altieri, Charles, "Ann Lauterbach's 'Still' and Why Stevens Still Matters" (*Wallace Stevens Journal* 19.2 [Fall 1995]: 219–233); Hume, Christine, "'Enlarging the Last Lexicon of Perception' in Ann Lauterbach's Framed Fragments," in *American Women Poets in the 21st Century: Where Lyric Meets Language*, ed. Claudia Rankine and Juliana Spahr (Middletown, CT: Wesleyan University Press, 2002, 367–399); Kallenberg, Garrett, "A Form of Duration" (*Denver Quarterly* 29.4 [Spring 1995]: 98–109); McCorkle, James, "Nimbus of Sensations: Eros and Reverie in the Poetry of John Ashbery and Ann Lauterbach," in *The Tribe of John: Ashbery and Contemporary Poetry*, ed. Susan M. Schultz (Tuscaloosa: University of Alabama Press, 1995, 101–125).

Amy Moorman Robbins

LAUX, DORIANNE (1952–)

Described by **Maxine Kumin** as an "archeologist of the everyday," Dorianne Laux implores us to dig beneath the mundane interactions between mothers and daughters, customers and grocery store cashiers, husbands and wives, and, finally, between the present and the past. Her poetry urges us, as she writes in "The Job" (*What We Carry*), to "pay attention to what's turning in the world." Weaving throughout Laux's poems are the enduring themes of love, loss, anger, betrayal, and, ultimately, profound gratitude and renewal, for Laux's poetry is at its core affirmative, imbued with the sort of human faith that is born only from the hard work of emotional excavation.

Dorianne Laux was born in Augusta, Maine, in 1952. She began writing poetry at age twelve, in mostly rhymed and metered verse. Through a marriage, a divorce, and the birth of a child, Laux continued to write, deciding, finally, to take a night class at Mesa College with the poet **Steve Kowit**, who in turn introduced Laux to multicultural and contemporary American women's poetry. Thus encouraged, Laux began reading her poetry in local venues and publishing in local magazines before moving with her daughter to the Bay Area, where she began writing in earnest and establishing ties with the West Coast literary community. At the Napa Valley Writer's Conference, which she attended for three years in a row, Laux met and studied with such established writers as **Carolyn Forché**, **Robert Hass**, and **Carolyn Kizer**. Laux went on to take another evening class, this time through the University of California–Berkeley's extension program, where she met fellow students **Jane Hirshfield** and Stefani Marlis. Laux began publishing her poems in Bay Area journals and other literary magazines, such as *Five Finger Review*, of which the poet **Kim Addonizio** was an editor. Her work in that publication caught the attention of the legendary **Philip Levine**, with whom Laux began a regular correspondence. Levine, having solicited Laux's poetry manuscript, sent the collection to Al Poulin at BOA, and it was accepted within a week of its submission. Laux's first book, *Awake*, was published in 1992 with an introduction by Levine. Eventually Laux resettled in Petaluma, California. Upon her daughter's graduation from high school and the publication of her second book, *What We Carry* (1994), Laux moved to Oregon to join the faculty at the University of Oregon–Eugene.

Central in Laux's work is a preoccupation with the fragility of things in the inevitable grasp of death, disillusion, and loss. In "Break" (*Awake*, 1990) a couple attempts to temper the pervasive forces of dissolution and decay from their small corner of the world. They "put the puzzle together piece / by piece," as their child "circles her room, impatient / with her blossoming," creating, literally and figuratively, a cohesive scene, however small, upon which "the world that is crumbling, a sky that is falling" cannot impinge. Finally, it is the cold reality of risk and loss in which we must live—hence the imperative to find bearings within the small details of "porch swings and autumn trees," a momentary stay against "the pieces we are required to return to." In "The Job" the speaker is reminded, via a friend's finger-severing mishap with a printing press, to come back to the passing and uneventful moment, "to pay attention / to what's turning in the world." Furthermore, it is with a blameless and sincere gratitude that the speaker's friend relates her disfigurement, maintaining that it is "a small price to pay" for her renewed appreciation of the tangible world. It is this same sincere gratitude with which the speaker inflects the lines of "Landrums's Diner, Reno" (*What We Carry*, 1994). After "seven years" recounted amid the joys and disappointments of the American holiday, the couple "have begun to love each other, to trust / the small favors, the daily gifts." Indeed, it is with the appreciation of the small gifts that the waitress appeals to our common humanity, "Asking / "what more we could want?" There is no airbrushing in the world Laux creates: The waitress is "round and clumsy," and the people and places bear the marks of habitual use.

Another thematic motif apparent in Laux's work is the necessary and inevitable process of reinvention and renewal. In "Late October" (*What We Carry*), the speaker, in a moment of clarity, sees the woman she has become, "forty-one years old, standing on a slab / of cold concrete," aware that something has been taken away from her, "valueless / and irreplaceable." Thus the speaker is cast into the flux between the present and the past where the reworking of identity is inescapable, and she approaches the process with fear, "afraid of what I might do next." The poems of *Smoke* (2000), Laux's third book, focus increasingly on the hard realities of grief, loss, and mortality; the poems, again, beg the question of how we may reconfigure the missing parts of ourselves and our separate and collective worlds, be they lost to death, romantic fallout, age, or disillusion. In "Ray at Fourteen," the speaker opens with a benediction, "Bless this boy, born with the strong face / of my older brother," and continues elegiacally, reflecting on the boy's uncanny resemblance to her brother Ray, who had died "at twenty-two on a roadside in Germany." Yet this poem ends not on a tone of lament but on one of hope; the speaker is enjoined to return to the fullness of the moment, where the boy constitutes, in his very likeness to the deceased brother, a junction of the past and the present, the hard work of grief and the possibility for regeneration and, in a sense, rebirth. The poem is contingent on her brother's very physicality, for it is in the solid here-and-now that the speaker must live: "He says, Feel my muscle, and I do."

This question of how we must live and love within the ever-present specter of mortality, fear, and loss is implicit in "The Line," in which a group of mothers wait to have their children fingerprinted and photographed in case they are abducted; in "Fear," a catalogue of worst-case scenarios; and in "The Student," which articulates the hard, insecurity-plagued road toward self-actualization.

Ultimately, Laux's poems articulate the ways in which we move from grief, fear, and desolation toward acceptance and reinvention, finding, all the while, fulfillment in the mundane physicality of the world. If the poems of *Smoke* give voice to the stages of grief, so then is the collection's final poem, "Life Is Beautiful," an anthem of gratitude and hope, representative of a world in which "Everywhere the good life oozes / from the waste we make when we create." Laux's vision, finally, is one of affirmation, wherein the fragmentation of death, loss, and betrayal is reshaped into a hard-won sense of gratitude: "Such abundance. We are gorged, engorging, and gorgeous."

Further Reading. *Selected Primary Sources:* Laux, Dorianne, *Awake* (Rochester, NY: BOA Editions, 1990); ———, *Facts About the Moon* (New York: Norton, 2005); ———, *Smoke* (Rochester, NY: Boa Editions, 2000); ———, *What We Carry* (Rochester, NY: BOA Editions, 1994). ***Selected Secondary Sources:*** Addonizio, Kim, and Dorianne Laux, *The Poet's Companion: A Guide to the Pleasures of Writing Poetry* (New York: W.W. Norton, 1997).

Robyn Art

LAX, ROBERT (1915–2000)

Robert Lax produced a distinctive body of startlingly simple, abstract **minimalist** poetry over his long writing career. Lax was a convert to Catholicism whose work was informed by his spiritual beliefs and the aesthetic principles of the painter Ad Reinhardt. Lax's poetry is visually striking, with short lines of one word or one syllable each, giving his poems a "vertical" appearance. He used an extremely restricted vocabulary, with many poems containing only one or two words—often the names of colors—repeated in a rhythmic pattern. The **visual** impact of his work led to his publication as a **concrete poet** in the 1960s. Lax achieved greater fame in Europe than in his native United States, and was the subject of a chamber film, *Why Should I Buy a Bed When All That I Want Is Sleep?*, and a video installation, *Three Windows*, by the German filmmakers Nicolas Humbert and Werner Penzel in 1999.

Lax was born in Olean, New York, in 1915. From 1934 to 1939 he attended Columbia University, where

Reinhardt, whom Lax had met in high school, was already a student. **Thomas Merton**, author of *The Seven Story Mountain*, in which Lax features prominently, was also at Columbia. Lax studied with Mark Van Doren, who remained a friend. Visits to **jazz** clubs in New York were a frequent activity for Lax and his circle. Merton became a Catholic in the 1930s, and Lax followed suit, converting from Judaism in 1943. In the 1940s, Lax wrote for and worked at the *New Yorker*, wrote film reviews for *Time*, worked as a scriptwriter in Hollywood, and attended Abstract Expressionist art exhibits and meetings of the New York Artists' Club with Reinhardt. In 1949 Lax traveled with the Cristiani Family Circus, sometimes appearing as a clown. In the 1950s Lax began collaborating with Emil Antonucci, who illustrated and published many of Lax's poems at his Journeyman Press over the next few decades. In the late 1950s, when Reinhardt was beginning to produce his famous black paintings, the painter's ideas began to have a profound effect on Lax's work, first evident in *New Poems* (1962). Lax moved to Greece in the early 1960s and settled on the island of Patmos, where he lived and continued to write until shortly before his death in 2000.

Circus of the Sun (1959) is a book of Christian poetry, based on Lax's travels with the Cristiani family circus. The book was begun in the summer of 1949 but not published until ten years later. Unlike Lax's later poems, those in *Circus* are not abstract or minimalist. In this book, the circus becomes a metaphor for the created world. Geometric shapes, especially spheres, feature prominently. The performers are in tune with the forces and rhythms of the universe. "The moment is a sphere moving with Mogador," the tightrope walker. The juggler Rastelli, who died at age thirty-three, is portrayed as a religious hero who "moved all things according to their natures." Among the admirers of *Circus* were **Denise Levertov**, **e.e. cummings**, and **Marianne Moore**.

New Poems proved somewhat of a shock even to Lax's friends Merton and Van Doren. Some poems in the book consist of repetitions of a single word, including "never," "death," "is," "life," and "go." Two others exhibit a pattern based on units of three and four that recurs (in various guises) in Lax's writing over the years. One of these is actually composed of the numbers, "1234," and the other solely of the letter "A." Although it is tempting to ascribe a mystical, Christian significance to Lax's use of the numbers 3 and 4 in this pattern, it can also be accounted for in terms of musical rhythm. Lax establishes a theme in the first line or stanza, repeats it in the second, provides a variation in the third, and returns to the initial theme in the final line or stanza. Lax's interest in such abstract patterns is, however, ultimately a spiritual one.

The *Lugano Review* published two long Lax poems in the 1960s: *Sea & Sky* (1965) and *Black & White* (1966). *Sea & Sky* displays the characteristic Lax vertical style, with one syllable to the line, and much repetition. The vocabulary is relatively varied for a Lax poem, but spare by other standards. Quite quickly the poem withdraws from an opening that suggests a troubled political situation, and turns to the underlying rhythms of natural phenomena, in keeping with Lax's interest in universal patterns. Lax's abstract approach to nature is not descriptive of particular scenes, but employs general nouns in repetitive schemes. A later poem, "Dark Earth Bright Sky" (1985), contains only the words in the title, plus "day" and "night." The contrasting terms and simple rhythm of the poem reflect the alternating light and dark that define and provide order to earthly existence, and thus train the focus on forces in the world that make patterns and provide regularity.

Black & White is much sparser than *Sea & Sky*. The entire poem, in twenty-one sections, is composed of the words "black," "white," and "stone" and an ampersand; "stone" drops out after the fifth section. As in Lax's many color poems, including others composed of "black" and "white," the words are used as contrasting elements in order to create a rhythmic pattern. Despite the extreme abstraction of these poems, there is evidence that they had a basis in actual events: Letters between Lax and Merton in 1963 indicate that the black and white poems were inspired by the Civil Rights Movement.

Lax experimented in a variety of ways, composing permutational poems, such as *Able Charlie Baker Dance* (1971), and poems made of marks or bars of color rather than words or letters, such as "Another Red Red Blue Poem" (1971) and "Cloning for Yellow" (1984). A performance of his *Black/White Oratorio*, with choir and solo voices, was staged at the Festival de la Bâtie in Geneva in 1997. Although he is not as widely known in the United States as in Europe, Lax's significance is grounded in his fusion of the experimental with the spiritual, and poetry with the visual arts.

Further Reading. ***Primary Sources:*** Lax, Robert, *Black & White* (*Lugano Review* 1.5–6 [1966]); ———, *Circus of the Sun* (New York: Journeyman, 1960); ———, *Love Had a Compass: Journals and Poetry*, ed. James J. Uebbing (New York: Grove, 1996); ———, *New Poems* (New York: Journeyman, 1962); ———, *Sea & Sky* (*Lugano Review* 1.3–4 [1965]); ———, *A Thing That Is: New Poems*, ed. Paul J. Spaeth (Woodstock, New York: Overlook, 1997); ———, *33 Poems*, ed. Thomas Kellein (New York: New Directions, 1988). ***Secondary Sources:*** Biddle, Arthur W., ed., *When Prophecy Still Had a Voice: The Letters of Thomas Merton and Robert Lax* (Lexington: University Press of Kentucky, 2001); Miller, David, "The Poetry of Robert

Lax: An Introduction" (*New Lugano Review* 2 [1975]: 46–48); Miller, David, and Nicholas Zurbrugg, eds., *The ABCs of Robert Lax* (Exeter, UK: Stride, 1999).

Karen Alexander

LAZARUS, EMMA (1849–1887)

Although Jewish American poet Emma Lazarus is difficult to categorize as a writer, the themes and genres of her poetry reflect both Hellenic and Hebraic traditions filtered through the mode of a Romantic aesthestic. Eleven years old when the South seceded and the Union declared war, she expressed in rhymed quatrains the sensitivity of a young girl hearing about the Civil War. Through her late teens and early twenties, she deployed through a range of traditional poetic genres the themes of high-Romantic idealism: heroism fighting against unjust tyranny and the beauty of nature and its effects on the poet. As her writing matures, it becomes more engaged taking up the issue of anti-Semitism and Jewish relocation.

The fourth of seven children, Lazarus was born in New York City on July 22, 1849, to Moses Lazarus, a descendant of Sephardic Jews, and Esther Nathan, a descendant of German Jews. Both sides of the family had immigrated to colonial America; at least one ancestor fought in the Revolutionary War. Established through his business as a sugar refiner, Lazarus's father saw that his children attended the Shearith Israel Synagogue and received an education in the classics. Lazarus was immersed in the rich cultural life of nineteenth-century New York, including concerts, art exhibits, and literary readings. Learning Greek, Italian, French, German, and later Hebrew, she translated into English poetic works by writers from Theocritus and Petrarch, to Coppée, Goethe, Heine, and German editions of medieval Spanish Hebrew poetry. Her first book, *Poems and Translations*, was published, through her father's encouragement and sponsorship, in 1866. She soon met literary mentor and lifetime friend **Ralph Waldo Emerson**, with whom she corresponded for a decade. Lazarus's *Admetus and Other Poems* (1871) received critical acclaim, and Ivan Turgenev praised Lazarus's third book, *Alide: An Episode of Goethe's Life* (1874). Because Emerson had assured her of the strength of her poetry, Lazarus challenged him when he failed to include her poems in his collection *Parnassus* (1874). Through her ties to Concord, the young Lazarus became acquainted with Thomas Wren Ward, **William Ellery Channing II**, **Walt Whitman**'s friend the naturalist John Burroughs, and **Bronson Alcott** and others in Alcott's "School of Philosophy." As she matured, she continued to read broadly in what she termed the literature of "the Greeks and Orientals," as well as the writings of literary contemporaries such as Carlyle, Browning, William Morris, and Mathew Arnold; Hugo, Dumas, Fromentin, and Sully-

Prudhomme; and Turgenev and Tolstoy. She conversed with intellectuals such as author and abolitionist **Thomas Wentworth Higginson**, and editors **Edmund Clarence Stedman** and Richard Watson Gilder. Gilder with his wife, Helena, established and hosted the Society of American Artists and the Authors' Club, and Lazarus sustained a lively correspondence with Helena for years. Lazarus also corresponded with **Nathaniel Hawthorne**'s daughter **Rose Hawthorne Lathrop**, whom she met in 1881. Shortly thereafter, Lazarus met Henry James, who shared her admiration for Turgenev and wrote letters introducing her into English literary circles, where she met William Morris and Robert Browning, among others. Lazarus also met distinguished members of England's Jewish community, such as Claude Montefiore and his great-uncle, philanthropist Sir Moses Montefiore, in addition to the Goldsmids, the Rothschilds, the Moscheles, and the Montalbas (Young, 107). She received correspondence from Laurence Oliphant, who, having served in British consulates and writing from Haifa, suggested that the American consulate in St. Petersburg press for the repeal of an edict prohibiting Russian Jews from immigrating to Palestine (259). Lazarus increasingly recognized, the need for a Jewish nation based on ethnicity rather than religion (Omer-Sherman 171). After the Russian pogroms of 1881, Lazarus wrote passionately for the immigrants fleeing Eastern Europe, and she advocated a Jewish homeland in Palestine. Her poetry of this period was collected in her book *Songs of a Semite* (1882), which includes her translations from the German of Hebrew poems written by medieval Spanish Sephardic scholars Solomon ibn Gabirol, Moses ibn Ezra, Judah Halevi, and Judah ben Solomon Al-Harizi. Her polemical works appeared in journals such as *Century Magazine* and *American Hebrew*. After her father's death in 1885, a difficult loss, she and her sisters began another tour of Europe. Weakened by cancer, however, Lazarus was compelled to return prematurely to America. She died on November 19, 1887.

Lazarus, like German Jewish poet Heinrich Heine, revered Hellenic and Hebraic literary traditions. She translated some of Heine's works in her book *Poems and Ballads of Heinrich Heine* (1881) and acknowledges his reverence for "Romanticism, Hebraism, Hellenism, Teutonism" in her essay "The Poet Heine" (Eiselein, 284). Lazarus developed a cosmopolitan knowledge of German, American, and English Romanticism and wrote in genres ranging from sonnets to blank-verse tragedy, and from *ottava rima* to free verse. Her early poetry is strongly Romantic. "Phantasies" (after Robert Schumann) reflects the theory and language of the Romantics while summoning associations with classical **pastoralism**. Opening at evening and evoking images of death, her second stanza recalls Wordsworth's "Ode: Intimations of Immortality from Recollections of Childhood":

The earth lies grave, by quiet airs caressed,
And shepherdeth her shadows, but each stream,
Freed to the sky, is by that glow possessed,
And traileth with the splendors of a dream.

She describes a nature made unfamiliar by the inward workings of the imagination. Whereas Schumann had titled the second movement of his composition "Aufschwung," Lazarus titles it "Aspiration," suggesting divine inspiration through "influence," "sways," "impulse," "whispers," and "nameless aspiration." Lazarus complicates this passage by incorporating Schumann's theme of "upswing" or "upturn," a sense of being lifted toward the evening star:

Exalted, thrilled, the freed soul fain would soar
unto that point of shining prominence,
. . .
To mount with daring flight, to hover o'er
Low hills of earth, flat meadows, level sea,
And earthly joy and trouble.

Lazarus develops Romantic topoi of transcendence, mourning, and flight established in earlier works such as Keats's "Ode to a Nightingale," Wordsworth's "To a Skylark," and Whitman's "Out of the Cradle Endlessly Rocking."

While Lazarus's early poetry emulates that of the largely Protestant Romantics, her sense of acceptance by that community may have been challenged as early as 1874, suggests Omer-Sherman, when Emerson omitted her poetry from *Parnassus* (186). At that moment, Lazarus, who never married, may have apprehended the significance of what scholar Diane Lichtenstein has described as "her Jewish, American, and female citizenships" (251) and what scholar Michael Weingrad has termed the "ironic fusions of Jewish and Christian allegiance" (108). Scholars cite Lazarus's poem "Echoes" (written in 1880) as her acknowledgment of a womanhood displaced in time and context: "Late-born and woman-souled I dare not hope, / . . . the might / Of manly, modern passion shall alight / Upon my Muse's lips." This poem not only verbalizes the difficulties faced by a woman whose abilities equal those represented in the male canon, but also, suggests Weingrad, indicates Lazarus's averions of a heritage in which a woman is "'screened' by the *mehitsah* of her sex" (110). Lazarus's empathy with her Jewish heritage appears poetically as early as 1867, when she wrote "In the Jewish Synagogue at Newport," a poem paralleling if not imitating Longfellow's "The Jewish Cemetery at Newport." As Lichtenstein has observed, Lazarus at eighteen years of age may have felt the need to adopt a subject and style "blessed" by an approved American male poet, but she chose a poem with Jewish theme (251). In 1877, writes scholar Gregory Eiselein, Lazarus translated from the German some medieval Sephardic poetry (17). Her earliest translations focus on poems of love and nature; these translations, such as "A Letter, from Judah Hallevi to His Friend Isaac," carry the sound of her early Romanticism. But others explicitly address a "Longing for Jerusalem," as her translations of that poem and "On the Voyage to Jerusalem" reveal. Like Heinrich Heine, Lazarus is torn between two cultures: In her own poem "The Venus of the Louvre," depicts Heine's pain as, kneeling before the statue, he confronts contradictions between his Hellenic and Hebraic identities. But Lazarus's Jewish voice strengthens as she matures, and her writings demonstrate an intellectual toughness, capable of meeting any philosophical challenge. This strength appears in her poem "An Epistle from Joshua Ibn Vives of Allorqui to His Former Master, Solomon Levi-Paul de Santa-Maria, Bishop of Cartagena, Chancellor of Castile, and Privy Councillor to King Henry III. of Spain," drawn from Heinrich Graetz's historical account of the conversion of a medieval Sephardic Jew to Catholicism. Choosing to write from the perspective of a young Jewish male who had followed Joshua Ibn Vives, Lazarus methodically analyzes and counters the reasons for conversion. In her efforts to aid imperiled Jews, Lazarus in 1883 established a Society for the Improvement and Colonization of East European Jews. The collapse of that organization has been attributed either to a broadening of Lazurus's interests, exemplified in her discussions of William Morris's humanitarian efforts to improve working conditions in factories (Young, 9), or to a loss of interest as Lazarus was swept back into her love of aesthetics as she toured Europe. However, examining Lazarus's poem "By the Waters of Babylon," the subtitle of which is a translation of Baudelaire's title *Petits poèmes en prose*, Michael Weingrad suggests that Lazarus experimented with **free verse** as an evocation of scriptural form and thus asserted her Jewish identity as never before.

By the late 1870s the focus of Lazarus's publications had shifted from aesthetics to political activism: The *New York Times* had reported Judge Henry Hilton's refusal to admit Joseph Seligman into the Grand Union Hotel in Saratoga (Young, 146), and Eastern European Jews were fleeing pogroms. Lazarus used her resources, language skills, and writings to aid immigrants on Ward's Island. When Russian immigrant Mme. Z. Ragozin defended the pogroms in "Russian Jews and Gentiles" (*Century*, April 1882), Lazarus immediately challenged Ragozin's "race-animosity or religious intolerance" in her own essay "Russian Christianity versus Modern Judaism" (Eiselein, 250). Even as Lazarus actively entered the political arena, however, she continued to work with European literary and mythological tradition, and synthesized it with the lamentation tradition of Judaism in her treatment of historical events. Her play *The Dance to Death: A Historical Tragedy in Five Acts,* dedicated to George Eliot in gratitude for *Daniel Deronda* and published in *Songs of a Semite* (1882), fuses Lazarus's artistry with immigrant witness to the pogroms. Lazarus bases this blank-verse tragedy on Richard Reinhard's *Der Tanz zum Tode* (1877), a narrative of the 1349 pogrom in Nordhausen, six centuries later a Nazi subcamp of Buchenwald. For documentation, Lazarus cites Heinrich Graetz's nineteenth-century, eleven-volume history *Geschichte der Juden von den Ältesten Zeiten bis auf die Gegenwart* (Eiselein, 131). A jeremiad opens the drama as a rabbi from France warns the Nordhausen Jews of impending catastrophe. Trusting in the good will of gentiles, however, the Jewish community remains in Nordhausen. Their trust proves fatal: the Jewish community is burned to death in the synnogogue. As Lazarus deploys the traditional European typing of gentile features as fair and Jewish as dark, she anticipates Holocaust survivor Paul Celan's "Todesfuge," in which the golden hair of Goethe's Margarete in *Faust* counters the now ashen hair of the Shulamite of *Song of Solomon*. But, whereas Lazarus suggests the possibility that gentiles might recognize the love and loyalty of the Jewish community, Celan describes an unbridgeable chasm between gentile and Jew enacted in the Shoah.

Lazarus, however, writing in the nineteenth century, hoped that the choices made in her moment of history would ensure freedom and provision not only for Jews but also for anyone persecuted on hostile shores. Her 1883 sonnet "The New Colossus," written to raise funds for the pedestal for Auguste Bartholdi's *Liberty Enlightens the World*, invokes her exhortation in "An Epistle to the Hebrews," essay XII: to provide a "home for the homeless, a goal for the wanderer, an asylum for the persecuted, a nation for the denationalized." In an iconoclastic and symbolic reconstruction of *Liberty*, writes Dan Marom, Lazarus implicitly contrasts the Colossus of Rhodes, representing the bronze might of European power, with the "Mother of Exiles," the Hebrew matriarch Rachel who weeps for her children (233). Lazarus recreates liberty as the measure by which a society relates to each of its members (237). Thus Lazarus hopes not only for freedom for the "huddled masses," but also for welcome and compassion.

Because of the millions of visitors to the Statue of Liberty, it is for this sonnet that Lazarus remains best known. The closing lines are often quoted:

> Give me your tired, your poor,
> Your huddled masses yearning to breathe free,
> The wretched refuse of your teeming shore,
> Send these, the homeless, tempest-tost to me.
> I lift my lamp beside the golden door.

Further Reading. *Selected Primary Sources:* Lazarus, Emma, *Admetus and Other Poems* (New York: Hurd and Houghton, 1871); ———, "By the Waters of Babylon. Little Poems in Prose" (*Century* [March 1887]: 801–803); ———, *Poems and Ballads of Heinrich Heine* (New York: R. Worthington, 1881); ———, *Poems and Translations* (New York: Hurd and Houghton, 1867); ———, *The Poems of Emma Lazarus*, 2 vols. (Boston: Houghton, Mifflin, 1888); ———, *Songs of a Semite: The Dance to Death and Other Poems* (New York: The American Hebrew, 1882). ***Selected Secondary Sources:*** Eiselein, Gregory, ed., *Emma Lazarus: Selected Poems and Other Writings* (Peterborough, ON: Broadview Press, 2002); Lichtenstein, Diane, "Words and Worlds: Emma Lazarus's Conflicting Citizenships" (*Tulsa Studies in Women's Literature* 6.2 [Autumn 1987]: 247–263); Marom, Daniel, "Who Is the 'Mother of Exiles'? Jewish Aspects of Emma Lazarus's 'The New Colossus'" (*Prooftexts* 20.3 [Autumn 2000]: 231–261); Omer-Sherman, Ranen, "Emma Lazarus, Jewish American Poetics, and the Challenge of Modernity" (*Legacy* 19.2 [2002]: 170–191); Vogel, Dan, *Emma Lazarus* (Boston: Twayne, 1980); Weingrad, Michael, "Jewish Identity and Poetic Form in 'By the Waters of Babylon'" (*Jewish Social Studies* 9.3 [Spring–Summer 2003]: 107–120); Young, Bette Roth, *Emma Lazarus in Her World: Life and Letters* (Philadelphia, Jerusalem: Jewish Publication Society, 1995).

Margaret Burton

LEA, SYDNEY (1942–)

It is impossible to separate the poetry of Sydney Lea from his love of the outdoors. Lea's work is imbued with his fascination with nature and his participation in the cycles of the seasons as husband and father, as environmentalist, and, perhaps surprisingly for a poet, as hunter. Subjects not usually associated with poetry—the training of bird dogs, the decision whether to shoot a prey, and the struggle between predator and quarry—are at the heart of his poetry, Lea's poems (as well as his stories and essays) are highly autobiographical and deeply meditative. They also tell the stories of other outdoorsmen: people who hunt and fish, who log for timber; people who live in harmony with the seasons; people who "inhaled the jab of air with the pine upon it, / took in the wail of loons that mourned for fish" ("The Dream of Sickness: Letter to LB in Vermont," *Hunting the Whole Way Home*, 1994).

At a deeper level, Lea's themes are those of all great poetry—man against man, man against nature, man against the universe, man against God, man against himself—and their reverse: man in harmony with man, nature, universe, God, and himself. Along with his nine volumes of poetry, Lea has published a novel, *A Place in Mind* (1989); and two collections of nonfiction, *Hunting the Whole Way Home* (1994) and *A Little Wildness: Some Notes on Rambling* (2005). He was the founder and for thirteen years editor of *New England Review*. Lea's first published poem appeared in 1976 in the *New Yorker* and was followed quickly by poems in the *Atlantic* and the *New Republic*. He has taught at Dartmouth, Yale, Middlebury, Wesleyan, Vermont College, and the National University of Hungary in Budapest, but he takes ample time off for writing. The collection *Pursuit of a Wound* (2000) was a Pulitzer Prize finalist, and his *To the Bone: New and Selected Poems* (1996) was co-winner of the Poets' Prize. His fame has been considerable for one who, from his earliest work, has aligned himself with the unlucky and the dispossessed.

Just as he chose to live with his wife and children and dogs in the flinty northern woods of Vermont's Connecticut River Valley, Lea was drawn to people whose existence was both doomed and heroic. He has often been called the poetic heir to **Robert Frost**. For Lea, that is the ultimate compliment. He told Marie Jordan Giordano in an interview for the *Writer's Chronicle* in September 2004 that he considers Frost "the great American poet. . . . You can take a Robert Frost poem into almost any venue and people will get something out of it. It's what I hope for in my writing" (Giordano).

Lea, like Frost, adopted Vermont as home, but there are great differences between them. "One thing Frost was able to do that I am constitutionally unable to do is to leave the almighty fetid, squalid 'I' out of the poem. I think when people call me an heir to Frost, what they're talking about is where I live, but I'm not really very much like Frost. Frost, God bless him, would never have written anything like my poem 'To The Bone,' which is kind of a blues rant," Lea remarks (Daley, 128).

You can hear the blues in much of Lea's writing. He has said if he had been 10 or 15 percent better a musician, he might have pursued music as a career rather than writing and teaching. "The rhythms and cadences of what I call Black classical music are probably more influential on my psyche than anything I've ever read," he says. "The heft of the old twelve bar blues is always in my mind to some extent" (Daley, 128).

The poem "To the Bone" from the collection of the same name (1996) exemplifies Lea's ability to weave personal and universal themes into recollections of real-life events, told in blues language. The poem records an incident in September 1994 when Lea cut his leg to the bone with a chainsaw while helping a friend whose husband had left her in a trailer with a couple of children, no car, and no heating wood. The reader joins Lea in the experience, beginning with the wound itself and the nurse who saved his muscle from rolling "up like a windowshade," through the delirium of the emergency room and surgery and painkillers to the eventual recovery. Lea presents the confusing yet somehow sane meanderings of his mind during the first few days after the accident. As worried family members penetrated the fog of shock and the morphine pump, a procession of friends, living and dead, also visited Lea's imagination. Among the latter, the most persistent was his old friend Earl Bonnett, "who had known more pain than any intern could conjure / his girlchild long since at seventeen having plain dropped dead."

As in so many of his poems, Lea presents Bonnett and a host of other sad-luck but valiant characters without distinction from the wife and children who gather at his bedside. Each has been challenged by life's worst—be it loss of limb, child, brother, or innocence. Yet, Lea ends the poem, like so many of his musings, on the side of optimism, writing "the wound sealing itself such that again I'd refer to me / as a being entire and such that this ceaseless current bearing every desire / we name life would come out all right."

Again, like Frost, Lea is deliberate about writing for the average person. He noted that some writers purposefully made their work too difficult for the average person to read, never mind comprehend, pointing out that **Ezra Pound** once said, "The man in the street is there because he doesn't deserve to be let in." Lea's feelings were "Well, the hell with that, I say! I want to invite as many people into my poetry or fiction as I can. Is that a lightweight aspiration? Not to my hero, Frost, it wasn't" (Giordano).

Born December 22, 1942, in Chestnut Hill, Pennsylvania, Lea grew up in the rural countryside nearby. He earned his bachelor's, master's, and doctorate degrees from Yale University. He came to writing late, having lived the first fifteen years of his adult life primarily as an academic. He "had dreams of being a writer since a child but never started writing until age 35. Writers were something different. I thought there was something magical about writing; I didn't know what it was" (Daley, 126). After graduate school, he was hired to teach at Dartmouth College. Seven years or so later, the chair of his department told Lea that if he ever wanted to be considered for tenure, he'd best publish some scholarly writing. Lea went to the Baker Library at Dartmouth and took a look at "my inscrutable Ph.D. dissertation on supernatural literature of the nineteenth century" (Daley, 126). He had thought he might turn some section of the thesis into an article for a scholarly journal. But as he stood in the stacks with the dissertation in his hand, he actually said out loud, "This is not what I want to do when I grow up" (Daley, 126).

He knew immediately what he wanted to write about and it had nothing to do with scholarly research and dissertation. "I was captivated by a generation of men and women I knew in New England, virtually all of them gone now, at least the ones that I knew well," he told Giordano. His narrative style grew as much out of his material as it did from instinct or design. His subjects "were essentially pre-industrial people who made their own entertainment, and the entertainment tended to take the shape of narrative, and I loved to hear those voices, male and female, as they rolled on and spun stories. I just loved the rhythms and the cadences of that language, and I said I'd like to write about them. I wanted to capture that quality," he told Giordano, explaining that he thought he could "better get a little bit of the heft of [his subjects'] language" in verse.

Lea's creative process is inextricably linked to his ramblings in the woods. "I'm an early riser," he said. "I get out of bed and head for the woods first thing—maybe 5 in the morning. I'm not necessarily looking for material for a poem. Things just seem to be given to me and I come back and write. Getting off by myself is part of my writing process" (Daley, 127). His friend the late poet **William Matthews** used to compare Lea's writing to the 1932 song "The Teddy Bears' Picnic," which has the line "If you go down in the woods today, you're sure of a big surprise." "It's that surprise that hooks you and what you find yourself writing about," Lea explained. "Last winter, for example, I was walking along and came across the carcass of a dead deer and I said to myself the words, 'winter kill.' Something in those words intrigued me and I played around with them when I got back home. Out of that came four poems in four days, all from going into the woods and encountering a big surprise" (Daley, 127).

Further Reading. *Selected Primary Sources:* Lea, Sydney, *The Floating Candles* (Urbana: University of Illinois Press, 1983); ———, *Ghost Pain: Poems* (New York: Sarabande Books, 2005); ———, *Hunting the Whole Way Home: Essays and Poems* (Hanover, NH: University Press of New England, 1994); ———, *A Little Wildness: Some Notes on Rambling* (Ashland, OR, Story Line Press, 2005); ———, *A Place in Mind* (New York: Scribner's, 1989); ———, *Prayer for the Little City* (New York: Charles Scribner's Sons, 1989); ———, *Pursuit of a Wound* (Urbana: University of Illinois Press, 2000); ———, *Searching the Drowned Man* (Urbana: University of Illinois Press, 1980); ———, *To the Bone: New and Selected Poems* (Urbana: University of Illinois Press, 1996). *Selected Secondary Sources:* Daley, Yvonne, *Vermont writers: A State of Mind* (Hanover, NH: University Press of New England, 2005); Giordano, Marie Jordan, "An Interview with Sydney Lea" (*Writer's Chronicle* [September 2004], http://www.mariejordan.com/publishedreviews).

Yvonne Daley

LEE, LI-YOUNG (1957–)

Li-Young Lee is one of the leading contemporary **Asian American poets** and arguably the one who has achieved the most literary recognition. Lee has won significant awards for his comparatively small literary output—three books of poems and a memoir. Lee's writing, largely autobiographical, is intimate, tender, and powerful. The power comes in part from his capacity to perceive life's paradoxes and to meditate on both the subject and object of memories by interweaving the real and the surreal, abstraction and details, philosophical considerations and personal narratives. The texture of Lee's poetry is rich and dense with images and reflections; the poems are, nonetheless, lyrical and accessible. Endowed with a diasporic consciousness, Lee speaks wistfully of the loss of his father, the displacement of his family, and the desire to make sense of his own identity. Some commentators think that Lee's experience as a Chinese immigrant shapes his poems and poetics, while others, refusing to confine his poetry to an ethnocentric reading, assert that Lee's thematic concerns are universal.

Lee was born to Chinese parents in Jakarta, Indonesia, on August 19, 1957. His father, the hero-figure of his work, was a personal physician to Chinese communist leader Mao Tse-tung. In Jakarta, Lee's father taught English and philosophy at Gamaliel University until, in 1958, he became a political prisoner of the anti-Chinese President Sukarno. In 1959 he escaped from prison and fled Indonesia with the family, for several years traveling through Hong Kong, Macau, and Japan; in 1964 Lee's family finally settled in the United States. Lee's father became a Presbyterian minister in a small town in Pennsylvania, where he died in 1981. Much of this history is recounted in Lee's poems and, more explicitly, in his memoir *The Winged Seed.* Lee attended grade school and high school in Pennsylvania, and he enrolled at the University of Pittsburgh in 1975, receiving his BA there in 1979. He later studied at the University of Arizona and the State University of New York at Brockport. Lee now lives in Chicago, Illinois, with his wife and their two children. When still pursuing undergraduate studies at the University of Pittsburgh, Lee met his mentor, Gerald Stern, who later introduced him to the poetry-reading public by writing the preface to his first book of poetry, *Rose.*

Rose was published in 1986 and won the Delmore Schwartz Memorial Poetry Award. Mostly written in early 1980s, shortly after Lee's father's death, the poems in *Rose* are emotionally intense, pervaded by poignant memories of his father: his suffering ("1949, he's 30 years old, / his toenails pulled out, / his toes beaten a beautiful / violet" ["Water"]), his love ("I was cold once. So my father took off his blue sweater, / He wrapped me in it" ["Mnemonic"]), and his death (he "lay down / to sleep like a snow-covered road / winding through pines older than him" ["Eating Together"]).

Many of the poems in *Rose* use simple objects as central images to invoke memories, introduce fragments of life, and suggest underlying messages. As Zhou Xiaojing points out, "Lee employs and develops a major technique which relies on a central image as the organizing principle for both the subject matter and structure of the poem" (117). In the **long poem** "Always a Rose," the encounter with a rose in the darkness triggers memories of various episodes associated with "rose." The poem begins with describing the ephemerality of life in nature: "Dead daisies, shriveled lilies" and "a rose / left for dead," and then shifts to the death of the speaker's father: "the roses burning in the coffin between my father's stiff hand." The image of the rose enables Lee to evoke and connect to all his loved ones—from the grandmother who ate black roses as a little girl to a brother who "inherited, / worm-eaten rose / of his brain." More importantly for the poet, it allows him to explore different facets of his father and his strong feelings toward him as a godlike figure: "My father the Godly, he was the chosen. / My father almighty, full of good fear."

Likewise, in "Persimmon," a widely anthologized poem from *Rose*, the central image of persimmons provides both freedom and restraint as the poem traverses the speaker's life, addressing particularly his growth and struggle between two languages and two cultures. The poem begins with the painful memory of the speaker being punished by his sixth-grade teacher for confusing "persimmon" with "precision," a "confusion" undermined later by the fact that though lacking a natural grasp of the pronunciation of the adopted language, this Chinese American child actually knows how to treat "persimmon" with more "precision" than his teacher and classmates. The poem then turns to a moment when the speaker is older, teaching Donna, a white girl, to learn Chinese, when he himself falters in the language. Eventually, the memory visits the now grown-up speaker, who finds the painting of two persimmons "so full they want to drop from the cloth." Here persimmons become a reminiscence of his father, who was able to paint these persimmons with such "precision" even after losing his eyesight, because, for him, as he hopes his son will bear in mind, "something never leaves a person: . . . the texture of persimmons, / in your palm, the ripe weight."

The City in Which I Love You, Lee's second poetry collection, was published in 1990 and awarded the Lamont Poetry Prize by the Academy of American Poets. Though the speaker still laments the loss of his father, the father is now more his equal than a godlike figure: "At the doorway, I watched, and I suddenly / knew he was one like me" ("My Father, in Heaven, Is Reading Out Loud"). Though still haunted by memories of the past ("Memory revises me" and "The past / doesn't fall away, the past / joins the greater / telling, and is" ["Furious Versions"]), the poet sheds more light on the present and on the potentiality of change for the future. Indeed, it seems that the speaker's grappling with the memories of his father is essential for him to understand his own making of a new home through marriage

and fatherhood, and his growth into a poet and a citizen of the world. In "Good Night," seeing his son going to sleep in his arms in a narrow bed, the speaker recalls a childhood incident when he fell off the roof while trying to break off "a petal decked branch" for his father, who in great worry and pain, "ran out to find me sprawled, dazed, gripping his crushed gift, thrust / at him in my bloody fist." Remembering this incident many years before when his father and he endured pain caused by their love for each other, now the speaker feels that he and his little boy are enjoying the discomfort of lying in the narrow bed, "comforted" by each other's presence. The poem ends "We suffer each other to have each other."

Lee realizes that suffering is inextricable from love and essential to growth, and in "Cleaving," the last poem of the collection, he has learned to accept more of life's paradoxes. The story is no longer centered on the father and speaker himself; it begins with his observation of and identification with a Chinese butcher in Chinatown. The speaker feels the power of "cleaving," cleaving of soul and body, cleaving as resolving obstacles and bringing about change, empowering the speaker and extending his love and sympathy beyond father and son, to Chinese immigrants, and to people of different races and ethnicities: "He is my sister, this/ beautiful Bedouin . . . this Jew, this Asian . . . this immigrant, / this man with my face."

In 1995 Lee published his memoir *The Winged Seed*. Since then, he has written another collection of poems, titled *Book of My Nights* (2001). As the title suggests, this collection is steeped in an atmosphere of dreams, sleeplessness, and darkness. Pursuing the themes of his earlier work, it is a book of questionings, often without answers. Even at the most peaceful and reassuring moment, as described in "The Hammock," in which the speaker holds his son in his lap as his mother once held him, he sees his life as if led "between two unknowns"; he asks "what's it like? / Is it a door, and good-bye on either side? / A window, and eternity on either side?" By inviting readers to contemplate such primal questions, the book constructs a resonant space, a sense of dark joy, of "singing between two great rests." that Lee's earlier collections did not achieve.

Further Reading. *Selected Primary Sources:* Lee, Li-Young, *Book of My Nights* (New York: BOA Editions, 2001); ———, *The City in Which I Love You* (New York: BOA Editions, 1990); ———, *Rose* (New York: BOA Editions, 1986): ———, *The Winged Seed: A Remembrance* (New York: Simon & Schuster, 1995). ***Selected Secondary Sources:*** Greenbaum, Jessica, "Memory's Citizen" (*Nation* 253.11 [October 1991]: 416–18); Yao, Steven G., "The Precision of Persimmons: Hybridity, Grafting and the Case of Li-Young Lee" (*LIT: Literature Interpretation*

Theory 12.1 [2001]: 1–23); Zhou, Xiaojing, "Inheritance and Invention in Li-Young Lee's Poetry" (*MELUS* 21.1 [Spring 1996]: 113–132).

Jun Lei

LEHMAN, DAVID (1948–)

David Lehman may be best remembered for two projects undertaken toward the end of the twentieth century: He created Scribner's *Best American Poetry* series (1988 to present) and he revitalized the popularity of the **New York School** of poets through *The Last Avant-Garde: The Making of the New York School of Poets* (1998) and through his own poetry, which continues the New York School's loose traditions of wit and whimsy.

Born in New York City in 1948, Lehman grew up in Inwood, Manhattan, just north of the George Washington Bridge. His childhood was marked by long walks in the city, time spent in the local public library, and baseball.

His early studies were in an Orthodox yeshiva, where secular studies occupied half of the day and Judaic studies the other half. Leaving the yeshiva in high school was the drama that shaped his teenage years. At seventeen he found himself writing poems every day (the first of many periods in his life when he would cultivate that practice); he decided then that he would be a poet.

As an undergraduate at Columbia University, he enrolled in **Kenneth Koch**'s yearlong imaginative writing course, later pursuing independent study with Koch. After earning a BA and MA from Cambridge University, he returned to Columbia for his Ph.D; mentors included thesis advisor Michael Wood, though he credits Lionel Trilling—with whom he worked as a graduate assistant—with being his strongest influence at that time.

Lehman's first collection of poems, *An Alternative to Speech*, was published in 1986, followed by *Operation Memory* (1990) and *Valentine Place* (1996). His first three collections are rife with sestinas, villanelles, and variant but recognizable sonnets (of special note is the thirty-sonnet sequence "Mythologies" that serves as centerpiece for *Operation Memory*). The mastery of form evinced by his early work is equally present, though in a jazz-influenced and improvisational way, in the daily poems that make up his latter two volumes of poems, *The Daily Mirror* (2000) and *The Evening Sun* (2002).

Because he is as much a cultural and literary critic as he is a poet, Lehman's nonfiction works bear examination alongside his poetry. Published in 1991, *Signs of the Times: Deconstruction and the Fall of Paul de Man* is a critique of deconstruction and an exploration of the downfall of one of the movement's first and strongest proponents, Paul de Man, who was revealed to be a Nazi apologist. The irony and sense of play in Lehman's work mark him a **postmodernist**, but he is careful to place postmodernism in opposition to deconstruction, arguing that postmodernism celebrates the literary impulses that poststructuralism and deconstruction denigrate.

Also noteworthy is *The Line Forms Here* (1992), a collection of essays and articles covering ground as diverse as the nature of verse, poets who work for a living, and individual poets ranging from **Elizabeth Bishop** to **John Hollander**. In 1998 Scribner released what many consider to be Lehman's finest work of nonfiction, a cultural history titled *The Last Avant-Garde: The Making of the New York School of Poets*.

Lehman's relationship with academe has been complex, thanks in part to *Signs of the Times* and in part to his long career in journalism (he spent seven years writing for *Newsweek* and reviewed books regularly for *People*). Lehman has also edited a range of anthologies, among them *Great American Prose Poems* (2003), and collections of critical essays on poets **James Merrill** and **John Ashbery**. In addition to serving as series editor for the *Best American Poetry* series, Lehman is also general editor of the University of Michigan Press's *Poets on Poetry* Series, a mantle he assumed when Donald Hall stepped down in 1994.

The themes that appear in Lehman's nonfiction—meaning (and the lack thereof), mysteries and film noir; the boundaries between prose and verse; an appreciation for the avant-garde sensibilities of the New York School—also permeate his poetry. His tenure in journalism led to the flair for reportage he displays in his two collections of daily poems, each named after a defunct or imaginary newspaper.

Lehman acknowledges that his daily poem practice was inspired in part by **William Stafford**, **Robert Bly**, **Emily Dickinson** (who wrote a poem every day in 1862 and 1863), and, most important, **Frank O'Hara**, a major New York School figure. For Lehman, writing a poem a day isn't an act of hubris, but rather an act of faith; inspiration, he writes in "January 1" (*The Daily Mirror*), is in the lungs and air and "comes / at my command like a turkey club sandwich." Each daily poem captures a moment, an afternoon, a snatch of conversation or song or dream; the book is a solution in which these captured moments float, and each poem gains new context from the poems alongside it.

An urbane and sometimes nostalgic relationship to Judaism is present in many of Lehman's poems, from *An Alternative to Speech*'s "Enigma Variations" ("We are the chosen people, choosing to laugh / At a practical joke that isn't all that funny") (90) to *The Evening Sun*'s "April 4," which paints a poignant picture of Passover. Although Lehman has moved far from his yeshiva upbringing, his work continues to embody a discernibly Jewish sense of humor, approaching the world with a rueful laugh and shrug. Perhaps it's no accident that in the poem "Peripheral Vision" (*An Alternative to Speech*) Lehman writes of "warding off panic with wit" (47).

Lehman's work is by turns poignant and ironic; he is at his most earnest when arguing, as he does in several *Best American Poetry* introductions, that poetry is alive and well in America today. For Lehman, the poetic impulse is deeply connected with pleasure, both the giving and the receiving thereof. His work argues (implicitly and explicitly) that art can have meaning, that poems can be fun, and that poetry is both important and relevant in today's world.

Further Reading. *Selected Primary Sources:* Lehman, David, *An Alternative to Speech* (Princeton, NJ: Princeton University Press, 1996); ———, *The Big Question* (Ann Arbor: University of Michigan Press, 1995); ———, *The Daily Mirror* (New York: Scribner, 2000); ———, *The Evening Sun* (New York: Scribner, 2002); ———, *The Last Avant-Garde* (New York: Doubleday, 1998); ———, *The Line Forms Here* (Ann Arbor: University of Michigan Press, 1992); ———, *Operation Memory* (Princeton, NJ: Princeton University Press, 1990); ———, *Signs of the Times: Deconstruction and the Fall of Paul de Man* (New York: Simon & Schuster 1991); ———, *Valentine Place* (New York: Scribner, 1996). ***Selected Secondary Sources:*** Scharf, Michael, "David Lehman: Lives of the Poets" (*Publisher's Weekly* [28 September 1998]: 68–72); Shoaf, Diann Blakely, "Valentine Place" (*Antioch Review*, 54.4 [Fall 1996]: 498); Steinman, Lisa M., "The Personal Lyric and the Physical World" (*Michigan Quarterly Review*, 43 [Winter 2004]: 117–132).

Rachel Barenblat

LEIB (BRAHINSKY), MANI (1883–1953)

Mani Leib was arguably the central poet of *Die Yunge* (the Young Ones), the Yiddish American literary movement that began in New York in 1907 and that focused on moving **Yiddish American poetry** away from the political didacticism of earlier "sweatshop" poets and toward a poetry of aesthetic beauty and **modernist** innovation. Influenced by Russian poets such as Pushkin and Lermontov, the French **Symbolists**, the German Romantics, and the "art for art's sake" movement, the *Yunge* poets—including Mani Leib; his key rival in the movement, Moishe Leib Halpern; his closest friend and group organizer, David Ignatoff; and fellow New York poets Zishe Landau and Reuben Iceland—attempted to write an introspective poetry exploring personal rather than communal concerns. It was an aesthetic poetry paradoxically written by poor immigrant workers. In following such ambitions, Leib and the *Yunge* risked being seen as decadent and even anti-Jewish; on the other hand, Leib, while a secular Jew, found inspiration for his poetry in Jewish folklore and religious motifs.

Mani Leib Brahinsky was born in 1883, the eldest of six brothers and two sisters, into a poor Jewish family in Nizhyn in the Ukraine. Leib's formal education ended at age eleven when, due to poverty, he was apprenticed to a boot maker. As a teen he became involved in labor strikes and was twice arrested, resulting in his decision to leave the Ukraine for London and then the United States. Upon arrival in New York in 1906, he began to work in a shoe factory and to publish almost immediately in small Yiddish-language journals and newspapers, dropping his last name in the process. Unlike most Jewish immigrants of the time, Leib had experienced relatively little oppression in Eastern Europe. He thus experienced a nostalgia for his Ukrainian home that was unusual among Jewish poets. As a result of his homesickness, Leib married a woman from Nizhyn for whom he was ill suited. They had five children, despite the fact that the marriage had quickly become unhappy.

In his 1914 poem "*Shtiler, shtiler*" (translated as "Hush" by Marie Syrkin), Mani Leib wrote an unofficial manifesto for the *Yunge* movement, which voiced his rejection of the hyperbole and invective of the "sweatshop" poets and issued a call for quiet contemplation. The poem ironically places Leib, a secular Jew, in the religious stream of earlier Jewish writing that advised Jews to wait patiently for the tardy Messiah: "Hush and hush—no sound be heard. / Bow in grief but say no word." Leib's call for patience was not hopeful, however, for the poem suggests that the Jews are waiting in vain. Leib's innovation is to adapt, secularize, and metaphorize these religious tropes for his own purposes, transforming the traditional Jewish motif of waiting with resignation for a Messiah who never comes into an emblem for the impossible quest he himself faced: that of creating a Yiddish literature for a people rapidly assimilating into American culture.

A key year for Mani Leib was 1918, for it was the year he edited *Der Inzel* (The Island), a collection of New York Yiddish poets, and published three books of his own poetry: *Lider* (Poems), *Baladn* (Ballads), and *Yidishe un slavishe motivnen* (Jewish and Slavic Motifs). These poems made Leib famous for his ability to deal with quotidian problems in a direct manner and in the speech of the common man. As had been the case with William Wordsworth in England, however, Leib's lyrical simplicity and use of common diction brought charges of sentimentality and childishness, accusations made worse when he began to write children's poems, sometimes set to music. Leib gained a reputation as a folk balladeer, his most famous ballad being the Yiddish Promethean fable *Yingl tsingl khvat* (Young Tongue Scamp).

Many critics thus missed the ironies and thematic seriousness of Leib's poetry. For example, his "Lullaby" (translated by Marie B. Jaffe) appears to be just that, but under the surface it presents an allegory of Jewish history, with the wind in the poem personifying the irrational force of anti-Semitism, a force that the speaker attempts to appease, trick, and finally rock to sleep with his song. The speaker's first attempt to deal with the wind, which wants to take his son, is to offer it a sheep—a scapegoat—instead. The trope of the scapegoat is troubling, since the Jews had once sacrificed animals at the Temple but were then transformed into the scapegoats of history. Moreover, the sheep too easily becomes a symbol of the Jews, sleeping soundly, as the poem says, without knowing its plight. The poem ends with the vain hope that the Jew's small song can somehow rock the wind into peace. Leib thus presents a modern variation on an old Jewish theme: that of the small, powerless Jew gaining power magically over the forces intent on destroying him.

The nostalgia for an idyllic childhood in the Ukraine, which permeates much of Leib's poetry, is a desire for a past doubly impossible to recover, given the growing anti-Semitism in Europe. Likewise, he realizes that his longing to escape the poverty and drudgery of his American life in order to become a Jewish prophet for poetry cannot be achieved, as is evident in his poem "Night and Rain" (translated by Ruth R. Wisse), in which the poet traces the ironic distance between that which is and that which should be. This distance is illuminated also in the self-portrait "I Am . . .," which begins in humorous Jewish American braggadocio—"I am Mani Leyb, whose name is sung / In Brownsville, Yehupets, and farther"—but soon turns to the harsh reality of one who, even less fortunate than the worm, whom God at least feeds, must creep back to his workbench to "sweat for bread."

Much of Mani Leib's best poetry was written later in his life. The experience of translating Russian and Ukrainian poetry for *Forverts* (the Jewish daily *Forward*) brought to his own work emotional intensity and a new prosodic complexity. Unfortunately, he contracted tuberculosis in 1919 and was forced to give up writing for five years. In 1932 he entered the Deborah Sanatorium in New Jersey, and there began to write some of his most powerful work, including "I Am . . .," a series of sonnets, and the play *Justice*. In the sonnets, many of which have been beautifully translated by **John Hollander**, Leib explores such complex topics as the Holocaust, anti-Semitism, and erotic relationships. As an example of the latter, in "Strangers," he describes the sense of painful alienation that follows sex with someone one is not suited for, such as his own wife. In "A Plum," on the other hand, reminiscent in theme of **William Carlos Williams**'s "This Is Just to Say," a husband gives a plum to his wife so that she can eat it out of his hands, "until those hands held only skin, / And pit, and flecks of overbrimming foam." Mani Leib's Holocaust sonnets, while few in number, are powerful. In "They . . .," for example, the poet moves from exploring the painful loss of a "nobly odd" language, to the horror at the image of a people "melted," and finally to their absence: "[T]hey

are what violence can remember, / Two or three trees left standing amid the fallen timber." In "To the Gentile Poet," Leib writes about the difficulties facing a Jewish poet writing in a Christian poetic tradition, a "dust-bearded nomad" who must chant of his desert ancestry "amid the alien corn."

Mani Leib died of lung cancer in 1953. In his sonnet "Inscribed on a Tombstone," he wrote of himself as going to his grave "like a good Jew," but he also described himself as a peddler of wind. Despite such a self-deprecating image, his poetry remains beautiful, original, and powerful.

Further Reading. *Selected Primary Sources:* Howe, Irving, and Eliezer Greenberg, eds., *A Treasury of Yiddish Poetry* (New York: Holt, Rinehart and Winston, 1969); Howe, Irving, Ruth R. Wisse, and Khone Shmeruk, eds., *The Penguin Book of Modern Yiddish Verse* (New York: Viking, 1987); Jaffe, Marie B., trans., *Ten for Posterity: An Anthology of Yiddish Poems* (New York: Exposition Press, 1972). ***Selected Secondary Sources:*** Chametzky, Jules, John Felstiner, Hilene Flanzbaum, and Kathryn Hellerstein, eds., *Jewish American Literature: A Norton Anthology* (New York: W.W. Norton, 2001); Wisse, Ruth R., *A Little Love in Big Manhattan* (Cambridge, MA: Harvard University Press, 1988).

Craig Svonkin

LEITHAUSER, BRAD (1953–)

Brad Leithauser is one of the most visible members of the **New Formalist** movement; his debut collection, *Hundreds of Fireflies* (1982), is thought to have drawn the first serious attention to the New Formalist trend. Leithauser has lamented the decline of "metrical literacy" in American poetry, and the primary feature of his poetry is a passion for prosodic experimentation (*see* **Prosody and Versification**). His writing, in which the influences of such poets as **Donald Hall**, **Robert Lowell**, and **Elizabeth Bishop** (as well as Gerard Manly Hopkins and A.E. Housman), may be discerned, displays formal mastery and a meticulous attention to form's possibilities, particularly the ways in which form relates to intonation and the sounds and cadences of spoken language.

Leithauser was born in Detroit, Michigan, and was educated at Harvard College (where he met his wife, **Mary Jo Salter**) and Harvard Law School. In addition to his volumes of poetry—*Hundreds of Fireflies* (1982), *Cats of the Temple* (1986), *The Mail from Anywhere* (1992), and *The Odd Last Thing She Did* (1998)—he has written six novels and a collection of essays. A book of light verse, *Lettered Creatures*, was published in 2004. He is also editor of the *Norton Anthology of Ghost Stories*. Among many awards and honors, he has received a MacArthur fellowship (1983). He is currently Emily Dickinson

Senior Lecturer in the Humanities at Mount Holyoke College.

An expansive poet who often finds metaphors in mathematics and natural science, and rhythms in everything from common speech to songs by George Gershwin, Leithauser writes with a wonderful combination of scholarship, a microscopic eye for detail, and a gentle but incisive sense of humor. Sensuous, naturalistic, frequently **pastoral** imagery is typical of his poems, and his painstakingly etched lyrics have reminded some critics of **Marianne Moore**'s animal poems. However, he is equally a deft chronicler of human characters, and human story intersects beautifully with natural phenomena in his best work. In "Plus the Fact of You" (*The Odd Last Thing She Did*, 1998), for example, a seamless interchange of personal and environmental details creates a sense of the sensuous and the cerebral as interchangeable, as the poem's speaker muses sleepily on a day of hiking and wonders, "Why at night do numbers clamor so?" as he finds himself counting his partner's breaths. This interplay, as much as his tireless attention to meter and intonation, is at the heart of what makes Leithauser's work inventive and captivating.

In "Small Waterfall" (*The Odd Last Thing She Did*), he neatly conveys the sense of a little waterfall with short phrases that tumble one into the next, breaking off in midstream and regathering. Rhymes splashed throughout bring continuity and likeness to the lines, as in "stumbling on this small, all-but-forest-swallowed waterfall." The poem also exemplifies his interest in correlating natural images and phenomena with the psychic "landscapes" of people, as it goes on to liken the waterfall to his wife, to whom the poem is addressed, calling both cataract and woman "a thing that flows and goes / and stays, self-propelled and -replacing."

Leithauser is often at his best as a storytelling poet. "The Odd Last Thing She Did" (1998), a sixteen-sonnet narrative of a young woman who leaves "The car running, the headlights on" to illuminate the spot where she has jumped to her death in the ocean, is a good example of the way lyric form and storytelling come together for Leithauser. The poem has, in a few lines, distinct characters and a discrete plot, but it does not sacrifice figurative language for them. In "Ghost of a Ghost" (*Hundreds of Fireflies*, 1982) Leithauser inhabits a first-person character—a dead man mourning the family that gradually resumes life without him: "You could scarcely start to comprehend / how queer it is, to have your touch / go unfelt." Here, his great prosodic gifts are harnessed to create a natural, speaking poetry, which some might find reminiscent of **Robert Frost**.

Such narrative drive makes sense in a poet who is also a novelist. In 2002 his novel and poetry interests dovetailed in the publication of *Darlington's Fall*, an ambitious novel-in-verse about a butterfly-obsessed Victorian natu-ralist, heralded by **John Updike** as "an amazing merger of art and science, verse and narrative." Written in ten-line rhyming stanzas, the book manages to be, equally, a poem and a novel—story-driven but also lyrical, erudite but accessible, grave and witty by turns. The verses rhyme in what he refers to as a "catch-as-catch-can" pattern, and the rhymes tend to be perfect ones (though he remarks in the author's note that he makes exceptions for *rime riche* [prays/praise] and pararhyme), but even over the course of this long narrative, rhyme never becomes cumbersome or unnatural, and it does not supplant plot or story. Rather, Leithauser has found a unique space where story and lyric fuse in a relationship that's as symbiotic as that of butterfly and flower.

With his exacting, elegantly conceived syllabics and fine descriptive sense, Leithauser proves that careful attention to form can liberate and give substance to an image or idea. His poems reveal a genuine delight in images, a genuine sympathy for humanity, and a tirelessly precise observation of the connectedness of man to nature and man to man.

Further Reading. *Selected Primary Sources:* Leithauser, Brad, *Darlington's Fall* (New York: Alfred A. Knopf, 2002); ———, "Metrical Illiteracy" (*New Criterion* 1.5 [January 1983]: 41–46); *The Mail from Anywhere* (New York: Random House, 1992); ———, *The Odd Last Thing She Did* (New York: Alfred A. Knopf, 1998). ***Selected Secondary Sources:*** Gwynn, R.S., "A Field Guide to Poetics of the '90s" (Expansive Poetry and Music Online [August 2002], http://home.earthlink.net/~arthur505/cult1096.html); Jarman, Mark, and David Mason, *Rebel Angels: 25 Poets of the New Formalism* (Ashland, OR, Story Line Press, 1998).

Amy Glynn Greacen

LELAND, CHARLES GODFREY (1824–1903)

Charles Godfrey Leland was an accomplished linguist and a prolific writer who published over fifty books in his lifetime, but he is remembered today chiefly for his studies of the occult. To his contemporaries, Leland was known as a humorist and dialect writer, whose ballads in the German American vernacular were imitated by **Oliver Wendell Holmes** and whose fictitious character Hans Breitmann was favorably compared to **James Russell Lowell**'s Hosea Biglow.

The son of a commission merchant, Leland was born in Philadelphia in 1824. He was briefly a pupil of **Bronson Alcott** before enrolling at Princeton (where his roommate was the future Civil War general George McClellan). He was an avid and eclectic reader, but was particularly influenced by Rabelais. While at Princeton, Leland began contributing to magazines such as the *Knickerbocker*. After graduating, he studied in Heidelberg, where he learned German and became an abolitionist.

He participated in the French Revolution of 1848, and upon his return to the United States in 1849 he studied to become a lawyer. Although he completed his training, Leland chose a career in publishing instead; he became the co-editor (with Rufus Griswold) of P.T. Barnum's *Illustrated News*, before leaving that publication for the Philadelphia *Evening Bulletin* and *Graham's Magazine*. Leland collaborated with George Ripley and Charles Dana on *Appleton's Encyclopedia* and began publishing monographs in the 1850s. Increasingly, Leland's professional life became tied to his political convictions. As a zealous member of the newly founded Republican Party, he became the editor of *Continental Magazine* in 1861. In his editorials (for which Harvard University later awarded him an honorary AM in recognition of "literary services rendered to the country"), Leland advocated emancipation as a political tool for winning the war, and he boasted that he influenced Lincoln's decision to issue the "Declaration of Emancipation" (*Memoirs*, 249). Dissatisfied with supporting the war effort only in writing, Leland joined the Union army as a "full private" in 1863. After the war Leland continued to advance the Republican cause, for example, through his hagiographic biography of Abraham Lincoln (1879). Yet he became chiefly interested in "liminal peoples and the religions at the margins of elite society" (Parkhill, 8), and published works such as *The Gypsies* (1882) and *The Algonquin legends of New England; or, Myths and folk lore of the Micmac, Passamaquoddy, and Penobscot tribes* (1884) on the traditions of European gypsies and Native Americans. In looking back on his accomplishments, Leland claimed that he was most proud of having introduced the industrial or minor arts into the curriculum of Philadelphia's public schools.

Leland's contributions to American poetry stemmed from his interest and skill in languages. As a schoolboy in Philadelphia, Leland had studied Spanish and French. He learned German while abroad, and during the Civil War he attained some skill in Native American languages. At a time when "there were not many linguists on the American press," he wrote "reviews in half-a-dozen languages" (*Memoirs*, 197). Leland was the first American to translate Heinrich Heine's *Reisebilder*, and *Pictures of Travel* (1855) remained in print into the twentieth century. Leland also compiled dictionaries of demotic languages, such as the *Dictionary of slang, jargon & cant embracing English, American, and Anglo-Indian slang, pidgin English, tinker's jargon and other irregular phraseology* (1889–1890).

Leland became best known for his creation of Hans Breitmann, a Rabelaisian German American who sang "ballads" in a pidgin language that blended German and English. Leland published his most famous poem, "Hans Breitmann's Barty," in *Graham's Magazine* in 1856, and the poem was reprinted in the *Knickerbocker*. In this poem,

Leland creates a gargantuan feast whose excesses extend beyond the bawdy scenes described, to the poem's language. A reviewer for *Harper's* observed that lines from the poem, such as "Hans Breitmann gife a barty, / Dey had biano-playin," when "rendered in good English" merely read "Hans Breitmann gave a party, They had piano-playing." He complained that the poem amounted to nothing other than "clownish vulgarity" (*Harper's New Monthly Magazine* [October 1869]: 795). On the contrary, another reviewer argued, "grotesque" effects such as "the softening-down of the hard labials and gutturals into the soft, represents the dilution of the hard Yankee sense with the plaintive German sentiment," and the "combination is a sharp satire on the most earthly materialism the world could produce" ("Spectator," in *The Living Age* [23 January 1869]: 241). Leland had found a distinctive way of writing that became solidified as he began to publish collections of Breitmann ballads. These collections also brought out the political dimension of Leland's work. In *Hans Breitmann's Party and Other Ballads* (1868), Leland made his character a soldier in the Civil War. In "Breitmann as a Bummer," the mock-hero participates in Sherman's (which in the dialect of the poem also doubles as "Germans") march to the sea. Driven by the hope for a reward in whiskey, Breitmann inadvertently holds a fort crucial to Sherman's success. The poem satirizes the common soldier's pursuit of physical comfort but also comments on the absurdity and fortuitousness of war. In the tradition of Washington Irving's "Rip Van Winkle," Breitmann is equally "drunk with the new world as with new wine" (*Atlantic Monthly* [October 1868]: 512). Leland followed the success of his collection with several volumes of Breitmann poems that quickly became formulaic: "Throughout the ballads, it is the same figure presented,—an honest Deutscher, and rioting in the expression of purely Deutsch nature and half-Deutsch ideas through a strange speech. It is a true figure enough, and recognizable; but it was fully developed in the original ballad, and sufficiently portrayed there" (ibid.). Yet the character maintained his appeal, and even gained popularity when he was made to serve other political causes. In *Hans Breitmann as an Uhlan* (1871), Leland resituated the character in the Franco-Prussian War of 1870–1871, and enlisted the "bummer" in the German army, where he individually captured the city of Nancy and demanded extravagant quantities of cigars from the citizens. This victory made the character newly popular in Germany and in Britain: When Leland returned to Europe in 1870, Hans Breitmann was appearing on three stages in London, and special cigars with his image were being sold in recognition of his feats. Despite the success he enjoyed in his lifetime, Leland's contribution to American poetry is largely forgotten today. As he himself recognized, "to be merely original in language is not to excel in everything—a fact very generally ignored—else my Pidgin-English ballads would take precedence of Tennyson's poems" (*Memoirs*, 336).

Further Reading. **Selected Primary Sources:** Leland, Charles Godfrey, *Abraham Lincoln and the abolition of slavery in the United States* (New York: G.P. Putnam's Sons, 1879); ———, *The Algonquin legends of New England; or, Myths and folk lore of the Micmac, Passamaquoddy, and Penobscot tribes* (Boston: Houghton Mifflin, 1884); ———, *Dictionary of slang, jargon & cant embracing English, American, and Anglo-Indian slang, pidgin English, tinker's jargon and other irregular phraseology* (London: Ballantyne Press, 1889–1890); ———, *The Gypsies* (Boston: Houghton Mifflin, 1882); ———, *Hans Breitmann as an Uhlan* (Philadelphia: T.B. Peterson, 1871); ———, *Hans Breitmann's Party and Other Ballads* (Philadelphia: T.B. Peterson and Brothers, 1868); ———, *Memoirs* (New York: D. Appleton and Co., 1893); ———, trans., *Pictures of Travel* [from the German of Henry Heine] (Philadelphia: J. Weik, 1855). **Selected Secondary Sources:** Pennell, Elizabeth Robins, *Charles Godfrey Leland: A Biography,* 2 vols. (New York: Houghton Mifflin, 1906); Parkhill, Thomas, *Weaving Ourselves into the Land: Charles Godfrey Leland, "Indians," and the Study of Native American Religions* (Albany, NY: SUNY Press, 1997).

Colleen Glenney Boggs

LEVERTOV, DENISE (1923–1997)

In the poem "Art," from her collection *With Eyes at the Back of Our Heads* (1960), Denise Levertov describes art's "best work" as being made "from hard, strong materials, / obstinately precise." These lines are indicative of Levertov's own aims and practices as a poet. Her powerful and obstinate lyricism takes shape from carefully wrought tensions—of both form and subject matter—and makes hers one of the most distinctive voices in twentieth-century American poetry. From her precise and discriminating poetic intelligence arises a haunting and difficult beauty, like no other in modern American poetry. Despite the singularity of her lyric voice, her influences are wide and remarkably varied. Most often she is associated with **William Carlos Williams**, **Robert Creeley**, and the **Black Mountain** poets, having learned from them that a poem's "strong materials" are paramount. Like these poets (and others associated with them, such as **Charles Olson**, **Jonathan Williams**, and **Paul Blackburn**) her **poetics** holds that there is no necessary gap between a poem's subject matter (materials in the world) and its poetic matter (as form, as words on a page). Indeed, her scrupulous poetic attention to the hard and strong "things" and particularities of the world allows her to render ideas about that world both concretely and passionately. But Levertov is also deeply indebted to other poets whose work, still obstinate in its precision, has space for mystery, the sacred, and the immaterial. The work of **Emily Dickinson, H.D., Wallace Stevens**, and, especially, her friend **Robert Duncan** showed her how poetry's glittering surfaces can reflect a reality beyond the

everyday and provide a connection to the numinous. If Levertov's work sustains a tricky balance between spirit and matter and—crucially—between moments of joy and suffering, this balance lends poetic weight to her political engagements (feminism, the anti-Vietnam movement and, in her latter years, ecology) for which she was well known. Levertov's best work is important for the obstinate precision with which it faces squarely the "hard, strong materials" of its own, and America's, engagement of the world, after modernity.

Denise Levertov was born in October 1923 in Ilford, Essex (in England). She was largely educated at home, along with her elder sister Olga, by her bookish and politically active parents. Her mother was of Welsh ancestry, descended from the tailor and mystic Angel Jones of Mold, while her father was a Russian Hassidic Jew who converted to Christianity and became an Anglican minister. The outbreak of World War II thwarted Levertov's plans to become a ballet dancer, and she worked instead as a nurse throughout the war. With the publication of her first collection, *The Double Image* (1946), she became associated with a set of young poets, the British New Romantics, centered around the figure of Dylan Thomas, and radically opposed to the "**Auden**-generation" that had immediately preceded them. In 1947 she met her husband, American writer Mitchell Goodman, in Geneva. They married in 1948, and lived in France and Italy before settling in New York at the end of that year. Their son, Nikolai, was born the following year. By this time, although her work was published in **Kenneth Rexroth**'s *New British Poets* (1949), Levertov was already feeling herself to be a poet in the American grain. She was now in correspondence with William Carlos Williams, Robert Creeley (whom her husband had known at Harvard), and Robert Duncan. Creeley introduced her to **Cid Corman**, who began publishing her work in his *Origin*, which was, at the time, the leading journal for experimental poetry. And Creeley himself began publishing her work in *Black Mountain Review* (hence her association with Black Mountain College, although she never set foot there). Between 1957 and 1958 she lived in Mexico and produced her first two American books, poems that respond particularly to the **open-form** poetics of Williams, Creeley, Duncan, and Olson. Although her poetry can be seen always to have been politically engaged, it was in the 1960s, with the collection *The Sorrow Dance* (1967), that her work became more explicitly political in focus. She and her husband became well-known anti-war campaigners during the Vietnam era, and she visited Hanoi to protest the war, with fellow poet **Muriel Rukeyser**, in the fall of 1972. Levertov taught in various universities throughout the 1960s and 1970s, including Vassar, City College of New York, Berkeley, and MIT, and she was poetry editor of the *Nation* in 1961 and again from 1963 to 1965.

After teaching at Tufts between 1972 and 1978, she taught at Brandeis and Stanford. In 1980 she was elected to the American Academy and Institute of Arts and Letters. Her final three collections, including the posthumous *The Great Unknowing: Last Poems* (1999), reflect the Catholic faith she found late in life, as well as her ecological responsiveness to the environment around Mt. Rainier and Lake Washington, where she spent her latter years. She died of complications due to lymphoma on December 20, 1997.

When Denise Levertov first moved to America, she knew very little about its poetry. Her first three American books, *Here and Now* (1957), *Overland to the Islands* (1958), and *With Eyes at the Back of Our Heads* (1960), show her rapid coming to poetic terms with the open-form, **experimental** poetics she was then encountering. In fact, the poetic pressure of these volumes is not simply a measure of Levertov's response to a different poetry and poetics; it also shows her conscious efforts to accommodate herself to a culture and idiom from which she initially felt estranged. In both respects, it was William Carlos Williams who showed Levertov the way. She has noted that "Williams gave me the use of the American language. He showed me how it and the American idiom could be used" (*Poet in the World*, 68). A poem such as "Laying the Dust" (1957) has obvious debts to Williams in its simple clarity of form and statement, and in its description of water that "flashes / each time you / make it leap." And throughout *Overland to the Islands*, Levertov tests her relationship to this older, male, poet. As with Williams's shorter lyrics, the title poem of this collection addresses a world of objective hardness and clarity with a conversational—apparently offhand—directness. This results from an "organic" poetics wherein the poetic imagination, like the dog described in this poem, is "engaged in its perceptions" such that it "keeps moving, changing / pace and approach but / not direction." But the often-explicit statements of her own poetics in *With Eyes at the Back of Our Heads* also see Levertov beginning to ease herself away from Williams's influence. This is especially evident in her developing notion of "organic form."

Levertov's famous and influential essay "Some Notes on Organic Form" (first published 1965 and reprinted in her first book of essays, *The Poet in the World*, 1973) makes clear the debates she initially had with contemporary American poetry and poetics. This essay, along with her poetry from the late 1950s on, leans heavily toward the open-form poetics of Olson (in his essay "**Projective Verse**," 1950) and Williams (in his dictum "no ideas but in things"), with its emphasis on the "exploratory" nature of one's poetic dealing with the world. But Levertov differs markedly from these models, too. According to her, a poem's engagement with the things of the world goes beyond them to a deeper reality. "For me," she writes, "back of the idea of organic form is the con-

cept that there is a form in all things which the poet can discover and reveal" (*Poet in the World*, 7). Thus, the poem "Illustrious Ancestors" (*With Eyes at the Back of Our Heads*) reveals Levertov's sense of connection to famous mystics in her family history—"The Rav / of Northern White Russia" and "Angel Jones of Mold." Following their example, Levertov wants to make "poems direct as what the birds said, / hard as a floor, sound as a bench, / mysterious as . . . silence." It is with this sense of poetry as discovering something that lies "back of" the everyday that Levertov finds her own particular voice. This can be seen in another successful poem from her 1960 volume, "Pleasures," which opens with the lines about the pleasure of finding what one doesn't see at once but that "lies / within something of another nature." The poem proceeds by revealing a delicate pattern of balances between senses of pleasure, pain, wonder, and fragility as Levertov describes her act of preparing squid for dinner. Stripping out the "bones of squid" from the flesh that surrounds them, she notes that they are "tapered as if for swiftness, to pierce / the heart, but fragile." Such carefully wrought thematic and formal balance is equally evident in Levertov's next three collections, all published in the 1960s, and which established her reputation. In these collections Levertov also discovers a political voice that lies behind her careful, exploratory, lyricism.

The title poem of *The Jacob's Ladder* (1961) provides another self-reflective examination of how a poem rises out of "solidly built" materials. However, as throughout this collection, this ascent is not without human—ultimately political—costs. Here it is felt in the scraped knees and numbed grip that suggest the physical difficulty of climbing. Still other poems in the collection imagine the poet having a "darkness in me" that turns the lyric "I" from "angel" to "tyrant" ("Three Meditations") or, famously, "During the Eichmann Trial: When We Look Up," a poem occasioned by the trial of the notorious Nazi, senses the ways in which political atrocity is implicated in—can be discovered "back of"—the poetic. *O Taste and See* (1964) is an especially important collection because it makes explicit Levertov's feminist concerns without diminishing her concentrated attention to her craft as poet. Throughout this collection Levertov is deeply troubled by a sense of splitting and doubleness that lies at the heart of her condition as a woman, as a poet, and as a woman poet. As though testing her place, as a woman, in poetic history, "Taste and See" and "September 1961" examine Levertov's relationship to illustrious poetic ancestors. In "Taste and See" Wordsworth's famous lines are revised to "The world is / not with us enough" as Levertov tests how her bodily experiences of the world—taste and vision—are rooted in poetic discrimination ("taste") and vision. And in "September 1961" Levertov considers the sorts of poetic language put "into [her] hands" by **modernist** poets **Ezra Pound**, William Carlos Williams, and H.D. Other poems, such as "Song for Ishtar," "Hypocrite Women," and "In Mind," express the difficult, often contradictory, forces of female creativity. Measuring herself against Ishtar, primitive female goddess and muse, Levertov feels that she is both "a pig and a poet." As critic Alicia Ostriker has pointed out, these poems, in which Levertov describes herself as both "a woman / of innocence, unadorned" and as a "turbulent, moon-ridden girl," reveal female identity to be a continual sundering. The sense of woman's essential doubleness that pervades this collection anticipates feminist theorist Luce Irigaray's *This Sex Which Is Not One* (1977) by over a decade. The justly famous "The Ache of Marriage" foreshadows Levertov's later work in two ways. First, its account of marriage as an ambiguous social institution (both an "ache" and an "ark" that might save us from the flood) articulates Levertov's sense of the inextricable link between the personal and the political. Second, its religious imagery (in marriage, she notes, "We look for communion") becomes a means of expressing and overcoming the doubleness that haunts her sense of being in the world.

The sequence of six poems called the "Olga Poems," which is physically and emotionally central to Levertov's next collection, *The Sorrow Dance*, is one of her greatest poetic achievements. Taking the spilt between Levertov's political and poetic selves as their focus, these poems are a moving **elegy** for Levertov's older sister, who died in 1964. Inspired by the memory of a sister who "wanted / to shout the world to its senses," Levertov is careful in these poems to avoid being seen as a **confessional poet** by giving extended consideration to the relationship between poetry and political action. In yet another image of the hidden resources that poetry might reveal, Olga's (and Levertov's own) political anger is depicted throughout the sequence as a burning inner light, "compassion's candle alight in you." The final section of *The Sorrow Dance* is its most politically powerful. Because of the palpable anger of their response to the conflict in Vietnam, poems such as "Life at War," "What Were They Like?" and "The Altars in the Street" are some of Levertov's most famous. "Life at War" is disturbingly graphic in its depiction of war's effects, with Levertov deliberately showing us the "breaking open of breasts whose milk / runs out over the entrails of still-alive babies." Despite such shocking immediacy (an excess that precipitated the bitter breakdown of Levertov's and Robert Duncan's friendship), Levertov remains profoundly troubled in these poems by the distance between herself and the horrors she describes: "burned human flesh / is smelling in Viet Nam as I write."

War poems also dominate Levertov's next two collections, *Relearning the Alphabet* (1970) and *To Stay Alive* (1971). The tone of these collections is now, however, one of bitter resignation, tempered by an increasing use of religious imagery. "Tenebrae," for example, juxtaposes the fact that "We are at war, / bitterly, bitterly at war" with the Roman Catholic ceremony during Holy Week for which the poem is named, a ceremony in which lights are gradually diminished. Similarly, "Advent 1966" overlays war and religious imagery. In this case, "flesh on fire" in Vietnam ends up "prefiguring / the Passion." These changes point to important new directions in Levertov's later work. Most important is her renewed religious faith. "Mass for the Day of St. Thomas Didymus," from *Candles in Babylon* (1982), and her poems in response to medieval English mystic Julian of Norwich's vision of Christ's suffering in *Breathing the Water* (1987) are delicately complex meditations on faith and poetry in a modern materalist, and largely atheist society. In her later collections, too, Levertov continues to assess her poetic influences: "Williams: An Essay" and "To R. D., March 4th 1988" are particularly fine elegies for her friends William Carlos Williams and Robert Duncan in, respectively, *Candles in Babylon* and *A Door in the Hive* (1989). Levertov's poetic interests and influences also broaden in her final collections to include more English and European poets. Rilke becomes especially important to her; in "To Rilke" (1989) she sees him as an "enabling voice" for her own sense of poetic mystery. Her final three books, *Evening Train* (1992), *Sands of the Well* (1996), and the posthumous *This Great Unknowing: Last Poems* (1999) develop a poetics of ecological responsibility toward the landscape where Levertov spent her last years, and which she loved. Mt. Rainier is as constant a presence in these last poems as it was in her actual daily sight. As with her poetry, so with Mt. Rainier: Via her obstinately precise vision, hardness and solidity come to reveal both mystery and wonder as the hidden form of all things. In one of the last poems she wrote, "The Mountain's Daily Speech Is Silence," Levertov likens the mountain to her own questioning poetics, asking whether its possible eruption will be an expression of its "own repressed voice" or that of the "fire" within it: "Does the mountain / harbor a demon distinct from itself?"

Further Reading. *Selected Primary Sources:* Brooker, Jewel Spears, ed., ———, *Conversations with Denise Levertov* (Jackson: University Press of Mississippi, 1998); *The Letters of Denise Levertov and William Carlos Williams* (New York: New Directions, 1998); ———, *The Letters of Robert Duncan and Denise Levertov* (Stanford, CA: Stanford University Press, 2004); Levertov, Denise, *Collected Earlier Poems 1940–1960* (New York: New Directions, 1979); *New and Selected Essays* (New York: New Directions, 1992);

———, *Poems 1960–1967* (New York: New Directions, 1983); ———, *Poems 1968–1972* (New York: New Directions, 1987); ———, *Poems 1972–1982* (New York: New Directions, 2001); *The Poet in the World* (New York: New Directions, 1974); ———, *Selected Poems*, ed. Paul A Lacey, intro. Robert Creeley (New York: New Directions, 2002); ———, *This Great Unknowing: Last Poems* (New York: New Directions, 1999); Wagner, Linda, ed., *Denise Lovertov: In Her Own Province* (New York: New Directions, 1979). **Selected Secondary Sources:** Kinnahan, Linda A., *Poetics of the Feminine: Authority and Literary Tradition in William Carlos Williams, Mina Loy, Denise Levertov and Kathleen Fraser* (Cambridge: Cambridge University Press, 1994); Little, Anne C., and Susie Paul, eds., *Denise Levertov: New Perspectives* (West Cornwall, CT: Locust Hill Press, 2000); Marten, Harry, *Understanding Denise Levertov* (Columbia: University of South Carolina Press, 1988); Rodgers, Audrey T., *Denise Levertov: The Poetry of Engagement* (London and Toronto: Fairleigh Dickinson University, 1993); Wagner-Martin, Linda, ed., *Critical Essays on Denise Levertov* (Boston: Hall, 1990).

Nick Selby

LEVIN, PHILLIS (1954–)

A meticulous and incandescent poet, Phillis Levin writes poetry that considers the philosophical and spiritual. Levin's work grows out of the ecstatic and sensual traditions of **Emily Dickinson** and **Wallace Stevens**; it also reminds one of such writers as **Czesław Miłosz**, with his poetry of praise and witness, and Jorge Luis Borges, with his baroque sensibility. Levin's poetry includes the metropolitan sensibility of **James Merrill** and **Marie Ponsot**, the fractured and spare quality of **Jean Valentine**, and, most significantly, as Levin has stated in conversation, **Charles Wright**'s revelatory nature of the line and landscape. Often a searing sensuality bursts from Levin's work, as in "The Temple Leopard," from *Temples and Fields*: "You taste my body's power when you run: / It carries you forward, a brutal hymn." A melancholy pervades her work as a poem, a relationship, or knowledge nears fulfillment only to separate and fail to resolve as in the final lines of her early poem "The Skaters," also from *Temples and Fields*: "Just as we part, the half-sun silhouettes / Two figures sailing close until they miss." This melancholy is balanced by the experience of the ecstatic, as enunciated in "Face to Face," from *Mercury*: "I sing of love, sacred and profane, / Of knowledge lost, strangely found again." Here we find Levin defining the major themes of her work as well as the commanding, almost oracular diction of her poetry.

Born on May 18, 1954, in Paterson, New Jersey, Levin was educated at Sarah Lawrence College (BA, 1976) and the Johns Hopkins University's Writing Seminars (MA, 1977). A recipient of fellowships from the Ingram Merrill Foundation and the Guggenheim Foundation, she also received a Fulbright fellowship to Slovenia and an Amy Lowell Traveling Scholar fellowship to Italy. Having taught at Baruch College and the University of Maryland, she is now professor of English and poet-in-residence at Hofstra University and teaches in the graduate writing program at New York University. Levin's first book, *Temples and Fields* (1988), received the Poetry Society of America's Norma Faber First Book Award; *The Afterimage* followed in 1995. In 2001 her collection *Mercury* was published, as was *The Penguin Book of the Sonnet: 500 Years of a Classic Tradition in English*, which she edited. Her work has been praised by such poets as James Merrill, **Richard Howard**, **Rachel Hadas**, and **William Matthews**.

For Levin, rhythm and form are rooted in the sacred, in aspects of ritual and the ceremonial. Her discussion of the origin of the sonnet, in her introduction to *The Penguin Book of the Sonnet*, focuses on the Platonic ideals of harmonics, proportion, and the golden mean, whereby a "precarious balance between necessity and chance" may be created, and the "poet can imitate the demiurge's artistic achievement and, by composing the poem, harmonize his, and perhaps the reader's, soul" (xlii). Similarly, Levin's own work reveals an architectural complexity. Stanzas serve as rhetorical and discursive rooms, defined by a variety of rhymes and metrical constructions. Perhaps equally significant is Levin's insistence on liminality, that is, the moment and space of relation, more often than not transient, as illuminative as it is mysterious.

Temples and Fields evokes these moments of mysterious balance. The poem "It Is Found," for example, refers to "sparks that carry strangers / Into realms of relation." The world seems defined for Levin by doubled or superimposed moments of communion and departure, as at the end of "Lunch After Ruins": "And ate bright fish / Just parted from the sea." Belonging to a tradition of American poets who consider the poet as tourist, such as **Richard Wilbur**, Charles Gullans, James Merrill, and **Elizabeth Bishop**, Levin evokes a certain solitude and a desire for elemental joy or comfort. The woman who leads the poet to the trattoria becomes "my momentary mother," and language moves from guidebook phrases to the rhythm of walking. Degrees of intimacy are considered in one of the collection's strongest poems, "A.D." During a long train ride, the poet notes ambiguously, "My love and I could love no better." From this moment of questioned love, Levin is able to evoke the disasters of Europe—"the dark music of empires scattered"—before settling her gaze upon a father who hoists up his family's only "trunk of possession." Set in quatrains with off-rhymed and perfect-rhymed couplets, the poem moves toward formal balance but also toward the awareness of our inextricable place in history: "We were wound in the wheels of the holy city / By the time the train pulled into anno Domini."

The role of the tourist is not the only means of mirroring the poet's uncertainty or the culture's failures. Levin writes in "Out of Chaos," one of her many poems on New York City, "Today I saw the usual human disaster." Seemingly callous, this observation in fact suggests that the repetition of life—"The doors close and open every day"—dehumanizes. At the end of the poem, Levin evokes the Augustinian city of God and the faltering of the human will to build it. The subway ride of "Out of Chaos" and the train journey of "A.D." find their counterparts in "Possessions," one of the central poems of Levin's second collection, *Afterimage*. Set in three-line stanzas, the poem depicts chance encounters that cannot resist allegory. Bearers of a "tiny Bible," a "miniature globe," and a "watch in a velvet box," somehow connect in their common mortality: "Together and apart at one time / In innocence, guilt, and poverty."

Although some have seen Levin's early work as exemplary of **New Formalism**, one should be wary of such labels, as Levin suggests in "The Lost Bee" from *Temples and Fields*. In this poem the returning bee struggles to find a sense of place: "I must have been exiled from habit / By a strange wind, a stray leaf." Levin's formalism lies in her practice of composition by rhythm and breath, her use of the coincidence of sound and off rhymes, and the role of memory in composition and diction. Form becomes a matter of the uncanny and the recurrent; as such it defines poetry as well as history, as she contends in *The Afterimage*'s "Prologue /Epilogue," with its culminating allusion to Troy: "Another horse rolled in yesterday. . . . can you smell / The sweat of those who wait inside?"

In *The Afterimage* Levin often compresses the lyric moment to the point of tautology, as in "The Third Day," where those first visiting Christ's tomb confront an emptiness that they must fill with their words, yet they "knew they could not / Say what they saw." The title poem of this book combines the autobiographical with a meditation on secular and mystical desire, in which Levin locates the necessity for writing. In the flame of a memorial candle, a child finds what she has always carried, "its meaning inscrutable yet clear." Poetry then is an afterimage of pure vision, or, as Levin puts it in Platonic terms, "the sun's plumage." In the insistence that life is a process of ecstatic revelation, Levin's significance as a poet resides.

Levin's third and most recent collection, *Mercury*, contains several longer poems, notably "Elegy for a Magnolia," "Beginning to Count," "Meditation on A and The," and the title poem. The poems of *Mercury* engage the poet's world and history, both personal and public, more fully and with less formal mediation than those of her previous collections. Set against a childhood memory of playing with a forbidden vial of mercury, Levin in her title poem reveals the impact of her father's revelation: "Do you think I will always be here?" The question initiates the awareness of another's mortality; the father's comment alters the world for the child and thereby divides him from her. Autobiographical and set in three-line stanzas like "Mercury," "Elegy for a Magnolia" eloquently folds childhood memories onto the larger tragedies of the past century: the Holocaust, racial prejudice, and the disavowal of history.

In her elegy "Beginning to Count," Levin again establishes the notion of chance; yet, chance now means not simply an illuminating encounter but rather that which informs history, defining the languages one knows and how and where one learns them. Levin again evokes the Holocaust and the layers of history both told and lost of those who, by chance, survived. A companion poem to "Elegy for a Magnolia," "Beginning to Count," suggests that language itself is a form of communion and yet also the means by which we learn what is irretrievable despite the power of a poet's invocation: "I have had to wait so long to call you back, / And am calling you now . . . To finish it for me."

In his *Letters to a Young Poet*, Rainer Maria Rilke, whose spare sacramental poetry Levin admires, advises his young correspondent "to try to love the *questions themselves* like locked rooms and like books that are written in a very foreign tongue" (35). Levin's poems, in their often lean, sculpted forms, arise from her tending to the questions that remain most mysterious, those of love, sacred or profane, of ends and of beginnings, and of the wit and spirit of language.

Further Reading. *Selected Primary Sources:* Levin, Phillis, *The Afterimage* (Providence, RI: Copper Beech, 1995); ———, *Mercury* (New York: Penguin, 2001); ———, ed., *The Penguin Book of the Sonnet: 500 Years of a Classic Tradition in English* (New York: Penguin, 2001); ———, *Temples and Fields* (Athens: University of Georgia Press, 1988). ***Selected Secondary Sources:*** Bawer, Bruce, "Borne Ceaselessly into the Past" (*Hudson Review* 54 [Autumn 2001]: 513–519); Macklin, Elizabeth, "It's a Woman's Prerogative to Change Her Mind," in *By Herself: Women Reclaim Poetry*, ed. Molly McQuade (St. Paul, MN: Greywolf, 2000, 9–29); McCorkle, James, "Elizabeth Bishop's Embracing Gaze: Her Influence on the Poetry of Sandra McPherson, Phillis Levin, and Jorie Graham," in *In Worcester Massachusetts: Essays on Elizabeth Bishop*, ed. Laura Menides and Angela Dorenkamp (New York: Peter Lang, 1999, 259–270); Rilke, Maria Rainer, *Letters to a Young Poet*, trans. M.D. Herter Norton (New York: Norton, 1954); Schneiderman, Jason, "Phillis Levin," *Dictionary of Literary Biography: New Formalist Poets*, Vol. 282 (Detroit: Gale, 2003, 195–200).

James McCorkle

LEVINE, PHILIP (1928–)

Philip Levine is one of the late twentieth century's most important poets. Working-class and liberal, Levine brings to his work material often shunned in traditional poetries. He most often writes about urban landscapes of desolation in industrial cities, such as the Detroit of his youth, and workers mired in hopeless jobs and poverty, assembly lines, and unemployment lines. His poetry is filled with rail yards and empty buildings, filled—like the factories and junkyards of neglected neighborhoods—with the detritus of the dispossessed. Though he is often criticized for a negative and depressing **poetics**, such criticism misses the hopeful undercurrent that runs throughout his poems. Again and again, Levine suggests that love and tenderness can exist despite oppressive circumstances. Levine is the natural heir to **Walt Whitman** and **William Carlos Williams** and their democratic, inclusive poetics, founded on the particulars of American lives. His poetry—grounded in narrative, speech-based diction, and personal experience—departs radically from the **New Criticism** and **modernism** from which he emerged, showing how politics and poetics can, and must, effectively live together. He is also heavily influenced by Spanish poets such as Vallejo, Lorca, and Machado. The result is a uniquely American voice that embodies an ultimate faith in the ability of individuals to stand against the odds that a capitalist, industrial society stacks against them.

Levine was born in Detroit, Michigan, the son of Russian Jewish immigrants. Growing up in Depression-era Detroit, he became engrossed in his parents' and his community's heated political debates about the Spanish civil war. He appears to have developed his anarchistic views early in his life. In fact, the Spanish civil war became the foundation of his political and poetic consciousness. Through the early 1950s, Levine worked at a variety of industrial jobs. He went on to study at Wayne University (now Wayne State University), graduating in 1954—the year he married Frances Artley. He then attended the University of Iowa Writers' Workshop (studying most notably with the poet **John Berryman**), from which he graduated in 1957. After Iowa, Levine became professor of English at California State University–Fresno, where he remained until 1992. During the same period he served as visiting writer at schools such as Tufts University, the University of Cincinnati, the National University of Australia, Vassar College, Columbia University, New York University, and Brown. From 1984 to 1985 he served as chair of the literature board for the National Endowment for the Arts (NEA). He has won numerous awards, including Stanford University's poetry fellowship, five NEA grants (one of which he refused in 1970), a National Institute of Arts and Letters grant, and two Guggenheim fellowships. *The Names of the Lost* (1976) was presented the Lenore Marshall Award for Best American Book of Poems. *Ashes: Poems New and Old* (1979) received both the National Book Award and the National Book Critics Circle Prize. The latter prize was also awarded to *7 Years from Somewhere* (1979). His work continued to be vital into the 1990s, when he published three works, *What Work Is* (1991), *The Simple Truth* (1994), which received the Pulitzer Prize, and *The Mercy* (1999), which stand among his finest. In 2004, he published *Breath.*

A self-described anarchist, Levine is one of America's most prolific poets, having consistently published volumes from 1968 into the new millennium. Although he published two prior collections, 1968's *Not This Pig* was where Levine truly found his voice and began to make his mark in American letters. The collection's title comes from his poem "Animals Are Passing from Our Lives," which stands as a manifesto of the individual's will and ability to live (or die) with dignity despite society's dehumanizing expectations. The speaker, a pig on his way to market, refuses to succumb to circumstance, refuses to "squeal / and shit like a new housewife / discovering television." Knowing that he is going to die a graceless death, the pig is supposed to lose all pride and fight back uselessly, to "hook his teeth with my teeth." But the pig stands firm, his pride and self-awareness intact: "No. Not this pig," he says at the end of the poem. The poem marks the belief in the individual that serves as the wellspring for all of Levine's work. In that same collection, the poem "Silent in America" marked another major theme—voicelessness—and showed Levine's continuing desire to give voice to society's dispossessed, the marginalized and forgotten, inviting them to "come with us tonight / drifters in the drifting crowd" where all shall arrive "beyond the false lights."

The title poem of 1972's *They Feed They Lion* stands as another of Levine's earlier seminal works, a rhythmic statement of an inarticulate anger, "the acids of rage, the candor of tar." The poem, influenced by Spanish surrealism, is distinct from much of Levine's work in that it is informed much more by rhythm and image than by story or character; much of the poem draws on the momentum of lists: "creosote, gasoline, drive shafts, wooden dollies." Yet at the core is the emotional weight of all his work, a stuttering, lurching cry that cannot be articulated in any other way. "Out of burlap sacks, out of bearing butter, / Out of black bean and wet slate bread," the poem begins as the speaker drives from "West Virginia to Kiss My Ass." The images accumulate centrifugally from "Mothers hardening like pounded stumps" to "all my white sins forgiven–spinning around the phrase "They Lion grow" until the final stanza, when the poem's force finally pushes the broken syntax toward an explosive conclusion: "From they sack and they belly opened / And all that was hidden burning on the oil-stained earth / They feed they Lion and he comes." The poem gives voice to a communal rage, an expression of "the sweet kinks of the fist" that has marked so much of his work as he explores what will move a people "from 'bow down' come 'rise up.'"

Although still mining this poetic terrain, his next three books—*1933* (1974), *The Names of the Lost* (1976), and *7 Years from Somewhere* (1979)—mark a change in tone. At the center of *1933* is an emotional exploration of the death of the father (marked by the year in the title). The poems become increasingly **elegiac**, turning their gaze more seriously toward the past, a gesture that has remained central to Levine's work ever since. In *The Names of the Lost*, however, this engagement with the past becomes a way for the poet to explore the connection between the personal and the historical. "The Lost" refers both to personal loss and to the historically neglected, the lost of society. And in *7 Years from Somewhere* Levine marks more directly his connection with history by aligning himself with Spanish anarchists Buenaventura Durruti and Francisco Ascaso, two martyrs of the Spanish civil war (the subject to which he has returned repeatedly) who struggled, and died, standing against injustice. Ascaso becomes the centerpiece of his poem "Francisco, I'll Bring You Red Carnations." In the poem, the speaker visits the cemetery in Barcelona "to see / the graves of my fallen," and to celebrate "the unbroken / promise of your life."

Figures such as Ascaso become the beacon of humanity for Levine, a benchmark against which lives are to be judged. Cipriano, in "To Cipriano, in the Wind" from 1981's *One for the Rose*, functions in much the same way. In the midst of 1941, when "Bataan would fall / to the Japanese and Sam Baghosian would make the long march / with bayonet wounds in both legs" and the speaker's brother has gone to war, the boy meets Cipriano, who says *Dignidad, . . . without is no riches.*" The speaker then wonders, "What could / a pants presser know of dignity?" But in the face of Bataan, of the Germans rolling into Russia where his cousins died, the speaker ends up spending his life searching for such a clear and elegant dignity: "tell me again that this / world will be ours." The collection as a whole works through this longing until by the end, in "One for the Rose," the speaker knows that the life he has lived is not the one it might have been in another time or other circumstances, but sees that he has made his way—despite circumstances—so deliberately that now he remembers every turn, "and each one smells like an overblown rose, / yellow, American, beautiful, and true."

This moment at the end of *One for the Rose* marks the turn toward another phase in his writing, in which the poet becomes increasingly concerned with a search for tenderness, mercy, and communion—in society and within himself. This quest leads him to a series of works, starting with *A Walk with Tom Jefferson* (1988) and leading toward three highly acclaimed collections in the 1990s—

What Work Is, The Simple Truth, and *The Mercy*—that function effectively as a single unit. The title poem of *What Work Is* stands as a quintessential Levine work, stylistically and thematically, as it wraps his concerns into one elegant meditation on the nature of work and love and dignity. The poem begins with a signature confrontational move: "You know what / work is, although you may not do it. / Forget you." Though he opens with this classic tone of indignation toward those who might not know of suffering and labor, by the end of the poem the speaker realizes that it is he who does not know what work is, because he is unable to act, to show affection for his brother. The notion of work has been transformed from the physical labor that is devalued by a capitalist society to the work of being human—which is likewise devalued. The tone has moved from confrontation to tenderness, to pity and mercy, a movement that mirrors the arc of his work as a whole as he works through rage toward empathy and self-criticism.

The book's opening poem, "Fear and Fame," also enacts this motion as the speaker descends into the Dante-esque hell of the acid vats in a plating plant to emerge having learned that work is only "half / what it takes to be known among women and men." The people of these poems are familiar—teachers, coaches, firefighters, and assembly workers—as are the scenes: the acid vats of the First-Rate Plumbing and Plating, the polishing wheel, Chevy Gear & Axle, the soap factory, and Ford Highland Park, where his brother stands amid other men waiting for jobs. But what emerges, along with these pained and elegiac portraits, is the sense that the work is not merely labor but is performed with tenderness and compassion.

The Simple Truth and *The Mercy* follow this emotional line as they move subtly from the political rage and cynicism of Levine's early work toward a state of grace. At heart, also, is the poet's continued examination of silence, of words that will slip away, of opportunities for communication that fail: "what he said came sideways out of his mouth / so the wind would blow it to tatters, words / that became nothing" ("Sundays with Lungo," *The Mercy*). The poems work to understand the silence and reach toward communion, until "We / are one, sharing whatever / you are as blindness descends" ("The Secret," *The Mercy*). But no answers are offered, as the title poem suggests. "The Mercy" refers both to the ship that brought his mother to the United States from Europe when she was a child and to that state of caring for which the speaker is endlessly searching. Ironically, the passengers of the *Mercy* were ravaged with smallpox and the survivors quarantined in a new land. The reader is left to wonder if there really is such a thing as mercy. *The Mercy* represents the mission of Levine's poetic project as a whole: the religious quest for grace and transcendence in the face of a world that repeatedly denies it.

Further Reading. *Selected Primary Sources:* Levine, Philip, *Breath* (New York: Knopf, 2004); ———, *The Mercy* (New York: Knopf, 1999); ———, *New Selected Poems* (New York: Atheneum, 1991); ———, *Not This Pig* (Middletown, CT: Wesleyan University Press, 1968); ———, *The Simple Truth* (New York: Knopf, 1994); ———, *Sweet Will* (New York: Atheneum, 1985); ———, *They Feed They Lion* (New York: Atheneum, 1972); ———, *A Walk with Tom Jefferson* (New York: Atheneum, 1988); ———, *What Work Is* (New York: Knopf, 1991). *Selected Secondary Sources:* Buckley, Christopher, ed., *On the Poetry of Philip Levine: Stranger to Nothing* (Ann Arbor: University of Michigan Press, 1991); Hirsch, Edward, "The Visionary Poetics of Philip Levine and Charles Wright," in *The Columbia History of American Poetry*, ed. Jay Parini (New York: Columbia University Press, 1993); Levine, Philip: *So Ask: Essays, Conversations and Interviews* (Ann Arbor: University of Michigan Press, 2002).

Glenn J. Freeman

LEVIS, LARRY (1946–1996)

Larry Levis's early work offers a primer on a prevalent style of North American poetry in the 1970s, whereas his later work stands as an exemplar of the kind of maturity and originality that are possible when a poet risks breaking away from a period style. Levis's first published poems, like much North American poetry of the early to mid-1970s, were influenced by the short-lined, image-based poetry of such poets as **W.S. Merwin**, **Robert Bly**, **James Wright**, **Galway Kinnell**, and Levis's mentor, **Philip Levine**, as well as by many of those poets' **translations** of French, South American, and Spanish surrealist poets. Beginning in the late 1970s, however, Levis began to work in an increasingly discursive, narrative, longer-lined style, and his poems began to draw more directly on his upbringing on a farm in California's Central Valley. These later poems, especially those in his final three books (the last published posthumously), embody a more original and compelling aesthetic, in which the postured mysteriousness of his earlier work is not so much eschewed as it is deepened in more meditative poems whose boundaries have widened to include not only the poet's own particular past but much of twentieth-century social history.

Levis was born in 1946 and grew up on his parents' farm near Fresno, California, where he often worked alongside Mexican American migrant workers in the fields. In 1968 he received a BA from California State University–Fresno, where he had taken poetry workshops with Philip Levine, who nurtured the young poet's talent and remained Levis's lifelong friend. Levis went on to receive an MA at Syracuse University in 1970, where he worked with **Donald Justice**, whose formalist aesthetic was to influence Levis's own experimentations with blank verse in the 1980s. Levis subsequently taught for two

years as a lecturer at California State University–Los Angeles, where he became friends with fellow teacher and noted Polish poet Zbigniew Herbert. After his first book, *Wrecking Crew*, which received the United States Award from the International Poetry Forum, was published in 1972, Levis received a fellowship to study creative writing at the University of Iowa, where he graduated with a Ph.D. in 1974. While at Iowa, Levis began working on his own translations of such Spanish-language surrealist poets as Miguel Hernández; this direct engagement with the surrealist tradition no doubt influenced the poems in his second book, *The Afterlife* (1977), which received the Lamont Award from the American Academy of Poets. Upon leaving Iowa, Levis embarked on a successful academic career, teaching at the University of Missouri, the University of Utah, the University of Iowa, Warren Wilson College, and, at the time of his death, Virginia Commonwealth University; he received National Endowment for the Arts, Guggenheim, and Fulbright fellowships, as well as many other prestigious awards and grants. His subsequent books—*The Dollmaker's Ghost* (1981), selected by **Stanley Kunitz** for publication in the National Poetry Series Open Competition; *Winter Stars* (1985); and *The Widening Spell of the Leaves* (1990)—received increasing acclaim. Levis also showed an interest in prose forms: In 1980 he and his wife, Marcia Southwick, co-authored *The Leopard's Mouth Is Dry and Cold Inside*, a book of prose poems, and in 1992 he published *Black Freckles*, a book of short stories. At the time of his death from a heart attack in 1996, he was much admired by poets senior to him, such as Levine and **Mark Strand**; by poets of his own generation, including **Robert Hass**, **David St. John**, **Tess Gallagher**, and Michael Ryan; and by two generations of younger poets, many of whom had studied with him in his twenty-plus–year teaching career. Levis was married three times and had one son, Nicholas, with his second wife, Southwick. The manuscript that was in progress at the time of his death was edited by Levine and published as *Elegy* (1997), with a foreword by Levine.

No doubt in part because of his initial success, Levis became a lightning rod for criticism of the period style his early poems exemplify. In his 1980 essay, "Eden and My Generation" (reprinted in the 2001 selection of his essays, *The Gazer Within*), Levis writes of his own early idolatry of poets such as Bly and Merwin, and suggests that "[t]hat imitative gesture began to feel faint, inauthentic, often simply insincere or naïve" (*Gazer Within*, 48). The poems in Levis's first two books exemplify that "inauthentic[ity]" for many readers, and thirty years later only a few of those poems—for example, "Fish"— have proven truly memorable. Although his transitional volume, *The Dollmaker's Ghost*, embodied a real leap forward in Levis's aesthetic, the last two books published in his lifetime—*Winter Stars* and *Widening Spell of the Leaves*, along with the posthumous *Elegy*—have proven most enduring for readers and critics. *Winter Stars* contains a masterful sequence of poems that serve as **elegies** both for Levis's father and for his own rural California childhood, in which "[t]he vineyards vanished under rain / And the trees held still or seemed to hold their breath" ("The Poet at Seventeen"). The qualification in the second line quoted above is typical of the meditative and digressive texture of Levis's later poems. These poems' sentences are long, almost prose-like, and they slowly unwind in a very loose blank verse broken up by shorter lines. "The Assimilation of the Gypsies" and "Sensationalism," both meditations on the work of Czech photographer Josef Koudelka, connect the poet's experience with the world of post–World War II Eastern Europe in a way that, as the latter poem's title implies, skirts—and somehow just narrowly avoids—the exploitative.

The Widening Spell of Leaves engages even more directly with historical material in poems whose settings shift in time and place from the central California of Levis's childhood to Renaissance Italy to North America in the 1960s. "Carravagio: Swirl and Vortex," one section of the longer poem "The Perfection of Solitude: A Sequence," for instance, begins "[i]n the Borghese [where] Caravaggio, painter of boy whores, street punk, exile & murderer, / Left behind his own face in the decapitated, swollen, leaden-eyed head of Goliath," and winds its way forward to the Haight-Ashbury district of San Francisco in 1970, where the speaker, "[a] man whose only politics [is] rage" remembers his "friend in high school who looked like Caravaggio" and who was subsequently drafted into the Vietnam War: "Two years later, thinking he heard someone call his name, he strolled three yards / Off a path & stepped on a land mine." Levis's posthumous collection, *Elegy*, extends the aesthetic of "The Perfection of Solitude: A Sequence" even further, in poems whose shifts in time and place are even more radical, and that are far too long to excerpt effectively. In these last poems the speaker often "just stand[s] there for a moment before he be[comes] something else / Some flyspeck on the wall of a passing & uninterruptible history" ("Elegy with a Bridle in Its Hand"). This inimitable combination of insouciance and gravity characterizes the attempt, articulated in "Caravaggio: Swirl and Vortex" to "enter . . . the wide swirl & vortex of history" that is Levis's unique and lasting contribution to North American poetry.

Further Reading. *Selected Primary Sources:* Levis, Larry, *Black Freckles* (Salt Lake City, UT: Peregrine Books, 1992); ———, *The Gazer Within*, ed. James Marshall, Andrew Miller, John Venable, and Mary Flinn (Ann Arbor: University of Michigan Press, 2001); ———, *The Selected Levis: Revised Edition*, ed. David St. John (Pittsburgh: University of Pittsburgh Press, 2003). ***Selected Secondary Sources:*** Buckley, Christopher, and Alexander Long, eds., *A Condition of the Spirit: The Life and Work of Larry Levis* (Spokane: University of Washington Press, 2004).

Eric Gudas

LEWIS, JANET (1899–1998)

Representative of many women writers and artists who produced and published significant works in the shadow of their more widely known husbands, Janet Lewis remains distinctly less visible than **Yvor Winters**, the renowned critic and poet. Much as Louis Untermeyer earlier did with his wife, Jean Starr Untermeyer, Winters singled out her poetry for inclusion in his discussion of strong lyricists of the era, albeit with a disclaimer—"The pleasure of skating over thin ice becomes even more dubious when the skater is both critic and husband and the ice is the public work of his private partner" (*American Poetry Since 1900* [New York: Henry Holt, 1923], 227)—and a dubious compliment: "one of the country's least spectacular and most unusual lyricists" (230). Winters begged the forgiveness of the reader, as well, when he praised his wife's poetry in *Forms of Discovery*, but his assessment of his wife's work was also reserved, as was his prose in general. Most together in the public light when they founded the short-lived journal *Gyroscope* (1929–1931), their lifelong mutual regard led Lewis to both concur with and veer from her husband's formulation of poetry as "a statement in words about a human experience . . . in which special pains are taken with the expression of feeling" (*In Defense of Reason* [New York: Swallow, 1947], 363), even as that mutuality may have played up against Elizabeth Isaacs's sense that Lewis was for Winters a source of calm in contrast to his extremes (Isaacs, 6).

Janet Lewis was born August 17, 1899, on the outskirts of Chicago to Elizabeth Taylor Lewis and Edwin Herbert Lewis, an English professor at the Lewis Institute. A poem she submitted in 1919 for a contest while enrolled at the University of Chicago led to an invitation to join the Poetry Club, where acquaintances with Pearl Andelson Sherwood, Kathleen Foster Campbell, Maurice Lesemann, Mark Turbyfill, Elizabeth Madox Roberts, **William Carlos Williams**, **Harriet Monroe**, and **Marianne Moore** developed. Three years later, however, Lewis was stricken with tuberculosis, and rather than remain bedridden in Chicago, she sought treatment and rest in New Mexico at the Sunmount Sanatorium. During those five years, her friendship with Yvor Winters, also a TB sufferer and whom she had just missed meeting in Chicago, where he too had been a member of the Poetry Club the year before, grew into engagement and marriage in 1926. Because of Winters's need to complete his doctoral work, the couple moved shortly thereafter to the Bay Area, to Los Altos, where they shared a long and fruitful marriage, both appreciating gardening and raising goats and champion Airedales. Both had teaching appointments at Stanford University, and she, from time to time, also taught at Berkeley. There she remained after her husband's death in 1968, and nearly to her own death thirty years later, on December 1, 1998.

Lewis earned a substantial reputation as a novelist, particularly as a writer of historical fiction. Perhaps her most lauded work, and the one taken up for a movie adaptation, was *The Wife of Martin Guerre* (1941). A Guggenheim fellowship in 1950 permitted her research in France for another historical novel, *The Ghost of Monsieur Scarron* (1959). Both of these novels, as well as a third, *The Trial of Sören Qvist* (1947), set the imperfections of human institutions against moral imperatives—in each case, mistaken identity, assumed identity, or false accusation places noble characters in moral dilemmas, each of these protagonists proving antithetical to the assumptions of modern, ostensibly sophisticated society. It can be of little surprise, given this framework of fiction, that Lewis was intrigued by uncorrupted Native American societies, such as she found in the Ojibwa people in her travels to Northern Michigan. A decade after her first book of poems, Lewis published her first novel, *The Invasion: A Narrative of Events Concerning the Johnston Family of St. Mary's* (1932), making evident for the first time her lifelong interest in Native American folklore and culture.

In 1922 she published *The Indians in the Woods*, initiating her first phase of poetry writing, which concluded around the middle of the 1940s. The second period was initiated after the death of her husband. Her earliest work, found in such collections as *The Indians in the Woods* and *The Earth-Bound*, exhibits not merely attentiveness to nature, but a plainspokenness that unhinges the anxiety-bound soul: "The quick dry spider / Ran across my hand" with its staccato internal resonances brings us closest to originary, unimpeded seeing, such that even the act of recollection itself almost vanishes—a berry plant, she writes, is "The berry leaf, remembered / Line for line." Both her poetry and that which Winters wrote in his early days in New Mexico depict a landscape of miraculous character in language stripped bare. During the first two decades of their married life, their exchange of poetry on domestic matters increased, with Lewis's work quickly being given the label "domestic," rather unfairly. Her lyric "Time and Music," drawing on a Winters quotation, is as complex a philosophical tract as any, pointing, as Helen Trimpi notes, to a pre-Kantian, pre-Cartesian consciousness that is "not 'primitive' but perennial" (252). Lewis's paean to human flight in "The Hangar at Sunnyvale, 1937," as well, is filled with no less delight about "a mathematic dream / Locked in

the hollow keel and webbed beam" than **Robert Frost** would later exhibit about the Wright Brothers in "Kitty Hawk."

Lewis's work in the second half of the twentieth century takes on fuller lines and darker phrasings, as is consonant with a spirit stripped of its companion; the verse turns toward memories of voices and friends, family members long since departed. "The dear past," she says, brings old enemies together and makes "[a]ll that we partly knew / . . . more completely grown," Yet some of the most affecting poems in the collection return to the brevity of her earliest work—the simple, devastating delight of a spider web caught in sunlight, for example.

Lewis has also been a frequent author of opera libretti; she has written six full-length works, which include *The Wife* (an adaptation of *The Wife of Martin Guerre*, scored by William Bergsma), *The Legend* (an adaptation of Lewis's *The Invasion*, scored by Bain Murray), *The Birthday of the Infanta* (based on Oscar Wilde's tale, scored by Malcolm Seagrave), *The Swans* (drawn from the Brothers Grimm, scored by Alva Anderson), *Mulberry Street* (after the O. Henry story, scored by Alva Anderson), and *The Manger* (scored by John Edmunds). Toward the end of her life, Janet Lewis continued her quest for the genuine, collaborating with illustrator DeLoss McGraw on a **small-press** book comprising Lewis's original work, as well as her **translations** from Japanese tankas by Tamiko Abe, Akitaka Uchimura, Keneko Murayama, and Isamu Nagase.

Further Reading. *Selected Primary Sources:* Lewis, Janet, *Against a Darkening Sky* (Athens: Swallow Press/Ohio University Press, 1943); ———, *The Ghost of Monsieur Scarron* (Garden City, NY: Doubleday, 1959); ———, *Good-bye, Son, and Other Stories* (Garden City, NY: Doubleday, 1946); ———, *The Invasion: A Narrative of Events Concerning the Johnston Family of St. Mary's* (Denver: University of Denver Press, 1932); *Keiko's Bubble* (Garden City, NY: Doubleday, 1961); ———, *Poems, 1924–1944* (Denver: Alan Swallow, 1950); ———, *Poems Old and New, 1918–1978* (Athens: Ohio University Press, 1981); ———, *The Selected Poems of Janet Lewis* (Athens: Swallow Press/Ohio University Press, 2000); ———, *The Trial of Sören Qvist* (Denver: Alan Swallow, 1947); ———, *The Wife of Martin Guerre* (San Francisco: Colt Press, 1941); Lewis, Janet, and DeLoss McGraw, *Poems and Pictures* (San Diego: Brighton Press, 1990). ***Selected Secondary Sources:*** Baxter, John, "Contrapuntal Voices: The Poetry of Yvor Winters and Janet Lewis" (*Literary Imagination: The Review of the Association of Literary Scholars and Critics* [Fall 2004]: 428–447); Isaacs, Elizabeth, *An Introduction to the Poetry of Yvor Winters* (Chicago: Swallow Press, 1981); Stern, Richard, "Janet Lewis" (*Virginia Quarterly Review* 69.3 [Summer 1993]: 532–543); Trimpi, Helen, "The

Poetry of Janet Lewis" (*Southern Review* 18.2 [Spring 1982]: 251–258).

Douglas Basford

LEWIS, RICHARD (CA. 1699–1783)

Richard Lewis was one of the most important poets of the American classical tradition of the early 1700s. His work is distinguished by a reliance on classical rather than British sources, by frequent declarations of **literary independence** from Britain and the Continent, and by attempts to discover an American identity distinct from that of the mother country. Lewis's poems were often long (many running from 200 to almost 400 lines) and took as their topics the natural scenery of early Maryland, literary aesthetics, the contemplative spiritual journey, and New World nation building.

Richard Lewis was born in Llanfair, Montgomery County, Wales, but emigrated to Maryland in 1718. Educated at the British Latin grammar school well enough to gain entrance to and matriculate at Balliol College, Oxford (beginning April 3, 1718, and continuing for only thirteen weeks), Lewis found employment in the Maryland Colony as a schoolmaster at King William's School (a Latin grammar school) in Annapolis, where he seems to have remained. Calling his teaching duties "very fatiguing" (preface to *Muscipula*, p. xii), he nonetheless managed to marry Elizabeth (Betty) Giles on March 15, 1723, father at least one child, and write a substantial quantity of poetry before his early death in March 1734.

The most important of Lewis's poems are the early *Muscipula: The Mouse Trap, or the Battle of the Cambrians [Welsh] and The Mice*, an English-language translation of a Latin poem by Edward Holdsworth, published in Annapolis (1728); "A Journey from Patapsco to Annapolis" (April or May 1730); "Food for Criticks" (May 1731); and *Carmen Seculare* (November 25, 1732), a state poem (after Horace) published as a folio pamphlet.

Muscipula, Lewis's first literary publication, suggests details of the poet's biography even as it addresses the aesthetic categories of beauty, the imagination, and the sublime, focusing particularly on the construction of "GOOD POETRY" (*Muscipula*, "Prologue," I: 17). In a discussion of the genre of *Muscipula*, Lewis calls the poem "Mock Heroic or Burlesque" (xi), of which he identifies "two Sorts." One describes a "ludicrous Action," of which Pope's *Rape of the Lock* is an excellent example. *Muscipula*, however, falls into the second sort, which has low characters and details some "great Event." In this instance Lewis chooses, not the usual "*odd, uncommon* Numbers" (irregular verse form), but heroic couplets in which to cast his translation; this form, Lewis claims, will effect a "more *truly comical*" production. Lewis is, nonetheless, careful to assert that he has "no intention to derogate . . . the Honour of the *Cambrians* [Welsh]" (xii).

Lewis's own Welsh origins account for his desire not to offend, despite the burlesque form. Lewis intended to ingratiate himself with his dedicatee, Maryland governor Benedict L. Calvert. Who, in fact, subscribed to ten copies of *Muscipula*, the largest number of any of the poem's 149 subscribers. The book's large subscription led to the immediate sale on publication of 233 copies, probably making possible the elaborate production of the volume in quarto with a rubricated title page, unique for the time until the appearance of the Massachusetts Bay Colony's still more elaborate *Pietas et Gratulatio* (1761; *Devotion and Gratitude*).

Muscipula celebrates the tenacity of Lewis's ancestors, the Cambrians who have "Their Antique Tongue and Freedom never lost," and who, as he says in one of his extensive footnotes, could not be induced "to endure . . . Servitude, nor could they be reconciled to the English Government" until the time of Henry VII, "descended from the Welsh" (93). In such passages, Lewis reveals his own love of freedom and perhaps his reason for immigration.

Lewis's "Notes" to *Muscipula* are remarkable for their erudition. Lewis quotes such sources as the Venerable Bede's *Historica Ecclessiastica*, or *Ecclesiastical History* (of Britain); Tacitus's *De Vit Iulii Agricolae,* or *Life of Agricola*; and Servius's *Commentarii Virgilium,* or *Commentary on Virgil* (fourth century). Elsewhere in the "Notes," Lewis observes that "history" connects "old Troy" to London as the "new Troy," and that Aeneas, who escaped Troy to become Virgil's founder of Rome , was the mythical grandfather of Camber, king of the Cambrians. In making these associations, Lewis appeals to those colonial Americans who possessed a classical education. During the eighteenth century, this practice of figuring parallels between early Americans and characters from Virgil's *Aeneid* became, among the intellectual elite, almost commonplace.

In the dedicatory poem to *Muscipula*, Lewis, reflecting early American conditions of literary production, maintains that "'*To raise the Genius*,' WE no time can spare, / *A bare Subsistence* claims our utmost Care" (II: 37–38). Despite this assertion, Lewis was able to execute in this translation the most intricate literary production of its time in the Maryland colony. In subsequent years Lewis continued to publish poetry in colonial newspapers, so that by the time of "A Journey from Patapsco to Annapolis" (1730), he was the author of a sizable body of poems. In "Journey" he indicates that he has thoroughly resettled himself as a loyal, enthusiastic citizen of his adopted colony. His portrait of "the *Monarch Swain*," for example, embodies a typical description of the early American farmer who reigns over "His Subject Flocks" and fecund fruits and vegetables, all "unbought," which "his well-till'd Lands afford" (II: 51–53).

The "Journey," printed at least four times in the colonies and five times in England during the eighteenth century, was surely Lewis's most popular poem. Pope alludes to it in his *Dunciad*, although the treatment is unflattering. More recently, this poem has provoked several critical essays, with some scholars interpreting it as a poem about nature and others seeing it as a spiritual account. "Journey" does contain stunning celebrations of Maryland's natural scenery. Lewis's portrait of the American Humming Bird, for example, is justly famous; he describes it as hardly larger than the bumble bee: "Like them, *He* sucks his Food, the Honey-Dew, / With nimble Tongue, and Beak of jetty Hue." Lewis relates that the bird's "gemmy Plummage strikes the Gazer's Sight"; its "vivid Green," scarlet, purple, blue and "golden Blaze" mock "the *Poet's* and the *Painter's* skill" (II: 92–105).

Recalling Virgil's *Georgics* and Thomson's *Seasons*, "Journey" actually belongs to the genre of the *meditatio*, a popular form in early America during the late seventeenth and eighteenth centuries. From Philip Pain's *Daily Meditations* and **Edward Taylor**'s *Preparatory Meditations* to **Roger Wolcott**'s *Poetical Meditations* and **Phillis Wheatley**'s "Thoughts on the Works of Providence," early American poets found this philosophical genre a convenient one in which to cast spiritual, contemplative responses to the American adventure. In such works as the Old English *Seafarer*, Dante's *La Commedia*, and John Donne's *Holy Sonnets*, this contemplative exercise of mind records a psychomachic or spiritual crisis; such a record of crisis dominates Lewis's "Journey."

Assuming a basic structure of memory (which encompasses the operation of both the senses and the imagination), understanding (or reason), and will, this meditatio opens with the line, "At length the *wintry* Horrors disappear." The use of the word "Horrors" is arresting: Following a long winter fraught with horrific consequences (perhaps the deaths of children from pneumonia resulting from their falling through a weak patch in an iced-over river), the speaker can at last be assured that the new season promises relief. Despite this promise, about a third of the way through the poem, an April storm wreaks a "dumb Horror thro' the Forest" (I: 145). This unwelcome intervention within an otherwise idyllic setting causes the speaker to exclaim, "How soon does Beauty fade!" (I: 180).

Earlier in the poem, pleasant memories of this April sojourn had led the speaker to remark: "Ten thousand Beauties [rise] to my View; / Which kindle in my Breast poetic Flame, / And bid me my *Creator's* praise proclaim" (II: 37–39). But the terror of the storm has, in "memory's mint," provoked him to give his reader the admonitory first line "At length the *wintry* Horrors disappear," horrors to be revisited in the destruction of the spring storm, which uproots trees and floods the valley. The speaker's memory, then, leads him to contemplate not just early spring's budding beauties but also the conflict between the promise of spring's pleasures and its painful threat of destruction. When the storm passes, as do eventually the "*wintry* Horrors," the "restless Thoughts" are calmed by April's "several Joys" (II: 197–198). Because the phrase "restless Thoughts" was, during the seventeenth and eighteenth centuries, a precise description of the active imagination (O.E.D.), it is clear that the memory here provides the speaker with a state of contrasting images and sensations, which brings him to the brink of a conflict within the soul.

The speaker then attempts to grasp this dynamic contrast, thereby bringing his understanding into play. For as his "wand'ring Thoughts aspire" toward a satisfying explanation, he turns to the vulnerable, human power of his mind to resolve the problem posed by his journey's "instructive Sight." His focus descends from contemplation of the heavens to his own "working Fancy" or imagination, once again enabling him to center on his own importance. He determines that what he lacks is calm "Content"; he wants to be allowed to share his "*leisure* Hours . . . With chosen *Books*, or a well-natur'd *Friend*," here echoing popular sentiments among the educated classes expressed earlier in the century by John Pomfret's "The Choice" (1700).

But the speaker finds again and again the return of the former horrors, especially fear "at th' Approach of *Death*" (I: 328). He cries out, "*Tremendous God*! May I not justly fear . . . that my Notions of" an afterlife "Are but creations of my own *Self-Love*!"—merely "*fancied* Feasts of *Immortality*!" (II: 350–357). Even though he is "Condemn'd to travel thro' a tiresome Way," as his understanding has taught him, "These active Thoughts that penetrate the Sky" lead him to entrust his fate to the "*Supreme of Beings*" and to conclude that "Whatever State" God chooses for him, he will "sustain thy wise Decree" with patience "And learn to know *myself*, and *honour* Thee" (II: 386–390).

While Lewis's "Journey" both emphasizes nature and traces the particulars of a spiritual odyssey, it is not principally the confession of a committed Christian. Rather, the form of the meditatio directs Lewis toward an analysis of the poet's principal faculty, the imagination.

In "Food for Criticks" (1731), Lewis again pursues his intense interest in aesthetics, here viewing Maryland's natural setting as a metaphor for art itself. So chauvinistic has Lewis become regarding his adopted "country" of Maryland that he claims this new land more able to provoke poetry than "The fam'd castalian or pierian well" of the ancient world of Greece and Rome. Indeed, the setting along the Skuylkill River would appear to have the power to turn the "rudest swains" into sages who can read "the wandering stars" like learned astrologers.

This hyperbole redefines the relatively innocuous pastoral of Virgil ("Food for Criticks" is preceded by a quote from Virgil's tenth *Eclogue*), peopled by urbane cosmopolites dressed in shepherd's garb, by suggesting that New World nature possesses a transformative capacity. In Maryland, "Each thicket seems a paradise renew'd" (I: 97). Even the Indian flies back here from "elyzium" because "He can't in death his native groves forget" (II: 108–109). In such phrases Lewis reinvents classical pastoral as a New World phenomenon. "Food for Critics"—the title striking a defiant chord to those who would attempt to denigrate the Maryland populace as culturally deprived—while it clearly indicates Lewis's fondness and respect for America's natural ambiance, also constitutes an enthusiastic statement of literary independence.

Carmen Seculare (1732) displays a similarly independent spirit. Lewis takes his title for this 300-line poem from Horace's state hymn *Carmen Saeculare*; both titles translate as "secular song." Horace's hymn was commissioned by the Roman emperor Augustus in 17 B.C. to celebrate the emperor's revival of the Secular Games, after an interval of about 130 years, and his rebuilding of Rome after a long season of civil wars. To Lewis the purpose of his *Carmen* was no less grave: He wished both to honor the centennial of the founding of the Maryland colony by Cecilius Calvert, the second Lord Baltimore, and to exploit the regenerative force of language to restore prosperity to an ailing economy (the staple crop tobacco was yielding to a failing market).

Beyond the celebratory and regenerative intentions of both Horace and Lewis, other parallels characterize the two works. Like Horace, but at greater length, Lewis extols the salubrious effect of Ceres, goddess of grain, as she "Clothes with her richest stores th' unfallow'd soil" (I: 19). Lewis goes on for almost thirty lines, praising sundry fruits, flowers, and game. In Maryland, indeed, "No earthquakes shock the soul with sad surprise" (I: 31).

On the one hand, Horace draws a spiritual connection between Aeneas, legendary founder of Rome, and Augustus as his descendant, emphasizing that Aeneas secured the course for that freedom which Augustus now bestows upon the Roman citizenry; on the other, Lewis celebrates Cecilius as the progenitor of Maryland's religious freedom (so long as colonists professed belief in the Christian trinity), enabling the colonists to "unite t'improve the public weal" (I: 103). The parallel suggests that Lewis hopes to locate a "better" Rome in the New World. Just as Horace concludes his *Carmen* with a prophecy that the children of Rome will experience new ages of prosperity, so Lewis ends his state poem by looking ahead to "those glorious Times" when "our Children" will enjoy "golden Days" (II: 298–300).

As in the other poems examined above, *Carmen Seculare* treats its sources not derivatively but re-creatively. Richard Lewis uses classical sources to create a new poetic world, designed to define the American adventure in freedom for those experiencing it. He writes a new, Maryland poetry for a new country. Lewis applies his considerable poetic talents to rearticulating classicism, the spiritual journey, and literary aesthetics in terms of the natural scenery and cultural imperatives of colonial Maryland, thus thoroughly Americanizing his poetic achievement.

Further Reading. *Selected Primary Sources:* Lewis, Richard, *Carmen Seculare, for the year M, DCC, XXXII . . . To the Right Honourable Charles . . . Lord Baron of Baltimore* (a folio pamplet) (Annapolis, 1732); ———, "A Journey from Patapsco" and "Food for Criticks," in *Early American Writings*, ed. Carla Mulford (New York: Oxford University Press, 2002, 572–579); ———, *Muscipula: The Mouse Trap*, in *Early Maryland Poetry*, ed. Bernard C. Steiner (Baltimore: Maryland Historical Society, 1900, 58–102). *Selected Secondary Sources:* Johnson, Christopher D., "A Spiritual Pilgrimage Through a Deistic Universe: Richard Lewis's 'A Journey from Patapsko [*sic*] to Annapolis, April 4, 1730'" (*Early American Literature* 27 [1992]: 117–127); Kropf, C.R., "Richard Lewis's 'Food for Criticks': an Aesthetic Statement" (*Early American Literature* 15 [1980/1981]: 205–216); Lemay, J.A. Leo, *Men of Letters in Colonial Maryland* (Knoxville: University of Tennessee Press, 1972); Marambaud, Pierre, "'At Once to Copy, —And the Original': Richard Lewis' 'A Journey from Patapsco to Annapolis'" (*Early American Literature* 19 [1984]: 138–152).

John C. Shields

LEYB, MANI. *SEE* LEIB, MANI

LIEBERMAN, LAURENCE (1935–)

Laurence Lieberman's poems appear straightforward enough in their meandering storytelling lines and flowing stanza forms, and as modern poems go they are easy to read. He travels to familiar places such as the Caribbean and Japan, and his verse takes the shape of a modern odyssey that involves his wife and children, usually accompanied by a trustworthy guide. One sees Lieberman with his Nikon and hiking boots tramping up the mountainside or riding in a hired taxi down to the shore. He has his notebook and he is jotting down whatever scenery or plant or animal strikes his attention. The persona of his poetry is a visitor and an outsider, two words he uses to describe himself in the final poem of *Flight from the Mother Stone* (2000), his twelfth book of poems.

Born in Detroit, Michigan, Lieberman graduated from the University of Michigan at Ann Arbor and the University of California at Berkeley. From 1964 to 1968 he taught at the College of the Virgin Islands, St. Thomas, where he discovered the world of the Caribbean that has become a major theme of his poetry. He has savored the waters and winds of so many Carib islands, his friend Franz, Bonaire's minister of culture, tells him, that no one may be more alive "to the best life of this region" ("Diving into the Stone"). Since 1970 Lieberman has been a professor of English at the University of Illinois at Urbana-Champaign and continues to serve as poetry editor of its press.

More often than not, in his poetry Lieberman plays the part of an honest, acute observer who records what he sees and hears of the everyday scene or the exotic tropical world, its flora, fauna, and people. In his desire to set down his experiences he has often been compared to **Whitman** with his open lines and all-encompassing vision, and rightly so, but in his almost total lack of ego he is the opposite of Whitman. Lieberman is rarely the central protagonist of his poems; he is always off on the sidelines, taking it all in and getting it straight. What he sees and hears, what happens to him, is more of a concern than who he is or where his ultimate destiny lies. The priests and nuns he meets along the way, with their sincere convictions and sure answers about eternal salvation, are treated with respect but kept at a safe distance. In "Four Sisters" he gives a priest and two nuns a copy of his 1980 collection, *God's Measurements* (an ironic title under the circumstances), but he does not accept their invitation to Sunday High Mass.

In their poetic form his stanzas are regular, though they repeat the same format, unique to each poem. Some poems have two different stanza shapes that again are repeated. Lines are indented in an unpredictable fashion, but with the same regularity for each verse. Words race along lines that mimic the narrative or descriptive pattern and receive unusual emphasis by their placement. It's a complex design but one that makes sense: **free verse** with its own rigorous, highly constricted rules of syllable counts and line lengths, like those of **Marianne Moore**, but having a wholly different result. Instead of density we get open-ended expansion and movement.

In "The Tilesmith's Hill Fresco" from *Eros at the World Kite Pageant: Poems 1979–1982*, Lieberman writes of "[a] mathematics that endures / (oh, steadfast cosmos!), / and survives—like inner light—." Like the Metaphysical poets, he is fascinated by shapes on the page, and he uses as his subjects Japanese craftsmen, Caribbean artists, builders, and storytellers to create the symmetry of his art. Poems take the shape of double helixes, mosaics, schools of fish, kites, or geese in flight to lead the reader from surface patterns to inner light. Like his children in "The Grave Rubbings," also from *Eros*, he traces "story-pictures of local sights" in the stone of poetry. Tombstone art becomes living language in imagery and sound. In a mea-

sured conversational beat, his voice conducts us in imitation of folk music, jazz, and classical quartets to lead us to hear what he sees, to get inside his skin and feel and touch this paradise that is also Eden after the fall.

From his first book of poems, *The Unblinding* (1968), with its description of "The Porcupine Puffer Fish," Lieberman has been fond of animals. In *Flight from the Mother Stone*, he includes a Guyana bestiary of Watras (Capybara or water rats), boa constrictors, jaguars, turtles, possum, and giant eagles called Harpies. But, in spite of the presence of these and many other animals, people matter most in Lieberman's poetry. In "Cactus Bride: The Rain Birth of Onima" from *The Regatta in the Skies* (1999), Winfred Dania, a seventeen-year-old deaf ex-convict, and his teacher Fritz embody two personages essential to this poet's world: the painter and the writer. His book *Hour of the Mango Black Moon* (2004) is inspired by his responses to the paintings of three Caribbean artists, Stanley Greaves, Ras Akyem, and Ras Ishi. In "Mapping the Sargasso City," black dogs preside over an empty neighborhood. The dogs are "Ourselves in canine skin." If we should forget who we are, we will fall "into *The Void*. / The doggy part of our psyche takes over." In a precolonial and subconscious world people and animals freely exchange places.

Lieberman's characters are always unique. In the first poem of *Flight from the Mother Stone*, "A Gift for Grandad Jacob," we meet an expatriated German, Klaus, an elderly restaurant owner, with his twenty-year-old native girlfriend, Christobel. Later we encounter Jolene and Eunice, elderly poachers who steal turtle eggs at great risk to themselves; Cecil and Jake, old friends who argue over eating possum; Nolly, a modern Johnny Appleseed who plants trees wherever he can; and Grande Dame Viola, a Haitian voodoo priestess who bites off a chicken head and tears out a goat's heart. Myths and legends of lost maidens unfold along our travels, such as the stories of the sea nymph Appolonia and of Alicia, a girl abducted by the Spirit of the Boiling Lake. A shaman or seer waits as guide and tale spinner to lighten and enliven the journey, as stories within stories interweave in the poet's odyssey.

Further Reading. *Selected Primary Sources:* Poetry: Leiberman, Laurence, *Compass of the Dying* (Fayetteville: University of Arkansas Press, 1998); ———, *The Creole Mephistopheles* (New York: Scribner's, 1989); ———, *Dark Songs: Slave House and Synagogue* (Fayetteville: University of Arkansas Press, 1996); ———, *Eros at the World Kite Pageant* (New York: Macmillan, 1983); ———, *Flight from the Mother Stone* (Fayetteville: University of Arkansas Press, 2000); ———, *God's Measurements* (New York: Macmillan, 1980); ———, *Hours of the Mango Black Moon* (Leeds: Peepal Tree Press, 2004); ———, *The Mural of Wakeful Sleep* (New York: Macmillan, 1985); ———, *New* *and Selected Poems 1962–92* (Urbana: University of Illinois Press, 1993); ———, *The Osprey Suicides* (New York: Macmillan, 1973); ———, *The Regatta in the Skies: Selected Long Poems* (Athens: University of Georgia Press, 1999); ———, *The Unblinding* (New York: Macmillan, 1968). *Criticism:* Leiberman, Laurence, *Unassigned Frequencies: American Poetry in Review 1964–77* (Urbana: University of Illinois Press, 1977); ———, *Beyond the Muse of Memory: Essays on Contemporary American Poets* (Columbia: University of Missouri Press, 1995).

James Finn Cotter

LIFSHIN, LYN (1944–)

Known as the "Queen of the Small Presses," Lyn Lifshin has been published by virtually every **small press** magazine since the late 1960s but has not sought publication by mainstream academic presses. Her poetry is important for anyone interested in understanding the role of small press writers in contemporary poetics. Although as prolific as Emily Dickinson, her approach to writing is in the tradition of **Charles Bukowski**.

Lyn Lifshin now lives near Washington, D.C., but she spent much of her life around Albany, New York. She was born in Burlington, Vermont, on July 12, 1944, and graduated with a BA in English from Syracuse University and an MA from the University of Vermont. Although she completed the majority of work toward a Ph.D. in English at SUNY–Albany, she did not finish the program.

Lifshin earns a living through selling books, teaching poetry and creative writing classes at various American colleges, and doing scores of readings each year. She has been a poet-in-residence at the University of Rochester, Colorado Mountain College, and Antioch College.

Lyn Lifshin: A Critical Study, written by Hugh Fox in 1985, provides an early assessment of her impact. Fox points to Lifshin's incompletion of her Ph.D. as a pivotal turning point in her poetic career. He argues that as she emerged as a personal poet who confessed her thoughts, she was in fact in a state of rebellion for being rebuffed by academia. Although this critical work provides insight into her earlier works and their possible motivation, Lifshin's poetic range and subject matter have matured in the decades since its publication. Her influence has spread in the 1990s and 2000s among a generation of young female poets who consider her a role model for retaining integrity and not "selling out." She has edited four anthologies showcasing contemporary women poets.

Her poems are readily accessible to a nonacademic audience, much in the same vein as the street poetry of Charles Bukowski. Like Bukowski, it is among the non-academic, underground writers that she is most respected.

Many young women poets cite Lifshin's work as a foundation in their poetic journey of discovery and growth. Lifshin's **feminism** is integrated into her poetry, which assumes that the reader empathizes with her struggles for love and direction. Her typical narrator is contemplative, strong, and feminine. In "Poet as Stripper" Lifshin exposes the vulnerability of poetry, writing of poets that "they assume more" and "they concentrate on your darkest places / they'll clap and holler / hoping to see something snap."

The content of Lifshin's poetry is what attracts her audience: Her love poems are uncommon, spiraling the reader down into analyses of human motivation, usually within twenty to forty lines of unrhymed, uncomplicated words.

Her poems often describe common objects and parallel their utility with a man or an emotion. In the poem titled "Men and Cars," she compares men and cars, describing some that "get you / Where you wanted to go" and others that "you have to / Lug out of a ditch / At great expense." In her poem "Most of the Dream I Don't Remember," she compares the comfort of a man's arm to a mark of punctuation: "except how his arm / held me like a comma." In the book *Cold Comfort*, Lifshin's poetry illustrates her struggles with losing parents and thinking about future generations. In the poem "The Daughter I Don't Have," she writes, "My girl wouldn't / vow to never have what / she could lose, hoard."

In several of her books of poetry, Lifshin uses the persona of the Madonna. The poem "Shifting for Herself Madonna" is a celebration of an independent woman who "wants to eat / power." In Lifshin's Madonna poems, a woman's actions are seen from a myriad of angles, but the woman is unapologetic about her desires, actions, or choices. (Documentary director Mary Ann Lynch captured this serene invulnerability of the Madonna poems in her film about Lifshin, *Not Made of Glass.*) Lifshin balances her Madonna moods with cause-and-effect phrases as if she were talking to a friend. In "Jealous Madonna" she writes, "he mentions a / stacked blond and / madonna can't sleep."

Some of Lifshin's books revolve around a single focal point or event, such as 2004's *When a Cat Dies*, in which Lifshin wrote hundreds of poems about the death of her twenty-year-old cat Memento and its effects on her. Likewise, in 1995's "Blue Tattoo: Poems of the Holocaust," Lifshin is focused on the emotions aroused by the Holocaust images and settings of Treblinka: "It is green and still / after forty years. / Then, nothing."

Further Reading. *Selected Primary Sources:* Lifshin, Lyn, *Blue Madonna* (Milwaukee: Shelter Press, 1974); ———, *Blue Tattoo* (Desert Hot Springs, CA: Event Horizon, 1995); ———, *Cold Comfort: Selected Poems, 1970–1996* (Santa Rosa, CA: Black Sparrow Press, 1997); ———, *Some Madonna Poems* (Buffalo, NY: White Pine Press, 1976); ———, *When a Cat Dies* (Tucson, AZ: The Moon,

2004); ———, "The Poetry of Lyn Lifshin," www.lynlifshin
.com. *Selected Secondary Sources:* Fox, Hugh, *Lyn Lifshin:
A Critical Study* (Troy, NY: Whitson Publishing Company,
1985).

Diane Marie Ward

LIGHT VERSE

Light verse is characterized by the absence of the seriousness one often attributes to or expects from poetry.
Light verse exists as a diversion by which to entertain its
readers. It emphasizes a sense of playfulness, finds its
subject in popular or current culture, and frequently
employs humor. Occasional poems, humorous forms
such as the limerick, dialect writing, **sentimental** verse,
and political and social satire are all examples of light
verse. These elements, however, are also often found in
what might be called "serious poetry," especially in the
latter part of the twentieth century, perhaps because
poets have been more willing after **modernism** to allow
playfulness in their work.

Collections of light verse often include a number of
poems written by anonymous authors, perhaps
because light verse comes more from a popular tradition than from a literary one. In the nineteenth and
early twentieth centuries, much light verse was published in newspapers—sometimes on editorial pages—
and in magazines such as the *Saturday Evening Post*, the
New Yorker, and *Vanity Fair*. Such verses may have been
written only to commemorate an occasion or holiday,
as was **Clement Clarke Moore**'s "A Visit from Saint
Nicholas." Early American light verse also includes
popular rhymes and verses that were set to music, such
as "Yankee Doodle Dandy" or **Francis Scott Key**'s
"The Star-Spangled Banner."

Light verse's most common association is with
humor and wit. In American poetry, such writers as
Ogden Nash and **Dorothy Parker** are prime examples. Nash's poems present characteristics of rhyming
light verse quite well. Though the poems rhyme, they
frequently run past or short of their metrical patterns.
Rhymes are often feminine (turtle/fertile), or mosaic
(hair up/bear up), or employ the use of made-up or mis-
pronounced words for the sake of humor (rhinoceros/
prepoceros). Breaking strict rules or principles of
rhyme, meter, and usage for the sake of playfulness
makes Nash's poems funny. Further examples of the
use of formal elements appear in limericks, often
bawdy and attributed to "anonymous"; the double dac-
tyl, at which **John Hollander** and **Anthony Hecht**
have shown proficiency; and the clarihew, recently
revived in a prize-winning volume of light verse by
Henry Taylor. Dorothy Parker, on the other hand, provides an example of acerbic criticism of the status quo,
which can also be a hallmark of light verse. Her poem
"One Perfect Rose," for example, suggests that a lim-

ousine would be a better and more useful token of affection from a lover than a flower.

Light verse may also include social commentary,
whether it be praise, such as **Robert Frost**'s poem for
the presidential inauguration of John F. Kennedy, or
mockery of an accepted social institution, as we see in
Gregory Corso's "Marriage." Additionally, light verse
often makes fun of the more serious verse on which it is
based, as we see in another of the twentieth century's
practitioners of both serious and light verse, **George
Starbuck**, who pokes fun at **Ezra Pound** and **T.S. Eliot**
by imagining a conversation (in rhyme) between their
personae Hugh Selwyn Mauberley and J. Alfred Prufrock. Pop culture also provides subject matter for light
verse, as can be seen in poems about popular sports
ranging from the well-known popular verse "Casey at
the Bat" to "Hometown Piece for Messrs. Alston and
Reese," about the Brooklyn Dodgers, by **Marianne
Moore**.

Though light verse can be literary and sophisticated, it
can also be used to reach an audience of children, as in
the hands of writers known for writing **children's
poetry**, such as **Dr. Seuss** or Shel Silverstein, as well as
"serious" poets such as Eliot, whose children's verses in
Old Possum's Book of Practical Cats became the basis for a
Broadway musical. Verse written to be set to music with
humorous effects, such as the lyrics of Ira Gershwin or
Cole Porter, often finds a place in collections of American light verse. Though the writings of Dr. Seuss or the
overall content of a musical drama may be serious or
address serious themes, because the writers use effects
such as concocted words or errant pronunciations for
the sake of metrically perfect verse or full rhyme, humor
is injected into the work, thus marking it for consideration as light verse.

Nonsense verse offers another subgenre of light verse.
Here humor or confusion replaces meaning in the poem.
One poet who often flirts with nonsense, it seems, is **e.e.
cummings**. Because his poems engage popular culture, use
typographical effects for humor, or play with the meanings
of words, they may all be considered, to some degree, light
verse. Many of his poems, such as "anyone lived in a pretty
how town" may seem on the surface nonsense, or mere
play with the sound of words. This poem, though, takes on
a serious meaning with "nobody loved anyone," showing
how, in the twentieth century, the lines that separate light
verse from serious poetry have been blurred.

Because of such blurring, many American poets of the
twentieth century, particularly its latter half, have written serious poems that utilize the characteristics of light
verse. In his *Dream Songs*, for example, **John Berryman**
uses rhyme, dialect, and topical—sometimes political—
references for comic and tragicomic effect. Poets in the
New York School likewise use humor, pop culture references, and an attention to the everyday experiences of

an individual to lighten up their poems, although no one would deny the seriousness of their work. Their playfulness is evident in their absurdity or campiness, qualities that can be seen clearly in **Frank O'Hara**'s work, whether he is writing a joking manifesto in "Personism" or addressing pop culture news in "Poem (Lana Turner Has Collapsed!)." Since such twentieth-century writers have written light verse or used its elements in their serious writing, the definition of poetry has been enlarged in this period.

Further Readings. Auden, W.H., *Oxford Book of Light Verse* (Oxford: Clarendon Press, 1938); Baker, Russell, *The Norton Book of Light Verse* (New York: W.W. Norton, 1986); Harmon, William, ed., *The Oxford Book of American Light Verse* (New York: Oxford University Press, 1979); Wallace, Ronald, *God Be with the Clown: Humor in American Poetry* (Columbia: University of Missouri Press, 1984).

Gary Leising

LILI'UOKALANI, QUEEN (LYDIA KAMAKA'EHA) (1838–1917)

Queen Lili'uokalani may be best known as the last monarch of Hawaii, but she is an important literary figure as well. Lili'uokalani composed over four hundred *mele*, or songs, including the traditional Hawai'ian love song "Aloha 'Oe" ("Farewell to Thee," 1877) and the poignant farewell to Crown Princess Ka'iulani, "Ke Aloha O Ka Haku" ("The Lord's Mercy," 1895). Her translation of the *Kumulipo*, published as *An Account of the Creation of the World according to Hawaiian Tradition* (1897), along with her extensive autobiography *Hawaii's Story by Hawaii's Queen* (1898), have served to preserve Hawai'ian arts, language, and culture.

Queen Lili'uokalani ("lily of the heavens") was born on September 2, 1838, in Honolulu, Hawai'i. As the third child of the royal couple, Lili'uokalani, or Lydia Kamaka'eha Paki, as she was often known in her younger years, was educated by Euro-American missionaries in the Royal School. In 1962 she married John Owen Dominis, son of a wealthy sea captain who later became governor of Oahu and Maui. When her brother, David Kalakaua, became monarch in 1874, he designated her his heir. In 1881 she began serving as regent while her brother toured the world on diplomatic and trade missions. Succeeding to the throne ten years later, she sought to restore to her office powers that American officials had taken from her brother. Her attempt to proclaim a new Hawai'ian constitution in 1893, however, resulted in her overthrow. Charged with treason against the United States, she spent eight months under house arrest in Iolani Palace.

Drawing upon her gifts as a lyricist and musician, Lili'uokalani used her long days of confinement to com-

pose some of the best-known pieces of her career. She began numerous creative projects, and music and writing became her consolation. Some of her music was published in secret; two of the most influential pieces associated with this period are "The Lord's Mercy," also referred to as "The Queen's Prayer," and "Farewell to Thee."

Gaining wide recognition upon its publication, "Farewell to Thee" remains one of Hawai'i's most familiar love songs. Though the song was likely composed after Lili'uokalani witnessed a romantic embrace between two young lovers, some of her opponents suggested that the lyrics of the song represent her acknowledgment of the Hawai'ian kingdom's demise. The lines "Farewell to you, farewell to you, / O fragrance in the blue depths / One fond embrace and I leave / To meet again," suggest to some that Lili'uokalani was referring to the state of the Hawai'ian kingdom, which was in danger of annexation by the United States. However, the last phrase of the song suggests not the queen's concession but her vision of a restored Hawai'ian state (Kualapai, 268).

Along with publishing over four hundred *mele*, Lili'uokalani translated the *Kumulipo*, the two thousand–line chant on Hawaiian cosmology and genealogy, into English. *An Account of the Creation of the World according to Hawaiian Tradition*, republished in 1997 as *The Kumulipo: An Hawaiian Creation Myth*, is important in that it illustrates Lili'uokalani's understanding of colonization. She realized that if the Hawai'ian islands were never restored to native control, Hawai'ians would have access to their history only through English and not their native Hawai'ian. In 1898 she ordered fifty-two copies of the translation printed at her own expense to be distributed among her friends and selected libraries (Kualapai, 268).

One of Lili'uokalani's final compositions, her autobiography, *Hawaii's Story by Hawaii's Queen*, was written during her visit to Washington, D.C., in 1897. There she argued against annexation while privately writing her autobiographical landmark. Despite her efforts, in the end Hawai'i was annexed by the United States, and Lili'uokalani was given an annual pension and treated as a relic. However, her writings succeeded in preserving traditional Hawai'ian language and culture, and she remains one of the most notable women of the late nineteenth century.

Further Reading. *Selected Primary Sources:* Lili'uokalani, "Aloha 'Oe," in *She Wields a Pen*, ed. Janet Gray (Iowa City: University of Iowa Press, 1997, 193–194); ———, trans., *An Account of the Creation of the World according to Hawaiian Tradition* (Boston: Lee & Shepard, 1897; republished as *The Kumulipo: An Hawaiian Creation Myth* [Kentfield, CA: Pueo Press, 1997]); ———, *Hawaii's Story by Hawaii's Queen* (Boston: Lee & Shepard, 1898); ———, *Island Fire: An Anthology of Literature from Hawai'i*, ed. Cheryl A. Harstad and James R. Harstad (Honolulu:

University of Hawai'i Press, 2002); ———, *The Queen's Songbook*, ed. Dorothy Kahanaui Gillett and Barbara Baruard Smith (Honolulu: Hui Hanai, 1999). ***Selected Secondary Sources:*** Allen, Helena, *The Betrayal of Liliuokalani, Last Queen of Hawaii, 1838–1917* (Glendale, CA: Arthur H. Clark, 1982); Korn, Alfred, and Barbara Peterson, "Lili'uokalani," in *Notable Women of Hawaii* (Honolulu: University of Hawai'i Press, 1984, 240–244); Kualapai, Lydia, "Queen Lili'uokalani," in *Dictionary of Literary Biography, Volume 221: American Women Prose Writers, 1870–1920* (Farmington Hills, MI: Gale Group, 2000).

Jennifer Englert

LINCOLN, ABRAHAM (1809–1865)

Assassinated a few short months into his second term as president, Abraham Lincoln died at age fifty-six. Yet five decades is a long time for a nineteenth-century writer, and Lincoln was a prolific writer long before he became president. Although he is best known for his brief address at the dedication of the Soldiers' National Cemetery at Gettysburg on November 19, 1863—the Gettysburg Address is just ten sentences long—the rest of Lincoln's letters, speeches, notes, and poems fill volumes. Lincoln is also well remembered for drafting the Emancipation Proclamation (January 1, 1863), which legally abolished slavery in the United States, and for his Second Inaugural Address, in which his words "with malice toward none; with charity for all" set forth in the midst of a bitter and bloody civil war the hope for a whole and healed nation (Sandburg, 544). A lover of poetry—his favorite poem was "Mortality," by the Scottish poet William Knox—Lincoln also wrote poetry, especially as a young man. His poems are primarily occasional verse that tends toward the **sentimental** and melancholy. Among his best pieces are "My Childhood Home I See Again" and "The Bear Hunt."

"I was born Feb. 12, 1809, in Hardin County, Kentucky. My parents were both born in Virginia, of undistinguished families—second families, perhaps I should say" (Steers, 14). So wrote Lincoln of his humble origins. In 1818 Lincoln's mother would die of milk sickness after the family had moved to Indiana, and his father would remarry one year later. As a child, Lincoln was an avid reader and writer; the following rhymes from Lincoln's school sum sheets are recorded in **Carl Sandburg**'s *Abraham Lincoln: The Prairie Years and the War Years* (the misspellings are Lincoln's):

> Abraham Lincoln is my name
> And with my pen I wrote the same
> I wrote in both hast and speed
> and left it here for fools to read (Sandburg, 25)

Plainspoken, brief, and showing some wit, these few lines reflect much of the adult Lincoln's character.

In 1830 Lincoln's family moved to Illinois. Just two years before, Lincoln had made the first of two flatboat trips down the Mississippi River to New Orleans, a bustling seaport and metropolis that the young Lincoln had never seen the like of before. After his second trip, Lincoln worked as a clerk in two stores and invested in two store ventures that ended in bankruptcy.

In the early spring of 1832, Lincoln announced his candidacy for the state legislature, and in April he was elected captain in the volunteer company that had been formed to resolve through force the aggressive incursion of Native Americans into Illinois to reclaim land they had lost through treaty. Through the following May, June, and July, Lincoln would serve in various units, suffering the hardships of a volunteer soldier. In August Lincoln's bid for a seat in the state legislature ended with his defeat at the polls.

President Jackson appointed Lincoln to be the postmaster of New Salem, Illinois, in 1833. Meanwhile, Lincoln spent late nights with his father trying to learn the craft of surveying. In 1834 Lincoln got his first surveying job, but greater success was to follow. In August Lincoln was elected to the Illinois General Assembly, where he would continue to serve until the spring of 1841.

Over the next twelve years Lincoln studied law to become a lawyer, married Mary Todd, and was admitted to practice before the United States Circuit Court. He and Mary had their first son in 1843 and their second in 1846; they would have two more sons before Lincoln was killed. Finally, in August of 1846, Lincoln won his bid for election as a member of Congress from Illinois. It was in 1846 during his term in office that Lincoln sent two of his poems to Andrew Johnston, a friend.

Lincoln's "My Childhood—Home I See Again" was delivered to Johnston, in whole or in part, at three different times: February 1846, April 1846, and September 1846. The February delivery consisted of twenty-four quatrains, nearly all with an *ABAB* rhyme scheme. This copy appears to be a draft of the first two cantos of a four-canto poem.

The April delivery consisted of the first ten quatrains of the February delivery. The topic of this first canto, as Lincoln referred to it, is the bittersweetness of memory meeting reality upon a visit to the Indiana town where he was raised after an absence of almost twenty years. Remarking on the poem and his visit, Lincoln said, "Its objects and inhabitants aroused feelings in me which were poetry; though whether or not my expression of those feelings is poetry is quite another question" (Fehrenbacher, 138).

The September delivery appears to be a revised second canto, a revision of the last fourteen quatrains of the February delivery down to thirteen. The topic of this canto is one Matthew Gentry, a man Lincoln had gone to school with who had become insane.

"The Bear Hunt" was delivered to Johnston in February 1847, and the title of the poem announces its topic. While Lincoln describes this poem as the third canto, its topic and tone are very different from the first (April 1846) and second (September 1846) cantos. The length of the poem is twenty-two quatrains, each with an *ABAB* rhyme scheme. Amusingly, Lincoln turns this lighthearted (albeit grisly) poem into a moral lesson about human conceit by having a mongrel dog who arrived late on the scene of the kill challenge the hunters for their prize, only to become the object of the hunters' laughter.

During the 1858 campaign, Lincoln wrote the brief "For Rosa" to the daughter of the proprietor of a hotel where he was staying, advising her to "Enjoy life, ere it grow colder," using the theme of many a carpe diem poem, and using the girl's name to invoke the familiar metaphor of a flower that smells sweet now but must fade and die:

The now's as good as any day—
To take thee, Rosa, ere she fade. (Basler et al., III, 203)

Although this poem, like others of Lincoln, uses a familiar quatrain form with *ABAB* rhyme, the fact that the poem was written at all for this young woman speaks volumes about Lincoln the man.

Lincoln ran for president in 1860, just two years after the Lincoln-Douglass debates. Opposition to slavery was a central part of his party platform; hence, his candidacy was not supported by the Southern states. Lincoln was elected president in November, and within two months the state of South Carolina seceded from the Union. A meeting was held on February 4, 1861, to form the Confederate States of America (Pratt, 10). Because Fort Sumter sat in the mouth of the harbor of Charleston, South Carolina, and flew the Union flag, this fort soon became a focal point between the Union and the Confederacy.

With the bombardment of Fort Sumter by Confederate forces, the nation was plunged into the Civil War. The war years were a bloody and tempestuous time, and Lincoln the president would write the prose he is most remembered for—the Emancipation Proclamation, the Gettysburg Address, and his Second Inaugural Address—before he was assassinated by John Wilkes Booth in Ford's Theatre. General Robert E. Lee of the Confederacy had surrendered to General Ulysses S. Grant at Appomattox Court House less than a week before.

Abraham Lincoln, president and poet, died April 15, 1865.

Further Reading. *Selected Primary Sources:* Lincoln, Abraham, *The Collected Works of Abraham Lincoln*, ed., Roy P. Basler, Marion Delores Pratt, and Lloyd A. Dunlap, 9 vols. (New Brunswick, NJ: Rutgers University Press, 1953); ———, *The Collected Works of Abraham Lincoln: Supplement, 1832–1865*, ed. Roy P. Basler (Westport, CT: Greenwood, 1974); ———, *Speeches and Writings 1832–1858: Speeches, Letters and Miscellaneous Writings: The Lincoln-Douglass Debates*, ed. Don E. Fehrenbacher (New York: Library of America, 1989). ***Selected Secondary Sources:*** Hollander, John, ed., *American Poetry: the Nineteenth Century*, vol. 1 (New York: Library of America, 1993); Pratt, Harry E., *Abraham Lincoln Chronology: 1809–1865* (Springfield: Illinois State Historical Library, 1957); Sandburg, Carl, *Abraham Lincoln: The Prairie Years and the War Years* (New York: Harcourt Brace Jovanovich, 1954); Steers, Edward, *Lincoln: A Pictorial History* (Gettysburg, PA: Thomas Publications, 1993).

Bruce A. Erickson

LINDSAY, VACHEL (1879–1931)

The one word used to describe Vachel Lindsay by his promoters and detractors alike is "original." Lindsay's poems were chant-laden, strange, mystical, musical, and utterly American in spirit. His work, the strongest of which appeared between 1912 and 1917, expressed a romanticized, heartfelt regard for common people and an equally strong hatred for business interests. Before most other poets, he wrote of new technologies—particularly movies and automobiles—accurately understanding their revolutionary implications. His poems, which mixed sound, word, and even artwork, were lauded for their exuberance and energy, and criticized for their sloppy craft and naive visions. Lindsay gained international fame during his lifetime, due in part to the popularity of his **performances**. By the mid-1920s, however, his performance style eclipsed consideration of his written work. As the complex, intellectual poems of the high **modernists** rose in academic esteem, Lindsay's poetry fell from critical favor. Lindsay as both a poet and a figure was and remains controversial.

Nicholas Vachel Lindsay, who was born and died in Springfield, Illinois, defined himself by his Midwestern upbringing. His obsession with Springfield—the home of Abraham Lincoln—is reflected in many of his poems (such as "Abraham Lincoln Walks at Midnight," a chestnut reprinted in children's books). His father, a physician, wanted Lindsay to take over his practice; his mother was an art teacher who encouraged her son to become an illustrator. To the disappointment of both parents, Lindsay was a mediocre student who preferred talking and daydreaming to studying. His earliest creative endeavors were in visual art. Lindsay attended Hiram College, left it for the Chicago Institute of Art, then left that program to attend the New York School of Art in Manhattan. There the modernist artist Robert

Henri advised him to give up his bad Beardsley-style drawings and concentrate on poetry. Lindsay quit school and embarked on the first of what he called "tramps" across the United States. On these walks he traded poems for lodging and food, seeing himself as an "American troubadour." It was during these tramps, and his later speaking engagements for the Anti-Saloon League, that Lindsay refined the performance skills that made him famous.

Although he wrote a number of poems as a young man, his career did not begin in earnest until 1912, when Lindsay was thirty-two. The next five years were to be his best and most productive years as a writer. In this period he published three critically and publicly praised books of poems (*General William Booth Enters into Heaven and Other Poems*, *The Congo and Other Poems*, and *The Chinese Nightingale and Other Poems*), a book of film criticism (*The Art of the Moving Picture*), and two books of travel essays (*Adventures While Preaching the Gospel of Beauty* and *A Handy Guide for Beggars*). None of his later books reached the literary or popular success of his first three poetry volumes.

Lindsay's writing career effectively ended around 1920, though he continued to perform throughout the United States and England. These performances reinforced the perception of Lindsay as a one-note poet: loud, bombastic, theatrical. His quieter poems and his prose were largely overlooked. Lindsay came to resent the domination of his public persona, even while he continued to go "on the road" to chant his performance pieces. Attempts to support himself as an academic by taking a job at Gulf Park College in Mississippi failed due to his lack of discipline and his growing mental and physical disabilities. Lindsay apparently had untreated epilepsy that exacerbated a tendency toward mania and depression. After leaving his teaching position, he moved to Spokane, where he met his future wife, Elizabeth Conner; he was forty-five, she was twenty-three.

While Lindsay had several romantic interests prior to Elizabeth—most importantly with poet **Sara Teasdale**—his requests for marriage had always been rebuffed. Lindsay claimed to be a virgin at the time of his marriage at age forty-five. After the birth of his two children, Lindsay and Elizabeth left Spokane for Springfield. Financially and emotionally destitute, exhausted by an endless series of speaking engagements and illnesses, unable to accept the demands of family life, Lindsay committed suicide in 1931.

Lindsay's career arc was unconventional: He emerged in middle age, did not live in a major city at the time of his fame, and made a sudden dramatic impact. In 1912 Lindsay's poem "General William Booth Enters into Heaven" appeared in *Poetry*. This one poem made his career; its rhythm-heavy, aural approach, which included directions for recitation, was praised, hated,

and—most important—noticed. Its popularity led to the publication of his best book, *General William Booth Enters into Heaven and Other Poems*, the following year. This volume includes a number of Lindsay's freshest and most spirited poems.

In 1913 Lindsay published his most notorious poem, "The Congo," which inspired heated debate in 1913 and continues to do so. A very long poem, "The Congo" begins with these lines:

Fat black bucks in a wine-barrel room,
Barrel-house kings, with feet unstable,
Sagged and reeled and pounded on the table,
Pounded on the table,
Beat an empty barrel with the handle of a broom,
Boom, boom, BOOM.
THEN I had religion. THEN I had a vision.
I could not turn from their revel in derision.

"The Congo" was lauded by **Langston Hughes** and **Arna Bontemps** and derided by **W.E.B. DuBois** (a schism that reflected a gulf between a number of African American artists and intellectuals of the time). Lindsay, who wrote the poem with what he believed to be good intentions following his witnessing of the Springfield race riots, appeared to be genuinely naive about the stereotypes he was perpetuating. In his view the poem was a fantasy about the ways that blacks had lived as royalty in Africa, where all was free, in comparison with their lives in America, where they were lynched. In 1913 it was considered to be unusual for whites to discuss African Americans in any kind of positive manner whatsoever. However, the poem, particularly when removed from its historical context, appears nearly a parody, presenting stereotypes of African life and African American heritage. Even T.R. Hummer, who defended Lindsay on other counts, called the poem "poetry in blackface," a reflection of the vaudevillian **minstrelsy** tradition and American arrogance. **Rachel DuPlessis** pointed out that "The Congo" reduces African Americans to symbols of primitivism.

Aside from the controversy surrounding "The Congo," most criticism of Lindsay addresses his populism and performance style. W.B. Yeats applauded the return to the poetic troubadour tradition and saw Lindsay as the first representative of a true American voice. **T.S. Eliot** found Lindsay crude and **Ezra Pound** found him laughable. The high modernists generally condemned him, while others in the New Poetry circles appreciated his interpretation of modern life. As for more recent criticism, Elizabeth Hardwick said Lindsay "had no more caution than a hobo hitching a ride," while Cary Nelson found Lindsay's vision of democracy to be an important reflection of American culture. Lindsay's name is even brought into debates about **slam poetry**, as writers continue to argue over the valuation of a poem's performance over its written artifice.

Because of his work's musical references, its evangelistic fervor, its obsession with popular culture, and his willingness to write about African Americans and other minority groups, Lindsay became known as a "**jazz** poet." His ability to pick up upon the sounds of modern life and the music of jazz and Tin Pan Alley influenced a number of later poets, among them Hughes and **Allen Ginsberg**. Over time, Lindsay came to hate the jazz poet label, because he felt that the audience was more interested in his chanting performances than in his writing. The taverns and clubs where jazz was played offended Lindsay's religious convictions, and he was never able to resolve the pull between freedom (as symbolized by jazz) and his rigid moral views.

Lindsay published one other book of generally well-considered poetry, *The Chinese Nightingale and Other Poems*, in 1917. While several other collections were later published, all were of declining quality. Over the course of his career, he published many poems of children's ephemera (such as "The Mysterious Cat" and "The Moon Is the North Wind's Cookie") that continue to be anthologized.

During the period when he should have been his most prolific, Lindsay focused his energies on a utopian novel, *The Golden Book of Springfield*. Seven years in the writing, *The Golden Book* presents a vision of a world in which all races and genders are provided equal consideration and justice. When *The Golden Book* was published in 1920, it met with nearly universal scorn. Its failure sent Lindsay into a spiraling decline. He became increasingly obsessed with arcane quests, such as research into hieroglyphic symbols that presages contemporary interests in visual text. His poetry became self-parody. Surprisingly, the material in *The Golden Book* and his theories about visual symbols have drawn recent critical attention, most notably from Ann Massa (in her book *Vachel Lindsay: Fieldworker for the American Dream*) and Paul Horgan (in an essay in *American Scholar*).

While even Lindsay's best poems are manic and sentimental, he remains an important figure in the development of American poetry and poetic performance. He mixed modern American music, machine sound, conversation, the spirit of rebellion, and the rhythm of word in a way that nobody had done before. Lindsay wanted to find a sound, a language, that reflected what he heard while walking the streets and roads—and, in that, he succeeded. He wanted to transmit a wide vision of American democratic possibilities and to convert everyone to his utopian dream—and, in that, he failed. His ability to make performance an integral part of the poem (to the point where the poem was meant to be performed and not read on the page) was unique in its period. Lindsay had an undeniably distinctive and original voice; nobody can imitate him.

Further Reading. *Selected Primary Sources:* Lindsay, Vachel, *The Art of the Moving Picture* (New York: Macmillan, 1915); ———, *The Chinese Nightingale and Other Poems* (New York: Macmillan, 1917); ———, *The Congo and Other Poems* (New York: Mitchell Kennerley, 1914); ———, *General William Booth Enters into Heaven and Other Poems* (New York: Mitchell Kennerley, 1913); ———, *The Poetry of Vachel Lindsay*, vols. 1 and 2, ed. Dennis Camp (Peoria: Spoon River Poetry Press, 1984). *Selected Secondary Sources:* DuBois, W.E.B., "The Looking Glass Literature" (*Crisis* 12.4 [August 1916]: 182–183); DuPlessis, Rachel Blau, "HOO, HOO, HOO: Some Episodes in the Construction of Modern Whiteness" (*American Literature* 67.4 [December 1995]: 667–700); Hardwick, Elizabeth, "Wind from the Prairie" (*New York Review of Books* [26 September 1991]: 9–16); Harris, Mark, *City of Discontent* (Indianapolis: Bobbs Merrill, 1952); Horgan, Paul, "Vachel Lindsay and the Book of the Dead" (*American Scholar* 62.4 [Autumn 1993]: 565–570); Hummer, T.R., "Laughed Off: Canon, Kharakter, and the Dismissal of Vachel Lindsay" (*Kenyon Review* 17.2 [Spring 1995]: 56–97); Massa, Ann, *Vachel Lindsay: Fieldworker for the American Dream* (Bloomington: Indiana University Press, 1970); Masters, Edgar Lee, *Vachel Lindsay* (New York: Scribner's, 1963); Ruggles, Eleanor, *The West-Going Heart* (New York: Norton, 1959).

Becky Bradway

LINE

The line is the defining characteristic of **verse**. While the association of verse with poetry is not absolute—we can identify "**prose poems**"—verse is and has always been the favored medium for poetry. Any written language must be written in lines, unless it runs lengthwise on an endless tape. In prose, however, we understand the lines to have been determined by the printer, and having to do with page-size and the justification of margins; in verse we recognize the divisions of the text into lines as decisions by the writer. As decisions they constitute means of expression, and so we take them—both the lines and the turning points that divide them—as implicated in the meaning of the text.

The status of "line" in poetry that is oral or received orally, as in preliterate **epic** or in song, may differ crucially from its status in poetry whose public home is the printed page. In oral contexts we can hear a line as a separable unit only if it is patterned in some auditorily prominent way: either by syntactical **closure** and the repetition of syntactical forms, as in the Psalms or, in the American nineteenth century, the poetry of **Walt Whitman**; or by the recurring patterns of stress and sound that we recognize (by ear) as meter and rhyme. It may therefore be tempting to say that in written poetry a line is a purely visual phenomenon, a fact for the eye only and not the ear. This is an argument made, in the 1920s and occasionally in recent decades, by critics of "free verse": that it is merely "prose cut into lines." However, it is more useful and more consistent to note that, like virtually everything else that can be thought of as distinctive about poetry, the written line is a cue to the ear, one of several instructions about how the language means to be heard.

It is this alliance of verse with poetry that motivates an examination of the nature and form of the line. Though different aspects of the functioning of lines are closely intertwined, it may be useful to isolate three of them for scrutiny: the line as an integral object in the poem; the relation of one line to those preceding and following it; and the measure by which a line's length is determined.

Integrity

For the idea of the line to justify its central place within our ideas of verse and poetry, many or most lines in a poem must claim some kind of semi-independent integrity. They not only further our attention, but also arrest it. When we consider lines in relation to the poetry that comprises a series of them, then, we notice a double function. Only by way of its accumulating lines can the poem proceed from its beginning to its end; it is made of nothing but accumulating lines. Yet the line, if it insists on integrity, simultaneously *resists* the continuation that the poem desires. A familiar metaphor is "flow": But the line's job is not to aid the gravitational inevitability of the poem's continuation, but rather to block and nuance and complicate it, like boulders and meanders in the stream.

In this sense the primal function of the line lies in the strain it mounts against the syntactical, discursive, and narrative momentum of the poem. The poem asks the line to further its projects of statement, argument, and storytelling; the line, although agreeing, asks first to be held up for individual inspection, to be savored for a moment that is always ready to expand. As the **lyric poem** is a moment excerpted (perhaps painfully) from time, the line may offer itself as an excerpt from the inexorable beginning-middle-end of the poem. The atemporal bent of lyric suggests that in some way the line is what the poem is for, that the poem keeps finding its whole reflection in a single line. A reader may quote "The fire that stirs about her when she stirs" and remember Yeats, but forget which particular poem's ecology threw up this brilliant specimen.

The question, then, is what can make a line—what we seem automatically to call "a good line"—feel like an integral utterance/object. Internal stress-rhythm (metrical or not) is only one factor, though even a free-verse line like "Maybe it's his wife" (**William Carlos Will-**

iams, "Exercise") may call our attention to the symmetry of its stresses, which is underscored—inverted and complicated—by the line that follows: "the car is an official car." Not only stress, however, but also all the many levels of our linguistic awareness are available for patterning and therefore cohesion.

The line may be syntactically closed; it may comprise a sentence, clause, or phrase whose urge toward extension into the next line is stilled, or at least lessened, by our sense that some piece of syntactical work has been completed. The one-line sentence is as tight an integral unit as the poem can contain: "I hear my being dance from ear to ear" (**Theodore Roethke**, "The Waking"). The effect of closure is subtly *lessened* when the line contains two sentences, as in, in the same poem, "We think by feeling. What is there to know?" While the variety of syntactical junctures is discussed below, a simple question to pose at each step in the poem's unfolding is whether a sentence that does not end at the end of the line *could* do so. **Elizabeth Bishop**'s "At the Fishhouses" includes the couplet, "The air smells so strong of codfish / that it makes one's eyes water and one's nose run." The sentence which the first line could have been, in which "so" is a mere intensifier, is revised by the adjoined line into a more cogent statement in which "so" is retrospectively revealed as analytic and as grounded in concrete, evidentiary experience. In that poem's first line, "Although it is a cold evening," the initial subordinating conjunction gives the line the forward impetus of syntactical incompleteness, and announces the poem's thematic concern with balancing observation (the quality of the time of day) with judgment (the hierarchically elaborated syntax). In contrast, "The Armadillo," also by Bishop, begins with a flat "This is the time of year," in which the minimal syntactical momentum signals the speaker's minimal engagement, at the outset, with the foreign customs she is observing. It is worth noting that of all the resources of integrity available to lines, syntactical closure is the one most easily exhausted. In a long run, sharply end-stopped lines almost cease to feel like lines, because line juncture fades into the sentence juncture central to prose, and loses any special function.

Many lines that we carry away separately from poems distinguish themselves by presenting an isolated image. (**Ezra Pound** at one point defined image as "that which presents an intellectual and emotional complex in an instant of time"; typically, the line is the instant.) A famous example is Andrew Marvell's image of oranges on the tree "Like golden lamps in a green night" ("Bermudas"). The line stands out not only because of its abrupt simile and sharp visual contrast, but also because the description is syntactically and discursively gratuitous within the ongoing stream of the poem, which it therefore interrupts even while continuing one of its sentences. A less obvious example, which may therefore represent a more common tendency among lines, is John Milton's "Of choicest flowers a garland to adorn" (*Pardise Lost,* ix. ln. 840). The two middle nouns present an image of gathered flowers, while the words that bracket them, not closely linked in sense or syntax, intimate both the selecting of the bouquet and its eventual disposition.

Sound patterns, too, when they do not belong to a continuing metric, can bind a line together internally at least as tightly as it is bound to the discourse it furthers. In the first line of John Keats's "Ode to Autumn," "Season of mists and mellow fruitfulness," hardly any phoneme fails to participate in an assonantal or consonantal pairing or larger pattern. The line plays with sound so richly as to make us hear it as a kind of auditory image, linked with the visual images the line otherwise presents more vaguely. Similarly, as Hugh Kenner has noted, the impression of visual sharpness most readers take from Pound's "While my hair was still cut straight across my forehead" ("The River-Merchant's Wife: A Letter") is probably traceable to the auditory distinctness of "still cut straight." The words' sounds enforce an articulatory care that readers translate unconsciously into a scene of quick, meticulous barbering which the poem has no leisure to notice explicitly.

Especially during the Augustan period—in America as in England—poets valued the integrity a line (or pair of lines) could gain from self-contained logical or rhetorical patterns: "Where change of favorites made no change of laws, / And senates heard before they judged a cause" (Samuel Johnson, "The Vanity of Human Wishes"); or, with greater stress on psychological complexity, "And when thou feel'st no grief, as I no harms, / Yet love thy dead, who long lay in thine arms" (**Anne Bradstreet**, "Before the Birth of One of Her Children"). A more general version of this method can be seen in lines as distant from each other in time as Chaucer's "And gladly would he learn, and gladly teach," and Roethke's "I wake to sleep, and take my waking slow." The repetition of words on which these semantic patterns depend also draws repetition of sound in its wake; as a result, such lines show how many resources of integrity can be brought to bear simultaneously.

It is common in some kinds of free verse for the line to combine tendencies toward isolation and openness. The contemporary English poet Geoffrey Hill's "September Song" includes this parenthetical stanza: "(I have made / an elegy for myself it / is true)." The arresting idea of an "elegy for myself" is countered immediately by the violent break after the momentarily unaccountable "it." The lines in their separation ask us to pause and demand that we push forward, and this is a main motivating force in such verse. More radically, in some twentieth-century verse the line acts out an apparent defiance of closure: "Yet if I should get married and it's

Connecticut and snow" (**Gregory Corso**, "Marriage"). The logical ellipsis at "it's" respects the poem's theme of stereotypical social inevitability in the face of which the poet stands bewildered; a more cogent surface logic of cause-and-effect would misrepresent this theme. Yet our cooperative response to such a line depends on recognizing its subversion of our long-standing expectation of verse-lines' integrity.

Finally, and from the beginning, the power of the poetic line often resides, or is realized only, in its relation to an accompanying line. The second half of one of our earliest English poems says, "Christ that my love were in my arms / And I in my bed again." As in the two halves of many proverbs, neither is very striking by itself (a wish for embrace; a wish for rest). Only the combination is astonishing, and the force would be dissipated without the delaying division between the lines.

Enjambment

The poem can never allow its lines complete self-containment. The most pervasive relation between lines emerges when we examine the breaks that occur at the ragged, decision-laden right margin of the poem. As noted earlier, a long sequence of one-line sentences ceases at some point to feel like verse at all. In almost any style of verse, a majority of lines are "enjambed": The sense of the language, or more precisely the syntax, runs over from one line to the next.

The vital contribution of enjambment to the whole rhythmic character of a poem, and to its meaning, arises from what has often been called "tension" or "counterpoint." A line's words belong simultaneously to two systems or grids or dimensions: that of the line's own measure (metrical or nonmetrical), and that of the sentence. Again, the sentence drives onward and the line holds back; it is at the line breaks, the points where one movement ceases while another continues, where one dynamic cuts across or counterpoints the other, that we feel the tension of being pulled in two directions. At the least this feeling contributes to the overall heightening of attention characteristic of poetry. In many cases this tension corresponds directly to semantic or affective events in the poem, as in the final lines of **Louise Bogan**'s "The Cupola":

Someone has thought alike of the bough and the wind
And struck their shape to the wall. Each in its season
Spills negligent death throughout the abandoned
  chamber.

The first of these lines terminates as calmly and meditatively as most of the lines preceding it in the poem; the next ends as if in mid-air, and the energy which enjambment supplies to our movement onward rushes us into a last line whose shock arises partly from the word "death," but still more from the sudden acceleration triggered by the line break.

Enjambment owes its effectiveness to being not a binary condition (end-stopped or not end-stopped) but a range of strengths. (This point is well explained in **John Hollander**'s classic essay "'Sense Variously Drawn Out': On English Enjambment," *Vision and Resonance.*) Roughly speaking, the more intimate the relation between successive words, the stronger an enjambment that divides them. The scale runs from zero (the end-stopped line that terminates the poem) to an extreme at which a single word is divided between lines, as in **Robert Creeley**'s "I Know a Man":

> the darkness sur-
> rounds us,

Between these extremes, the weaker enjambments divide clauses within the sentence or phrases within the clause. Breaks between a verb and its object are more noticeable; those between an adjective or possessive pronoun and the nouns they modify register as very abrupt and potentially dramatic; those between an article and its noun, or a phrasal verb and its prepositional component ("give / up") threaten the sentence with disruption. While it is tempting to see weak enjambments as allowing the line the greatest degree of integrity—because syntactical self-sufficiency supplements other kinds of containment—it is equally true that strong enjambments highlight the presence of verse-lines in general, and may therefore help to emphasize the line's resistance to syntactical pressure.

At its most prominent, the effect of enjambment is revelation, as at the end of **James Wright**'s "A Blessing": "Suddenly I realize / That if I stepped out of my body I would break / Into blossom." It is the special genius of enjambment to reveal a semantic discovery (in this case a spiritual insight linking dissolution with rebirth) through a linguistic one (that "break" alters its meaning radically when it becomes part of the phrasal verb "break into"). Poets whose favored mode is wit, such as **Heather McHugh** and **William Matthews**, rely on this device, but so do meditative poets such as **T.S. Eliot**: "words or music reach / The stillness, as a Chinese jar still / Moves perpetually in its stillness" ("Burnt Norton").

Enjambment is by no means the only kind of link between lines. Especially in American poetry (Whitman's, **James Weldon Johnson**'s) that reflects a Biblical rhetorical tradition, syntactical parallelism binds lines together as much as syntactical continuity does. Rhyme, too, is a relation between lines even more particularly associated with poetry. In eighteenth-century heroic couplets, the rhyme is so constant, and end-stopping (at least of the couplet, often of the line) so regular, that

rhyme can be thought of as replacing enjambment in organizing the relation between lines. On a more expansive scale, rhyme may define stanzaic forms. The stanza resembles the line in being an organization of language unique to verse. In stanzaic poems, one line is related not only to others in its stanza, but also to lines in the same position in other stanzas. The short final lines of a series of Sapphic stanzas, for example, enter into a kind of community a little separate from the rest of the poem. In **Marianne Moore**'s arbitrary syllabic structures, fully accounting for a line entails checking it against corresponding lines in other stanzas.

Measure. The line might seem to be completely defined by what it contains and by how its end-points react with adjoining lines. Yet the study of lines in poetry has usually focused on a different question: what determines the length of the line? (This means both what controls the poet's decision about where to end a line and a reader's expectations about its length.) When poetry was almost entirely metrical—in English, very roughly until the twentieth century—this question revolved around the choice of metrical "feet" (groups of stressed and unstressed syllables) and the number of feet in the line. From this view, the whole topic of "measure" could be summarized, with an accuracy of perhaps 75 percent, in the two words "iambic pentameter": A line of verse is ten syllables long, the even-numbered ones stressed, with a set of allowable variations. (In recent decades, linguists have proposed more exact and explanatory accounts of the iambic pentameter.) The minority of English poetry omitted from this summary differed from it either by the use of falling ("trochaic") rather than rising ("iambic") feet, or three- rather than two-syllable feet; or by adopting a different or sometimes varying number of feet in the line (occasionally one or two, often three or seven, most often four or six).

With the advent of free verse (q.v.) the whole topic grew more complicated and perhaps more central. If no metrical norm measures the line, or measures it out, what does? One valid but not very helpful answer is that in the absence of predetermined metrical form, local phenomena govern the line's termination, as when the force of an enjambment is the main effect the poet seeks, as often in the work of **Nikki Giovanni**. Yet few poems read as if the poet simply continued horizontally until a good occasion for enjambing came along. Most poems are consistent enough in measure that when we look at the page from a distance we already know something about a steady rhythm in which it will move.

If non-metrical line length is not unboundedly arbitrary, it is vitally arbitrary nonetheless. What strikes us as arbitrary—not as governed by preordained rule, nor merely contingent on context, nor inhumanly random— gives us a sense of the will of its maker. For this reason, lines' measure embodies voice. In this sense measure is the poet's hallmark as "touch" is the pianist's; an experienced reader may recognize a line as belonging to some one poet's work even in the absence of its context.

At this point, probably more than at any other within the topic of line, we may identify a specifically American sensibility at work. Despite the many complex prehistories critics have offered for it, free verse is largely an American invention, and an American obsession. Whitman's cardinal example, programmatically individualistic, stands behind the vast array of styles and experiments that typifies the majority of American poetry in the twentieth century. Williams's lifelong investigation of what he called "the American idiom and the variable foot" leads to a very different sense of measure from Whitman's, but grows from the same root: "**Prosody** means the rhythm of the poet's personal speech as it partakes of the rhythm of a cultural idiom" (Mary Ellen Solt, interview in *Massachusetts Review* [1962]: 38). It could be argued that the long process of American cultural differentiation from Britain made poets especially aware of linguistic differences, especially rhythmic ones. For Williams this was a motive for rejecting the pentameter measure he identified as fundamentally British. Since Williams, much American poetry has aimed at a measure for the line that acknowledges, embraces, or even duplicates the cadences of American speech.

Yet if "measure" has been a particularly American concern, by the same token there is no one American measure. There are styles that entail expectations about the length and structure of lines: **Allen Ginsberg**'s (long), **George Oppen**'s (short), **Charles Olson**'s (typographically scattered). There are also, especially in the last four or five decades, recognizable norms. Wright, **Philip Levine**, **Mary Oliver**, and **Gary Snyder** differ in many stylistic choices; but in the work of all of them and countless others, a non-metrical line about three or four accents long sustains whole collections. This kind of cultural consensus can, in turn, become the basis for further distinctions: If **Rita Dove**'s poems contract the typical line toward a more song-like measure, **Galway Kinnell**'s and **Amiri Baraka**'s expand it toward a more spacious rhetoric. A poet's decision to occupy any point in this wide range is ultimately founded on what she or he needs each line to contain, to do, and to sound and feel like. These choices, driven basically by the constant need to build and measure one line after another, define for us the poet's voice.

Further Reading. *Selected Primary Sources:* Attridge, Derek, *The Rhythms of English Poetry* (New York: Longman, 1982); Frank, Robert, and Henry Sayre, *The Line in Postmodern Poetry* (Urbana: University of Illinois Press, 1988); Hanson, Kristin, and Paul Kiparsky, "The Nature of Verse and Its Consequences for the Mixed Form," in *Prosimetrum: Cross-Cultural Perspectives on Narrative in Prose and Verse*, ed. Joseph Harris and Karl Reichl (Rochester, NY: D.S. Brewer, 1997, 17–44); ———, "A Parametric Theory of Poetic Meter" (*Language* 72.2 [1996]: 287–335); Hartman, Charles O., *Free Verse: An Essay on Prosody* (Evanston, IL: Northwestern University Press, 1996); Hollander, John, *Vision and Resonance: Two Senses of Poetic Form*, 2nd ed. (New Haven, CT: Yale University Press, 1985); Kinzie, Mary, *A Poet's Guide to Poetry* (Chicago: University of Chicago Press, 1999); Smith, Barbara H., *Poetic Closure: A Study of How Poems End* (Chicago: University of Chicago Press, 1968).

Charles O. Hartman

LINEAR FALLACY

The notion of linear fallacy originated with American critic Marjorie Perloff in 1981. As the title of a landmark essay on the nature of the poem in the age of **free verse**, the expression conveys the puzzlement one may experience in front of poems which are by and large defined as "a series of words, phrases, or clauses divided into line lengths and arranged on the page with a fixed left margin" (Linear, 855). After discarding traditional versification, lineation as a visual element is what denotes the poetic status of a text. Questioning the definitions of free verse as bringing focus on the action, rather than how it is expressed, or as shifting the definition of the poetic from rhythm to tone, Perloff shows the discrepancy between lines that are artificially imposed on otherwise indeterminate text to create "a set of expectations and conventions that determine how a verbal sequence is to be read" (Linear, 857) and lines that provide complex aural and visual patterning. The issue is at the heart of the return to form brought about by the post-Williams insistence on measure, and the failure of some poets (and critics) to conceive of these forms as versatile and plural, not limited to lineation, and least of all to the fallacy of "chopped up prose" (Linear, 858).

Referring to the etymology of verse as *versus* (what turns back) and to Oswald Ducrot and Tzvetan Todorov's definition of verse (185–186), Perloff stresses the importance of parallelism: "some form of regular recurrence in time among the elements of the speech chain" (Linear, 859), be it metrical (John Milton), quantitative (**Ezra Pound**), accentual (**William Carlos Williams**), or syntactic (**Walt Whitman**). She suggests that the line has become "a surface device," which has produced "a tolerance among us for various kinds of imprecise and sloppy writing" (Linear, 861). There ensue a number of examples where linear fallacy is at work, illegitimately asserting the poetic nature of commonplace or weak statements, on the assumption that "lineation spells elevation" (Linear, 864). Grounding her conclusions on the close reading of a poem by **George Oppen**, Perloff defines the free verse poem as weaving intricate patterns of visual and metrical connections that definitely forbid their being "rewritten as . . . prose paragraph[s]" (Linear, 866). For Oppen, as well as other poets, line (or no line) becomes "the graph of consciousness" (Linear, 867). Lineation is not a convention for poetry *per se*; the necessity of lineation has to be proven in each and every poem: "The nonlineation of prose may [also] function as poetry," "when prose foregrounds marked patterns of recurrence (whether phonic, syntactic or verbal), calling attention to itself as language art" (Linear, 867).

Coming into play as **David Antin** performs talk poems or as the **Language poets** start working on the "new sentence" as a rhythmic unit for the poem, the notion of linear fallacy is one that allows the integration of a more comprehensive definition of the poetic, in terms of formal experimentation, individual determination, and reflexivity. It allows the substitution of the more operative notion of **prosody** for that of metrics in the analysis of contemporary poetry. It underlies any assessment of **performance** or procedural work as being not formless or aleatory but, on the contrary, extremely formal and rule governed. The notion returns throughout Marjorie Perloff's work on twentieth-century poetry as the *locus* for the emergence of **New Forms**.

Further Reading. *Selected Primary Sources:* Perloff, Marjorie, *The Dance of the Intellect: Studies in the Poetry of the Pound Tradition* (Evanston, IL: Northwestern University Press, 1996); ———, *Differentials: Poetry, Poetics, Pedagogy* (Tuscaloosa: University of Alabama Press, 2004); ———, "The Linear Fallacy" (*Georgia Review* XXXV.4 [1981]: 855–869); ———, *Radical Artifice: Writing Poetry in the Age of Media* (Chicago: University of Chicago Press, 1991); ———, "Symposium on the Line" (*Epoch* 29 [1980]: 163–221). ***Selected Secondary Sources:*** Davidson, Michael, *Ghostlier Demarcations: Modern Poetry and the Material Word* (Berkeley: University of California Press, 1997); Ducrot, Oswald, and Tzvetan Todorov, *Encyclopedic Dictionary of the Sciences of Language*, trans. Catherine Porter (Baltimore: Johns Hopkins University Press, 1979); Fredman, Stephen, *Poet's Prose: The Crisis in American Verse* (Cambridge: Cambridge University Press, 1990); Kirby-Smith, H.T., *The Origins of Free Verse* (Ann Arbor: University of Michigan Press, 1998).

Hélène Aji

LITERARY INDEPENDENCE POEM

The literary independence poem, an American genre of the eighteenth century, always holds that America, or significant geographical regions of America, has begun to rival the literary achievements of ancient Greece and Rome; that America or a part of it will advance as a principal center of learning; that literary and/or cultural independence from Britain becomes a consistent claim,

the earlier examples registering their claims long before political and economic declarations begin to dominate; and that, in line with eighteenth-century America's turn toward secularism, this new literary accomplishment will come from an anthropocentric, secular ambiance. Many of these poems are exhortatory in tone, urging others to emulate the example of their American superiors, or they predict authors of great genius to come. Echoing the rhetoric of the rising rebellion, the later poems of this genre come to speak of a liberating moment in which all the Atlantic colonies will participate. The most dramatic characteristic each example of this genre displays is a universal urgency or even anxiety to bring about a palpable cultural separation from the Mother country and hence to encourage the discovery of an identity that eventually comes to be called American.

Numbering over twenty, this group of poems constitutes a genre of its own. As well, most of these poems participate in the eighteenth century's on-going identity discourse wherein the American character, one clearly not British, becomes identifiable. What is perhaps the first example of this genre occurs appropriately in the prefatory material to *Magnalia Christi Americana* (1702), **Cotton Mather**'s prose **epic** wherein he delineates the American self in terms of Virgil's *pietas*, devotion to God, Mother (family and friends), and Country.

In a Latin poem by **Henricus Selyns**, Dutch Reformed Church minister of New York, the poet quotes Aeneas's exclamation, "Quantum mutatus ab illo" (How changed from what he was!), taken from the passage in Book II of the *Aeneid* introducing Aeneas's vision of battle-ravaged Hector, whom Virgil calls the "light of Troy," coming to warn Aeneas to leave Troy. At the same time Hector imparts the virtue of *pietas* to him by advising him to take with him his household deities and his family and companions in order to found a new city to the West. Selyns has indeed chosen his quotations well, for they subtly prepare the reader for Mather's appropriation of *pietas* to the American character. Selyns also takes the opportunity here to register the claim that, even though wisdom may teem in the "Veterem . . . Orbem" (Old World), "Sat est Academia nostra" in the "*Novus Orbis*"; that is, our college is the Old World's equal, though now located in the New World. Selyns is even emboldened to assert that "Forte novas, pluresque artes *Novus Orbis* haberet" (As it so happens, the New World has many new things and [even] the many arts), thus presenting a formidable challenge to all of Europe (iii).

Selyns's claim that Cambridge's Harvard University has now become the educational equal of the Old World's institutions of higher learning (whether true or not is beside the point) and his assertion that new things along with the many arts have now arisen in the New

World captures the spirit of all subsequent independence poems, all of which celebrate New World possibilities while suggesting the Old World may be lapsing into, or has already lapsed into, a state of decline. The sentiments in Selyns's Latin poem receive considerable elaboration by other hands as the eighteenth century presses toward political, military, and economic independence.

These poems have been confused with the "Westward the course of Empire" motif supposedly initiated by George Berkeley, the British theologian and philosopher who, as part of his Bermuda Project, sailed for America in September 1728 and returned to Britain in October 1731. David Berman, one of Berkeley's most recent biographers, notes that he had written a version of his famous poem, "On the Prospect of Planting Arts and Learning in America" (here Berkeley is unaware of Selyns's earlier testimony), as early as 1726 but did not allow the piece to appear in print until 1752. While it may be argued that this early 1726 version could have circulated in manuscript, Berman says that Berkeley was "secretive" about it, "even to the extent of denying his authorship." Berman also points out that a century earlier the English poet George Herbert had in "The Church Militant" emphasized "the westward movement of religion and Christianity: 'The course was westward, that the Sun might light / As well our understanding as our sight'" and that "Religion stands on tip-toe in our land, / Readie to pass to the American strand."

To be sure, Berkeley and even Herbert may have taken this notion of westward movement from Virgil's *Aeneid* and Aeneas's journey from Troy in the east to the promised land in the west. Of course neither Selyns nor the later authors of literary independence poems needed Herbert or Berkeley. Their grammar school's required reading of the first book of the *Aeneid* in Latin would have given these early American poets all the instruction they would have wanted regarding their own relocation in a land to the west, and the possible political and social implications of that relocation. Literary independence poems begin to surface with some regularity in early America during the 1720s, as poet after poet declares separation from Britain and/or Europe.

A cluster of such poems appears to have been motivated by the example of Philadelphia's Aquila Rose, who flourished as printer, poet, and politician from about 1719 into the early 1720s. In "An Encomium to Aquila Rose, on His Art in Praising" Joseph Breintnall, writing as if Rose were still alive, penned these startling lines:

Go on, and find more Candidates for Praise,
Our infant Country's Reputation raise;
Doubt not but Strangers far remote will come
For what they are so much in Want at Home,

And visit us as ancient *Greece* or *Rome*.

These lines characterize a mind anxious to see his "Country," which Breintnall, a more senior member of the literary coterie that surrounded Rose, probably thought of as the colony of Pennsylvania, receive recognition on the world scene. That recognition, Breintnall significantly maintains, should come from his country's literary achievements, not necessarily, yet, from its political, economic, or military exploits.

While he does cite both Greece and Rome as glorious precedents to be emulated, the triple (sight) rhyme "come," "Home" and "Rome" clearly gives weight to the Roman example. So exhilarating has been Rose's effect, at least on this author, that it has emboldened him to view his own "Country's Reputation" not only as rivaling that of England but also as even surpassing it. So far reaching appears to be the spread of this reputation that "Strangers far remote" will soon visit this New World for the same sort of intellectual sustenance the Old World once sought from the ancient Greeks and Romans. Selyns's earlier, more modest claim waxes bold here.

Just as striking is a 1729 poem by **Richard Lewis**, which he offers as from "a distant Muse" (from Annapolis) but publishes in Philadelphia's *American Weekly Mercury*, wherein he declares: "Westward from Britain shall an *Athens* [seat of wisdom and the arts] rise, / Which soon shall bear away the learned prize." Echoing Breintnall's earlier comparison, Lewis apparently inspired another Philadelphia poem published a year later. As J.A. Leo Lemay has asserted, "The poem was immediately imitated in Philadelphia, for George Webbe's poem in Titan Leeds' almanac for 1730 contains the same theme and echoes phrases from this poem" (132). In any event, Webbe issues his own challenge when he states that "*Europe* shall mourn her ancient Fame declin'd / And *Philadelphia* be the *Athens* of Mankind," for "Here / Sweet Liberty her gentle Influence sheds." Note Webbe's extension of literary independence into the area of politics.

Another example of this independence genre, hailing from Boston, presents one of the most aggressive declarations of American literary self-sufficiency to appear in print before **Ralph Waldo Emerson**'s famous Phi Beta Kappa address delivered on August 31, 1837, and known to all serious readers of American letters as *The American Scholar*. This remarkable document is nothing like or as well known as Emerson's *Scholar*, nor is its probable author, John Perkins, Harvard graduate of the class of 1695 and known to his contemporaries not for his ability as a poet, but for his skill as a physician. Perkins is the first native-born author of an American literary independence poem. Born in Ipswich, Massachusetts, on August 28, 1676, Perkins prepared for his admission to Harvard at the Ipswich grammar school. After leaving Harvard, Perkins studied medicine, returned to Ipswich to practice for a time, and a few years after his marriage in 1697 seems to have permanently located in Boston, where his wife held some property. This same John Perkins enjoyed the support of Mather in his promotion of inoculation for smallpox. Little is known of his activities after this time until his death on December 26, 1740, while on a journey to South Carolina to restore his health.

Not much is known of Perkins after 1720 or so, that is, except for his publication on August 4, 1728, in the *New England Weekly Journal* of "On Reading the *Poem* to His Excellency, by Mr. Byles." Earlier, **Mather Byles**, literary editor of the *New England Weekly Journal*, had published a creditable poem on the arrival in Boston of Governor William Burnet, not in the *Weekly* but as a pamphlet. Perkins's perhaps over-enthusiastic appreciation of Byles's Burnet piece appeared in print at least one other time in one of the first volumes that can be called an anthology of American poems; this anthology, *A Collection of Poems by Several Hands*, was published in Boston in 1745 and contains a majority of poems by Byles that did not appear in his *Poems on Several Occasions*, issued in the same year. In the anthology, Perkins's poem is the fourth selection, where it is given the title "To _____ _____." For the convenience of easy reference, as the person to whom the poem is addressed is most certainly Mather Byles, modify the poem's title to read simply "To Mather Byles."

"To Mather Byles" compels our attention, however, not because of what it observes about Byles's poetic performance, but because of what it asserts about New England's literary independence. This twenty-four–line poem written in iambic pentameter couplets and triplets opens with these tense lines:

> Long has New-England groan'd beneath the load,
> Of too too just reproaches from abroad,
> Unlearn'd in arts, and barren in their skill,
> How to employ the tender muses quill.

Despite past failings, now the young poet Byles binds his name "on the radiant wings of fame." From such a height, others who might aspire to such achievement, so says Perkins, can only "fondly gaze" after Byles's example, for he "Has lost th' attracting world, and shines among the stars." This last line is an alexandrine (an iambic pentameter line with an extra foot), surely cast for effect. The imagery here of winged fame shining among the stars echoes that of the poet **John Adams**'s translation of Horace's first ode.

Whether or not Byles deserves such hyperbolic praise is finally not the point of Perkins's verses. For the author clearly directs the young poets of New England to observe Byles's example "With anxious care" in order

that that example may "Inspire our imitation, as it does our praise." Notice that Perkins zealously recommends that native New Englanders emulate another native New Englander—not a figure from Old England or from Europe. For such aspiration will lead other native poets, as Byles already does, to proclaim loudly and "in harmonious lines" that "*New England*'s sons, e'rewhile of barb'rous name" have lately become "A match for *Albion*, or the *Graecian* fame." Perkins's unabashed objective in this poem is not merely to separate New England's literary accomplishment, but indeed to declare that his country can now boast itself the equal of England and even of Greece, whose example has lighted the way of letters within the civilization of the West. Today it is easy enough to argue that Perkins's "saying it" does not "make it so," but to do so is once again to miss the point. Simply put, Perkins insists that a divergence from British and/or European literary tradition is, in 1728, in place, and he appears to be most impatient to ascertain this divergence, this new identity, to the world. As well, Perkins's naming of New England underscores **Benjamin Tompson**'s earlier identification of this region as a new country—one clearly separated from Great Britain.

While not approaching the greater substance of Emerson's *The American Scholar*, "To Mather Byles" deserves brief comparison with the later essay, if only because of its zeal. Written over 110 years after Perkins's verses, Emerson's *Scholar* opens with a complaint resembling Richard Lewis's earlier claim that Colonial Americans have no time "To raise the Genius." In Emerson's words Americans are "a people too busy to give to letters any more . . . [than] simply a friendly sign." Both Emerson and Perkins exaggerate the dearth of exemplary works within their respective literary scenes, each expressing in his own way exasperation. Perkins asserts, for example, that the accusations that American authors are "Unlearn'd in arts, and barren in their skill" have heretofore proved all too true, ignoring the works, for example, of **Anne Bradstreet**, Tompson, and Mather. Emerson maintains that "exertions of mechanical skill . . . [have] postponed expectation of the world" that America would produce first-rate writers—choosing not to acknowledge the critically acclaimed writings of Washington Irving, James Fenimore Cooper or **William Cullen Bryant**. Such close parallels of thought are repeated as Perkins declares that now Byles's example surely leads the way toward establishing literary separation from England and Europe, and Emerson urges that "our day of dependence, our long apprenticeship to the learning of other lands, draws to a close" (Miller, I:898).

The largely forgotten *Pietas et Gratulatio* (1761) gives the site of the next significant independence poem; as well it springs from a most unlikely source, Francis Bernard, whose tenure as royal Governor of Massachusetts

Bay began in 1760 with great fanfare but concluded in ignominy. In fact it was Bernard, hounded out of office because of his support of British policy in the late 1760s, who suggested the construction of *Pietas et Gratulatio* (Devotion and Congratulations). Noting that several British universities had presented similar volumes to George III at his accession, Bernard urged that recent graduates of Harvard College gather three poems in Greek, sixteen in Latin, and twelve in English to celebrate Britain's new monarch. Finely tooled as a rubricated quarto volume, this book represented the most sophisticated printing and collective intellectual venture of eighteenth-century America.

Bernard was given the honor of composing the final poem, an ode of almost perfect Latin sapphics which project, far into the future, a moment when "the uncultivated Muse" of America "will sound a grander and a better song" than that of Great Britain (Shields, 93). As well, this poem, and indeed the entire contents of the *Pietas* volume, signals the intersection of politics and literary/cultural concerns. For when Bernard points out the importance of civic devotion (or "*pietas civica*" in the poem), along with his insistence that the intellectual arts are now thriving in such American institutions as Harvard, he identifies *pietas* in a manner closely paralleling that of Mather in *Magnalia Christi Americana*, wherein he had earlier declared in the "Life of William Phips" that Phips's life represented devotion (*pietas*) to secular virtue. In other words, Bernard's "Epilogue" not only perpetuates the inclination of those on the American strand to seek and express cultural freedom from Britain but also celebrates as well the American devotion to the secular way of life.

John Trumbull's 1770 Yale College commencement address, "An Essay on the Use and Advantages of the Fine Arts," in many ways constitutes the most provocative example within the literary independence genre. Employing such phrases as "the most noble extravagance of imagination," "sublimity of conception," and "fire the imagination of the Artist and raise to sublimity the aspiring Muse," this tract of combined prose and poetry reads like a preamble to the Romantic movement.

Within a litany of the future glories of America, Trumbull predicts the coming of a new "lofty Milton" and the arrival of "Some future Shakespeare" who will "charm the rising age, / And hold in magic chains the listening stage." Trumbull even goes so far as to insist that women too will make contributions to the arts. Indeed "With fancy blooming and with taste refin'd, / Some Rowe [a prominent British woman poet of the eighteenth century] shall rise and wrest with daring pen, / The pride of genius from assuming men." Could Trumbull here have predicted the phenomenon of **Phillis Wheatley**?

A year later, in 1771, yet another commencement address provided the occasion for one of the last literary independence poems preceding the American Revolution. The well-known poet **Philip Freneau**, with the assistance of his friend and fellow classmate **Hugh Henry Brackenridge**, composed for the College of New Jersey (later Princeton) commencement "The Rising Glory of America." This poem, showing many affinities for classical **pastoral**, presents a history of America from Columbus to the mid-eighteenth century. As Greece and Rome no more detain the Muses "who have now located on American shores," Freneau extends America's cultural achievement into the sciences citing Franklin and his experiments with electricity.

The final third of "Rising Glory" is given over to mention of the Boston Massacre (of March 1770), to condemnation of British trampling on the Colonies' inchoate struggle for political liberty, to recollection of Bernard's infamy, and to the new, blatantly patriot resolve to achieve "independent power." With this poem, which exposes the British inclination "To rob the hive, and kill the industrious bee!" (the metaphor for British aggression against the Colonies is taken from Virgil's fourth *Georgic*), the literary independence poem has now become a form of political independence discourse.

Further Reading. *Selected Primary Sources:* Bernard, Francis, "Epilogue," in J.C. Shields, *The American Aeneas* (Knoxville: University of Tennessee Press, 2001, 92–93); Freneau, Philip, "The Rising Glory of America," in *The Literature of Colonial America*, ed. Susan Castillo and Ivy Schweitzer (Oxford, UK: Blackwell, 2001); Lewis, Richard, "To His Excellency Benedict Leonard Calvert" (includes "'To raise the Genius'" passage), in *Muscipula* (Annapolis, 1728); Perkins, John, "To Mather Byles" (*New England Weekly Journal* [4 August 1728]); Rose, Aquila, *Poems on Several Occasions* (includes Breintnall's "Encomium") (Philadelphia: New Printing Office, 1740); Selyns, Henricus, "That Great and Most Learned Man, Mr. Cotton Mather," in Cotton Mather, *Magnolia Christi Americana* (London, 1702); Trumbull, John, *An Essay on the Use and Advantages of the Fine Arts* (New Haven, CT: T. and S. Green, 1770); Webbe, George, "A Poem," in Titan Leeds, *Almanac* (Philadelphia: 1730). ***Selected Secondary Sources:*** Berman, David, *George Berkeley: Idealism and the Man* (Oxford, UK: Oxford University Press, 1994); Lemay, J.A. Leo, *Men of Letters in Colonial Maryland* (Knoxville: University of Tennessee Press, 1972); Miller, James E., Jr., *Heritage of American Literature: Beginnings to the Civil War* (includes Emerson's *American Scholar*) (New York: Harcourt Brace Jovanovich, 1991); Shields, John C., *The American Aeneas: Classical Origins of the American Self* (Knoxville: University of Tennessee Press, 2001).

John C. Shields

LITERARY MAGAZINES

From the beginnings of American literature to the present, literary magazines have played a vital role in forming literary communities and in disseminating poetry to the larger public. Nearly every major American poet has featured in one or more of the thousands of literary magazines that have been published over the past three centuries and nearly every literary movement has boasted its own literary magazine. Judging from the limited number of scholarly publications on this subject, the importance of literary magazines is a neglected feature of literary history. Literary magazines can be defined as journals and magazines that appear periodically—usually weekly, monthly, or quarterly—and are primarily devoted to printing literary texts and literary criticism. A subcategory of literary magazines consists of poetry magazines, which focus almost exclusively on publishing poetry or articles on poetry. Daily newspapers are not considered literary magazines, although especially in the nineteenth and early twentieth century major poets regularly published poems in newspapers. After the 1940s poetry all but disappeared in American newspapers. General-interest magazines—for instance, the *Atlantic* or the *New Yorker*—usually do not appear under the rubric of literary magazines because printing literary texts has not been their principal aim. Yet since they have consistently featured poetry in their pages and have introduced major poets, their function as literary magazines should not be underestimated.

The history of literary magazines in the United States shows various stages and phases in which certain types of magazines gained and subsequently lost their popularity. The little magazines of the 1910s and 1920s reacted against the lack of literary experimentation in major nineteenth-century magazines. The quarterlies of the 1930s, 1940s, and 1950s, which were often edited from university campuses, emphasized the formalist tenets of the **New Criticism**, while the multitude of magazines that sprung up during the mimeograph revolution from the late 1950s through the late 1970s rebelled against the predictability and staidness of those quarterlies (*see also* **Post–World War II Avant-Garde Poetry Magazines**). Like the magazines that came up during the mimeograph revolution, e-zines of the 1990s and beyond also emerged because of a technological innovation—the rise of the Internet. The huge number of literary magazines and the ephemeral nature of many of them make it hard to discern which are significant and which are not. Still, the endurance of this publishing phenomenon shows that literary magazines will continue to play a central role in American poetry.

Up until the twentieth century there were relatively few literary magazines, let alone poetry magazines. Most of the literature in periodical publications appeared in newspapers or magazines that also printed articles on art, politics, religion, and science. The first magazine to speak of, the *Royal American Magazine*, founded in 1774 to further the cause of the nascent American republic, printed a number of patriotic poems, but except for two minor poems by **Phillis Wheatley**, the quality was poor. After independence, the *Columbian Magazine*, publishing out of Philadelphia, continued the tone of the *Royal American Magazine*. Elizabeth Graeme Fergusson and Francis Hopkinson were the *Columbian*'s most prolific poets. Hopkinson's symbolic poem "The Birds, the Beasts and the Bat," published in 1787 and modeled on one of Aesop's fables, in which the birds become Americans and the beasts British, is a typical example of the verse published in those post-revolutionary years. Most of the eighteenth-century magazines had strong regional alliances and published some poetry, much of it political or sentimental. Noah Webster's short-lived *American Magazine*, which lasted from 1787 to 1788, was a first attempt to create a national magazine. **Timothy Dwight** published his poems sporadically in *American Magazine*, but the focus was more on the politics of the fledgling nation.

During the nineteenth century the *North American Review* became the country's premier intellectual magazine and the first to be respected abroad. Like *American Magazine*, it consciously presented itself as a national publication, but unlike its predecessor, it did remarkably well both in sales and longevity. Founded in 1815, the *North American Review* lasted until 1940, when a scandal involving propaganda for Japanese expansion led to the magazine's demise. At its height, in the 1890s, the magazine boasted a circulation of over 75,000 copies. While criticized by some for being too conservative and dry, the *North American Review* at its best provided a forum that helped bring about an awareness of an autonomous American literature. Whereas *Harper's Magazine*, which started in 1850, earned a reputation by pirating fiction by Charles Dickens and William Makepeace Thackeray, the *North American Review* opened up its pages to American authors, even if it also printed European literature. In this sense the *North American Review* was similar to the *Knickerbocker* (1833–1862), although that monthly was even more vigorous in endorsing an American tradition. The *North American Review* printed **William Cullen Bryant**'s "Thanatopsis," "To a Waterfowl," and many of his influential essays on American literature. The success of *Harper's* indirectly led to the downfall of two political magazines that printed some of the most characteristic poetry of the nineteenth century. The *American Whig Review* ran **Edgar Allan Poe**'s "The Raven" and "Ulalume" as well as works by **Walt Whitman** and **James Russell Lowell**. Ironically, its political adversary, the *United States Magazine and Democratic Review*, published many of the same poets.

Nearly all of the renowned poets of the nineteenth century, with the exception of **Emily Dickinson**, were involved in editing or running magazines. This urge is in part reflective of their impatience with the overtly commercial and political magazines of their time. Bryant, for instance, edited the *Atheneum* and Poe was literary editor of the *Southern Literary Messenger, Burton's Gentleman's Magazine, Graham's Magazine,* and the *Broadway Journal.* Poe's personal tastes often clashed with those of the magazines' owners and he made far-reaching plans to start up his own magazine, in which he could publish high-class literature and criticism. Yet this magazine never materialized. Lowell, who later became editor of the *Atlantic* from 1857 to 1861 and the *North American Review* from 1863 to 1872, had similar aspirations and started *The Pioneer* in 1842. Even though it folded after only three issues, *The Pioneer* published Poe's "Lenore" and short stories by **Nathaniel Hawthorne**. Shortly before that, in 1840, members of the Transcendental Club, including **Ralph Waldo Emerson** and **Margaret Fuller**, founded the *Dial* as an outlet of their circle's writing because they felt that other publications were either too conservative or unsympathetic to Transcendentalism. Fuller edited the *Dial* for two years, but Emerson took over in 1842 when Fuller had to resign on account of her bad health. Emerson sought to include more Transcendentalist poets, including **William Ellery Channing** and **Henry David Thoreau**. The *Dial*'s circulation never exceeded three hundred copies, and in 1844 it had to close. Despite the poor sales and lack of durability of the *Dial* and the *Pioneer*, these magazines had a great influence in fostering literary experimentation and strengthening a literary community. In this sense these short-lived magazines were the precursors of the little magazines of the twentieth century.

It was out of discontent with the complacency exemplified by the established periodicals, such as the *Atlantic* and *Harper's*, that many little magazines were started. Rather than set the highest standards of literature, these magazines, along with others like the *Literary Digest, Collier's,* and the *Saturday Evening Post,* were content to follow the literary taste of their readers. The editors of little magazines rebelled not only against the traditional patterns of literature and the current doctrines of taste, but also to the lack of poetry that appeared in magazines. Although the *Atlantic* was considered the best literary magazine of the second half of the nineteenth century, it printed only six or seven poems in each issue. **Harriet Monroe**, who established *Poetry* in 1912, thought that most magazines neglected or ignored serious poetry. Unlike other editors of little magazines, Monroe also paid for printing poems. Another Chicagoan, Margaret Anderson, was bothered that as a periodical reviewer she was supposed to give moral instead of literary judgments. She started the *Little Review* in 1914. *Poetry* and the *Little Review* emerged as the two most successful little magazines during and after World War I. In the wake of these magazines, a number of other magazines were started that also primarily focused on poetry, including *Contemporary Verse* (1916–1929), the *Fugitive* (1922–1925), *Glebe* (1913–1914), the *Measure* (1921–1926), *Others* (1915–1919), and the *Poetry Journal* (1912–1918). As with nearly all little magazines, their financial position was unstable, but they published artistic masterpieces that no other magazine dared to print at the time, which had a lasting influence on the development of literature. *Poetry* was the first of these and has outlasted all of them. What must have seemed impossible for Poe—to publish a journal that would be devoted to vanguard poetry—was made a reality in the first few decades of the twentieth century.

The embarrassment of riches that *Poetry* presented in the first decades after its inception is unrivaled in magazine history and ensured that *Poetry* was the prime medium through which the **modernist** poetry renaissance was conducted. As adviser and foreign editor to *Poetry*, **Ezra Pound** had much to do with its distinguished performance. Not only did Pound bombard Monroe with manuscripts from London by Richard Aldington, **H.D.**, **T.S. Eliot**, John Gould Fletcher, **Robert Frost**, Rabindranath Tagore, **William Carlos Williams**, and W.B. Yeats, but Monroe also published **Vachel Lindsay**, **Edna St. Vincent Millay**, **Carl Sandburg**, **Wallace Stevens**, and many others on her own account. The open-door policy of *Poetry*, which Monroe unfolded in its first issues, never really changed throughout the years and under its various editors. During its first years *Poetry* published the American avant-garde in London alongside British, Irish, and occasionally Indian poets, experimentalists of **free verse** at home, cowboy ballads, regional verse, and more conventional versifiers. Herself a fairly conservative poet, Monroe was usually receptive to the work Pound sent her, but reserved her greatest sympathy for quintessentially American poems. Much to Pound's chagrin, the local poets Lindsay and Sandburg, whose work was devoid of Old World sophistication, picked up *Poetry*'s most important prizes. Bothered by *Poetry*'s promiscuity, which also welcomed Edwardian and Victorian voices, Pound threatened to resign and sought a different outlet for his friends' poems. Arguments over censorship and copyright further deteriorated Pound's relationship with Monroe, and in 1917 Pound became foreign correspondent of the *Little Review*—*Poetry*'s Chicago neighbor. Although Pound's departure meant that *Poetry*'s heyday was over, the magazine survived and became, in Eliot's words, an institution.

While *Poetry*'s approach has been criticized for being noncommittal and pusillanimous, it has had spells in its publication history when its influence seems undeniable.

During **Karl Shapiro**'s brief tenure as editor, from 1950 to 1955, for instance, poets as different as **Philip Booth**, **James Dickey**, **John Logan**, **Frank O'Hara**, **Adrienne Rich**, **Charles Tomlinson**, and **James Wright** made their debut, while **Anthony Hecht**, **James Merrill**, and **W.S. Merwin** were among those who had poems accepted by *Poetry* during their formative periods. Shapiro's successor, Henry Rago, was perhaps even more successful in pursuing *Poetry*'s aim of presenting nearly all schools. Rago was quick to include not only **John Ashbery** and other members of the **New York School**, but also **Robert Creeley** and **Charles Olson** of the **Black Mountain School** as well as **Louis Zukofsky**. Even though Creeley and Olson also published in more experimental magazines, such as **Cid Corman**'s *Origin*, they were not wary of appearing in the nation's premier poetry magazine. **Beat poetry** was not well represented in the pages of *Poetry*. Poets affiliated with the Beat generation considered *Poetry* a powerful institution but a lackluster publication, and they preferred to publish in new little magazines that cropped up since the 1950s.

By the 1930s and 1940s *Poetry* magazine had lost much of its prestige of Monroe's days. The most prominent journals of these decades were the literary quarterlies that surfaced at campuses around the United States. Their formula and aesthetic emphasis were in some way modeled on the *Dial*, *Hound & Horn*, and the *Symposium*. The *Dial*, led by Scofield Thayer, James Sibley Watson, and, later, **Marianne Moore**, steered a middle course between the avant-garde and the commercial literary magazines. The *Dial* could offer payment to contributors and regularly awarded prizes, which many of its little contemporaries could not afford. Its criticism, which featured Eliot, Pound, Kenneth Burke, and Van Wyck Brooks, was particularly strong, but the *Dial* was also noteworthy for its fiction, poetry, art, and cultural commentary.

The vacuum created by the disappearance of the *Dial*, *Hound & Horn*, and the *Symposium* was initially filled by the *Southern Review*, which was started at Louisiana State University in 1935. The *Southern Review* had a special interest in Southern history and, though waning, in **agrarianism**, but this did not limit the scope of the magazine. Criticism was its most significant feature, although its fiction and poetry sections were also important. **Randall Jarrell** and **John Berryman** were in their twenties when the editors Cleanth Brooks and **Robert Penn Warren** chose their poems for publication. Reviews and articles were written by **R.P. Blackmur**, Brooks, Donald Davidson, **John Crowe Ransom**, **Allen Tate**, and others. The *Southern Review* therefore became the first house organ of the New Criticism. Despite its critical success, Brooks and Warren failed to retain the support of their university. In 1942 the *Southern Review* was discontinued by Louisiana State University, but it proved a model for similar academically sponsored ventures that were more broadly literary and cultural than scholarly journals.

Tate was the impetus behind the renaissance of the *Sewanee Review*. Established at the University of the South in Sewanee, Tennessee, in 1892, it is now the oldest quarterly in the United States. Although Tate was editor only from 1944 to 1946, he changed the face of the journal. During its first fifty years the *Sewanee Review* had confined itself to general culture, but in the 1940s it dished up an attractive mix of modern poetry, prose, and criticism, which Tate's successors continued. Ransom's quarterly was established in 1939 and operated from Kenyon College. It soon rivaled *Partisan Review* as the leading American literary review. Like other quarterlies, the *Kenyon Review* was dedicated to criticism. Yet the magazine's space allocated to poetry was filled in well during his editorship. **Howard Nemerov**, Jarrell, **Robert Lowell**, and Wright were among Ransom's favorites, but his taste was fairly broad.

Partisan Review is usually bracketed together with the literary quarterlies, although it was more urban, more overtly political, and initially not supported by a university. The reason is that *Partisan Review* also took an interest in serious cultural and literary criticism. Founded in 1934 by William Phillips and Philip Rahv, *Partisan Review* wanted to create a cultural and intellectual magazine on Marxist principles. Arguments over the Spanish Civil War, the Moscow Trials, Trotsky's assassination, and American participation in World War II split the magazine and made many hard-core communists leave. When Dwight Macdonald left the editorial board in 1943 to start *Politics*, Phillips and Rahv hired **Delmore Schwartz** to replace him. Schwartz served as poetry editor from 1946 to 1955 and dished up an attractive mix of established and new poets. Ashbery, Merrill, Nemerov, **Louis Simpson**, and **May Swenson** appeared alongside **Elizabeth Bishop**, Lowell, Stevens, and Dylan Thomas. After Schwartz's departure, this policy was continued with interesting early work by Dickey, **Donald Hall**, **John Hollander**, **Denise Levertov**, **Sylvia Plath**, Rich, and **Anne Sexton**.

The wealthiest magazine with literary aspirations was probably the *New Yorker*. After a wobbly start in 1925, Harold Ross's brainchild soon attracted an audience that in number far exceeded the readership of *Poetry* and the quarterlies. By 1950 the *New Yorker* was selling four hundred thousand copies a week, which makes *Poetry*'s thirty-five hundred a month look pale by comparison. As a consequence, the *New Yorker* was able to pay its writers much more than other magazines. Its favorite authors even received a lucrative first reading contract that ensured the right of first refusal. Bishop was one of the poets who had such a first reading contract and therefore nearly all of her poems first appeared in this monthly. The *New Yorker* concentrated on fiction with a sophisticated and comical slant its poetry also known for its lightness, elegance, and wit. **Howard Moss**, who became the *New Yorker*'s first poetry editor in 1950, made the poetry more serious, but the weekly remained true to its particular taste. The *New Yorker* steered clear of experiment and concentrated on respectable and polished poems. Its policy did not differ all that much from the *Atlantic* and *Harper's*, although its actual record of published poems was better.

The 1940s saw the publication of *Ark* and *Circle*; subsequently, the late 1950s and early 1960s gave rise to a host of little magazines that consciously avoided the larger magazines' dependence on criticism. *Big Table*, *Contact*, the *Floating Bear*, *Folder*, *Kayak*, *Measure*, *Poetry New York*, and *Yugen* are just a few examples of the proliferation of new small magazines that contributed to a period of intense activity, particularly in poetry. Small magazines are often able to publish work that better-established quarterlies refuse; for example, *Big Table* was started in response to the refusal by the editors of *Chicago Review* to publish excerpts of William Burroughs's *Naked Lunch*. Some of these magazines had a circulation of less than a hundred copies and most disappeared within a few years. The late 1950s and 1960s also saw the flourishing of the "mimeo revolution"; with the use of the mimeograph machine, it was possible to create a magazine or booklet in small editions over the course of days. The impact of these small magazines and mimeo magazines was considerable and made visible by the publication of *The New American Poetry*, an anthology edited by Donald Allen and published by Grove Press in 1960. Allen had culled poems affiliated with the Beat movement, Black Mountain School, and the New York School from several of these obscure magazines as well as from other sources. Even though they represented heterogeneous tendencies in American poetry, they all rejected academic verse as appeared in the quarterlies. While this opposition to academic verse is significant, perhaps more importantly, these small magazines expanded the possibilities of poetry and revealed its complexity and astounding variety.

A newly founded quarterly that certainly enlivened the magazine scene was the *Paris Review*. Unlike nearly all other quarterlies, the *Paris Review* opted to emphasize fiction and poetry and excluded criticism. The *Paris Review* did not publish reviews or articles, although their interviews with poets, novelists, and dramatists about their trade created a fad in magazine history. Hall undertook many of the interviews with poets, such as Eliot and Moore, during the first years of the *Paris Review*'s existence. Moreover, he acted as poetry editor and printed not only many of his contemporaries, including **Robert Bly**—whose magazine the *Fifties / Sixties* was also a welcome change from the New Criticism—Merwin, and Wright, but also poets whose careers were more

advanced, which underlines the fact that the *Paris Review* was not dedicated to new poetry only. The first three editors, Hall (1953–1961), **X.J. Kennedy** (1961–1964), and Tom Clark (1964–1974), published lively poetry, but they were not innovative editors. Clark emphasized New York poets more clearly than did his predecessors and was a little more daring than Hall and Kennedy, but at a time when they were already well established.

Another new influential quarterly that was even less like a traditional academic review was *Evergreen Review*, which began publication in 1957 under Barney Rossett. Using **James Laughlin**'s New Directions as a model, Rossett had founded Grove Press in 1951, which initially focused on editions of out-of-print classics. Realizing that he had to pass on a great number of exciting manuscripts, he founded *Evergreen Review*. *Evergreen Review*'s second issue was a "landmark" for bringing many members of the Beat generation to the fore, including **Allen Ginsberg**, with "Howl," **Jack Kerouac**, **Michael McClure**, and **Gary Snyder**. Soon Creeley, **Kenneth Koch**, O'Hara, and Olson were also published. The *Evergreen Review* would later move away from its origin as a cutting-edge avant-garde publication as Rossett changed the publication from a quarterly to a bi-monthly with glossy covers and, in the late 1960s, put on the market as many as one hundred thousand copies, many of which were sold at newsstands. In this sense *Evergreen Review* bodied forth, along with *New World Writing* and *discovery*, which had a similar appeal, a new sort of literary magazine. *Evergreen Review* folded after ninety-six issues in 1973.

Important to note is the role of colleges and universities in the creation and support of literary magazines. While the *Kenyon Review* set the precedent, such journals as *Field*, *Northwest Review*, *Ploughshares*, *Seneca Review*, and *Shenandoah*, for example, emerged in the 1970s as important venues for poetry. Published quarterly or bi-annually, many of these journals serve as extensions of academic and mainstream publishing. Some included criticism and reviews as well as fiction, while others strictly published poetry. **Translation** also came to be a regular and notable feature of some of these magazines, such as *Field* and *Seneca Review*. Arguably, the presence of many these journals is the result of the rapid growth of creative writing courses and graduate **creative writing programs** during this period, and indeed some such as *Columbia: A Magazine of Poetry and Prose* is edited and published by the graduate students of Columbia University.

Other magazines emerging in the early 1970s to prominence, but not associated with universities, include the *American Poetry Review*, founded in 1972 and published in a newspaper format six times a year and including poetry, photographs of the featured poets, and essays on **poetics**. *APR* has the same broad range as *Poetry* but is livelier. Like many poetry magazines, *APR* now offers an annual book prize. The elegant but now closed *Antaeus*, edited by the poet Daniel Halpern, published poetry, essays, and fiction, often with special thematic or genre-defined issues. *Antaeus* also published books of poems under the imprint Ecco Press, including the work of **Louise Glück**, **Jorie Graham**, **Robert Hass**, and **Sandra McPherson**, introduced **Czesaw Miłosz,** and reissued earlier collections of Ashbery.

With second-wave **feminism**, the emergence of women's studies programs, and the prominence of such poets as Rich, **June Jordan**, and **Barbara Guest**, the 1960s and 1970s saw the emergence of women-centered magazines, such as *Sinister Wisdom*, *13th Moon*, and *Conditions*, and in the early 1980s *Raddle Moon* and *HOW(ever)*. Some were separatist in nature, whereas others such as *HOW(ever)* sought to incorporate experimental writing often neglected by mainstream, academic feminism.

Literary magazines continue to be important as a forum for poets to keep up to date with the latest trends and for introducing new poetic modes. The poetry and poetic theories of **Language poetry**, for instance, were also initially communicated through magazines in the 1970s and 1980s. Early examples by Language poets and theories aligning their work to Pound, **Gertrude Stein**, Zukofsky, the Black Mountain School, and the New York School appeared in *This*, *Roof*, and *L=A=N=G=U=A=G=E* in the early 1970s, introducing the works of **Bruce Andrews**, **Charles Bernstein**, **Ron Silliman**, and others. (For a fuller discussion of the magazines associated with Language poetry as well as earlier **experimental poetry**, see **Post–World War II Avant-Garde Poetry Magazines**.)

While little magazines are constantly being founded and disbanded, literary quarterlies and established poetry journals also continue to ensure that poets have a dependable channel through which they can be heard. Funded by universities, many quarterlies, such as the *Kenyon Review*, the *Missouri Review*, and *Prairie Schooner*, have carried on printing poetry for decades. In general, they have been less experimental than little magazines, but they remain important outlets for up-and-coming and established poets. There are also dozens of journals primarily devoted to poetry, of which *Poetry* magazine is now the oldest and one of the most esteemed. Due to a multimillion-dollar gift in 2002, *Poetry* was able to expand its educational programs, create seminars to help teachers teach poetry in schools all over the country, and offer more grants and fellowships, as well as publish more books, thereby becoming an ever more active promoter of poetry. In contrast to *Poetry*, web-based journals are expanding, perhaps fueling another blossoming of poetry akin to the proliferation of **small presses** and mimeo magazines in the 1960s. *See also* **Periodicals, Pre–Twentieth-Century.**

Further Reading. ***Selected Primary Sources:*** Anderson, Elliott, and Mary Kinzie, eds., *The Little Magazine in America: A Modern Documentary History* (Yonkers: Pushcart, 1978); Chielens, Edward E., ed., *American Literary Magazines: The Eighteenth and Nineteenth Centuries* (Westport, CT: Greenwood Press, 1986); ———, *American Literary Magazines: The Twentieth Century* (Westport, CT: Greenwood Press, 1992); Clay, Steven, and Rodney Phillips, *A Secret Location on the Lower East Side: Adventures in Writing, 1960–1980* (New York: New York Public Library, 1998); Hoffman, Frederick J., Charles Allen, and Carolyn F. Ulrich, *The Little Magazine: A History and a Bibliography* (Princeton, NJ: Princeton University Press, 1946); Marek, Jayne E., *Women Editing Modernism* (Lexington: University Press of Kentucky, 1995); Perelman, Bob, *The Marginalization of Poetry: Language Writing and Literary History* (Princeton, NJ: Princeton University Press, 1996).

Diederik Oostdijk

LIVINGSTON, WILLIAM (CA. 1723–1790)

If remembered at all, William Livingston is most often cited for his service to the British colonies in America and his subsequent patriotic devotion to the young United States. He was a lawyer, statesman, and politician, an early spokesman for the rights of the colonies. He was, however, a gentleman-poet as well, his major work being the **long poem** *Philosophic Solitude*, which was one of the most popular and enduring literary works in eighteenth-century America.

Livingston was born into a prominent family in the city of Albany in colonial New York on November 30 sometime in the period from 1723 to 1725. He attended Yale College as a young man, and after graduating with top honors in 1741, he studied law for a time and eventually gained admission to the bar in 1748. As a politician working for the rights of the American colonies, he became a spokesman during the revolutionary move toward liberty from British rule. He was a leader in the crucial years both before and after the Revolution, ultimately serving as the elected governor of New Jersey from independence until his death on July 25, 1790.

In 1778 Livingston wrote his "Ode to General Washington," a blank verse poem published in the *New-Jersey Gazette*. In 1770 he had published *America: Or, A Poem on the Settlement of the British Colonies.* But his most significant contribution to the history of American poetry had come much earlier. *Philosophic Solitude: Or, the Choice of a Rural Life* was initially published in 1747 as a small book issuing from the press of publisher-printer James Barker of New York. The poem was reprinted as a stand-alone work several times and in several American towns during Livingston's lifetime. In addition, it was the oldest and longest of only six American poems to appear in all three of the first major poetry anthologies that were printed in

America and included works by American poets—Mathew Carey's *The Beauties of Poetry, British and American* (1791), Elihu Hubbard Smith's *American Poems, Selected and Original* (1793), and James Carey's *The Columbian Muse: A Selection of American Poetry, from Various Authors of Established Reputation* (1794).

Philosophic Solitude represents, perhaps, the best example of Augustan poetry composed in early America. The work is prefaced by "The Argument," which lists the topics to be presented; these include "Situation of the Author's House," "His Love of Retirement, and Choice of his Friends," "Contemplation of the Heavens," "The Vanity of Riches and Grandeur," and, eventually, "The Author's Exit." These topics are then taken up in 684 lines of heroic couplets in reverent, if sometimes plodding, imitation of Alexander Pope. While the form is Pope's, Livingston also follows John Milton's example, drawing many allusions from classical and biblical sources. In contrast to these honored English poets, Livingston's imagery often seems flat. And yet it is sometimes fresh and vivid. The reader is offered the stock "rosiate bow'rs" and "refreshing Zephyrs" and then rewarded with a rich description of the season of harvest in a rural setting: "AUTUMN bends beneath the golden grain; / The trees weep amber."

The poem's theme, "the pleasures of a *rural* life," is announced in the fifth line and followed by a list of all the speaker wishes to escape:

> the painted belle, and white-glov'd beau,
> The lawless masquerade, and midnight show:
> . . . ladies, lap-dogs, courtiers, garters, stars,
> Fops, fiddlers, tyrants, emperors, and czars.

Livingston's speaker wants to retreat from the vain corruptions of life. He wants a wife; he wants nothing more of her than that "in her breast let moral beauties shine, / Supernal grace and purity divine." Although Livingston's speaker longs for his rustic hideaway, he is ultimately unable to leave his duty to the public good. The entire poem is in the subjunctive mood; he is never really in his longed for solitude, only thinking about it, wishing for it, but all the while still in the world he wants to escape and doing his duty.

Philosophic Solitude teaches by contrasts: war and peace, the court and the rustic grove, the garish women of society and the simple country maid. But it also teaches by example: The friends the speaker would have visit him in his solitude are honored for their great virtues; his reading lists for the books he would have with him in his retreat, even when pleasant to read, are for spiritual and intellectual edification—Milton, Pope, Dryden, Watts, Locke, Cato, Socrates, Raleigh, Derham, and Newton.

The lessons the poem teaches are those necessary for the creation of a viable social order in the American wilderness. The civic virtue and moral character of the people could be formed without the involvement of "priestcraft," or the social and cultural domination of religion. The achievement of political freedom and the creation of upright citizens depended not on an established church but rather on how the individual could engage in society in some useful way that was without the taint of religious oppression, be that from Puritanism or Anglicanism. In Livingston's poem, the reality of rural solitude is not the most necessary component of a good and stable life, but the topics the poem takes up—civic virtue, frugality, the company one keeps, individual awareness of God and goodness, the destructive power of vanity and luxury, efficacious instruction—serve the citizen in all walks of life from the rural to the urban.

The need for such lessons, however, seemingly decreased after independence was established and the country became busy. *Philosophic Solitude* maintained its popularity long after its initial publication because the language and form of the poem strongly echo Milton and Pope, the great English poet-heroes in America throughout the eighteenth century. As the nineteenth century progressed, however, the United States was making headway in establishing its own literature. By the middle of the 1800s Livingston's poem had so fallen out of favor among American literati that Rufus W. Griswold would print only a portion in his historical introduction to *The Poets and Poetry of America* (1842), referring to it as "a specimen of elegant mediocrity."

Further Reading. *Selected Primary Sources:* Livingston, William, *America: Or, A Poem on the Settlement of the British Colonies* (New Haven: Thomas & Samuel Green, 1770); ———, *Philosophic Solitude: Or, the Choice of a Rural Life. A Poem* (New York: James Parker, 1747). ***Selected Secondary Sources:*** Shuffleton, Frank, "'Philosophic Solitude' and the Pastoral Politics of William Livingston" (*Early American Literature* 17.1 [Spring 1982]: 43–53); Wilson, Rob, "William Livingston's *Philosophic Solitude* and the Ideology of the Natural Sublime" (*Early American Literature* 24.3 [1989]: 217–236).

Michael Cody

LOCKLIN, GERALD (1941–)

For the past four decades, Gerald Locklin has been an active and defining poet in the turbulent and ever evolving community of American small presses and little literary magazines. Able to cut through pretense with slicing, ironic humor, the wisecracking Locklin has become a dominant and preeminent figure in this literary subculture. He is an outlaw, underground poet, and college professor, who has published more than one hundred books of poetry and prose. Seeking clarity without complexity, his poetry is sometimes obtuse and sometimes sentimental but never artless. Commanding a wide spectrum of literary tools, informed with voracious reading, and a deep understanding of art and jazz, Locklin's poetic vision demands direct imaginative and intellectual responses to everyday circumstances. A master of the music of spoken language, Locklin's candid poems focus upon literary accessibility and common sense. His is truly poetry of the people and for the people.

Locklin was born in Rochester, New York, on February 17, 1941. He was an only child. During World War II his father spent four years in the service. His mother was an Irish-American, Catholic schoolteacher and from a large family. Locklin found himself the center of attention in this extended family. He took tap dance lessons, and he attended parochial schools where he was instructed by nuns and Jesuit and Basilian priests. By his junior year he was writing poems. He was also a first-class athlete. By all accounts, Locklin's environment was stable and supportive. The deep affection Locklin exhibits in his poems about his children is testament to the loving family life he experienced. While nurturing, the matricentric and parochial world had its limits, and when he received a sport scholarship, he left for the College of Holy Cross.

While away from Rochester, Locklin became disenchanted with sports and intoxicated with writing and literature. After his freshman year, disillusioned, he left Holy Cross and enrolled in Rochester's St. John Fisher College. He completed his BA in English, graduating summa cum laude in 1961. On the day he was married, at age twenty-one, he left Rochester for the University of Arizona. Locklin was determined to be a writer. Graduate school and the West provided more than a physical distance between the burgeoning writer and his conservative roots. He wrote his dissertation on the novels of Nathaniel West and earned a Ph.D. at age twenty-three. Leaving his wife and Arizona, Locklin eventually located a teaching position at California State University in Long Beach. He remains active at CSU, although he is semi-retired.

Locklin published his first book, *Sunset Beach*, in 1967, and in 1968 his work appeared in Marvin Malone's *Wormwood Review* as a special section titled "Star Trek & Such." By the mid-1970s Locklin was firmly entrenched in southern California's literary milieu. He associated with underground poets like Steve Richmond and **Charles Bukowski**. He developed several personae, among them the lascivious drunk Jimmy Abby and the self deprecating Toad. It was an era of grassroots, **small press publishing** and an evolving, post-1960s populace poetry. Hardly a street poet, working man, or active revolutionist, Locklin was, nevertheless, an intimate part of this literary uprising.

Informed by the simple yet tightly controlled language of Ernest Hemingway and the rich cadences of spoken language in the poetry of **Edward Field**, Locklin's matter-of-fact poetry and prose allowed him to be both a rabble-rousing poet and a proficient, polished literary artist. He had an uncanny ability to locate truth via sarcasm and humor in poetry. Writing contrary to the academic avant-garde's necessity to distance poetry from the common, Locklin embraced and refined the rhythms of his poetry and focused on pedestrian themes. For example, in his book *Go West, Young Toad* (1998) is a poem titled "Beer" in which Locklin outlines the simple pleasures of beer and the conversations it inspires among men in bars; and in his collection *The Firebird Poems* (1999) is a poem titled "Meditation Occasioned by a Midnight Snack" in which Locklin praises French's mustard as opposed to the haughty Grey Poupon. In his book *The Iceberg Theory* (2000) the title poem defines Locklin's poetic stance. In it Locklin compares ordinary iceberg lettuce to his own poetic language, "i guess the problem is / it's just too common. . . . It just isn't different enough, and / it's too goddamn american." Locklin's poems read without the impediment of literary ornaments and are a form of literary entrainment that offers insight into the obvious.

Throughout the 1980s and the 1990s Locklin continued to publish prolifically. In 1992 **Donna Hilbert**'s Event Horizon Press published *The Firebird Poems*, a substantial collection that offered Locklin's work to an audience greater than the insular network of the literary small press. This substantial collection remains a key text in his oeuvre because it brings together disparate works that exemplify the many themes and forms of Locklin's poetry. During the 1990s Locklin made the acquaintance of Mark Weber, a small press poet and editor, whose Zerx Press has issued many collections of Locklin's jazz-related and travel poems. Weber edited a second substantial anthology of Locklin's prose and poems. The book was titled *Go West, Young Toad* (1998) and was published by Jeffery Weinberg's Water Row Press. Weinberg has become Locklin's principal publisher and has published substantial collections, including *Candy Bars: Selected Stories* (2000) and *The Life Force Poems* (2002).

Now in his sixties, Locklin continues to write with a singularly bright, clear, and committed literary vision—a vision that while it has matured has not varied from its roots in the idea that poetry can not be confined by literary canonization, college classrooms, critical barbs, or powerful publishing houses. His poetry remains independent and untainted. Locklin's first published poem appeared in the *Wormwood Review* (vol. 3, no. 1, issue 9, 1963) and was titled "Johnny Rigoletto." The poem's final two lines summarize Locklin's literary career: "an archetype of the Fool / musing on the great evil."

Further Reading. ***Selected Primary Sources:*** Locklin, Gerald, *The Firebird Poems* (Desert Hot Springs, CA: Event Horizon Press, 1992); ———, *Go West, Young Toad* (Sudbury, MA: Water Row Press, 1998); ———, *Charles Bukowski: A Sure Bet* (Sudbury, MA: Water Row Press, 1996). ***Selected Secondary Sources:*** Brantingham, John Michael, Mick Haven, Robert Headley, Michael Basinski, Normal Friedman, and Tricia Cherin, "The Gerald Locklin ALA Panel" (*Spring—Journal of the E.E. Cummings Society* n.s. 10 [October 2001]: 112–142).

Michael Basinski

LODEN, RACHEL (EDELSON) (1948–)

Rachel Loden, writing in the last quarter of the twentieth century and the early part of the twenty-first, has developed an approach to political poetry that is unique in American letters. Rather than writing poetry that pursues or supports a political agenda, she has found a way to inhabit the personae of some of the most controversial public figures of her time, in a manner that is partisan but strangely nonjudgmental, probing but boisterously comic, in order to examine the social and moral soul of her country and her era.

Loden was born Rachel Edelson on June 27, 1948, in Washington, D.C., at the same time that her father, an actor and radio announcer, was blacklisted. After her parents' divorce and her mother's mental illness, she spent time in foster families. Loden has been married to mathematician Jussi Ketonen (a second marriage) since 1973. Her great-great-aunt was muckraking novelist Rebecca Harding Davis, and she has credited this family connection with giving her the conviction that, even without much formal education, she could be a writer and produce meaningful work.

Her first book, *The Last Campaign*, won the Hudson Valley Writers' Center Chapbook Competition in 1998. Her second, *Hotel Imperium*, the Contemporary Poetry Series Competition winner for the University of Georgia Press, 1999, was named one of the Ten Best Poetry Books of 2000 by the *San Francisco Chronicle* and was a Poetry Book Club selection of the Academy of American Poets in 2000. She received a Pushcart Prize in 2001 and a fellowship in poetry from the California Arts Council in 2002.

The American poetic tradition has always had difficulty with political poetry. **Walt Whitman** in the nineteenth century and **Carl Sandburg** and **Stephen Vincent Benét** in the twentieth took on American history and the American character as their themes, but neither Sandburg nor Benet became a model for succeeding generations, and Whitman's expansive line and personal honesty were more of an influence than his approach to politics. **Robinson Jeffers**'s polemical poems were perhaps more of an influence, but not always a positive one.

The lack of a distinctive American political voice became particularly apparent in the post–World War II era, when other cultures had produced poets like Pablo Neruda (strongly influenced by the political style of Whitman), Yevgeny Yevtushenko, and Vladislava Szymborska, and most Americans were eschewing political engagement in favor of the personal **lyric**. The Vietnam era drove many poets to express opposition to government policies, and movements like **feminism** and Black Power produced strong poetic voices such as **Adrienne Rich** and **Amiri Baraka**, who found ways to blend the personal with the political. But there remained a sense that American literary culture and political poetry were antithetical, although **W.D. Snodgrass** in the 1970s and **Carolyn Forché** in the last two decades of the century made significant contributions. Eastern European émigré **Charles Simic** is one of the few who, like Loden, has incorporated the political into a seriocomic worldview.

Loden was a "red diaper baby"—a child of parents who came from the political cauldron of the 1930s and 1940s. She has described them, in an interview with Lance Phillips, as having "a rather thoroughgoing political philosophy," which did not, however, "seem . . . to be serving them particularly well as people." Loden remembers seeing the FBI camped out on her doorstep when she returned from a day in second grade. She has described her childhood as a vantage point from which she could see normal middle-class life (mostly on television) and the chaotic life of radical politics and mental illness, the boisterous Jewishness of her father's family, and the refined WASPishness of her mother's.

Loden's own era for coming of age was the 1960s, when she substituted the street life and ferment of New York's East Village and Berkeley, California, for formal education. At the same time, she became a fierce autodidact, reading what excited her over a wide range of traditions. She credits the variety of both her life and reading experiences with forging her style and sensibility, which began to coalesce in the 1990s. She wrote her first poem about Richard Nixon, "Premillennial Tristesse," in 1994, as the former president lay on his deathbed. The poet places him on that deathbed; her poem begins "Nixon is slipping / in and out of consciousness." But Nixon was never to slip far from her consciousness. He appears in many of the poems in her first chapbook, *The Last Campaign*, and emerges as a full-blown troubled hero in *Hotel Imperium*. His presence is unsettling and challenging on a number of levels.

First, he's dead; but that scarcely seems to slow him down. He speaks from the grave, or beyond the grave, or in his will, which he writes while "reposing in the Borough / of disposing mind and memory." The poem gives him a humanity in death that he lacked in life.

Nixon was not a popular figure to the American left, nor to much of the literary community, but Loden never uses him simply as the butt of jokes or diatribes. She is his amanuensis, he her muse, her id, even her lover. In the poem "Bride of Tricky D." she marries him, letting neither his being dead nor his being already married stand in the way of their wedded bliss: Gazing at Nixon "Asleep with Pat and Checkers / by his side," Loden finds "his fierce beard lovely and the shadows / long."

If Nixon is not the comic villain of Watergate or the serious villain of the blacklists, who is he? Loden's answers, over a series of poems and books (he is also the hero of *The Richard Nixon Snow Globe*), make him ourselves as much as the other, demon lover as much as scourge of the *zeitgeist*. With Nixon at the center, Loden spins out her web to ensnare other icons of his era, from Jayne Mansfield to Svetlana Stalin (in the manner of G.M. Hopkins: "it is / the blight you were born for, / it is a century you mourn for") to Little Richard to Philip Larkin—a complex, interconnected, and richly comic universe.

Further Reading. *Selected Primary Sources:* Loden, Rachel, *Hotel Imperium* (Athens: University of Georgia Press, 1999); ———, *The Last Campaign* (Sleepy Hollow, NY: Slapering Hol Press, 1998); ———, *The Richard Nixon Snow Globe* (Bray, Ireland: Wild Honey Press, 2005). *Selected Secondary Sources:* Johnson, Kent, "Interview with Rachel Loden" (*Jacket* [February 2003], http://www.jacketmagazine.com/); Phillips, Lance, "Interview with Rachel Loden" (*Here Comes Everybody*, http://herecomeseverybody.blogspot.com/, 2005); Van Cleave, Ryan G., "Welcome to the Twenty-first Century: An Email Interview with Rachel Loden" (*Iowa Review* 33:3 [Winter 2003/4]: 127).

Tad Richards

LODGE, GEORGE CABOT (1873–1909)

George Cabot Lodge wrote five collections of poetry and one work of verse drama between 1898 and his death in 1909. He began publishing poetry in the 1890s as part of a well-respected coterie surrounding Harvard University and the undergraduate literary magazine, the *Harvard Monthly*. The so-called "Harvard School" of poets included Lodge as well as **George Santayana**, **William Vaughn Moody**, and **Trumbull Stickney**. The poetry produced by Lodge and the "Harvard School" did not attempt the kind of stylistic innovation realized by their Harvard peers **Robert Frost** or **Wallace Stevens**. Instead, Lodge is best remembered as a **genteel versifier** whose writing largely resembles the language and form of its Victorian predecessors. While his reputation would later diminish almost to obscurity, his work exerted some influence over its small New England audience at the turn of the twentieth century.

Lodge was born in 1873 at Nahant, Massachusetts, into a prominent Boston family. His father, the statesman Henry Cabot Lodge, introduced him to Theodore Roosevelt and Henry Adams, both of whom served as important mentors throughout Lodge's life. After launching his literary career at Harvard, Lodge spent the better part of two years publishing poems in literary magazines while studying in Paris and Berlin. Just as his first collection, *The Song of the Wave and Other Poems* (1898), appeared, Lodge entered the military to serve as a gunman in the Spanish-American War. When he returned from the war, Lodge continued writing poetry, but was unable to win much critical notice. That same year his life and work took a dramatic turn when his close friend Stickney died suddenly of a brain tumor. Grief-stricken, Lodge produced what is perhaps his finest work, *The Great Adventure* (1905), a pensive collection of sonnets inspired by Stickney's death. While Lodge was preparing *The Soul's Inheritance and Other Poems* (1909), he too met with a sudden and premature death, brought on by heart trouble. As an attempt to rescue his son's reputation, Henry posthumously issued the collected *Poems and Dramas of George Cabot Lodge* (1911) with an introduction by Roosevelt, and persuaded Adams to write a companion volume of biography.

Throughout his poetry, Lodge demonstrates a deep indebtedness to American Transcendentalism, most notably the writings of **Ralph Waldo Emerson**. Inspired by Emerson's doctrine of innate, human divinity, the title poem of Lodge's first collection, "The Song of the Wave" uses the crashing and rising of the wave as a metaphor for the human soul's struggle for autonomy. Bound by the rhythm of the tide, the wave glories "in the lust of attainment," but, ultimately, "rises to fall." Like the human soul, the wave crests toward ecstasy, but always comes crashing back toward death. Lodge's first collection thus establishes the dominant theme of his entire corpus: the conflict between the transcendental potential of the soul and the limiting mortality of the individual.

Lodge's poem "Youth" epitomizes this struggle between hope and despair. Its two stanzas are perfectly balanced in opposition to one another, the first beginning "If I must die," and the second opening, "If I must live." The metaphysical lesson of "Youth," as much of Lodge's poetry, lies in its recognition that suffering and melancholy enrich the soul by connecting the individual more perfectly to the ebb and flow of the natural world. His poem "Passing Days" warns of the dangers of forgetting one's mortality: "In the fire of hopeless love / . . . I half forget / My soul shall wake and find the days a dream." In Lodge's estimation, the more acutely one feels the certainty of death, the more fully one may appreciate life.

His reflections on mortality represent an attempt to couple Transcendentalism with the determinism of Arthur Schopenhauer, a philosophical inspiration Lodge fostered during his studies in Berlin. This pessimistic vision reveals his close affinity with French and American Naturalism more broadly and the poetry of his friend **Edwin Arlington Robinson**, in particular. While a similar skepticism toward individual freedom and metaphysical doubt would soon become hallmarks of **modernism**, Lodge's genteel rhetoric and style have prevented his sensibility from being compared to more aesthetically innovative poets like **T.S. Eliot**.

Lodge's later work, *The Great Adventure*, transforms his youthful pessimism into a more overt celebration of life. Divided into three sections, "Life," "Love," and "Death," the sonnets meditate on the soul's quest for meaning. The final section, "Death," dedicated to Stickney, offers a developed sonnet cycle that documents the chronology of Stickney's life. While traces of whimsical pessimism remain, "Death" carefully affirms a type of mystical faith. As he asserts in "Death XXVI," "We now keep sure faith with things transcendent, true / and untransmissable." By his final collection, *The Soul's Inheritance*, Lodge had begun to connect his increasingly subtle philosophy to experiments with aesthetic form. His most complex poem, "The Noctambulist," attempts to innovate poetic form by using dramatic dialogue. The poem represents a shift away from antiquated diction and toward a sparser, economical precision. Lodge's last work suggests that he may have begun the transition toward modernism.

In the 1970s the critic John W. Crowley edited a new edition of Lodge's poetry and verse drama, which includes, for the first time, his short fiction. Crowley's work attempts to recuperate Lodge as an aesthetic precursor to modernism and an important representative of the cultural and intellectual life of early twentieth-century New England.

Further Reading. *Selected Primary Sources:* Lodge, George Cabot, *The Great Adventure* (Boston: Houghton Mifflin, 1905); ———, *Poems and Dramas of George Cabot Lodge* (Boston: Houghton Mifflin, 1911); ———, *Selected Fiction and Verse*, ed. John W. Crowley (St. Paul, MN: John Colet Press, 1976); ———, *The Song of the Wave and Other Poems* (New York: Scribner's, 1898); ———, *The Soul's Inheritance and Other Poems* (Boston: Houghton Mifflin, 1909). ***Selected Secondary Sources:*** Adams, Henry, *The Life of George Cabot Lodge* (Boston: Houghton Mifflin, 1911); Crowley, John W., *George Cabot Lodge* (Boston: G.K. Hall & Co., 1976).

Melissa Girard

LOGAN, JOHN (1923–1987)

John Logan was admired by poet-critics, from **John Crowe Ransom** to **Paul Carroll**, but neglected by the wider reading public. In spite of the musical mastery, stark sensuality, and intense emotionality of his verse, he is little known, partly because he never was a member of any school of poetry. Furthermore, his first book, *Cycle for Mother Cabrini* (1955), was pigeonholed as the work of a religious poet writing about Catholic saints and obscure philosophical notions, and he never lost that reputation, although he later forsook Catholicism. Logan continued to address issues of community and communion, becoming, like a number of his contemporaries, ever more personal and less formalistic. He remained, however, first and foremost, a **lyric** poet who regarded poetry as "a ballet for the ear."

A month after Logan's birth in Red Oak, Iowa, in 1923, his mother died. This haunted him all through his life and in his poetry he tried to recreate his mother's presence. He started out a scientist, receiving his BA in biology from Coe College, earned his MA in English from the University of Iowa, and went on to do graduate work in philosophy at Georgetown and Notre Dame. He married in 1945, converted to Catholicism in 1946, and fathered nine children. Anguished by religious and metaphysical questions, as well as by his confused sexuality, he went into analysis in 1955, and Freud came to inspire his writing. Logan taught at many universities and colleges, the longest at Notre Dame and SUNY–Buffalo. He was poetry editor of *Critic* and the *Nation* and co-founder and editor of *Choice*. His many honors include Rockefeller and Guggenheim grants, and the **William Carlos Williams**, Morton Dauwen Zabel, and Lenore Marshall awards. In later life, divorced from his wife, Logan drank heavily and experimented with different kinds of sexual encounters. His death, in 1987, was variously attributed to suicide, surgery, and a heart ailment.

From the first, Logan emphasized the importance of music in his verse and we find his operatic lyricism in *Cycle for Mother Cabrini*, the title poem of which commemorates Chicago's sainted nun, while others deal with Catholic concerns like Good Friday, St. Augustine, or St. Athanasius. The influences on his early poetry are not American, but classical, devotional, and European authors, particularly Rilke. In *Ghosts of the Heart* (1960) the saints have been displaced by poet-heroes such as Byron and Shelley, and by Logan himself. Most personal in *Ghosts* is "On the Death of the Poet's Mother Thirty-three Years Later," a breakthrough poem after which Logan could look at relationships with others, though he remained inordinately preoccupied with her. In this book he identified strongly with poets dying young, such as Heine and Rimbaud, who were obsessed by their mothers and unable, in Logan's far-fetched view, to build their mothers' lower body in verse, to confront their sexuality. In spite of Logan's probing, personal voice, his unsettling images, his stark detail, *Ghosts* was little noticed beyond Catholic magazines, though **Robert Bly** praised his vigor and originality and **James Dickey**, despite his aversion to religious themes in poetry, cautiously pronounced him, in potential, one of America's best poets.

In *Spring of the Thief* (1960) the poet's voice is less insistent than in his earlier books, and almost melancholic. Here Logan becomes outspoken about sex. Whereas earlier sexuality involved feelings of shame, in this, as in Logan's later work, the sensual and the sexual, the sacred and the profane are merged. In the title poem, the poet feels God's "terrible, aged heart / moving under mine" and can "tell the faint press and hum / of his eternal pool of sperm." With the publication of *The Zig Zag Walk* (1969), a collection of colloquial, direct, intimate poems, reviewers realized that Logan was not a dry intellectual poet, dishing up clever Catholic and classical allusions, but an uninhibitedly honest writer of natural ease, loving, in "Homage to Rainer Maria Rilke," "the poor, weak words / which starve in daily use." Images of fluids recur in Logan's work, from the sea and lakes in the many landscape poems in this collection to mother's milk, sperm, and urine. More and more, too, Logan obsesses about androgyny, merging male and female. In the key-poem "The Search," he transforms the sexes. Desperately cruising bars and brothels, the speaker does not even know whom he looks for: "Father? Mother? / The father who will be the mother?" He ends with: "The limbs of my poems / come within your reach. / Perhaps it is you whom I seek."

More than most **confessional poets**, Logan wants to build a relationship with the reader. In his important essay "On Poets and Poetry" he stated that the "poet is an anonymous lover . . . and his poetry is an anonymous reaching out, which occasionally becomes personal." His next collection, *The Anonymous Lover* (1973), demonstrates this desire to seduce the reader. Formally, it is a radical departure from his earlier verse, in that all poems have broken lines. The break often occurs in the middle of a word, surprising the reader into rethinking its meaning, while simultaneously exploiting internal rhymes to heighten the music. "New Poem" recalls the poet's wedding day and failed marriage, recording with immediacy, yearning to make the reader care: their new gold rings, shining "in the sun, seemed to make the fing- / er lighter: we hoped / they'd be seen by others." "Poem: Tears, Spray, and Steam" exhibits the hallmarks of Logan's poetry. Water is its main element as the poet and his friends sit naked in a sulphur spring bath, reading Keats, touching each other. The poem has an unusual, implausibly idyllic ending: "and we all bathe and sing together / in the new waters of brother, sister."

It clarifies the author's exhaustive and exhausting emphasis on sex, expressing his yearning for joining, for love rather than lust.

The Anonymous Lover was widely reviewed, praised for its photographic view and sharp sensibility, and it gained Logan a wider reading public. However, his next volume, *The Bridge of Change* (1981), contained sloppy writing and clichés instead of specificity. But the new poems in the posthumously published *Collected Poems* (1989) unexpectedly show a rejuvenation of his gifts, many poems picturing his childhood with bright moments of perception. They bring Logan's concerns full circle, forming a worthy conclusion to his career as a scrupulously honest melodious poet.

Further Reading. ***Selected Primary Sources:*** Logan, John, *A Ballet for the Ear: Interviews, Essays, and Reviews,* ed. A. Poulin, Jr. (Ann Arbor: University of Michigan Press, 1983); ———, *The Collected Fiction* (Brockport, NY: BOA, 1991); ———, *The Collected Poems* (Brockport, NY: BOA, 1989). ***Selected Secondary Sources:*** Chaplin, William, "Identity and Spirit in the Recent Poetry of John Logan" (*American Poetry Review* 2.3 [May–June 1973]: 19–24); Mazzaro, Jerome, "Integrities" (*Kenyon Review* 32.1 [1970]: 163–169); Waters, Michael, ed., *Dissolve to Island: On the Poetry of John Logan* (Houston: Ford-Brown, 1984).

Marian Janssen

LOGAN, WILLIAM (1950–)

Best known as an unflinching literary critic in the vein of **Randall Jarrell** and **Delmore Schwartz**, William Logan has established his reputation as a longtime contributor of reviews and essays to *Parnassus*, the *Southwest Review*, the *New Criterion*, *Salmagundi*, the *New York Times Book Review,* and elsewhere. In his biannual "Verse Chronicle" for the *New Criterion*, Logan has been unsparing in his exposure of what he believes to be the catastrophic flaws in current American and British poetry. Even if he lends a few poets the keys to his kingdom, what may remain most memorable to a reader of his critical prose is his vitriol and dismissal of his favorite targets, such as **John Ashbery** and **Sharon Olds**, whose verse he declares in a tellingly titled review "No Mercy" is "headlong, hell-for-leather hubris—you never know what's coming next, but you're sure it's going to be a disaster." It is small wonder that he has come to be known widely as the scourge of American poetry.

William Logan was born on November 16, 1950, in Boston, Massachusetts. His father, William Donald Logan, was a businessman of many stripes, a salesman and manager, as well as a real estate broker, the last being an occupation he shared with Nancy Damon Logan, the poet's mother. Logan's childhood was spent in Massachusetts (Braintree and Westport), Pittsburgh, and Huntington, New York. After completing his BA in literature at Yale University in 1972 and an MFA through the University of Iowa Writers' Workshop in 1975, he and his partner, poet **Debora Greger**, eventually arrived together on the faculty at the University of Florida, where he has since taught creative writing and contemporary poetry. His awards for criticism include the Citation for Excellence in Reviewing from the National Book Critics Circle, and he has received fellowships and grants from the Ingram Merrill Foundation and National Endowment for the Arts, among others.

The majority of Logan's positive-leaning reviews and essays call forth the voices of Geoffrey Hill, whose "absolute unreasonableness" he finds suitable to his own tastes (*Reputations of the Tongue*, 217) and the middle generation of American poetry, **Elizabeth Bishop**, **Anthony Hecht**, **W.D. Snodgrass**, **James Merrill**, and particularly **Donald Justice**. Sensing facile reactions against Justice's use of nostalgia, Logan presents it as a matter of necessity determined by contemporary conditions: "nostalgia isn't necessarily a wish to return to the past . . . it is a gesture of counter-sentiment. Nostalgia is the refuge of poets for whom the current modes of reminiscence have been irremediably stained with sentiment" (Gioia and Logan, 87). His criticism advocates deliberateness, thorough comprehension of the tradition, elision of showiness, and the sanctity of a poet's voice.

Logan's own poetic production—comprising six full-length books to date, and a seventh, *The Whispering Gallery*, due out in Fall 2005—can be divided into two stages. The first stage involves a trio of books, *Sad-Faced Men* (1982), *Difficulty* (1985), and *Sullen Weedy Lakes* (1988), all three of which establish, in greater or lesser terms, his poetry of decorous sensibility and unsmiling sarcasm. *Sad-Faced Men* commences with "Deception Island," where the lines "She represents what blinds and what forgets, / The tropic sun that might rise anywhere" call to mind the unsettling *noir* of Justice's "A Tourist from Syracuse," who could as well be a car salesman or an assassin, the threat bound up in the slipperiness of identity. Extension on the theme of what could bring about arbitrary trouble, if not extinction, Logan shows moth unaware of the poet's hands that could kill it but are stayed by a luminescence of the wing: "Qualities unmastered / By it keep it alive." The verbal and thematic trouble of *Difficulty* emanates from Logan's nod to, and heedlessness toward, the "old conspiracy" of those who would have him lighten his tone, marked with an epigraph from Charles Dickens's *Bleak House*: "Everyone seemed to be in it!" His third book, *Sullen Weedy Lakes*, takes aim at populist, too-easy political stances, such as those that would examine obsessively racial prejudice in Imperial Rome or take offense at treasonous jokes delivered while the source "relieved himself in the garden."

The second cluster is comprised by *Vain Empires* (1998), *Night Battle* (1999), and *Macbeth in Venice* (2003), all of which display a clarity and quickness absent in the first phase. *Vain Empires*, like *Difficulty*, displays interest in logic taken to its absurd extremes ("The English out of England"), or to the reflexive ("The Rule of the Rule of Law"), forever reminding us of the violence not of the endeavor, the blood that "repays / such sanctity," but also the idleness, "such boredom, such cigarettes." Time, Logan's "slender chariot," forms the elegant framework of moral existence. *Night Battle* turns toward the **elegiac** as Logan never had done before, his poems of mourning and remembrance for Merrill, **Amy Clampitt**, **Howard Moss**, Bishop, and his father occupying center stage. The final book of this trio is itself four-part, each necessarily a shortening and refiguring of received texts, "The Shorter Aeneid," "Punchinello in Chains," "Venetian Hours," and the title sequence, "Macbeth in Venice." Logan takes pains to set his reworkings apart from others who would merely rewrite into their own lives those legends: For example, his *Macbeth* is one written at the request of King James, and which levels accusations at our core complacencies and self-satisfaction: "Which of you," he has the witches sneer, "would raise a hand if resurrected Christ / were crucified before the shopping mall?" The sentiment is itself hardly new but the scaffolding of the dramatic moment mingles with doggerel rhyming: the falling night being "spent" and the square "quiet" have "paid its rent / and gone on a diet."

Further Reading. ***Selected Primary Sources:*** Logan, William, *All the Rage* (Ann Arbor: University of Michigan Press, 1998); ———, *Desperate Measures* (Gainesville: University Press of Florida, 2002); ———, *Difficulty* (Boston: David R. Godine, 1985); ———, *Macbeth in Venice* (New York: Penguin, 2003); ———, *Night Battle* (New York: Penguin, 1999); ———, "No Mercy" (*New Criterion* 18.4 [December 1999], http://www.newcriterion .com/archive/18/dec99/logan.htm); ———, *Reputations of the Tongue: On Poets and Poetry* (Gainesville: University Press of Florida, 1999); ———, *Sad-Faced Men* (Boston: David R. Godine, 1982); ———, *Sullen Weedy Lakes* (Boston: David R. Godine, 1988); ———, *Vain Empires* (New York: Penguin, 1998); Gioia, Dana, and William Logan, eds., *Certain Solitudes: Essays on the Poetry of Donald Justice* (Fayetteville: University of Arkansas Press, 1997). **Selected Secondary Source:** Ruddick, Bill, "Ending What at First Began: Themes of Time and Distance in Some Recent Poetry" (*Critical Quarterly* 27.3 [Autumn 1985]: 79–83).

Douglas Basford

LONG POEM

Throughout most of Western literary history, the epitome of poetic achievement has been the **epic** heroic poem, usually a long **narrative** work with a single pro-tagonist, certain conventions including beginning *in media res* with a call to the muses, a trip to the under-world, and long descriptions of battles and war games as can be seen in the works of Homer, Virgil, Dante, and Milton. The American contribution to this tradition is twofold: until the mid-nineteenth century, American poets were all too comfortable working within these parameters and produced numerous instances thereof on distinctively American themes, but after that, the epic was transformed in ways that will be made clear below, forcing critics to let go of the term "epic" and use the more loosely defined "long poem" to refer to them.

Lynn Keller notes that "narrative poems, **verse** nov-els, sonnet sequences, irregular lyric medleys or cycles, collage long poems, meditative sequences, extended dramatic monologues, **prose** long poems, serial poems, heroic epics" are all what "may legitimately be identified as long poems" (3). Keller suggests, especially in regard to twentieth-century poetry, the long poem is less a reac-tion to epic traditions than to late Romantic lyricism with its dependence on landscape and the solitary "I." The recourse to the long poem, in all its hybridity and restless multiplicity, notes Keller, is an attempt for poetry to regain its cultural importance. The long poem, as opposed to the epic and in counterpoint to the senti-mentalized **lyric**, is a re-visioning of gender-defined genres. What becomes clear especially as we move toward **postmodern poetics** is that the structure of the long poem does not depend on a single thematic or compositional feature.

One of the first epic poems to be written on or directly about the North American continent was **Ben-jamin Tompson**'s *New Englands Crisis. Or a Brief Narra-tive, of New-Englands Lamentable Estate at Present, Compar'd with the Former Years of Prosperity* of 1676. The seven-hundred–line account of King Philip's War is full of classical allusions and recounts battles between set-tlers and Native Americans, favoring the former. Two years later, in 1678, the Puritan **Anne Bradstreet**, often considered the first truly American poet, came out with a 231-line poem titled "Contemplations." This poem may be said to inaugurate the tradition of meditative long poems by Americans; broken into thirty-three numbered seven-line stanzas, it distinctly moves toward the idea of a long poem as a sequence of discrete sec-tions. **Edward Taylor**'s devoutly religious *Gods Determi-nation* of 1680 has been compared to the morality plays of England during the same period, but Roger Walcott's (1679–1767) historical epic in rhyming couplets of Con-necticut's foundation and war with the Pequot Indians, *A Brief Account of the Agency of the Honorable John Winthrop, Esquire, in the Court of King Charles the Second, A.D., 1662* (published in his *Poetic Meditations* of 1725), best exempli-fies the epic standards of seventeenth-century America in a poem on an American topic, while simultaneously opening the genre to the eighteenth century. These poems, taken as a whole and apart from their rather tra-ditional formal properties, show a split in what these early American writers believed an epic poem ought to be about, a split that would mark epic and long poems for the next two centuries: Should they, following the example of Milton in *Paradise Lost*, interrogate or explore religious topics, or should they promote the ide-als of what was soon to become the American republic? The revivalist and Universalist orator Elhanan Winches-ter's (1751–1797) *The Process and Empire of Christ* (1805) exemplifies the religious line in this debate. **Joel Bar-low**'s *The Columbiad* (1807), Daniel Bryan's (1795–1866) *The Mountain Muse* (1813) on the life of Daniel Boone, **James Kirke Paulding**'s (1778–1860) *The Backwoodsman* (1819), and Richard Emmons's (1788–1834) *The Fre-doniad* (1827) adhere to the more political and idealistic vein of American epic poetry; their subjects range from Western expansion, the wars of an empire, to the birth of a nation. Most critics agree that, all in all, these poems represent more of an aspiration to be the great Ameri-can epic rather than a fulfillment of that goal: Con-strained by the epic conventions of the time, the treatment of American topics combined with retention of British literary standards prevented these writers from achieving any striking originality.

However, with the coming of the American Civil War halfway through the nineteenth century, a profound change in the consciousness of American poets seems to have taken effect. **Walt Whitman**'s *Leaves of Grass*, a long poem, or rather a collection of shorter poems that form a whole, as the title suggests, gives the most experi-mental and prominent account of this transformation, a prime example from it being the poem-within-a-poem "Song of Myself." The book went through many editions from 1855 until Whitman's death in 1892, growing and reflecting the ever-changing face of the United States during that period. Whitman introduces a colloquial style: loose, personal, and open, thus distinctly free from the classical models. One long poem that has received relatively little critical recognition but is self-evidently one of the achievements of the genre in the late nine-teenth century is **Herman Melville**'s *Clarel: A Poem and Pilgrimage to the Holy Land* (1876), which took the author of *Moby Dick* the last sixteen years of his life to write. About a group of American pilgrims site-seeing in the Holy Land, its overarching theme is disillusionment with religious idealism in the face of present reality, con-tinuing in the vein of religious long poems of the seven-teenth and eighteenth centuries. It could be argued that each of **Emily Dickinson**'s forty fascicles are indeed sequences that comprise a long poem parallel to Whit-man's accumulative sequence of shorter narratives and lyrics.

The nineteenth century also saw the rise of the first epics and long poems by African Americans: James Monroe Whitfield's (1822–1871) "America" (1853) is a long poem highly critical of American domestic policies concerning African Americans; James Madison Bell (1833–1901) wrote a series of long poems on slavery-related topics, including "A Poem" (1862) on Emancipation and "The Progress of Liberty" (1866) on the meaning of the Civil War; James Ephraim McGirt (1874–1930) wrote three epics in the pastoral and military styles of Virgil, including *Avenging the Maine Siege of Manila* (1898); and George Marion McClellan's (1860–1934) intricate *The Legend of Tannhauser* (1896) is often accredited with being the most accomplished work of nineteenth-century African American narrative epic. Though now critically neglected, they offer a complement to the Whitmanian vision of the United States.

But there is no doubt that the twentieth century has seen the greatest flourishing of the long poem. Discarding almost completely, as Whitman did, the constraining aspects of traditional epic poetry, poets in the "new" genre managed to reinvent the written word in an entirely new aesthetic. As Roy Pearce argues, American poets, especially from Whitman on, have not written about history so much as seeing that the epic is history itself, and the epic hero becomes the poet, as evidenced by Whitman's self-portrait in the 1855 *Leaves of Grass* (133–136). The unease with the European models of culture and politics thus destabilized the narrative parameters of the epic, thereby creating or necessitating a new genre.

Early **modernists'** works such as: **T.S. Eliot**'s "The Love Song of J. Alfred Prufrock" (1915), *The Waste Land* (1921), *Burnt Norton* (1941), and *Four Quartets* (1943), which won him the Nobel Prize; **Stephen Vincent Benét**'s *John Brown's Body*, for which he received the Pulitzer Prize in 1929, and which was to become one of the few long poems to achieve commercial success; and **Hart Crane**'s lyrical long poem mythologizing America, *The Bridge* (1930) are all prime examples of this new genre. The former **Imagist H.D.** wrote three complex poems on classical themes, including *Trilogy* (1946), *Helen in Egypt* (1961), and *Hermetic Definition* (1972). Nearly fifty years in the making, *The Cantos* of **Ezra Pound** is widely considered to be one of the most complex, beautiful, and troubling (due to instances of blatant anti-Semitism) poems ever written, and is perhaps the greatest achievement in the genre by an American, albeit one who spent most of his life in Europe. Written in dozens of languages, dealing from topics ranging from World Wars I and II to economic policies and the founding of nation-states in America and under Fascist Italy, the poem works as an accumulative sequence, almost an open-ended encyclopedic palimpsest.

African Americans have also played an important role in the transformation of the long poem: **Gwendolyn Brooks**'s formal mock epic *Annie Allen* (1949); **Langston Hughes**'s *Montage of a Dream Deferred* (1951); **Jay Wright**'s *The Double Invention of Komo* (1980); **Rita Dove**'s *Thomas and Beulah* (1986), which fuses lyric and narrative in a historical chronicle; Brenda Marie Osbey's *Desperate Circumstance, Dangerous Woman* (1991); **Harryette Mullen**'s *Muse & Drudge* (1995); and C.S. Giscombe's 1998 book *Giscome Road,* a profound meditation between and beyond cultures, geographies, and races, are just a few examples.

Locality has been an important thread in twentieth-century long poems, including **William Carlos Williams**'s five-part *Paterson* (1963), which explores the relationship between a man and a city of the same name, and **Charles Olson**'s *Maximus Poems* (written 1960–1975), concerning the history of his home town, Gloucester. Olson's formulation of the **open form** or **projective verse** extended Pound's palimpsestic processes, giving rise to the visual possibilities of the long poem composition. Drawing from Whitmanian tradition, **Allen Ginsberg**'s "Howl" (1956) has become the defining poetic text of **Beat poetry** and the aesthetic of the immediate perception fused with political vision. **James Merrill**'s *The Changing Light at Sandover* (1982) invokes distinct cosmological spaces that fuse with voices. Merrill's poem fuses the dramatic with the very process and space of transcription. Other poets whose work includes substantial examples and innovations in the long poem include: **Wallace Stevens, Jean Toomer, A.R. Ammons, Judy Grahn, Marilyn Hacker, Derek Walcott, Jorie Graham, W.S. Merwin,** and **Clark Coolidge**—indeed, many of the most significant recent poets have explored this form.

The **postmodern** long poem may offer the most compelling innovations to this highly diverse genre. The long poem may be described as either a finite or infinite series or a procedural form, according to Joseph Conte. The procedural form employs lexical and semantic modes of recurrence, as found in the work of **John Cage**. Exemplifying a finite series, **Louis Zukofsky**'s hermetic long poem *"A"* was written upon the counterpoint principles of Bach's fugues. During the 1950s **Jack Spicer** and **Robin Blaser** were instrumental in the propagation of "serial poems," which Conte defines as demanding "neither summation nor exclusion. It is instead a combinative form whose arrangements admit a variegated set of materials"; furthermore, "each element of the series is a module that asserts its position in combination with other elements; its place is not assigned by any external schema" (21). Conte's description is a cogent summary of the innovations of the long poem after the Modernists. **Robert Duncan**'s *Passages* is perhaps the exemplary infinite serial poem, as Conte writes, it "aspires to constant motion and the self-description of form" (48).

By the close of the twentieth century, experimental poets such as **Ronald Johnson** in his quotation-driven, cosmological poem *Ark* (1996), **Rachel Blau DuPlessis's** *Drafts* (2001), **John Ashbery's** book-length poem *Flow Chart* (1991) or "The Skaters" (1966), as well as the works of **Beverly Dahlen**, **Lyn Hejinian**, and **Susan Howe** give ample evidence that the long poem is far from disappearing from the American literary landscape in the twenty-first century. In many ways these poems institute a new turn in the form of the long poem: Unlike Whitman's orientation toward the personal, these poets are interrogating if not countering the dominance of the confessional or lyric "I." Against this form of interiority, the texture of language or its material form on the page becomes a focal point.

Further Reading. ***Selected Primary Sources:*** Conte, Joseph, *Unending Design: The Forms of Postmodern Poetry* (Ithaca, NY: Cornell University Press, 1991); Dickie, Margaret, *On the Modernist Long Poem* (Iowa City: University of Iowa Press, 1986); Keller, Lynn, *Forms of Expansion: Recent Long Poems by Women* (Chicago: Chicago University Press, 1997); McHale, Brian, *The Obligation toward the Difficult Whole: Postmodernist Long Poems* (Tuscaloosa: University of Alabama Press, 2004); McWilliams, John P., *The American Epic: Transforming a Genre, 1770–1860* (Cambridge: Cambridge University Press, 1989); Miller, James E., *The American Quest for a Supreme Fiction: Whitman's Legacy in the Personal Epic* (Chicago: University of Chicago Press, 1979); Murphy, Francis, "The Epic in the 19th Century," in *The Columbia History of American Poetry*, ed. Brett C. Millier and Jay Parini (New York: Columbia University Press, 1993); Pearce, Roy Harvey, *The Continuity of American Poetry* (Middletown, CT: Wesleyan University Press, 1987).

Antony Adolf

LONGFELLOW, HENRY WADSWORTH (1807–1882)

Henry Wadsworth Longfellow, a poet of enormous popularity during his own time, continues to be celebrated as one of America's most respected and beloved poets. Longfellow's works were some of the first to evoke native subject matter, drawing on what would become the icons of America's landscape, history, and people as primary themes. He was an essential contributor to the infancy of American literature, and along with contemporaries such as **Nathaniel Hawthorne**, **Ralph Waldo Emerson**, and **Henry David Thoreau,** helped to establish credibility and interest in nineteenth-century American culture. Though some modern-day critics consider Longfellow's work to be **sentimental**, and feel that he does not capture the spirit of American poetry so

well as **Walt Whitman**, the universal and accessible nature of Longfellow's poems, combined with his gift for rhyme and melody, and his evocation of the American wilderness allow his works to linger in the reader's consciousness long after the poems have been read.

Longfellow was born in Portland, Maine, in 1807. Growing up in the seaside harbor town of Portland allowed him to be a native of New England and yet to be slightly removed from its bustling center. The active Atlantic seaboard, the virtual edge of America, fostered within young Longfellow a desire to travel and embrace new experiences. Though his father was eager to have him follow in his footsteps as a lawyer, Longfellow's gift for language and writing prompted Bowdoin College to offer him a position as their first professor of Modern Languages. Longfellow, only nineteen years old at the time, agreed under the condition that he first be allowed to travel and study in Europe, and in 1826 set out on a journey that would take him through Spain, Italy, France, Germany, and England. The bulk of his travel was experienced on foot, allowing him ample time to take in the local traditions and people. When he returned to America in 1829, he began his notable teaching career, at Bowdoin and later moved on to Harvard. He strove to enlighten his students to many of the same themes and subjects that appear in his poetry. His career as an academic was a compromise between the man of law and action that his father wanted him to be and the dreamy poet that Longfellow himself longed to be; this very same conflict of ideals is seen in some of his best poetry, coloring the verse with fraught action and grand romance. A great tragedy in Longfellow's life, was the death of his first wife, Mary Storer Potter, in 1834, after only three years of marriage. Another great loss occurred much later when his second wife, Frances Appleton, died of burns in 1861. Despite these events, Longfellow's poems rarely failed to inspire joy and optimism within his faithful readers.

This same spirit is present in the now-iconic landscape of Longfellow's verse. It is a landscape of vast and untamed wilderness, evoking the thirst for adventure embodied by America's early settlers and explorers. It is as imaginary and wondrous as the Acadians' primeval forest, and as real and familiar as the village blacksmith. Concerned with both history and myth, this landscape is suggestive of Longfellow's interest in mixing the practical and fantastic. It is highlighted by an appreciation of the gothic style that he saw in the work of fellow New England writer Washington Irving. The most significant and notable poems in Longfellow's vast body of work illustrate this landscape particularly well. They include his two most popular pieces, "Evangeline" (1847) and "The Song of Hiawatha" (1855). In addition to showcasing the quintessential Longfellow landscape, these poems demonstrate the long **narrative** form that Longfellow became known for, as well as his enormous, seemingly effortless gift for music, meter, and composition.

The legend behind Evangeline and the Acadians was originally passed on to Longfellow by his friend and fellow Bowdoin alumnus Hawthorne, who prompted the Reverend Horace Lorenzo Conolly, a rector at St. Matthew's Episcopal Church in Boston, to tell Longfellow the story at a dinner party that all three attended. The legend of Evangeline is itself rooted in the 1755 expulsion of the Acadian people from Nova Scotia (an event known historically as *Le Grand Dérangement*), who were then dispersed across America's Atlantic seaboard and the southern Gulf Coast. Though Evangeline herself is said to have never existed, Longfellow transformed her into a mythic figure after hearing Conolly's fascinating story of an Acadian bride and bridegroom whose marriage was impeded by deportation. Separated from her lover, the bride wandered the wilds of America and did not reunite with her groom until both were aged and he lay upon his deathbed. Perceiving the bride as an archetypal faithful woman, Longfellow dubbed her "Evangeline."

The popularity of "Evangeline" stemmed from its appeal as an exotic, fantastical tale of romance and innocence lost, and as a reminder of the power that can be found in faith and steadfastness. A perhaps lesser-known fact about the poem is that "Evangeline" was especially appealing to those readers with anti-British leanings, who judged the deportation of the Acadians to be a tragedy committed by the same tyrannical monarchy that the colonies had fought during America's own Revolutionary War. Indeed, Longfellow heightened the Anglophobic sentiment within his poem and downplayed New England's own considerable role in the actual Acadian deportation (over fifteen thousand New England soldiers were directly involved). This oversight was likely intentional, as Longfellow was, like many New England citizens, distressed by the irony of southern slaves escaping to Canada via the underground railroad, seeking out freedom under the British monarchy. As such, the Anglophobic quality of "Evangeline" is also suggestive of the unique tensions that were brewing in the years before America's Civil War.

Written in the same hexameters that characterized the epics of Homer and Virgil, "Evangeline" represents Longfellow's first attempt at the long narrative form that would become his trademark. Longfellow's opening description of Acadia and the village of Grand-Pré conjures up a rich landscape that resembles an un-touched Eden, "darkened by shadows of earth, but reflecting an image of heaven." The "shadows of earth" are, appropriately enough, indicative of the very real political unrest that threatened this Northern Utopia in the decades leading up to the Acadian deportation. In the seventeenth century the region was passed back and forth between Britain, New England, and France, falling first into Britain's hands after Scottish entrepreneur Sir William Alexander was granted a trade monopoly for the region. After renaming the region "Nova Scotia," England gave Acadia over to France by the Treaty of Saint-Germain-en-Laye (1632), thus ushering in an era of French colonization. Britain, France, and America continued to juggle claim to Acadia throughout the rest of the seventeenth century, but in 1713 the Treaty of Utrecht finally placed the region in Britain's possession. It was this very same treaty that gave the Acadians a year in which to take an oath of Allegiance to Britain or to face removal by force—a force that Longfellow imagines as a powerful wind storm that will leave the Acadians "Scattered like dust and leaves, when the mighty blasts of October / Seize them, and whirl them aloft, and sprinkle them far o'er the ocean."

Longfellow's characterization of Acadia as a paradise threatened by political unrest, particularly by British tyranny, continues beyond the poem's introduction and into Part One. Part One's thorough description of the village of Grand-Pré features details that further contribute to Longfellow's fantastic and **pastoral** vision of the landscape. Through his verse Acadia is rendered a "happy valley" where villagers live in communal harmony, dwelling "in the love of God and of man." Even more important, Acadia is "free from / Fear, that reigns with the tyrant, and envy, the vice of republics." Longfellow stresses the peaceful and harmonious nature of Acadia several times throughout the poem, referring to the village as a place where "Peace seemed to reign upon earth." In fact, so harmonious is Acadia and its people that some villagers, such as Evangeline's father, Benedict, naively underestimate the threat of the British tyrant, believing that the arriving English ships might be seeking "some friendlier purpose." In describing the Acadians in such a way, Longfellow establishes them not only as a peaceful people, but also as people of incomparable faith.

Longfellow imagines his heroine Evangeline to be the sort of mythical woman who could only be born of an otherworldly place such as Acadia; as such, his thorough rendering of the landscape as a place of sheer, heavenly joy serves the dual purpose of providing contrast to Britain's threatening presence, as well as illustrating how the landscape itself is bound up within the spirit of Evangeline. Hailed as "the pride of the village," Longfellow's description of Evangeline creates overt connections between her physical presence and the landscape itself, for "Black were her eyes as the berry that grows on the thorn by the wayside" and "Sweet was her breath as the breath of kine that feed in the meadows." Though she is portrayed as the archetypal fair maiden, Longfellow identifies spirituality and faith as the most compelling aspects of Evangeline's beauty, declaring that "a celestial brightness—a more ethereal beauty— / Shone on her face and encircled her form, when, after confession, / Homeward serenely she walked with God's benediction upon her." Like the Acadian village from which she hails, Evangeline is extraordinary not only for her beauty, but also for the spirit, that she radiates.

This same spirit, residing in both Evangeline and her fellow Acadians, is nearly destroyed by Britain's forced deportation. For Evangeline, the pain of having to part from her village is doubled when she must also part from her groom, Gabriel. Despite this wrenching separation, Longfellow once again emphasizes Evangeline's enduring faithfulness when she whispers to Gabriel "be of good cheer! for if we love one another / Nothing, in truth, can harm us, whatever mischances may happen!" Not even the sight of her father, utterly broken in spirit and "with the weight of a heavy heart," can sap her steadfastness. Evangeline continues to possess a deep sense of faith into Part Two of the poem, which finds her searching for Gabriel in the years following the burning of Grand-Pré. Though challenged by an unfamiliar countryside, numerous false leads, and one particularly poignant moment in which her boat passes Gabriel's in the darkness, Evangeline continues her search for Gabriel. Even while others ask "why dream and wait for him any longer?" she persists in her journey and travels down the mythic path Longfellow forges for her—for "patient endurance is godlike."

In many ways, Evangeline's search for Gabriel amounts to a rediscovery of Acadia—if not literally, then spiritually. For even though they have been displaced and "scattered like dust and leaves," Evangeline is reunited with many of her fellow villagers as she carries out her journey, which plays out like a travelogue in its rich description of the American landscape. In each of Evangeline's encounters with her fellow Acadians, readers see how the people of Grand-Pré persist as best they can in establishing their new homes and communities, still clinging to the spirit of faith that colored their daily lives prior to the deportation. Though their pastoral Eden has been lost, the Acadians' faith is renewed within the sanctuary of America, where "lands may be had for the asking" and "No King George of England shall drive you away from your homesteads." By characterizing the Acadians as nothing but accepting and grateful of their new American home, Longfellow both maintains the anti-British undertones of the poem while demonstrating that the deplorable actions of the British tyrant have been unsuccessful in destroying the Acadian spirit.

In old age, Evangeline's spiritual and divine nature has transformed her into a "Sister of Mercy"—one who comforts the ill and forsaken, bringing them flowers so that "the dying once more might rejoice in their fragrance and beauty." In reward for her kindness, patience, and faith, Evangeline is finally reunited with Gabriel on his deathbed. At the moment of their long-awaited reunion, Acadia seems to spring to life around them once more, and the lovers are surrounded by the "Green Acadian Meadows, with sylvan rivers among them, / Village, and mountain, and woodlands." Though Evangeline suffers "the constant anguish of patience" in her long and arduous search for Gabriel, Longfellow makes it clear that the extent of her suffering and patience is precisely why she is deserving of reward in the end.

Though not the first American writer to evoke the iconic "noble savage" in a literary context, Longfellow's "The Song of Hiawatha" endures as one of the most notable evocations of the Native American. "Hiawatha" is a thoroughly researched and grand vision of American archaeology and anthropology, two of Longfellow's interests, which were likely intensified by his scholarly travels in Europe. His experiences abroad developed within him a certain amount of the wonder and curiosity that many Europeans felt toward the more fascinating aspects of an emerging American culture, which certainly included the mysterious figure of the vanishing Native American. Though he invested years of research into the writing of "Hiawatha," this research was primarily utilized for creating a sense of authenticity within the poem, and as such reaffirms Longfellow's preference for imaginative re-creation over stark, historical realism. By imbuing his hero with a familiar Apollonian fate, and wisely avoiding overly deep and tragic themes, Longfellow keeps his poem successfully rooted in the grand tradition of mythmaking and folklore, thus assuring its appeal and relevance for generations to come.

Though arguably the work that Longfellow is best known for today, and though it was wildly popular in his own time, "Hiawatha" was not without controversy at the time of its publication in March of 1855. Longfellow was accused by some of having plagiarized the Finnish poem "Kalevala," and indeed, he openly admitted to having used the meter of "Kalevala" in "Hiawatha." In fact, before he became a professor at Harvard, Longfellow traveled throughout England, Sweden, Denmark, Holland, and Germany, an experience that most certainly drew his attention to the literary traditions of Northern Europe.

There are numerous reasons why Longfellow might have bypassed more traditional meters and arrangements in favor of modeling his verse after that of "Kalevala." First, it seems possible that in dealing with subject matter that was relatively new to literature Longfellow was interested in experimenting with an equally new and unfamiliar meter in "Hiawatha." Second, the meter of "Kalevala" appropriately evokes the shamanistic quality that makes "Hiawatha" so unique and memorable—a sing-song melody that Longfellow felt uncannily similar to the descriptions of Native chanting that he had read about in his researches. Regarding his borrowing of the trochaic tetrameter of "Kalevala," most critics eventually agreed that however consciously or unconsciously the Finnish poem inspired Longfellow, the form and meter of "Hiawatha" was not the sole property of Finland—Longfellow was merely working in the tradition of many authors before him, much the same way as the Homer-inspired Virgil did when he wrote the *Aeneid.*

However, it was not just the meter of "Hiawatha" that inspired controversy; the themes and events in the epic poem resembled those in "Kalevala" to such an extent that they too raised suspicions of plagiarism. Hiawatha's parents, for example, have mythic qualities paralleling those of Väinämöinen, the hero of "Kalevala"; likewise, many of Hiawatha's adventures are of an epic flavor similar to those that Väinämöinen experiences. A few weeks after the initial publication of "Hiawatha," a Washington newspaper charged Longfellow with having borrowed "the entire form, spirit, and many of the most striking incidents" of "Kalevala." Longfellow responded by writing: "I know the Kalevala quite well; and that some of its legends resemble the Indian stories preserved by Schoolcraft is very true. But the idea of making me responsible for that is too ludicrous."

As for the actual Native American legends that appear in the poem, Longfellow gave credit to American anthropologist Henry Rowe Schoolcraft, a historian and explorer who headed Indian Affairs for Michigan from 1836 to 1841. Other primary sources Longfellow consulted include George Caitlin's *Letters and Notes on the Manners, Customs, and Condition of the North American Indians* (1841) and J.G.E. Heckewelder's *Account of the History, Manners, and Customs of the Indian Nations, Who Once Inhabited Pennsylvania and the Neighbouring States* (1819). In 1856 Schoolcraft's *Algic Researches* was republished as *The Myth of Hiawatha*, the bulk of which was complied by Schoolcraft's half-Ojibway wife, Jane, and her mother, O-shau-gus-coday-way-qua ("The Woman of the Green Prairie"). The legends and stories described in *The Myth of Hiawatha* served as the basis for "Hiawatha." Claims of plagiarism subsided when it became clear that the poem, though inspired by and based on the Finnish "Kalevala," was rooted in a distinctly American folklore and history. Gifting the American people with an **epic** hero of their own was such a significant contribution to the country's culture and identity that the poem's Finnish roots hardly mattered to most readers and critics. Longfellow's defense was aided when, in 1899, Nathan Haskell Dole published a focused, scholarly discussion of the relations between "Hiawatha" and "Kalevala," in which Longfellow was completely vindicated.

Like Evangeline, Hiawatha is a hero whose fate and character is bound up in the landscape that he traverses. In Hiawatha's case this is a definite and familiar American landscape, located centrally in the Great Lakes region of Michigan. Hiawatha himself is based on a semi-divine Native American culture hero known by the Algonquins as Manabozho and, according to Schoolcraft, by the Iroquois as Tarenyawagon or Hiawatha. Hiawatha is quite literally born of the land in that his father is the immortal west wind, Mudjekeewis, who woos the beautiful Wenonah with "words of sweetness" and "soft caresses." Wenonah soon bears a son and "child of wonder," Hiawatha, but dies of a broken heart after being cruelly abandoned by the "false and faithless" Mudjekeewis. Young Hiawatha is raised on his grandmother Nokomis's tales of "the stars that shine in heaven" and the "Warriors with their plumes and war clubs," and soon grows into a remarkable youth, learning the languages of birds and beasts, "their names and all their secrets," and yet hunts with sublime expertise. Even in his youth Hiawatha's potential for heroism and leadership is recognized by the villagers, who hail him as "Strong Heart, Soan-ge-taha!" and feast in his honor. Longfellow's inclusion of authentic Ojibway language and customs is vital to the creation of a genuine folklore within the poem; though these elements were unfamiliar to readers in the mid-1800s, this same unfamiliarity was nonetheless suggestive of a very real Native American authenticity that no doubt intrigued and captivated Longfellow's audience.

Hiawatha grows into a young man with all the characteristics one would expect of a hero who is destined for legends and folklore. He has the abilities of a young God, able to "shoot an arrow from him / And run forward with such fleetness, / that the arrow fell behind him!" In addition to possessing magic tools which provide him with even more tremendous skills, such as mittens which "smite the rocks" and moccasins which allow him to take mile-long strides, Hiawatha can also "shoot ten arrows upward, / Shoot them with such strength and swiftness, / That the tenth had left the bow-string / Ere the first to earth had fallen!" Hiawatha's abilities not only amaze readers, but also serve as indication that his adult life will be abundant with the sort of fantastical adventures any well-prepared hero would be destined to encounter. Interestingly, it is his "false and faithless" father who provides Hiawatha with his heroic calling. Though initially seeking out Mudjekeewis to avenge his mother's death, Hiawatha's battle with his father is thwarted when Mudjekeewis calls out "you cannot kill the immortal. / I have put you to this trial, / But to know and prove your courage." It is in this moment that Mudjekeewis assigns Hiawatha the task of returning to his people to "Cleanse the earth from all that harms it." If he does so, Hiawatha will be rewarded with immortality in the days before his death, invited to share Mudjekeewis's kingdom as "the Northwest-Wind, Keewaydin."

Hiawatha's immortality is assured in the scope and
grandeur of his legend, which grows in accordance to
the loyalty and leadership he shows his people. After
marrying the beautiful Minnehaha to unite the warring
Ojibway and Dacotah tribes in peace, Hiawatha rids his
village of the mischievous Pau-Puk-Keewis, and teaches
his people to mourn the dead so they will no longer
"lack the cheerful firelight" and "grope about in darkness." When it becomes apparent to Hiawatha's people
that there is "a flower unknown" among them, Hiawatha
encourages his tribe to welcome them, the "people with
white faces." At this climactic moment, seen in Part
XXI, "The White Man's Foot," and Part XXII, "Hiawatha's Departure," readers are presented with a transitional moment in both Hiawatha's life and America's
history.

The transitional moment that appears in Parts XXI
and XXII of "Hiawatha" is that moment when the history and culture of the Ojibway people are altered forever by the arrival of the white man, which Longfellow
casts as a moment to embrace rather than mourn. At
times it can seem difficult to comprehend why Longfellow would write so many lines of verse in celebration of
Native American culture, only to imply that the fate of
Hiawatha's people will be altered in the hands of a
"Black robe chief, the Prophet / He the Priest of Prayer,
the Pale-face . . . With the cross upon his bosom." However, the sheer volume of Longfellow's painstaking
research on Native culture suggests that he was not *deliberately* trying to undermine its significance in the context
of Anglo-Christian culture, but rather hoped to honestly
portray that transitional moment in history when America was discovered and claimed by the Western world.
The common belief at the time was that this claim was
"natural" and justified. It is unsurprising, then, that when
Hiawatha bids farewell to his tribe in order to join his
father as the Northwest-Wind, he asks them to "Listen to
their words of wisdom, / Listen to the truth they tell
you." As such, "Hiawatha's Departure" signifies a poignant end to the rich and vivid world of the Native people, while "Hiawatha" exists as a memorial to it.

This very same premise is evident in much of Longfellow's poetry, which memorializes the events and themes
in American culture that we have long cherished and
reserved within the collective American conscience. The
American readers' love of Longfellow is not merely a
love for his gift for verse and meter, but a love for his
ability to render the American landscape differently,
more ideally, than history would or could. While Longfellow's idealized, iconic landscape may not be the
America that readers know from history, it *is* the America they have often loved in literature.

Further Reading. *Selected Primary Sources:* Longfellow,
Henry Wadsworth, *The Complete Poetical Works of Henry*

Wadsworth Longfellow (Boston: Houghton Mifflin, 1893);
———, *Evangeline and Selected Tales and Poems*, ed.
Horace Gregory (New York: New American Library,
1964); ———, *The Song of Hiawatha, by Henry Wadsworth
Longfellow* (New York: T.Y. Cromwell, 1898). ***Selected
Secondary Sources:*** Evans, James Allan, "Longfellow's
Evangeline and the Cult of Acadia" (*Contemporary Review*
[February 2002]); Osborn, Chase S., and Stellanova
Osborn, *Schoolcraft, Longfellow, Hiawatha* (Lancaster, PA:
Jacques Cattell Press, 1942); Wagenknecht, Edward,
Henry Wadsworth Longfellow, His Poetry and Prose (New
York: Ungar, 1986).

Leslee Wright

LONGFELLOW, SAMUEL (1819–1892)

Samuel Longfellow is probably most widely known
today for his multi-volume 1886 biography of his older
brother, *The Life of Henry Wadsworth Longfellow.* He
carefully removed any unpleasant, irreverent passages
from his brother's manuscript journals so that the published journal extracts would present a very favorable
image. Longfellow achieved literary distinction, not
only as a biographer, but also as a philosopher, hymn
writer, and poet. He published theological papers,
especially in Unitarian periodicals. Longfellow graduated from Harvard University in 1839 and entered
Harvard Divinity School in 1842. Under the teaching
of Convers Francis and the preaching of **Theodore
Parker**, he developed an enthusiasm for Transcendentalism. Francis Christie, writing in the 1933 edition of
the *Dictionary of American Biography*, claimed that Longfellow was the clearest and most methodical of the
transcendental thinkers. When one recalls that **Amos
Bronson Alcott, Ralph Waldo Emerson, Margaret
Fuller**, and Parker, among others, were Transcendentalist thinkers publishing in the same period, that is
high praise for Longfellow. In his *Emerson among the
Eccentrics* (1996), Carlos Baker mentions that Alcott
once held a talk in Longfellow's home. Emerson and
the poet **Walt Whitman** were among those present.
Although Longfellow associated himself with quite radical Protestant thinkers, he was always moderate in his
philosophical speculations. His philosophical essays,
especially those published in the *Radical*, display his
independence and intellectual depth.

In 1848 Longfellow became a Unitarian minister in
Fall River, Massachusetts. In 1853 he accepted the min-
istry of the Second Unitarian Church in Brooklyn, New
York, and served in Germantown, Pennsylvania, from
January of 1878 to 1882. His warm and generous tem-
perament was reflected in his sermons.

During the nineteenth century Longfellow was known
for publishing hymns—some original and others collected and edited by him. With his classmate Samuel

Johnson, he edited and published *A Book of Hymns* in 1846. Among the hymn writers in that collection were Harriet Beecher Stowe, **Jones Very**, and **John Greenleaf Whittier**. Longfellow's selections for the hymnal were those that were, generally, more mystical, tender, devout, and reflective over Johnson's more intellectual, aspiring, heroic and passionate choices. *Thalatta, A Book for the Seaside* is an anthology of poetry edited and published in 1853 by Longfellow in collaboration with **Thomas Wentworth Higginson**, a Divinity School classmate. Longfellow published a vesper service book in 1859, *A Book of Hymns and Tunes* in 1860, and *Hymns of the Spirit* in 1864. Among his original hymns are "Bless Thou the Gifts Our Hands Have Brought," "Now, on Land and Sea Descending," "Again as Evening Shadows Fall," and "Holy Spirit, Truth Divine."

Longfellow was also a poet. After his death, Edith Longfellow, daughter of **Henry Wadsworth Longfellow**, published some of her uncle's hymns and poems in a collection titled *Hymns and Verses* (1894). His poem "I Will Trust and Not Be Afraid" compares us to our forefathers through the image of sailing unknown seas. It asks us to search for Truth wherever that search may lead: "Afloat, but not adrift upon the tide, / Dare Truth's broad seas." We should place our faith in God on the personal inner spirit we each possess, rather than accept an uninspired faith: "He must be safe who sails where God doth guide." The image affirms that our ships will be different from those of our forefathers as we sail different seas. In his "The Golden Sunset," a boat "Hangs silently" in the midst of a golden glow created by the evening sky being mirrored in the sea: "The sea is but another sky, / The sky a sea as well." The poet hopes that when his "latest hour" of life arrives, the transition to heaven will be as smooth and seamless as that image: "Where earth ends and heaven begins / The soul shall scarcely know." His poems, like his hymns, are paeans of faith to a God who listens with a tender heart and soul to the prayers of men.

In 1882 Longfellow retired from the ministry to write a biography of his brother, Henry Wadsworth Longfellow, who had died in March of that year. Longfellow's strength as a poet was known mainly through his hymn lyrics. His images are usually from nature and his themes are promises that his God is not an angry forbidding God, but rather a God of generosity and love.

Further Reading. ***Selected Primary Sources:*** Longfellow, Samuel, *Hymns and Verses*, ed. Edith Longfellow (Boston: Houghton Mifflin, 1894); ———, *A Book of Hymns*, ed. Samuel Johnson (Boston: Ticknor, Reed, and Fields, 1846); ———, *A Book of Hymns and Tunes* (1860); ———, *Hymns of the Spirit* (Boston: Ticknor and Fields, 1864); ———, *The Life of Henry Wadsworth Longfellow, with extracts from his journals and correspondence,* 2 vols. (Boston:

Fields, Osgood & Co., 1886); ———, *The Life of Henry Wadsworth Longfellow, with extracts from his journals and correspondence,* 3 vols. (Boston: Houghton Mifflin,1891); Longfellow, Samuel, and Thomas Wentworth Higginson, *Thalatta, A Book for the Seaside* (Boston: Ticknor, Reed, and Fields, 1853). ***Selected Secondary Sources:*** Baker, Carlos, *Emerson Among the Eccentrics* (New York: Viking, 1996); Garrity, J.A., and M. Carnes, eds., "Longfellow, Samuel," in *American National Biography* (New York: Oxford University Press, 1999); Malone, Dumas, ed., "Longfellow, Samuel," *Dictionary of American Biography*, Vol. VI (New York: Scribner's Sons, 1933; reprint 1961); Christensen, Paul S., et al., Amos Bronson Alcott Network, "Samuel Longfellow," http://www.alcott.net/alcott/home/champions/Longfellow.html.

Carle Johnson

LORDE, AUDRE(Y) (GERALDINE) (1934–1992)

After World War II, women found themselves in the position of an inferior social group, as the "second sex," as Simone de Beauvoir claimed in 1949. Postwar American women faced the emergence of an ideology about femininity that marginalized their social position and reduced them to the roles of housewife, wife, and mother. This ideology of femininity was for the first time clearly and publicly stated by Betty Friedan in her influential book *The Feminine Mystique* (1963), with which she provoked the rise of consciousness among many women and brought about the beginning of a change in the reflection on women's social position. In the 1960s the Women's and Civil Rights movements gained new momentum. Audre Lorde was one of the first African Caribbean American women writers to achieve public recognition as both a writer and an activist and to reject openly the dominance of white middle-class women in feminism. Like other black women poets, such as **Rita Dove**, **Nikki Giovanni**, Gloria I. Joseph, and Ntozake Shange, Lorde broke the silence about black women's double marginalization and discrimination and discussed key issues in her autobiographical poetry.

As the American-born daughter of immigrant parents from Barbados and Grenada, Audre Lorde experienced a childhood of discrimination against otherness, in her case both as a black and as a woman in a male- and white-dominated American society. She grew up in Harlem, graduated from Hunter College (1959), and received an MLS from Columbia University (1961), which helped her secure a professorship in English at John Jay College for Criminal Justice (1970) and Hunter College (1981–1987). She was married in 1962, had a daughter (Elizabeth-Lorde Rollins [b.1963]) and a son (Jonathan F.A. Rollins [b.1965]), and was divorced in 1970. For Lorde the 1960s was a period of racial, social, sexual, and poetical awakening. Having written poetry early in her life, she published her first collection, *The*

First Cities, in 1968. Like **Adrienne Rich**, **Anne Sexton**, and to some extent **Sylvia Plath**, Lorde realized that being a woman and wanting to become a poet were not easily compatible. She subsequently called herself "Gamba Adisa" (Warrior—she who makes her meaning known) and came out as a lesbian and feminist activist. She was one of the founders of Kitchen Table: Women of Color Press, a small feminist publishing house. Because of her struggle with cancer, she retired to St. Croix in the U.S. Virgin Islands, where she, together with her friend and partner Gloria I. Joseph, initiated the Women's Coalition and continued to support SISA (Sisterhood in Support of Sisters in South Africa) and CAFRA (Caribbean Association for Feminist Research and Action). She was Poet Laureate of New York State from 1991 until her death of cancer on November 17, 1992.

In her teaching and life, as well as in her prose and poetry, Lorde was a radical feminist, an outspoken lesbian, and a political activist. In addition to her fight against any form of discrimination, another one of the underlying themes in her work, is the representation or re-creation of herself, of a multiple identity that had undergone major changes, which she painfully recorded. To find or present herself was not only a purpose but also a means to overcome a crisis or the more general feeling of being marginalized in a white, male, and heterosexual society. Lorde used her writing as a personal and political therapy in which she spoke about herself and others. In her work three main issues recur that were constitutive of the development of herself in writing. First, being the daughter of black Caribbean immigrants in the United States motivated Lorde to redefine motherhood and search for mirror images in her children, her African origins, and her lesbianism. Second, poetry was her most essential means for expressing the intimate relationship she saw between her life, her body, and the public world. Third, her textual representation works through mirroring; the material world of the poet and the textual world of the poem and persona constantly reflect each other.

In addressing the first issue, Lorde saw herself to a large extent connected to her mother and her mother's influences and heritage. When she started to write about her mother—from the perspective of a daughter and then as a mother herself—and to create an image of her, she did so with the intention of establishing the missing links between the generations in order to achieve a harmonious unity and mutual reflection that would help her find her own place in society and in a community of women. In many of her poems, and particularly in "Black Mother Woman" (in *From a Land Where Other People Live*), Lorde explores mother-daughter relationships as determined by the mother's weakness because of her fear of discrimination and the daughter's desire for her mother's love. What the mother teaches her daughter instead is how to survive. In contrast to her mother, however, Lorde always believed in affirming one's blackness and womanhood.

To stay in touch with the political development of her time was important for Lorde's survival because of the dominant power of racism. She recognized two different kinds of racism in American society: inter- and intra-ethnic racisms. Lorde's response to overt racism in the United States was anger, which she gradually learned to turn into a creative force, as seen in her 1981 essay "The Uses of Anger," published in *Sister Outsider*. In poems such as "Cables to Rage" (in *New York Head Shop and Museum*), "Every Traveler Has One Vermont Poem" (in *Our Dead Behind Us*), and "The Day They Eulogized Mahalia" (in *From a Land Where Other People Live*), she describes various forms of racism that climax for her in white women's racism, as for example, in "Who Said It Was Simple" in *From a Land Where Other People Live* and "A Meeting of Minds" in *Our Dead Behind Us*. Lorde experienced intra-ethnic racism in 1990 on a trip from St. Croix to Virgin Gorda, an island in the Caribbean, when she was told at immigration that she could not enter with her braided hair, as she interrogates in her 1990 essay "Is Your Hair Still Political?" and her poem "A Question of *Essence*" in *Our Dead Behind Us*.

Lorde's experiences of discrimination through both inter- and intra-ethnic racism made her turn toward the idea of African heritage, which, for her, transformed blackness into a strong and superior social category. The connection to her African heritage was possible for Lorde through a global community of women, as exemplified by her poem "Sisters in Arms" in *Our Dead Behind Us*, based on mythic mother figures who represent female strength, and through the re-writing of white Western master narratives, for example, the title poem of *The Black Unicorn*. Both finally result in the celebration of a female (mythic) principle, as in the poem "Call" from *Our Dead Behind Us*. Lorde was constantly in search of myths that transgress the boundaries of generations—such as those of Mawu-Lisa, Seboulisa, Mother Yemanjá, Oshun, Shango, Oya, Eshu, Afrekete, and Aido Hwedo—to connect the female members of each generation with each other. She established connections of these mythic figures with, among others, Rosa Parks, Fannie Lou Hamer, Assata Shakur, Yaa Asantewaa, and Winnie Mandela. The rewriting of these myths in her poetry helped Lorde to connect her African-ness and American-ness with her sexuality.

Lorde's experiences of her own sexuality were shaped by her recognition of her lesbianism and by her suffering from cancer. Her *Cancer Journals* (1980) and her poetry show how she was able to overcome the physical, psychological, and social limitations imposed by society on a woman with breast cancer because of her rootedness in a community of women and because of her writing. For Lorde it was a matter of survival to break the silence about her illness, as she describes in her essay "The Transformation of Silence into Language and Action" (from *The Cancer Journals*) and in her poem "Restoration: A Memorial—9/18/91" (in *The Marvelous Arithmetics of Distance*). Lorde identified completely with lesbianism as derived from her mother's Caribbean origins, which she related in *Zami: A New Spelling of My Name. A Biomythography* (1982), with "Zami" as a patois word for "lesbian." To a large extent, *Zami* is Lorde's coming-out story, describing her sensations in childhood, her first careful relationships with other women, and her ultimate whole-hearted embracement of African mythology and lesbianism. Most of her poems that deal with woman-to-woman relationships are openly erotic in presentation. For Lorde eroticism was a form of power for women and therefore needed to be expressed, as in "Love Poem" from *New York Head Shop and Museum*, "Woman" from *The Black Unicorn*, "Outlines" from *Our Dead Behind Us*, and her 1978 essay "Uses of the Erotic: The Erotic as Power." Poetry helped her integrate life and text; poems became her looking glasses.

Turning to the second issue, like the recognition of her lesbianism, Lorde's development as a writer was intimately connected with her mother. In order to express her multiple identities, Lorde used and mixed various genres and frequently inserted poems into her prose. Since her "Poetry Is Not a Luxury" (essay in *Sister* Outsider [1977]), she metapoetically thematized the relevance of poetry in many poems, as in the poems "Power" and "Therapy," both from *The Black Unicorn*. Lorde did not speak until she was four or five years old, and then she began to communicate through poems she had read and memorized. At twelve or thirteen she realized that there were many things she wanted to talk about but could not find the right poems. Thus, she began to write poems herself. For Lorde, poetry subsequently meant empowerment and reconnection to herself as a black mother woman, thus a necessity for the survival of humanity. Frequently, Lorde compared the process of lesbian lovemaking to the process of writing poetry. For her, poetry served two functions: on a personal level, she found expression of feelings otherwise hidden and allowed her poems to influence her life; on a political level, her poems were meant to criticize social conditions (in particular of black women) and to stimulate and motivate personal action. Lorde considered writing poetry a political activity and traced the existence and significance of poetry on both levels back to the particular life circumstances of herself as a black female lesbian mother, locating the origins of poetry deep inside a woman's and a mother's body. Because of this intimate connection between poetry and the female body, her poetry necessarily is autobiographical and gendered.

Addressing the third thematic issue, Lorde frequently used the image of the mirror to further emphasize her search for identity as a black lesbian mother and poet. Many of the mirror images in her poems reflect the desire for a clear vision, as in "Good Mirrors Are Not Cheap" in *From a Land Where Other People Live*, as well as the fighting and often ambiguous social forces within the female viewers with regard to womanhood, as in "The One Who Got Away" from *The Marvelous Arithmetics of Distance*; motherhood, as in "What My Child Learns from the Sea" in *The First Cities*; race, as in "Who Said It Was Simple" in *From a Land Where Other People Live*; sexuality, as in "Meet" from *The Black Unicorn*; and poetry, as in "Coal" from *The First Cities*. The mirrors shed light on Lorde's private and public activities, but in particular on the way in which she translated her life experience into poetry. She needed to see herself reflected in her environment by making her various selves visible in a society that sanctioned difference with rejection or even total denial.

Lorde's poetry and prose can be seen as indicative and expressive of women's positions in American society from the 1950s to the 1990s. Her poetry is rooted in a post-war patriarchal society governed by the feminine mystique. She experienced the tension between herself as an individual and as a member of social groups and of society as a whole, and translated this experience into autobiographical poetry through which she exposed gender and race and the rules and values connected to them as cultural constructs meant to support a white heterosexual patriarchal American society. (*See also* **African American Poetry**, **Feminist Poetics**, and **Gay and Lesbian Poetry**.)

Further Reading. *Selected Primary Sources:* Lorde, Audre, *The Audre Lorde Compendium: Essays, Speeches and Journals* (London: Pandora, 1996); ———, *Between Our Selves: Poems* (Point Reyes: Eidolon Editions; Berkeley, CA: Book People, 1976); ———, *The Black Unicorn: Poems* (New York: Norton, 1978); ———, *A Burst of Light: Essays* (Ithaca, NY: Firebrand Books, 1988); ———, *Cables to Rage* (London: Paul Breman, 1970); ———, *The Cancer Journals* (San Francisco, CA: Spinsters / aunt lute, 1980); ———, *Chosen Poems, Old and New* (New York: Norton, 1982); ———, *Coal* (New York: Norton, 1976); ———, *The Collected Poems of Audre Lorde* (New York: Norton, 1997); ———, *The First Cities* (New York: Poets Press, 1968); ———, *From a Land Where Other People Live* (Detroit, MI: Broadside Press, 1973); ———, *The Marvelous Arithmetics of Distance: Poems 1987–1992* (New York: Norton, 1993); ———, *New York Head Shop and Museum* (Detroit, MI: Broadside Press, 1974); ———, *Our Dead Behind Us: Poems* (New York: Norton, 1986); ———, *Sister Outsider: Essays and Speeches* (Trumansburg, NY: The Crossing Press Feminist Series, 1984); ———, *Undersong: Chosen Poems Old and New Revised* (New York:

Norton, 1992); ———, *Zami: A New Spelling of My Name: A Biomythography* (Freedom, CA: The Crossing Press, 1982). **Selected Secondary Sources:** Birkle, Carmen, *Women's Stories of the Looking Glass: Autobiographical Reflections and Self-Representations in the Poetry of Sylvia Plath, Adrienne Rich, and Audre Lorde* (Munich: Fink, 1996); Keating, AnaLouise, *Women Reading Women Writing: Self-Invention in Paula Gunn Allen, Gloria Anzaldúa, and Audre Lorde* (Philadelphia, PA: Temple University Press, 1996); Kley, Antje, *"Das erlesene Selbst" in der autobiographischen Schrift: Zu Politik und Poetik der Selbstreflexion bei Roth, Delany, Lorde und Kingston* (Tübingen; Narr, 2001); Ricciardi, Gabriella, *Autobiographical Representation in Pier Paolo Pasolini and Audre Lorde* (Tübingen: Stauffenburg, 2001); Tate, Claudia, *Black Women Writers at Work* (New York: Continuum, 1983).

Carmen Birkle

LOUIS, ADRIAN C. (1946–)

Adrian C. Louis is one of the most important, yet highly controversial, **Native American poets**. Writing about life on the reservation with a gritty, honest realism, Louis has been equally praised and condemned. Criticism has suggested that such realism should focus on the positive side of Native American experience, but Louis has attempted to write a poetry large enough to confront and explore the complexities of contemporary America and to grapple with some of the harsh realities of Indian life: alcoholism, violence, poverty, and loss. His poems struggle to portray contemporary life while not forgetting or denying a rich past, searching for a tradition or way of life that will sustain him and his culture. He stands simultaneously inside and outside of the culture he examines; he becomes, as Leslie Ullman has said in "Betrayals and Boundaries," "both an observer and a prime example of a condition . . . both the accuser and the accused" (188). His poems, then, paint a highly complex portrait of an individual's search for redemption in the midst of a harrowing world. His work has inspired and served as a model for many younger Native American poets such as **Joy Harjo** and **Sherman Alexie**.

Louis, a mixed-race Indian and enrolled member of the Lovelock Paiute tribe, was born in Nevada in 1946, the eldest of twelve children. He studied at Brown University where he received an MA in creative writing, and has worked as a journalist, edited four tribal newspapers—including the award-winning *Talking Leaf* in Los Angeles, the *Lakota Times* in Pine Ridge, South Dakota, and *Indian Country Today*—and founded the Native American Press Association. He taught for many years at the Oglala Lakota College on the Pine Ridge Indian Reservation and at Southwest Minnesota State University. He has received grants from the South Dakota Arts Council, the Bush Foundation, the National Endowment of the Arts, and is in the Nevada Writers Hall of Fame.

Besides ten collections of poems, he has published two highly acclaimed books of fiction, the novel *Skins* (1995)—which was turned into a movie in 2002—and a collection of short stories *Wild Indians and Other Creatures* (1996).

Louis's early collection *Fire Water World* (1989) demonstrated a fully matured and unique voice, a romantic lyricism and meditation mixed with a hard-edged cynicism and world weariness. The voice is rough and streetwise at the same time that it sings with a graceful rhythm, a constant tension between the sacred and the profane that allows a large and complex emotional range, which he continued to mine in his next three collections: *Among the Dog Eaters* (1992), *Bloodthirsty Savages* (1994), and *Vortex of Indian Fevers* (1995). While these books certainly confront white America's culpability in the degradation and disenfranchisement of native communities, they are most notable for their hard-edged examination of the communities themselves. Louis trains his gaze on self-destructive behavior as Native Americans have frequently turned to become their own worst enemies. In *Fire Water World* we can see this mixture of blame and self-recrimination (and the ever-present subject of alcohol) in a poem such as "Pabst Blue Ribbon at Wounded Knee." The poem confronts the genocidal nature of American history but admits that "We wait and wonder and don't ask why / we sit in our cars drinking Pabst Blue Ribbon." The reservation has become, as he notes in *Vortex of Indian Fevers*, a landscape littered with "used Pampers, dead cars, punctured tires, and empty beer cans" ("Notes from Indian Country"). The reservation, though, becomes not merely a bleak landscape but a metaphor for human boundaries and limitations that Louis is always attempting to transcend.

Ceremonies of the Damned (1997) takes on the tone of a more personal **elegy** as the poet grapples with his wife's decline into the darkness of Alzheimer's, most notably in the title poem and his lengthy meditation "Earth Bone Connected to the Spirit Bone." "Darling, it seems my only reason / for living is to help you remember" he says, and, indeed, the book elegizes as a way to memorialize what is being lost and to transform memory into a form of sustenance. Alzheimer's becomes not only a central subject for his poetry but also a rich metaphorical terrain for cultural consciousness; the vacancy of a mind without memory becomes a metaphor for the wasteland that Louis sees as America and its cultural amnesia.

As if in response to this cultural forgetfulness, *Ancient Acid Flashes Back* (2000) is a meditation on memory and American history embodied in a journey through the Haight-Ashbury district in the late 1960s. The book, working as a single poem constructed out of vignettes, recounts the adventures of semi-autobiographical character Naatsi from his vantage in the 1990s, when "*Naatsi is middle-aging gracelessly / smackdab in the middle of America.*" The book examines the ways in which both Naatsi and his nation have failed to live up to the promise of the 1960s. In the late 1990s, faced with AIDS, drugs, welfare, and gangs, "*the future looks / mind-dead & televised, / grim, greedy & goofy*" ("April 24, 1971").

Louis's latest books, *Bone & Juice* (2001) and *Evil Corn* (2004), return to a more elegiac tone, and a somber exploration of loss. At the same time, the poems become more bitingly angry—at himself and at society. In *Bone & Juice* everything but his love for his wife is dying away, and American culture has been reduced to "Cowturdville," the mythic midwestern town in which the speaker lives. Composed completely of prose poems, *Evil Corn* carries his disgust at American culture even further. He has seemingly abandoned the romantic lyricism that marked his earlier work, leaving the language stripped down in a harsher, more cynical indictment. The book becomes an assault on self, reader, and culture. But beneath this assault there still lies the wit and tenacity that has marked his work as a whole. At the heart of these poems, beneath the bitterness, anger, and sorrow, Louis still seems to be struggling to say that "*Because all things return / to their source, / grace is possible*" ("Indian Summer Gives Way to the Land of the Rising Sun," *Bone & Juice*).

Further Reading. ***Selected Primary Sources:*** Louis, Adrian, *Among the Dog Eaters* (Albuquerque, NM: West End Press, 1992); ———, *Ancient Acid Flashes Back* (Reno: University of Nevada Press, 2000); ———, *Blood Thirsty Savages* (St. Louis, MO: Time Being Books, 1994); ———, *Vortex of Indian Fevers* (Evanston, IL: TriQuarterly Books, 1995); ———, *Bone & Juice* (Evanston, IL: TriQuarterly Books, 2001); ———, *Ceremonies of the Damned* (Reno: University of Nevada Press, 1997); ———, *Evil Corn* (Granite Falls, MN: Ellis Press, 2004); ———, *Fire Water World* (Albuquerque, NM: West End Press, 1989). ***Selected Secondary Sources:*** Nelson, Cary, ed., "Adrian Louis" (*Modern American Poetry Online*, http://www.english.uiuc.edu/maps/poets/g_l/louis/louis.htm); Ullman, Leslie, "Betrayals and Boundaries: A Question of Balance" (*Kenyon Review* 15.3 [Summer 1993]: 182–197).

Glenn J. Freeman

LOWELL, AMY (1874–1925)

Amy Lowell was a tireless writer and promoter of poetry whose accomplishments extend well beyond her association with **Imagism**. She created new forms, edited anthologies, gave memorable readings of her work to packed audiences, lectured widely, and produced volumes of poetry, translations, critical prose, and biography. She was one of the most important and influential poets of the early twentieth century—allied with some of her contemporaries, at odds with others, but always engaged with the development and circulation of **modernist** poetry.

Lowell was born in 1874, the youngest child of Augustus and Katharine Bigelow Lowell of Boston, Massachusetts. The family helped develop the region's textile industry in the early nineteenth century and was recognized for its financial prominence and philanthropic interests. Lowell's oldest brother, Percival, was a noted traveler to and writer about East Asia; and her brother, Abbott Lawrence, was the president of Harvard University from 1909 to 1933. Significantly younger than her five siblings—she was nineteen years younger than Percival—Lowell grew up at the family estate in Brookline, "Sevenels," which was named for the seven members of the Lowell family. She later inherited the family home and lived there with her partner, Ada Dwyer Russell. Lowell was a prolific writer. She contributed work to leading magazines such as the *Atlantic Monthly* and to literary journals such as *Poetry*. She also edited three volumes of the Imagist anthology *Some Imagist Poets* (1915, 1916, and 1917). She published eleven books during her lifetime, including the following collections of original poetry: *A Dome of Many-Coloured Glass* (1912); *Sword Blades and Poppy Seed* (1914); *Men, Women and Ghosts* (1916); *Can Grande's Castle* (1918); *Pictures of the Floating World* (1919); *Legends* (1921); and *A Critical Fable* (1922). Lowell also published *Fir-Flower Tablets* (1921), a selection of Chinese poems that she co-translated with Florence Ayscough. Her two books of critical prose, *Six French Poets* and *Tendencies in Modern Poetry*, appeared in 1915 and 1917, respectively, and she published essays and reviews in addition to giving lectures. *John Keats* (1925), her two-volume biography of the romantic poet, consumed much of her time and energy in her last years to the point of compromising her health. Over the years, Lowell had a number of health-related conditions, including neuralgia, gastritis, and a hernia that required four surgeries. On May 12, 1925, Lowell suffered a stroke and died at Sevenels. *What's O'Clock* (1925), *East Wind* (1926), and *Ballads for Sale* (1927) appeared posthumously, as did a collection of Lowell's unpublished lectures and essays, *Poetry and Poets* (1930). In 1926 *What's O'Clock* received the Pulitzer Prize.

After her death Lowell's reputation revolved for many years around her affiliation with Imagism. In 1913 she traveled to London to meet with some of the Imagist poets, a group of writers initially organized by T.E. Hulme but ultimately directed by **Ezra Pound**. Their approach to writing poetry emphasized the direct treatment of the poetic subject, used only the words absolutely necessary to the poem, and structured lines around the rhythm of the poetic line rather than existing meters and rhyme schemes. Lowell's poem "In a Garden" appeared in the first anthology of Imagist poetry, *Des Imagistes*, in 1914. Pound edited this anthology; however, differing opinions between Pound and Lowell, Pound's goals for his own writing, and Lowell's decision to edit her own anthology led Pound to rename Imagism as "Amygism" and to disassociate himself from the group. Lowell organized, edited, and funded the anthologies *Some Imagist Poets*, *Some Imagist Poets II*, and *Some Imagist Poets III* as venues for her own poetry and the poems of her colleagues. She also incorporated Imagist poetry into her books, including *Sword Blades and Poppy Seed* and most notably *Pictures of the Floating World*.

The **Chinese**- and **Japanese**-style poems in the first section of *Pictures of the Floating World* reflect the formal similarities between Lowell's Imagist work and East Asian poetry, especially given that some of these poems had previously appeared in the Imagist anthologies. The brevity and natural images in the two-line poems "To a Husband" and "Autumn Haze" suggest the poetic techniques found in haiku, while the mention of Edo (now Tokyo) and courtesans in "Streets" and to a samurai in "Spring Dawn" are direct references to Japanese history. The expression of love, loss, and longing found in "The Fisherman's Wife" and "Vicarious" recall similar expressions found in the Japanese poetic form, tanka. The visual and tactile imagery as well as the tone of "Spring Longing," on the other hand, recall Chinese poetry, and "Li T'ai Po" directly addresses one of the great poets from the T'ang dynasty. While there are very few Chinese-influenced poems in this book, Lowell later pursued this interest in *Fir-Flower Tablets*, a collection of classical Chinese poems by Li T'ai-Po, Tu Fu, and other poets as co-translated by Lowell and Ayscough. Ayscough, who was born in China and lived there for much of her childhood and most of her adult life, knew Chinese. She wrote out the English transliterations of the poems and provided lists of the many possible meanings for each word. Lowell, who did not know any Chinese, selected words from these lists in order to create her versions of the poems.

Cadenced verse, or *vers libre*, represents another connection between Lowell's work with Imagism and its impact on her poetics. While Imagists disregarded conventional meter and rhyme, they focused on rhythm for structuring the poetic line. Lowell used the term "cadenced verse" to refer to *vers libre* or **free verse** because it emphasized the importance of rhythm. In Lowell's work, such as the short poem "White and Green" or the much longer poem "Lilacs," this rhythm was based on the intake and exhalation of breath. The exact pacing of Lowell's cadenced verse was made especially clear to audiences who attended her well-publicized and dramatic poetry readings because people could hear exactly how she had crafted the rhythm of each line.

Lowell's poetic innovations extended beyond her work with Imagism, East Asian poetic forms, and cadenced verse. She, with John Gould Fletcher, developed a style of poetry that she named "polyphonic prose." To some extent this style incorporates elements of her experimental poetry with more traditional techniques. Polyphonic prose, literally a prose-style poem in many voices, integrates seemingly opposite approaches to poetry. The phrase "many voices" refers not to multiple speakers but rather to a multiplicity of forms and subjects within one poem. For instance, "Guns as Keys: And the Great Gate Swings" contains internal rhyme as well as cadenced verse. It combines narrative passages, such as the description of a U.S. naval ship sailing down the Mississippi on its way to Japan, with lyric passages, such as the lines describing three Japanese men measuring a pine tree by hand. The poem also presents the speaker's personal observations and exclamations while simultaneously addressing a large-scale historical event: Commodore Perry's trip to Japan to establish, under the threat of military force, trade treaties between Japan and the United States.

Lowell's versatility as a writer also took the form of parody. In 1922 she anonymously published *A Critical Fable*, a humorous and pointed overview of her contemporaries and of herself. She imitated the rhymes and puns used by her great-cousin, **James Russell Lowell**, in his *A Fable for Critics*, a consideration of the poets of his own day. Although many people suspected that she had written the poem, and some, including **Conrad Aiken**, actually accused her of doing so, Lowell publicly denied her authorship until finally including *A Critical Fable* in her entry for Britain's *Who's Who* in 1923.

Recognized for her innovative writing and for championing the new poetry, Lowell was, however, equally accomplished at using established structures and forms. A poem such as "On Looking at a Copy of Alice Meynell's Poems, Given Me, Years Ago, by a Friend" demonstrates her adeptness with stanzas such as the quatrain. It also reflects her skill with traditional rhyme schemes and with end rhyme. Lowell used many of these formal techniques when writing in traditional forms as well. For instance, she wrote sonnets, including "Eleonora Duse," a six-poem sonnet sequence written about and titled after the famous stage actress. Even when she took a new approach to an existing form, as in her monologue "The Sisters," she did so by drawing on her knowledge of standard forms such as the dramatic monologue and occasional poem in order to develop something new.

Lowell's poems, whether formally experimental or traditional, covered a wide range of topics, including love, war, and history as well as poems written to or about other poets and artists. She described a Japanese print in "A Coloured Print by Shokei," considered the brutalities of war in "A Ballad of Footmen," and contemplated the marriage of William Blake and Catherine Bourchier in "An Incident." She also embraced a diverse array of speakers, and many of her poems contained a lesbian subtext as well. For instance, in "Madonna of the Evening Flowers," a poem Lowell acknowledged was written for her partner, Ada Dwyer Russell, the speaker searches for her lover in the garden and longs to kneel in worship at her feet. Other poems, such as "The Weather-Cock Points South," include descriptions that are more blatant in their suggestion of lesbian sexuality (*see also* **Gay and Lesbian Poetry**).

One of the best-known poets of her day, Lowell received very little critical attention in the decades following her death. Her work was largely out of print and references to her were often limited to discussions of Imagism or disparaging remarks made about her by Pound. Late in the twentieth century, however, a growing number of articles and books addressed Lowell's role in American poetry. An edition of her selected poems appeared in 2002 and a book of critical essays was published in 2004, both of which added considerably to the available amount of information on Lowell's life and work. Collectively, the new studies delineate her accomplishments in terms of poetic craft and the lesbian subtext of many of her poems, and they locate Lowell as a major poet and an important figure in the history of American modernism.

Further Reading. *Selected Primary Sources:* Lowell, Amy, *The Complete Poetical Works of Amy Lowell* (Boston: Houghton, Mifflin, 1955); ———, *Selected Poems of Amy Lowell*, ed. Melissa Bradshaw and Adrienne Munich (New Brunswick, NJ: Rutgers University Press, 2002). ***Selected Secondary Sources:*** Damon, S. Foster, *Amy Lowell: A Chronicle with Extracts from Her Correspondence* (Boston: Houghton Mifflin, 1935); Gould, Jean, *Amy: The World of Amy Lowell and the Imagist Movement* (New York: Dodd, Mead, 1975); Heymann, C. David, *American Aristocracy: The Lives and Times of James Russell, Amy, and Robert Lowell* (New York: Dodd, Mead, 1980); Munich, Adrienne, and Melissa Bradshaw, eds., *Amy Lowell, American Modern* (New Brunswick, NJ: Rutgers University Press, 2004).

Ce Rosenow

LOWELL, JAMES RUSSELL (1819–1891)

Famous in his day as a poet, essayist, abolitionist, editor, lecturer, professor, and diplomat, James Russell Lowell has been neglected by later generations, particularly our own. It is difficult to pinpoint exactly why he has been almost entirely excised from recent anthologies of nineteenth-century American literature, for he excelled in multiple genres and was a key player in national culture for almost half a century, usually sup-

porting or condemning crucial ideas of his era. His most successful poems appeared as separate volumes in 1848—*The Biglow Papers, First Series*, *The Vision of Sir Launfal*, and *A Fable for Critics*—and garnered popularity and critical acclaim, establishing Lowell as an influential poet. Lowell's "Ode Recited at the Commemoration of the Living and Dead Soldiers of Harvard University, July 21, 1865" (commonly known as the "Commemoration Ode") and *The Biglow Papers, Second Series* (1867) were seen as major cultural statements on the Civil War. Both collections of *The Biglow Papers* gave Lowell his reputation as a skilled satirical poet who could write in a biting Yankee vernacular. But for modern critics, Lowell is usually seen as a minor figure. He was not as skeptical or adventuresome as **Herman Melville**, not as psychologically sophisticated as **Nathaniel Hawthorne**, and not as philosophical as **Ralph Waldo Emerson**. And Lowell disparaged **Walt Whitman**'s attempts to be so original and nationalistic. Lowell had definite conservative streaks and many of his **lyrics** were sentimental and derivative, but he was a writer of great congeniality, wit, and optimism.

Born to an old Cambridge, Massachusetts, family in a patrician mansion called Elmwood, where he also died, Lowell enjoyed many social advantages. He once dryly remarked that anyone living in Elmwood could not help but become conservative. He received one of the best educations available in his day and locale, studying with an older sister, Mary, who was an extraordinary linguist, and attending William Wells' Private School and Harvard University. Lowell's father, a doctor of theology, wanted Lowell to go into the ministry, but Lowell chose the law, completing degrees at Harvard (BA, 1838; LLB, 1840; MA, 1841) and gaining admission to the bar in 1842. Unambitious as a lawyer, Lowell happily abandoned that career once he began to sell poetry and essays to newspapers and magazines. For a short period in 1843, Lowell and Robert Carter were the editors of *The Pioneer: A Literary and Critical Magazine*, which received good reviews while Lowell had complete control of editorial selections. Lowell's first volumes of poetry, *A Year's Life* (1841) and *Poems* (1843), along with his contributions to the *Dial, Graham's, National Anti-Slavery Standard*, and *Pennsylvania Freeman* gave him the modest income on which in 1844 he finally married Maria White (1821–1853) the beautiful, frail, and passionate activist he had long sought. But his genuine literary success came with the satirical Yankee dialect collection *The Biglow Papers*, the first installments of which appeared in anti-slavery newspapers in 1846. Lowell's reputation continued to rise when he took on editing responsibilities with the *National Anti-Slavery Standard* (1848–1852).

After White's death from consumption in 1853, Lowell's productivity slowed, but in 1855 Lowell was commissioned to give the Lowell Institute lectures on "The English Poets." He studied intensely to develop his material and his witty and winsome style gained him enough popularity so that he was asked to succeed Longfellow as the Smith Professor of Modern Languages at Harvard. After a year of preparatory study abroad, Lowell taught at Harvard from 1857 through 1872, his lackadaisical style irritating many, but his wide learning and unguarded informality also endeared him to many students. In this period he balanced his professorial duties with a temporary position as the first editor of the *Atlantic Monthly* (1857–1861), which serialized *The Biglow Papers, Second Series* during the Civil War. From 1863 through 1872 he served as joint editor with Charles Eliot Norton of the influential *North American Review*. Lowell's pro-Union writings during the Civil War and support for the presidential candidate Rutherford B. Hayes led to appointments as minister to Spain (1877–1880) and thereafter England (1880–1885). In 1885 after the death of his second wife, Frances Dunlap, who had been a tutor to his daughter, Lowell retired to Elmwood and became the second president (1887–1891) of the Modern Language Association, a post he held until the year of his death.

Lowell's notebooks and letters from 1838 and 1839 indicate a growing social consciousness concerning egalitarian and humanitarian issues. Claire McGlinchee points out that Lowell's interest in the "suffering poor and . . . [his] Abolitionist spirit [were] well-rooted in him even before the eventful date of December 2, 1839, when he met Maria White" (29), who is often seen as awakening Lowell's passion for social reform. Through White, Lowell became an active member of a literary and philosophical group known as "the Band," who idealized the attractive couple and promoted Lowell's literary ambitions by giving eager attention to his extempore macaronic verses and impressionistic cultural criticism. Once Lowell unleashed his wit on the Mexican War, which he believed was a ploy to extend slavery west, he produced some of his strongest verses. In *The Biglow Papers, First Series*, which first entered anti-slavery newspapers in 1846, Lowell seizes a place for himself as an innovator in satirical dialect poetry and prose; he anticipates by decades some of Mark Twain's dark humor and satirical dialect writing, which has since become a mainstay in American literature. The collection of essays and poems pilloried the Mexican War "fer the spreadin' o' slavery," as Hosea Biglow observes. It is a complex work that showcases multiple voices through three main personas: a wordy, incompetent, and solipsistic Yankee minister, Wilbur Homer; a common, ranting farmer poet, Hosea Biglow; a racist, opportunistic, and eventually disillusioned young Yankee soldier, Birdofredum Sawin. Lowell reveals his disgust for the national stain of slavery and war through linguistic agitation; the urbane

Lowell is concealed behind personas from different classes who revile the war. He makes an appeal that readers in the age of "the common man" will find to be amusing and insightful. In *The Biglow Papers, First Series* laughter is meant to disrupt vapid justifications better than formal argumentation. Hosea Biglow stands in the tradition of American cracker-barrel philosophers who freely voice cutting-edge views on national issues. Emmanuel Gomes calls this kind of philosophy a "group of literary creations which flourished in the earlier years of American letters [and] represented the average man on the street, or behind the plow, who, by means of common sense, ridicule, and an occasional tall tale, got to the heart of the political, social, or economic problem being debated" (254). Cracker-barrel philosophers are wise fools who subject not-so-wise fools to censure.

Lowell's humor, seriousness, and moral conviction combine in powerful indictments of slavery, war, and expansionism. The satirical vigor of the *First Series* caused them to be "copied everywhere," Lowell comments in his "Introduction" to the *Second Series*; "I saw them pinned up in workshops. . . . I once even, when rumor had at length caught up my name in one of its eddies, had the satisfaction of overhearing . . . that *I* was utterly incompetent to have written anything of the kind." His poetry could escape his Brahmin status, even if he could not. In "Letter I," *First Series*, Hosea Biglow points out that the leadership of America has been taken over by narrow interests: "Them thet rule us, them slave traders, / Haint they cut a thunderin' swarth, / (Helped by Yankee renegaders,) / Thru the vartu o' the North!" Slave masters, in other words, have taken over national politics, which implies that many Northerners have lost or relinquished their freedom of independent thought and action. At the behest of the wealthy and powerful slavocracy, some Yankees also submitted to immoral opportunism, damaging the traditional New England respect for conscience, which Lowell, speaking from a solid ministerial background, says will have to be accounted for: "But it's curus Christian dooty / Thise ere cuttin' folks's throats." Slavery and its extension require satanic compacts and rationalizations that a common, independent-minded farmer like Hosea Biglow cannot stomach, nor should any other honest American.

In contrast, Birdofredum Sawin, a caricature of a self-interested Yankee, thought that he would gain glory and wealth through the Mexican War and enlisted out of bigotry; he wanted to revel in and pillage "the halls of Montezumy." Birdofredum displays rampant and outrageous Anglo-American pomposity that contributes to a sense of expansionistic entitlement: "I hed a strong persuasion / Thet Mexicans worn't human beans,—an ourang outang nation, / . . . I'd an idee thet they were built arter the darkie fashion all, / An' kickin' colored folks about, you know, 's a kind o' national." A case study in racist indoctrination, Birdofredum bases his sense of innocence on a belief in the sub-humanity of other races, as if he performs a national service by abusing, injuring, and killing non-whites.

Offering valuable criticism of the kind of Anglo-American nationalism that takes pride in debasing non-white races, both series of *The Biglow Papers* are also odd and difficult at times because of obscure references, and rhetorical complexity. Texts are found within texts; Hosea translates politicians' and soldiers' writings into verse; and Homer Wilbur edits and translates Hosea for readers. The work can be read as a meditation on perspectives, filtering, and translation, which are vital for understanding and coming to conclusions on any contentious subjects. But at the core of the *Papers* is the idea that vernacular is the best and clearest way to frame and view politics. Lowell certainly pokes fun at dialect, but he seriously uses its strengths to cut through cant and indefensible behavior. He articulates how common language and perspectives can expose sham justifications and, he identifies the real sufferers from the overreaching of the slaveholding class: common men, like Hosea, and racial others. The Mexican War was not, for Lowell, a war for the common citizen, but for the plantation owners. Wanting to appeal to a wide audience and stir them, Lowell relied on language from his youth when he worked with farmhands, and he captured an air of practicality and homespun that extended back to Ben Franklin. In the *Second Series*, Lowell famously mocks Jefferson Davis's speeches. In an important *Atlantic* essay titled "The Election of November" (1860), Lowell emphasized how slavery had damaged American democracy and needed to be dealt with once and for all through the ballot.

If *The Biglow Papers, First Series* gained notoriety, *A Fable for Critics* did even better, running through three editions in one year. It sold more copies than all Lowell's earlier books combined. Lowell gives sharp judgment of writers of his day, along with charity and praise. He appreciates while he belittles and suggests that his barbs cannot harm any valuable writers: "All the critics on earth cannot crush with their ban / One word that's in with the nature of man." In *A Fable* Lowell distills within a few lines insightful summations of contemporary writers in an effort to track down genuine strengths and qualities in American writers. He ventures to find great literature and reveals the ironic position of a critic who seeks too much; there is disappointment and pleasure to be had in such a search. One of Lowell's best biographers, Martin Duberman, recognizes that Lowell wrote the poem "impulsively and rapidly, and though this helped to give it all the dash of a *jeu d'esprit*, its hasty constructions led also to forced rhymes, painful puns, rambling digressions" (96). Despite *A Fable*'s quite visible weaknesses, the poem itself reflects the flaws of America's ardent literati, hungry for recognition; the poem critiques writers and itself for expecting too much too soon. Lowell is not merely critiquing himself, a view that is commonly seen in the poem: "if you have manfully struggled thus far with me, / You may e'en twist me up and just light your cigar with me." Lowell emblematically opens *A Fable* with the dangers of eager aesthetic pursuits. Hence, when beginning with Apollo's ardent attempts to capture Daphne, who to escape her pursuer transformed herself into a laurel tree, Lowell writes with multi-faceted, comedic punning rhymes. After pursuing Daphne, a figure for poetry, Apollo opines, "you've less chance to win her the more she is wood[.] / Ah! it went to my heart and the memory still grieves, / To see those loved graces all taking their leaves." Potential gets lost because of overzealous actions; lack of caution and sympathy hold American writers back, and Lowell wishes to trace the effects.

Lowell could ridicule writers and their self-importance to a mainstream audience who might not be deeply versed in literature. But almost all readers would know precisely what is meant by a tempered judgment of **Edgar Allan Poe**: "There comes Poe, with his raven, like Barnaby Rudge, / Three fifths of him genius and two fifths sheer fudge, / Who talks like a book of iambs and pentameters, / In a way to make people of common sense damn metres." Poe's metrical regularity and idiosyncratic subject matter are still subjects that interest modern readers. Similarly, Lowell's appraisal of Cooper reveals what still intrigues and discourages critics: "He has drawn you one character, though, that is new, / One wildflower he's plucked that is wet with the dew / Of this fresh Western world, and, the thing not to mince, / He has done naught but copy it ill ever since." Highbrow and common readers could appreciate the tongue-in-cheek trenchant comments on many of the other notable American writers of the time, including **Amos Bronson Alcott**, **William Cullen Bryant**, **Lydia Maria Child**, Emerson, Hawthorne, **Oliver Wendell Holmes**, **Henry David Thoreau**, and **John Greenleaf Whittier**.

Readers might be tempted to critique Lowell for being too lukewarm in his poetry, too restrained and genteel, but this would be an underestimate of his stance. He did much to legitimize writing as a profession for Americans at a time when **Thomas Wentworth Higginson**, whom Lowell first met at Wells's School, remarked that such a career choice caused "much shaking of heads among the elders" (Duberman, 30). Years before *A Fable* tainted his attitude toward Lowell, Poe announced that Lowell's *Poems* made him one of the leading poets in America. Writing at the end of the nineteenth century in a sort of literary obituary, Horace Traubel estimated Lowell's poetic accomplishments and temperament: "He does not announce fresh determinations with reference to the whole range of life" (24). Traubel suggests that Lowell was not inclusive enough, and so instead reserves most of his praise for Whitman's broad subject matter. But unlike Traubel, readers can recognize crossovers between Lowell's perception of the function of the poet and Whitman's. While Whitman sees the poet as a guide, and a breaker of traditions, a door opener and a nationalist, we can see in Lowell similar messages in subdued tones: "Till America has learned to love art, not as an amusement, not as the mere ornament of her cities . . . but for its humanizing and ennobling energy, for its power of making men better by arousing in them a perception of their own instincts for what is beautiful, and therefore sacred and religious, and an eternal rebuke of the base and worldly, she will not have succeeded in that high sense which alone makes a nation out of a people, and raises it from a dead name to a living power" (quoted in McGlinchee, 23). Lowell's vernacular poetry definitely reached beyond just refined city dwellers, but he wanted to spread ideals that raise men above tawdry and corrupt worldly affairs. Lowell departed company with literary trends because he did not go in for the common life for common life's sake, like Whitman. Instead, Lowell wanted to push people toward moral idealism that overlapped with common sense; his moralizing, which was unpopular among **modernist** critics and **New Critics**, was his main poetic impetus, which is why he was a strong political essayist and diplomat. Lowell's combination of social critique with experiments in vernacular warrants careful reconsideration by cultural and literary critics.

Further Reading. *Selected Primary Sources:* Lowell, James Russell, *The Biglow Papers, First Series*, ed. Thomas Wortham (DeKalb: Northern Illinois University Press, 1977); ———, *The Biglow Papers, Second Series. The Complete Poetical Works of James Russell Lowell*, ed. Horace E. Scudder (Cambridge, MA: Riverside Press, 1925); ———, *A Fable for Critics. The Complete Poetical Works of James Russell Lowell*, ed. Horace E. Scudder (Cambridge, MA: Riverside Press, 1925); ———, *The Writings of James Russell Lowell*, 12 vols., ed. James Russell Lowell and Charles Eliot Norton (New York: Houghton Mifflin, 1890–1892). ***Selected Secondary Sources:*** Bell, Michael J., "'The Only True Folk Songs We Have in English': James Russell Lowell and the Politics of the Nation" (*Journal of American Folklore* 108 [1995]: 131–155); Duberman, Martin, *James Russell Lowell* (Boston: Houghton Mifflin, 1966); Gomes, Emmanuel, "The Crackerbox Tradition and the Race Problem in Lowell's *The Biglow Papers* and Hughes's *Sketches of Simple*" (*College Language Association Journal* 3 [1984]: 254–269); McGlinchee, Claire, *James Russell Lowell* (New York: Twayne, 1967); Sedgwick, Ellery, *The Atlantic Monthly: Yankee Humanism at High Tide*

and Ebb (Amherst: University of Massachusetts Press, 1994); Traubel, Horace, "Lowell—Whitman: A Contrast" (*Poet-Lore* 4 [1892]: 22–31); Voss, Arthur, "Background of Satire in *The Biglow Papers*" (*New England Quarterly* 23 [1950]: 47–64); Wagenknecht, Edward, *James Russell Lowell: Portrait of a Many-Sided Man* (New York: Oxford University Press, 1971).

Roland Finger

LOWELL, MARIA WHITE (1821–1853)

Thomas Wentworth Higginson once suggested to **Emily Dickinson** that Dickinson's own poetry could be greatly improved if she read the work of Maria Lowell. This praise, along with the admiration of relatives and associates, seems the only deep attention that Lowell's poetry has received. Overshadowed, perhaps, by the poetic career and fame of her poet husband, **James Russell Lowell**, and a life of sadness and sickness, Lowell nevertheless contributed fine poetry to the American tradition. Lowell shows, through her poetry, that the images and experiences gleaned from a women's role in the domestic sphere can offer powerful arguments, both emotional and logical, in regard to freedom and racial equality.

Lowell was born Anna Maria White on July 8, 1821, and later attended the Ursuline Convent school in Charleston, Massachusetts, until the school was burned to the ground in 1834. Due in part to her Unitarian upbringing, Maria had strong leanings toward social issues and reforms. A strong abolitionist, she also associated with women such as **Margaret Fuller** and **Lydia Child**. All of Maria's sixteen published poems appeared in abolitionist publications such as the *Liberty Bell* and *Putnam's Monthly*.

In 1844 Maria was engaged to James Russell Lowell after meeting him in a group of young Harvard students called The Band. Although happy together, the marriage was marred by Maria's own sickness and a string of family tragedies. Between the years of 1845 and 1850, the Lowell's gave birth to four children—only one of which survived infancy. As a result of this tragedy, Maria's physical and mental health declined, leading the Lowells to relocate to Italy in the hope that the air would aid Maria's persistent cough and deep depression. The Lowells returned to Boston in 1852 after the death of their third child. Later in the same year, Maria also died, most likely from tuberculosis.

Fuller argues in her *Women in the Nineteenth Century* that men fear that if women were involved in politics, government meeting chambers would be packed with strollers and baby carriages. Packing a forum with strollers and carriages, though, is precisely what Lowell does concerning the issue of slavery.

The most powerful domestic and motherly themes and images occur in "The Slave-Mother." The poem begins with the title character holding her newborn daughter in her lap. The scene, however, is infused with sadness as the mother realizes that, in truth, the child "is not here but his who can out bid her in the mart." Here Lowell brings to the surface the underlying motive behind slavery—avarice. In this case, however, the sin is doubled as the avarice leads to thievery—but not of goods or possessions, but rather of one's own child.

This thievery motif is again echoed in Lowell's other abolitionist poem "Africa." In this work Lowell personifies the African continent as both queen and mother. From her breast, Africa's children "sucked Wisdom's dew," but the white man, she opines, "took my free / My careless one's and the great sea / Blew back their endless sighs to me." The once stately queen now sits "dreary, desolate" waiting "Till the slow moving hand of fate / Shall lift me from my sunken state."

The optimism of the African continent is nowhere apparent in the slave mother. There is no joy even when "the little arms steal upward, and upon her breast / She feels the brown and velvet hands that are never at rest." Instead, there is only the slave mother's continued prayer: "God grant my little helpless one in helplessness may die!" That a mother would wish death upon her infant is poignant enough, but when one considers that the poet herself had three children "stolen" from her, it becomes all the more powerful.

The pain that Lowell herself felt concerning the loss of her children is made apparent in the "The Morning Glory." The bereaved speaker finds solace in the belief that "in the groves of paradise, full surely we shall see / Our morning-glory beautiful twine round our dear Lord's knee." The image of the child twining around the knee is also used in "Africa" when the personified continent proclaims that "my children round my knees upgrew."

Through both these thematic connections regarding the avarice and thievery of slavery as well as the repeated imagery of the grieving mother, Lowell creates a seeming web of meaning. By associating the pain of the loss of her children with the pain experienced by both a mother country and a slave mother, Lowell shows that there is no great gulf between the white mother, the slave mother, or the love of a mother country. In regard to loss, the feelings and emotions, the grief and the sadness, are the same. This obviously is intended to "humanize" the female slave and to thus raise the moral question whether it is right to enslave another human being, and not a member of a sub-race, which was part of the justification for slavery by the slave-owners. These connections, one could argue, also add weight to nineteenth-century women's belief that, in truth, women were no more than slaves with regard to rights. Again, Fuller decries the white men who "steal their children" from their own wives "to frighten the poor woman, to who, it seems, the fact that she alone had borne the pangs of their birth, and nourished their infancy, does not give an equal right to them."

Lowell's poetry, then, becomes much more than the saccharine and **sentimental** poetry that most of those critics that have looked at Lowell claim. Instead, she stands in the field of American poetry as a strong example of domestic imagery being used to effect social change.

Further Reading. *Selected Primary Sources:* Lowell, Maria, *American Women Poets of the Nineteenth Century*, ed. Cheryl Walker (New Brunswick, NJ: Rutgers University Press, 1992); ———, *The Poems of Maria Lowell* (Cambridge, MA: Riverside Press, 1907). *Selected Secondary Sources:* Fuller, Margaret, *Women in the Nineteenth Century* (New York: Norton, 1998); Loeffelholz, Mary, "Poetry, Slavery, Personification: Maria Lowell's 'Africa'" (*Studies in Romanticism* 38.2 [Summer 1999]: 171–202); Rodier, Katharine, "'What Is Inspiration?' Emily Dickinson, T.W. Higginson, and Maria White Lowell" (*Emily Dickinson Journal* 4.2 [1995]: 20–43).

Raymond Yanek

LOWELL, ROBERT (1917–1977)

Robert Lowell, viewed by many of his contemporaries as the pivotal poet of his time, changed the way poetry was written in Cold War America. From the outset of his career, Lowell was noted for the public dimensions of his poetry. He addressed the political questions of his time from a position of conscience, without descending into the predictability and bombast that often characterize public poetry. Beginning with *Life Studies* in 1959, Lowell also initiated and propelled a poetic journey to the interior. He established a new poetics of self-exploration and self-disclosure, channeling a diverse range of cultural forces then shaping and elevating the individual psyche, and inventing **free verse** forms that concealed their own subtle artistry. Generations of poets have followed his leads. Lowell thus changed poetry by expanding both its public and personal spheres while inventing a series of surprising new styles suited to his every purpose. He helped make American poetry influential in ways it has rarely been before or since— as a moral voice in social and political issues, as an ironic eye on familial and communal behaviors, as a realm of psychological probing and self-discovery, and as a vital creative space hospitable to acts of creative recuperation and renovation.

Robert Traill Spence Lowell IV was born on March 1, 1917, in Boston, Massachusetts, the only child of Robert Traill Spence Lowell III, an engineer in the U.S. Navy, and Charlotte Winslow Lowell. Lowell's ancestors on his father's side include poets **James Russell Lowell** and **Amy Lowell**, as well as Harvard President Abbott Lawrence Lowell and astronomer Percival Lowell. On his mother's side were Colonial patriarchs Edward Winslow and Josiah Winslow and Revolutionary War General John Stark. Lowell belonged to a collateral branch of these families, financially and emotionally strained, and the ancestors functioned more as rebuke than as support. Later, Lowell satirically termed James Russell Lowell a poet "pedestalled for oblivion" and Amy Lowell "a scandal, as if Mae West were a cousin." Recognizing that Josiah Winslow had committed brutally aggressive acts against Native Americans, Percival Lowell had discovered non-existent canals on Mars, and Abbott Lawrence Lowell had helped send Sacco and Vanzetti to their deaths, he found the past to be a burden and, at best, a source of deep ambivalence.

Lowell's father failed in both his naval career and his subsequent career as a stockbroker. Moreover, Lowell's parents quarreled incessantly. Young Lowell endured the irony of possessing a celebrated family name but a conflicted and ignominious family reality. He grew up haunted and horrified by his family, feelings he ultimately transferred to his country and the world. After brief moves to Washington, D.C., and Philadelphia, the family settled for good in Boston. At the Episcopalian prep school St. Mark's, Lowell's sullen and angry behavior earned him the sobriquet of "Cal," short for both "Caligula" (the mad Roman tyrant) and "Caliban" (the beast-man of Shakespeare's *Tempest*). Lowell then matriculated for two years at Harvard University (1935–1937), where his poetic and intellectual gifts went unnoticed. After a violent altercation with his father—memorialized in a series of guilt-ridden poems written throughout his career with titles such as "Rebellion," "Father," and "Mother and Father"—Lowell drove to Clarksville, Tennessee, to introduce himself to the **fugitive** poet and critic **Allen Tate**. Tate became Lowell's first important poetic mentor, changing and perhaps saving his life. Recognizing Lowell's talent, he gave that talent direction. Lowell bought a tent at the local Sears, camped out on Tate's lawn for the summer, and spent his days composing poems and talking poetry with the elder poet. In the fall of 1937 he enrolled at Kenyon College in Ohio to study with Tate's friend and fellow poet **John Crowe Ransom**. Among the other students there, Lowell met **Randall Jarrell**, who was to become his best friend and a noted poet-critic himself. Lowell now excelled in his classes, wrote impassioned poems on Classical and Christian themes, and graduated summa cum laude in Classics in 1940.

Soon after graduation, Lowell married his first wife, Jean Stafford, then just beginning her illustrious career as a writer of fiction. The couple moved to Baton Rouge, where Lowell studied for a year at Louisiana State University. He took graduate courses in English with two of the leading **New Critics** of the day, Cleanth Brooks and **Robert Penn Warren**. At about the same time, he formally converted from his inherited Episcopalian faith to Roman Catholicism, influenced by the writings of Gerard Manley Hopkins, Etienne Gilson, and other Catholic poets and philosophers—and impelled as well by his dark moods and what his wife termed "fire-breathing righteousness." His newfound and fervent religious belief would strongly shape the character of his first two books of poetry. Lowell left graduate school in 1941 to work briefly at the Catholic publishing house Sheed & Ward in New York. His poetic career resumed when he returned with his wife for a year's stay with Tate and his wife, the novelist Caroline Gordon, in Monteagle, Tennessee. Living with Tate, Lowell wrote most of the highly wrought—some would say overwrought—religious and social poems that would appear in his first published book, the privately printed *Land of Unlikeness* (1944). Although the book received positive reviews from such prominent critics as **R.P. Blackmur**, Elizabeth Drew, and **Randall Jarrell**, Lowell almost immediately felt that the poems were inadequate, and he never consented to have them reprinted in his lifetime.

In 1942 Lowell volunteered and was rejected for U.S. military service in World War II. Nevertheless, when inducted in 1943 he refused to serve. He based his refusal partly on a new-found but principled pacifism, partly on his horror of the bombing of civilians, partly on opposition to President Roosevelt's demand for Germany's unconditional surrender, and perhaps partly on barely conscious fascist sympathies he had acquired both from his upbringing and from the **modernist poetics** and thought exemplified by **Ezra Pound**. His mentors Tate and Ransom also adamantly opposed the United States' participation in the war, though his friend Jarrell served willingly in the U.S. armed forces, writing some of the most famous poems to emerge from the war. As a conscientious objector, Lowell was sentenced to a year in prison; he served five and a half months—first in West Street Jail in New York City and then in federal prison at Danbury, Connecticut. He later depicted his experience of incarceration in such memorable poems as "In the Cage" and "Memories of West Street and Lepke." Upon release Lowell returned to his poetic vocation, filled with renewed inspiration and dedication. He composed thirty-two new poems, revised ten of his earlier poems, and published them all in the book that made him famous, *Lord Weary's Castle* (1946). This volume earned Lowell the first of his two Pulitzer Prizes, and it won rave reviews from many of the most notable poets and critics of the time. **Louise Bogan** observed that his technique was "remarkable" and his impact "often overwhelming." Jarrell, by now the nation's leading poetry reviewer, recalled that in commenting on Lowell's first book, he had predicted that Lowell would write some of the best poems of the future. Now, he said, *Lord Weary's Castle* "makes me feel less like Adams or Leverrier than like a rain-maker who predicts rain and gets a flood which drowns everyone in the country."

Lord Weary's Castle, moderating and perfecting Lowell's earlier rhetoric, lambastes the violence, greed, and egotism that Lowell sees pervading the American past and present. According to "Children of Light," our Puritan ancestors "fenced their gardens with the red man's bones." In "At the Indian Killer's Grave," the seventeenth-century Indian King Philip arises from the dead to condemn his Puritan murderers for having hurled "anathemas at nature and the land." In "Concord" Lowell scorns twentieth-century Americans who have only managed to replace Puritan zealotry with consumerist conformity: "Ten thousand Fords are idle here in search of a tradition." The volume's longest and most wrenching poem, "The Quaker Graveyard in Nantucket," laments all that nineteenth-century Americans lost "in the mad scramble of their lives," and it even more deeply mourns present-day losses, implicitly those resulting from the unimaginable violence of World War II. The poem echoes and alters imagery from a wide range of traditional texts, including John Milton's "Lycidas," **Henry David Thoreau**'s *Cape Cod*, Hopkins's "The Wreck of the Deutschland," and especially **Herman Melville**'s *Moby-Dick*: "The bones cry for the blood of the white whale." "Quaker Graveyard" ends in a chilling evocation of God's abandonment of humankind. As human beings devolve into ever more chaotic violence, "the Lord survives the rainbow of His will."

Throughout *Lord Weary's Castle*, Lowell presents the Virgin Mary and Jesus Christ as sources of salvation. But it is the prolonged anguish of the narrating subject and his harrowing vision of human beings at war, rather than the occasional half-visions of redemption, that dominate the poetic discourse. For all of its rhetorical flash and fire and for all of its redemptive yearning, the volume predicts Lowell's lonely confrontations with self and history that were to come. In the final poem, "Where the Rainbow Ends," the poet calls himself a "red arrow" on the graph "of Revelations," a position he would keep, come what may. Considered from a formal perspective, *Lord Weary's Castle*, with its elaborate metrics and highly condensed imagery, moves American poetry to a new plateau of verbal energy and complexity. Brilliantly deploying an array of new critical techniques such as tension, irony, allusion, plurisignation, and symbolism, the volume brings late modernism to a triumphant climax.

For all of its enduring power, however, *Lord Weary's Castle* was more the end of something than a beginning. Lowell's modernist aesthetic and Christian faith consumed themselves in the process of articulation, leaving his career in a quandary. His poetic drive sputtered on to produce one additional volume, *The Mills of the Kavanaughs* (1951), and then was reduced to an eight-year silence. That book includes several interesting narrative poems and monologues, such as "Mother Marie Therese" and "Falling Asleep over the Aeneid," but the aimless title poem all but announces that Lowell is at a dead end.

Mid-century generated very few poems but tumultuous personal changes. Lowell, no longer a Catholic, divorced Stafford in 1948 and married the essayist and novelist Elizabeth Hardwick the following year. He spent several years with Hardwick in Europe and then a year in Iowa, teaching at the Writers' Workshop at the University of Iowa (where his students included **W.D. Snodgrass**). Beyond losing his faith and his aesthetics, he lost his political certitudes as well. His views now became increasingly ambiguous and ambivalent, striated with conservative, moderate, liberal, and radical tendencies. In times of mental normality, he opposed the brinkmanship of President Eisenhower's foreign policy, and he supported civil rights and other social reform movements. In times of mental distress, however, he would sleep with Hitler's *Mein Kampf* hidden under his pillow and imagine that he himself was Napoleon. Perhaps the most striking change to occur in his life, which accounted for his occasional identification with tyrants, was the onset of a full-blown mood disorder that would leave him for the rest of his life periodically disabled, hospitalized, and medicated. This mental illness, in which manic highs were followed by paralyzing lows, was undoubtedly exacerbated by the death of both of his parents. Lowell's remote, ineffectual, ambivalently loved father died in 1950, and his demanding, frustrated, and even more ambivalently loved mother died in 1954. Lowell spent much of 1955 in mental hospitals. By 1957 he was back in Boston, living with Hardwick and their newborn daughter, Harriet Winslow Lowell, and teaching poetry part-time at Boston University (where his students included **Sylvia Plath** and **Anne Sexton**). Although he was attempting to write a prose autobiography, he was finishing nothing and publishing nothing. On a West Coast reading tour, he compared the poems he was presenting to audiences, all written years before, with those being read by the young **Beat** poet **Allen Ginsberg**. He thought that his own poems seemed in comparison like "prehistoric monsters." Feeling the aching emptiness of not writing poetry, and convinced that most of what he knew about writing was now a hindrance, he determined to start over.

As the 1950s wore on, Lowell deemphasized his modernist models, such as Pound, **T.S. Eliot**, Ransom, and Tate, in favor of a new set of influences. He became interested in the work of his new mentor **William Carlos Williams** (especially his more personal, recent poems such as "Asphodel, That Greeny Flower"); his longtime friend **Elizabeth Bishop** (especially a poem such as "The Armadillo," which he carried around in his wallet); his former student Snodgrass (who was then drafting the poetic sequence that would become "Heart's Needle"); and perhaps, though he denied it, his friendly rival Ginsberg (who was receiving great popular acclaim from the 1956 publication of *Howl*). Reflecting in different ways the impact of all four of those contemporaries, Lowell began writing free-verse poems about himself and his family.

Lowell collected these rueful new poems in *Life Studies* (1959). They portrayed his parents, his upbringing, his marriage, and his mental breakdown. They were more consistently and revealingly autobiographical than any major poem had ever been before. Lowell had come down off of his rhetorical stilts, discovering a language that could touchingly convey the sadness and humor of his personal experience. He wanted, he later explained, to see "how much of my personal story and memories I could get into poetry." He hoped that "each poem might seem as open and single-surfaced as a photograph." Gone was the prophetic and highly condensed discourse of *Lord Weary's Castle*. In its place were **lyrics** that, as he said, "sounded a little like conversation" yet were written "with hidden artifice," blurring the boundary between "actual experience" and "something invented." Despite their off-hand manner, the poems were replete with complex social and psychological implications, and they possessed a verbal artistry that registers immediately but only becomes fully apparent through rereading. The poems mark a breakthrough in the representation of subjectivity and alterity, at the same time that they manifest new kinds of linguistic ingenuity. As the speaker remembers, the language plays.

Chronicling a family's decline while commenting on the ironies of class, race, gender, sexuality, and nationality, *Life Studies*, so different from *Lord Weary's Castle*, was, if anything, an even greater success. The volume caused a sensation and won, among other honors, the National Book Award. A. Alvarez called the book "something really new," Bishop termed it "heart-breaking," Bogan praised its "balance, detachment, and consistent moral courage," Donald Davie thought it "hair-raising," **John Hollander** called it "unbelievably moving," and M.L. Rosenthal said Lowell had made himself into "the damned speaking-sensibility of his world." The volume ushered out an era in which poems consisted of a "symbol hanging on a hatrack," as Lowell sardonically said. It ushered in the family plot and what Harold Bloom has called "the trope of vulnerability." The book's key "Life Studies" sequence commences with memory poems about a family whose dominant notes were conflict, failure, separation, loss, and death. The sequence concludes with poems depicting the narrator's own discordant marriage, his descent into mental illness, and his partial

and perhaps temporary recovery. The final poem, "Skunk Hour," breaks with chronological order to show the very moment of the poet's mental collapse. It also breaks irretrievably with the modernist principles of objectivity and impersonality: "I myself am hell; nobody's here." The poem's ambiguous conclusion depicts a mother skunk who, like the narrating subject himself, refuses to "scare." Astutely interweaving the signs of his own life with those of his culture, Lowell accomplished a memorable and influential de-centering of personal being, family, nation, and the institution of poetry.

In the years that followed, Lowell modified and expanded the personal lyric without ever quite abandoning it. He felt that after *Life Studies* "continuous autobiography was impossible." Having moved with his wife and daughter from Boston to New York, he began to focus instead on historical, intellectual, and cultural issues. He published a volume of creative translations of European poets, ranging from Homer to Pasternak, titled *Imitations* (1960). Then he produced a volume of new poems, *For the Union Dead* (1964). Although neither as cohesive nor as compulsively readable as *Life Studies*, the latter volume includes such memorable personal lyrics as "Eye and Tooth" and "Night Sweat." It concludes with Lowell's most justly celebrated public poem, "For the Union Dead." Employing an astonishing array of reverberating images and motifs, this poem effortlessly merges personal observation, historical imagination, and cultural critique. It juxtaposes a courageous black Union Army regiment with the integration battles in the 1950s, and it counterpoises the horror of Hiroshima with present-day social amnesia. It celebrates a select group of American heroes, such as Colonel Robert Gould Shaw and his Union Army regiment, the sculptor Augustus St. Gaudens, and the black children who integrated Little Rock schools. But it also meditates on the darker aspects of the American scene, summed up in the poem's final image of a "savage servility" that "slides by on grease." On the basis of this poem, Richard Poirier labeled Lowell "our truest historian."

Lowell continued to compose resistant historical texts throughout the rest of the 1960s. His dramatic trilogy, *The Old Glory* (performed in 1964 and published in 1965), revises stories by **Nathaniel Hawthorne** and Melville in order to critique what Lowell saw as an uneasy alliance of idealism and violence in the American character. The trilogy depicts a self-righteous drive for domination that Lowell believed stretched from Puritan times through the Revolution and the slave trade to Vietnam. Regarding violence as "*the* hellfire," Lowell dramatized crucial seventeenth-, eighteenth-, and nineteenth-century moments as filtered through a keen moral awareness of contemporary events.

In 1965 about six months after *The Old Glory* was produced, Lowell protested the start of the Vietnam War by publicly declining President Lyndon Johnson's invitation to a White House arts festival. This controversial act plunged him into active politics for the first time since he had refused the draft during World War II. He participated in such anti-war demonstrations as the 1967 March on the Pentagon, and he accompanied Senator Eugene McCarthy in his anti-war presidential campaign of 1968. His next collection of poems, *Near the Ocean* (1967), reflects and extends this political engagement, as does his updating of Aeschylus's *Prometheus Bound* (performed in 1967 and published in 1969). Both texts question the modes of patriarchal authority that generate war abroad and inequity at home. In *Near the Ocean*, for example, "Central Park" portrays an America wracked by poverty, crime, and class division. "Waking Early Sunday Morning" turns to global problems. Employing Marvellian couplets, it depicts President Johnson publicly justifying war yet secretly "sick" of his "ghost-written rhetoric." This poem concludes with an unforgettable lament for the earth, condemned to wars until the end of time, orbiting forever lost in "our monotonous sublime."

Now teaching at Harvard (where his students included **Frank Bidart** and **Jane Shore**), Lowell began his next writing project still caught up in the political and moral concerns of the late 1960s. But as he rewrote and revised it, the project changed character, ultimately turning into his epic, his *Cantos* or *Paterson*. It began as a modest, experimental volume of unrhymed sonnets titled *Notebook 1967–68* (1969). The plot "rolls with the seasons" as it mixes "the day-to-day with the history." The sonnets refer to private moments as well as to protest marches, presidential campaigns, assassinations, uprisings, and, looming behind everything, the Vietnam War. But after the book was published, the sonnet form would not let Lowell alone, and he found he "couldn't stop writing." In 1970 he published an expanded version of the sequence, containing ninety new sonnets and now called simply *Notebook* (1970). The seasonal organization of the earlier version was, if not quite abandoned, then certainly loosened. Both versions ended, however, with the same self-obituary, which emphasized his love for his wife, Hardwick. After "loving you so much," he asked, how can I "forget you for eternity"?

In the years following that publication, Lowell continued to compose yet more sonnets. Finally, he divided his accumulated sonnets in two, publishing the historical ones in *History* (1973) and the personal ones in *For Lizzie and Harriet* (1973). In *History* the sonnets now appear in chronological order according to subject. The volume plunges readers into a verbal labyrinth of tyrants, heroes, artists, wars, art-works, and quotations, all tied together with bent epigrams and by the insistent sounds of death. The book sums up and concludes the poet's obsession with the public life and the cultural past. *For Lizzie and Harriet*, addressed to his wife and daughter, conversely suggests a very personal drama of domestic life and marital discord. It concludes with Lowell's self-obituary, but now prefaced by a new, downcast address to his wife: "Our love will not come back on fortune's wheel."

While completing the aforementioned two volumes, Lowell composed his final sonnet sequence titled *The Dolphin* (1973). This volume, in counterpoint to *For Lizzie and Harriet*, tells an elliptical story of love and remarriage. Lowell moved to England in 1970, where he taught at Essex University and lived with the novelist and essayist Caroline Blackwood. In 1971 the couple had a son, Robert Sheridan Lowell. The following year Lowell divorced Hardwick and married Blackwood. While evoking these tumultuous personal events, *The Dolphin* also provides a metapoetic commentary on the complex interactions between human experience and poetic language. The "dolphin" of the title is alternatively erotic desire and artistic vocation. Thus, if *History* caps Lowell's public meditations, *The Dolphin* culminates his personal and aesthetic musings: "my eyes have seen what my hand did." **Adrienne Rich** and others criticized the volume for its disturbing violations of Hardwick's privacy. For many readers, *The Dolphin* is the limit test of Lowell's autobiographical mode. But for other readers, the volume, which earned Lowell his second Pulitzer Prize, remains a haunting fusion of lament and celebration, autobiography and meditation.

In his final years Lowell was plagued by worsening physical and psychic debilities. His heart was failing, his third marriage dissolving, and his periods of depression growing more frequent. In 1977 he returned to the United States and to Hardwick. On September 12 of that year he died of congestive heart failure in a New York taxi on his way back from a last, unhappy visit with Blackwood in Ireland. After a traditional Episcopalian funeral service in Boston, Lowell was buried in the family gravesite at Dunbarton, New Hampshire. Weeks before his death, his final book of poetry, *Day by Day* (1977), had appeared. This volume, written in what Jeffrey Gray, in his essay "Memory and Imagination in *Day by Day*" (in *The Critical Response to Robert Lowell*), has termed a "notational style" corresponding to a "drifting" life, centers on a poignant sequence called "Day by Day," which haltingly describes Lowell's downward personal descent. The volume also includes a complex Homeric narrative of domestic conflict called "Ulysses and Circe," a final political poem (about Richard Nixon and mad King George) titled "George III," and an ars poetica titled "Epilogue." This last summary poem has become one of Lowell's classic texts. The poet, who had devoted his life to exploring the boundaries between literature and life, left as his final words a prayer for the "grace of accuracy" that permits artists to give every depicted figure his "living name."

Although Lowell was widely considered the foremost American poet of his time, his reputation became fiercely contested in the decades following his death. That controversy burns brightly today. Yet Lowell will be remembered as a poet powerful enough to shape the course of English-language poetry. His poems, as vital and untamable now as ever, continue to affect readers in profound ways. His names for things endure.

Further Reading. *Selected Primary Sources:* Lowell, Robert, *Collected Poems*, ed. Frank Bidart and David Gewanter (New York: Farrar, Straus and Giroux, 2003); ———, *Collected Prose*, ed. Robert Giroux (New York: Farrar, Straus and Giroux, 1987); ———, *Notebook* (New York: Farrar, Straus and Giroux, 1970); ———, *Notebook 1967–68* (New York: Farrar, Straus and Giroux, 1969); ———, *The Old Glory* (New York: Farrar, Straus and Giroux, 1965; rev. ed. 1968); ———, *Prometheus Bound* (New York: Farrar, Straus and Giroux, 1969). ***Selected Secondary Sources:*** Axelrod, Steven Gould, *Robert Lowell: Life and Art* (Princeton, NJ: Princeton University Press, 1978); ———, ed., *The Critical Response to Robert Lowell* (Westport, CT: Greenwood Press, 1999); Axelrod, Steven Gould, and Helen Deese, eds., *Robert Lowell: New Essays on the Poetry* (New York: Cambridge University Press, 1986); Bloom, Harold, ed., *Robert Lowell* (New York: Chelsea House, 1987); Ferguson, Suzanne, ed., *Jarrell, Bishop, Lowell, & Co.* (Knoxville: University of Tennessee Press, 2003); Mariani, Paul, *Lost Puritan: A Life of Robert Lowell* (New York, W.W. Norton, 1994); Meyers, Jeffrey, ed., *Robert Lowell: Interviews and Memoirs* (Ann Arbor: University of Michigan Press, 1988); Perloff, Marjorie, *The Poetic Art of Robert Lowell* (Ithaca, NY: Cornell University Press, 1973); Tillinghast, Richard, *Robert Lowell's Life and Work: Damaged Grandeur* (Ann Arbor: University of Michigan Press, 1995).

Steven Gould Axelrod

LOY, MINA (1882–1966)

For a decade after World War I, Mina Loy's status as one the most exciting modernist poets was acknowledged by her fellow writers, and her aura of vivid innovation was felt by a wider circle of readers and cultural journalists. But by World War II she and her work were little noted, receding in subsequent decades to footnote status. In the 1990s Loy's work came back into print and, due to its increasing impact, seems likely to remain a central fact in the history of **modernism**. It has a unique combination of qualities. It is rapid, terse, witty, at times direct, at times slyly sarcastic, always impassioned; Loy writes frankly from her situation as a woman, a mother, a lover, a social activist, and a cultural "mongrel" (her own self-descriptive term). Such a mix-

ture both gives her work its interest and accounts for the earlier fluctuation in its reception. The writing remains difficult to classify. It does not display the salient exploration of poetic propositions that the writing of **Gertrude Stein** or **Marianne Moore** does, nor does it use an acknowledged body of myth to narrate a psychosocial position as happens with **H.D.** Unlike many of the better-known modernists, Loy barely entered the arena of criticism, polemics, and artistic entrepreneurship, and thus her reputation depended solely on the reception of the poems. The frank eroticism of "Songs to Johannes" (1915–1917) could be read as a shocking example of the emerging social identity of the New Woman (cf. **Rachel Blau DuPlessis**); but a poem like "Parturition" (1914), arguably the first poem to describe the experience of giving birth, was a more confusing shock for its first readers. "Anglo-Mongrels and the Rose" (1923–1925), a sixty-page poem that uses the framework of autobiography to stage a profound exploration of the clash of British and Jewish cultural histories that Loy herself embodied, was initially published only in bits and pieces. Its immediate impact was slight, though by the end of the twentieth century it was beginning to be recognized as a major modernist **long poem** comparable to contemporary and near-contemporary works like *The Waste Land*, "Hugh Selwyn Mauberley," and *The Bridge*.

Loy was born in London in 1882 in a repressive home where her lower-middle-class British mother attempted to ignore the Jewishness of Loy's father, a Hungarian émigré and tailor whose surname was Lowy. In unpublished memoirs and in "Anglo-Mongrels" Loy makes it clear that her mother was unhappy with her own marriage and its outcome—her daughter. As the poem puts it, her mother "flaunt[ed] the whole of England in [her father's] foreign face." Her father was a more sympathetic presence: he encouraged her artistic ambitions, though he rejected any foray outside of respectability. As a young woman Loy studied art at John Wood's School, the Women's Academy in Munich, and the Académie Colarossi in Paris—unadventurous institutions all. At the latter she met Stephen Haweis, a man with some claim to an aristocratic background. In her subsequent descriptions of him, this was his only positive quality. He was pretentious, selfish, unattractive, and short. Moreover, his art was not at all interesting. Nevertheless, he seems to have seduced her and gotten her pregnant. In hindsight, it seems remarkable that Loy, who by all accounts was extraordinarily beautiful and who as she emerged into her writing career appeared to be culturally and emotionally fearless, would have married such a man. Her rejection by her mother and her own unease over her "mongrel" origins might well account for this.

Loy and Haweis stayed together for an unhappy decade, during which Loy had two children, one of whom Haweis fathered. At first they remained in Paris, where Loy began exhibiting her art (and at that point changed her birth name, Lowy, to Loy). In 1907 they moved to Florence, falling in with a motley set of British and American expatriates, intellectuals, artists, and poseurs. During her years with Haweis she was solely an artist and stood in his shadow socially and emotionally, receiving bits of modest acclaim for paintings and watercolors that were, it must be said, only of modest interest. In the meantime, however, Loy gradually met people who would help her escape her crippling situation: Mabel Dodge, **Gertrude Stein**, Carl Van Vechten, and the Italian futurists Giovanni Papini and Filippo Marinetti. By 1912 Haweis had left. In 1914 Loy had brief affairs with Marinetti and then Papini, beginning a wide-ranging transformation. She was plunged into the midst of the ferment of Italian futurism, with Papini and Marinetti as rivals for leadership of the coalescing movement as well as for Loy's attentions. Despite the futurists' public iconoclasm (hyperbolic praise for the energy of war, airplanes, and machine-guns; scorn for the malaise of culture, convention and, often enough, for women), the erotic skirmishing of Loy, Marinetti, and Papini was commonplace. But the affairs did propel Loy out of her marriage, and her exposure to the cultural extremism of futurism was crucial to her becoming a writer.

Nothing in Loy's past prepared her for her new identity. She had two children and no money outside of a small stipend from her father, half of which went to Haweis, absent but still legally her husband. She came from a non-intellectual lower-middle-class family; her art education was mediocre; for a decade she had only sporadic access to the excitement of modernism occurring in Paris, London, and Berlin. Unlike almost every other modernist writer of note (with **Jean Toomer** possibly an exception) she had no years of apprentice writing and reading behind her. She had to invent her writing on the spot out of whatever the present offered. Stein had recently become a valued acquaintance and Loy had read a few of her portraits. She knew the futurist manifestos and Marinetti's doctrine of *parole-in-libertà* (words-in-liberty). She took the possibility of typographical liberty from the manifestos and in Stein's practice and Marinetti's doctrine she had models that encouraged anti-conventional word-by-word construction. She later told her son-in-law that she "was trying to make a foreign language, because English had already been used." But formal experiment was not a sufficient accomplishment: Her situation between marriage and some as-yet-unknown mode of being a woman put her in social, emotional, and economic limbo. Her writing explored this territory with great penetration.

Her earliest work (1914–1919)—poems such as "Virgins Plus Curtains Minus Dots," "Sketch of a Man on a Platform," "The Effectual Marriage," and "Lions' Jaws";

and other writing such as "Aphorisms on Futurism" and the "Feminist Manifesto"—used futurist and other modernist formal means to exult in the opportunities for breakthrough that futurism offered, while at the same time critiquing, with acerbic wit, what now would be known as the sexism of her lovers. But her criticism was far from dismissive: it was interwoven with her desire for transformed relations between men and women. While the futurist males—along with many other Italian men—were successfully agitating for Italy to enter World War I, Loy's writing centered around a more unresolvable conflict she called the "sex war." In "Songs to Johannes," her major statement on this, she wrote of the physical side of sexual relations with unheard-of directness. The opening lines struck their first readers as brashly vulgar—thirty years later, **William Carlos Williams** quoted them in his autobiography: "Pig Cupid his rosy snout / Rooting erotic garbage / 'Once upon a time' / Pulls a weed white star-topped / Among wild oats sown in mucous-membrane." But ultimately "Songs to Johannes" is much more complex than it is scandalous: physicality, critique of contemporary sexual ideology, eroticism, empathetic solicitude, sarcasm, and the visionary are packed tightly together. In the opening lines Williams quotes, Loy takes "wild oats," a Victorian euphemism that cordons off illicit male lust in a vague haven of **pastoral** imagery, and juxtaposes the intimate reality of the female body. The innocuously agricultural act of "sowing" becomes, when placed "in mucous-membrane," sexual at the most physical level. However, Loy is not simply debunking prudery and writing frankly about sex: She is allowing a wide range of emotional, social, and physical reaction to sound, almost simultaneously. One can focus on "Pig" and "snout"; but one cannot ignore "rosy" and "Cupid." Pig Cupid's salacious act of "Rooting erotic garbage" is placed in the context of a fairy tale with "Once upon a time," bringing in connotations of domesticity, the nursery, and childhood innocence. Irony and utopian earnestness are impossible to separate out; they are atomized, as it were, both occurring throughout the antithetical phrases. What from a Victorian perspective is "garbage" might be the food of the (new) gods.

It is hard to avoid calling Loy's work feminist, but as her "Feminist Manifesto" makes clear (1914, but unpublished during her life), she is not interested in gender equality: "leave off looking to men for what you are **not**—seek within yourselves to find out what you **are**." For Loy, marriage offers nothing beyond "parasitism" and "prostitution"; the "only point at which the interests of the sexes merge—is the sexual embrace." But such a merger of interests does not bring men and women closer—quite the reverse. In "Songs for Johannes" she writes: "Evolution fall foul of / sexual equality / Prettily miscalculate / Similitude / Unnatural selection / . . . /

Let them clash together / From their incognitoes / In seismic orgasm / For far further / Differentiation." The syntax is gnomic, but the opposite is clear: a quasi-futurist "Evolution" is pitted against the status quo, which produces men and women who are not intelligible to one another—"jibber[ing] / Uninterpretable cryptonyms"; the way out of this impasse is via sex—"seismic orgasm," which produces not unity but greater "Differentiation."

Thanks to her connections with Dodge and Van Vechten among others, Loy's poems were published in small magazines in America alongside work of Stein, Williams, and **Wallace Stevens**. The utopian complexity of Loy's work seems to have been lost on most of her contemporaries, but its eventual impact was considerable. By 1916, when she traveled to America, she had begun to gain a reputation her biographer Carolyn Burke describes as "a free-verse 'radical'" whose poetics were as radical as her political and social beliefs. In New York she met Williams, Moore, Man Ray, **Djuna Barnes**, Marcel Duchamp, and, most crucial to her personally, Arthur Cravan. He was notorious for his size, loud public drunkenness, and boxing (he had fought an exhibition bout against Jack Johnson, then world heavyweight champion). Cravan and Loy fell in love and married; in 1917 as America entered the war and was gripped by xenophobic, anti-experimental patriotic fervor, he escaped conscription by fleeing to Mexico, and Loy soon followed. They lived haphazardly with little money and were planning to move to South America, but Cravan drowned while testing a boat. His death marked the rest of Loy's life. Distraught and pregnant with his child, she traveled to Buenos Aires, to London (where her daughter was born), then to Geneva, to Florence, and back to New York, before settling in Paris for most of the 1920s and 1930s.

In the first years of her Paris sojourn, she was a noted member of the international modernist scene. Sections of "Anglo-Mongrels and the Rose" appeared, as did her first book, *Lunar Baedecker* (1923), which included many of her earlier poems, as well as poem-appreciations of Stein, James Joyce, Wyndham Lewis and Constantin Brancusi. Loy's trope figuring Stein as a Madame Curie who "crushed / the tonnage / of consciousness / congealed in phrases / to extract / a radium of the word" was used, without acknowledgment, as a metaphor for the basic process of poetry by Williams in *Paterson*. Loy's book was well received, but this marked the apogee of her reputation during her life.

From the later 1920s on, she produced few poems, writing a number of unfinished prose memoirs and a quasi-autobiographical novel, *Insel* (1991), about complex relations with a German expatriate painter. Much of her attention during this period was taken up by attempts to make money. With the intermittent backing of Peggy Guggenheim, she and her eldest daughter opened a shop selling artistic lamps and lampshades. This was ultimately more a social than a financial success. In 1937 Loy moved to New York. She was no longer publishing, and her vagabond ways had left her with little economic viability. For the rest of her life she was dependent on her daughters. She lived near or at poverty level in the Bowery, occasionally writing poems, some of them concerning world events, others about the poor in her neighborhood. "Hot Cross Bum" is the most notable of the latter. Her last decade was spent in Aspen, Colorado, where she died in 1966.

Loy's reception is a complex matter. For most of the twentieth century, poets were her best readers. In 1918, when most American poets and critics were struck by the scandalous physicality of her work, **Ezra Pound** was acute in registering its demanding intellectuality: Loy and Moore, he claimed, were creating a new kind of writing, which he termed "logopoeia" (in a later slogan he explained this as "the dance of the intellect among the words"). Peter Nicholls suggests that Loy's work was "in some way pivotal" to Pound's own development of logopoeia in "Hugh Selwyn Mauberley"; he also comments that Pound was not able to grasp Loy's complexity, which showed "the 'logos' of 'logopoeia' to be embedded in the very body it was supposed to rise above." Williams consistently praised Loy and it seems likely that the verbal dexterity and erotic content of her poetry was a major influence on his work from *Spring and All* through *Paterson*. Writing at mid-century, **Kenneth Rexroth** placed her among the best American poets. But the fact that her work fell out of print for decades has delayed wider influence and critical reception. A **small-press** edition of her work was published in 1958 and a critical book came out in 1980; however, it was not until her (more or less) complete works were issued in 1986 that the full impact of her writing began to be felt. She became a major focus for feminist reevaluations of modernism, though her formal affinity with high modernism and her early connection with futurism made for troubled categorization. Recent pieces by DuPlessis and Nicholls and Carolyn Burke's excellent biography are fully alive to the challenging pleasures of her work.

Loy was ahead of her time, to say the least. In "Anglo-Mongrels" she describes her parents' courtship as follows: "She / simpering in / ideological pink / He / loaded with Mosaic / passions . . . / has no notion / of offering other than the bended knee / to femininity." It is remarkable to find so early in the last century such emotional and sociological analysis compressed so precisely. In the description of her own birth—a most unusual subject—the humor, physical frankness, verbal playfulness, and rueful insight into her own painful relations with her mother make it seem that few poets, critics, or readers have yet caught up with Loy: "They pull /

A clotty bulk of bifurcate fat / out of her loins . . . then mop up . . . / their golden residue."

Further Reading. ***Selected Primary Sources:*** Loy, Mina, *Insel,* ed. Elizabeth Arnold (Santa Rosa, CA: Black Sparrow, 1991); ———, *The Last Lunar Baedecker,* ed. Roger Conover (Highlands, NC: Jargon Society, 1982); ———, *The Lost Lunar Baedecker,* ed. Roger Conover (New York: Farrar, Straus and Giroux, 1996); ———, *Lunar Baedecker & Time-Tables* (Highlands, NC: Jonathan Williams, 1958). ***Selected Secondary Sources:*** Benstock, Shari, *Women of the Left Bank: Paris, 1900–1940* (Austin: University of Texas Press, 1986); Bronstein, Hilda, "Mina Loy: A Symposium" (*How2* 1.5 [2001], http://www.scc.rutgers.edu/however/v1_5_2001/current/index.html); Burke, Carolyn, *Becoming Modern: The Life of Mina Loy* (Berkeley: University of California Press, 1997); DuPlessis, Rachel Blau, *Genders, Races, and Religious Cultures in Modern American Poetry, 1908–1934* (Oxford: Oxford University Press, 2001); Galvin, Mary E., *Queer Poetics: Five Modernist Women Writers* (Westport, CT: Greenwood Press, 1999); Kinnahan, Linda A., *Poetics of the Feminine: Authority and Literary Tradition in William Carlos Williams, Mina Loy, Denise Levertov, and Kathleen Fraser* (Cambridge: Cambridge University Press, 1994); Kouidis, Virginia M., *Mina Loy, American Modernist Poet* (Baton Rouge: Louisiana State University Press, 1980); Nicholls, Peter, "'Acid Clarity': Ezra Pound, Mina Loy, and Jules Laforgue" (*How2* 1.5 [2001], http://www.scc.rutgers.edu/however/v1_5_2001/current/index.html); Rexroth, Kenneth, *American Poetry in the Twentieth Century* (New York: Herder and Herder, 1971); Scott, Bonnie Kime, ed., *The Gender of Modernism* (Bloomington: Indiana University Press, 1990); Shreiber, Maeera, and Keith Tuma, eds., *Mina Loy: Woman and Poet* (Orono, ME: National Poetry Foundation, 1998).

Bob Perelman

LUMMIS, SUZANNE (1951–)

Suzanne Lummis has been, for more than two decades, one of the most distinctive and influential poets in Los Angeles. As poet, performer, editor, teacher, and poetic impresario—in 1989 she founded, and she continues to co-direct, the Los Angeles Poetry Festival—Lummis has worked to bridge the poetic worlds of **performance** and "the page." This concept came to be known as **stand-up poetry**, after the anthology of that title (1990) she co-edited with **Charles Harper Webb**. With or without the humor that the term implies, stand-up poetry aims to unite the vividness and immediacy that performance demands with the subtlety and depth we expect of a printed work. Lummis exemplifies that union in word and deed. She is a performer, an actress, for many years a member of the poetry performance troupe Nearly Fatal Women, and a playwright, her two produced plays,

October 22, 4004 B.C., Saturday and *Night Owls,* won Drama-Logue Awards. Finally, to understand what she has meant to Los Angeles, it should be said that, in her master class in poetry at UCLA Extension, she has taught a significant number of the poets now practicing in the city and that she is an instantly recognizable personage there, with her signature beret and dark clothes, her slinky, winning manner of a wit and raconteur.

Lummis was born in 1951, funny and *noir*: both her parents were working for the Secret Service, and, while their home was in San Francisco, she was actually born in Oakland, narrowly missing being born on the Bay Bridge. Her earliest memories are of Sicily, where her father was then working for the U.S. Foreign Service; and she spent formative years in the Sierra Nevada mountains, where her father managed a ski lodge. She returned to Berkeley for high school and split her college education between Fresno State University, where she studied with **Philip Levine**, and the University of California–Berkeley, where the poet William Dickey read to her class one day. She credits Dickey as the writer who first gave her the idea that humor could play a role in significant poetry. Los Angeles attracted her in her late twenties. "I came to Los Angeles to be in the movies," she has said half jokingly. "I think all of this goes into the kind of poetry I write."

Lummis and Webb have edited a sequel to their first anthology, *Grand Passion: The Poetry of Los Angeles and Beyond* (1995), picked by the *Los Angeles Times* as one of its Hundred Best Books of the Year. She has published three books of poems: *Idiosyncracies* (1984), *Falling Short of Heaven* (1990), and *In Danger* (1999).

As indicated above, Lummis's work exemplifies the stand-up attitude. Her poems are accessible and enormously entertaining, and they usually begin with a "hook," as if to grab the attention of the crowd in a comedy club. One can see all this at work in one of her finest poems, "Letter to My Assailant," from her book *In Danger*. The title's implied premise, an intimate epistolary communication with her attempted rapist, immediately spotlights her text, which like most of her poems is a written monologue. Its artistic problem becomes the transformation of this "talk" into a poem that stands up on the page. She accomplishes this transformation with wit, an economy of language, and a sense of cadence that makes her riveting flow of language equally powerful as patter for the ear and form for the eye. The imagery of the poem is at once funny, dark, and apt, as when she conjures a man's mother: "Even in her grave / her hopes kept shrinking. / Now she's thin as a spindle." Perhaps the central image comes when the speaker screams, he lets her go, and "We leapt from each other / like two hares released from a trap." This image calls up at once the feral sense of the encounter, the idea of sexual frustration and miscommunication as a "trap," and the larger theme of the poem, that "something's not right between men and women." "Letter" also shows off the noir tendency in Lummis's work, its focus on the underbelly of the city, its poverty, threat, and darkness. *In Danger* ends with the poem "When in Doubt Have a Man Come Through the Door with a Gun in His Hand," the title of which is advice to aspiring mystery writers from Raymond Chandler, the famous Los Angeles detective novelist. Following the attacks on the World Trade Center in New York in 2001, Lummis commented in the *Los Angeles Times* (September 17, 2001, E4), "What poetry tries to do is bear the harsh and luminous world into language."

Further Reading. *Selected Primary Sources:* Lummis, Suzanne and Charles H. Webb, Eds., *Grand Passion: The Poets of Los Angeles and Beyond* (Los Angeles: Red Wing Books, 1995); Lummis, Suzanne, *Falling Short of Heaven* (Santa Fe, NM: Pennywhistle Press, 1990); ———, *Idiosyncrasies: Poems* (Los Angeles: Red Wing Books, 1989); ———, *In Danger* (Berkeley: Roundhouse Press, 1999).

Richard Silberg

THOMAS LUX (1946–)

Thomas Lux began writing poetry in the late 1960s. By 1980 he had published three full-length collections and four chapbooks, and critics had labeled him a neo-surrealist and surrealist. Lux currently refers to himself as a "recovering surrealist." Praised for its descriptions of middle-class America, Lux's fourth volume, *The Drowned River* (1990), marked the poet's emergence into realism and broke new ground with syntax-splitting examinations of daily life that "rock and break it down to sand." *Split Horizon* (1995) received the prestigious $50,000 Kingsley Tuft Award, and Lux became recognized for his adroit manipulation of language and tone, ironic descriptions of the human condition, and satirical wit.

Lux was born in Northhampton, Massachusetts, on December 10, 1946. He spent most of his childhood on a dairy farm owned by his uncle and grandfather. Lux recalls that both of his parents were supportive of his career as a poet; however, neither parent graduated from high school, and he acknowledges that his work does not concern their daily lives. Even as a young boy he had an early love for language and was a voracious reader, but it was not until he attended Emerson College in the late 1960s that he began to pursue a career in poetry. Helen Chasin was the first poet to formally instruct Lux, and it was during this time that he met **Robert Lowell** and discovered contemporary poets such as **James Wright**, **Adrienne Rich**, **Bill Knott**, and **James Tate**.

While at Emerson College he began publishing poems, and Jim Randall Press published the chapbook *The Land Sighted* (1970). It wasn't until *Memory's Handgrenade* (1972) that Lux became an established poet known for his zany depictions, imagistic juxtapositions of the sane and insane, and psychological snapshots of human distress. Over the course of the next thirty years, Lux published eight more full-length collections and eight chapbooks, and he received three National Endowment of the Arts awards and a Guggenheim fellowship. He has taught at Sarah Lawrence College, Columbia University, Boston University, the Warren Wilson low-residency program, and the University of Houston. He is currently the Bourne Chair in Poetry at Georgia Tech University. His popularity continues to grow alongside his teaching reputation.

Lux's surrealistic roots are evident in *Memory's Handgrenade* (1972). His verse is disjunctive with syncopated phrasing that exemplifies a nightmarish, sordid world. Reminiscent of the work of **John Ashbery**, "The Day of the Lacuna," a ten-part poem, exemplifies the discontinuity in Lux's verse while chronicling a man's "shattered profile" and the dissolution of an intimate relationship with a woman. The poem becomes a metaphor for Lux's work, for many of his poems attempt to articulate how humans negotiate psychological voids in social situations. The speakers in these poems "feel closer to zero," "find a worthless machine gun in the tub," and ask "Who am I in this picture?" The poems "How to Find Love," "Ten Notes to M—," and "The Handkerchief Trick" signal the beginning of Lux's preoccupation with memory, regret, desire, and portrayal of human vulnerability.

Sunday (1979) continues with similar themes of life's torments and tortures, and the poems "Solo Native," "The Bitterness of Children," "Miserable Time," and "Song of Darkness" highlight these concerns and reiterate the sentiment that "Fate has beaten you: for the lighthearted another life." His verse combines human bitterness with the comic in celebration of the aberrant human psyche, but in *The Drowned River* (1990) Lux begins moving toward a softer, slightly hidden narrative portrayal of raw realism and historical references, and the poems aptly titled "Postmortem Menu," "On Visiting Herbert Hoover's Birth and Burial Place," and "Walt Whitman's Brain Dropped on Laboratory Floor" exhibit this departure. He begins using longer more narrative lines and examines a gentler human psyche. "Fever Ship" chronicles a ship where the majority of the men have died from the plague, and the captain remarks, "We're sailing, boys, we're sailing, sort of, home." The insertion of the colloquial "sort of" indicates human uncertainty and hope. In "Upon Seeing an Ultrasound Photo of an Unborn Child" Lux addresses the child and moves from sarcasm—"it's not time yet to nag you about college"—toward the jovial—"I'm waiting . . . You'll recognize me . . . I'll have your nose." Lux does not abandon his uncompromising use of the grotesque and brutal, but the syntax of this poem illuminates a terser and more understated depiction of the human condition.

Split Horizon (1994) received widespread critical acclaim for its examination of contemporary lifestyles and pop-culture trends. With its publication coming in mid-career, Lux was praised for sticking to the hard-edge truths and signature saturnine voice he invented nearly two decades earlier. The poems highlight lonely characters who "bear a lot" and "shoot people—revolutionaries, whether earnest, sincere, or just thugs." Whether examining the "brain matter beneath the brain stem" or performing self analysis ("I've always been curious, born that way—why this, why that.") Even when "results are unpleasant" Lux never strays from his satirical voice.

In a later collection, *The Cradle Place* (2004), Lux makes a turn for slightly more philosophical conceits and intellectual concerns. The odd scenarios and acerbic wit are still present in the poems, and "Monkey Butter," "Birds Nailed to Trees," and "The Devil's Beef Tub" bear a striking resemblance to the work of **Stephen Dobyns**. Lux's verse juxtaposes rhythm and music with biological and scientific matter. The poems examine the microscopic eyelash and the life of ants, dung beetles, flies, locust, and remora. The poems are not solipsistic; they are "less lost than" those of earlier collections. Lux "leads them all, quick cunning, and assisted," acknowledging that he has passed "the time to add guilt and fear" in his poems. He demonstrates his "probe me, rather numbness" technique. He is now infamous for his dissection of human emotions, his shrewd narration, and his journeys from the banal to "the invisible point of the pyramid." His prolific career has spanned thirty-five years and his influence on contemporary American poetry, strengthens with each passing year.

Further Reading. ***Selected Primary Sources:*** Lux, Thomas, *The Blind Swimmer: Selected Early Poems, 1970–1975* (Easthampton, MA: Adastra Press, 1996); ———, *The Cradle Place* (Boston: Houghton Mifflin, 2004); ———, *The Drowned River: New Poems* (Boston: Houghton Mifflin, 1990); ———, *Half Promised Land* (Boston: Houghton Mifflin, 1986); ———, *Memory's Handgrenade* (Cambridge: Pym Randall Press, 1972); ———, *New and Selected Poems, 1975–1995* (Boston: Mariner Books, 1997); ———, *Split Horizon* (Boston: Houghton Mifflin, 1994); ———, *The Street of Clocks* (Boston: Houghton Mifflin, 2001); ———, *Sunday* (Boston: Houghton Mifflin, 1979). ***Selected Secondary Sources:*** Lux, Thomas, *The Land Sighted* (Cambridge: Pym Randall Press, 1970); Ryan, Michael, "A Symposium of Young Poets" (*Iowa Review* 4.4 [1973]: 52–112); Spalding, J.M.,

Interview with Thomas Lux (*Cortland Review* [August 1999], http://www.cortlandreview.com/issue/8/lux8i.htm).

Ashley Nicole Montjoy

LYRIC ESSAY

The lyric essay, a term popularized in the mid-1990s, is a hybrid form of writing that draws on both poetic and non-fictional techniques. The lyric essay, like the **lyric poem**, is marked by linguistic density, expressive form, distilled ideas, and the pronounced use of figurative language, imagery, and musicality. At the same time, it remains loyal to the original French intention of the word "essay" as a test or quest, an attempt at making sense, and shares with the traditional essay a deliberate analytic weightiness and an overt desire to engage with facts. Nonetheless, the lyric essay gives primacy to artfulness over the conveying of information, employing free-wheeling meditation and poetic language and form in place of the conventional essay's discursive logic and persuasive rhetoric. Furthermore, though ruminative, the lyric essay often leaves pieces of experience and observation undigested and tacit; while it seemingly seeks answers as it explores a topic, it is content to seldom find them, and its subject, as with a poem's, is not readily paraphrasable.

Indeed, in examples such as Annie Dillard's "Total Eclipse," John McPhee's "The Search for Marvin Gardens," and Susan Griffin's "Red Shoes," we see an experience, a place, or a memory contemplated from multiple viewpoints and time frames, a circular exploration that dwells, in the end, in uncertainties and mysteries—as Keats would have it—rather than relying on an "irritable reaching after fact and reason." Instead, as Helen Vendler says of the lyric poem, the lyric essay "depends on gaps. . . . It is suggestive rather than exhaustive" (6).

Structurally, the lyric essay tends to advance by association (meandering from one line of thought to another via imagery or connotation), by juxtaposition, or by a kind of sidewinding poetic logic, without a conventional narrative shape or climax. It often accretes by fragments, taking shape mosaically—its import visible only when one stands back and sees it whole. Or as Phillip Lopate describes the fragmentary essay, it is "a mirror to the unconnectable, archipelago-like nature of modern life" (xliii). The discrete parts of a fragmentary essay can at times stand alone and function much as prose poems, but on the whole, the lyric essay resists the coherence and quick closure of the **prose poem**.

The lyric essay is **postmodern** in the way it incorporates other genres when they serve its purpose: recombinant, it samples the techniques of fiction, drama, journalism, song, and film, along with poetry, and draws on science and sociology as easily as history and literature. **Ralph Waldo Emerson**'s 1834 definition of the essay, in fact, sounds remarkably close to what many lyric essayists do: Emerson calls essays the form of literature in which "everything is admissible—philosophy, fun, ethics, divinity, criticism, poetry, humor, mimicry, anecdotes, jokes, ventriloquism. All the breadth and versatility of the most liberal conversation, highest and lowest local topics—all are permitted, and all may be combined into one speech."

Dillard writes similarly of the essay in 1988: "There's nothing you can't do with it. No subject matter is forbidden, no structure is proscribed." She specifically points to its poetic possibilities: "Nonfiction prose can also carry meaning in its structures and, like poetry, can tolerate all sorts of figurative language, as well as alliteration and even rhyme" (74–75).

Historical precursors of the lyric essay can be traced as far back as the earliest aphorisms, about five thousand years ago in Sumer Akad, in which arguments—the essay's propelling force—are sieved concisely down to a single metaphor. It was in Sumer, as well, that scribes began gathering various aphorisms together under individual themes—"Family Life," "Work," "Friendship," "Death"—so that the previously discrete "sayings" on a particular subject cohered as a series of thoughts on a single, sustained theme. There is no literary "missing link" that helps bridge the crucial leap from these early anthologies of aphorisms to what we'd recognize today as essays, yet this custom of compiling one's varied thoughts on broadly fundamental subjects remained a common essayistic strategy in all subsequent periods. The Hebrew Book of Ecclesiastes, for example, which dates to around 950 B.C.E., is essentially a collection of poetic aphorisms, as is *The Analects* by Confucius, which dates to about 470 B.C.E.; the *Meditations* by Marcus Aurelius, from about the year 180; and Sei Shonagon's *The Pillow Book*, which dates back to about 1000.

Even as the essay evolved and gained literary status—especially in the work of Michel de Montaigne, who named the genre in 1580—its loose structure and diverse subjects allowed the essay to slowly accrue the weight of an argument through a series of anecdotes and reflections rather than the sharpened point of a thesis. As Montaigne put it in a 1588 essay, "Could my mind find a firm footing, I would not be making essays, but coming to conclusions; it is, however, always in its apprenticeship and on trial." Among more recent examples, Elias Canetti's *The Agony of Flies* continues the tradition of employing concise but varied images, observations, and anecdotes in order to pursue a single thought, as does Edmond Jabes's *The Book of Questions,* **John Ashbery**'s *The Vermont Notebook,* **Joe Brainard**'s *I Remember*, and even David Shields's compilation of bumper stickers in his essay "Life Story" in *Remote* or Joe Wenderoth's catalogue of "Things to Do Today" in *It Is If I Speak.*

Today the aphoristic strategy of such notebooks or compilations sometimes results in a "fragmented essay," "braided essay," or simply "collage," but the form of a lyric essay is one that is in fact deeply rooted in the essay's instinctively exploratory nature. What the lyric essay employs is an impressionistic, speculative approach from a variety of angles, one that is empirically less sure of itself than the essay's traditionally processional form, but one, on the other hand, that pursues its subjects multi-dimensionally.

In recent times there are writers, such as **Anne Carson**, who deliberately try to elude the genre boundary between poetry and nonfiction. Carson's first three books are billed as nonfiction, and they largely fit the definition of the lyric essay. But Carson went on to make a name for herself as a poet when she decided that a long prose work she was writing was "too dense" and "didn't move," so she divided its sentences into alternating short and long lines and published it as *The Autobiography of Red*, one of the best-selling books of poetry in recent times (D'Agata, 1). On the poetry side of the genre border, one finds poets such as **Jorie Graham** and **Robert Hass** pursuing philosophical, historical, scientific, and artistic ideas essayistically in long, exploratory poems. Other contemporary writers are similarly hard to pin down. Jenny Boully's innovative *The Body,* written entirely as a series of footnotes for an absent text, has been included in both essay and poetry anthologies. Eliot Weinberger and Terry Tempest Williams also frequently inhabit this ambiguous territory between essay and poem.

What has pushed some essayists so close to poetry? Perhaps these writers are drawn to the lyric essay because the supposedly value-free objectivity of conventional nonfiction seems a less plausible or rewarding way to approach the post-modern world. Or perhaps, given the extent to which we are bombarded in contemporary culture with information, the lyric essayist, to get our attention, feels the need to stylistically shock and tether our attention through overtly literary, poetic devices. The lyric essay, with its malleability, subtlety, complexity, and use of poetic language, seems to offer a fresh way to make music of the world of facts.

Further Reading. *Selected Primary Sources:* Ashbery, John, *The Vermont Notebook* (Calais, VT: Z Press, 1975); Aurelius, Marcus, *The Meditations*, trans. Gregory Hays (New York: Modern Library, 2002); Boully, Jenny, *The Body* (Londonderry, NH: Slope Editions, 2002); Brainard, Joe, *I Remember* (New York: Granary Books, 2001); Canetti, Elias, *The Agony of Flies: Notes and Notations*, trans. H.R. Broch De Rotherman (New York: Farrar, Straus and Giroux, 1994); Carson, Anne, *Autobiography of Red* (New York: Alfred A. Knopf, 1998); D'Agata, John, *The Next American Essay* (St. Paul, MN:

Graywolf Press, 2003); Dillard, Annie, *Teaching a Stone to Talk* (New York: Harper & Row, 1982); Graham, Jorie, *The Dream of the Unified Field* (Hopewell, NJ: Ecco Press, 1995); Griffin, Susan, *The Eros of Everyday Life* (New York: Doubleday, 1995); Hass, Robert, *Praise* (Hopewell, NJ: Ecco Press, 1979); Jabes, Edmond, *The Book of Questions*, trans. Rosemarie Waldrop (Hanover, NH: University Press of New England, 1991); McPhee, John, *Pieces of the Frame* (New York: Noonday Press, 1992); Montaigne, Michel de, *Essays*, trans. J.M. Cohen (New York, Penguin Books, 1993); Shields, David, *Remote* (New York: Alfred A. Knopf, 1996); Shonagon, Sei, *The Pillow Book of Sei Shonagon*, trans. Ivan Morris (New York: Columbia University Press, 1991); Weinberger, Eliot, *Works on Paper* (New York: New Directions, 1986); Wenderoth, Joe, *It Is If I Speak* (Hanover, NH: University Press of New England, 2000); Williams, Terry Tempest, *Refuge: An Unnatural History of Family and Place* (New York: Vintage Books, 1991). ***Selected Secondary Sources:*** D'Agata, John, "A _____ with Anne Carson" (*Iowa Review* 27.2 [1997]); Dillard, Annie, "To Fashion a Text," in *Inventing the Truth: The Art and Craft of Memoir*, ed. William Zinsser (Boston: Houghton Mifflin, 1987); Lopate, Phillip, *The Art of the Personal Essay* (New York: Anchor Books, 1994); Vendler, Helen, *Soul Says: On Recent Poetry* (Cambridge, MA: Harvard University Press, 1995).

John D'Agata
Deborah Tall

LYRIC POETRY

Lyric poetry is the dominant mode of poetry in the United States as well as in the literary history of Europe and the West. In many ways the term "lyric" has lost its specificity—there is a sense that all poetry is "lyric." Such a conflation is suggested by not atypical statements by two contemporary poets of the United States. **Jane Hirshfield** describes "poetry" in terms that might best describe "lyric" poetry: "The cadences and music a poem makes within us join to create its feeling-tone . . . under every poem's music, whether in form or free verse, lies the foundational heartbeat, its drum and assurance accompanying us through our lives" (8–9). **Gary Snyder** writes, "Poetry must sing or speak from authentic experience. . . . Poetry is the vehicle of the mystery of voice" (118). Music, voice, and authenticity seem to form the ethical core of poetry in these statements, which echo much of the recorded practice of lyric poetry for the past four thousand years as well as its critical definitions.

Traditionally, the lyric is one of several modes of poetry, including **narrative** and dramatic poetry. The term derives from the Greek word *lyra,* or the musical instrument the lyre, and has its earliest expressions in chanting and recitation to musical accompaniment. This is not to suggest that lyric poetry is strictly organized according to a musical frame, nor that it must be performed with music; rather, lyric poetry's performative value exists in its ability to convey emotional states through a language in which the musical element is intrinsic. W.R. Johnson places the focus on the singularity of the poet's voice when distinguishing lyric poetry from other acts of language: "What distinguishes the lyric poet from people who are not lyric poets is perhaps, in part, his extreme sensitivity to emotion; but even more important here is his ability to arrange his perceptions of emotion into clear patterns by means of precise language" (33).

Discussions of the lyric typically fall into several different categories. Lyric poetry may be considered as a genre, distinct from dramatic and **epic** or **narrative** poetry; as such it includes such forms and sub-genres as the aubade, **elegy**, epithalamion, hymn, ode, **pastoral**, and sonnet. The lyric may also refer to a general sense of expressiveness; thus the description of a passage, whether of a film, novel, or painting, for example, may be termed "lyrical"; such expressiveness may also indicate an intensity and temporal brevity. In addition, the lyric may be considered the domain of the voice or a specialized form of address. Finally, the lyric may be considered ideologically, with a view toward the ways in which a mode of discourse becomes dominant or codified.

The earliest lyrics that come to us in written form are Egyptian, from 2600 B.C.E., including funeral song or elegy, praise to the king, invocation of the gods, hymns and work songs of shepherds and fisherfolk. Love songs and epitaphs are recorded from 1550 B.C.E. in Egypt. **Ezra Pound** and Noel Stock translated examples of love poems from this period, which give evidence to the immediacy of voice and, often hyperbolic, address: "Or flowers of Mekhmekh, give us peace! / For you I will follow my heart's dictation" or "I would be willing to settle for less / And be her ring, the seal on her finger."

The ideal example of lyric, as word and music wedded together, is the work of the Greek poet Sappho (ca. 630 B.C.E.). As classicist and poet **Anne Carson** notes in her translation of Sappho's work, Sappho was both a musician and a poet. While her music is lost, her poetry survives in fragments. In fragment 118, Sappho addresses her lyre: "yes! radiant lyre speak to me / become a voice" (trans. Carson). Here Sappho makes the explicit connection between voice and music, although it is a complicated one, since one may ask whose voice it is that the poet assumes and whether that voice is inward or outward. Here, too, we have the apostrophe or direct address to her lyre, which represents the Muse.

What we now call lyric is vastly different than what the Greeks before the fourth century B.C.E. termed lyric compositions. As Johnson and William Waters note, the pre-Hellenistic performance of the lyric was embedded in social contexts, whether religious or celebratory events at festivals. Gradually, as these social events fell into disuse, the lyric moved from the realm of performance to the activity of scholar poets who wrote detached from any social occasion. These detachments were compounded with the separation of the lyric from music and the advent of print culture. Timothy Bahti observes that since the rise of European vernacular literatures, and probably as early as Roman literature, "there is no lyric without reading" and "the role of the silent reader that the lyric aims at is for him or her to be the recipient, the goal and end, of the lyric" (7).

In English-language literary tradition, the inception of the lyric is most commonly associated with the anonymous fifteenth-century poem "Western Wind," which fuses the immediacy of the lover's address with the religious invocation: "Western wind, when will thou blow, / The small rain down can rain? / Christ, if my love were in my arms / And I in my bed again!" The tradition of the sonnet, with its origins in music and mathematics, as exemplified by Sidney and Shakespeare, is perhaps the best instance of the continued insistence upon the connection between music and poetry as well as its direct address of an absent other—whether a lover or God or language itself.

In the early English-language poetry of the United States we see the use of apostrophe, as in these examples from **Anne Bradstreet**'s work. In her 1678 poem "A Letter to Her Husband, Absent upon Public Employment," Bradstreet opens with a direct address to her husband: "My head, my heart, mine eyes, my life, nay more." In her lyric sequence, "Contemplations," Bradstreet begins by invoking the landscape and myth, "Sometime now past in the autumnal tide, / When Phoebus wanted but one hour to bed," in the lyric mode of an overheard monologue. Very much akin to the English metaphysical poets writing half a century earlier, **Edward Taylor** apostrophizes and questions God in his religious lyrics, as in his Prologue to his *Preparatory Meditations*: "Lord, can a crumb of dust the earth outweigh, / Outmatch all mountains, nay the crystal sky?" (ca. 1682). Like its British counterparts, lyric poetry in the American colonies follows the genre conventions.

Theoretical discussions of the lyric are often conflated with discussions of poetry—its definition, value, and purpose. Plato's *Ion* states that all good poets compose their works not by art but because they are possessed or inspired. While it is debated whether Plato was speaking ironically, the sensibility of the lyric and inspiration, having fallen under the spell of the irrational or Dionysus, became a consistent element defining lyricism since the advent of Romanticism. Aristotle spoke generally of poetry as an imitation of action and considered expression at best secondary. Dante, in his *Convivio* (1316–1319), considered poetry as a unity of thought and the adornment of words; Sir Philip Sidney, following Aristotle and his commentators in the Italian Renaissance such as Castelvetro and Mazzoni, argues in his *The Defense of Poesie* (1595) that poetry is "an art of imitation, for so Aristotle termth it in the word *mimesis*, that is to say, a representing, counterfeiting, or figuring forth—to speak metaphorically, a speaking picture; with this end, to teach and delight." It is the lyric poet, according to Sidney, who with his "tuned lyre and well-accorded voice giveth praise, the reward of virtue, to virtuous acts."

Edward Phillips, in his preface to *Theatrum Poetarum* (1675), defined lyric poetry thematically as "songs or airs of love . . . most apt for musical composition." Northrup Frye notes that the insistence by poets that their expression was song not verbal expression reveals two elements of importance: First, "the lyric turns away, not merely from ordinary space and time, but from the kind of language we use in coping with ordinary experience"; secondly, the lyric's "turning away from ordinary experience means that the words do not resonate against the things they describe, but against other words and sounds" (34–35). "The poet," writes Frye, "in the ancient phrase, unlocks the word-hoard, but the word horde is not a cupboard: it is something more like a world that our senses have filtered out, and that only poets can bring to awareness" (35). This suggests something of the special role assigned to the lyric poet—indeed, Frye notes that Rilke and Mallarmé both saw the aim of lyric poetry as one of praise of the mysteries of this world.

It is with William Wordsworth, in his 1800 preface to his *Lyrical Ballads*, that the expressive became the dominant mode rather than the imitative. Wordsworth stated famously that "all good poetry is the spontaneous overflow of powerful feelings," and sought to bring poetic "language near to the language of men." Wordsworth's poetics thus underscores the epiphanic and the seeming lack of rhetorical mediation. Amplifying this, John Stuart Mill described lyric poetry as speech in overheard soliloquy in his 1833 essay "What Is Poetry," distinguishing poetry from "eloquence [which] presupposes an audience." Thus the main strands of lyricism, and indeed of poetry in general, are voice, the sense of possession or inspiration, and directness. **Ralph Waldo Emerson**, however, differentiates *poetry* from *lyric* in his central essay "The Poet," as he describes the writer of lyrics as having a mind like a "music-box of delicate tunes and rhythms" whereas a poet "has a new thought: he has a whole new experience to unfold" and is able to bring forth the "universality of symbolic language" and thus are "liberating gods."

The persistence of viewing lyric poetry as a distinct form and even epistemology is evidenced by **T.S. Eliot**'s

1953 lecture "The Three Voices of Poetry," where he distinguishes lyric poetry from didactic and dramatic poetry, and designates it as meditative verse, stating that the poet "has something germinating in him for which he must find words; but he cannot know what words he wants until he has found the words; he cannot identify this embryo until it has been transformed into an arrangement of the right words in the right order" (106). Eliot continues by stating that the poet is "haunted by a demon, a demon against which he feels powerless, because in its first manifestation it has no face, no name, nothing; and the words, the poem he makes, are a kind of form of exorcism of this demon" (107). Eliot's discussion expands the definition of the lyric explicitly to include the psychological state of the poet, as lyricism's purpose is "to gain relief from acute discomfort" (107). Eliot's description of poetry as a form of wrestling with the demonic has its parallels with Goethe's claim that poetry always has something of the Daemonic or vital force. We should note also the Spanish poet Garcia Lorca's discussion in his essay "The Duende: Theory and Divertissement" (1930) of *duende*, or that which is "oldest in culture: of creation made act."

In terms of linguistic structures, it is perhaps the use of pronouns that is most distinctive about the lyric. W.R. Johnson notes that the lyric uses three types of pronominal addresses. The first is the I-you poem, where "the poet addresses or pretends to address his thoughts and feelings to another person." Here, the "you" is often the implied reader or listener. The second form follows Eliot's description of the meditative poem, where the "poet talks to himself or to no one in particular or, sometimes, calls on, apostrophizes, inanimate or nonhuman entities, abstractions, or the dead." The third category is "the poem cast as a dialogue, dramatic monologue, or straight narrative, in which the poet disappears entirely" (3). In this sense, the audience—as listener or reader—is as central as the voice. Jonathan Culler has argued in his essay "Apostrophe" that the apostrophe or address is essential to the lyric itself; here, the poet has turned away from any actual listener. In his essay "Changes in the Study of the Lyric," Culler notes that the apostrophe is a figure of voicing, but ironically, as a *figure*, it signals a resistance to treating the poem as a fictive or literal voicing or utterance.

Waters, however, argues that while "Saying *you*, and the irreplaceable particularity of that addressee, can be the center of a poem's gravity," we should be mindful that address "is the meridian of all discourse, the plumb line without which pragmatics [in linguistics, the study of the interpenetration of language and its context], and so language, are strictly unthinkable . . . it is the fiber of language's use and being, inseparable from every word in every sentence" (4–5). The problem that lyric poetry embodies, confronts, and in some ways defines, as

Waters writes, is that it is "not so much a stable communicative situation as a chronic hesitation, a faltering, between monologue and dialogue, between 'talking about' and 'talking to,' third and second person, indifference to interlocutors and the yearning to have one" (8). The problem then with the lyric is its duplicity—it is both an utterance and the fiction of speech; it is this double vision or dialectic quality that makes, argues Daniel Tiffany, the lyric inherently modern in a theoretical sense rather than a historical perspective. It is the lyric's inherent instability, the tension between its invisibility as "air" or "song" and its materiality, its use of imagery and representation, that makes the lyric, as Paul de Man argues, inherently modern and a representation of the very intrinsic problems of language.

While the beginning of a poem often signals its adherence to lyric conventions, the ending is also significant. As written texts demanding reading and re-reading, lyric poems, writes Bahti, "are to be understood, and direct their reading toward understanding, but at the end of reading . . . they have inverted the attempts at interpretation into discoveries of where reading has to rebegin, never end, or sometimes even realize its own threshold of unreadability" (13). Despite a lyric poem's often revelatory ending, that ending becomes a self-reflexive moment necessitating a re-commencement with the poem. A lyric resists **closure** as much as it presumes to present itself as an immediate address.

A discussion of lyric poetry in relation to the poetry of the United States might best begin with Pound's reflections on the nature of poetry, as his essays typically draw from the past and seek to configure the possibilities for poetry. In his 1934 statement of poetic theory and primer for poetry, *ABC of Reading*, Pound described three means of achieving the aim "to charge language with meaning to the utmost possible degree": *phanopoeia*, or "throwing the object (fixed or moving) on to the visual imagination"; *melopoeia*, or "inducing emotional correlations by the sound and rhythm of the speech"; and *logopoeia*, or "inducing both of the effects by stimulating the associations (intellectual or emotional) that have remained in the receiver's consciousness in relation to the actual words or word groups employed" (63). Pound posits that great literature is "language charged with meaning to the utmost possible degree"; poetry concentrates this energy, as Pound formulates, "Dichten = condensare," or poetry equals concentration (36). **Lorine Niedecker** would later echo Pound's dictum in her 1962 poem "Poet's Work" by describing her "trade" as "condensary." Pound's description, and Niedecker's example of his dictum followed, underscores the lyric not only as a brief or short poem, but also more importantly as a use of highly concentrated language.

Pound's comments are not new, as Andrew Welsh has pointed out in his *Roots of Lyric*. Similar distinctions are to be found, for example, in Samuel Coleridge's 1813 "On the Principles of Genial Criticism," which describes as general artistic distinctions a poetry of eye, ear, and language; these may have their roots in Aristotle's *Poetics*, which lists three of the six elements of tragedy as melos, opsis, and lexis. While not definitive of either the lyric or poetry, they do draw our attention to the centrality of the question of the poet's language. Welsh's study suggests origins and affinities of the lyric with basic structures of poetic language, especially the phanopoetic with such language events as the riddle and kenning, and later elevated to the Renaissance use of the emblem and **Ernest Fenollosa**'s theory of the ideogram. Melopoeia, Welsh argues, stems from uses of rhythmic languages, such as communal chants, the use of charms, and in dance-songs. He notes, importantly, that the "rhythmical situation in a lyric poem, then, is somewhat more complex than just the syncopation of metrical pattern and speech rhythm. There are also present other rhythms derived from other uses of language—old, compelling forces whose purpose was to move. . . . The distinctive rhythm of lyric, I suggest, is actually a complex interplay of rhythms in language, a syncopation that crosses the rhythms of speech-melos, charm-melos, and song-melos. The modern poets who break the metrical patterns to explore other rhythms are working not to invent something new but to recover something old in the poet's language" (196–197).

One of the central issues of lyric poetry is its implicit sense of an authentic voice or expression. The lyric is then not only a concentrated event in language, but also a "charged" one, to use Pound's term, evoking a technological image, one that electrifies or brings about some transformation within the reader. A half-century earlier, **Emily Dickinson**, in an 1870 conversation with the poet and editor **Thomas Wentworth Higginson**, would describe poetry as something that "makes my whole body so cold no fire ever can warm me. . . . If I feel physically as if the top of my head were taken off, I know *that* is poetry. These are the only ways I know it." Dickinson's comments point to an emotional connection between the poem and the reader, yet one that is interior and private, as well as implicitly unified. Dickinson's comments also seek to define an authentic moment of response as corresponding to an authentic text. Dickinson's own poems are perhaps the quintessence of the modern lyric as they assume a complex immediacy of voice while addressing themes—powerful foundational themes, such as love and death, as in "Wild Nights—Wild Nights!" (Poem 249) or "I should not dare to leave my friend" (Poem 205). Echoing Sappho, Dickinson calls upon her music to sustain her: "Bind me—I can still sing" (Poem 1005).

Expression of self, of the private, and the closed text tend to mark much of lyric poetry. The solo lyric, writes Johnson, situates the I and the world; the choral lyric situates we and the world; thus, it does not define an opposition or the limitations of the private self but "imagines those emotions which lead us to want to understand both the possibility of the communion with each other and the possibility of our communion with the world" (177). The lyric as hymn or choral is best exemplified by **Walt Whitman**. The choral lyric erases the dislocation of time through the sense of plurality or inclusiveness of address.

Edgar Allan Poe's "The Poetic Principle" (1850) was perhaps the seminal American essay that sought to define an authentic poetry, claiming that the lyrical was the authentically poetic mode, for it alone is capable of the "rhythmical creation of Beauty." Indeed, the value of the poem increases only to the degree that it "elevates the soul" and as such effects are transient, only the lyric poem can provide a unified experience. Poe claimed that the **long poem** could not sustain such a meditation and thus was a contradiction in terms; in fact, Poe claimed it was composed of lyric fragments. Poe's insistence that a poem's language must be "simple, precise, terse . . . cool, calm, unimpassioned" prefigures the language of the **modernists**, such as Pound, Eliot, and **William Carlos Williams**. The image or representation becomes foregrounded in modernist poetry as a means of conveying precision and immediacy that marks the lyric. Pound's "In a Station of the Metro," that exemplar of **Imagism**, is also a study in a complex musicality. **H.D.**'s "Oread" may also serve, as in this brief poem's opening lines: "Whirl up, sea— / whirl your pointed pines." This use of the image as the nodal point of music and logos would be developed by the **Objectivists**, such as **George Oppen** and Niedecker, and a range of poets exploring **Deep Image** poetics, including **Jerome Rothenberg** and **W.S. Merwin**. Regardless of the poem's outward form and ideological project, there remains an insistence on the authenticity of the voice, either as the voice of a community or the individual's voice. The text itself is considered transparent or secondary to the vocative presence.

Drawing from Eliot's essays, the New Criticism, while not emphasizing genre definitions, particularly valorized the poem in that the poem could be understood as an independent entity. As New Criticism desired to eschew scientific methodology in the study of literature, it sought to authorize the idea of poetry as mimesis: The poet represents the world of objects in order for us to understand it; a poem does not yield abstract knowledge, information, or ideology. The lyric, insofar as it is a relatively short text, fits well into the New Criticism's procedures and emphasis on the unity of the text. As many of its most astute practitioners were poets, including **John Crowe Ransom**, **Robert Penn Warren**, **Allen Tate**, and **R.P. Blackmur**, a case could be made that the rise of the lyric in the United States, especially within the academy, was due to the New Criticism. While not rejecting the use of history in the process of interpretation, New Criticism saw poems as organized around humanly significant themes and meanings, not social, political, or biographical concerns.

In discussions, distinctions between poetry and the lyric are difficult to discern; equally important is the question of the authenticity of the voice and the presence of the self. **Wallace Stevens**'s comments about poetry in his 1943 essay "The Figure of the Youth as Virile Poet" in his *The Necessary Angel* are typical. Whereas Aristotle said that the poet should say little *in propria persona*, Stevens argues that there "can be no poetry without the personality of the poet" (45–46). Lyric poetry is intrinsically bound up in the issue of the poet's voice, self, and address. The critic Helen Vendler, in her *The Given and the Made*, argues that the lyric in post–World War II poetry of the United States is still a nonsocial genre, citing as examples **Robert Lowell**, **John Berryman**, **Rita Dove**, and **Jorie Graham**. The purpose of the lyric as a genre, Vendler writes, "is to represent an inner life in a manner that it is assumable by others." As "assumable," the lyric poem "is a script written for performance by the reader—who as soon as he enters the lyric, is no longer a reader but rather an utterer, saying the words of the poem *in propria persona*, internally and with proprietary feeling" (xi).

In recent innovative poetry of the United States, the lyric has come under intense scrutiny. In part this is due to the apparent dominance of the first-person direct address reflecting the daily in language, which falls back on Romanticism's apparent privileging of the experience of the isolated individual. Critics such as Charles Altieri and Robert Von Hallberg have termed such poetry as scenic or akin to the disengaged tourist. The lyric, in this view, is ideologically compromised, as it presents on the one hand an unexamined but dominant point of view and on the other hand assumes the veracity of the presence of the self. There is a tacit refusal within the conventional lyric to acknowledge the productive forces shaping discourse and thereby to question the authenticity of the self. Much innovative or language-based **poetics** reject the lyric or the voiced poem because of the implicit illusion of voice the lyric creates. The issue in question, as Culler points out in his essay "Changes in the Study of the Lyric," is in part "the fundamental aspect of lyric writing, which is to produce an apparently phenomenal world through the figure of the voice" (50). This position, Culler suggests, argues that the lyric is no longer a genre but a figure or poetic device akin to prosopopoeia. Similarly, Harold Bloom, with his theory of misreading and the **anxiety of influence**, suggests that poems are intertextual spaces and that poets, far from being the idealized

voices postulated by the New Critics, are products of traditions of reading.

The **confessional** voices of poets such as **Sylvia Plath** or **Gerald Stern**, as well as the more recent self-reflective voices of **Robert Hass** or **Frank Bidart**, insist on the ability to communicate an emotion or inner life, suggesting that such an act indicates an authentic identity which is also representative of the idea of self. The insistence of the primacy of the "I" or the interiorized self, as well as an emotive response to the landscape, the reliance on the present tense, and the use of images to evoke meaningfulness, argue such critics as Altieri or Marjorie Perloff, reflects a profound social failure to engage in the world. Against this model of interiority, one could place the work of such recent poets as **John Ashbery**, **Ann Lauterbach**, **Michel Palmer**, or **Susan Schultz**. Here the poem, rather than presenting meaning or epiphany, engages the reader in the creation of meaning.

The lyric tradition is also problematic in its gendered position, as **Rachel Blau DuPlessis** writes: "To talk about the lyric, one must say something about beauty, something about love and sex, something about Woman and Man and their positionings, something about active agency versus malleability. This is a cluster of foundational materials with a gender cast built into the heart of the lyric." DuPlessis continues, noting that there is often "an overtly male 'I,' speaking as if overheard in front of an unseen but postulated, loosely male 'us' about a (Beloved) 'she'" (71). Furthermore, the norms of the lyric, as traditionally defined, parallel the social construction and marginalization of women: private, subjective, personal, and emotional. While the confessional or autobiographical poem—or lyric—may have provided a sense of community, such poems inversely come to represent, if not stereotype, members or features of that community. Yet the critique of privacy, for example, is complex, especially if read against the culture and political climate in the United States from the Cold War era and the rise of confessional poetry, to the present interest in surveillance technologies and the rise of the security-state in the United States. Is a lyric poetry that insists upon the autonomy of the private self finally gendered, consumeristic, or narcissistic, or is it, as Deborah Nelson has argued, instrumental as forming an oppositional poetics for those most marginalized—women, people of color, or sexually marginalized people—for whom the dominant society and state most deprive of autonomy and privacy?

The lyric, as a brief poem or sequence, continues to be a site of interrogating the possibilities of language. The conflation of the terms "lyric" and "poetry" present problems if viewed strictly as genres. Rather, the lyric points to a hybridity of form and function, as suggested by the attempts to rename the lyric as meditative verse or, more recently, as applied to the work of Lauterbach, Graham, and others, as critical lyric. The foregrounding of the fragment as a lyric marker or the inverse, the parodic use of the lyric apostrophe, are yet other instances of the re-visioning of the lyric. Certainly the interest in spoken word poetries begins a redefinition of the connection between voice and lyric. Theories of the lyric seem inevitably to discover insufficiencies in our reading practices as well as our need or necessity for astonishment in the face of our world and our selves.

Further Reading. *Selected Primary Sources:* Bahti, Timothy, *The Ends of the Lyric: Direction and Consequence in Western Poetry* (Baltimore: Johns Hopkins University Press, 1996); Carson, Anne, trans., *If Not Winter: Fragments of Sappho* (New York: Knopf, 2002); Culler, Jonathan, "Apostrophe," in *The Pursuit of Signs* (Ithaca, NY: Cornell University Press, 1981); ———, "Changes in the Study of the Lyric," in *Lyric Poetry: Beyond New Criticism,* ed. Chaviva Hosek and Patricia Parker (Ithaca, NY: Cornell University Press, 1985); de Man, Paul, "Lyric and Modernity" in his *Blindness and Insight* (Minneapolis: University of Minnesota Press, 1983); DuPlessis, Rachel Blau, "'Corpses of Poesy': Some Modern Poets and Some Gender Ideologies of Lyric," in *Feminist Measures: Soundings in Poetry and Theory,* ed. Lynn Keller and Cristanne Miller (Ann Arbor: University Michigan Press, 1994); Eliot, T.S., *On Poetry and Poets* (New York: Farrar, Straus and Giroux, 1961); Frye, Northrop, "Approaching the Lyric," in *Lyric Poetry: Beyond New Criticism,* ed. Chaviva Hosek and Patricia Parker (Ithaca, NY: Cornell University Press, 1985); Hirshfield, Jane, *Nine Gates: Entering the Mind of Poetry* (New York: HarperCollins, 1998); Hosek, Chaviva, and Patricia Parker, eds., *Lyric Poetry: Beyond New Criticism* (Ithaca, NY: Cornell University Press, 1985); Johnson, W.R., *The Idea of Lyric: Lyric Modes in Ancient and Modern Poetry* (Princeton, NJ: Princeton University Press, 1982); Nelson, Deborah, *Pursuing Privacy in Cold War America* (New York: Columbia University Press, 2002); Pound, Ezra, *ABC of Reading* (New York: New Directions, 1960); Pound, Ezra, and Noel Stock, trans., *Love Poems of Ancient Egypt* (New York: New Directions, 1962); Snyder, Gary, *Earth House Hold* (New York: New Directions, 1969); Stevens, Wallace, *The Necessary Angel: Essays on Reality and the Imagination* (New York: Vintage, 1951); Tiffany, Daniel, *Toy Medium: Materialism and Modern Lyric* (Berkeley: University of California Press, 2000); Vendler, Helen, *The Given and the Made: Strategies of Poetic Redefinition* (Cambridge, MA: Harvard University Press, 1995); Walsh, Andrew, *Roots of Lyric: Primitive Poetry and Modern Poetics* (Princeton, NJ: Princeton University Press, 1978); Waters, William, *Poetry's Touch: On Lyric Address* (Ithaca, NY: Cornell University Press, 2003).

James McCorkle